PHILIPS' MODERN SCHOOL ATLAS

ASTRONOMICAL GEOGRAPHY

THE SOLAR SYSTEM

The Solar System is a tiny part of one of the countless galaxies that make up the Universe. It consists of the Sun at the centre with nine planets and various moons, comets, dust particles and gases revolving around it. All the planets revolve around the Sun in the same direction, anti-clockwise when viewed from the Northern Heavens, and almost in the same plane.

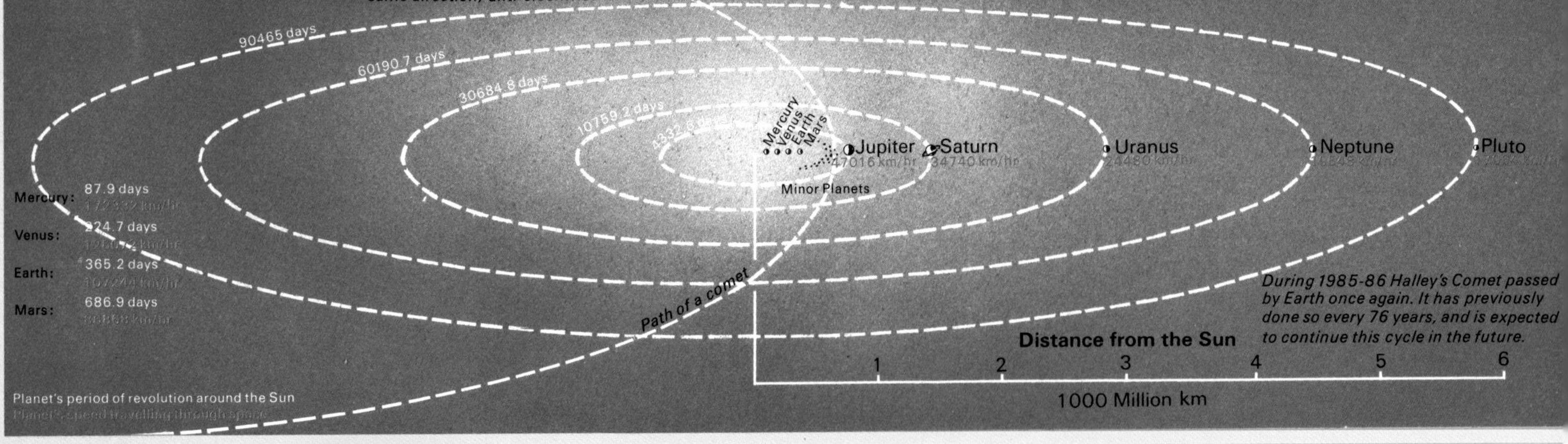

90465 days
60190.7 days
30684.8 days
10759.2 days
4332.6 days

Mercury Venus Earth Mars
Jupiter 47016 km/hr
Saturn 34740 km/hr
Uranus 24480 km/hr
Neptune
Pluto
Minor Planets

Mercury: 87.9 days
Venus: 224.7 days
Earth: 365.2 days
Mars: 686.9 days

Path of a comet

During 1985-86 Halley's Comet passed by Earth once again. It has previously done so every 76 years, and is expected to continue this cycle in the future.

Distance from the Sun
1 2 3 4 5 6
1000 Million km

Planet's period of revolution around the Sun
Planet's speed travelling through space

THE PLANETS IN RELATION TO THEIR SIZE

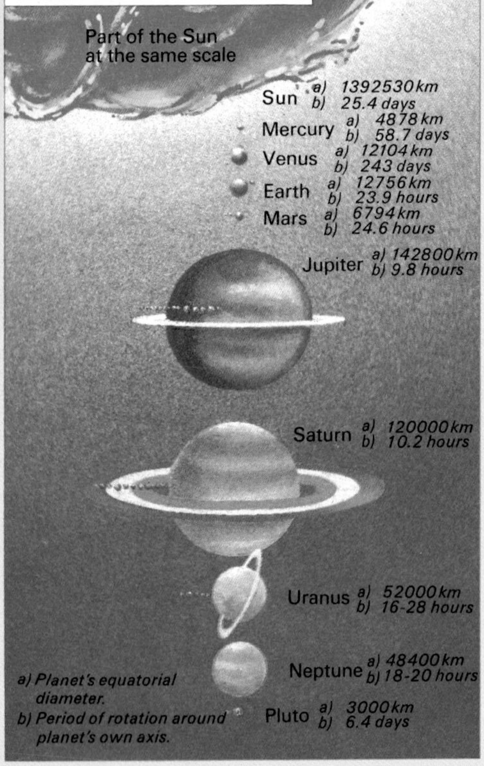

Part of the Sun at the same scale

	a)	b)
Sun	1392530 km	25.4 days
Mercury	4878 km	58.7 days
Venus	12104 km	243 days
Earth	12756 km	23.9 hours
Mars	6794 km	24.6 hours
Jupiter	142800 km	9.8 hours
Saturn	120000 km	10.2 hours
Uranus	52000 km	16-28 hours
Neptune	48400 km	18-20 hours
Pluto	3000 km	6.4 days

a) Planet's equatorial diameter.
b) Period of rotation around planet's own axis.

ECLIPSES

Direction of moon's orbit
Direction of earth's orbit

When the Moon passes between the Earth and the Sun it blots out the sunlight over part of the Earth's surface. This is called a partial eclipse of the Sun.

Partial eclipse

EARTH
MOON
SUN

When the Earth passes between the Moon and the Sun it casts a shadow over the whole surface of the Moon. This is a total eclipse of the Moon.

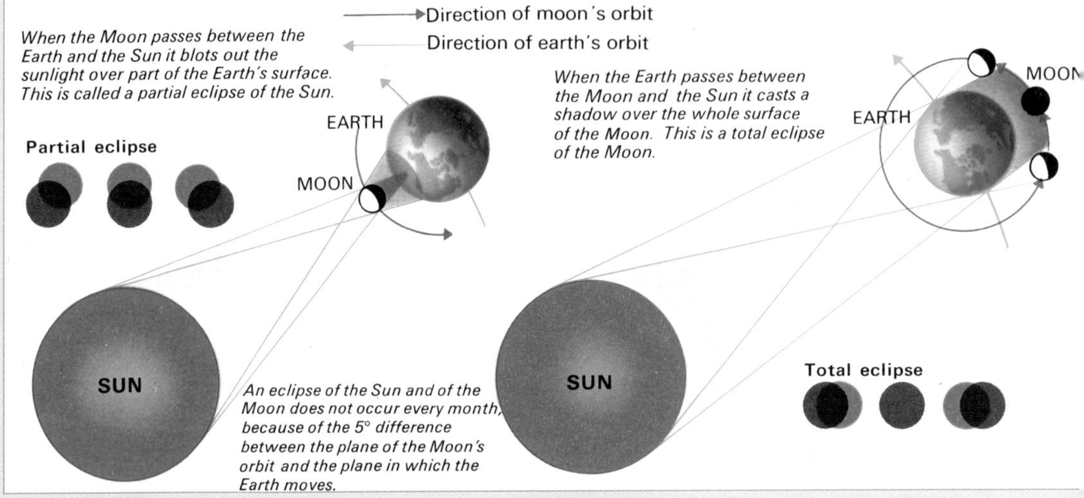

EARTH
MOON
SUN

Total eclipse

An eclipse of the Sun and of the Moon does not occur every month, because of the 5° difference between the plane of the Moon's orbit and the plane in which the Earth moves.

TIDES

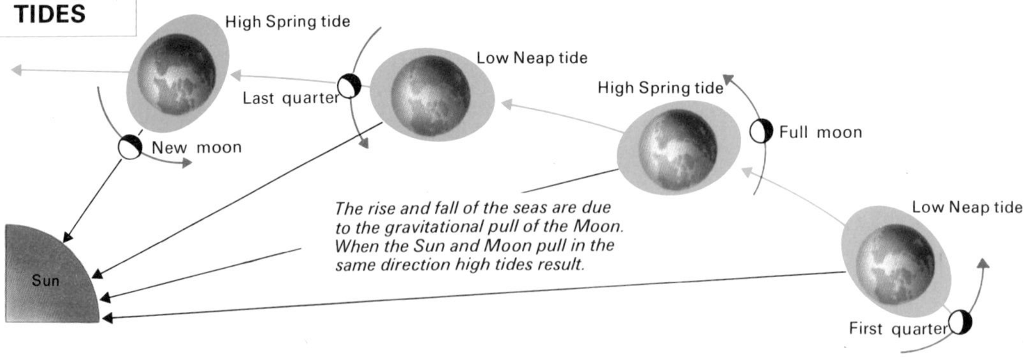

High Spring tide
Low Neap tide
Last quarter
High Spring tide
Full moon
New moon
Low Neap tide
First quarter
Sun

The rise and fall of the seas are due to the gravitational pull of the Moon. When the Sun and Moon pull in the same direction high tides result.

THE PHASES OF THE MOON

The Moon, like the planets, has no light of its own and shines only by reflecting sunlight.

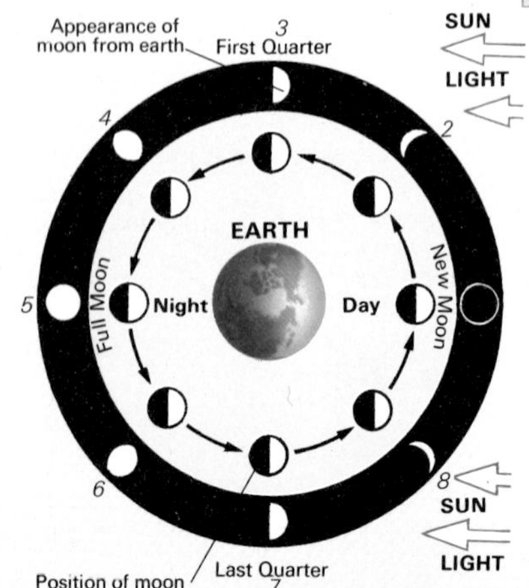

The Moon rotates on its own axis in just over 27 days, which is the same as its period of revolution around the Earth, so that it always presents the same face (hemisphere) to us. Because the Earth has moved on its own orbital plane around the Sun, while the Moon is revolving around it, the time from one full Moon to the next is 29½ days.

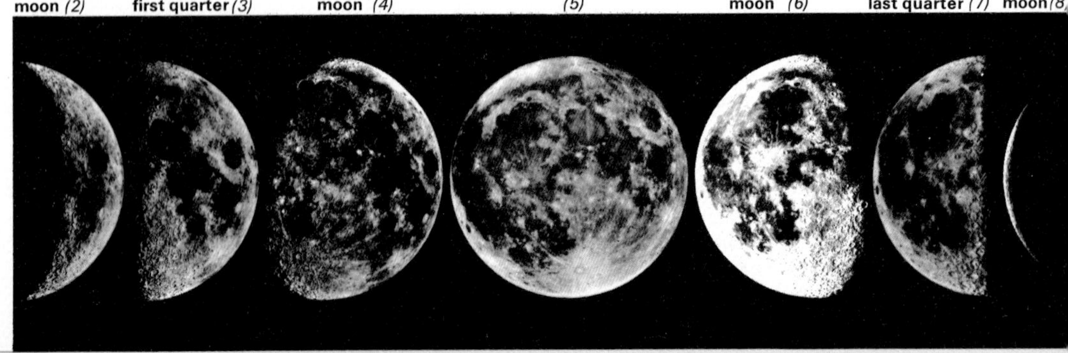

THE SEASONS

The earth revolves around the sun once a year in an anti-clockwise direction. The earth is tilted at an angle of $66\frac{1}{2}$ degrees to the plane of its orbit and always points into space in the same direction. In June the northern hemisphere is tilted towards the sun and it is the northern summer – days are longer and it is generally warmer. The southern hemisphere is pointing away from the sun. It is cooler and the days are shorter – the southern winter. In December the reverse is the case.

Equinox – One of the two times in the year when day and night are of equal length, owing to the Sun being overhead at the Equator.

Solstice – One of the two times in the year, midway between the two equinoxes, when the Sun is overhead at one of the Tropics (Cancer or Capricorn) and is at its highest latitude from the Equator (23½° North or South).

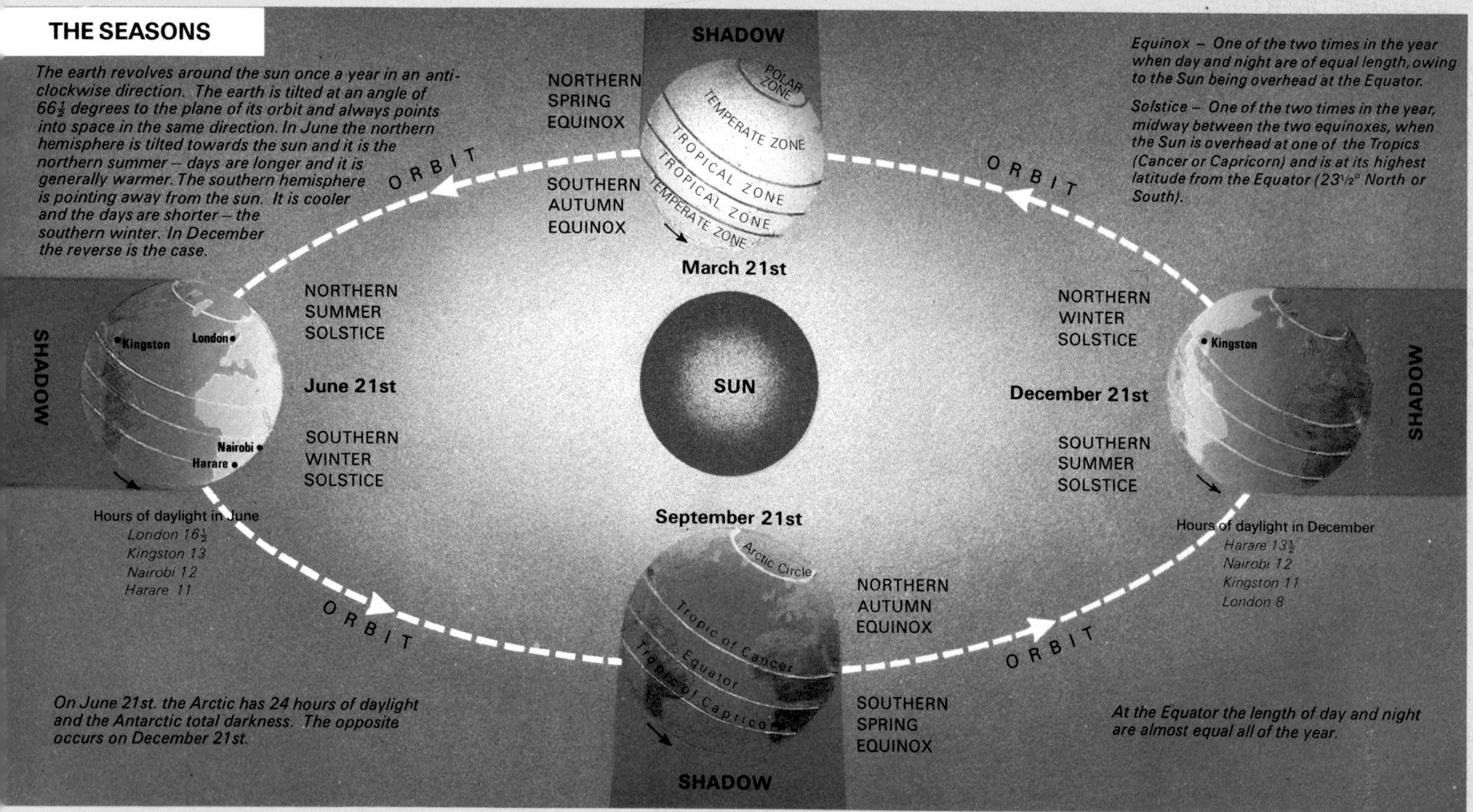

SHADOW

NORTHERN SPRING EQUINOX

SOUTHERN AUTUMN EQUINOX

POLAR ZONE

TEMPERATE ZONE

TROPICAL ZONE

TROPICAL ZONE

TEMPERATE ZONE

March 21st

ORBIT

ORBIT

NORTHERN SUMMER SOLSTICE

June 21st

SOUTHERN WINTER SOLSTICE

SHADOW

Kingston

London

Nairobi

Harare

SUN

NORTHERN WINTER SOLSTICE

December 21st

SOUTHERN SUMMER SOLSTICE

Kingston

SHADOW

Hours of daylight in June
London $16\frac{1}{2}$
Kingston 13
Nairobi 12
Harare 11

Hours of daylight in December
Harare $13\frac{1}{2}$
Nairobi 12
Kingston 11
London 8

September 21st

Arctic Circle

Tropic of Cancer

Equator

Tropic of Capricorn

NORTHERN AUTUMN EQUINOX

SOUTHERN SPRING EQUINOX

SHADOW

ORBIT

ORBIT

On June 21st. the Arctic has 24 hours of daylight and the Antarctic total darkness. The opposite occurs on December 21st.

At the Equator the length of day and night are almost equal all of the year.

LENGTH OF DAY AND NIGHT ON THE EARTH

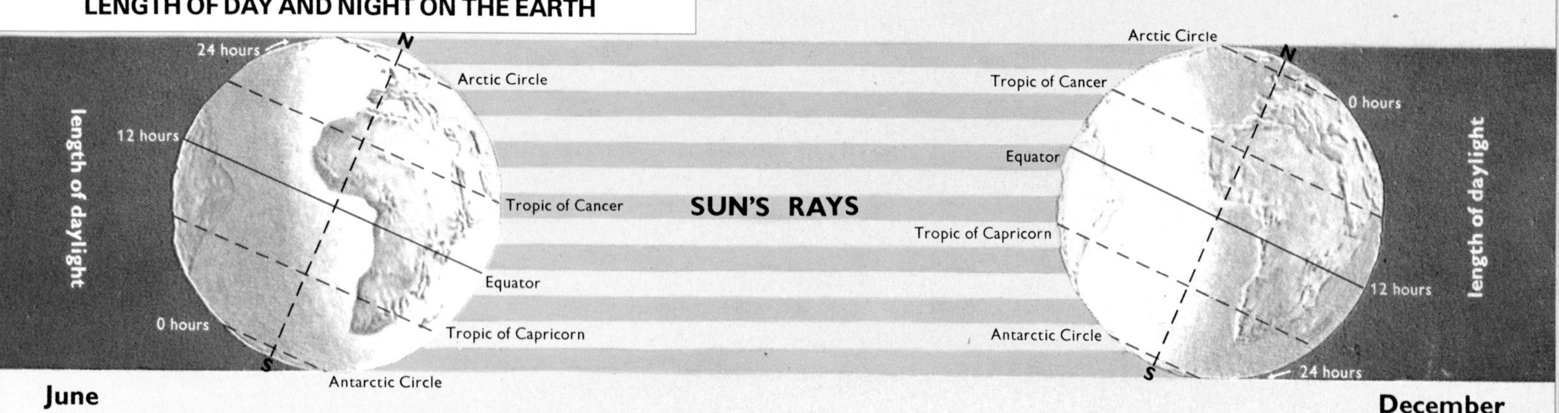

TIME

The Year *– the time taken by the Earth to revolve around the Sun, or 365¼ days.*

The Month *– the approximate time taken by the Moon to revolve around the Earth. The twelve months of the year in fact vary from 28 (29 in a Leap Year) to 31 days.*

The Week *– an artificial period of 7 days, not based on astronomical time.*

The Day *– the time taken by the Earth to complete one rotation on its axis.*

The Hour *– 24 hours make one day. Usually the day is divided into hours A.M. (ante meridiem or before noon) and P.M. (post meridiem or after noon), although most timetables now use the 24-hour system, from midnight to midnight, for example, 1p.m. = 13.00 hours.*

SUNRISE AND SUNSET

From the diagrams below it is possible to find out the time of sunrise or sunset on a given date and for latitudes between 60°N and 60°S.

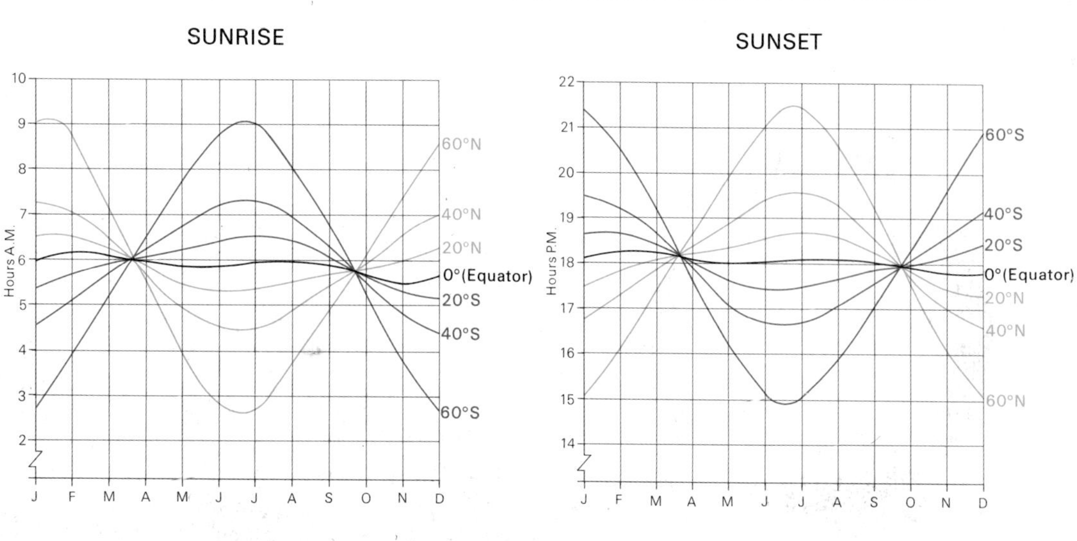

PHILIPS'
MODERN
SCHOOL
ATLAS

Contents

Front Endpaper: Astronomical Geography

British Isles

4 Physical ~ 1:4M
Geology ~ 1:16M
5 Administrative ~ 1:4M
6 Climate
7 Transport
8 Population
9 Agriculture
10 Energy and Industry
11 Employment, Leisure and Trade
12-13 Climate Graphs
14-15 South and South-East England ~ 1:1M
16 South-West England ~ 1:1M
17 Wales ~ 1:1M
18-19 Northern England ~ 1:1M
20-21 Scotland: South ~ 1:1M
22-23 Scotland: North ~ 1:1M
24-25 Ireland ~ 1:1,25M

Europe

26 Physical ~ 1:20M
27 Political ~ 1:20M
28 Climate and Natural Vegetation ~ 1:40M
29 Economic ~ 1:20M
30-31 Themes
32-33 Statistics
34-35 France and Western Europe ~ 1:4M
36 Low Countries and Lower Rhine ~ 1:2M
37 Spain and Portugal ~ 1:5M
38-39 Mediterranean Lands ~ 1:10M
40-41 Italy and the Balkan States ~ 1:5M
42-43 Central Europe ~ 1:5M
44-45 Scandinavia and the Baltic Lands ~ 1:6M
46-47 European Russia and Turkey ~ 1:10M
48-49 Union of Soviet Socialist Republics ~ 1:20M

Asia

50 Physical ~ 1:50M
51 Political ~ 1:50M
52 Climate and Natural Vegetation ~ 1:100M
53 Economic ~ 1:50M
54-55 Statistics (*including Oceania*)
56-57 South-West Asia ~ 1:15M
The Holy Land ~ 1:1,5M
58-59 South Asia ~ 1:10M
60-61 China and Korea ~ 1:15M
62 Japan ~ 1:7,5M
63 South-East Asia ~ 1:15M
64-65 Pacific Ocean ~ 1:54M

Australia and New Zealand

66-67 Australia ~ 1:12M
Political ~ 1:80M
68 Climate and Natural Vegetation ~ 1:60M
69 Economic ~ 1:20M
70 South-East Australia ~ 1:4,5M
71 New Zealand ~ 1:6M
Samoa, Fiji and Tonga Islands ~ 1:12M

Africa

72 Physical ~ 1:40M
73 Political ~ 1:40M
74 Climate and Natural Vegetation ~ 1:80M
75 Economic ~ 1:40M
76-77 Statistics
78-79 Northern Africa ~ 1:15M
80-81 Central and Southern Africa ~ 1:15M

Edited By
B.M. Willett, *Cartographic Editor*
D. Gaylard, *Assistant Cartographic Editor*
and L. Prince-Smith, J. Russell, R. Smith and A. Wells
George Philip and Son Ltd., London.

Maps prepared by
George Philip Cartographic Services Ltd., London under the direction of A.G. Poynter, *Director of Cartography*.

Eighty-third Edition
ISBN 0 540 05528 X (Educational Edition)
0 540 05529 8

Printed in Great Britain by Redwood Offset, Trowbridge

Contents

North America

82 Physical ~ 1:35M
83 Political ~ 1:35M
84 Climate and Natural Vegetation ~ 1:70M
85 Economic ~ 1:32M
86-87 Statistics (*including South America*)
88-89 Canada ~ 1:15M
Alaska ~ 1:30M
90-91 United States ~ 1:12M
Hawaiian Islands ~ 1:10M
92-93 Basin of the St Lawrence and North-East United States ~ 1:6M
94-95 Mexico, Central America and the West Indies ~ 1:15M
Panama Canal ~ 1:1M
Jamaica, Trinidad and Tobago, Leeward and Windward Islands ~ 1:5M

South America

96 Physical ~ 1:30M
97 Political ~ 1:30M
98 Climate and Natural Vegetation ~ 1:70M
99 Economic ~ 1:30M
100-101 South America: North ~ 1:16M
102 South America: South ~ 1:16M

The World

103 Polar Regions ~ 1:50M
104-105 Physical ~ 1:80M
106-107 Structure, Volcanoes and Earthquakes
108-109 Climatic Regions, Soils and Vegetation
110-113 Climate Statistics
114 Temperature and Ocean Currents
115 Pressure, Winds and Annual Precipitation
116-117 Density of Population
118-119 Population of Cities
120 Languages and Religions
121 International Organisations
122-123 Population Trends
124-125 Quality of Life
126-127 Economic Facts of Life
128-129 Political ~ 1:80M
130-131 Time and Distance

Index

Back Endpaper: Map Projections

General Reference

Settlement symbols in order of size

SETTLEMENTS

LONDON Osaka Venice Andropov *Toledo* *Cromer* *Interlaken*

Settlement symbols and type styles vary according to the scale of each map and indicate the importance of towns on the map rather than specific population figures.

ADMINISTRATION

International Boundaries

International Boundaries
(Undemarcated or undefined)

Internal Boundaries

International boundaries show the 'de facto' situation where there are rival claims to territory.

COMMUNICATIONS

Motorways in UK
Principal Roads
Tracks and Seasonal Roads
Road Tunnels
Principal Railways
Railways under construction
Railway Tunnels
Passes
Principal Canals
Principal Oil Pipelines
Principal Airports

PHYSICAL FEATURES

Perennial Streams
Seasonal Streams
Seasonal Lakes and Salt Flats
Swamps and Marshes
Permanent Ice and Glaciers
Wells in Desert
▲ 8848 Elevations in metres
▼ 8050 Sea Depths in metres
1134 Height of Lakes

BRITISH ISLES : Physical

1:4 000 000

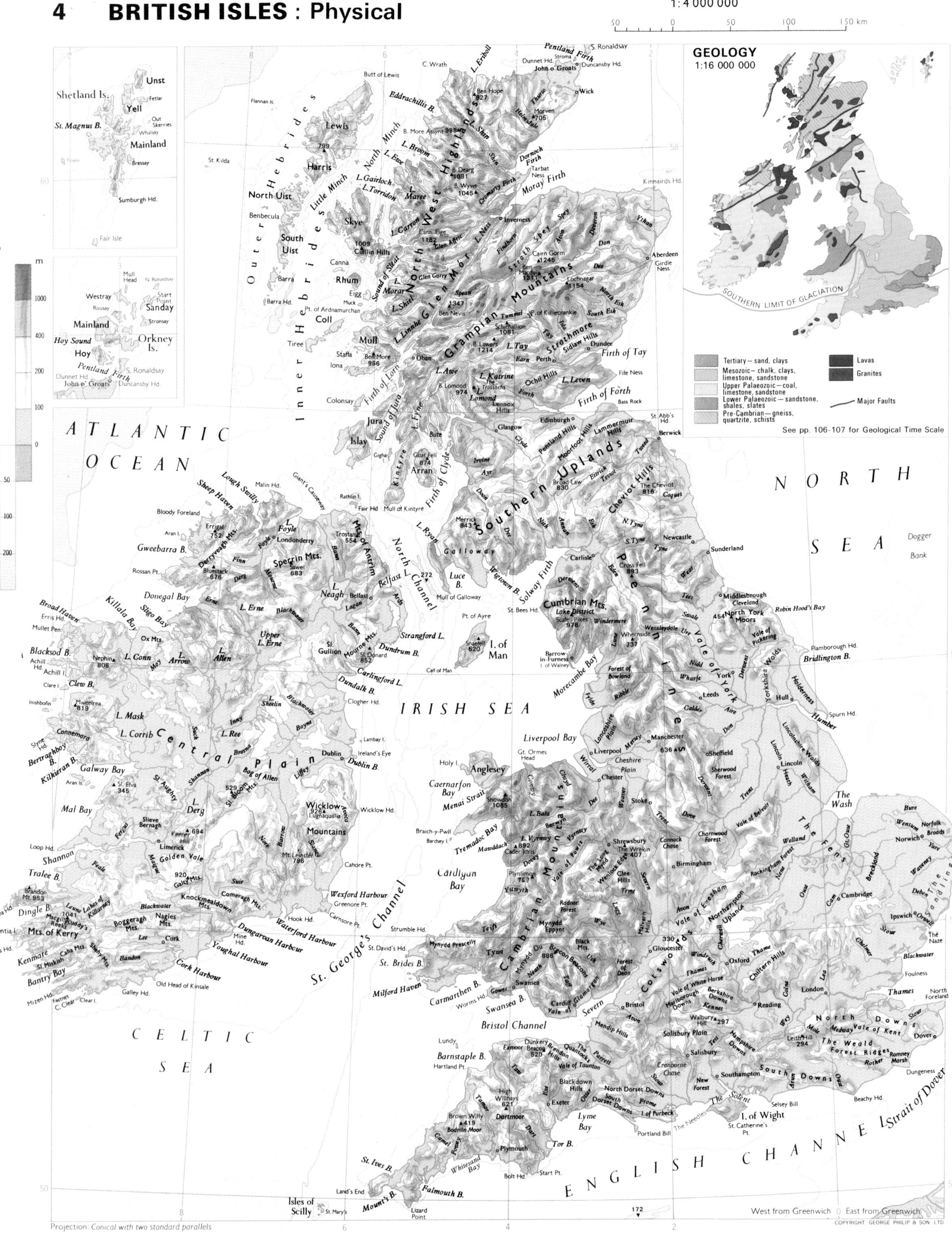

1:4 000 000
50 0 50 100 150 km
The DISTRICTS of Northern Ireland have been numbered and can be identified by reference to this table.
1 Londonderry
2 Limavady
3 Coleraine
4 Ballymoney
5 Moyle
6 Larne
7 Ballymena
8 Magherafelt
9 Cookstown
10 Strabane
11 Omagh
12 Fermanagh
13 Dungannon
14 Craigavon
15 Armagh
16 Newry & Mourne
17 Banbridge
18 Down
19 Lisburn
20 Antrim
21 Newtownabbey
22 Carrickfergus
23 North Down
24 Ards
25 Castlereagh
26 Belfast
Metropolitan Counties :-
On 1st April 1986 the administrative functions of the six metropolitan counties such as planning, education, transportation, libraries and social services were transferred to the city and town boroughs and various non-elected residuary bodies.
ORKNEY
Kirkwall
HIGHLAND
SHETLAND
Lerwick
WESTERN ISLES
Stornoway
HIGHLAND
Inverness
GRAMPIAN
Aberdeen
SCOTLAND
TAYSIDE
Dundee
FIFE
Glenrothes
CENTRAL
Stirling
Edinburgh
LOTHIAN
Glasgow
STRATHCLYDE
Newtown St. Boswells
BORDERS
DUMFRIES AND GALLOWAY
Dumfries
NORTHUMBERLAND
Newcastle
TYNE AND WEAR
Durham
Carlisle
DURHAM
CLEVELAND
Middlesbrough
CUMBRIA
Northallerton
NORTH YORKSHIRE
ISLE OF MAN
Douglas
ATLANTIC OCEAN
North Channel
NORTH SEA
IRISH SEA
St. George's Channel
CELTIC SEA
ENGLISH CHANNEL
Lifford
DONEGAL
Londonderry
Antrim
NORTHERN IRELAND
Tyrone
Belfast
Down
Fermanagh
Armagh
Sligo
LEITRIM
SLIGO
Monaghan
MONAGHAN
Carrick-on-Shannon
Cavan
CAVAN
Dundalk
LOUTH
MAYO
Castlebar
ROSCOMMON
Roscommon
Longford
LONGFORD
Mullingar
WESTMEATH
An Uaimh (Navan)
MEATH
DUBLIN
Dublin
GALWAY
Galway
OFFALY
Tullamore
KILDARE
Naas
IRELAND
Port Laoise
LAOIS
Wicklow
WICKLOW
CLARE
Ennis
Limerick
Kilkenny
Carlow
CARLOW
TIPPERARY
KILKENNY
LIMERICK
WEXFORD
Wexford
Clonmel
Tralee
KERRY
WATERFORD
Waterford
CORK
Cork
LANCASHIRE
Preston
WEST YORKSHIRE
Wakefield
HUMBERSIDE
Hull
GREATER MANCHESTER
Barnsley
SOUTH YORKSHIRE
MERSEYSIDE
Manchester
Liverpool
ENGLAND
Lincoln
LINCOLNSHIRE
DERBYSHIRE
NOTTINGHAMSHIRE
Nottingham
Chester
CHESHIRE
Matlock
Caernarfon
Mold
CLWYD
GWYNEDD
Stafford
STAFFORDSHIRE
Shrewsbury
SHROPSHIRE
Leicester
LEICESTERSHIRE
NORFOLK
Norwich
WEST MIDLANDS
Birmingham
WALES
POWYS
WARWICKSHIRE
Warwick
NORTHAMPTONSHIRE
Northampton
CAMBRIDGESHIRE
Cambridge
SUFFOLK
Ipswich
HEREFORD AND WORCESTER
Worcester
Llandrindod Wells
Bedford
BEDFORDSHIRE
DYFED
Carmarthen
Gloucester
GLOUCESTERSHIRE
BUCKINGHAMSHIRE
Aylesbury
Hertford
HERTFORDSHIRE
ESSEX
Chelmsford
Oxford
OXFORDSHIRE
WEST GLAMORGAN
Swansea
GWENT
Cwmbran
MID GLAMORGAN
Cardiff
Bristol
SOUTH GLAMORGAN
AVON
GREATER LONDON
Reading
Kingston
BERKSHIRE
WILTSHIRE
Trowbridge
SURREY
Maidstone
KENT
SOMERSET
Taunton
HAMPSHIRE
Winchester
WEST SUSSEX
EAST SUSSEX
Lewes
Chichester
DEVON
Exeter
DORSET
Dorchester
Newport
ISLE OF WIGHT
CORNWALL
Truro
FRANCE
o Norwich Administrative headquarters
MERSEYSIDE Metropolitan counties
Antrim Former Northern Ireland counties
Projection: Conical with two standard parallels
West from Greenwich 0 East from Greenwich

January Temperature

Actual surface temperature

°C: 7, 6, 5, 4, 3, 2, 1, 0

Sunshine

453 Average duration of bright sunshine in hours November - April

January isotherms reduced to sea-level °Celsius

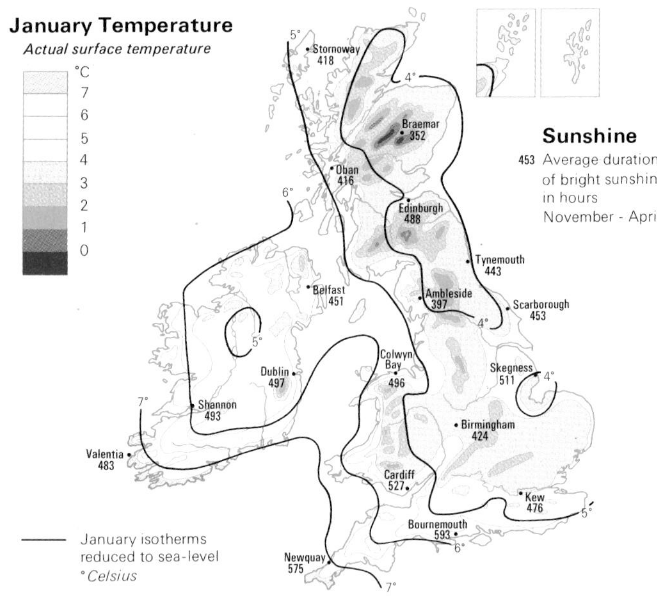

July Temperature

Actual surface temperature

°C: 17, 16, 15, 14, 13, 12, 11, 10

Sunshine

944 Average duration of bright sunshine in hours May - October

July isotherms reduced to sea-level °Celsius

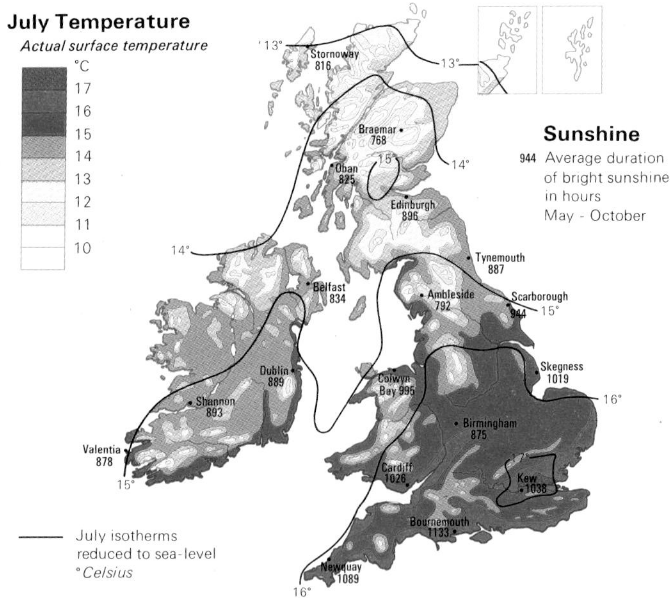

Annual Rainfall

mm: 2500, 2000, 1500, 1000, 750, 625

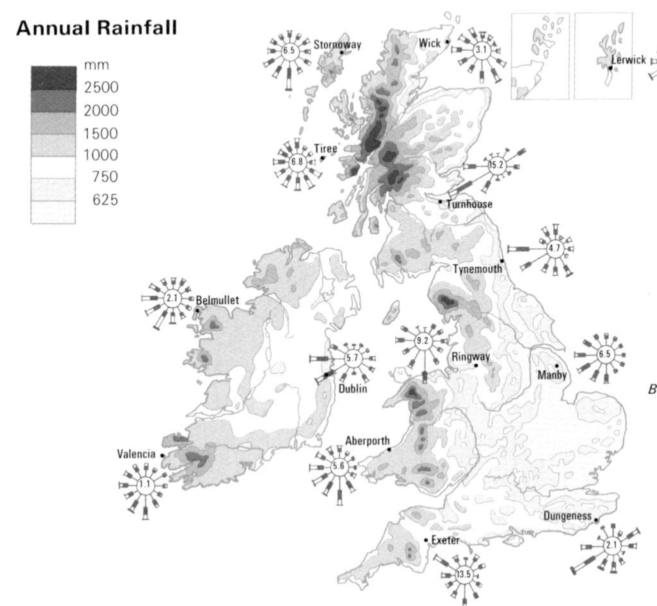

Wind

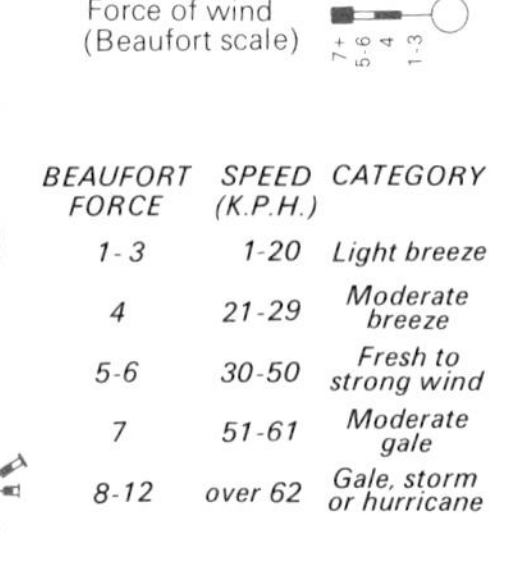

BEAUFORT FORCE	SPEED (K.P.H.)	CATEGORY
1-3	1-20	Light breeze
4	21-29	Moderate breeze
5-6	30-50	Fresh to strong wind
7	51-61	Moderate gale
8-12	over 62	Gale, storm or hurricane

Snow

Average number of mornings with snow cover per year

more than 50, 20-50, 15-20, 10-15, 5-10, less than 5

(after Manley, 1970)

Frost

—5— Mean length of frost free period in months

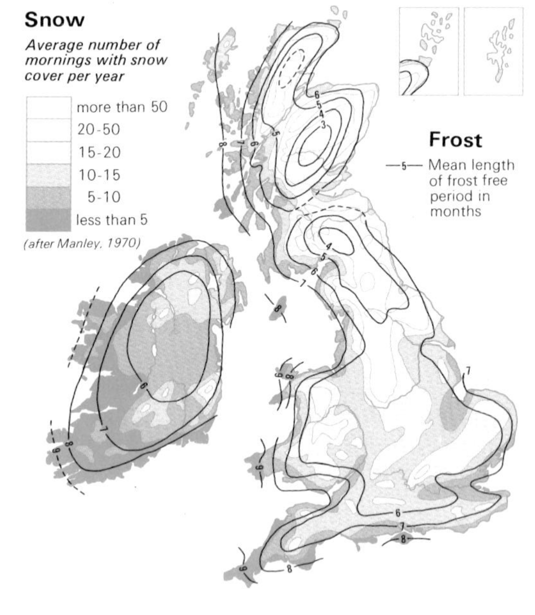

Variability of Rain

The percentage frequency with which rainfall varies from the normal rainfall regime in an area: the higher the percentage figure, the more variable the rainfall.

over 20%, 18-20%, 16-18%, 14-16%, 12-14%, 10-12%, under 10%

(after Gregory, 1955)

Rainfall is least variable in the wetter northern and western areas and most variable in the drier eastern and southern areas

Regions of reliably high rainfall (more than 1250mm in at least 70% of the years)

Regions of occasionally low rainfall (less than 750mm in at least 30% of the years)

Synoptic Chart for a Typical Winter Depression

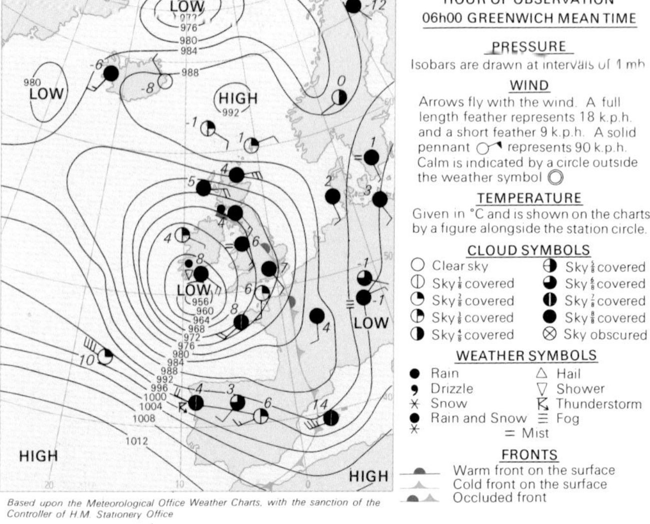

HOUR OF OBSERVATION 06h00 GREENWICH MEAN TIME

PRESSURE

Isobars are drawn at intervals of 1 mb

WIND

Arrows fly with the wind. A full length feather represents 18 k.p.h. and a short feather 9 k.p.h. A solid pennant represents 90 k.p.h. Calm is indicated by a circle outside the weather symbol

TEMPERATURE

Given in °C and is shown on the charts by a figure alongside the station circle.

CLOUD SYMBOLS

Clear sky; Sky ⅛ covered; Sky ¼ covered; Sky ⅜ covered; Sky ½ covered; Sky ⅝ covered; Sky ¾ covered; Sky ⅞ covered; Sky covered; Sky obscured

WEATHER SYMBOLS

Rain; Drizzle; Snow; Rain and Snow; Hail; Shower; Thunderstorm; Fog; Mist

FRONTS

Warm front on the surface; Cold front on the surface; Occluded front

Based upon the Meteorological Office Weather Charts, with the sanction of the Controller of H.M. Stationery Office

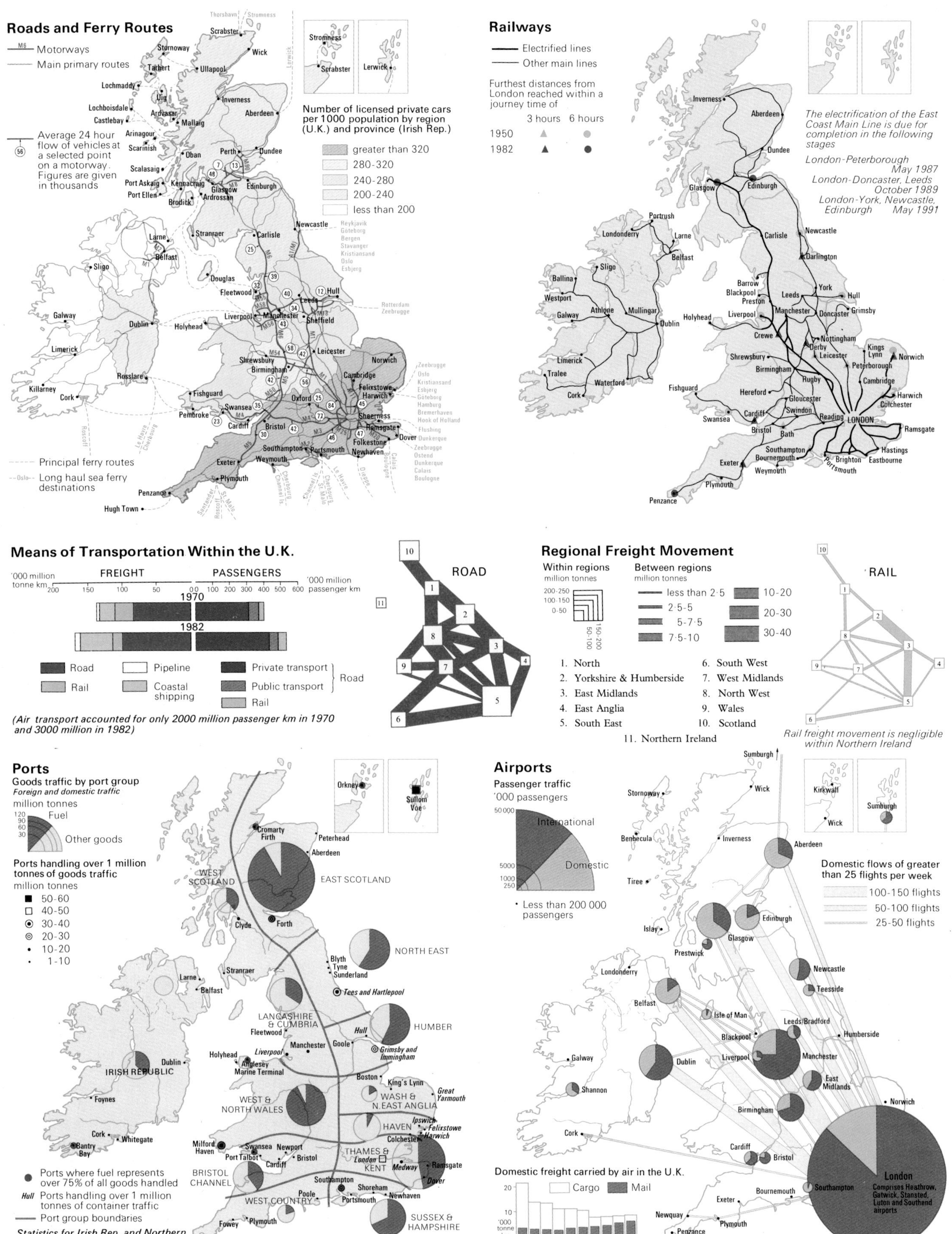
Roads and Ferry Routes
M6 Motorways
Main primary routes
Average 24 hour flow of vehicles at a selected point on a motorway. Figures are given in thousands
Principal ferry routes
Oslo Long haul sea ferry destinations
Number of licensed private cars per 1000 population by region (U.K.) and province (Irish Rep.)
greater than 320
280-320
240-280
200-240
less than 200
Railways
Electrified lines
Other main lines
Furthest distances from London reached within a journey time of
3 hours 6 hours
1950
1982
The electrification of the East Coast Main Line is due for completion in the following stages
London-Peterborough May 1987
London-Doncaster, Leeds October 1989
London-York, Newcastle, Edinburgh May 1991
Means of Transportation Within the U.K.
'000 million tonne km
FREIGHT
PASSENGERS
'000 million passenger km
1970
1982
Road
Rail
Pipeline
Coastal shipping
Private transport
Public transport
Rail
Road
(Air transport accounted for only 2000 million passenger km in 1970 and 3000 million in 1982)
ROAD
Regional Freight Movement
Within regions
million tonnes
Between regions
million tonnes
less than 2·5
2·5-5
5-7·5
7·5-10
10-20
20-30
30-40
1. North
2. Yorkshire & Humberside
3. East Midlands
4. East Anglia
5. South East
6. South West
7. West Midlands
8. North West
9. Wales
10. Scotland
11. Northern Ireland
RAIL
Rail freight movement is negligible within Northern Ireland
Ports
Goods traffic by port group
Foreign and domestic traffic
million tonnes
Fuel
Other goods
Ports handling over 1 million tonnes of goods traffic
million tonnes
50-60
40-50
30-40
20-30
10-20
1-10
Ports where fuel represents over 75% of all goods handled
Hull Ports handling over 1 million tonnes of container traffic
Port group boundaries
Statistics for Irish Rep. and Northern Ireland do not include domestic traffic
EAST SCOTLAND
WEST SCOTLAND
NORTH EAST
LANCASHIRE & CUMBRIA
HUMBER
IRISH REPUBLIC
WEST & NORTH WALES
WASH & N.EAST ANGLIA
HAVEN
THAMES & KENT
BRISTOL CHANNEL
WEST COUNTRY
SUSSEX & HAMPSHIRE
Airports
Passenger traffic
'000 passengers
International
Domestic
Less than 200 000 passengers
Domestic flows of greater than 25 flights per week
100-150 flights
50-100 flights
25-50 flights
London
Comprises Heathrow, Gatwick, Stansted, Luton and Southend airports
Domestic freight carried by air in the U.K.
Cargo
Mail
'000 tonne km
1974 '75 '76 '77 '78 '79 '80 '81 '82 '83

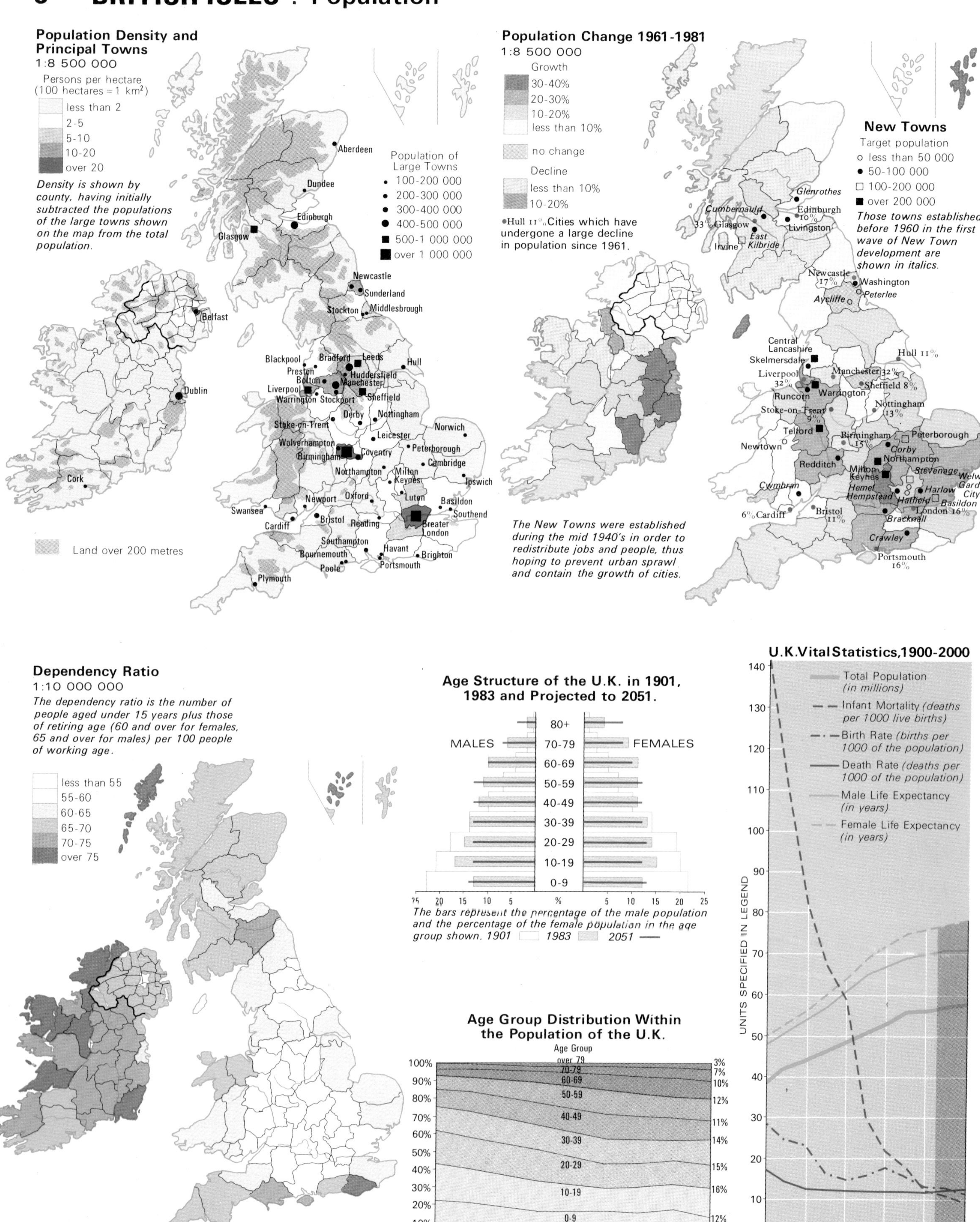
Population Density and Principal Towns
1:8 500 000
Persons per hectare (100 hectares = 1 km²)
less than 2
2-5
5-10
10-20
over 20
Density is shown by county, having initially subtracted the populations of the large towns shown on the map from the total population.
Population of Large Towns
100-200 000
200-300 000
300-400 000
400-500 000
500-1 000 000
over 1 000 000
Land over 200 metres
Aberdeen
Dundee
Edinburgh
Glasgow
Belfast
Dublin
Cork
Newcastle
Sunderland
Stockton
Middlesbrough
Blackpool
Bradford
Leeds
Hull
Preston
Bolton
Huddersfield
Manchester
Liverpool
Warrington
Stockport
Sheffield
Derby
Nottingham
Stoke-on-Trent
Norwich
Leicester
Wolverhampton
Peterborough
Birmingham
Coventry
Cambridge
Northampton
Milton Keynes
Ipswich
Newport
Oxford
Luton
Basildon
Swansea
Bristol
Reading
Southend
Cardiff
Greater London
Southampton
Havant
Bournemouth
Brighton
Portsmouth
Poole
Plymouth
Population Change 1961-1981
1:8 500 000
Growth
30-40%
20-30%
10-20%
less than 10%
no change
Decline
less than 10%
10-20%
Hull 11% Cities which have undergone a large decline in population since 1961.
The New Towns were established during the mid 1940's in order to redistribute jobs and people, thus hoping to prevent urban sprawl and contain the growth of cities.
New Towns
Target population
less than 50 000
50-100 000
100-200 000
over 200 000
Those towns established before 1960 in the first wave of New Town development are shown in italics.
Glenrothes
Cumbernauld
Edinburgh 10%
33% Glasgow
Livingston
East Kilbride
Irvine
Newcastle 17%
Washington
Peterlee
Aycliffe
Central Lancashire
Skelmersdale
Hull 11%
Liverpool 32%
Manchester 32%
Sheffield 8%
Runcorn
Warrington
Stoke-on-Trent 9%
Nottingham 13%
Telford
Birmingham 15%
Peterborough
Newtown
Corby
Northampton
Redditch
Milton Keynes
Stevenage
Welwyn Garden City
Hemel Hempstead
Harlow
Hatfield
Basildon
Cwmbran
London 16%
6% Cardiff
Bristol 11%
Bracknell
Crawley
Portsmouth 16%
Dependency Ratio
1:10 000 000
The dependency ratio is the number of people aged under 15 years plus those of retiring age (60 and over for females, 65 and over for males) per 100 people of working age.
less than 55
55-60
60-65
65-70
70-75
over 75
Age Structure of the U.K. in 1901, 1983 and Projected to 2051.
MALES
FEMALES
80+
70-79
60-69
50-59
40-49
30-39
20-29
10-19
0-9
25 20 15 10 5 % 5 10 15 20 25
The bars represent the percentage of the male population and the percentage of the female population in the age group shown. 1901 1983 2051
Age Group Distribution Within the Population of the U.K.
Age Group
over 79
70-79
60-69
50-59
40-49
30-39
20-29
10-19
0-9
100%
90%
80%
70%
60%
50%
40%
30%
20%
10%
3%
7%
10%
12%
11%
14%
15%
16%
12%
1983
1901 1911 1921 1931 1941 1951 1961 1971 1981
U.K. Vital Statistics, 1900-2000
Total Population (in millions)
Infant Mortality (deaths per 1000 live births)
Birth Rate (births per 1000 of the population)
Death Rate (deaths per 1000 of the population)
Male Life Expectancy (in years)
Female Life Expectancy (in years)
UNITS SPECIFIED IN LEGEND
140
130
120
110
100
90
80
70
60
50
40
30
20
10
1900 1920 1940 1960 1980 2000

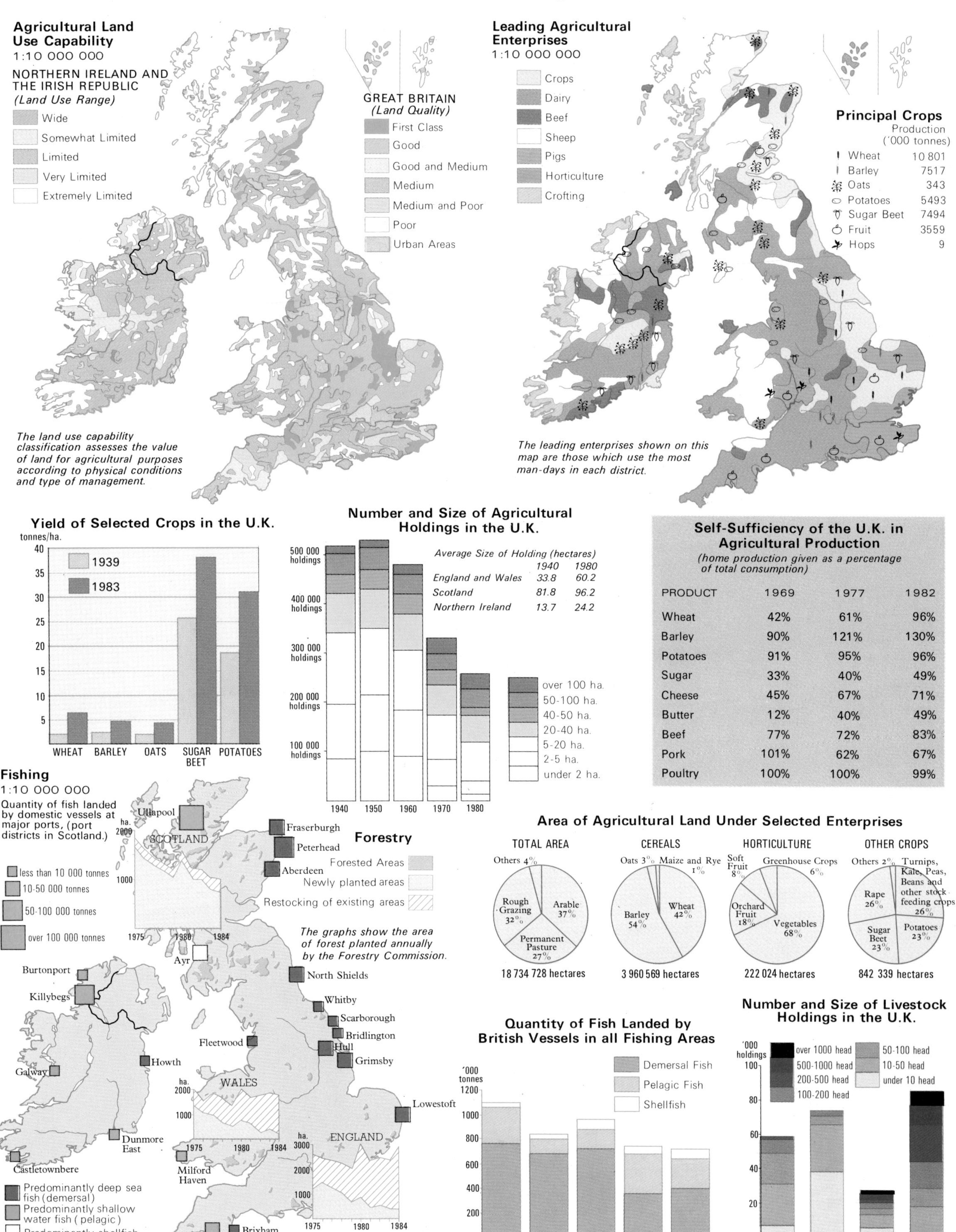

Self-Sufficiency of the U.K. in Agricultural Production

(home production given as a percentage of total consumption)

PRODUCT	1969	1977	1982
Wheat	42%	61%	96%
Barley	90%	121%	130%
Potatoes	91%	95%	96%
Sugar	33%	40%	49%
Cheese	45%	67%	71%
Butter	12%	40%	49%
Beef	77%	72%	83%
Pork	101%	62%	67%
Poultry	100%	100%	99%

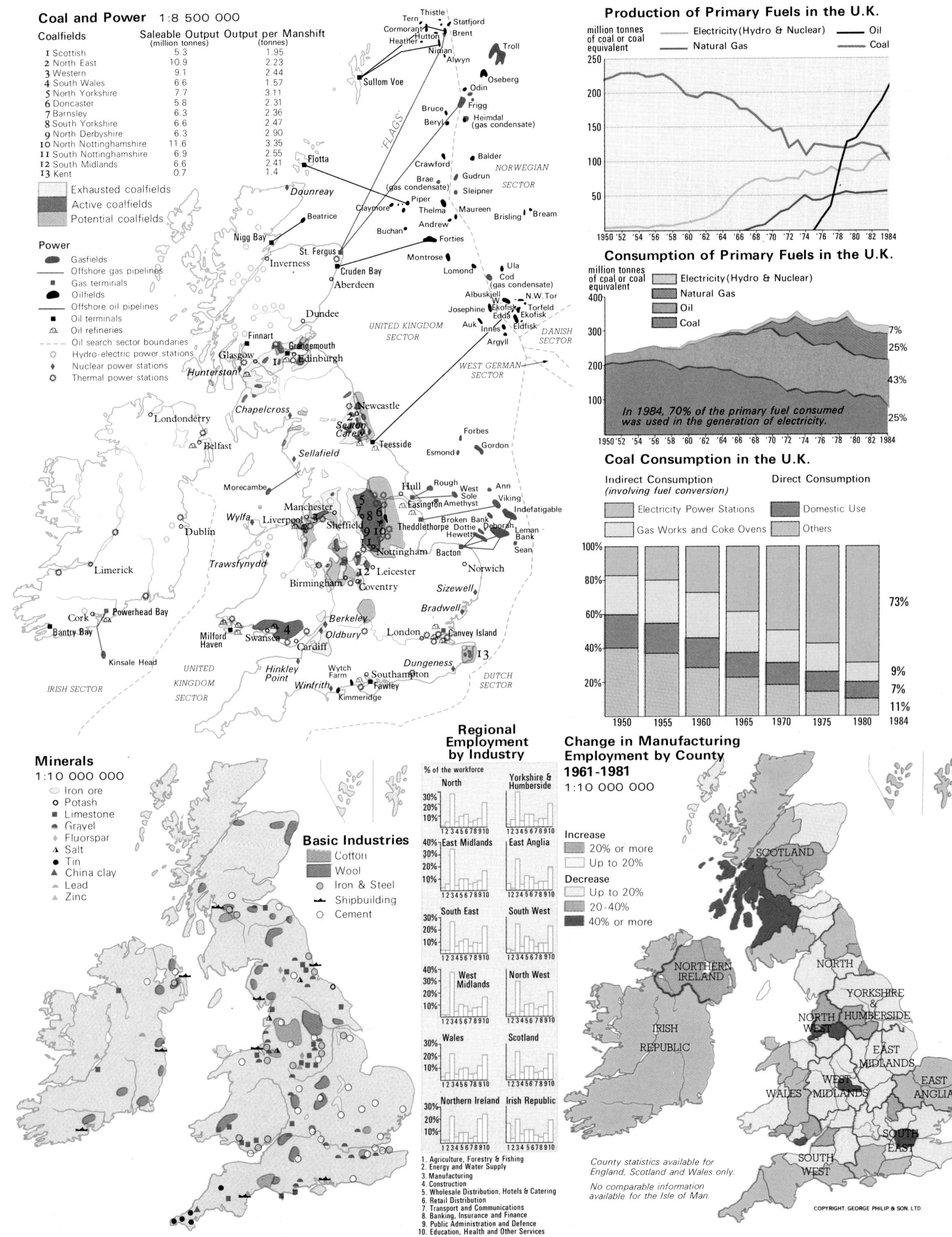

Coalfields	Saleable Output (million tonnes)	Output per Manshift (tonnes)
1 Scottish	5.3	1.95
2 North East	10.9	2.23
3 Western	9.1	2.44
4 South Wales	6.6	1.57
5 North Yorkshire	7.7	3.11
6 Doncaster	5.8	2.31
7 Barnsley	6.3	2.36
8 South Yorkshire	6.6	2.47
9 North Derbyshire	6.3	2.90
10 North Nottinghamshire	11.6	3.35
11 South Nottinghamshire	6.9	2.55
12 South Midlands	6.6	2.41
13 Kent	0.7	1.4

Employment in the U.K. by Industry

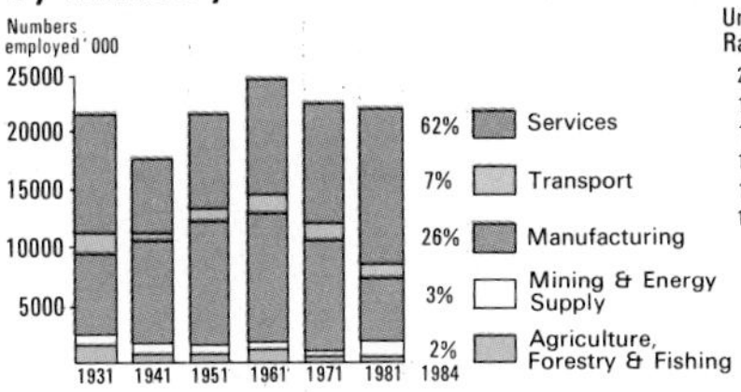

Numbers employed '000
25000
20000
15000
10000
5000
1931 1941 1951 1961 1971 1981 1984
62% Services
7% Transport
26% Manufacturing
3% Mining & Energy Supply
2% Agriculture, Forestry & Fishing

Unemployment Rates for Selected Regions

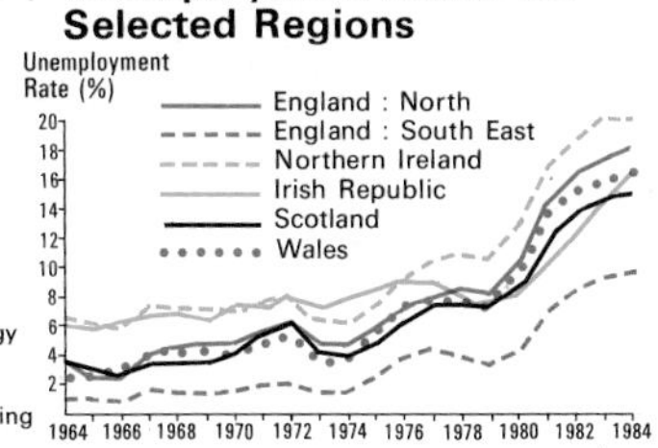

Unemployment Rate (%)
England : North
England : South East
Northern Ireland
Irish Republic
Scotland
Wales
1964 1966 1968 1970 1972 1974 1976 1978 1980 1982 1984

Leisure

1:8 500 000

National Parks
National Park Direction Areas (Scotland)
National Forest Parks
Areas of Outstanding Natural Beauty (England & Wales)
National Scenic Areas (Scotland)
Coastal Conservation Zones (Scotland)
Heritage Coasts (England & Wales)
Long Distance Footpaths
Navigable Waterways
Canals
Loch Torridon
Glen Affric
Speyside Way
GLENMORE
Cairngorm
Glen Nevis and Glencoe
Trossachs
QUEEN ELIZABETH
ARGYLL
West Highland Way
Southern Upland Way
GLEN TROOL
BORDER
Northumberland
Pennine Way
Lake District
Yorkshire Dales
North York Moors
Cleveland Way
Wolds Way
Millenium Way
Forest of Bowland
Peak District
Lincolnshire Wolds
The Broads
Snowdonia
Offa's Dyke Path
Brecon Beacons
FOREST OF DEAN
Cotswolds
Ridgeway
Chilterns
North Downs Way
South Downs Way
NEW FOREST
Exmoor
Dartmoor
South-West Peninsula Path
Pembrokeshire Coast
Pembrokeshire Coast Path
Glenveagh
The Ulster Way
Connemara
Wicklow Way
South Leinster Way
Killarney
Kerry Way
Shannon
Trent
Great Ouse
Thames

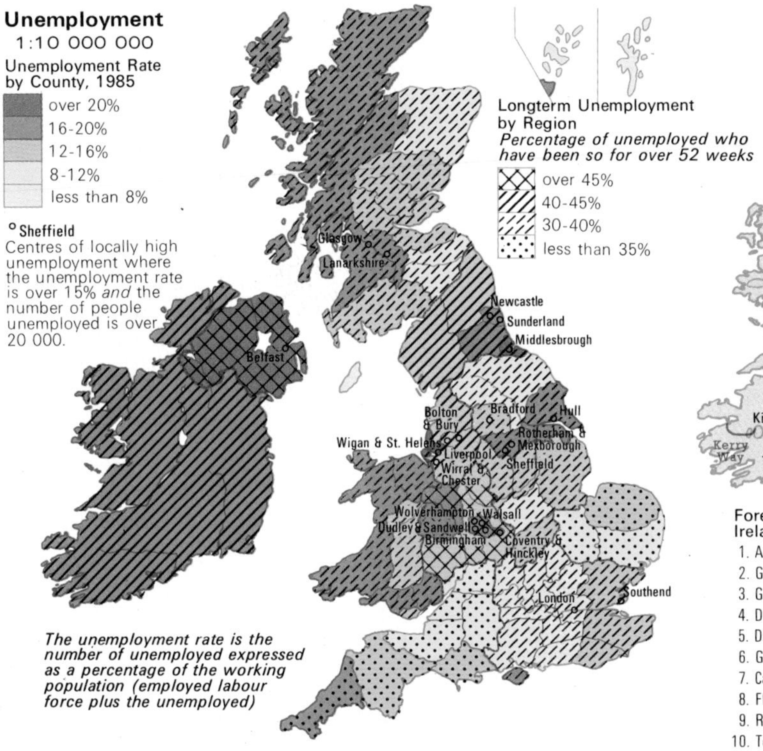

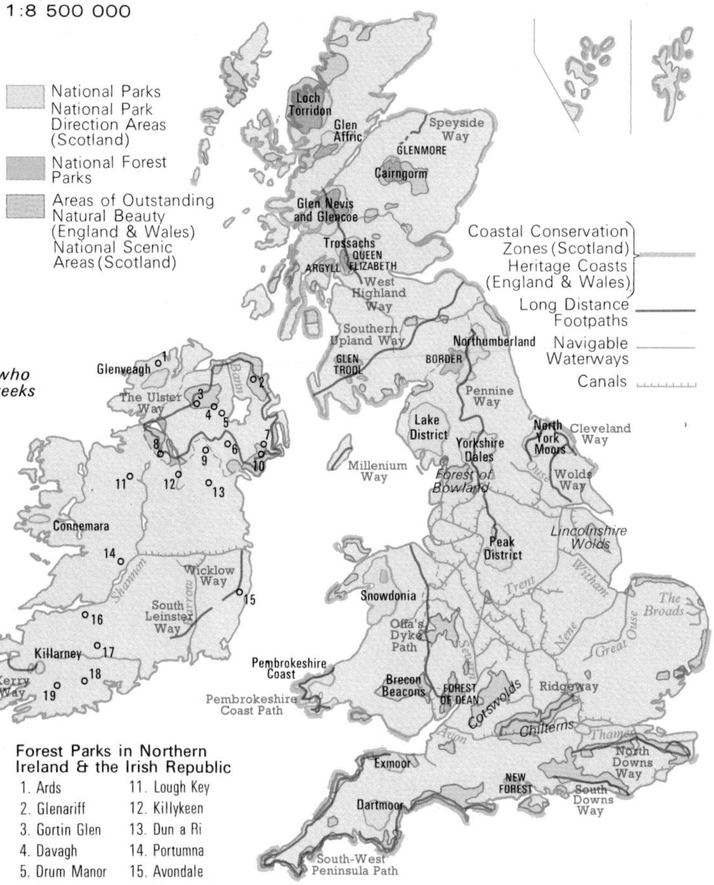

Forest Parks in Northern Ireland & the Irish Republic

1. Ards
2. Glenariff
3. Gortin Glen
4. Davagh
5. Drum Manor
6. Gosford
7. Castlewellan
8. Florence Court
9. Rossmore
10. Tollymore
11. Lough Key
12. Killykeen
13. Dun a Ri
14. Portumna
15. Avondale
16. Curraghase
17. Doneraile
18. Farran
19. Gougane Barra

Unemployment

1:10 000 000

Unemployment Rate by County, 1985
over 20%
16-20%
12-16%
8-12%
less than 8%
Sheffield
Centres of locally high unemployment where the unemployment rate is over 15% *and* the number of people unemployed is over 20 000.
Longterm Unemployment by Region
Percentage of unemployed who have been so for over 52 weeks
over 45%
40-45%
30-40%
less than 35%
Glasgow
Lanarkshire
Belfast
Newcastle
Sunderland
Middlesbrough
Bolton & Bury
Bradford
Hull
Wigan & St. Helens
Liverpool
Wirral & Chester
Rotherham & Mexborough
Sheffield
Wolverhampton
Walsall
Dudley & Sandwell
Birmingham
Coventry & Hinckley
London
Southend

The unemployment rate is the number of unemployed expressed as a percentage of the working population (employed labour force plus the unemployed)

Top Ten Trading Partners with the U.K. by Value of Goods

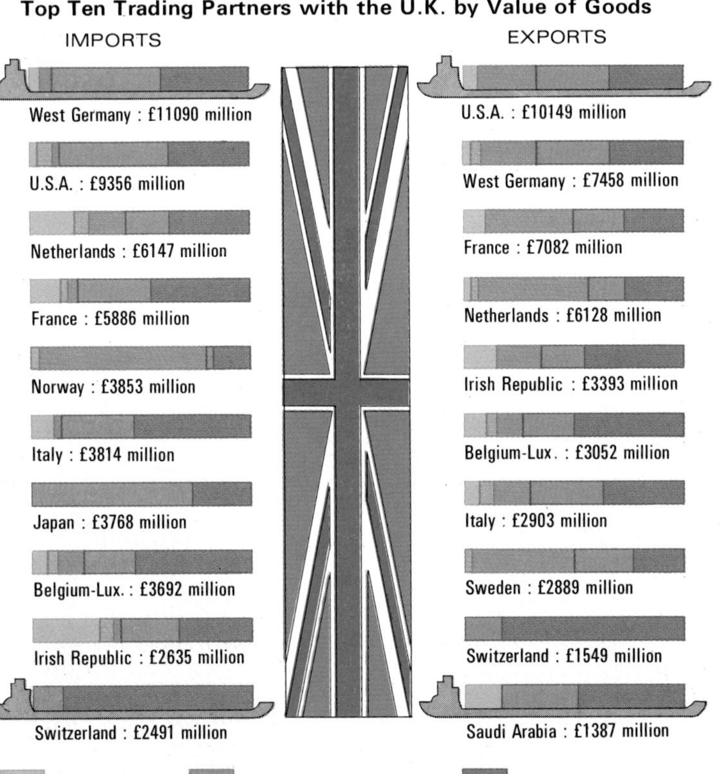

IMPORTS
West Germany : £11090 million
U.S.A. : £9356 million
Netherlands : £6147 million
France : £5886 million
Norway : £3853 million
Italy : £3814 million
Japan : £3768 million
Belgium-Lux. : £3692 million
Irish Republic : £2635 million
Switzerland : £2491 million
EXPORTS
U.S.A. : £10149 million
West Germany : £7458 million
France : £7082 million
Netherlands : £6128 million
Irish Republic : £3393 million
Belgium-Lux. : £3052 million
Italy : £2903 million
Sweden : £2889 million
Switzerland : £1549 million
Saudi Arabia : £1387 million
Food and drink
Raw materials
Fuel
Machinery and equipment
Manufactured goods

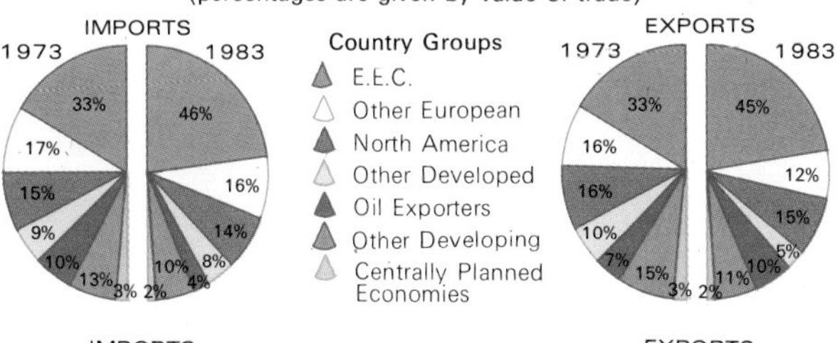

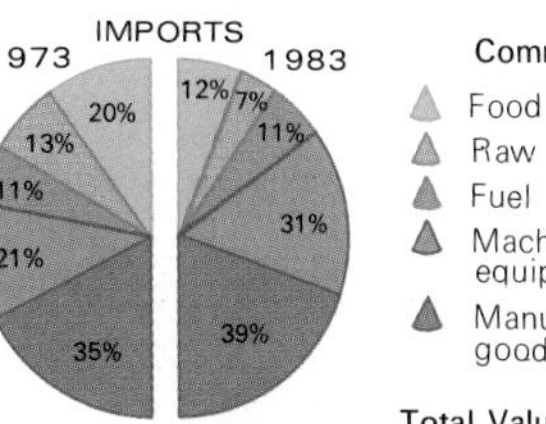

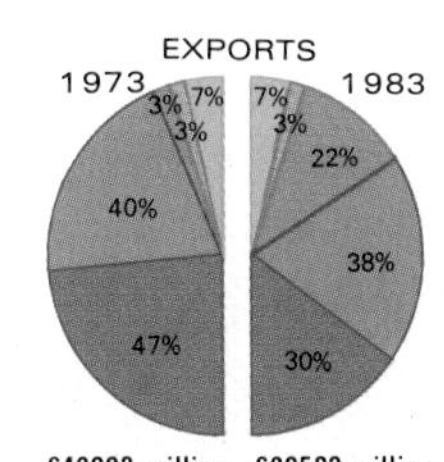

U.K. Trade by Country Group and Commodity Type

(percentages are given by value of trade)

IMPORTS
1973
1983
33%
17%
15%
9%
10%
13%
3%
46%
16%
14%
8%
4%
10%
2%
EXPORTS
1973
1983
33%
16%
16%
10%
7%
15%
3%
45%
12%
15%
5%
10%
11%
2%
Country Groups
E.E.C.
Other European
North America
Other Developed
Oil Exporters
Other Developing
Centrally Planned Economies
IMPORTS
1973
1983
20%
13%
11%
21%
35%
12%
7%
11%
31%
39%
EXPORTS
1973
1983
3%
7%
3%
40%
47%
7%
3%
22%
38%
30%
Commodity
Food and Drink
Raw materials
Fuel
Machinery and equipment
Manufactured goods
Total Value of Trade
(at current prices)
£59841 million
£65993 million
£46002 million
£60533 million

Balance of Payments (£ million)

		1963	1973	1983
CREDITS	Visibles *(Exports)*	4331	11937	60625
	Invisibles	2515	8506	34975
	Total	6846	20443	95600
DEBITS	Visibles *(Imports)*	4450	14523	61341
	Invisibles	2271	6899	31343
	Total	6721	21422	92684
BALANCE		+125	−979	+2916

Visible trade involves transactions of goods while invisible trade involves transactions of money and services.

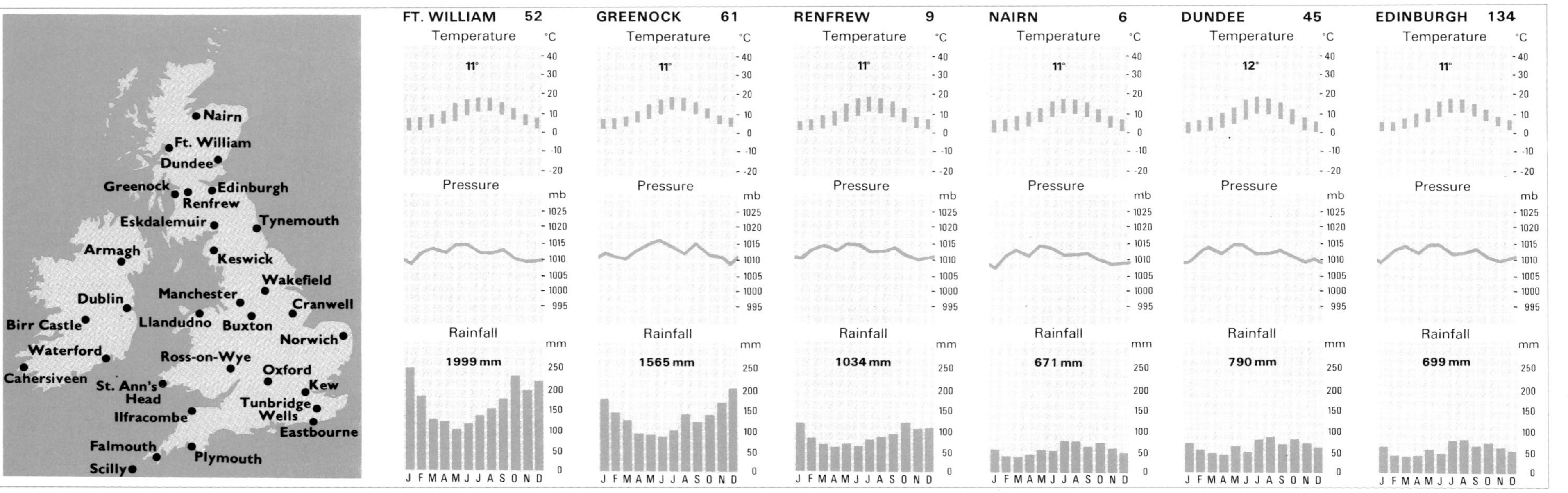

The climate graphs should be used in conjunction with the maps illustrating the climate of the British Isles on page 6. The stations have been selected to show climatic variations throughout the British Isles. On each graph the name of the station is followed by its height in metres above sea level, so that comparisons between stations can be made allowing for elevation. Temperature is shown by a bar, the top of the bar representing the mean monthly maximum and the bottom of the bar the mean monthly minimum temperature. A mid point between these is the mean monthly temperature; the mean annual range of temperature (in degrees Celsius) is given above the graph. The line on the pressure graphs shows the mean monthly pressure (in millibars and reduced to sea level). The rainfall graphs show the average monthly rainfall and above them is given the average total annual rainfall (in millimetres).

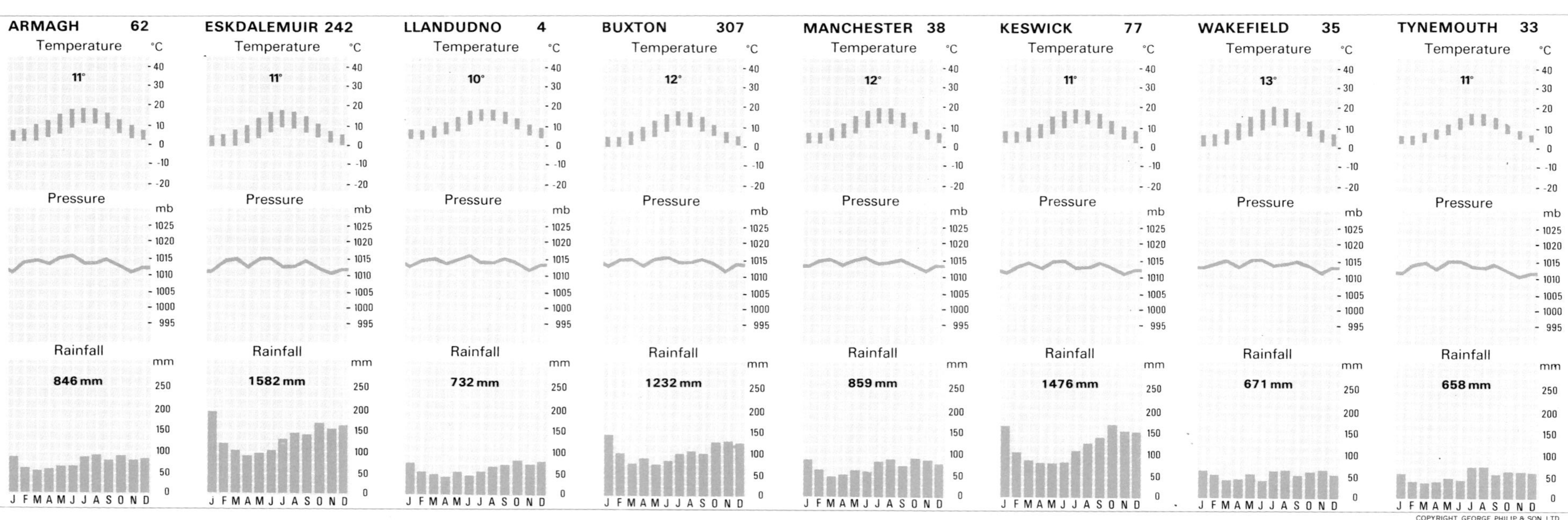

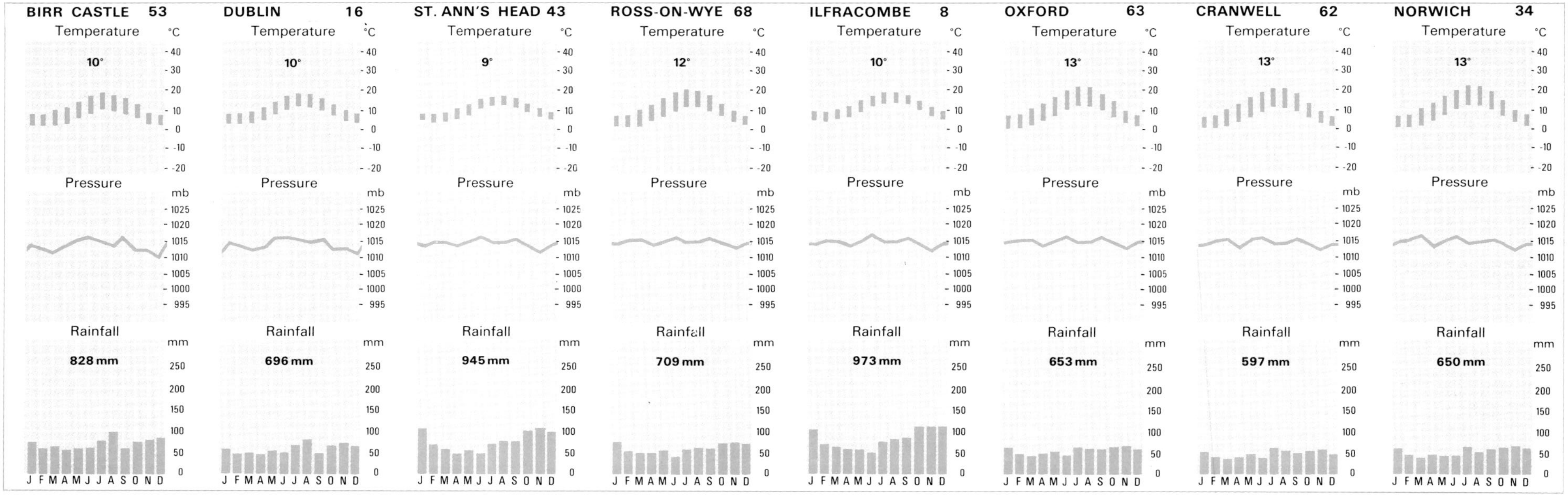

Station	Height	Mean temperature	Annual rainfall
BIRR CASTLE	53	10°	828 mm
DUBLIN	16	10°	696 mm
ST. ANN'S HEAD	43	9°	945 mm
ROSS-ON-WYE	68	12°	709 mm
ILFRACOMBE	8	10°	973 mm
OXFORD	63	13°	653 mm
CRANWELL	62	13°	597 mm
NORWICH	34	13°	650 mm
CAHERSIVEEN	9	8°	1412 mm
WATERFORD	42	10°	1044 mm
SCILLY	50	9°	826 mm
PLYMOUTH	27	10°	960 mm
FALMOUTH	51	10°	1100 mm
KEW (LONDON)	5	13°	610 mm
EASTBOURNE	11	12°	782 mm
TUNBRIDGE WELLS	107	13°	770 mm

Temperature °C: 40, 30, 20, 10, 0, -10, -20
Pressure mb: 1025, 1020, 1015, 1010, 1005, 1000, 995
Rainfall mm: 250, 200, 150, 100, 50, 0
J F M A M J J A S O N D

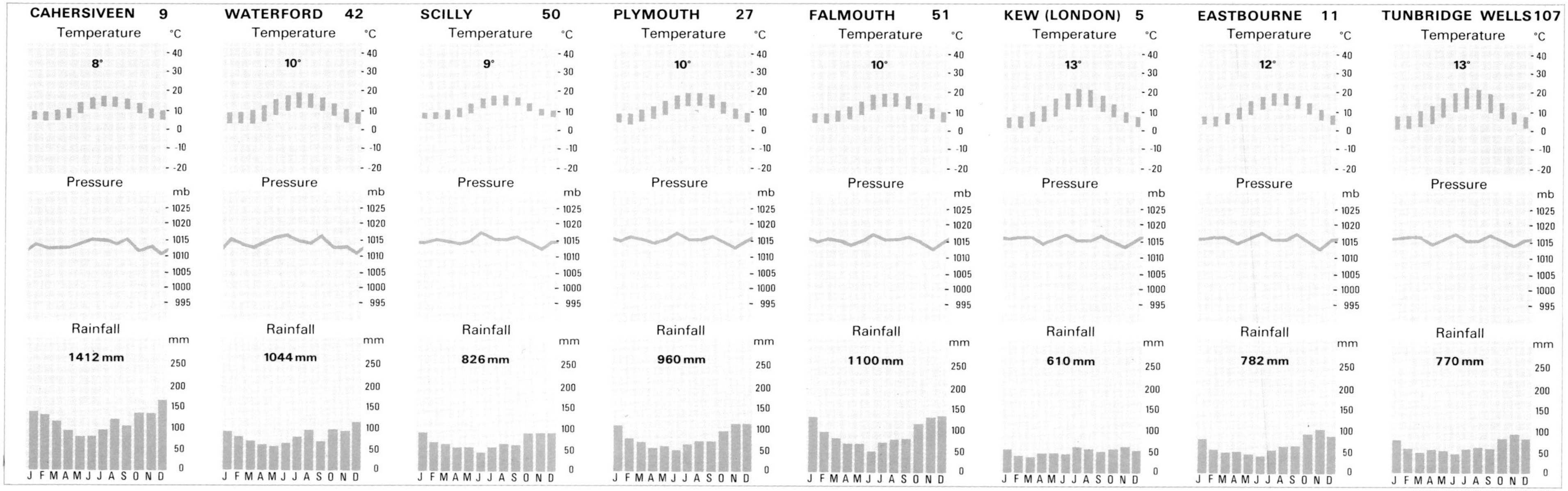

GWYNEDD
Oswestry
Shrewsbury
Telford
Stafford
STAFFORDSHIRE
Burton upon Trent
Long Eaton
Loughborough
Coalville
Welshpool
Machynlleth
Dolgellau
Newtown
Wellington
Cannock
Lichfield
Tamworth
WOLVERHAMPTON
Walsall
Sutton Coldfield
Nuneaton
Hinckley
Dudley
West Bromwich
Smethwick
BIRMINGHAM
Solihull
Bedworth
COVENTRY
Rugby
Kidderminster
Bromsgrove
Redditch
Kenilworth
Warwick
Royal Leamington Spa
SHROPSHIRE
POWYS
WARWICKSHIRE
Stratford-upon-Avon
Knighton
Ludlow
Leominster
HEREFORD AND WORCESTER
Worcester
Droitwich
Evesham
Banbury
Great Malvern
Hereford
DYFED
Llandrindod Wells
Builth Wells
Brecon
Black Mountains
Ross-on-Wye
Tewkesbury
Cheltenham
Gloucester
GLOUCESTERSHIRE
Cirencester
Stroud
Oxford
Abergavenny
Monmouth
Ebbw Vale
Merthyr Tydfil
GWENT
Pontypool
Cwmbran
Newport
Chepstow
Abingdon
Didcot
Wantage
Swindon
Neath
Swansea
Port Talbot
MID GLAMORGAN
WEST GLAMORGAN
Rhondda
Caerphilly
Bridgend
SOUTH GLAMORGAN
CARDIFF
Barry
Penarth
AVON
BRISTOL
Bath
Chippenham
Marlborough
Newbury
Hungerford
BERKSHIRE
Bristol Channel
Weston-super-Mare
Bridgwater Bay
Mendip Hills
Wells
Trowbridge
WILTSHIRE
Salisbury Plain
Devizes
Basingstoke
Andover
Exmoor
Minehead
Quantock Hills
Bridgwater
Glastonbury
SOMERSET
Taunton
Yeovil
Sherborne
Shaftesbury
Salisbury
Winchester
HAMPSHIRE
Eastleigh
SOUTHAMPTON
Portsmouth
Gosport
Tiverton
Blackdown Hills
DEVON
Exeter
Exmouth
Sidmouth
DORSET
Blandford Forum
Wimborne Minster
Ringwood
Christchurch
Poole
Bournemouth
Dorchester
Weymouth
I. of Portland
Bridport
Lyme Regis
Swanage
ISLE OF WIGHT
Newport
Ryde
Shanklin
Ventnor
The Solent
New Forest
Projection: Conical with two standard parallels

1:1 000 000

Based upon the Ordnance Survey Map with the permission of the Controller of Her Majesty's Stationery Office. Crown Copyright Reserved.

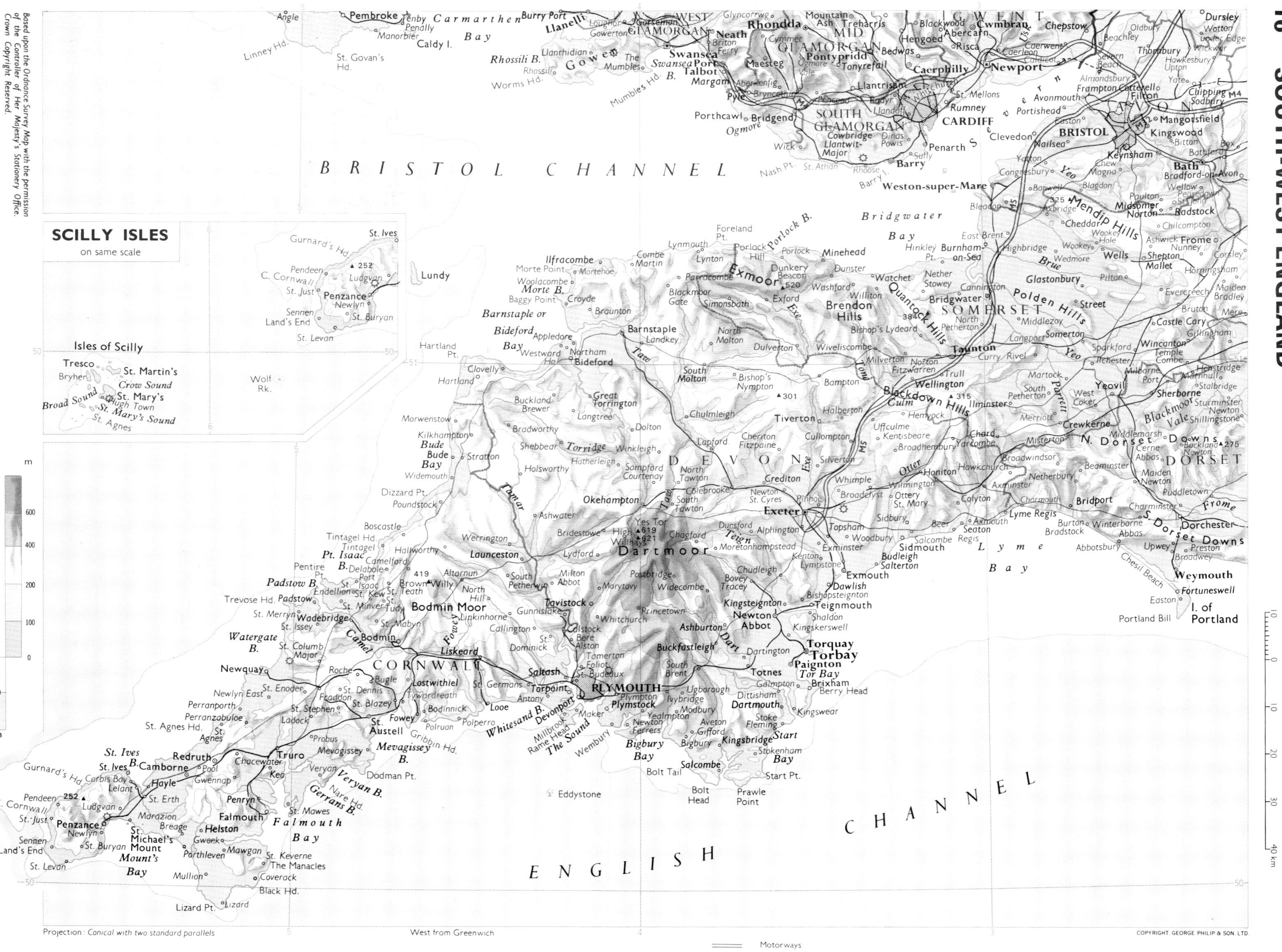
1:1 000 000
10 0 10 20 30 40 km
SCILLY ISLES
on same scale
Isles of Scilly
BRISTOL CHANNEL
ENGLISH CHANNEL
Bridgwater Bay
Lyme Bay
CORNWALL
DEVON
SOMERSET
DORSET
AVON
SOUTH GLAMORGAN
BRISTOL
CARDIFF
PLYMOUTH
Exeter
Dartmoor
Exmoor
Bodmin Moor
Lundy
Projection: Conical with two standard parallels
West from Greenwich
COPYRIGHT GEORGE PHILIP & SON, LTD
Motorways
Motorways under construction

1:1 000 000

10 0 10 20 30 40 km

Projection: Conical with two standard parallels

West from Greenwich

DUMFRIES AND GALLOWAY
Galloway
Cree
Corsock
Maxwelltown
Dumfries
Collin
Dalton
Ecclefechan
Canonbie
Eaglesfield
Crocketford
Newton Stewart
Minnigaff
710
L. Ken
Haugh of Urr
New Abbey
Bankend
Annan
Ruthwell
Gretna Green
Gretna
Cummertrees
Longtown
Roadhead
Smithfield
Brampton
Gilsland
Irthing
HADRIAN'S WALL
Greenhead
Haltwhistle
NORTHUMB
Colwell
Humshaugh
Chollerton
Stamfordham
Haydon Bridge
Tyne
Hexham
Corbridge
Prudhoe
New Luce
Laurieston
Dalbeattie
Criffell
569
Kirkbean
Creetown
Gatehouse of Fleet
Castle Douglas
Ringford
Kirkcowan
Wigtown
Glenluce
Caulkerbush
Solway Firth
P. Carlisle
Bowness-on-Solway
Rockcliffe
Stanwix
Carlisle
Hayton
Wetherall
Cumwhinton
Cold Fell
622
Lambley
S. Tyne
Allen
Catton
Allendale Town
Derwent
Silloth
Kirkbride
Newton Arlosh
Sandhead
Kirkinner
Auchencairn
Kirkcudbright
Dundrennan
Luce Bay
Whauphill
Sorbie
Garlieston
The Machars
Port William
Wigtown Bay
Port Logan
Drummore
Whithorn
Isle of Whithorn
Burrow Hd.
Mull of Galloway
Kirkcudbright B.
Beckfoot
Abbey Town
Wigton
Red Dial
Thursby
Caldew
Croglin
High Hesket
Alston
Allenheads
Collier Law
516
Allonby
Aspatria
Mealsgate
Crosby
Maryport
Ellen
Bothel
High Pike
658
Caldbeck
Lazonby
Kirkoswald
Eden
Melmerby
Cross Fell
893
St. John's Chapel
Wearhead
Weardale
Stanhope
Wolsingham
Fothergill
Flimby
Seaton
Dearham
Broughton
Cockermouth
Skelton
Greystoke
Workington
Harrington
Distington
Parton
Bassenthwaite L.
Great Clifton
Thornthwaite
Skiddaw
931
Greta
Penrith
Pooley Bridge
Threlkeld
Temple Sowerby
Kirkby Thore
Mickle Fell
790
Teesdale
Middleton in Teesdale
Mickleton
Bishop
Whitehaven
Rowrah
Lowes Water
Crummock Water
Keswick
Derwent Water
CUMBRIA
Appleby
Hackthorpe
Ullswater
Hoff
Cotherstone
Frizington
Cleator Moor
Buttermere
Lake
Thirlmere
950
Helvellyn
Patterdale
Shap
M6
Crosby Ravensworth
Brough
St. Bees Head
St. Bees
Ennerdale Water
Egremont
Borrowdale
Kirkstone Pass
Haweswater
Orton
Bowes
Stainmore Forest
Beckermet
Calder Bridge
Scafell Pikes
978
Wast Water
Grasmere L.
Grasmere
Rydal
High Borrow Bridge
Ambleside
District
Gosforth
Boot
Kirkby Stephen
Ravenstonedale
671
Rogans Seat
Arkle
Seascale
Irt
Hawkshead
Windermere
Tebay
Keld
Swale
Reeth
Esk
Coniston
Staveley
Grayrigg
Aisgill
Gt. Shunner Fell
713
Ravenglass
Coniston Water
Bowness-on-Windermere
Torver
Windermere
Kendal
Sedbergh
Askrigg
Garsdale Head
Hawes
Broughton-in-Furness
Bootle
Black Combe
600
Gawthwaite
Newby Bridge
Dent
Wensleydale
Whicham
Millom
Grizebeck
Greenodd
Lindale
Crooklands
Milnthorpe
Whernside
737
Langstrothdale Chase
Kidstones
Great Whernside
704
Haverigg
Ulverston
Cartmel
Kirkby Lonsdale
Ingleborough
693
Pen-y-Ghent
Kettlewell
Duddon R.
Dalton-in-Furness
Cark
Grange-over-Sands
Arnside
Burton
Ingleton
723
Horton in Ribblesdale
Greta
Aldingham
Morecambe
Carnforth
Austwick
Malham Tarn
Vickerstown
Barrow-in-Furness
Furness B.
Bolton-le-Sands
Lune
High Bentham
Settle
Threshfield
Grassington
I. of Walney
Rampside
Morecambe
Caton
Giggleswick
Long Preston
Hellifield
Ribble
Hilpsford Pt.
Heysham
Lancaster
Ward's Stone
560
Bolton Abbey
Galgate
Forest of Bowland
Hodder
Slaidburn
Bolton-by-Bowland
Gargrave
Skipton
Cockerham
Knott End
Pilling
Preesall
Fleetwood
Rossall Pt.
Bleasdale Moors
Garstang
Gisburn
Earby
Silsden
Cleveleys
Thornton
Wyre
Clitheroe
Barnoldswick
Poulton-le-Fylde
LANCASHIRE
Pendle Hill
558
Barrowford
Colne
Keighley
Longridge
Whalley
Brierfield
Nelson
Blackpool
M55
Fulwood
Padiham
Burnley
Haworth
BRADFOR
Queensbury
Kirkham
Preston
Gt. Harwood
Rishton
Accrington
Freckleton
Penwortham
Bamber Bridge
Blackburn
Lytham St. Anne's
Longton
R. Ribble
Oswaldtwistle
Haslingden
Todmorden
Darwen
Rawtenstall
Bacup
Tarleton
Leyland
Croston
Euxton
Southport
Birkdale
Rufford
Burscough Bridge
Chorley
Adlington
Whitworth
Ainsdale
Ormskirk
Coppull
Standish
Horwich
Ramsbottom
Rochdale
Littleborough
Formby
Formby Pt.
Skelmersdale
Wigan
Westhoughton
Bolton
GREATER
Bury
Heywood
Farnworth
Royton
Shaw
Radcliffe
MERSEYSIDE
Maghull
Ashton-in-Makerfield
Hindley
Prestwich
Oldham
Mossley
Crosby
Litherland
Haydock
Atherton
Tyldesley
Middleton
MANCHESTER
Bootle
LIVERPOOL
Kirkby
St. Helens
Leigh
Salford
Ashton under Lyne
Stalybridge
Dukinfield
Glossop
Hyde
New Brighton
Prescot
Newton le Willows
Urmston
Stretford
Wallasey
Hoylake
Huyton
M62
Warrington
Irlam
Sale
Gatley
Marple
West Kirby
Birkenhead
Garston
Widnes
Partington
Altrincham
Cheadle
Stockport
Hazel Grove
New Mills
Heswall
Bebington
Speke
Lymm
Hale
Cheadle Hulme
Whaley Bridge
Port Sunlight
Bromborough
Mersey
Frodsham
Runcorn
M56
Wilmslow
Poynton
Bollington
Neston
Ellesmere Port
Willaston
Knutsford
Alderley Edge
Macclesfield
Weaver
Helsby
Weaverham
Northwich
Connah's Quay
Upton
CHESHIRE
Axe Edge
552
Chester
Kelsall
Winsford
Holmes Chapel
Tarporley
Middlewich
Congleton
Buglawton
Elworth
Sandbach
Biddulph
Dane
Wardle
Crewe
Alsager
Kidsgrove
Leek
Cheddleton
Nantwich
Newcastle-under-Lyme
STOKE ON TRENT
Keele
Cheadle
Audlem
Madeley
Trentham
Blythe Bridge
STAFFORDSHIRE
Rocester
Market Drayton
Stone
Uttoxeter
SHROPSHIRE
Prees
Ellesmere
Whittington
Whitchurch
Malpas
Overton
Chirk
Oswestry
Wrexham
Holt
Hope
Buckley
Mold
Mynydd Isa
Treuddyn
Caergwrle
Brymbo
Minera
Rhosllanerchrugog
Ruabon
Cefn-mawr
Llangollen
Glyn Ceiriog
Llanarmon Dyffryn Ceiriog
Berwyn Mts.
827
Dee
CLWYD
Clwydian Ra.
Ruthin
Llanarmon
Denbigh
Llandyrnog
Llansannan
Bylchau
Flint
Holywell
Mostyn
Northop
Prestatyn
Rhyl
Kinmel Bay
Rhuddlan
Clwyd
St. Asaph
Henllan
Llanfair Talhaiarn
Llangerniew
Abergele
Old Colwyn
Colwyn Bay
Rhos-on-Sea
Llandudno
Gt. Ormes Hd.
Lit. Ormes Hd.
Deganwy
Conwy
Conwy B.
Penmaenmawr
Llanfairfechan
Puffin I.
Red Wharf B.
Beaumaris
Menai Bridge
Bangor
Bethesda
Carnedd Llewelyn
1062
Dolgarrog
Trefriw
Llanrwst
Capel-Curig
Betws-y-coed
Pentrefoelas
Cerrigydrudion
Gwyddelwern
Corwen
Llandrillo
Bala
Bala L.
L. Tegid
Arenig Fawr
Trawsfynydd
853
Maentwrog
Ffestiniog
Blaenau Ffestiniog
Penmachno
Dolwyddelan
GWYNEDD
Snowdon
1085
Llanberis
Caernarfon
Waunfawr
Menai Str.
Penygroes
Llanllyfni
Clynnog-fawr
Talysarn
Beddgelert
Tremadog
Porthmadog
Criccieth
Llanystumdwy
Llannor
Pwllheli
Talsarnau
Harlech
Llanaelhaiarn
564
Nefyn
Lleyn Peninsula
Tudweiliog
Caernarfon Bay
Malltraeth B.
Newborough
Aberffraw
Llanfaelog
Gwalchmai
Gaerwen
Llangefni
Anglesey
Valley
Bodedern
Holy I.
Holyhead
Holyhead B.
Llanerchymedd
Benllech
Pentraeth
Moelfre
Dulas B.
Parys Mt.
128
Amlwch
Llanfechell
Cemaes Bay
Wylfa Head
The Skerries
Carmel Head
IRISH SEA
Pt. of Ayre
Andreas
Bride
Jurby Hd.
Sulby
Ramsey B.
Ramsey
Ballaugh
Maughold
Maughold Hd.
Kirk Michael
Snaefell
620
Glen Helen
Peel
Laxey
Patrick
St. John's
Clay Hd.
Glenmaye
Baldrine
ISLE OF MAN
S. Barrule
483
Foxdale
Douglas
Douglas Hd.
Bradda Hd.
Colby
Ballasalla
Port Erin
Castletown
Port St. Mary
Langness
Calf of Man
55
54
53
4
3
2
m
1000
800
600
400
200
100
0
50
Projection: Conical with two standard parallels

1:1 000 000

10 0 10 20 30 40 km

Based upon the Ordnance Survey Map with the permission of the Controller of Her Majesty's Stationery Office. Crown Copyright Reserved.

Pt. of Ardnamurchan
Ardnamurchan
Sorisdale
Kilchoan
Mingary
527
Salen
Sunart
888
Strontian
Corran
North Ballachulish
L. Leven
Blackwater Res.
Kinlochleven
Kinloch Rannoch
Rannoch Sta.
Coll
Clabhach
L. Sunart
Glen Coe
South Ballachulish
Laroch
L. Laidon
L. Rannoch
Rannoch Moor
Arinagour
Caliach Pt.
Tobermory
Drimnin
Calgary
Dervaig
Morvern
Kingairloch
1146
Clach Leathad 1098
Glen Etive
Glen Lyon
Caoles
Passage of Tiree
L. Frisa
Sd. of Mull
Loch Linnhe
Portnacroish
Tiree
Scarinish
Hynish B.
Hynish
Treshnish Isles
Gometra
Ulva
L. Tuath
Lochaline
Salen
Lismore I.
L. Tulla
1079
B. Dorain 1074
Br. of Orchy
L. na Keal
Ben More 966
Mull
Loch Etive
Killin
Staffa
Lochdonhead
Connel
B. Cruachan 1124
Glen Orchy
Tyndrum
Ardchyle
Kerrera
Oban
Taynuilt
Pass of Brander
Ben Lui 1130
Crianlarich
Dalmally
L. Spelve
L. Scridain
Lochbuie
Iona
Fionnphort
Ross of Mull
Bunessan
Firth of Lorn
L. Buie
Seil
Kilninver
Loch Awe
Cladich
1174
Ben More
Lochearnhead
Balquhidder
L. Voil
Ardlui
Balvicar
L. Avich
Kilmelford
Stronachlachar
The Trossachs
Torran Rocks
Garvellachs
Luing
Inveraray
1011
L. Katrine
729
Callander
Tarbet
Arrochar
974
B. Lomond
B. Venue
Aberfoyle
Scarba
L. Melfort
Ford
Argyll
Strachur
Lochgoilhead
Dubh Artach
G. of Corryvreckan
L. Craignish
Kilmartin
779
L. Goil
Loch Lomond
Buchlyvie
Colonsay
Scalasaig
Crinan Can.
Finnart
Luss
Passage of Oronsay
Lochgilphead
Cowal
Dunans
L. Eck
Coulport
Garelochhead
Faslane
Drymen
Balfron
ATLANTIC
Killchianaig
Ardentinny
Oronsay
Ardrishaig
Otter Ferry
Rosneath
Helensburgh
578
Campsie Fells
L. Tarbert
Jura
Sound of Jura
Loch Fyne
L. Striven
Strone
Kilcreggan
Balloch
Alexandria
Rubha a'Mhail
Lagg
Kilfinan
Sandbank
Gourock
Dumbarton
Paps of Jura 784
Knapdale
Tighnabruaich
Kyles of Bute
Dunoon
Greenock
Port Glasgow
Old Kilpatrick
Milngavie
Ardnave Pt.
561
Tarbert
Kames
Innellan
Wemyss Bay
Kilmacolm
Bearsden
Clydebank
L. Caolisport
Port Askaig
Sound of Islay
Craighouse
Port Bannatyne
Rothesay
Skelmorlie
Br. of Weir
Renfrew
GLASGOW
Paisley
Johnstone
Rutherglen
Bridgend
Islay
W.L. Tarbert
Bute
Cumbrae Is.
Largs
522
Barrhead
Port Charlotte
Bowmore
L. Indaal
Clachan
Skipness
Sd. of Bute
Kingarth
Millport
Kilbirnie
Lochwinnoch
Neilston
490
B. Bheigeir
Gigha I.
Beith
Fairlie
Hunterston
Dalry
Eaglesham
Portnahaven
Laggan B.
Ardbeg
Ardmore Pt.
Lochranza
West Kilbride
Dunlop
Stewarton
Port Ellen
OCEAN
Killean
Kintyre
Kilbrannan Sound
Goat Fell 874
Corrie
Stevenston
Kilwinning
Kilmaurs
Fenwick
Cunninghame
Ardrossan
Saltcoats
The Oa
Carradale
Irvine
Kilmarnock
Darvel
Mull of Oa
Arran
Brodick
Dreghorn
Newmilns
Glenbarr
Barassie
Hurlford
Galston
Lamlash
Troon
Kyle
Saddell
Holy I.
Monkton
Mauchline
Sorn
Prestwick
Tarbolton
Catrine
Auchinleck
Ayr
Inishtrahull
Machrihanish
Campbeltown
Firth of Clyde
Pladda
Heads of Ayr
Drongan
Ochiltree
Ballygorman
446
Dalrymple
New Cumnock
Connel Park
Malin Pen.
Glengad Hd.
Malin
Maybole
Patna
Doon
Dalmellington
Culdaff
Rathlin
Kirkoswald
Crosshill
Turnberry
Carndonagh
Benbane Hd.
Southend
Milton
Bellsbank
Giants Causeway
Mull of Kintyre
Sanda I.
Gleneely
Inishowen Hd.
The Skerries
Ballintoy
Ballycastle B.
Ailsa Craig 334
Dailly
Girvan
L. Doon
Drumjohn
Inishowen
Stroove
NORTH CHANNEL
Magilligan Pt.
Portrush
Fair Hd.
Girvan
Greencastle
Moville
615
Portstewart
Bushmills
Ballycastle
Ballyvoy
Stinchar
Barr
Carrick
Carsphairn
Lendalfoot
Pen.
Magilligan
Knocklayd 517
Runabay
Carrowkeel
Lough Foyle
Downhill
Derrykeighan
Cushendun
Bennane Hd.
Pinwherry
Coleraine
Armoy
Ballybogy
Colmonell
843
Merrick
Rhinns of Kells
Bellarena
Ballantrae
Drenagh
Macosquin
Ballymoney
Cushendall
Barrhill
Glentrool Village
Clatteringshaws Loch
Muff
Mountains of Antrim
Trostan 554
Red B.
Benerairp
439
Creeside
Limavady
Ringsend
Garron Pt.
DUMFRIES
Londonderry
Roe
Finvoy
Dunloy
Newtown Crommelin
Milleur Pt.
Mark
Cree
Ballynameen
Garvagh
Carnlough
Corsewall Pt.
LONDONDERRY
Bann
Clough
Glenarm
Kirkcolm
Cairnryan
Galloway
Claudy
Dungiven
Kilrea
ANTRIM
Leswalt
L. Ryan
New Luce
Newton Stewart
Minnigaff 710
NORTHERN
Feeny
Carncastle
Creetown
Dunamanagh
Sperrin Mts.
Inishrush
Portglenone
Agnews Hill 476
Larne
Larne Lough
Stranraer
Kirkcowan
Gatehouse of Fleet
ULSTER
Ballymena
Wigtown
Maghera
Tobermore
L. Beg
Main
Kells
The Gobbins
Island Magee
Lochans
Glenluce
The Rhins
683
Sawel
Draperstown
Castledawson
Bellaghy
Black Hd.
Portpatrick
Kirkinner
Plumbridge
Desertmartin
Ballyclare
Glenoe
Ballynure
Sandhead
Whauphill
Garlieston
Owenkillew
Magherafelt
Randalstown
Whitehead
Luce Bay
Rousky
The Loop
Eden
Sorbie
The Machars
Wigtown Bay
Gortin
Moneymore
Ballyronan
Antrim
Greenisland
Carrickfergus
Port William
IRELAND
Port Logan
Whithorn
Glengormley
Belfast Lough
Copeland I.
272
Drummore
Mountfield
Creggan
Cookstown
Coagh
Lough Neagh
Newtownabbey
Bangor
Groomsport
Isle of Whithorn
Omagh
Ballinderry
Crumlin
Legoniel
Holywood
Donaghadee
Burrow Hd.
Pomeroy
Tullaghoge
Glenavy
BELFAST
Millisle
Mull of Galloway
TYRONE
Stewartstown
Newtownards
Sixmilecross
Dunmurry
Dundonald
Beragh
Donaghmore
Coalisland
Drumbeg
Comber
Ballywalter
Seskanore
Dungannon
Aghalee
Greyabbey
m
1000
800
600
400
200
100
0
50
100
m
56
55
6
5
Projection: Conical with two standard parallels
West from Greenwich

1:1 000 000

10 0 10 20 30 40 km

Based upon the Ordnance Survey Map with the permission of the Controller of Her Majesty's Stationery Office. Crown Copyright Reserved.

SHETLAND ISLANDS
on same scale
Herma Ness
Haroldswick
Baltasound
Bluemull Sd.
Unst
Balta
Cullivoe
Uyeasound
Mu Ness
Ramna Stacks
Whale Firth
Point of Fethaland
Fetlar
North Roe
The Faither
Ronas Hill
450
Mid Yell
Yell
Colgrave Sd.
The Snap
Yell Sound
Esha Ness
Burravoe
Hillswick
Sullom Voe
Sullom
Lunna Ness
St. Magnus Bay
SHETLAND
Brae
Skaw Taing
Out Skerries
Muckle Roe
Papa Stour
Whalsay
Voe
The Haa
Sd. of Papa
Sandness
S Nesting Bay
Walls
Easter Skeld
Vaila
Gruting Voe
Score Hd.
Lerwick
I. of Noss
Scalloway
Bressay
Hamnavoe
West Burra
Bard Hd.
Clift Sound
293
Bressay Sd.
Kettla Ness
Helli Ness
Hoswick
Mousa
St. Ninian's I.
Scousburgh
Fitful Hd
Boddam
B. of Quendale
Sumburgh Hd.
Butt of Lewis
Port of Ness
South Dell
Ness
Borve
Cellar Hd.
Barvas
North Tolsta
Tolsta Hd.
Shawbost
Carloway
Back
Broad Bay
291
Newmarket
Tiumpan Hd.
Gallan Hd.
Great Bernera
Stornoway
Melbost
Portaguiran
Eye Peninsula
Uig
Callanish
Bayble
L. Roag
Chicken Hd.
575
Lewis
Aird Brenish
Gisla
Crossbost
Lochs
Loch Langavat
Balallan
Cromore
L. Erisort
Park
Kintaravay
Gravir
Kebock Hd.
Scarp
Husinish
N.Harris
Husinish Pt.
Ardvourlie Castle
571
Beinn Mhor
L. Shell
799
W. L. Tarbert
Ardhasig
Sd. of Shiant
Shiant Is.
Taransay
L. Seaforth
Tarbert
Sd. of Taransay
WESTERN
Harris
Scalpay
Toe Hd.
E. L. Tarbert
Scarastavore
S.Harris
Sound of Harris
Pabbay
Leverburgh
Sd. of Pabbay
Berneray
Rodel
Renish Pt.
Haskeir Is.
ISLES
Rubha Hunish
Griminish Pt.
Sollas
Kilmaluag
North Uist
Lochmaddy
L. Maddy
Vaternish Pt.
Paible
Sound of Monach
Clachan
L. Eport
Loch Snizort
Uig
Rona
Carinish
347 Eaval
Dunvegan Head
Waternish
Trotternish
Monach Is.
Baleshare
Grimsay
Stein
The Storr
719
Gramisdale
Ronay
Benbecula
Milovaig
Lephin
Dunvegan
Roskhill
Sound of Raasay
Inner Sound
Ardivachar Pt.
Portree
Wiay
L. Bee
488
Raasay
Toscaig
Bagh nam Faoileann
Bracadale
Coillore
Crowlin Is.
Howmore
South Uist
L. Harport
Narrows
Fernilea
605 Hecla
L. Bracadale
Carbost
Drynoch
Scalpay
Kyle of Lochalsh
Rubha Ardvule
Sligachan
Minginish
Kyleakin
L. Alsh
620 B. Mhor
Cuillin Hills
Bla Bheinn
928
L. Eynort
Glenbrittle
Broadford
1009
Daliburgh
Lochboisdale
Rubh'an Dunain
Soay Sd.
Elgol
L. Boisdale
Soay
L. Scavaig
L. Eishort
Eilean Iarmain
Sound of Barra
Sd. of Eriskay
Cuillin Sound
Teangue
Eriskay
Canna
Armadale
Ardvasar
Sound of Sleat
Greian Hd.
Sanday
Sd. of Canna
Kinloch
Barra
384
Rhum
Pt. of Sleat
Castlebay
810
Mallaig
Bruernish Pt.
Morar
Vatersay
Sound of Rhum
Eigg
Arisaig
Sandray
394
Pabbay
Sd. of Eigg
Sd. of Arisaig
Mingulay
Muck
Shona I.
Berneray
Barra Head
L. Moidart
241
Pt. of Ardnamurchan
Ardnamurchan
Kilchoan
Mingary
Salen
527
Sorisdale
Coll
Clabhach
Arinagour
Caliach Pt.
Tobermory
Calgary
Dervaig
L. Frisa
Caoles
Passage of Tiree
Treshnish Isles
L. Tuath
Tiree
Scarinish
Hynish B.
Hynish
Outer Hebrides
Little Minch
Inner Hebrides
North Minch
Skye
Sd. of Mull
Drimnin
Morvern
Lochaline
Kingairloch
Loch Linnhe
Lismore I.
Salen
C. Wrath
L. Inchard
Kinlochbe
L. Laxford
Handa I.
Scourie
Eddrachillis Bay
Pt. of Stoer
Drumbeg
Quinag
Stoer
Assynt
Enard Bay
Lochinver
Canisp
847
Rhu Coigach
Summer Isles
Elphin
L. Lurgainn
Cromalt Hills
Gruinard B.
Greenstone Pt.
L. Broom
Coigach
Ullapool
Mellon Charles
Aultbea
An Teallach
1062
L. Ewe
Melvaig
L. na Sealga
Fionn Loch
Poolewe
Braemore
Longa I.
L. Gairloch
Gairloch
Henderson
Kerrysdale
Talladale
981
Slioch
L. Maree
L. Fannich
Kinlochewe
L. Torridon
1053
Torridon
Achnasheen
Fasag
Shieldaig
Achnashellach
Applecross Forest
Applecross
Coulags
Carron
1052
Monar Forest
L. Monar
L. Kishorn
Lochcarron
Stromemore
Plockton
Stromeferry
L. Carron
1150
L. Mullardoch
Auchtertyre
Dornie
Carn Eige
1182
Glen Affric
Glenelg
Invershiel
A' Chralaig
1120
The Saddle
1010
Glen Shiel
L. Cluanie
L. Hourn
L. Quoich
Tomdoun
Ladhar B.
1019
Knoydart
Inverie
Glen Garry
L. Nevis
1040
Sgurr na Ciche
Tarbet
983
L. Arkaig
Gairlochy
Loch Morar
Culvain
Caledonian Canal
Lochailort
Glenfinnan
Kinlocheil
882
Moidart
Kinlochmoidart
Loch Shiel
L. Eil
Fort William
1347
Ben Nevis
Ardgour
Corran
L. Leven
Sunart
888
Strontian
North Ballachulish
L. Sunart
South Ballachulish
Glen Coe
1148
Portnacroish
Loch Etive
Projection: Conical with two standard parallels
m
1000
800
600
400
200
100
0
50
100
m

1:1 000 000

10 0 10 20 30 40 km

ORKNEY ISLANDS
on same scale

West from Greenwich

DISTRICTS IN NORTHERN IRELAND
1 Londonderry
2 Limavady
3 Coleraine
4 Ballymoney
5 Moyle
6 Larne
7 Ballymena
8 Magherafelt
9 Cookstown
10 Strabane
11 Omagh
12 Fermanagh
13 Dungannon
14 Craigavon
15 Armagh
16 Newry and Mourne
17 Banbridge
18 Down
19 Lisburn
20 Antrim
21 Newtownabbey
22 Carrickfergus
23 North Down
24 Ards
25 Castlereagh
26 Belfast
NORTHERN IRELAND
ULSTER
IRELAND
CONNACHT
DONEGAL
LONDONDERRY
ANTRIM
TYRONE
FERMANAGH
ARMAGH
DOWN
MONAGHAN
CAVAN
LOUTH
MEATH
WESTMEATH
LONGFORD
ROSCOMMON
SLIGO
LEITRIM
MAYO
BELFAST
DUBLIN
Lough Neagh
Donegal Bay
Clew Bay
Dundalk Bay
Sligo Bay

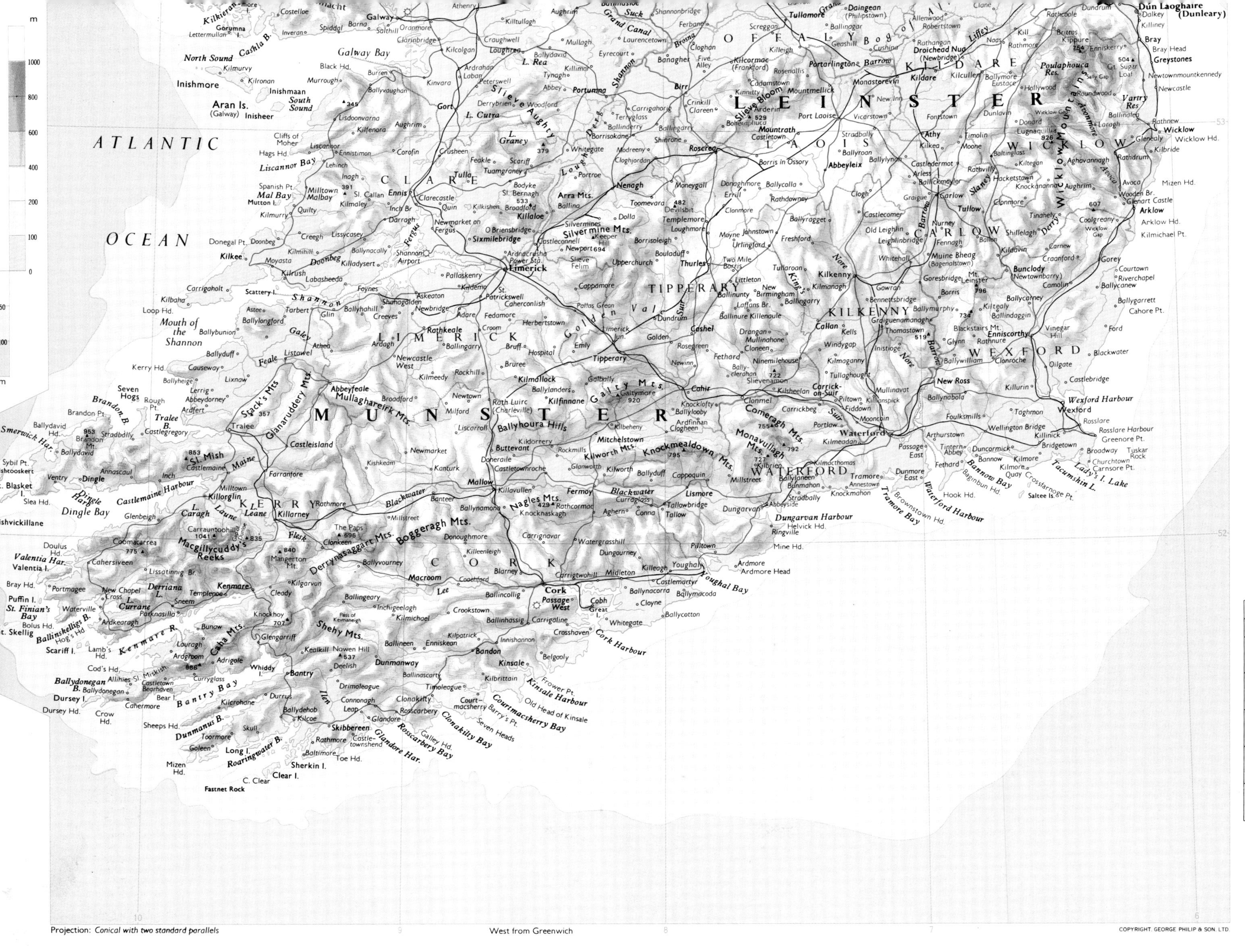

1:1 250 000

10 0 10 20 30 40 50 km

Projection: *Conical with two standard parallels*

West from Greenwich

1:20 000 000

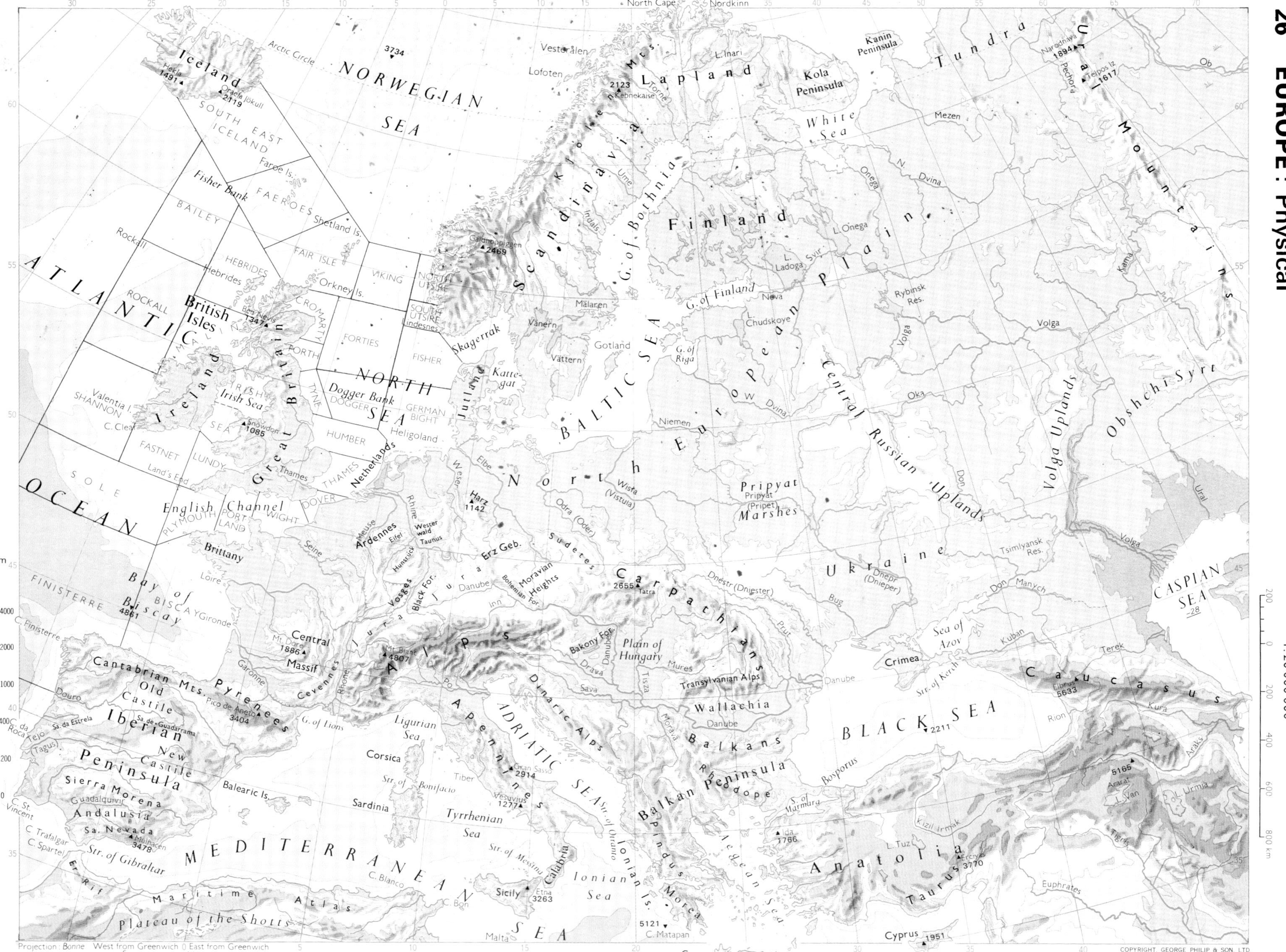
200 0 200 400 600 800 km
NORWEGIAN SEA
NORTH SEA
BALTIC SEA
ADRIATIC SEA
BLACK SEA
CASPIAN SEA
-28
MEDITERRANEAN SEA
Aegean Sea
Ionian Sea
Tyrrhenian Sea
Ligurian Sea
White Sea
Sea of Azov
ATLANTIC OCEAN
Bay of Biscay
English Channel
Irish Sea
G. of Bothnia
G. of Finland
G. of Riga
G. of Lions
Skagerrak
Kattegat
Str. of Gibraltar
Str. of Otranto
Str. of Messina
Str. of Bonifacio
Str. of Kerch
Bosporus
S. of Marmara
Ural Mountains
Obshchi Syrt
Volga Uplands
Central Russian Uplands
North European Plain
Tundra
Caucasus
Carpathians
Transylvanian Alps
Balkans
Alps
Apennines
Pyrenees
Dinaric Alps
Sudetes
Pindus
Maritime Atlas
Er Rif
Plateau of the Shotts
Scandinavia
Kjølen Mts.
Lapland
Finland
Kola Peninsula
Kanin Peninsula
Iceland
British Isles
Great Britain
Ireland
Brittany
Massif Central
Cevennes
Cantabrian Mts.
Iberian Peninsula
Old Castile
New Castile
Andalusia
Sierra Morena
Sa. Nevada
Balkan Peninsula
Rhodope
Morea
Anatolia
Taurus
Crimea
Ukraine
Pripyat Marshes
Plain of Hungary
Wallachia
Ardennes
Black For.
Harz
Erz Geb.
Moravian Heights
Bohemian For.
Jura
Corsica
Sardinia
Sicily
Calabria
Crete
Cyprus
Malta
Volga
Don
Dnepr (Dnieper)
Dnestr (Dniester)
Danube
Rhine
Elbe
Wisła (Vistula)
Odra (Oder)
Loire
Seine
Rhône
Garonne
Po
Tiber
Tejo (Tagus)
Douro
Pechora
Mezen
N. Dvina
Onega
Kama
Ural
Ob
Kura
Tigris
Euphrates
North Cape
Nordkinn
C. Finisterre
C. St. Vincent
C. Trafalgar
C. Spartel
C. Matapan
C. Bon
C. Blanco
Arctic Circle
Elbrus 5633
Mt. Blanc 4807
Pico de Aneto 3404
Etna 3263
Galdhøpiggen 2469
Kebnekaise 2123
Oraefa Jökull 2119
Ben Nevis 1347
Snowdon 1085
Harz 1142
Tatra 2655
Projection: Bonne West from Greenwich 0 East from Greenwich
ROCKALL Sea areas named in
COPYRIGHT GEORGE PHILIP & SON LTD

1:20 000 000

200 0 200 400 600 800 km

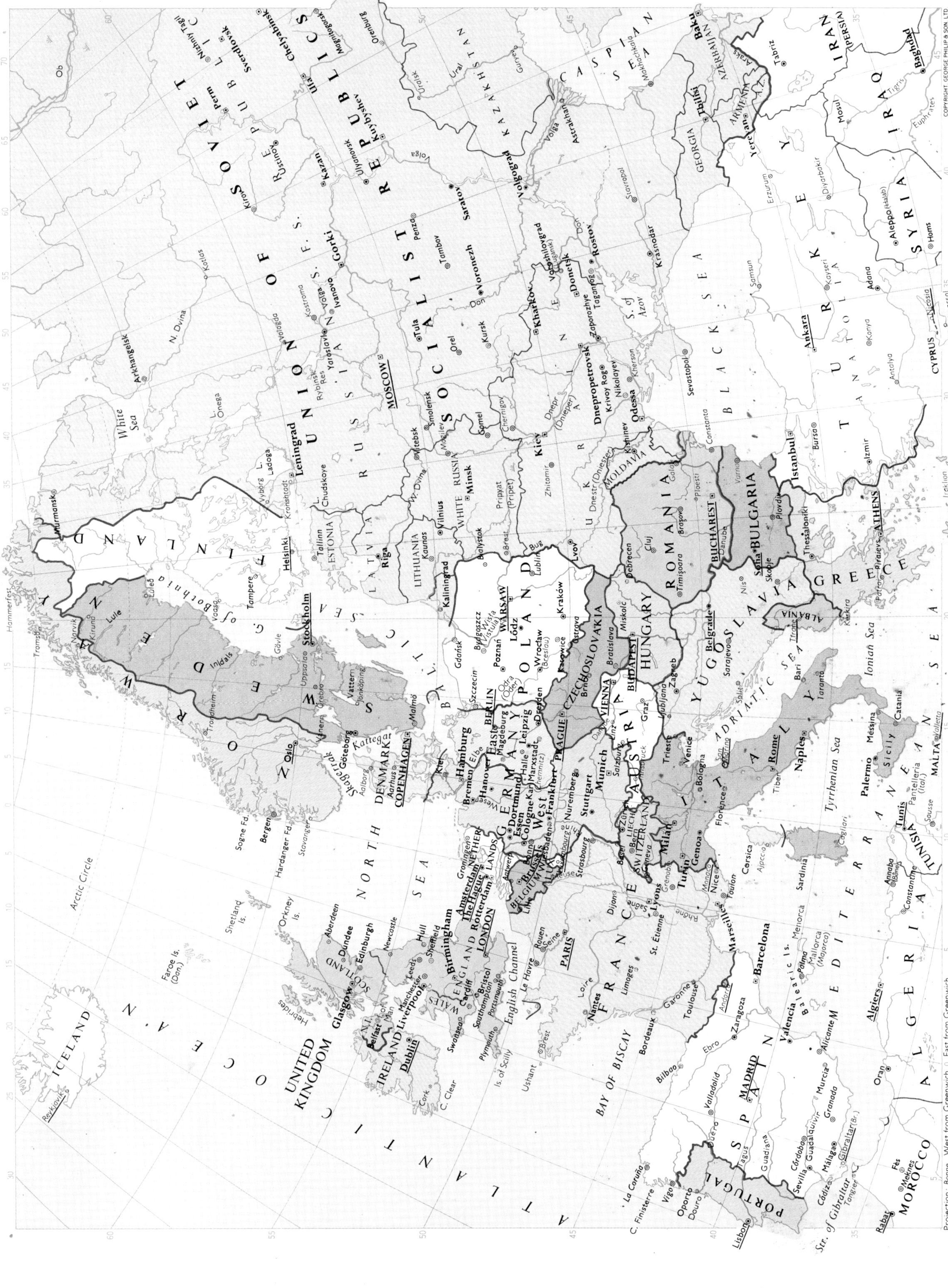

LONDON Capital Cities

Projection: Bonne West from Greenwich 0 East from Greenwich

UNION OF SOVIET SOCIALIST REPUBLICS

R. S. F. S. R.

FINLAND SWEDEN NORWAY DENMARK ICELAND UNITED KINGDOM IRELAND FRANCE SPAIN PORTUGAL ITALY GERMANY POLAND CZECHOSLOVAKIA AUSTRIA SWITZERLAND HUNGARY ROMANIA BULGARIA YUGOSLAVIA GREECE ALBANIA TURKEY SYRIA IRAQ IRAN (PERSIA) CYPRUS ALGERIA TUNISIA MOROCCO MALTA

ATLANTIC OCEAN NORTH SEA BALTIC SEA BLACK SEA CASPIAN SEA MEDITERRANEAN SEA ADRIATIC SEA Ionian Sea Tyrrhenian Sea BAY OF BISCAY English Channel White Sea Kattegat Skagerrak G. of Bothnia S. of Azov Str. of Gibraltar Arctic Circle

1:40 000 000

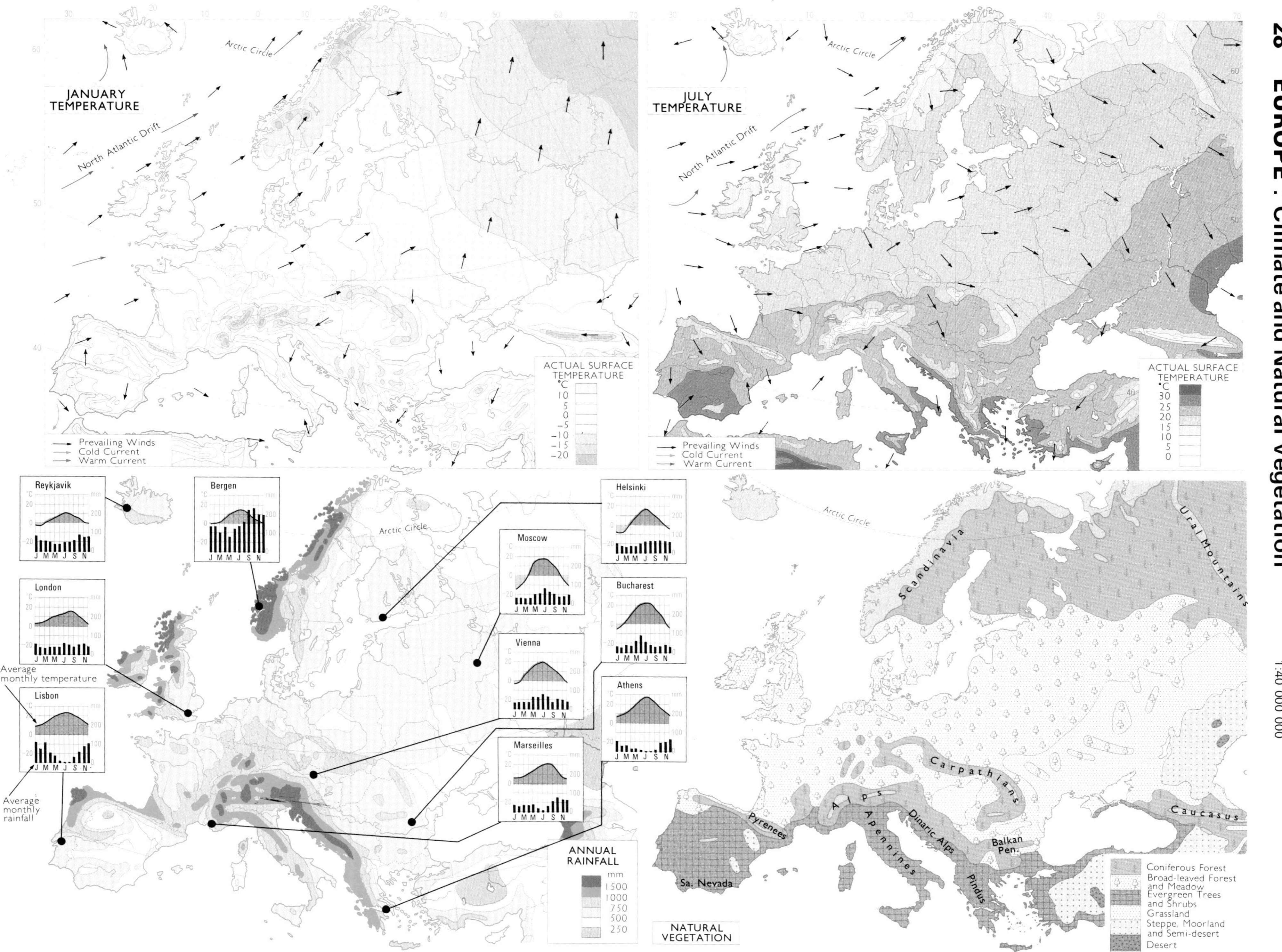
JANUARY TEMPERATURE
North Atlantic Drift
Arctic Circle
ACTUAL SURFACE TEMPERATURE
°C
10
5
0
−5
−10
−15
−20
Prevailing Winds
Cold Current
Warm Current
JULY TEMPERATURE
North Atlantic Drift
Arctic Circle
ACTUAL SURFACE TEMPERATURE
°C
30
25
20
15
10
5
0
Prevailing Winds
Cold Current
Warm Current
Reykjavik
Bergen
Helsinki
Moscow
Bucharest
Vienna
Athens
London
Lisbon
Marseilles
Average monthly temperature
Average monthly rainfall
Arctic Circle
ANNUAL RAINFALL
mm
1500
1000
750
500
250
Arctic Circle
Scandinavia
Ural Mountains
Carpathians
Caucasus
Pyrenees
Alps
Apennines
Dinaric Alps
Balkan Pen.
Pindus
Sa. Nevada
NATURAL VEGETATION
Coniferous Forest
Broad-leaved Forest and Meadow
Evergreen Trees and Shrubs
Grassland
Steppe, Moorland and Semi-desert
Desert

1:20 000 000

200 0 200 400 600 800 km

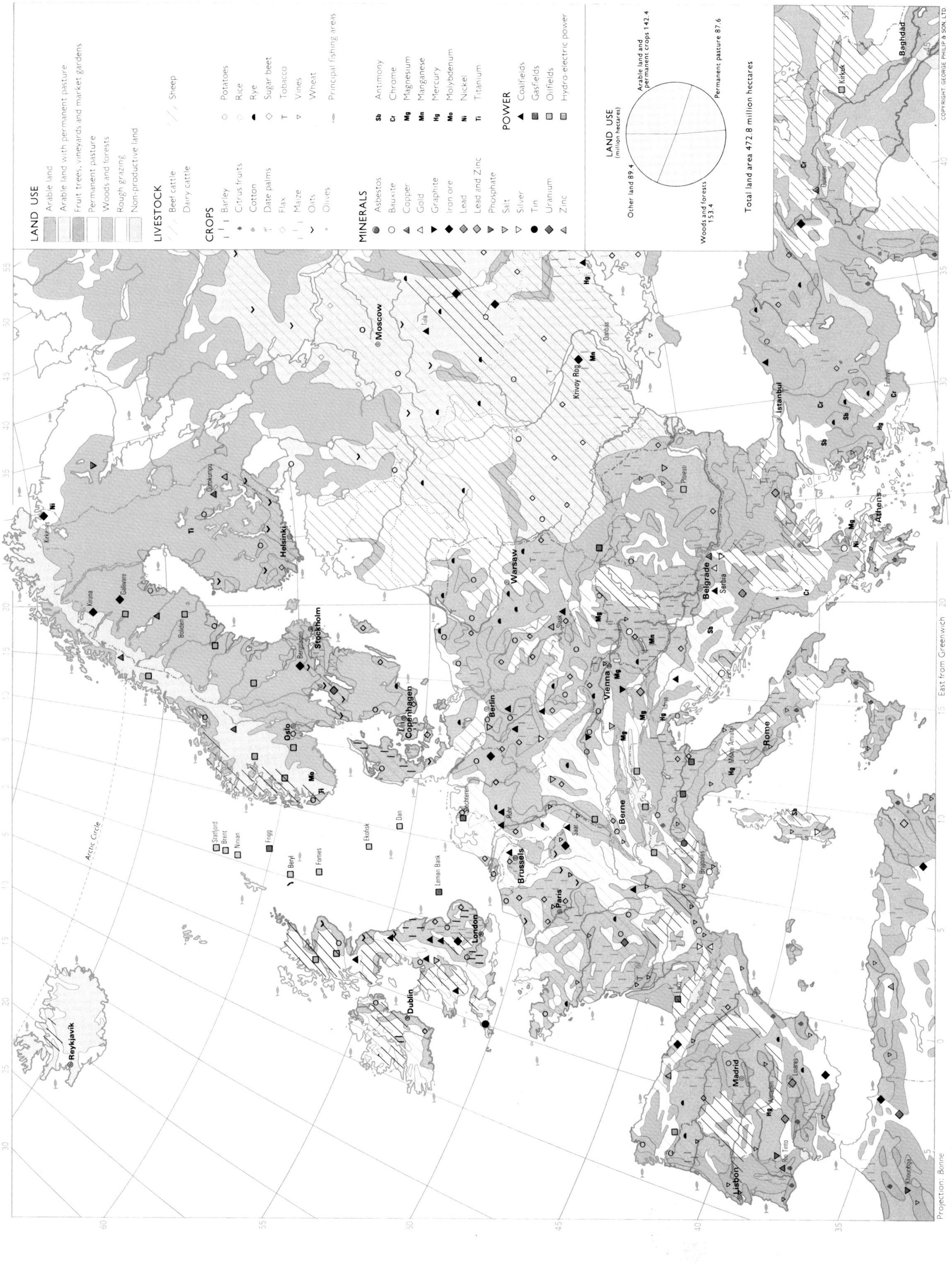

LAND USE

- Arable land
- Arable land with permanent pasture
- Fruit trees, vineyards and market gardens
- Permanent pasture
- Woods and forests
- Rough grazing
- Non-productive land

LIVESTOCK

- Beef cattle
- Dairy cattle
- Sheep

CROPS

- Barley
- Citrus fruits
- Cotton
- Date palms
- Flax
- Maize
- Oats
- Olives
- Potatoes
- Rice
- Rye
- Sugar beet
- Tobacco
- Vines
- Wheat
- Principal fishing areas

MINERALS

- Asbestos
- Bauxite
- Copper
- Gold
- Graphite
- Iron ore
- Lead
- Lead and Zinc
- Phosphate
- Salt
- Silver
- Tin
- Uranium
- Zinc
- Sb Antimony
- Cr Chrome
- Mg Magnesium
- Mn Manganese
- Hg Mercury
- Mo Molybdenum
- Ni Nickel
- Ti Titanium

POWER

- Coalfields
- Gasfields
- Oilfields
- Hydro-electric power

LAND USE
(million hectares)

Other land 89.4
Arable land and permanent crops 142.4
Woods and forests 153.4
Permanent pasture 87.6

Total land area 472.8 million hectares

Reykjavik
Arctic Circle
Kirkenes
Kiruna
Gällivare
Boliden
Outokumpu
Helsinki
Bergslagen
Stockholm
Oslo
Statfjord
Brent
Ninian
Frigg
Beryl
Forties
Ekofisk
Dan
Copenhagen
Moscow
Tula
Dublin
London
Leman Bank
Slochteren
Berlin
Warsaw
Brussels
Ruhr
Paris
Saar
Slask
Krivoy Rog
Donbas
Vienna
Berne
Idrija
Ploiesti
Lacq
Brignoles
Belgrade
Serbia
Lisbon
Madrid
Almadén
Rio Tinto
Linares
Monte Amiata
Rome
Istanbul
Guleman
Kirkuk
Baghdad
Athens
Fethiye
Khouribga

Projection: *Bonne*

East from Greenwich

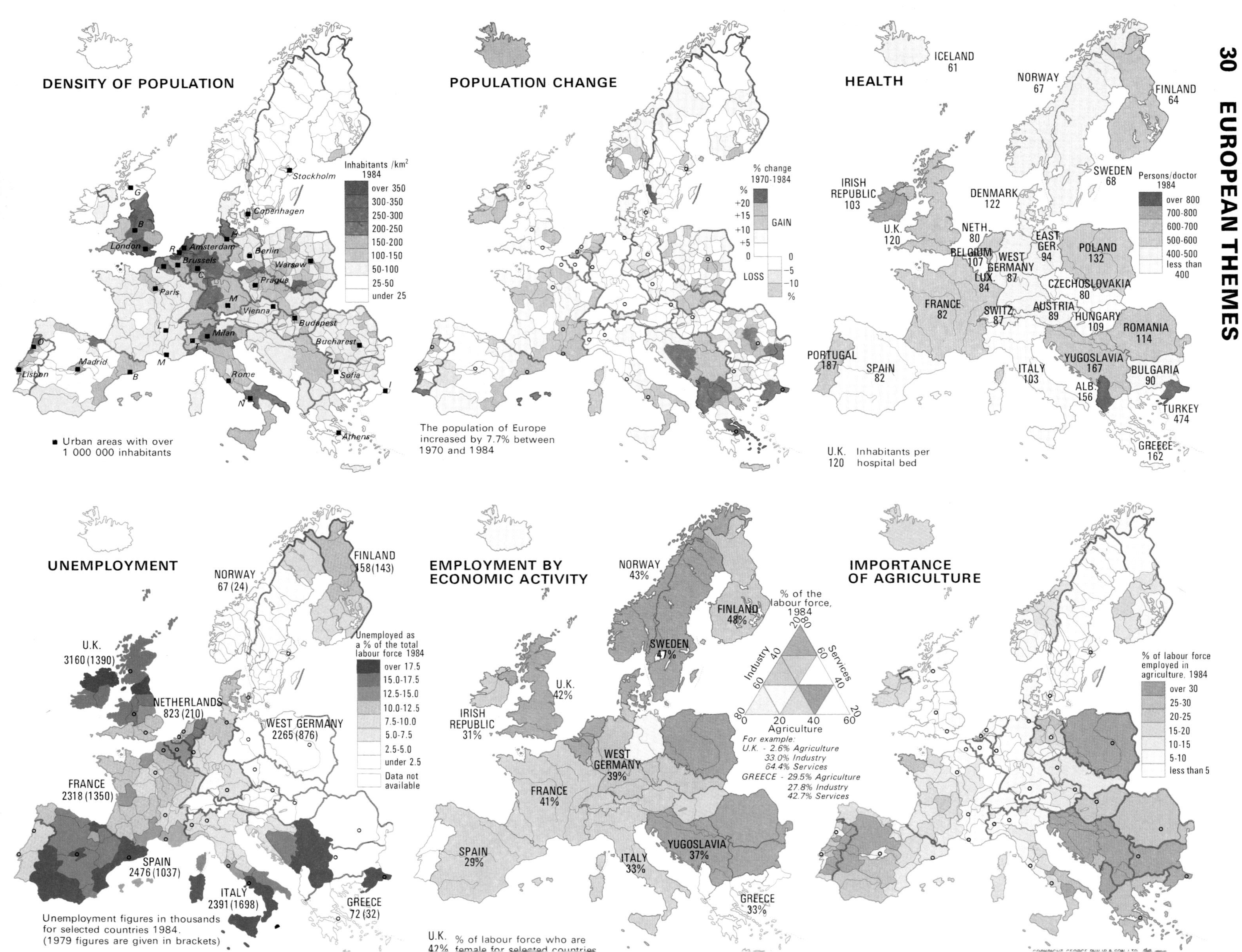
DENSITY OF POPULATION
Inhabitants /km² 1984
over 350
300-350
250-300
200-250
150-200
100-150
50-100
25-50
under 25
Stockholm
Copenhagen
Berlin
Warsaw
Prague
Vienna
Budapest
Bucharest
Sofia
Athens
Amsterdam
Brussels
London
Paris
Milan
Rome
Madrid
Lisbon
Urban areas with over 1 000 000 inhabitants
POPULATION CHANGE
% change 1970-1984
%
+20
+15
+10
+5
0
GAIN
LOSS
0
-5
-10
%
The population of Europe increased by 7.7% between 1970 and 1984
HEALTH
ICELAND 61
NORWAY 67
FINLAND 64
SWEDEN 68
IRISH REPUBLIC 103
DENMARK 122
U.K. 120
NETH. 80
EAST GER. 94
POLAND 132
BELGIUM 107
WEST GERMANY 87
LUX. 84
CZECHOSLOVAKIA 80
FRANCE 82
SWITZ. 87
AUSTRIA 89
HUNGARY 109
ROMANIA 114
PORTUGAL 187
SPAIN 82
ITALY 103
YUGOSLAVIA 167
BULGARIA 90
ALB. 156
TURKEY 474
GREECE 162
Persons/doctor 1984
over 800
700-800
600-700
500-600
400-500
less than 400
U.K. 120 Inhabitants per hospital bed
UNEMPLOYMENT
NORWAY 67 (24)
FINLAND 158 (143)
U.K. 3160 (1390)
NETHERLANDS 823 (210)
WEST GERMANY 2265 (876)
FRANCE 2318 (1350)
SPAIN 2476 (1037)
ITALY 2391 (1698)
GREECE 72 (32)
Unemployed as a % of the total labour force 1984
over 17.5
15.0-17.5
12.5-15.0
10.0-12.5
7.5-10.0
5.0-7.5
2.5-5.0
under 2.5
Data not available
Unemployment figures in thousands for selected countries 1984. (1979 figures are given in brackets)
EMPLOYMENT BY ECONOMIC ACTIVITY
NORWAY 43%
FINLAND 48%
SWEDEN 47%
U.K. 42%
IRISH REPUBLIC 31%
WEST GERMANY 39%
FRANCE 41%
SPAIN 29%
ITALY 33%
YUGOSLAVIA 37%
GREECE 33%
% of the labour force, 1984
Industry
Services
Agriculture
For example:
U.K. - 2.6% Agriculture
33.0% Industry
64.4% Services
GREECE - 29.5% Agriculture
27.8% Industry
42.7% Services
U.K. 42% % of labour force who are female for selected countries
IMPORTANCE OF AGRICULTURE
% of labour force employed in agriculture, 1984
over 30
25-30
20-25
15-20
10-15
5-10
less than 5

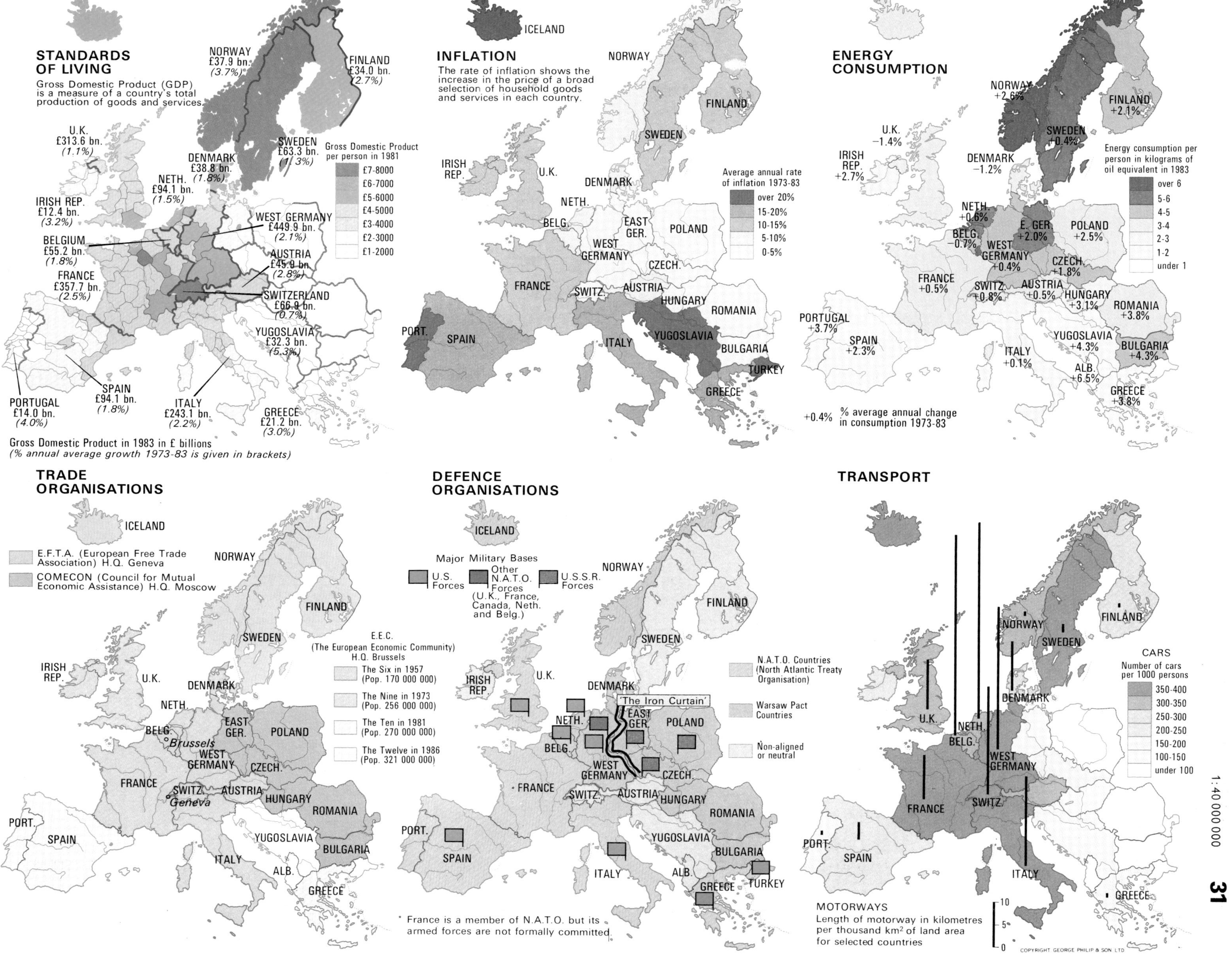
STANDARDS OF LIVING
Gross Domestic Product (GDP) is a measure of a country's total production of goods and services.
NORWAY £37.9 bn. (3.7%)
FINLAND £34.0 bn. (2.7%)
U.K. £313.6 bn. (1.1%)
SWEDEN £63.3 bn. (1.3%)
DENMARK £38.8 bn. (1.8%)
NETH. £94.1 bn. (1.5%)
IRISH REP. £12.4 bn. (3.2%)
WEST GERMANY £449.9 bn. (2.1%)
BELGIUM £55.2 bn. (1.8%)
AUSTRIA £45.9 bn. (2.8%)
FRANCE £357.7 bn. (2.5%)
SWITZERLAND £66.9 bn. (0.7%)
YUGOSLAVIA £32.3 bn. (5.3%)
SPAIN £94.1 bn. (1.8%)
PORTUGAL £14.0 bn. (4.0%)
ITALY £243.1 bn. (2.2%)
GREECE £21.2 bn. (3.0%)
Gross Domestic Product per person in 1981
£7-8000
£6-7000
£5-6000
£4-5000
£3-4000
£2-3000
£1-2000
Gross Domestic Product in 1983 in £ billions
(% annual average growth 1973-83 is given in brackets)
INFLATION
The rate of inflation shows the increase in the price of a broad selection of household goods and services in each country.
ICELAND
NORWAY
FINLAND
SWEDEN
IRISH REP.
U.K.
DENMARK
NETH.
BELG.
EAST GER.
POLAND
WEST GERMANY
CZECH.
FRANCE
SWITZ.
AUSTRIA
HUNGARY
ROMANIA
PORT.
SPAIN
ITALY
YUGOSLAVIA
BULGARIA
TURKEY
GREECE
Average annual rate of inflation 1973-83
over 20%
15-20%
10-15%
5-10%
0-5%
ENERGY CONSUMPTION
NORWAY +2.6%
FINLAND +2.1%
U.K. −1.4%
SWEDEN +0.4%
IRISH REP. +2.7%
DENMARK −1.2%
NETH. +0.6%
E. GER. +2.0%
POLAND +2.5%
BELG. −0.7%
WEST GERMANY +0.4%
CZECH. +1.8%
FRANCE +0.5%
SWITZ. +0.8%
AUSTRIA +0.5%
HUNGARY +3.1%
ROMANIA +3.8%
PORTUGAL +3.7%
SPAIN +2.3%
YUGOSLAVIA +4.3%
BULGARIA +4.3%
ITALY +0.1%
ALB. +6.5%
GREECE +3.8%
Energy consumption per person in kilograms of oil equivalent in 1983
over 6
5-6
4-5
3-4
2-3
1-2
under 1
+0.4% % average annual change in consumption 1973-83
TRADE ORGANISATIONS
ICELAND
E.F.T.A. (European Free Trade Association) H.Q. Geneva
COMECON (Council for Mutual Economic Assistance) H.Q. Moscow
NORWAY
FINLAND
SWEDEN
E.E.C. (The European Economic Community) H.Q. Brussels
The Six in 1957 (Pop. 170 000 000)
The Nine in 1973 (Pop. 256 000 000)
The Ten in 1981 (Pop. 270 000 000)
The Twelve in 1986 (Pop. 321 000 000)
IRISH REP.
U.K.
DENMARK
NETH.
BELG.
Brussels
EAST GER.
POLAND
WEST GERMANY
CZECH.
FRANCE
SWITZ.
Geneva
AUSTRIA
HUNGARY
ROMANIA
PORT.
SPAIN
YUGOSLAVIA
BULGARIA
ITALY
ALB.
GREECE
DEFENCE ORGANISATIONS
ICELAND
Major Military Bases
U.S. Forces
Other N.A.T.O. Forces (U.K., France, Canada, Neth. and Belg.)
U.S.S.R. Forces
NORWAY
FINLAND
SWEDEN
IRISH REP.
U.K.
DENMARK
'The Iron Curtain'
NETH.
EAST GER.
POLAND
BELG.
WEST GERMANY
CZECH.
FRANCE
SWITZ.
AUSTRIA
HUNGARY
ROMANIA
PORT.
SPAIN
YUGOSLAVIA
BULGARIA
ITALY
ALB.
GREECE
TURKEY
N.A.T.O. Countries (North Atlantic Treaty Organisation)
Warsaw Pact Countries
Non-aligned or neutral
* France is a member of N.A.T.O. but its armed forces are not formally committed.
TRANSPORT
NORWAY
FINLAND
SWEDEN
DENMARK
U.K.
NETH.
BELG.
WEST GERMANY
FRANCE
SWITZ.
PORT.
SPAIN
ITALY
GREECE
CARS
Number of cars per 1000 persons
350-400
300-350
250-300
200-250
150-200
100-150
under 100
MOTORWAYS
Length of motorway in kilometres per thousand km² of land area for selected countries
10
5
0

	Population									Land			Agriculture		
						Growth									
	Total	Density	Birth Rate	Death Rate	Life Expectancy	1965-73	1973-83	Urban		Area	Arable	Forest	Agricultural Population	Index of Production	Food intake
	th.	persons per km²	per th. popn.		yrs.	av. % per annum		%		th. km²	th. km²	th. km²	% of total popn.	1974-76 = 100	calories per day
Albania	2 901	107	26	6	71	2.6	2.1	38		27	7	12	58	130	3 063
Austria	7 552	91	12	12	73	0.4	0.2	56		83	16	33	7.9	113	3 426
Belgium*	9 877	329	12	11	73	0.4	0.1	89		30	8.3	7.0	2.7	104	3 774
Bulgaria	8 961	81	14	11	70	0.6	0.1	67		111	42	39	30	118	3 622
Czechoslovakia	15 459	124	15	12	70	0.3	0.6	65		125	52	46	8.8	117	3 395
Denmark	5 112	122	10	11	74	0.7	0.2	85		42	27	4.9	6.1	120	3 548
Finland	4 882	16	14	9	73	0.2	0.4	60		305	24	233	11	115	3 079
France	54 947	101	14	10	75	0.8	0.4	80		546	186	146	7.5	115	3 530
Germany, East	16 671	157	14	13	71	0.5	0.1	76		106	50	30	8.7	102	3 689
Germany, West	61 181	251	10	11	75	0.7	0.1	86		244	75	73	3.3	113	3 351
Greece	9 896	76	14	9	75	0.5	1.1	64		131	39	26	35	105	3 668
Hungary	10 665	116	12	14	70	0.3	0.3	55		92	53	16	14	126	3 484
Iceland	239	2.3	18	7	77	1.6	0.8	89		100	0.1	1.2	10	108	3 274
Ireland	3 535	51	19	9	73	0.8	1.3	56		69	9.7	3.3	19	106	3 699
Italy	56 983	194	11	10	76	0.6	0.3	71		294	124	64	9.5	113	3 688
Luxembourg*	363	140	12	11	69	0.9	0.2	78		2.6					
Malta	380	1 267	15	8	71	0.1	1.8	85		0.3	0.1		4.5	152	2 843
Netherlands	14 420	424	12	8	76	1.1	0.7	52		34	8.6	2.9	4.7	123	3 618
Norway	4 140	13	12	10	77	0.8	0.4	55		308	8.4	83	6.7	117	3 392
Poland	36 914	121	19	10	71	0.7	0.9	59		305	148	87	28	97	3 479
Portugal	10 164	110	14	9	71	0.2	1.1	30		92	36	36	24	84	3 205
Romania	22 897	100	15	10	71	1.2	0.8	51		230	105	63	45	117	3 346
Spain	38 717	76	13	7	75	1.0	1.0	76		499	205	156	15	108	3 296
Sweden	8 337	20	11	11	78	0.7	0.2	85		412	30	264	4.3	102	3 146
Switzerland	6 442	161	11	9	79	1.2	0.2	59		40	4.1	11	4.6	116	3 455
U.K.	55 624	230	13	12	74	0.4	0.1	91		242	70	21	1.8	120	3 249
Yugoslavia	22 963	90	17	10	69	0.9	0.8	45		255	78	93	34	116	3 550
U.S.S.R.	275 000	12	20	10	69	0.9	0.9	65		22 272	2 323	9 200	15	108	3 360

*Many figures for Luxembourg included in Belgium.

Population. This is the United Nations' estimate for the mid-year 1984 (thousands).

Population density. This is the quoted population total divided by the quoted land area (persons per square kilometre).

Birth Rates and Death Rates. These are the registered or United Nations' estimated rates per thousand population.

Life Expectancy. This figure indicates the number of years that a child born today can expect to live if the levels of death of today last throughout its life. The figure is an average of that for men and women. The figure for women is usually higher than that for men (U.K. male 70, female 76 years).

Population Growth. This shows the average annual percentage change in population for two periods 1965-1973 and 1973-1983.

Urbanization. This is the percentage of the total population living in urban areas. The definition of urban is that of the individual nation and usually includes quite small towns.

Land Area. This is the total area of the country minus the area covered by major lakes and rivers (thousand square kilometres).

Arable Land and Permanent Crops. This excludes fallow land but includes temporary pasture (thousand square kilometres).

Forest and Woodland. This includes natural and planted woodland and land recently cleared of timber which will be replanted (thousand square kilometres).

Agricultural Population. This is the percentage of the economically active population working in agriculture. It includes those people working also in forestry, hunting and fishing.

Index of Agricultural Production. The base period for this index is 1974-1976 and it shows the level of production in each country in 1983 in comparision with that of the earlier period. Only edible crops and meat are included.

Food Supply. The figures are the average intake per person in calories per day in the period 1979-1981.

Trade		Education		Health	Energy	Consumer Price Index	G.N.P		G.D.P. Part formed by		Loans & Debt		
Imports	Exports	Primary	Secondary					Growth per capita	Agric.	Indust.			
US$ per capita		% of age group		Popn. per doctor	Consumption in kgs of oil equiv. per capita	1970 = 100	US$ per capita	% per yr. 1973-82	%		end 1983 US$ millions	as % of GNP	
		100	66		982								Albania
2 598	2 083	99	74	400	3 083	234	9 210	2.7	4	31	181	0.3	Austria
5 395	5 049	98	94	400	4 401	286	9 160	1.6	2	28	410	0.6	Belgium*
1 414	1 432	100	82	410	4 390		3 800		19	48			Bulgaria
1 105	1 112	89	46	360	4 691	123	5 000		7	61			Czechoslovakia
3 322	3 196	98	100	480	3 061	376	11 490	1.2	5	18	449	0.9	Denmark
2 549	2 768	98	98	530	4 649	443	10 440	2.2	8	29	178	0.4	Finland
1 888	1 698	100	87	580	3 429	398	10 390	2.2	4	28	3 790	0.8	France
1 376	1 490	94	88	520	5 370		6 800		9	73			Germany,East
2 489	2 758	100	94	450	4 156	199	11 420	2.3	2	36	2 767	0.5	Germany,West
960	486	100	81	430	1 790	959	3 970	2.4	16	21			Greece
760	803	100	73	400	2 968	216	2 150	5.6	15	37			Hungary
3 417	3 033	100		488	3 364	9 898	10 270	1.7					Iceland
2 730	2 720	100	95	780	2 354	640	4 810	1.3	11	35			Ireland
1 414	1 292	100	74	340	2 458	708	6 350	2.0	6	35	1 105	0.3	Italy
		100		495	9 000	266	12 190	2.3	2	33			Luxembourg*
1 887	1 037	100		383	1 180	99	3 710	9.1	3	37			Malta
4 309	4 569	98	98	540	5 397	249	9 910	0.9	4	26	1 268	1.0	Netherlands
3 355	4 568	99	95	520	8 087	346	13 820	3.2	4	35	526	1.0	Norway
269	304	100	75	570	3 133	383	3 700		30	42			Poland
767	510	100	50	540	1 194	637	2 190	1.9	8	32			Portugal
435	578	100	71	680	3 305		2 500		16	57			Romania
744	608	100	88	450	1 858	732	4 800	0.8	7	27			Spain
3 159	3 518	99	85	490	5 821	373	12 400	0.8	3	24	737	0.8	Sweden
4 577	4 016	100		410	3 794	200	16 390	0.8			286	0.3	Switzerland
1 775	1 628	100	83	650	3 461	515	9 050	1.0	2	29	1 432	0.3	U.K.
522	447	100	83	550	1 903	3 368	2 570	4.3	14	42			Yugoslavia
293	333	100	97	270	4 505		5 300		15	51			U.S.S.R.

Andorra, Land 0.5/Popn. 34; Faeroe Is. 1.4/45; Gibraltar 0.01/28; Liechtenstein 0.2/27; Monaco 0.0015/27; San Marino 0.06/22; Svalbard 62/3.

Trade. The trade figures are normally for the year 1983 or 1984. The total trade figures have been divided by the population and are a measure of the country's external trade (U.S. $ per capita).

Education. The ages of primary school are taken to be 6-11 years and secondary school 12-17 years. The percentage of the total school age group in this type of education is shown.

Energy. All forms of energy have been converted to their equivalent in oil. Firewood and other traditional forms used in developing countries are not included and so the energy consumption in those countries is understated (kilograms of oil equivalent per capita).

Consumer Price Index. The base year is 1970 which is 100 and the level of consumer prices in 1984 or 1985 are shown in relation to the base year. It is a measure of inflation.

G.N.P. (Gross National Product) This figure is an estimate of the average production per person measured in U.S. dollars and for 1983. The G.N.P. measures the value of goods and services produced in a country, plus the balance, positive or negative, of income from abroad, for example investments, interest on capital, money returned from foreign labour, etc. The rate of change is the average annual percentage change during the period 1973-1982 in the G.D.P. The G.D.P. (Gross Domestic Product) is the G.N.P. minus the foreign balances. The adjoining two columns show the percentage contribution to the G.D.P. made by the agricultural and mining and manufacturing sectors.

Loans and Debt. This figure in millions of U.S. dollars shows the external public debt at the end of 1983. This is then shown as a percentage of the annual G.N.P. The figures in red show official development assistance made by the developed countries and also as a percentage of the donor country's G.N.P.

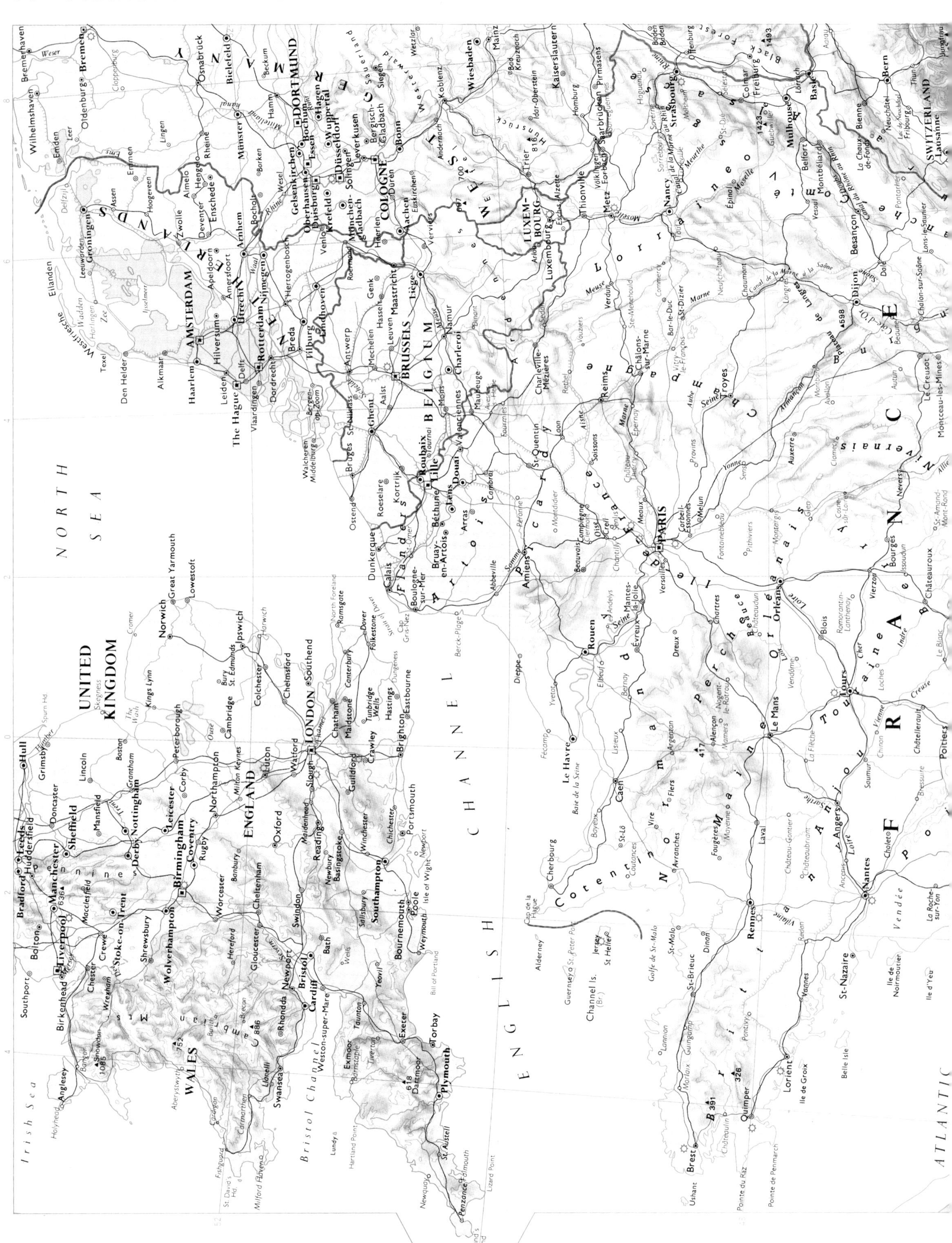
NORTH SEA
UNITED KINGDOM
ENGLAND
WALES
ENGLISH CHANNEL
Bristol Channel
Irish Sea
BELGIUM
LUXEMBOURG
SWITZERLAND
FRANCE
ATLANTIC
LONDON
PARIS
BRUSSELS
AMSTERDAM
COLOGNE
DORTMUND

1:4 000 000

20 0 20 40 60 80 100 120 km

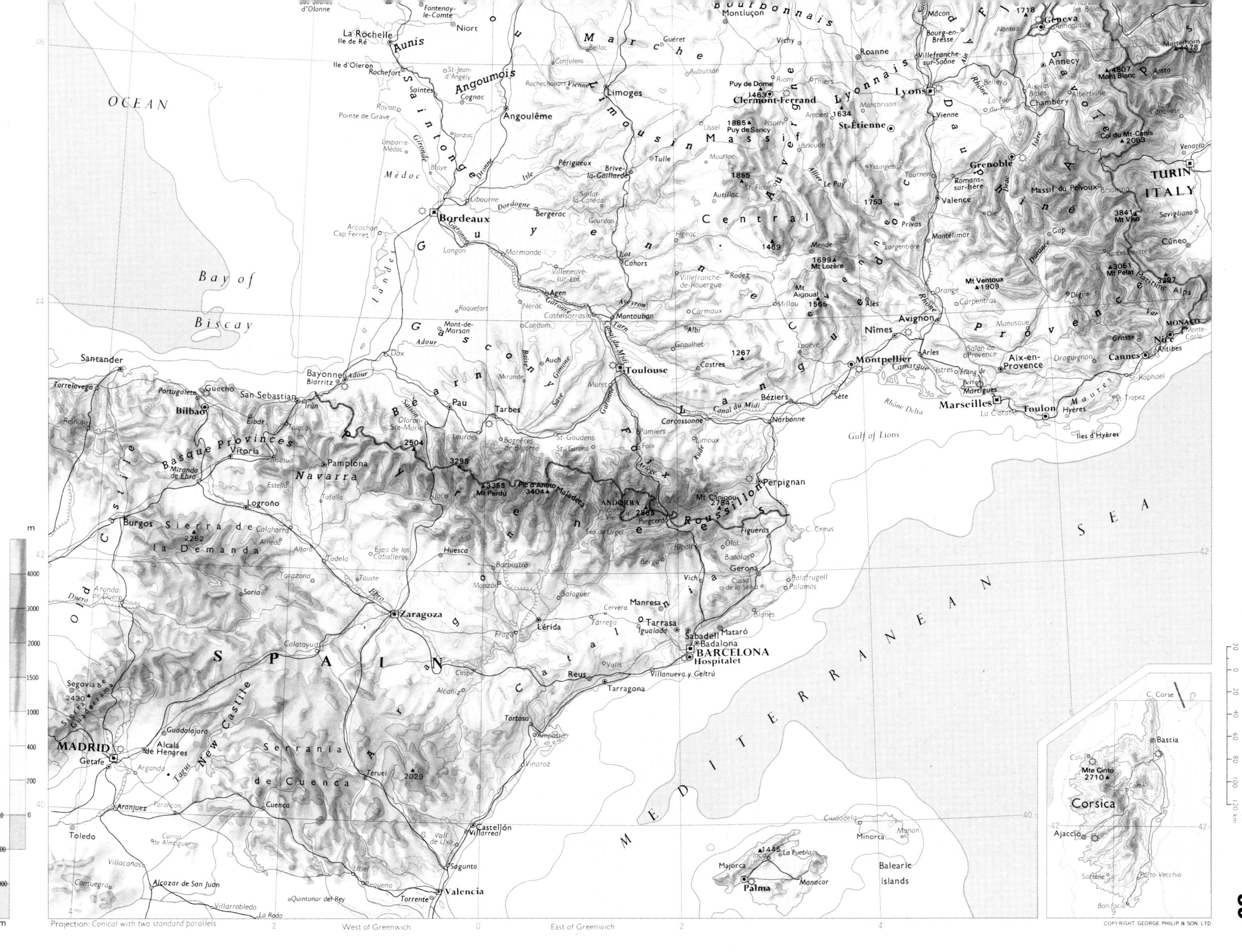

LOW COUNTRIES AND LOWER RHINE

1:2 000 000

10 0 10 20 30 40 50 60 70 80 km

m

400

200

0

Projection: Conical with two standard parallels

East from Greenwich

1:5 000 000

50 0 50 100 150 200 km

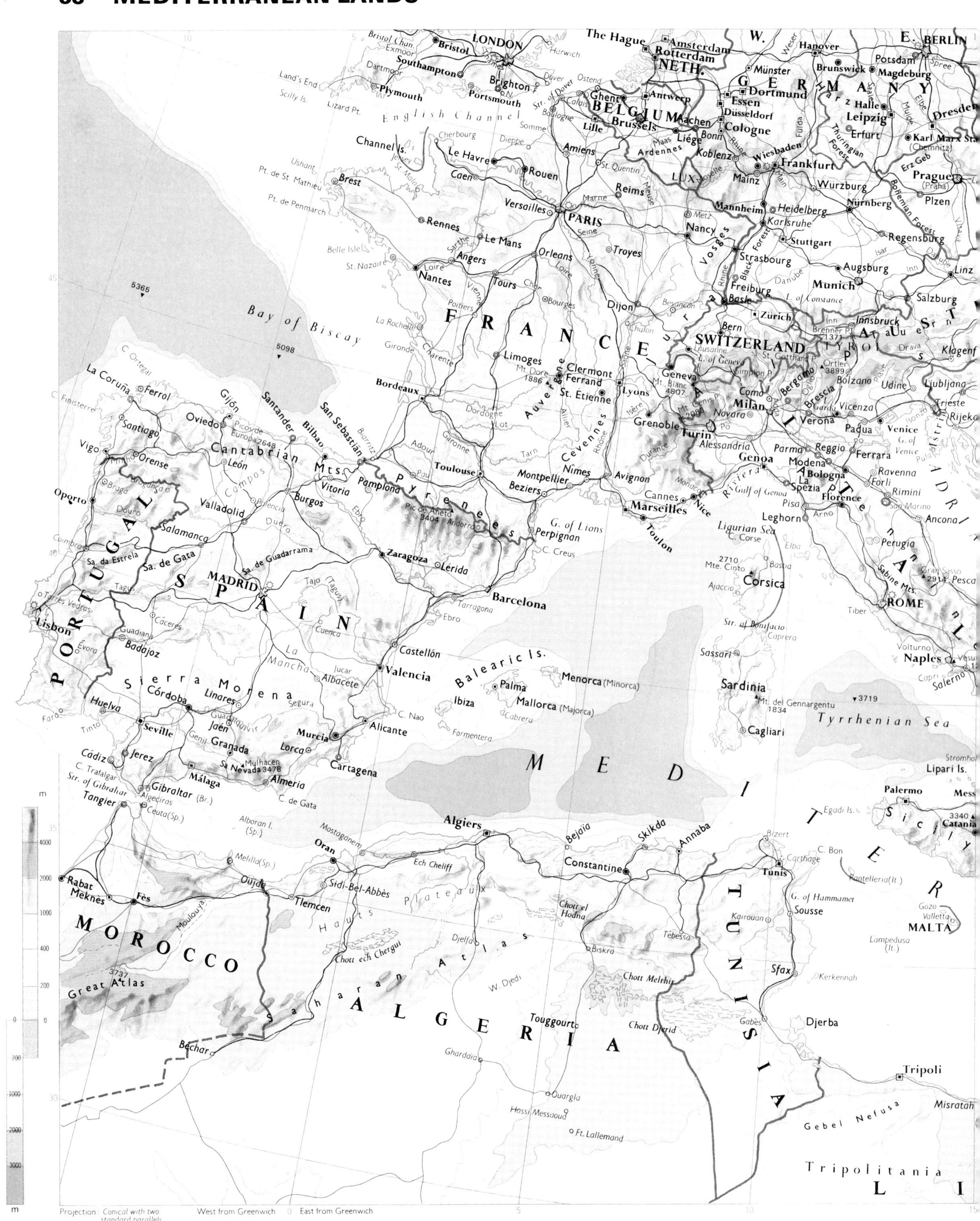
LONDON
Bristol
Bristol Chan.
Exmoor
Dartmoor
Southampton
Plymouth
Brighton
Portsmouth
Harwich
Dover
Ostend
Str. of Dover
Calais
Boulogne
Land's End
Scilly Is.
Lizard Pt.
English Channel
Channel Is.
Jersey
St. Malo
Cherbourg
Dieppe
Somme
Le Havre
Caen
Rouen
Ushant
Pt. de St Mathieu
Brest
Pt. de Penmarch
Rennes
Le Mans
Angers
Belle Isle
St. Nazaire
Loire
Nantes
Tours
Orleans
Versailles
PARIS
Seine
Marne
Amiens
St. Quentin
Reims
Meuse
Troyes
Yonne
Dijon
Besançon
Bourges
Cher
Vienne
Poitiers
La Rochelle
Gironde
Charente
Bay of Biscay
5365
5098
FRANCE
Limoges
Mt. Dore 1886
Clermont Ferrand
Auvergne
St. Étienne
Lyons
Bordeaux
Dordogne
Lot
Garonne
Adour
Tarn
Toulouse
Cevennes
Allier
Rhône
Isère
Grenoble
Montpellier
Nîmes
Avignon
Beziers
Durance
Marseilles
Toulon
Cannes
Nice
Monaco
Riviera
G. of Lions
Perpignan
C. Creus
Biarritz
The Hague
Amsterdam
Rotterdam
NETH.
Antwerp
Ghent
BELGIUM
Brussels
Lille
Liège
Aachen
Maas
Ardennes
LUX.
Moselle
Metz
Nancy
Vosges
Strasbourg
W.
Weser
Hanover
Münster
Essen
Dortmund
Düsseldorf
Cologne
Bonn
Koblenz
Rhine
Wiesbaden
Mainz
Frankfurt
Main
Fulda
GERMANY
Brunswick
Magdeburg
Harz
Halle
Leipzig
Erfurt
Thuringian Forest
Saale
Mulde
Elbe
E.
BERLIN
Potsdam
Spree
Dresden
Karl Marx Stadt (Chemnitz)
Erz Geb.
Prague (Praha)
Plzen
Bohemian Forest
Würzburg
Nürnberg
Regensburg
Mannheim
Heidelberg
Karlsruhe
Stuttgart
Black Forest
Danube
Isar
Inn
Augsburg
Munich
Linz
Salzburg
Freiburg
Basle
L. of Constance
Zürich
Jura
Bern
SWITZERLAND
Lausanne
L. of Geneva
Geneva
St. Gotthard
Simplon P.
Mt. Blanc 4807
Mt. Cenis P.
Innsbruck
Brenner P. 1371
TYROL
Drava
Ortler 3899
Bolzano
Piave
Udine
Klagenfurt
Ljubljana
Trieste
Rijeka
Istria
ALPS
Bergamo
Brescia
Como
Milan
Garda
Verona
Vicenza
Padua
Venice
G. of Venice
Isonzo
Novara
Turin
Po
Alessandria
Parma
Reggio
Modena
Ferrara
Bologna
Ravenna
Forli
Rimini
San Marino
Genoa
La Spezia
Gulf of Genoa
Pisa
Arno
Florence
Leghorn
Ancona
Ligurian Sea
C. Corse
Elba
Perugia
ITALY
APENNINES
Gran Sasso 2914
Pescara
Sabine Mts.
ROME
Tiber
Bastia
2710 Mte. Cinto
Corsica
Ajaccio
Str. of Bonifacio
Caprera
Sassari
Sardinia
Mt. del Gennargentu 1834
Cagliari
Volturno
Naples
Vesuvius
Capri
Salerno
ADRIATIC SEA
Tyrrhenian Sea
3719
Stromboli
Lipari Is.
Palermo
Messina
Egadi Is.
Sicily
3340
Catania
C. Bon
Pantelleria (It.)
Gozo
Valletta
MALTA
Lampedusa (It.)
C. Ortegal
La Coruña
Ferrol
C. Finisterre
Gijón
Oviedo
Picos de Europa 2648
Santander
Bilbao
San Sebastián
Santiago
Cantabrian Mts.
León
Vigo
Orense
Miño
Braganza
Braga
Oporto
Douro
Campos
Burgos
Vitoria
Pamplona
Pyrenees
Pic de Aneto 3404
Andorra
Palencia
Valladolid
Duero
Ebro
Salamanca
Coimbra
Sa. da Estrela
Sa. de Gata
Sa. de Guadarrama
MADRID
Zaragoza
Lérida
Barcelona
Tarragona
Tajo (Tagus)
Tagus
Torres Vedras
Lisbon
PORTUGAL
SPAIN
Cáceres
Guadiana
Badajoz
Évora
Cuenca
La Mancha
Jucar
Albacete
Castellón
Valencia
Balearic Is.
Menorca (Minorca)
Palma
Mallorca (Majorca)
Ibiza
Cabrera
Formentera
Sierra Morena
Linares
Córdoba
Segura
Guadalquivir
Huelva
Faro
Tinto
Seville
Genil
Jaén
Granada
Murcia
Lorca
Alicante
C. Nao
Cartagena
Cádiz
Jerez
Mulhacen Sa. Nevada 3478
Almeria
C. Trafalgar
Str. of Gibraltar
Gibraltar (Br.)
Algeciras
Málaga
C. de Gata
Tangier
Ceuta (Sp.)
Alboran I. (Sp.)
MEDITERRANEAN
Mostaganem
Oran
Algiers
Bejaïa
Skikda
Annaba
Bizert
Carthage
Tunis
Constantine
Ech Cheliff
Melilla (Sp.)
Oujda
Sidi-Bel-Abbès
Tlemcen
Hauts Plateaux
Rabat
Meknès
Fès
Moulouya
MOROCCO
3737
Great Atlas
Chott el Hodna
Djelfa
Chott ech Chergui
Saharan Atlas
Biskra
Tébessa
Kairouan
G. of Hammamet
Sousse
Chott Melrhir
W. Djedi
ALGERIA
TUNISIA
Sfax
Kerkennah
Touggourt
Chott Djerid
Gabès
Djerba
Béchar
Ghardaïa
Ouargla
Hassi Messaoud
Ft. Lallemand
Tripoli
Misratah
Gebel Nefusa
Tripolitania
LI
m
4000
2000
1000
400
200
0
200
1000
2000
3000
m
Projection: Conical with two standard parallels.
West from Greenwich
East from Greenwich

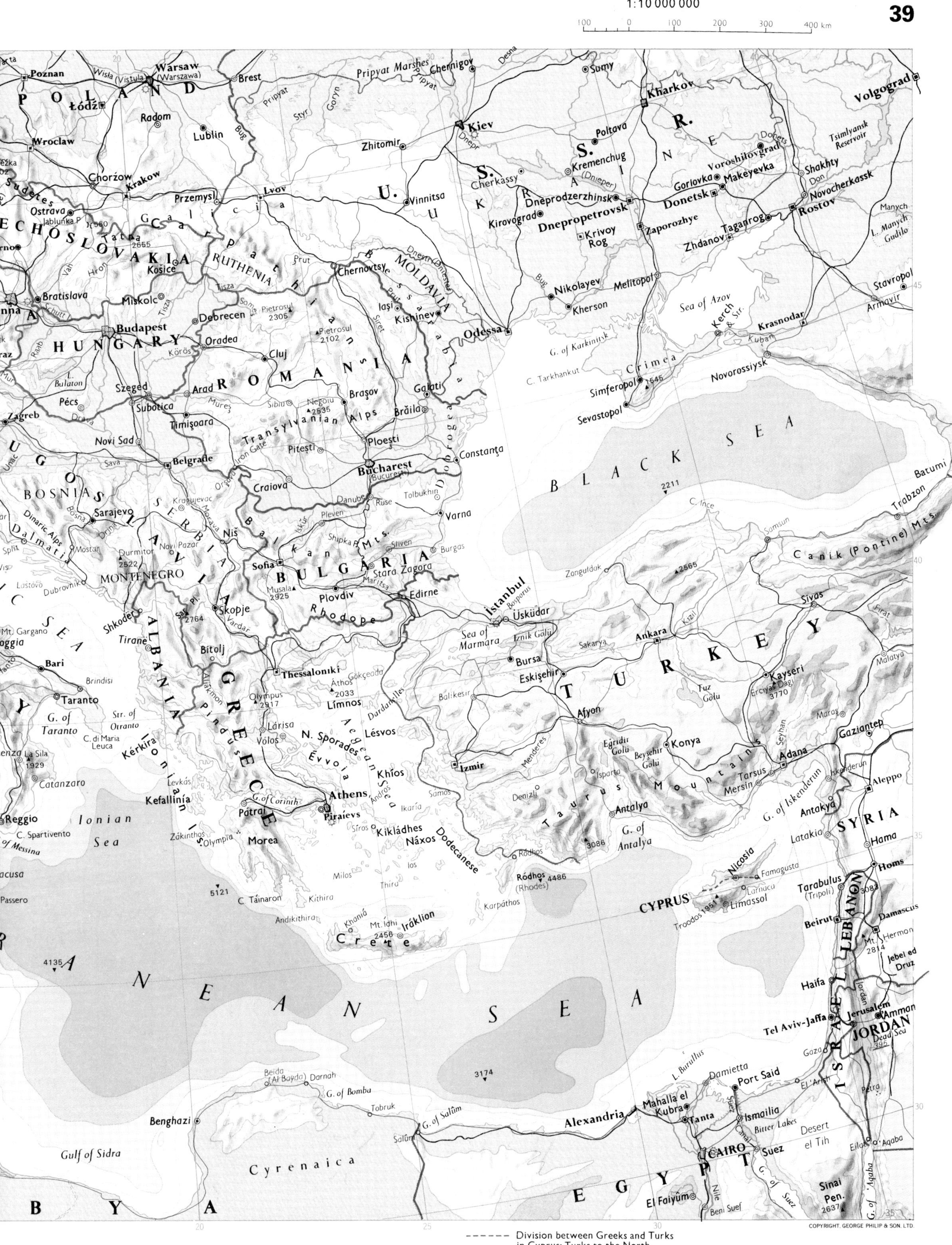

------ Division between Greeks and Turks in Cyprus; Turks to the North.

ITALY AND THE BALKAN STATES

50 0 50 100 150 200 km

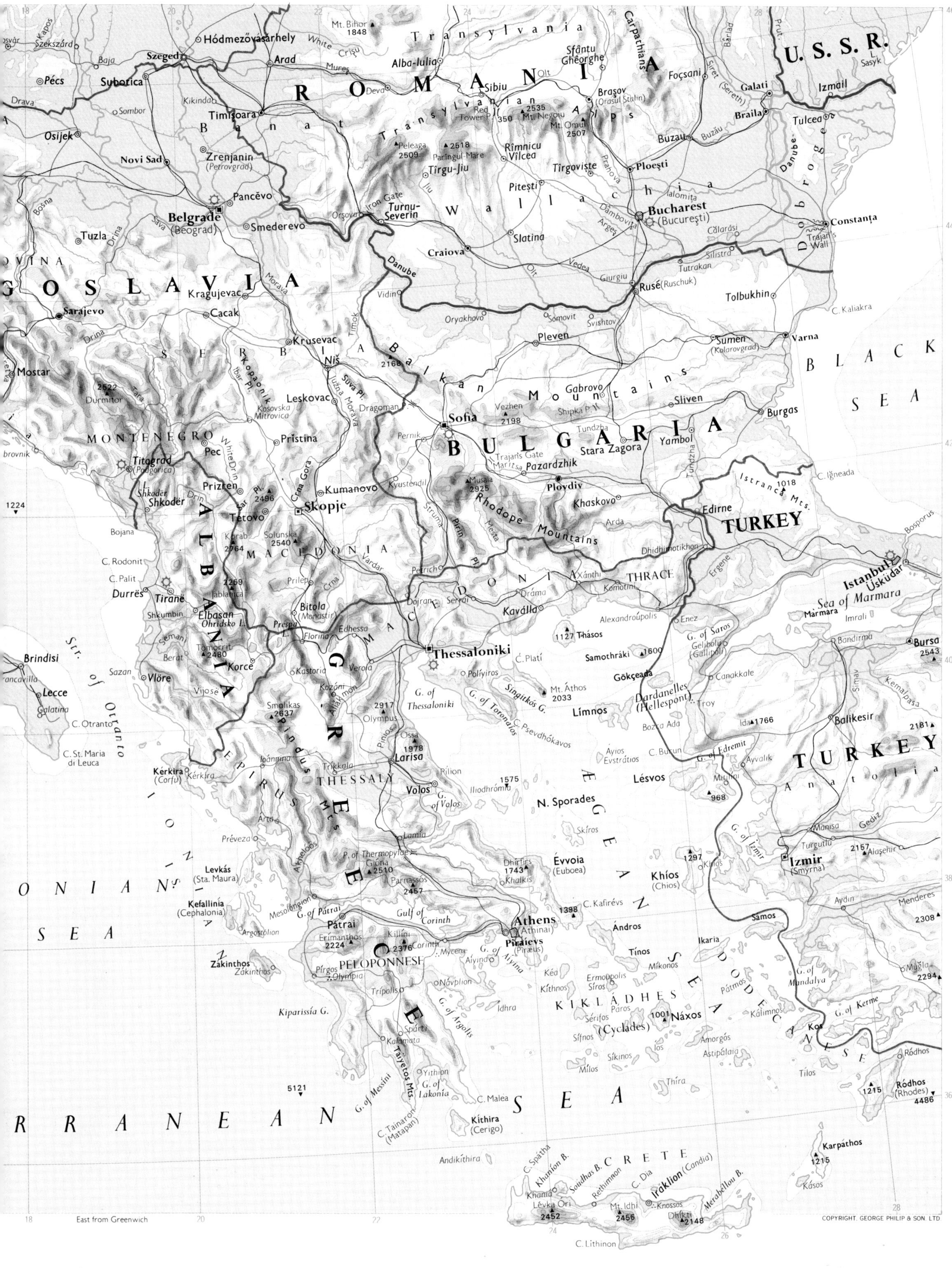

Hódmezővásárhely
Szeged
Arad
Alba-Iulia
Transylvania
Mt. Bihor 1848
White Crişu
Mureş
Sfântu Gheorghe
Carpathians
Focşani
Siret (Sereth)
Bârlad
Prut
U. S. S. R.
L. Sasyk
Izmail
Galati
Braila
Tulcea
Szekszárd
Kapos
Baja
Pécs
Subotica
Drava
Kikinda
Sombor
Osijek
Timişoara
ROMANIA
Deva
Sibiu
Olt
Braşov (Oraşul Stalin)
Transylvanian Alps
Red Tower P. 350
2535 Mt. Negoiu
Mt. Omul 2507
Banat
Novi Sad
Zrenjanin (Petrovgrad)
Peleaga 2509
2518 Paringul Mare
Tîrgu-Jiu
Rîmnicu Vîlcea
Tîrgovişte
Prahova
Buzau
Ploeşti
Danube
Dobrogea
Pancĕvo
Belgrade (Beograd)
Sava
Bosna
Smederevo
Orşova
Iron Gate
Turnu-Severin
Jiu
Walachia
Piteşti
Dâmboviţa
Argeş
Ialomiţa
Bucharest (Bucureşti)
Constanţa
Călăraşi
Trajan's Wall
Tuzla
Drina
Slatina
Craiova
Silistra
Tutrakan
Danube
Vedea
Giurgiu
Olt
Vidin
Ruse (Ruschuk)
Tolbukhin
C. Kaliakra
YUGOSLAVIA
BOSNIA
Kragujevac
Morava
Sarajevo
Cacak
Timok
Oryakhovo
Somovit
Svishtov
Pleven
Sumen (Kolarovgrad)
Varna
Drina
Krusevac
SERBIA
Niš
Balkan Mountains
2168
BLACK SEA
Mostar
Kopaonik Pl.
Ibar
2522 Durmitor
Tara
Kosovska Mitrovica
Leskovac
Suva Pl.
Južna Morava
Dragoman
Gabrovo
Shipka P.
Sliven
Burgas
Vezhen 2198
Sofia
MONTENEGRO
Priština
Pernik
BULGARIA
Tundzha
Yambol
Stara Zagora
Dubrovnik
Titograd (Podgorica)
Pec
White Drin
Trajan's Gate
Maritsa
Pazardzhik
C. Iğneada
Istranca Mts. 1018
L. Shkoder
Shkodër
Prizren
Sar Pl. 2496
Crna Gora
Kumanovo
Kyustendil
Musala 2925
Plovdiv
Khaskovo
Tundzha
Edirne
1224
Drin
Tetovo
Skopje
Struma
Pirin Pl.
Rhodope Mountains
Mesta
Arda
TURKEY
Bosporus
Bojana
ALBANIA
Korab 2764
Solunska 2540
MACEDONIA
Vardar
Dhidhimotikhon
C. Rodonit
C. Palit
2269
Jablanica
Prilep
Crna
Petrich
Xánthi
THRACE
Ergene
Komotini
Istanbul
Üsküdar
Durrës
Tiranë
Shkumbin
Elbasan
Ohridsko L.
Bitola (Monastir)
Dojran
Sérrai
Dráma
Kavála
Alexandroúpolis
Enez
Sea of Marmara
Marmara
Imrali
Prespa L.
Florina
Edhessa
MACEDONIA
1127 Thásos
G. of Saros
Gelibolu (Gallipoli)
Bandirma
Bursa 2543
Brindisi
Str. of Otranto
Semani
Tomorrit 2480
Berat
Korçe
GREECE
Veroia
Thessaloniki
C. Platí
Samothráki 1600
Sazan
Vlörë
Kastoria
Kozáni
Aliákmon
Polýiyros
Singitikós G.
Mt. Áthos 2033
Gökçeada
Çanakkale
Simav
Kemalpaşa
Francavilla
Lecce
Galatina
Vijosë
Smolikas 2637
2917 Olympus
G. of Thessaloniki
G. of Toronaíos
C. Psevdhókavos
Límnos
Dardanelles (Hellespont)
Troy
Ida 1766
Balikesir
2181
C. Otranto
Pindus Mts.
Piniós
Óssa 1978
Bozca Ada
C. St. Maria di Leuca
Ioánnina
EPIRUS
Lárisa
Tríkkala
THESSALY
Áyios Evstrátios
C. Burun
G. of Edremit
Ayvalik
TURKEY
Kérkira (Corfu)
Kérkira
Pílion
Volos
G. of Vólos
Iliodhrómia 1575
Lésvos
Mitilíni
968
Anatolia
N. Sporades
IONIAN SEA
Árta
AEGEAN SEA
Skíros
Manisa
Gediz
Préveza
Lamía
G. of Izmir
Turgutlu
Izmir (Smyrna)
2157 Alaşehir
P. of Thermopylae
Giona 2510
Dhírfis 1743
Khalkis
Évvoia (Euboea)
1297
Khíos
Khíos (Chios)
Levkás (Sta. Maura)
Akhelóos
Parnassós 2457
Kefallinía (Cephalonia)
Mesolóngion
G. of Pátrai
Gulf of Corinth
1398 C. Kafirévs
Aydin
Menderes
Argostólion
Pátrai
Erímanthos 2224
Killíni 2376
Corinth
Athens (Athínai)
Piraievs (Piræus)
Ándros
Samos
2308
Ikaria
Tínos
Mýkonos
Zákinthos
PELOPONNESE
Mycenæ
Aíyina
G. of Aíyina
Kéa
Kíthnos
Ermoúpolis Síros
Pátmos
G. of Mandalya
Muğla
2294
Pírgos
Olympia
Tripolis
Návplion
G. of Argolis
Ídhra
KIKLÁDHES (Cyclades)
Páros
Sérifos
Náxos 1001
DODECANESE
Kálimnos
Kos
G. of Kerme
Kiparissía G.
Spárti
Kalámata
Sífnos
Íos
Amorgós
Astipálaia
Míkinos
Síkinos
Mílos
Ródhos
Tílos
Taíyetos Mts.
Yíthion
G. of Lakonía
G. of Messíni
5121
C. Malea
Thíra
Ródhos (Rhodes) 1215
4486
MEDITERRANEAN SEA
C. Tainaron (Matapan)
Kíthira (Cerigo)
Kárpathos 1215
Kásos
Andikíthira
C. Spátha
Khanion B.
Soudhas B.
CRETE
C. Dia
Rethimnon
Iráklion (Candia)
Merabéllou B.
Khaniá
Lévka Óri 2452
Mt. Ídhi 2456
Knossós
Díkti 2148
C. Lithinon

East from Greenwich

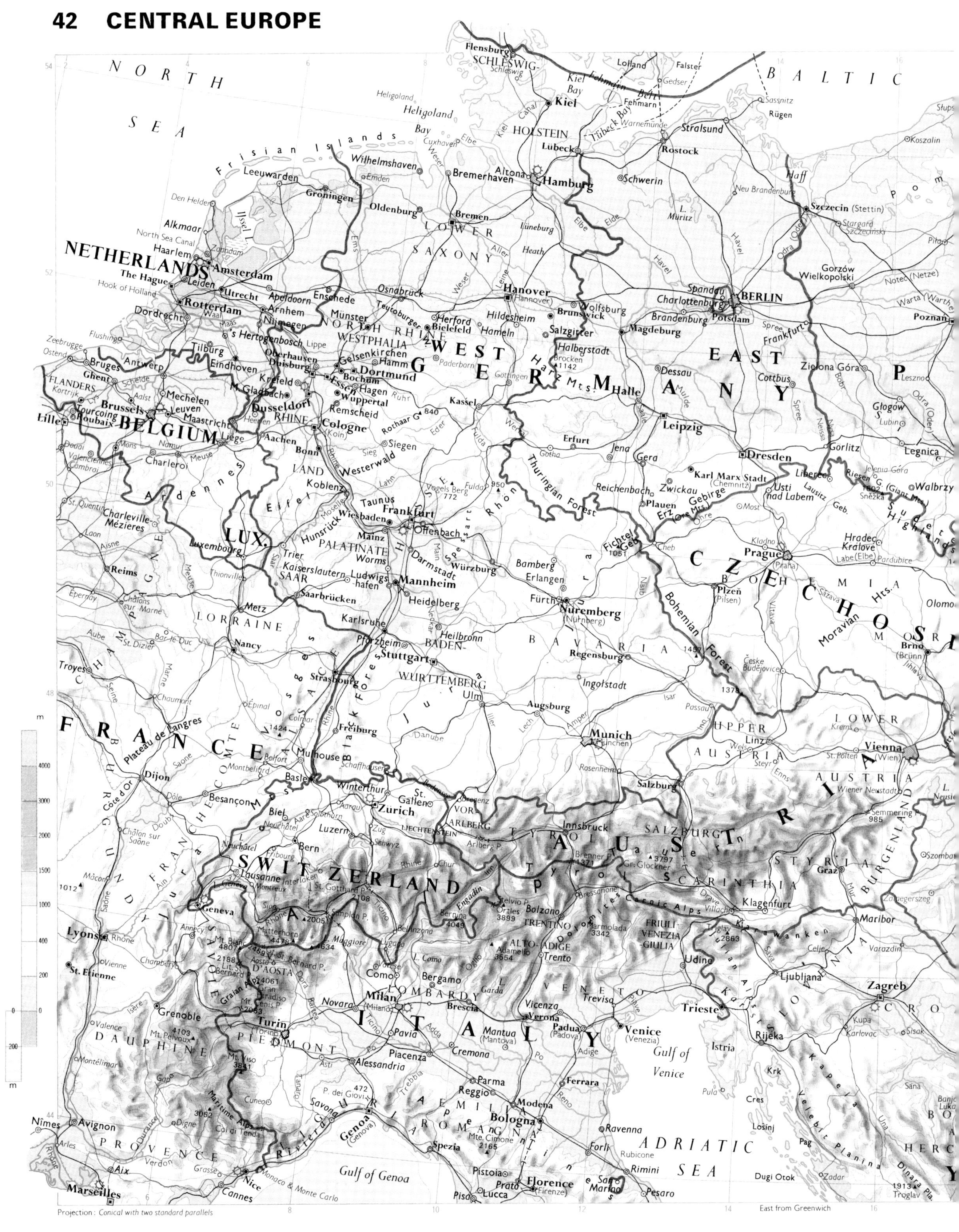
NORTH SEA
BALTIC
Frisian Islands
NETHERLANDS
BELGIUM
LUX.
WEST GERMANY
EAST GERMANY
CZECHOSLOVAKIA
FRANCE
SWITZERLAND
AUSTRIA
ITALY
Amsterdam
The Hague
Rotterdam
Brussels
Luxembourg
BERLIN
Hamburg
Bremen
Hanover
Cologne
Frankfurt
Munich
Nuremberg
Stuttgart
Prague
Vienna
Zürich
Bern
Geneva
Milan
Turin
Venice
Genoa
Bologna
Florence
Marseilles
Lyons
Dijon
Strasbourg
Leipzig
Dresden
Szczecin (Stettin)
Poznan
Zagreb
Ljubljana
Trieste
Gulf of Genoa
Gulf of Venice
ADRIATIC SEA
Projection: Conical with two standard parallels
East from Greenwich

1:5 000 000

50 0 50 100 150 200 km
CENTRAL EUROPE POLITICAL
1:25 000 000
DENMARK
Copenhagen
Amsterdam
Hamburg
Berlin
WEST GERMANY
EAST GERMANY
POLAND
Warsaw
U.S.S.R.
Kiev
Lvov
BELGIUM
Brussels
Bonn
LUX.
FRANCE
Prague
CZECHOSLOVAKIA
Vienna
Budapest
AUSTRIA
HUNGARY
Bern
SWITZ.
Liechtenstein
Trieste
ROMANIA
ITALY
Bucharest
Belgrade
YUGOSLAVIA
Monaco
San Marino
BULGARIA
Sofia
Rome
Gdańsk Bay
Kaliningrad
Pregel
Chernyakhovsk
Vilnius
LITHUANIA S.S.R.
Gdynia
Sopot
Gdańsk
329
Tczew
Elblag
Lyna
309
Suwałki
WHITE RUSSIA S.S.R.
Olsztyn
Grodno
Neman
238
Masurian Lakes Plateau
Grudziadz
Shchara
Slonim
Lomza
Ostrołęka
Białystok
Volkovysk
Torun
Narew
Noteć
Ciechanów
Inowrocław
Wkra
Bug
Włocławek
Wisła
Płock
(Vistula)
Gniezno
Warsaw
(Warszawa)
Siedlce
Biała Podlaska
Brest
Konin
Pripyat
Kalisz
Łódź
Pabianice
Tomaszów Mazowiecki
Sieradz
Pilica
Warta
Piotrków
Radom
Pripyat Marshes
316
Uzh
Desna
Sluch
Kovel
Styr
Korosten
Lublin
Chełm
Zamość
Vladimir Volynski
Lutsk
Rovno
Kiev
Kielce
612
Ostrowiec Swietokrzyski
Częstochowa
Opole
Teterev
Zhitomir
Shepetovka
Stalowa Wola
Tarnobrzeg
San
390
Fastov
Belaya Tserkov
Zabrze
Bytom
Gliwice
Sosnowiec
Chorzów
Katowice
Tychy
Kraków
Wisła (Vistula)
Tarnov
Rzeszów
Berdichev
Kazatin
Starokonstantinov
Opava
Ostrava
Bielsko
Przemyśl
Lvov
Zolochev
UKRAINE S.S.R.
Nowy Sącz
Krosno
Dukla P.
502
1725
471
Ternopol
Khmelnitsky
384
Vinnitsa
Frýdek Místek
Jablunka P.
550
West Beskids
East Beskids
Dnestr
Drogobych
U. S. S. R.
Carpathian Mountains
High Tatra
2655
Žilina
Gottwaldov
Váh
Prešov
Zhmerinka
Uman
SLOVAKIA
Low Tatra
Banská Bystrica
Košice
Ivano Frankovsk
Kamenets Podolski
Bug
White Mts.
Nitra
Slovakian Ore Mts.
Uzhgorod
Mukachevo
Ruthenia
1881
Khotin
Pervomaisk
931
of the Tartars
Chernovtsy
2061
Hron
Salgótarján
Sajó
Hernád
Bodrog
Miskolc
Botoșani
Beltsy
MOLDAVIA S.S.R.
Prut
Kotovsk
Eger
Nyíregyháza
Satu Mare
Baia Mare
Pietrosul
2305
Suceava
Győr
Tatabánya
Forest
Újpest
BUDAPEST
Tisza
Debrecen
Someș
429
Iași
Kishinev
Tiraspol
Bendery
Székesfehérvár
Cegléd
Szolnok
2102
Bistrița
Pietrosu
Bistrita
Zalău
Oradea
Piatra Neamț
Vaslui
Odessa
HUNGARY
Balaton
Kecskemét
Cluj
Bacau
Körös
Békéscsaba
Tîrgu Mureș
Black Crișu
1848
Mt. Bihor
Miercurea Ciuc
Belgorod Dnestrovski
Siret (Sereth)
Kaposvár
Szekszárd
Hódmezővásárhely
White Crișu
Transylvania
Szeged
Arad
Alba-Iulia
Mureș
Sasyk
Pecs
Subotica
Senta
Deva
Sibiu
Olt
Sfîntu Gheorghe
Brașov
Focșani
Galati
Izmail
Drava
Sombor
Kikinda
Timișoara
ROMANIA
Hunedoara
Red Tower P.
350
Transylvanian Alps
Mt. Negoiu
2535
Mt. Omul
2507
Braila
467
Tulcea
Osijek
Banat
Peleaga
2509
2518
Parîngul Mare
Buzau
Novi Sad
Tisa
Zrenjanin
(Petrovgrad)
Resița
Rîmnicu Vîlcea
Prahova
Ploesti
Danube
Dobrogea
Sremska Mitrovica
Vršac
Porta Orientalis
Tîrgu-Jiu
Tîrgoviste
Slobozia
Jiu
Pitești
Wallachia
Ialomița
Bela Crkva
Iron Gate
Turnu-Severin
Dîmbovița
Argeș
Bucharest
(București)
BLACK SEA
Constanta
Belgrade
Sava
(Beograd)
Smederevo
Slatina
Calarași
Trajan's Wall
Tuzla
Craiova
Morava
Olt
Vedea
Alexandria
Timok
1346
YUGOSLAVIA
Danube
Giurgiu
Ruse (Ruschuk)
BULGARIA
Tolbukhin
Sarajevo
Kragujevac
18
20
22
24
26
28
30
44
46
48
50
52
54

BARENTS SEA
NORWEGIAN SEA
U.S.S.R.
GULF OF BOTHNIA
FINLAND
NORWAY
SWEDEN
FINNMARK
TROMS
NORRBOTTEN
VÄSTERBOTTEN
OULU
KUOPIO
VAASA
KESKI-SUOMI
POHJOIS-KARJALA
MIKKELI
JÄMTLAND
VÄSTERNORRLAND
N.-TRØNDELAG
SØR-TRØNDELAG
MØRE OG ROMSDAL
Lappland
Arctic Circle
West from Greenwich
ICELAND
At the same scale as main map
Murmansk
Kandalaksha
Kandalaksha Gulf
Pechenga
Nikel
Kirkenes
Vadsø
Varanger Fjord
Hammerfest
North Cape
Porsangen
Lopphavet
Kvænangen
Tromsø
Senja
Vesterålen
Lofoten
Narvik
Kiruna
Kebnekaise
Gällivare
Luleå
Boden
Piteå
Skellefteå
Umeå
Haparanda
Tornio
Kemi
Rovaniemi
Oulu
Kajaani
Kokkola
Pietarsaari
Vaasa
Kvarken
Örnsköldsvik
Kramfors
Härnösand
Sundsvall
Östersund
Storsjön
Trondheim
Steinkjer
Levanger
Namsos
Mo i Rana
Mosjøen
Bodø
Vest Fjorden
Kristiansund
Molde
Ålesund
Jyväskylä
Kuopio
Joensuu
Savonlinna
Varkaus
Nurmes
Inari L.
Reykjavík
Keflavík
Akranes
Hafnarfjörður
Akureyri
Húsavík
Ísafjörður
Sauðárkrókur
Seyðisfjörður
Vopnafjörður
Faxaflói
Breiðafjörður
Húnaflói
Vatnajökull
Langjökull
Hofsjökull
Mýrdalsjökull
Hekla 1491
Vestmannaeyjar
Surtsey

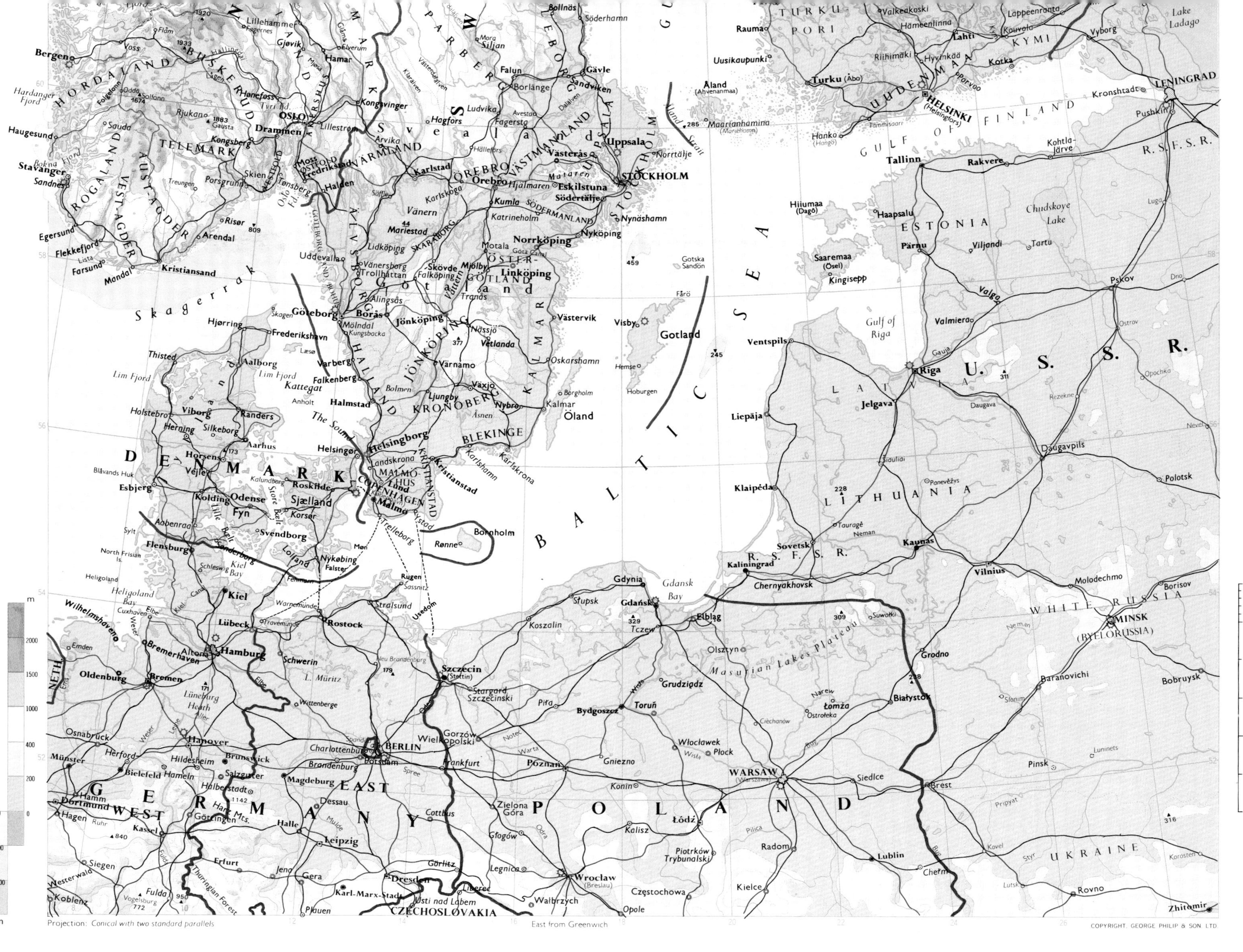

LENINGRAD
HELSINKI (Helsingfors)
GULF OF FINLAND
ESTONIA
Tallinn
Riga
LATVIA
LITHUANIA
Vilnius
Kaunas
MINSK
WHITE RUSSIA (BYELORUSSIA)
U. S. S. R.
UKRAINE
Brest
WARSAW
POLAND
Gdańsk
Gdynia
Kaliningrad
BALTIC SEA
Gotland
Visby
STOCKHOLM
Uppsala
Gulf of Riga
Saaremaa (Ösel)
Hiiumaa (Dagö)
Åland
OSLO
Göteborg
Skagerrak
Kattegat
COPENHAGEN
DENMARK
Malmö
Bornholm
Rønne
Szczecin (Stettin)
BERLIN
EAST GERMANY
WEST GERMANY
Hamburg
Bremen
Kiel
Rostock
Poznań
Wrocław (Breslau)
Łódź
CZECHOSLOVAKIA
1:6 000 000
50 0 50 100 150 200 250 km
Projection: Conical with two standard parallels
East from Greenwich
COPYRIGHT GEORGE PHILIP & SON LTD

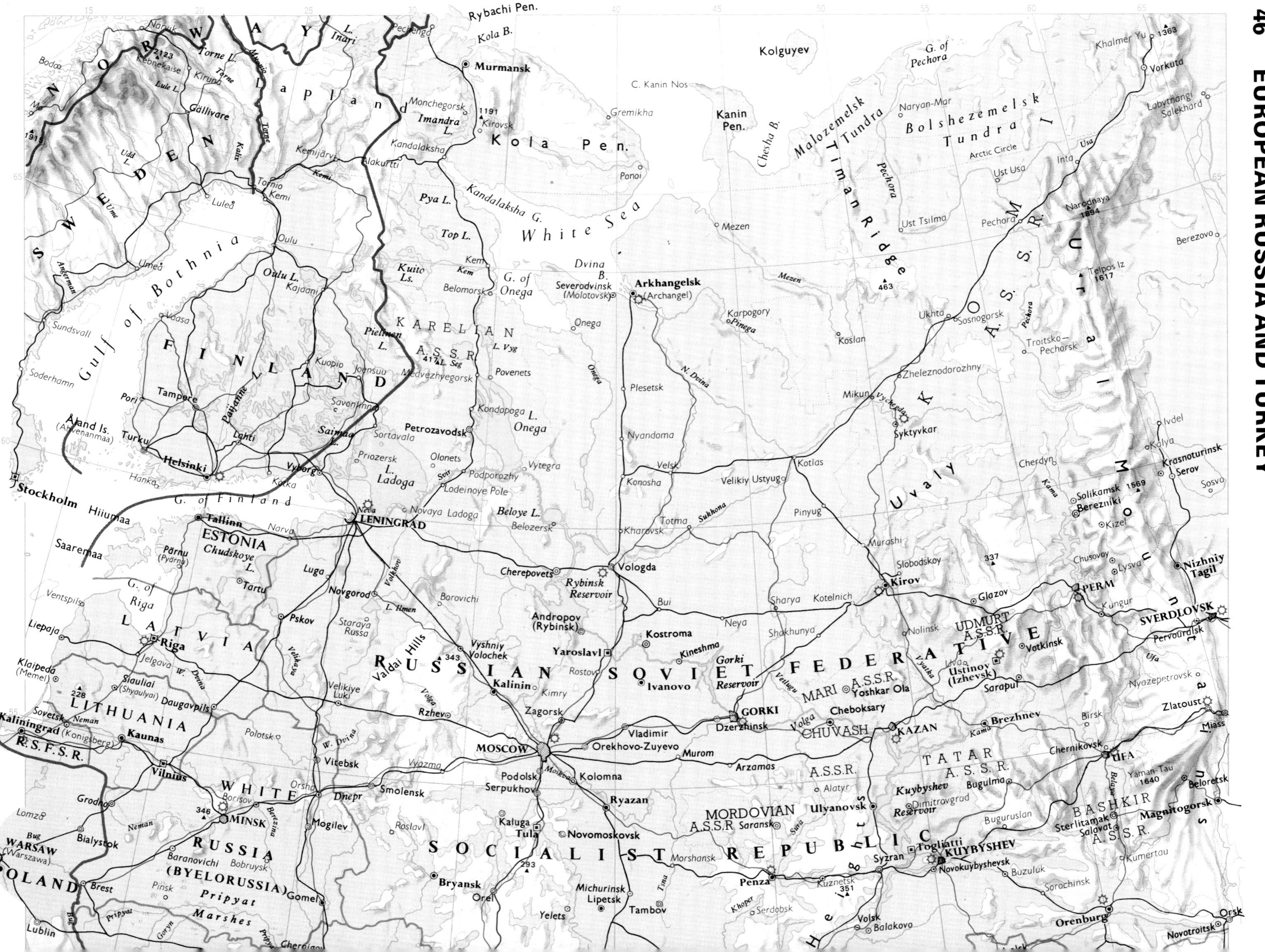
Rybachi Pen.
Kola B.
Murmansk
Kola Pen.
Kandalaksha G.
White Sea
C. Kanin Nos
Kanin Pen.
Chesha B.
Kolguyev
Malozemelsk Tundra
Timan Ridge
Bolshezemelsk Tundra
G. of Pechora
Pechora
Arctic Circle
Naryan-Mar
Ust Tsilma
Ust Usa
Inta
Vorkuta
Labytnangi
Salekhard
Narodnaya 1894
Telpos Iz 1617
Ural Mts.
Ukhta
Sosnogorsk
Troitsko-Pechorsk
Syktyvkar
Kotlas
Uvaly
Kirov
Glazov
PERM
Berezniki
Solikamsk
Serov
Krasnoturinsk
Nizhniy Tagil
SVERDLOVSK
Pervouralsk
Zlatoust
Magnitogorsk
Beloretsk
UFA
BASHKIR A.S.S.R.
Sterlitamak
Salavat
Orenburg
Orsk
Novotroitsk
UDMURT A.S.S.R.
Ustinov (Izhevsk)
Votkinsk
Sarapul
Brezhnev
TATAR A.S.S.R.
KAZAN
Bugulma
Buzuluk
KUYBYSHEV
Togliatti
Novokuybyshevsk
Syzran
Kuybyshev Reservoir
Ulyanovsk
CHUVASH
Cheboksary
MARI A.S.S.R.
Yoshkar Ola
GORKI
Dzerzhinsk
Gorki Reservoir
Arzamas
MORDOVIAN A.S.S.R.
Saransk
Penza
Tambov
Michurinsk
Lipetsk
Yelets
Ryazan
Novomoskovsk
Tula
Kaluga
Orel
Bryansk
Smolensk
Vitebsk
Mogilev
Gomel
MINSK
WHITE RUSSIA (BYELORUSSIA)
Pripyat Marshes
Brest
Grodno
Bialystok
WARSAW (Warszawa)
POLAND
Lublin
Vilnius
Kaunas
LITHUANIA
Kaliningrad (Königsberg)
R.S.F.S.R.
Klaipeda (Memel)
Sovetsk
Liepaja
Ventspils
G. of Riga
Riga
LATVIA
Daugavpils
Pskov
Tartu
ESTONIA
Tallinn
Pärnu
Saaremaa
Hiiumaa
G. of Finland
Narva
Novgorod
Luga
LENINGRAD
L. Ladoga
L. Onega
Petrozavodsk
Valdai Hills
Kalinin
MOSCOW
Podolsk
Serpukhov
Kolomna
Orekhovo-Zuyevo
Vladimir
Ivanovo
Kostroma
Yaroslavl
Andropov (Rybinsk)
Rybinsk Reservoir
Cherepovets
Vologda
Beloye L.
Velikiy Ustyug
Arkhangelsk (Archangel)
Severodvinsk (Molotovsk)
Dvina B.
Onega
G. of Onega
Mezen
Plesetsk
KARELIAN A.S.S.R.
RUSSIAN SOVIET FEDERATIVE SOCIALIST REPUBLIC
FINLAND
Helsinki
Tampere
Turku
Pori
Vaasa
Oulu
Oulu L.
Kemi
Tornio
Lapland
L. Inari
Kuopio
Joensuu
Saimaa
Vyborg
Lahti
Kotka
Gulf of Bothnia
Åland Is. (Ahvenanmaa)
SWEDEN
NORWAY
Stockholm
Luleå
Umeå
Sundsvall
Gällivare
Kiruna
Kebnekaise 2123
Narvik
Bodø

1 Kabardino-Balkar A.S.S.R.
2 North Ossetian A.S.S.R.
3 Nakhichevan A.S.S.R. (Azer.)
4 Checheno-Ingush A.S.S.R.
-132 Karagiye Depression
-28m below sea-level
CASPIAN SEA
BLACK SEA
Sea of Azov
MEDITERRANEAN SEA
Levant
KAZAKHSTAN
Kirgiz Steppe
UKRAINE
MOLDAVIA
ROMANIA
BULGARIA
TURKEY
Anatolia
GEORGIA
ARMENIA
AZERBAIJAN
DAGESTAN
ABKHAZ
ADZHAR
IRAN (PERSIA)
IRAQ
SYRIA
LEBANON
CYPRUS
KALMYK A.S.S.R.
Caucasus Mountains
Taurus Mountains
Canik (Pontine) Mts.
Elburz
Syrian Desert
Ergeni Heights
KIEV
KHARKOV
DONETSK
DNEPROPETROVSK
ODESSA
BUCHAREST (Bucureşti)
ISTANBUL
ANKARA
TBILISI
YEREVAN
BAKU
TEHRAN
BAGHDAD
DAMASCUS (Esh Sham)
Volgograd (Stalingrad)
Voroshilovgrad (Lugansk)
Astrakhan
Rostov
Krasnodar
Sevastopol
Simferopol
Crimea
Trabzon
Samsun
Izmir (Smyrna)
Bursa
Konya
Adana
Aleppo (Halab)
Mosul
Tabriz
Rasht
Hamadan
Kara Bogaz Gol.
Ródhos (Rhodes) 4486
Demavend 5604
Elbrus 5633
Kazbek 5047
Ararat 5165
Dodecanese
Projection: Conical with two standard parallels
Division between Greeks and Turks in Cyprus, Turks to the North
East from Greenwich
1:10 000 000
100 0 100 200 300 400 km

R.S.F.S.R.
1. Daghestan A.S.S.R.
2. Kabardino-Balkar A.S.S.R.
3. Mari A.S.S.R.
4. Mordovian A.S.S.R.
5. North Ossetian A.S.S.R.
6. Tatar A.S.S.R.
7. Udmurt A.S.S.R.
8. Chuvash A.S.S.R.
9. Checheno-Ingush A.S.S.R.
AZERBAIJAN
10. Nakhichevan A.S.S.R.
GEORGIA
11. Abkhaz A.S.S.R.
12. Adzhar A.S.S.R.
NORWAY
SWEDEN
FINLAND
DENMARK
POLAND
ROMANIA
TURKEY
IRAQ
IRAN (PERSIA)
AFGHANISTAN
CHINA
North Sea
Skagerrak
Kattegat
Baltic Sea
Gulf of Bothnia
G. of Finland
G. of Riga
Barents Sea
White Sea
Kara Sea
Black Sea
Sea of Azov
Caspian Sea
Aral Sea
L. Balkhash
L. Ladoga
L. Onega
Franz Josef Land
Novaya Zemlya
Kolguyev I.
Vaigach I.
Yamal Pena.
Gyda Pena.
Gulf of Ob
Yenisey Gulf
Pechora G.
Arctic Circle
RUSSIAN SOVIET FEDER
KOMI A.S.S.R.
KARELIAN A.S.S.R.
BASHKIR A.S.S.R.
KALMYK A.S.S.R.
KARAKALPAK A.S.S.R.
ESTONIA
LATVIA
LITHUANIA
WHITE RUSSIA
UKRAINE
MOLDAVIA
GEORGIA
ARMENIA
AZERBAIJAN
KAZAKHSTAN
UZBEKISTAN
TURKMENISTAN
KIRGIZIA
TADZHIKISTAN
West Siberian Plain
Kara Kum
Kyzyl Kum
Ust Urt Plateau
Pamirs
Dzungaria
Tarbagatai Ra.
Elburz Mts.
Zagros Mts.
Dasht-i-Kavir
Oslo
Stockholm
Helsinki
Copenhagen
Hamburg
Berlin
Warsaw
Kaliningrad (Königsberg)
Riga
Tallinn
Vilnius
Minsk
Leningrad
Moscow
Kiev
Kharkov
Odessa
Dnepropetrovsk
Donetsk
Rostov
Volgograd
Saratov
Kuybyshev
Kazan
Gorki
Perm
Sverdlovsk
Chelyabinsk
Ufa
Orenburg
Astrakhan
Tbilisi
Yerevan
Baku
Arkhangelsk
Murmansk
Omsk
Novosibirsk
Tomsk
Karaganda
Alma Ata
Frunze
Tashkent
Samarkand
Dushanbe
Ashkhabad
Tehran
Tabriz
Urumqi
Mt. Blednaya 1053
Communism Pk. 7495
Pk. Pobedy 7439
Projection: Conical Orthomorphic with two standard parallels
East from Greenwich

1:20 000 000
200 0 200 400 600 800 km
Boundaries of U.S.S.R.
Boundaries of S.S.R.
Boundaries of A.S.S.R.

1:50 000 000

500 0 500 1000 1500 2000 km

m 6000 4000 2000 1000 400 200 0

0 200 2000 4000 6000 8000 m

Projection: Bonne

East from Greenwich

1:50 000 000

500 0 500 1000 1500 2000 km

1:100 000 000

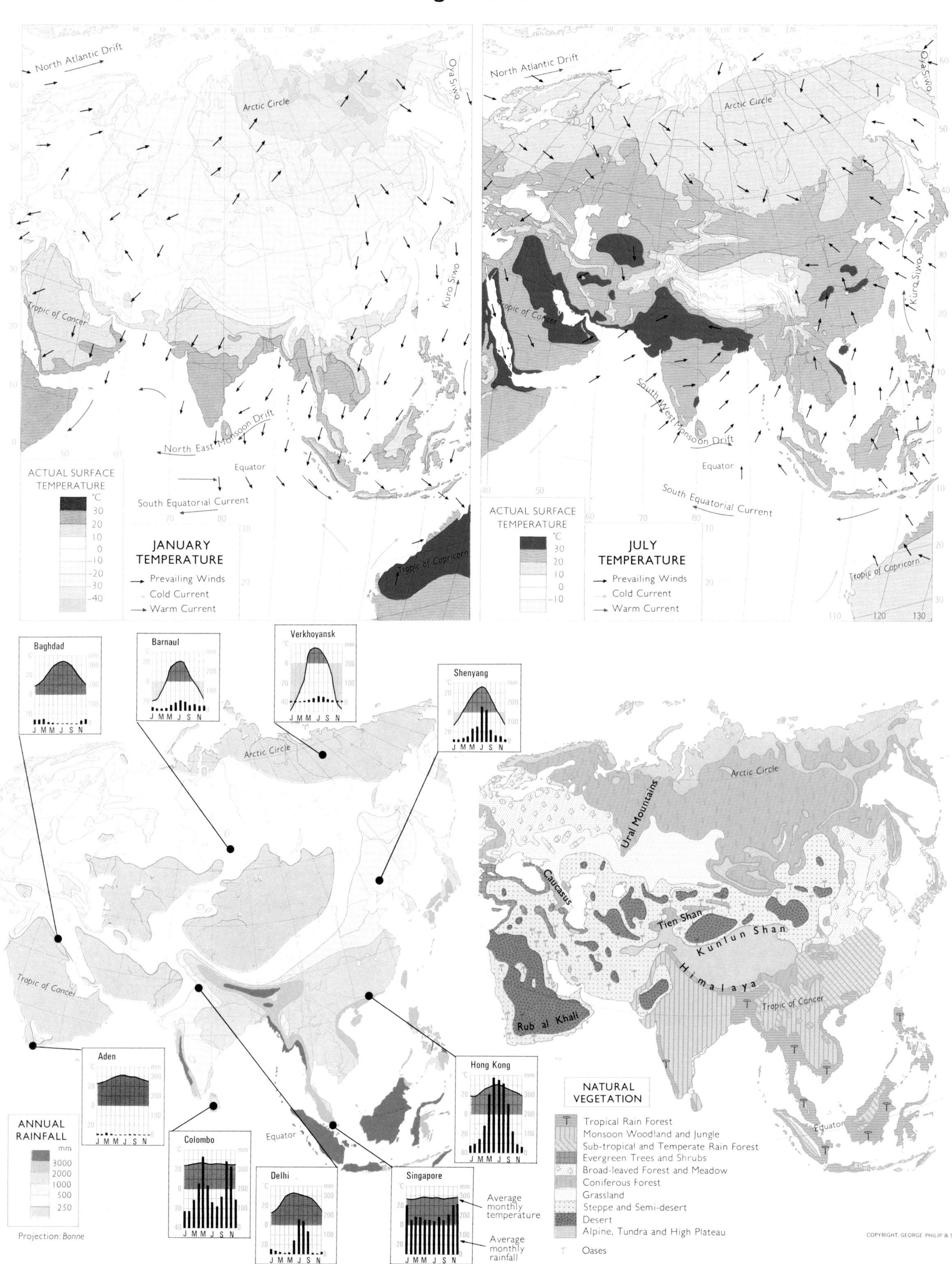
North Atlantic Drift
Arctic Circle
Oya Siwo
Kuro Siwo
Tropic of Cancer
North East Monsoon Drift
Equator
South Equatorial Current
Tropic of Capricorn
ACTUAL SURFACE TEMPERATURE
°C
30
20
10
0
−10
−20
−30
−40
JANUARY TEMPERATURE
Prevailing Winds
Cold Current
Warm Current
South West Monsoon Drift
JULY TEMPERATURE
Baghdad
Barnaul
Verkhoyansk
Shenyang
Aden
Colombo
Delhi
Singapore
Hong Kong
ANNUAL RAINFALL
mm
3000
2000
1000
500
250
Average monthly temperature
Average monthly rainfall
J M M J S N
Ural Mountains
Caucasus
Tien Shan
Kunlun Shan
Himalaya
Rub al Khali
NATURAL VEGETATION
Tropical Rain Forest
Monsoon Woodland and Jungle
Sub-tropical and Temperate Rain Forest
Evergreen Trees and Shrubs
Broad-leaved Forest and Meadow
Coniferous Forest
Grassland
Steppe and Semi-desert
Desert
Alpine, Tundra and High Plateau
Oases
Projection: Bonne

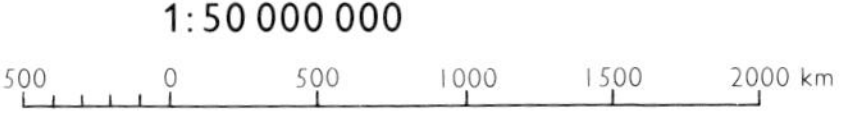

1:50 000 000

500 0 500 1000 1500 2000 km

Arctic Circle
Tropic of Cancer
Equator
Stockholm
Warsaw
Moscow
Donbas
Istanbul
Beirut
Kirkuk
Tehrān
Urals
Kuzbas
Tashkent
Delhi
Calcutta
Peking
Chungking
Daye
Hong Kong
Tōkyō
Rangoon
Bangkok
Ho Chi Minh City
Manila
Singapore
LAND USE
Arable land
Arable land with permanent pasture
Fruit trees, vineyards and plantations
Permanent pasture
Woods and forests
Rough grazing
Rough grazing with trees
Non-productive land
LIVESTOCK
Cattle
Sheep
MINERALS
Asbestos
Bauxite
Copper
Diamonds
Gold
Iron ore
Lead
Lead and Zinc
Mica
Silver
Tin
Zinc
Sb Antimony
Cr Chrome
Co Cobalt
Mg Magnesium
Mn Manganese
Hg Mercury
Ni Nickel
Ti Titanium
POWER
Coalfields
Gasfields
Oilfields
Hydro-electric power
CROPS
Bananas
Barley
Citrus fruits
Coffee
Cotton
Date palms
Groundnuts
Maize
Millet
Potatoes
Rice
Rubber
Soybeans
Sugar beet
Sugar cane
Tea
Tobacco
Vines
Wheat
Principal fishing areas
LAND USE
(million hectares)
Arable land and permanent crops 713.6
Permanent pasture 911.7
Woods and forests 1 523.6
Other land 1 754.9
Total land area 4 903.8 million hectares
Projection: Bonne
East from Greenwich

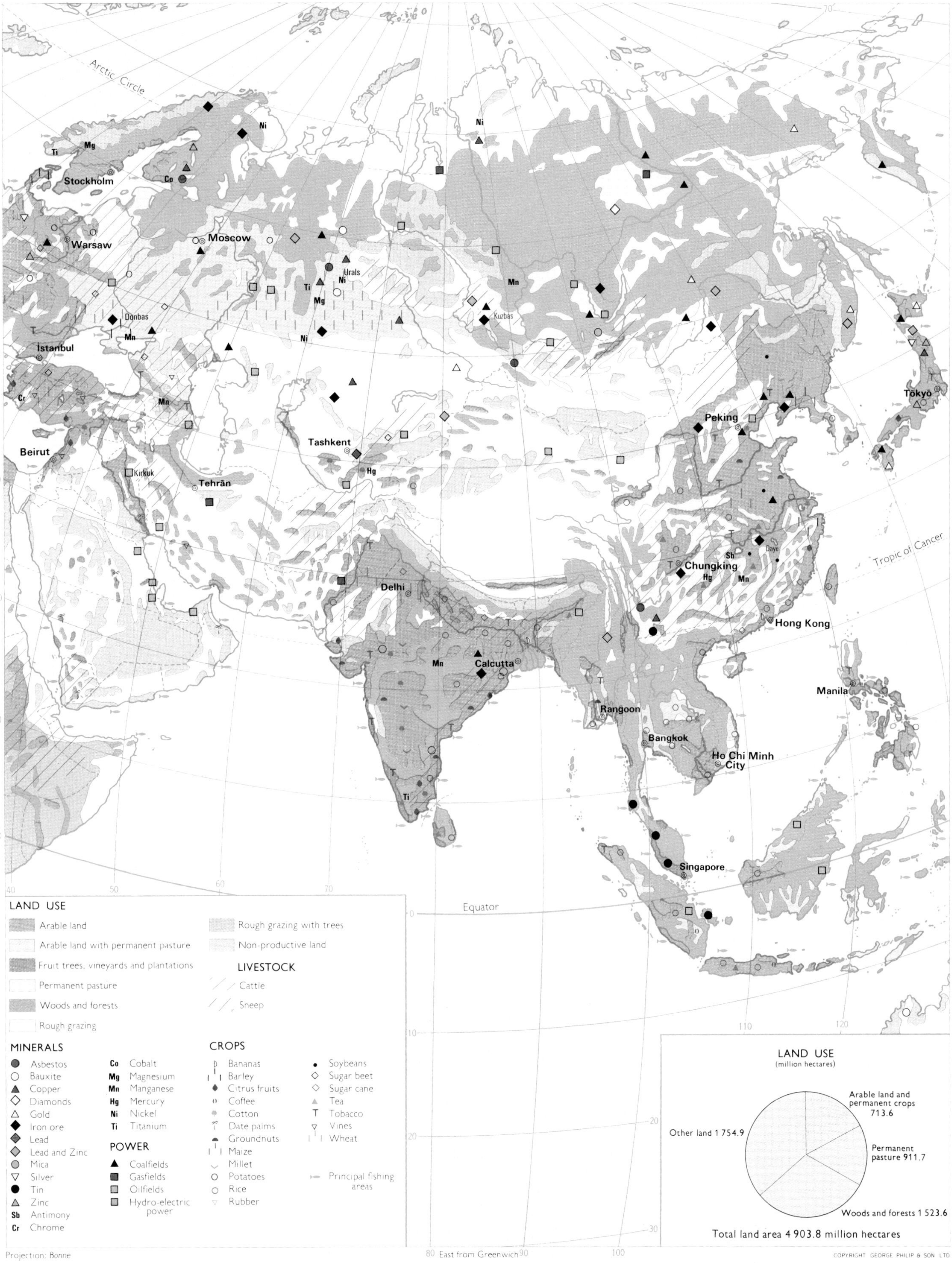

	Population								Land			Agriculture		
	Total	Density	Birth Rate	Death Rate	Life Expectancy	Growth 1965-73	Growth 1973-83	Urban	Area	Arable	Forest	Agricultural Population	Index of Production	Food intake
Asia	th.	persons per km²	per th. popn.	per th. popn.	yrs.	av. % per annum	av. % per annum	%	th. km²	th. km²	th. km²	% of total popn.	1974-76 = 100	calories per day
Afghanistan	17 672	27	48	22	36	2.3	2.6	17	648	81	19	77	115	2 055
Bangladesh	96 730	722	47	19	50	2.6	2.4	17	134	91	21	83	125	1 837
Burma	37 614	57	39	14	55	2.3	2.0	29	658	101	322	50	150	2 420
Cambodia	7 149	40	30	40	31	1.8			177	30	134	72	104	1 922
China	1 051 551	113	22	8	67	2.7	1.5	21	9 326	1 009	1 282	57	145	2 426
Cyprus	657	73	20	9	74		0.6		9	4.3	1.7	33	113	3 378
Hong Kong	5 364	5 364	14	5	76	2.0	2.5	92	1	0.1	0.1	2.1	67	2 771
India	746 742	251	34	12	55	2.3	2.3	24	2 973	1 695	675	61	132	2 056
Indonesia	159 895	88	36	15	54	2.1	2.3	24	1 812	196	1 218	57	140	2 373
Iran	43 414	27	43	12	60	3.3	3.1	53	1 636	137	180	36	116	2 834
Iraq	15 158	35	47	13	59	3.3	3.6	69	434	55	15	38	136	2 789
Israel	4 194	210	24	7	74	3.1	2.3	90	20	4.2	1.2	6.2	121	3 062
Japan	120 018	323	13	6	77	1.2	0.9	76	371	48	252	9.2	99	2 852
Jordan	3 375	35	48	10	64	3.0	2.7	72	97	4.1	0.4	24	136	2 498
Korea, North	19 630	164	33	8	65	2.8	2.5	62	120	23	90	43	138	2 995
Korea, South	40 578	414	23	6	67	2.2	1.6	62	98	22	66	35	122	3 056
Laos	4 315	19	43	17	44	1.4	2.2	15	231	8.9	128	72	150	1 927
Lebanon	2 644	264	30	9	65	2.6	0.3	78	10	2.9	0.7	7.9	123	2 995
Malaysia	15 204	46	31	7	67	2.6	2.4	31	329	43	219	45	127	2 518
Mongolia	1 820	1.1	37	8	63	3.1	2.8	54	1 565	13	152	45	111	2 757
Nepal	16 107	118	45	21	46	2.0	2.6	7	137	23	45	92	117	1 933
Pakistan	93 286	120	42	10	50	3.1	3.0	29	779	203	29	52	132	2 180
Philippines	53 351	179	34	8	64	2.9	2.7	39	298	118	122	44	133	2 405
Saudi Arabia	10 824	5	46	14	56	4.0	4.7	71	2 150	11	16	58	36	2 947
Singapore	2 529	4 215	16	5	73	1.8	1.3	100	0.6	0.007	0.003	1.9	75	3 165
Sri Lanka	15 606	240	26	6	69	2.0	1.7	26	65	22	24	52	124	2 255
Syria	9 934	54	46	9	67	3.4	3.3	48	184	58	4.9	46	166	3 010
Taiwan	19 012	528	20	5	72				36	8.9	1.9	22	121	2 811
Thailand	50 396	98	31	8	63	2.9	2.3	18	512	190	158	74	134	2 330
Turkey	48 265	63	35	10	63	2.5	2.2	45	771	273	202	50	121	3 002
Vietnam	58 307	179	39	12	64	3.1	2.7	20	325	61	102	69	136	2 034
Yemen, North	6 386	33	49	24	44	2.6	2.9	18	195	28	16	74	79	2 478
Yemen, South	2 225	6.6	48	21	46	2.1	2.2	37	333	2	24	57	101	2 276
U.S.S.R.†														
Oceania														
Australia	15 544	2	16	7	76	2.1	1.3	86	7 618	465	1 060	5.2	122	3 055
New Zealand	3 233	12	16	8	74	1.4	0.6	83	269	4.7	100	8.6	117	3 572
Papua New Guinea	3 601	8	43	16	54	2.5	2.1	14	452	3.7	322	81	122	2 074

† See in Europe

Population. This is the United Nations' estimate for the mid-year 1984 (thousands).

Population density. This is the quoted population total divided by the quoted land area (persons per square kilometre).

Birth Rates and Death Rates. These are the registered or United Nations' estimated rates per thousand population.

Life Expectancy. This figure indicates the number of years that a child born today can expect to live if the levels of death of today last throughout its life. The figure is an average of that for men and women. The figure for women is usually higher than that for men (U.K. male 70, female 76 years).

Population Growth. This shows the average annual percentage change in population for two periods 1965-1973 and 1973-1983.

Urbanization. This is the percentage of the total population living in urban areas. The definition of urban is that of the individual nation and usually includes quite small towns.

Land Area. This is the total area of the country minus the area covered by major lakes and rivers (thousand square kilometres).

Arable Land and Permanent Crops. This excludes fallow land but includes temporary pasture (thousand square kilometres).

Forest and Woodland. This includes natural and planted woodland and land recently cleared of timber which will be replanted (thousand square kilometres).

Agricultural Population. This is the percentage of the economically active population working in agriculture. It includes those people working also in forestry, hunting and fishing.

Index of Agricultural Production. The base period for this index is 1974-1976 and it shows the level of production in each country in 1983 in comparision with that of the earlier period. Only edible crops and meat are included.

Food Supply. The figures are the average intake per person in calories per day in the period 1979-1981.

Trade: Imports (US$ per capita)	Trade: Exports (US$ per capita)	Education: Primary (% of age group)	Education: Secondary (% of age group)	Health: Popn. per doctor	Energy: Consumption in kgs of oil equiv. per capita	Consumer Price Index: 1970 = 100	G.N.P.: US$ per capita	G.N.P.: Growth per capita, % per yr. 1973-82	G.D.P. Part formed by: Agric. %	G.D.P. Part formed by: Indust. %	Loans & Debt: end 1983 US$ millions	Loans & Debt: as % of GNP	Asia
41	42	35	12	16 730	46				63	20			Afghanistan
21	10	60	15	7 810	36	642	130	3.2	48	8	4 185	38	Bangladesh
6	8	84	20	4 680	65	327	180	3.6	47	11	2 226	36	Burma
				20 000	2 093								Cambodia
19	21	100	35	1 740	455		290	4.5	42	43			China
2 067	871	84		1 060	2 000	182	3 720		9	20			Cyprus
5 329	5 283	100	67	1 210	1 647	350	6 000	6.8	1	27	224	0.8	Hong Kong
18	11	79	30	3 690	182	323	260	1.8	32	19	21 277	11	India
87	137	100	33	11 530	204	159	560	4.6	24	36	21 685	29	Indonesia
283	476	97	40	6 090	976	699			17	22			Iran
	668	109	59	1 800	763				7	53			Iraq
2 036	1 190	95	74	370	1 932	683th	5 630	0.2	6	29	15 149	70	Israel
1 137	1 148	100	92	780	2 929	271	10 100	3.3	3	34	4 319	0.4	Japan
824	222	100	77	900	790	130	1 710	7.8	6	18	1 940	48	Jordan
		100		430	2 093								Korea, North
755	721	100	89	1 440	1 168	634	2 010	5.6	17	32	21 472		Korea, South
31	81	97	18	20 000	76								Laos
1 364	334	100	58	540	610				9	18	182		Lebanon
963	958	92	49	4 000	702	126	1 870	4.9	25	28	10 665	39	Malaysia
388	258	106	89	450	1 137		1 500		15	29			Mongolia
27	6	73	21	30 060	13	210	170	0.3	63	4	346	14	Nepal
63	35	44	14	3 480	197	184	390	2.9	27	18	9 755	31	Pakistan
153	96	100	64	7 970	252	351	760	2.9	23	29	10 385	30	Philippines
3 763	4 505	67	32	1 670	3 536	370	12 180	6.2	1	67			Saudi Arabia
11 394	9 567	100	66	1 150	4 757	220	6 620	6.5	1	32	1 244	7.6	Singapore
118	93	100	54	7 170	143	411	330	3.2	27	19	2 205	44	Sri Lanka
414	187	100	51	2 240	847	507	1 680	4.9	18	24	2 305	14	Syria
1 163	1 613	100	95	1 242		331	2 570						Taiwan
203	147	96	29	7100	269	320	810	4.0	24	23	7 060	18	Thailand
224	147	100	39	1 630	599	269	1 230	1.4	21	28	15 396	30	Turkey
		100	48	4 190	90		170						Vietnam
250	6	59	7	11 670	116		510	3.5	28	8	1 574	38	Yemen, North
332	212	64	18	7 120	934		510	6.4	10	13	1 263	119	Yemen, South
													U.S.S.R.†
													Oceania
1 507	1 529	100	90	560	4 811	387	10 780	0.9	6	30	773	0.5	Australia
1 860	1 659	100	81	640	3 808	568	7 410	0.3	11	27	59	0.3	New Zealand
305	247	65	13	13 590	223	299	790	0.7	36	19	911	40	Papua New Guinea

† See in Europe

Bahrain Land 0.6/Popn. 400; Bhutan 47/1 338; Brunei 5.3/269/Kuwait 17.8/1 787;Macau 0.02/343; Maldives 0.3/173; Oman 212.5/1 181; Qatar 11/291; U.A.E. 83.6/1 255. American Samoa 0.2/34; Cocos Is.0.01/0.5; Cook Is 0.2/19; Fiji 18.3/686; Fr. Polynesia 3.7/160; Guam 0.6/112; Johnston I. 0.001/1; Kiribati 0.7/62; Midway I. 0.005/2; Nauru 0.02/8; New Caledonia 18.8/152; Niue I. 0.26/3; Norfolk I. 0.036/2; Pacific Is. 1.8/149; Samoa 2.9/159; Solomon Is.27.5/269; Tokelau 0.01/1.6; Tonga 0.7/107; Tuvalu 0.2/8; Vanuatu 14.8/128; Wake Is.0.008/2; Wallis & Futuna 0.2/10

Trade. The trade figures are normally for the year 1983 or 1984. The total trade figures have been divided by the population and are a measure of the country's external trade (U.S. $ per capita).

Education. The ages of primary school are taken to be 6-11 years and secondary school 12-17 years. The percentage of the total school age group in this type of education is shown.

Energy. All forms of energy have been converted to their equivalent in oil. Firewood and other traditional forms used in developing countries are not included and so the energy consumption in those countries is understated (kilograms of oil equivalent per capita).

Consumer Price Index. The base year is 1970 which is 100 and the level of consumer prices in 1984 or 1985 are shown in relation to the base year. It is a measure of inflation.

G.N.P. (Gross National Product) This figure is an estimate of the average production per person measured in U.S. dollars and for 1983. The G.N.P. measures the value of goods and services produced in a country, plus the balance, positive or negative, of income from abroad, for example investments, interest on capital, money returned from foreign labour, etc. The rate of change is the average annual percentage change during the period 1973-1982 in the G.D.P. The G.D.P. (Gross Domestic Product) is the G.N.P. minus the foreign balances. The adjoining two columns show the percentage contribution to the G.D.P. made by the agricultural and mining and manufacturing sectors.

Loans and Debt. This figure in millions of U.S. dollars shows the external public debt at the end of 1983. This is then shown as a percentage of the annual G.N.P. The figures in red show official development assistance made by the developed countries and also as a percentage of the donor country's G.N.P.

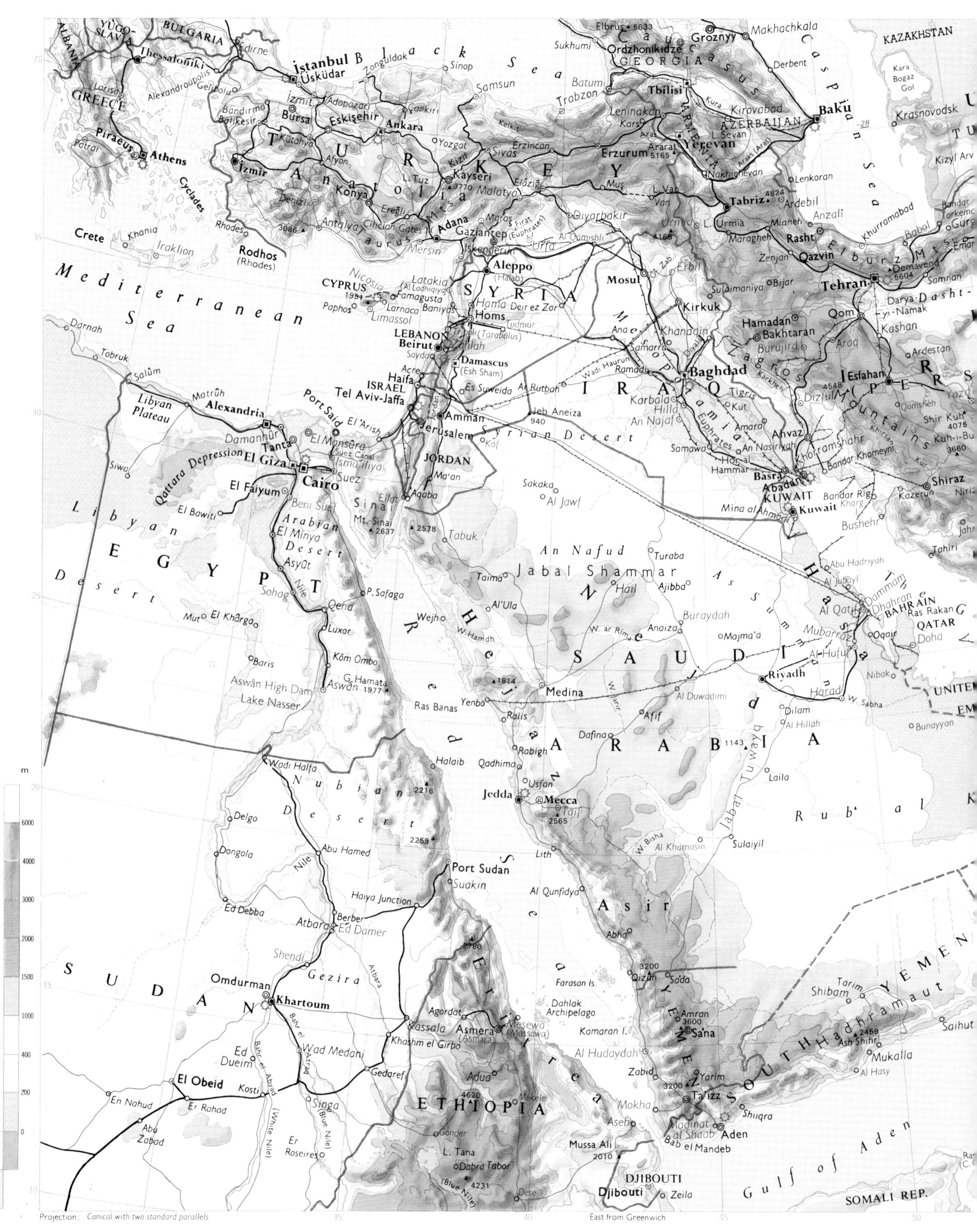

BULGARIA
ALBANIA
GREECE
Thessaloniki
Edirne
Istanbul
Üsküdar
Black Sea
Sinop
Samsun
Zonguldak
Izmit
Adapazari
Bursa
Eskişehir
Ankara
Bandirma
Balikesir
Kütahya
Afyon
Izmir
Athens
Piraeus
Patrai
Cyclades
Crete
Khania
Iraklion
Rhodes
Rodhos
(Rhodes)
TURKEY
Anatolia
Konya
Denizli
Antalya
Eregli
Cilician Gates
Taurus Mts
Kayseri
Yozgat
Kizil
L. Tuz
Sivas
Malatya
Adana
Mersin
Maraş
Gaziantep
Iskenderun
Elazig
Diyarbakir
Erzincan
Erzurum
Trabzon
Batumi
Sukhumi
Elbrus 5633
Caucasus
Ordzhonikidze
Groznyy
Makhachkala
Derbent
GEORGIA
Tbilisi
Leninakan
Kars
ARMENIA
Yerevan
L. Sevan
Ararat 5165
Kirovabad
AZERBAIJAN
Baku
Caspian Sea
KAZAKHSTAN
Kara Bogaz Gol
Krasnovodsk
Nakhichevan
Lenkoran
Tabriz
Ardebil
L. Van
Van
Muş
L. Urmia
Urmia
Maragheh
Mianeh
Anzali
Rasht
Qazvin
Zenjan
Elburz Mts
Demavend 5604
Tehran
Semnan
Babol
Mediterranean Sea
CYPRUS
Nicosia
Famagusta
Larnaca
Limassol
Paphos
Latakia
(Al Ladhiqiya)
Aleppo
(Halab)
SYRIA
Hama
Homs
Deir ez Zor
Baniyas
Tudmur
Tripoli (Tarabulus)
LEBANON
Beirut
Zahlah
Sayda
Damascus
(Esh Sham)
Es Suweida
Acre
Haifa
ISRAEL
Tel Aviv-Jaffa
Jerusalem
Amman
JORDAN
Ma'an
Aqaba
Mosul
Erbil
Kirkuk
Sulaimaniya
IRAQ
Mesopotamia
Ana
Samarra
Ramadi
Baghdad
Karbala
Hilla
An Najaf
Kut
Amara
An Nasiriyah
Samawa
Basra
Abadan
Khorramshahr
Ahvaz
Dizful
Euphrates
Tigris
Zagros Mountains
Hamadan
Bakhtaran
Qom
Kashan
Arak
Esfahan
Ardestan
Shiraz
Kazerun
Bushehr
Bandar Khomeyni
PERSIA
Syrian Desert
Ar Rutbah
Jeb Aneiza 940
Kaf
Sakaka
Al Jawf
KUWAIT
Kuwait
Mina al Ahmadi
Dammam
Dhahran
BAHRAIN
QATAR
Doha
Al Qatif
Al Hufuf
Riyadh
An Nafud
Jabal Shammar
Hail
Taima
Tabuk
Al 'Ula
Buraydah
Anaiza
Medina
Yenbo
Rabigh
Jedda
Mecca
Taif
SAUDI ARABIA
Rub' al Khali
Asir
Abha
Sulaiyil
Lith
Al Qunfidya
Hejaz
Red Sea
Dahlak Archipelago
Kamaran I.
Al Hudaydah
Zabid
Sana
Ta'izz
Mokha
Aden
Bab el Mandeb
Gulf of Aden
YEMEN
SOUTH YEMEN
Hadhramaut
Shibam
Tarim
Mukalla
Shuqra
DJIBOUTI
Djibouti
Zeila
SOMALI REP.
Alexandria
Port Said
El 'Arish
El Mansura
Tanta
Damanhur
El Giza
Cairo
Suez
Suez Canal
Ismailiya
Qattara Depression
Siwa
El Faiyum
El Bawiti
Beni Suef
El Minya
Asyut
Sohag
Qena
Luxor
Kôm Ombo
Aswan
Aswân High Dam
Lake Nasser
Libyan Desert
Libyan Plateau
Arabian Desert
EGYPT
Sinai
Mt. Sinai 2637
Mut
El Khârga
Baris
Salûm
Matrûh
Tobruk
Darnah
P. Safaga
Ras Banas
Halaib
Wadi Halfa
Nubian Desert
Delgo
Dongola
Abu Hamed
Nile
Port Sudan
Suakin
Haiya Junction
Ed Debba
Berber
Atbara
Ed Damer
Shendi
Gezira
Omdurman
Khartoum
SUDAN
Kassala
Agordat
Asmera
(Asmara)
Mesewa
(Massawa)
Eritrea
Wad Medani
Ed Dueim
Gedaref
Kosti
El Obeid
En Nahud
Er Rahad
Abu Zabad
Singa
Er Roseires
ETHIOPIA
Adua
Mekele
Gonder
L. Tana
Dabra Tabor
Dese
Asab
Mussa Ali 2010
Projection: Conical with two standard parallels
East from Greenwich

1:15 000 000

THE HOLY LAND
Armistice boundaries between Arab States and Israel, 1949-1974
1:1 500 000
East from Greenwich
CHINA
TADZHIKISTAN
UZBEKISTAN
AFGHANISTAN
PAKISTAN
INDIA
OMAN
Arabian Sea
Gulf of Oman
Gulf of Masira
Tropic of Cancer
Samarkand
Dushanbe
Bukhara
Chardzhou
Ashkhabad
Mashhad
Herat
Kabul
Peshawar
Rawalpindi
Srinagar
Kashmir
Hindu Kush
Lahore
Sialkot
Multan
Qandahar
Quetta
Hyderabad
Karachi
Makran
Kerman
Zahidan
Muscat
Abu Dhabi
Socotra (South Yemen)
The Brothers
Kuria Muria Is.
Dhofar
Salala
Marbat
Saugra Bay
Ras al Madraka
Ras al Hadd
BEIRUT (Bayrut)
Saydā (Sidon)
Tyre (Sur)
LEBANON
SYRIA
JORDAN
ISRAEL
EGYPT
Damascus (Esh Sham)
Ba'labakk (Baalbek)
Anti Lebanon
Lebanon Mts
Beka'a Valley
Hermon
Al Qunaytirah
GALILEE
SAMARIA
JUDAEA
NEGEV
Acre
B. of Haifa
Haifa
Nahariya
Tsefat (Safad)
L. Kinneret (Sea of Galilee)
Tiberias
Nazareth
Afula
Beit Shean
Irbid
Dar'a
Hadera
Netanya
Herzliya
TEL AVIV-JAFFA
Petah Tiqva
Ramat Gan
Holon
Bat Yam
Rishon Le-Zion
Lod (Lydda)
Ramla
Rehovot
Ashdod
Ashqelon
Gaza (Ghazzah)
Gaza Strip
Khan Yūnis
Beersheba
Dimona
Jerusalem
Bethlehem
Hebron (El Khalil)
Jericho
Ram Allah
Nabulus
Tul Karm
Janin
Qumran
Masada
Dead Sea
Jordan
Amman
Az Zarqa
As Salt
Madaba
Al Karak
Jebel 'Ajlun

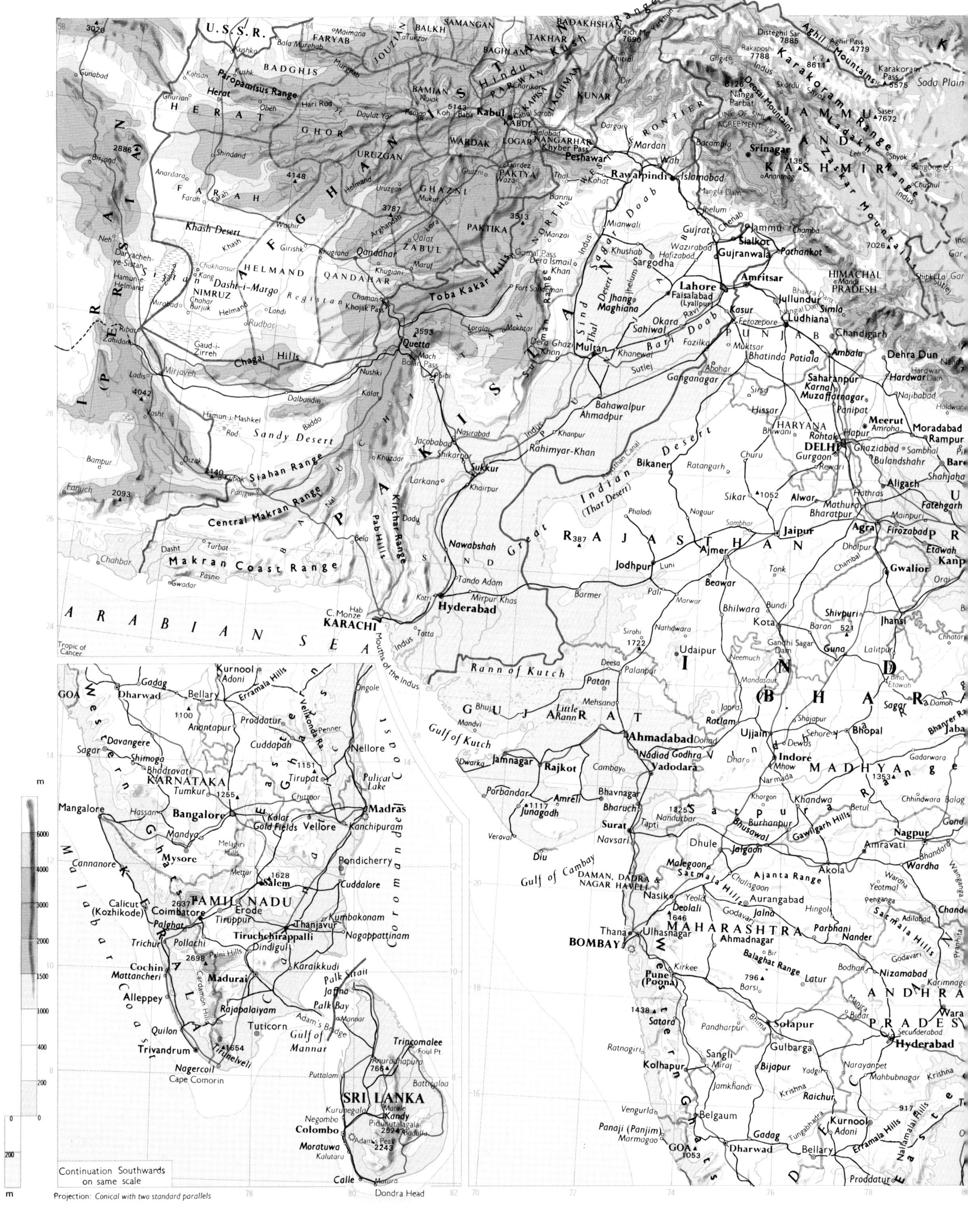

Continuation Southwards on same scale

Projection: *Conical with two standard parallels*

m
6000
4000
3000
2000
1500
1000
400
200
0
0
200
m

1:10 000 000

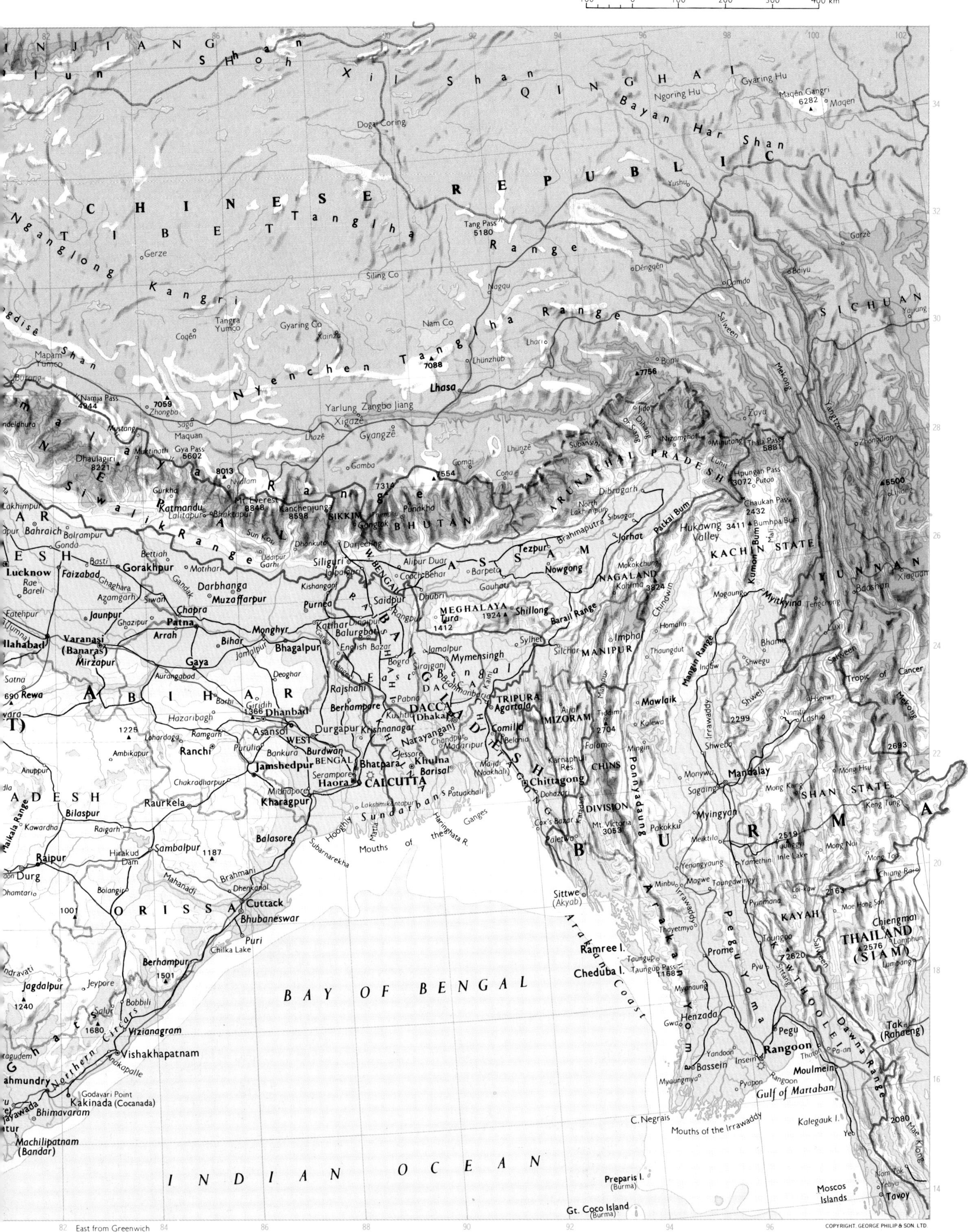
BAY OF BENGAL
INDIAN OCEAN
CHINESE REPUBLIC
TIBET
QINGHAI
BHUTAN
SIKKIM
ASSAM
BANGLADESH
BURMA
THAILAND (SIAM)
ORISSA
BIHAR
WEST BENGAL
Lhasa
CALCUTTA
DACCA
Rangoon
Mandalay
Chittagong
Gulf of Martaban
Mouths of the Ganges
Mouths of the Irrawaddy
East from Greenwich

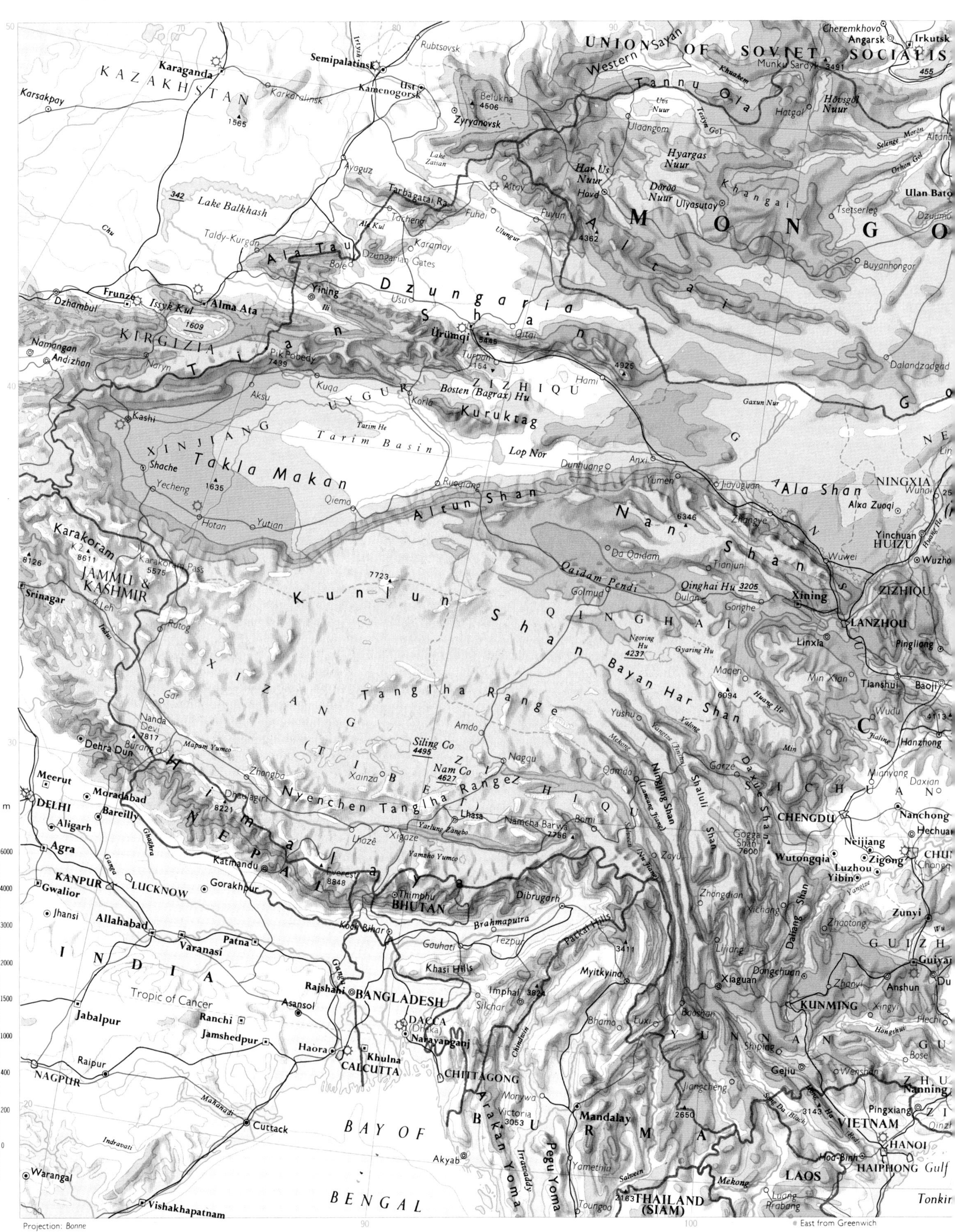
UNION OF SOVIET SOCIALIS
KAZAKHSTAN
Karaganda
Karsakpay
Semipalatinsk
Rubtsovsk
Ust-Kamenogorsk
Karkaralinsk
Zyryanovsk
Belukha 4506
Lake Zaisan
Ayaguz
Lake Balkhash
342
Chu
Taldy-Kurgan
Tarbagatai Ra.
Tacheng
Ala Kul
Ala Tau
Dzungarian Gates
Karamay
Bole
Frunze
Dzhambul
Issyk Kul
1609
Alma Ata
KIRGIZIA
Namangan
Andizhan
Naryn
Pik Pobedy 7439
Yining
Ili
Usu
Dzungaria
Tian Shan
Ürümqi
5445
Qitai
Turpan
154
Fuhai
Ulungur
Altay
Fuyun
4362
4925
Hami
Kuqa
Aksu
Korla
Bosten (Bagrax) Hu
Kuruktag
UYGUR ZIZHIQU
XINJIANG
Kashi
Tarim He
Tarim Basin
Lop Nor
Takla Makan
Shache
Yecheng
1635
Hotan
Yutian
Qiemo
Ruoqiang
Altun Shan
Dunhuang
Anxi
Yumen
Jiayuguan
Ala Shan
Alxa Zuoqi
Nan Shan
6346
Zhangye
Wuwei
Da Qaidam
Tianjun
Qaidam Pendi
Golmud
Qinghai Hu
3205
Xining
Dulan
Gonghe
LANZHOU
QINGHAI
Ngoring Hu
4237
Gyaring Hu
Linxia
Maqen
Min Xian
Tianshui
Baoji
Pingliang
Karakoram
K2 8611
8126
Karakoram Pass 5575
JAMMU & KASHMIR
Srinagar
Leh
Indus
Rutog
7723
Kunlun Shan
Bayan Har Shan
6094
Huang He
Tanglha Range
XIZANG
(TIBET)
ZIZHIQU
Gar
Nanda Devi 7817
Burang
Mapam Yumco
Amdo
Siling Co
4495
Nam Co
4627
Nagqu
Yushu
Zhongba
Xainza
Nyenchen Tanglha Range
Dhaulagiri 8221
Lhasa
Yarlung Zangbo
Namcha Barwa 7756
Lhazê
Xigazê
Yamzho Yumco
Everest 8848
Himalaya
NEPAL
Katmandu
Thimphu
BHUTAN
Dibrugarh
Brahmaputra
Dehra Dun
Meerut
DELHI
Moradabad
Bareilly
Aligarh
Agra
Ghaghra
Ganga
KANPUR
LUCKNOW
Gorakhpur
Gwalior
Jhansi
Allahabad
Varanasi
Patna
INDIA
Tropic of Cancer
Jabalpur
Ranchi
Jamshedpur
Asansol
Rajshahi
BANGLADESH
DACCA (Dhaka)
Narayanganj
Khulna
Haora
CALCUTTA
Raipur
NAGPUR
Mahanadi
Cuttack
Indravati
Warangal
Vishakhapatnam
BAY OF BENGAL
Koch Bihar
Gauhati
Tezpur
Khasi Hills
Imphal
3824
Silchar
Patkai Hills
3411
Myitkyina
Bhamo
Chindwin
CHITTAGONG
Monywa
Victoria 3053
Arakan Yoma
Akyab
Irrawaddy
Pegu Yoma
Mandalay
BURMA
Yametinn
Toungoo
Salween
2163
THAILAND (SIAM)
Mekong
Luang Prabang
LAOS
Qamdo
Ningjing Shan
Shaluli Shan
Zayü
Garzê
Daxue Shan
Gongga Shan 7600
Zhongdian
Lijiang
Xichang
Daliang Shan
Xiaguan
Dongchuan
KUNMING
Baoshan
Luxi
YUNNAN
Shiping
Gejiu
Jiangcheng
2650
3143
Wenshan
Yalong
Min
Jialing
Hanzhong
Mianyang
Daxian
CHENGDU
SICHUAN
Nanchong
Hechuan
Neijiang
Zigong
Luzhou
Yibin
Wutongqiao
Yangtze
Zhaotong
Zunyi
GUIZHOU
Guiyang
Anshun
Zhanyi
Xingyi
Hongshui
Hechi
Bose
GUANGXI ZHUANG
Nanning
Pingxiang
VIETNAM
HANOI
Hoa Binh
HAIPHONG
Gulf of Tonkin
Song Da (Black)
Red
Irkutsk
Cheremkhovo
Angarsk
Munku Sardyk 3491
455
Western Sayan
Tannu Ola
Uvs Nuur
Ulaangom
Tesiyn Gol
Hövsgöl Nuur
Hatgal
Selenge Mörön
Orhon Gol
Ulan Bator
Hyargas Nuur
Har Us Nuur
Hovd
Dörgön Nuur
Uliastay
Khangai
Tsetserleg
Dzuunmod
MONGOLIA
Altai
Buyanhongor
Dalandzadgad
Gaxun Nur
GOBI
NINGXIA HUIZU ZIZHIQU
Yinchuan
Wuhai
Wuzhong
Wudu
4113
Projection: Bonne
East from Greenwich

Lake Baykal
REPUBLICS
Chita
Ulan Ude
Nerchinsk
Yablonovyy Range
Borzya
Argun
Manzhouli
Hulun Nur
Hailar
Buir Nur
Choybalsan
Kerulen
Great Khingan Mts.
HEILONGJIANG
Oroqen Zizhiqi
Amur
Svobodny
Blagoveshchensk
Aihui
Little Khingan Mts
Nenjiang
Bei'an
Yichun
Butha Qi
Nen
Qiqihar
Anda
Suihua
Song Hua
Hegang
Jiamusi
Shuangyashan
Chegdomyn
Aleksandrovsk
Komsomolsk
L. Bolon
Birobidzhan
Khabarovsk
Bikin
Sikhote Alin Ra.
Poronaysk
C. Terpeniya
Sakhalin
Yuzhno-Sakhalinsk
La Perouse Str.
Wakkanai
Asahigawa
2290
Hokkaido
Otaru
SAPPORO
Kushiro
C. Erimo
Hakodate
L I A
Horqin Youyi Qianqi
HARBIN
Manchuria
Jixi
Mishan
Lake Khanka
Mudanjiang
Ussuriysk
Tao'an
JILIN
CHANGCHUN
Jilin
Vladivostok
Nakhodka
Saynshand
Dzamin Üud
Erenhot
Abagnar Qi
1949
INNER MONGOLIA
Gobi
Shuangliao
Tongliao
Siping
Liaoyuan
Songhua Lake
Yanji
LIAONING
Chifeng
Fuxin
FUSHUN
SHENYANG (Mukden)
Tonghua
2744
Chongjin
Chaoyang
Liaoyang
Benxi
NORTH
Yalu
KOREA
Jinzhou
Yingkou
ANSHAN
Dandong
Hungnam
Hohhot
Jining
Zhangjiakou
Chengde
G. of Liaodong
Qinghuangdao
Xuanhua
Baotou
Datong
PEKING (Beijing)
Tangshan
Liaodong Pen.
Korea Bay
PYONGYANG
Wŏnsan
Ordos
GREAT WALL
Baoding
TIENTSIN (Tianjin)
DALIAN (Lüda)
3058
HEBEI
Cangzhou
G. of Chihli (Bo Hai)
Haeju
Kaesong
SEOUL
INCHON
TAIYUAN
Shijiazhuang
Yangquan
Yantai
Weihai
SHANXI
Fenyang
Yuci
Dezhou
Ye Xian
Huang He
Weifang
JINAN
Zibo
SHANDONG
YELLOW SEA
Taejon
SOUTH
TAEGU
PUSAN
Handan
Anyang
Tai'an
QINGDAO
Kwangju
Masan
1915
Changzhi
Huang He (Yellow)
Jining
Xinxiang
Tongchuan
Grand Canal
Lianyungang
Sanmenxia
Luoyang
Kaifeng
SIAN (Xi'an)
ZHENGZHOU
Shangqiu
Xuzhou
Qingjiang
Pingdingshan
HENAN
Nanyang
Shangshui
Hongze Hu
JIANGSU
Ankang
Han Shui
Zhumadian
Bengbu
Huainan
NANKING (Nanjing)
Zhenjiang
Changzhou
Nantong
Xiangfan
Dabie Shan
ANHUI
Hefei
Wuxi
Suzhou
Wuhu
SHANGHAI
HUBEI
WUHAN
Tongling
Yichang
Shashi
Anqing
Yangtze
Hangzhou
Hangzhou Wan
Huangshi
Tunxi
Shaoxing
Ningbo
Jiujiang
ZHEJIANG
Changde
Dongting L.
Poyang L.
Jingdezhen
Jinhua
Yiyang
Nanchang
Shangrao
HUNAN
Changsha
JIANGXI
Xiangtan
Zhuzhou
Wuyi Shan
2120
Wenzhou
Shaoyang
Hengyang
Jian
Min
Nanping
Sanming
Fuzhou
Xiang
Gan
Ganzhou
FUJIAN
Guilin
Nan Ling
Quanzhou
Shaoguan
Zhangzhou
Xiamen (Amoy)
Mei Xian
Chao'an
GUANGXI
Wuzhou
GUANGDONG
CANTON (Guangzhou)
Shantou
Xi Jiang
Bei
Foshan
Jiangmen
HONG KONG (Br.)
Macau (Port.)
Maoming
Zhanjiang
Hainan Str.
Haikou
Hainan
1879
SEA OF JAPAN
Sado
Niigata
Sendai
Koriyama
Utsunomiya
Toyama
Kanazawa
Honshu
TOKYO
KAWASAKI
YOKOHAMA
NAGOYA
Fuji-san
3776
Yokosuka
KYOTO
KOBE
OSAKA
Sakai
Shizuoka
Hamamatsu
Wakayama
Okayama
Hiroshima
Shimonoseki
Korea Str.
Tsugaru Strait
Aomori
Hachinohe
Morioka
Akita
JAPAN
Shikoku
Kochi
Matsuyama
KITAKYUSHU
FUKUOKA
Sasebo
Nagasaki
Kumamoto
Kyushu
Kagoshima
Tanega
Cheju Do
1950
EAST CHINA SEA
Amami-ō-Shima
Ryukyu Islands
Okinawa
Naha
Sakashima Gunto
Formosa Strait
Chilung
TAIPEI
Taichung
Chiai
Yu Shan
3997
TAIWAN
Tainan
KAOHSIUNG
Tropic of Cancer
PACIFIC OCEAN
Batan Is.
Babuyan Is.
SOUTH CHINA SEA
110
120
130
140
50
40
30
20

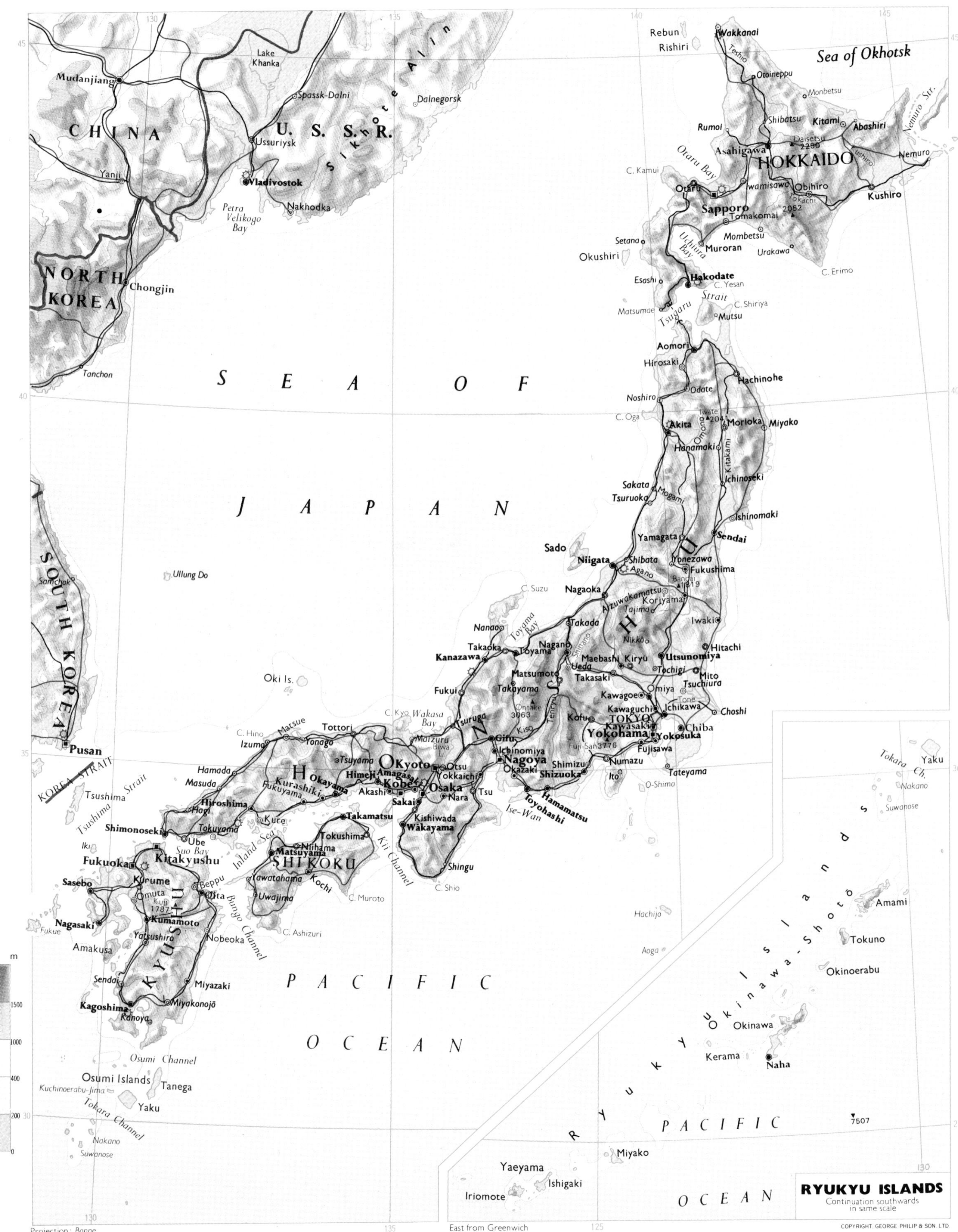
1:7 500 000
50 0 50 100 150 200 250 300 km
CHINA
U.S.S.R.
NORTH KOREA
SOUTH KOREA
Sikhote Alin
Lake Khanka
Mudanjiang
Spassk-Dalni
Dalnegorsk
Ussuriysk
Yanji
Vladivostok
Nakhodka
Petra Velikogo Bay
Chongjin
Tanchon
SEA OF JAPAN
Ullung Do
Samchok
Pusan
KOREA STRAIT
Tsushima
Tsushima Strait
Iki
Sea of Okhotsk
Rebun
Rishiri
Wakkanai
Teshio
Otoineppu
Monbetsu
Nemuro Str.
Shibetsu
Rumoi
Kitami
Abashiri
Daisetsu 2290
Asahigawa
HOKKAIDO
Nemuro
Otaru Bay
C. Kamui
Otaru
Iwamisawa
Obihiro
Kushiro
Sapporo
Tomakomai
Tokachi
2052
Setana
Uchiura Bay
Mombetsu
Muroran
Urakawa
Okushiri
C. Erimo
Esashi
Hakodate
C. Yesan
Tsugaru Strait
C. Shiriya
Matsumae
Mutsu
Aomori
Hirosaki
Hachinohe
Odate
Noshiro
C. Oga
Iwate 2041
Akita
Morioka
Miyako
Hanamaki
Kitakami
Ichinoseki
Sakata
Mogami
Tsuruoka
Ishinomaki
Yamagata
Sendai
Sado
Niigata
Shibata
Yonezawa
Fukushima
Agano
Bandai 1819
Nagaoka
C. Suzu
Aizuwakamatsu
Koriyama
Tajima
HONSHU
Iwaki
Nanao
Toyama Bay
Takada
Shinano
Nikko
Hitachi
Takaoka
Toyama
Nagano
Utsunomiya
Kanazawa
Maebashi
Kiryu
Tochigi
Mito
Matsumoto
Ueda
Takasaki
Tsuchiura
Oki Is.
Fukui
Takayama
Ontake 3063
Kawagoe
Omiya
Tone
C. Kyo
Wakasa Bay
Tenryu
Kofu
Kawaguchi
Ichikawa
Choshi
TOKYO
Tottori
Tsuruga
Kiso
Kawasaki
Chiba
C. Hino
Matsue
Maizuru
Biwa
Gifu
Yokohama
Yokosuka
Izumo
Yonago
Fuji-San 3776
Fujisawa
Tsuyama
Kyoto
Ichinomiya
Otsu
Nagoya
Numazu
Shimizu
Tateyama
Hamada
Himeji
Amagasaki
Yokkaichi
Okazaki
Shizuoka
Masuda
Okayama
Kobe
Osaka
Ito
Kurashiki
Fukuyama
Akashi
Tsu
O-Shima
Sakai
Nara
Hamamatsu
Hiroshima
Toyohashi
Hagi
Ise-Wan
Kure
Takamatsu
Kishiwada
Shimonoseki
Tokuyama
Inland Sea
Wakayama
Ube
Tokushima
Suo Bay
Niihama
Kii Channel
Fukuoka
Kitakyushu
Matsuyama
SHIKOKU
Shingu
Kurume
Kochi
C. Shio
Sasebo
Beppu
Yawatahama
Omuta
Oita
Uwajima
Kuju 1787
C. Muroto
Bungo Channel
Nagasaki
Kumamoto
Fukue
Yatsushiro
Nobeoka
C. Ashizuri
KYUSHU
Amakusa
Sendai
Miyazaki
Kagoshima
Miyakonojo
Kanoya
PACIFIC OCEAN
Osumi Channel
Osumi Islands
Tanega
Kuchinoerabu-Jima
Yaku
Tokara Channel
Nakano
Suwanose
Hachijo
Aoga
Tokara Ch.
Yaku
Nakano
Suwanose
RYUKYU ISLANDS
Okinawa-Shoto
Amami
Tokuno
Okinoerabu
Okinawa
Kerama
Naha
7507
PACIFIC OCEAN
Miyako
Yaeyama
Ishigaki
Iriomote
RYUKYU ISLANDS
Continuation southwards in same scale
m
1500
1000
400
200
0
200
m
Projection: Bonne
East from Greenwich
COPYRIGHT. GEORGE PHILIP & SON. LTD.

1:15 000 000

100 0 100 200 300 400 500 600 km

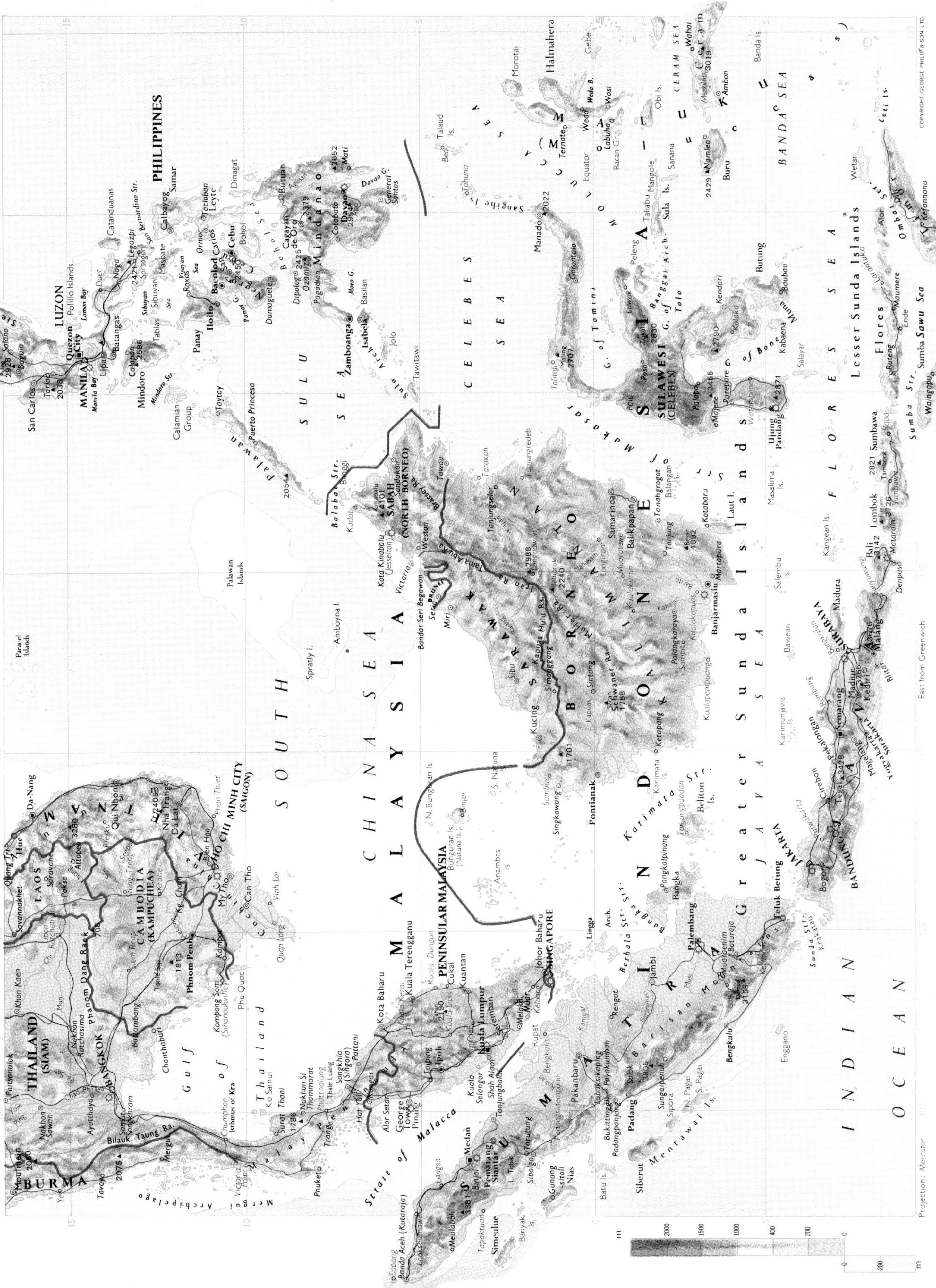

Projection: Mercator

East from Greenwich

EUROPE
U. S. S. R.
ASIA
CHINA
MONGOLIA
INDIA
Moskva
Leningrad
Sverdlovsk
Novosibirsk
Irkutsk
Ulan Bator
Peking
Tientsin
Shenyang
Changchun
Harbin
Vladivostok
Khabarovsk
Sea of Okhotsk
Kamchatka
Sakhalin
Sea of Japan
JAPAN
Tōkyō
Yokohama
Kyōto
Ōsaka
Nagoya
Sendai
Hakodate
KOREA
Seoul
Dalian
Qingdao
Shanghai
Yellow Sea
East China Sea
Taipei
Taiwan (Formosa)
HONG KONG
Canton
Hanoi
Chungking
Wuhan
Nanking
Lanzhou
Kunming
TIBET
Lhasa
Mt. Everest 8848
Delhi
Lahore
Kanpur
Calcutta
Dacca
Bay of Bengal
Madras
Hyderabad
Colombo
SRI LANKA
BURMA
Rangoon
THAILAND
Bangkok
CAMBODIA
Phnom Penh
Ho Chi Minh City
South China Sea
PHILIPPINES
Manila
Mindanao
Sulu Sea
Celebes Sea
MALAYSIA
Kuala Lumpur
SINGAPORE
Sumatra
Borneo
Celebes
Java Sea
Jakarta
Surabaya
Java
INDONESIA
Banda Sea
Timor
Arafura Sea
Irian Jaya
PAPUA NEW GUINEA
Port Moresby
Bismarck Arch.
SOLOMON IS.
Coral Sea
VANUATU
New Caledonia
FIJI
TONGA
TUVALU (Ellice Is.)
NAURU
Gilbert Is.
Marshall Is.
Caroline Islands
Micronesia
Melanesia
Fed. States of Micronesia
Belau
Guam (U.S.)
Northern Marianas
Mariana Trench
11,022
U.S. TRUST TERR. OF THE PACIFIC ISLANDS
Marcus Necker Ridge
Wake I. (U.S.)
International Date Line
Emperor Seamount Chain
Aleutian Trench
Kuril Is.
Kuril Trench
Japan Trench
Midway Is.
AUSTRALIA
WESTERN AUSTRALIA
NORTHERN TERRITORY
QUEENSLAND
SOUTH AUSTRALIA
NEW SOUTH WALES
VICTORIA
TASMANIA
Perth
Darwin
Alice Springs
Brisbane
Sydney
Canberra
Melbourne
Adelaide
Hobart
Great Australian Bight
Great Divide
Tasman Sea
Lord Howe Ridge
NEW ZEALAND
Auckland
Wellington
Christchurch
Dunedin
Invercargill
Kermadec Trench
Tonga Trench
INDIAN OCEAN
Mid-Indian Ridge
Kerguelen (Fr.)
Crozet Is. (Fr.)
Amsterdam I. (Fr.)
St. Paul I. (Fr.)
Heard Is. (Aust.)
Cocos (Keeling) Is. (Austral.)
Christmas I. (Austral.)
Java Trench
7450
Projection: Mollweide's Homolographic
East from Greenwich

CANADA
NORTH AMERICA
UNITED STATES
MEXICO
Rocky Mountains
Sierra Madre
Gulf of California
Gulf of Mexico
Gulf of Alaska
Hudson Bay
Labrador
Newfoundland
NORTH ATLANTIC OCEAN
West Indies
Caribbean Sea
CENTRAL AMERICA
SOUTH AMERICA
BRAZIL
PERU
BOLIVIA
ARGENTINA
COLOMBIA
VENEZUELA
ECUADOR
PARAGUAY
URUGUAY
Andes
Patagonia
SOUTH ATLANTIC OCEAN
East Pacific Ridge
Pacific–Antarctic Ridge
Chile Rise
FRENCH POLYNESIA
Tuamotu Archipelago
Hawaiian Is. (U.S.A.)
Tropic of Cancer
Equator
Tropic of Capricorn
West from Greenwich
Tierra del Fuego
C. Horn
Falkland Is. (U.K.)
South Georgia

Java Trench
6389
TIMOR SEA
Ashmore Reef
Scott Reef
Bonaparte Archipelago
C. Londonderry
C. Bougainville
Admiralty G.
Cambridge G.
Joseph Bonaparte Gulf
Drysdale
Wyndham
Kununurra
L. Argyle
Ord
Mt. Hann
776
Kimberley
Collier B.
King Sd.
C. Levêque
Lacepede Is.
King Leopold Ras.
Mt. Ord
1007
Durack Range
Derby
Broome
Roebuck B.
Fitzroy
Fitzroy Crossing
Hall's Creek
Rowley Shoals
Eighty Mile Beach
P. Hedland
Mount Goldsworthy
De Grey
Great Sandy Desert
Sturt
Gregory Lake
Dampier Archipelago
Karratha
C. Dampier
Roebourne
Barrow I.
Pilbara
Marble Bar
Throssell Ra.
Nullagine
Fortescue
Hamersley Ra.
Mt. Bruce
1235
Ophthalmia Ra.
Tom Price
Paraburdoo
Ashburton
Mount Whaleback
Newman
Robertson Ra.
Onslow
N.W. Cape
Exmouth
Learmonth
Exmouth G.
L. Dora
L. Mackay
L. Disappointment
Gibson Desert
Rawlinson Ra.
WESTERN AUSTRALIA
L. McLeod
Lyons
Mt. Augustus
1105
Geographe Chan.
Carnarvon
Gascoyne
Wooramel
Shark B.
Dirk Hartog I.
Denham
Murchison
Robinson Ra.
Peak Hill
L. Carnegie
Meekatharra
Wiluna
L. Wells
661
L. Yeo
Great Victoria Desert
INDIAN OCEAN
Tallering Peak
453
Mt. Magnet
Sandstone
L. Austin
Laverton
Leonora
L. Carey
L. Minigwal
Houtman Abrolhos
Northampton
Mullewa
Geraldton
L. Monger
L. Barlee
L. Ballard
Menzies
Dongara
L. Moore
Kanowna
Kalgoorlie-Boulder
Bonnie Rock
Bencubbin
Coolgardie
Southern Cross
Darling Range
Swan
Northam
Kellerberrin
The Johnston Lakes
L. Lefroy
L. Cowan
Norseman
L. Dundas
Perth
York
Fremantle
Kwinana
Pinjarra
Narrogin
Collie
Wagin
Bunbury
Geographe B.
Katanning
Stirling Ra.
Busselton
Bridgetown
Manjimup
Mt Barker
Albany
Augusta
C. Leeuwin
Flinders B.
C. Knob
Esperance
C. Pasley
Archipelago of the Recherche
Nullarbor Plain
Hampton Tableland
Rawlinna
Eyre
Deakin
Ooldea
Tarcoola
Great Australian Bight
Head of Bight
C. Adieu
Nuyts Archipelago
Streaky B.
Anxious B.
Coffin B. Penin.
Port Lincoln
Penong
Ceduna
L. Everard
L. Gairdner
Nukey Bluff
Coober Pedy
Stuart
SOUTH AUSTRALIA
Warrina
Oodnadatta
Alberga
Hamilton
Everard Ras.
Musgrave Ranges
1549
Mt. Woodroffe
Blackstone Ra.
L. Amadeus
Mt. Olga
1069
Ayers Rock
868
James Ra.
Palmer
Finke
Hugh
Alice Springs
Macdonnell Ras.
Mt. Ziel
1510
L. Macdonald
Reynolds Ra.
998
Mt. Singleton
808
Hordern Hills
NORTHERN TERRITORY
Murchison Ra.
Davenport Ra.
Sandover
Tennant Creek
Tanami Desert
Gordon Downs
Wave Hill
Newcastle Waters
L. Woods
Barkly
Daly
Birdum
Victoria
Mataranka
Roper
Katherine
Daly
Batchelor
Rum Jungle
Anson B.
Arnhem Land
Darwin
P. Darwin
Clarence Str.
Van Diemen Gulf
Melville I.
Bathurst I.
Cobourg Pen.
Croker I.
Crocodile Is.
Projection: Bonne
East from Greenwich
115
120
125
130
135
2000
1500
1000
400
200
0
200
2000
4000
6000
m

1:12 000 000

100 0 100 200 300 400 500 km

AUSTRALIA AND NEW ZEALAND : Climate and Natural Vegetation

1:60 000 000

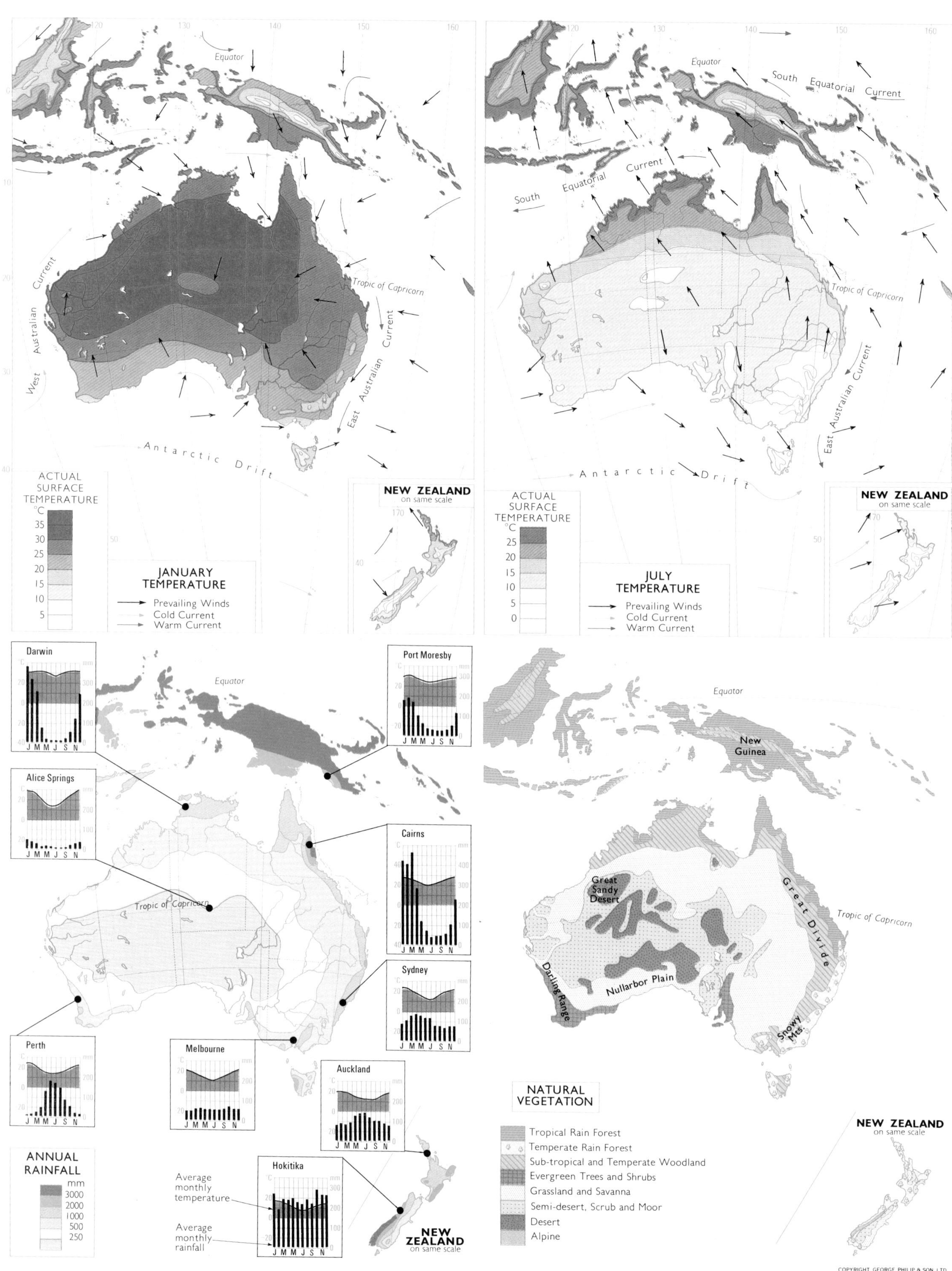

1:20 000 000

200 0 200 400 600 800 km

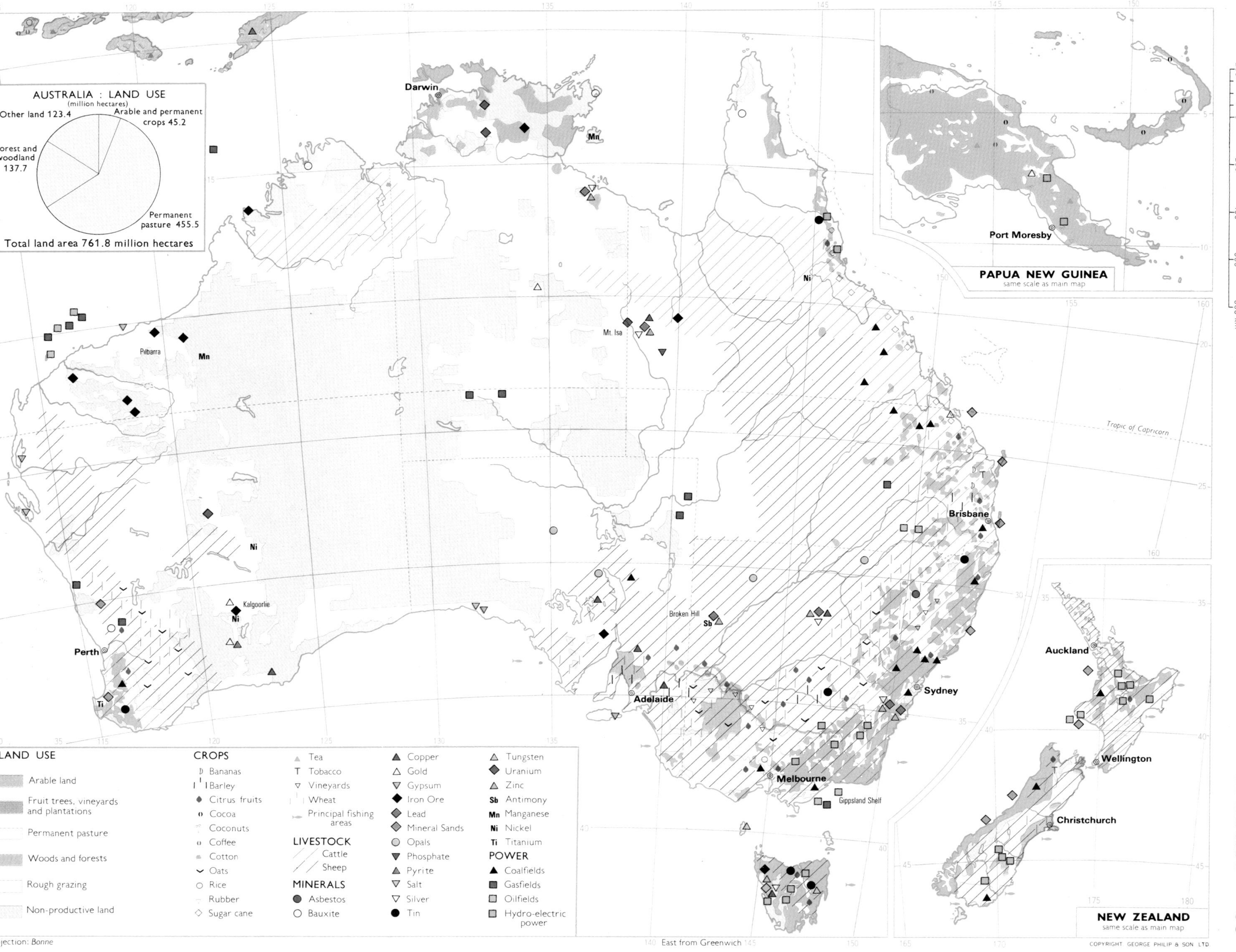

1:4 500 000

25 0 25 50 75 100 125 150 175 200 km

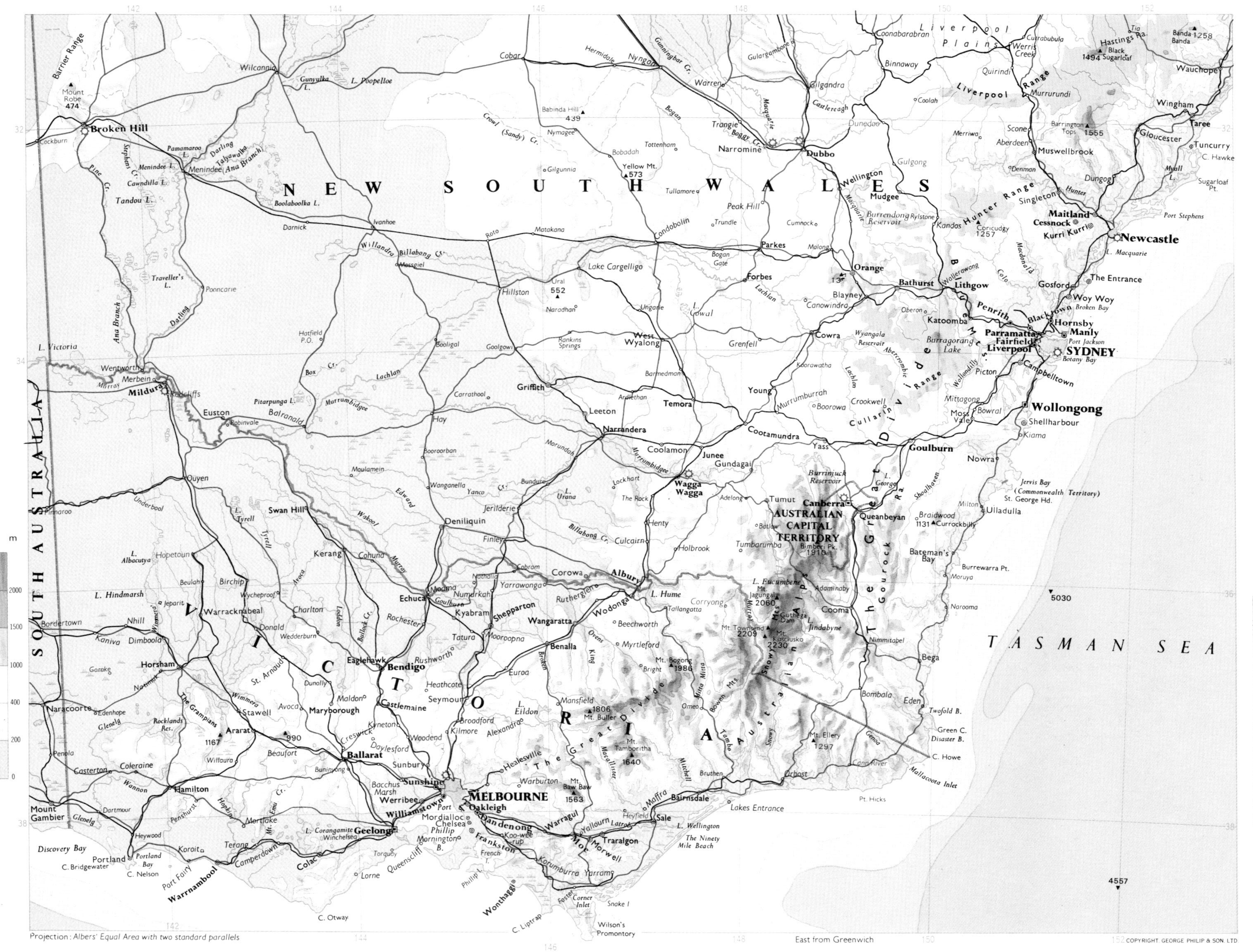

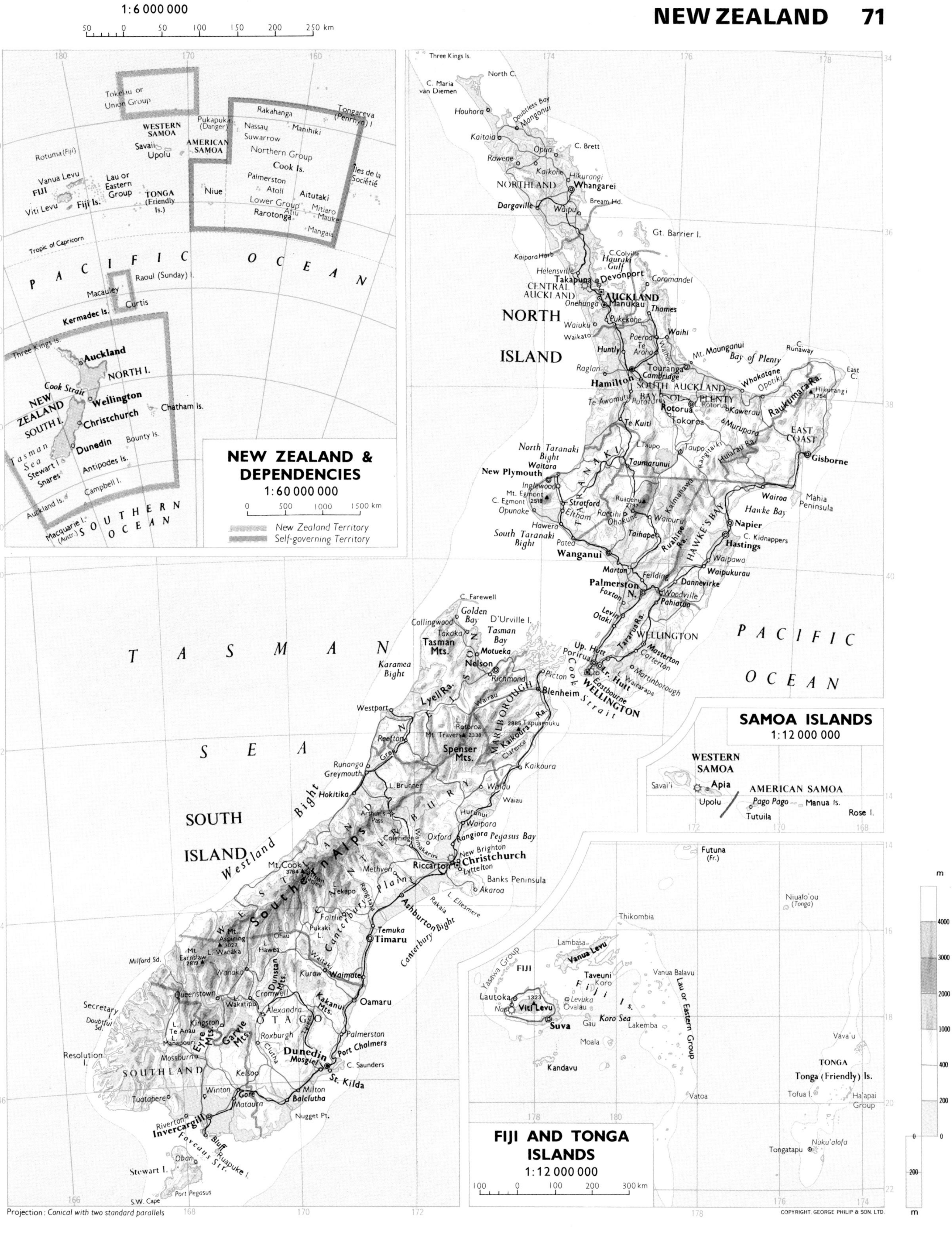

1:6 000 000

50 0 50 100 150 200 250 km

NEW ZEALAND & DEPENDENCIES

1:60 000 000

0 500 1000 1500 km

New Zealand Territory
Self-governing Territory

Tokelau or Union Group
WESTERN SAMOA
Savaii
Upolu
AMERICAN SAMOA
Pukapuka (Danger)
Rakahanga
Tongareva (Penrhyn) I.
Manihiki
Nassau
Suwarrow
Northern Group
Cook Is.
Îles de la Société
Rotuma (Fiji)
Vanua Levu
FIJI
Viti Levu
Fiji Is.
Lau or Eastern Group
TONGA (Friendly Is.)
Niue
Palmerston
Atoll
Aitutaki
Lower Group
Mitiaro
Atiu
Mauke
Rarotonga
Mangaia
Tropic of Capricorn
PACIFIC OCEAN
Raoul (Sunday) I.
Macauley
Curtis
Kermadec Is.
Three Kings Is.
Auckland
NORTH I.
Cook Strait
NEW ZEALAND
Wellington
Chatham Is.
SOUTH I.
Christchurch
Dunedin
Bounty Is.
Tasman Sea
Stewart I.
Snares
Antipodes Is.
Campbell I.
Auckland Is.
Macquarie I. (Austr.)
SOUTHERN OCEAN

Three Kings Is.
North C.
C. Maria van Diemen
Houhora
Doubtless Bay
Mangonui
Kaitaia
C. Brett
Opua
Rawene
Kaikohe
Hikurangi
NORTHLAND
Whangarei
Dargaville
Waipu
Bream Hd.
Gt. Barrier I.
Kaipara Harb.
C. Colville
Hauraki Gulf
Helensville
Coromandel
Takapuna
Devonport
CENTRAL AUCKLAND
AUCKLAND
Onehunga
Manukau
Thames
NORTH ISLAND
Waiuku
Pukekohe
Waikato
Waihi
Paeroa
Te Aroha
Huntly
Mt. Maunganui
Bay of Plenty
C. Runaway
Raglan
Tauranga
Cambridge
Whakatane
Opotiki
East C.
Hamilton
SOUTH AUCKLAND
BAY OF PLENTY
Raukumara Ra.
Hikurangi 1754
Te Awamutu
Putaruru
Rotorua
L. Rotorua
Kawerau
Te Kuiti
Tokoroa
Murupara
EAST COAST
North Taranaki Bight
L. Taupo
Taupo
Huiarau Ra.
Waitara
Taumarunui
Gisborne
New Plymouth
TARANAKI
Kaimanawa
Inglewood
Mt. Egmont 2518
C. Egmont
Ruapehu 2797
Stratford
Opunake
Eltham
Raetihi
Ohakune
Waiouru
Wairoa
Mahia Peninsula
Hawke Bay
Hawera
Taihape
Napier
South Taranaki Bight
Patea
Ruahine Ra.
HAWKE'S BAY
C. Kidnappers
Hastings
Wanganui
Waipawa
Waipukurau
Marton
Feilding
Dannevirke
Palmerston N.
Foxton
Woodville
Pahiatua
Levin
Otaki
Tararua Ra.
WELLINGTON
Masterton
Carterton
Martinborough
Wairarapa
Up. Hutt
Porirua
Lr. Hutt
Eastbourne
WELLINGTON
Cook Strait
Picton
Blenheim
C. Farewell
Golden Bay
D'Urville I.
Collingwood
Takaka
Tasman Bay
Tasman Mts.
Motueka
Nelson
Richmond
Karamea Bight
Westport
Lyell Ra.
Wairau
L. Rotoroa
Mt. Travers 2338
2885 Tapuaenuku
MARLBOROUGH
Kaikoura Ra.
Reefton
Spenser Mts.
Clarence
Kaikoura
Runanga
Greymouth
Grey
L. Brunner
Waiau
Hokitika
Arthur's Pass
Hurunui
Waipara
Coleridge
Oxford
Rangiora
Pegasus Bay
Waimakariri
New Brighton
Riccarton
Christchurch
Lyttelton
Banks Peninsula
Akaroa
Mt. Cook 3764
Methven
Rangitata
Canterbury Plains
Rakaia
L. Ellesmere
L. Tekapo
Ashburton
Fairlie
Temuka
Timaru
Canterbury Bight
Pukaki L.
Ohau
Mt. Aspiring 3027
L. Wanaka
L. Hawea
Mt. Earnslaw 2819
Milford Sd.
Wanaka
Dunstan Mts.
Waitaki
Kurow
Waimate
Queenstown
Cromwell
L. Wakatipu
Alexandra
Kakanui Mts.
Oamaru
Secretary I.
Doubtful Sd.
Kingston
L. Te Anau
L. Manapouri
Eyre Mts.
Garvie Mts.
OTAGO
Roxburgh
Palmerston
Port Chalmers
Clutha
Dunedin
Mosgiel
Resolution I.
Mossburn
C. Saunders
St. Kilda
SOUTHLAND
Kelso
Winton
Gore
Milton
Balclutha
Tuatapere
Mataura
Riverton
Invercargill
Nugget Pt.
Bluff
Ruapuke I.
Foveaux Str.
Oban
Stewart I.
Port Pegasus
S.W. Cape
TASMAN SEA
SOUTH ISLAND
Westland Bight
WESTLAND
Southern Alps
CANTERBURY
PACIFIC OCEAN

SAMOA ISLANDS

1:12 000 000

WESTERN SAMOA
Savai'i
Apia
Upolu
AMERICAN SAMOA
Pago Pago
Manua Is.
Tutuila
Rose I.

FIJI AND TONGA ISLANDS

1:12 000 000

100 0 100 200 300 km

Futuna (Fr.)
Niuafo'ou (Tonga)
Thikombia
Lambasa
Vanua Levu
Yasawa Group
FIJI
Taveuni
Koro
Fiji Is.
Vanua Balavu
Lau or Eastern Group
Lautoka
1323
Levuka
Ovalau
Nandi
Viti Levu
Koro Sea
Suva
Gau
Lakemba
Moala
Kandavu
Vatoa
Vava'u
TONGA
Tonga (Friendly) Is.
Tofua I.
Ha'apai Group
Tongatapu
Nuku'alofa

m 4000 3000 2000 1000 400 200 0 200 m

Projection: *Conical with two standard parallels*

1: 40 000 000

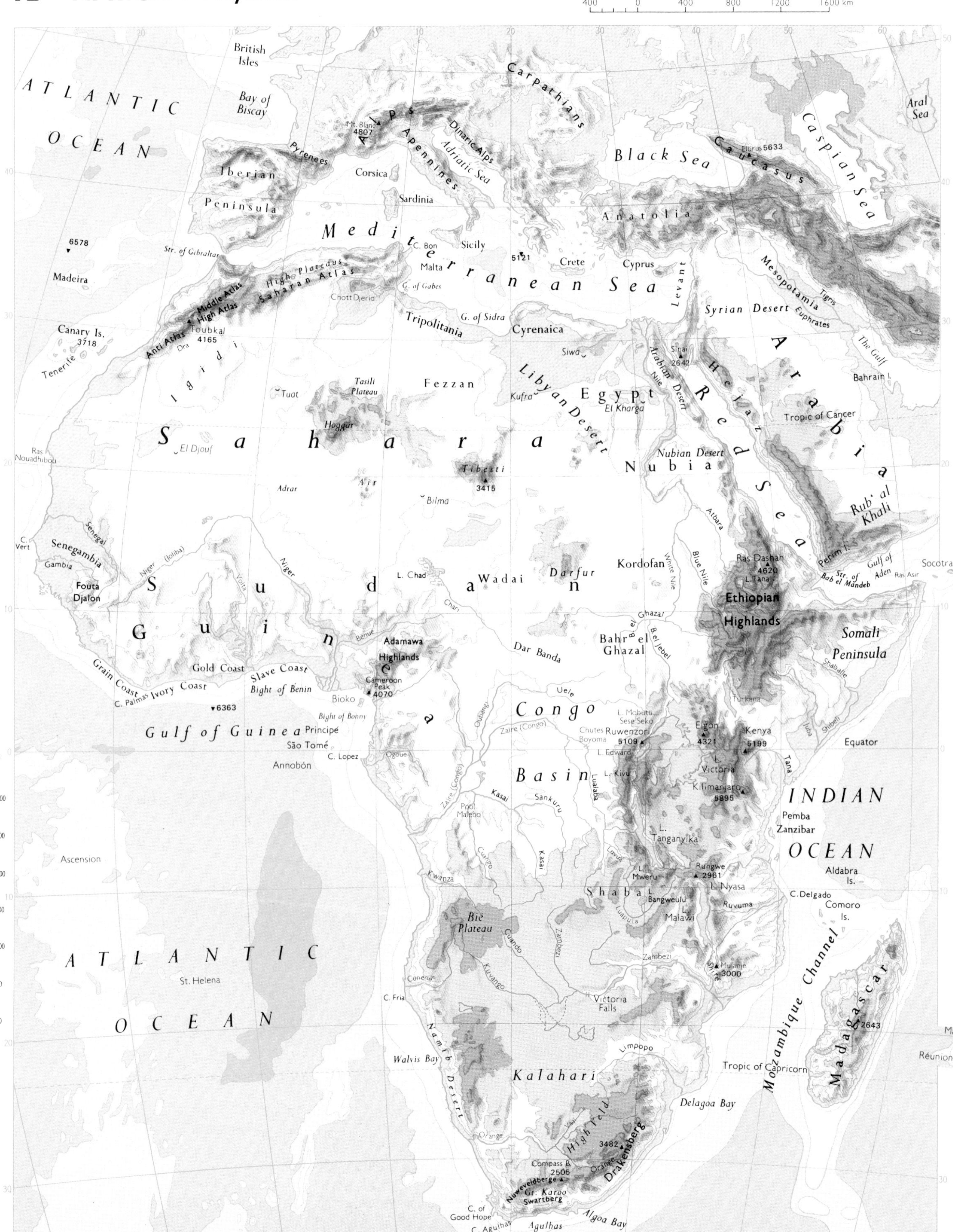

Projection: Zenithal Equidistant. West from Greenwich East from Greenwich

1: 40 000 000

400 0 400 800 1200 1600 km

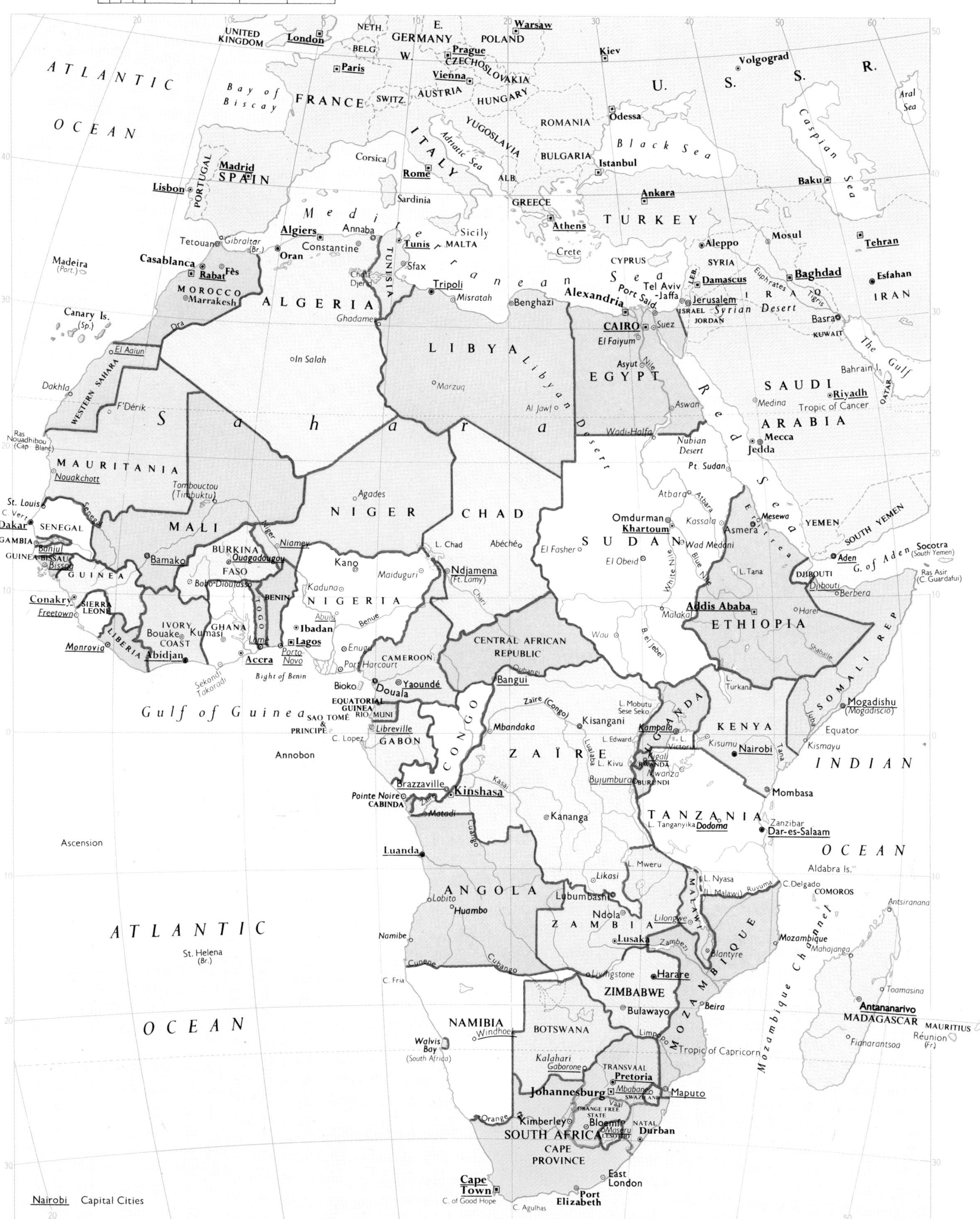

Projection: *Zenithal Equidistant.* West from Greenwich East from Greenwich

1:80 000 000

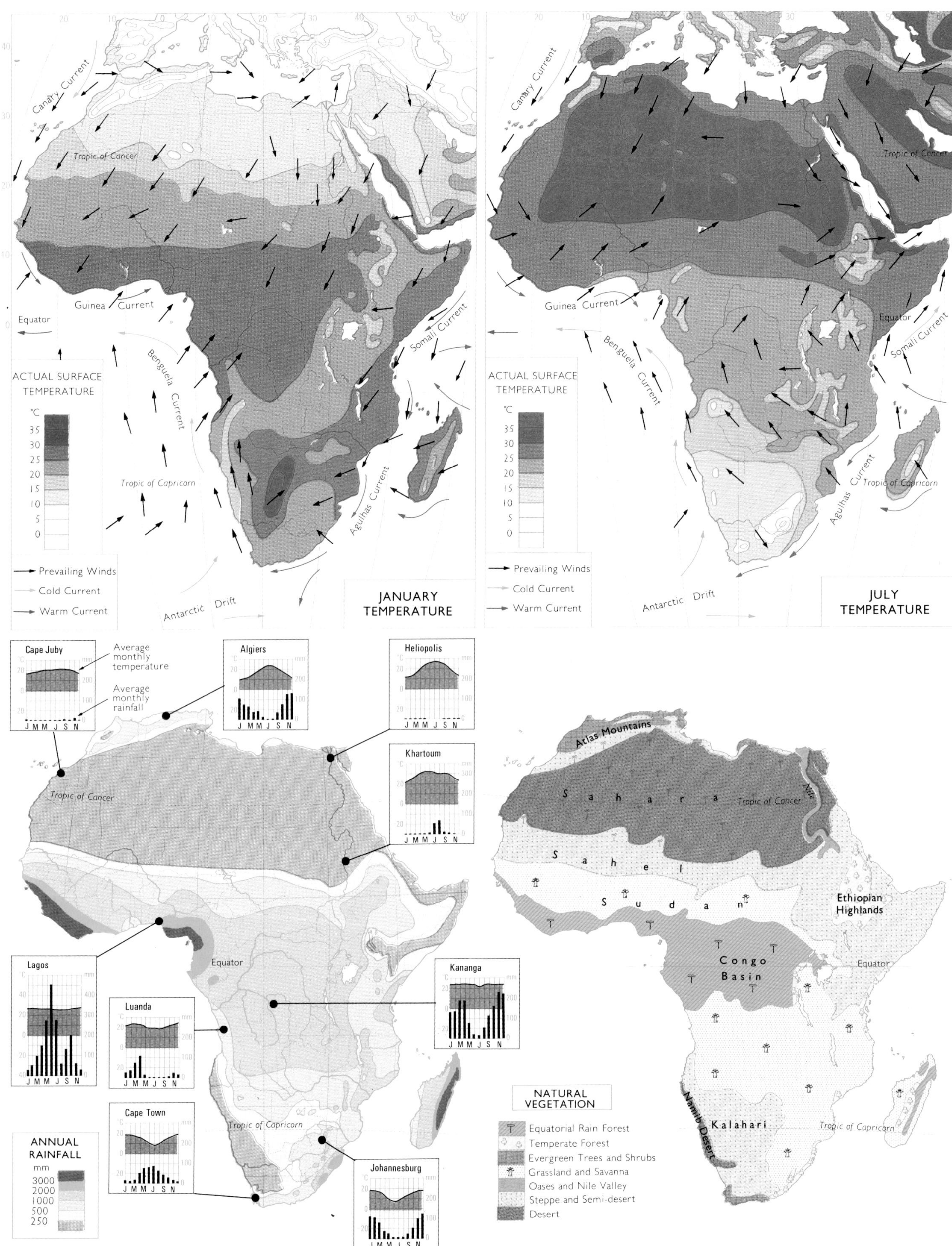

Projection: *Sanson-Flamsteed's Sinusoidal*

1:40 000 000

400 0 400 800 1200 1600 km

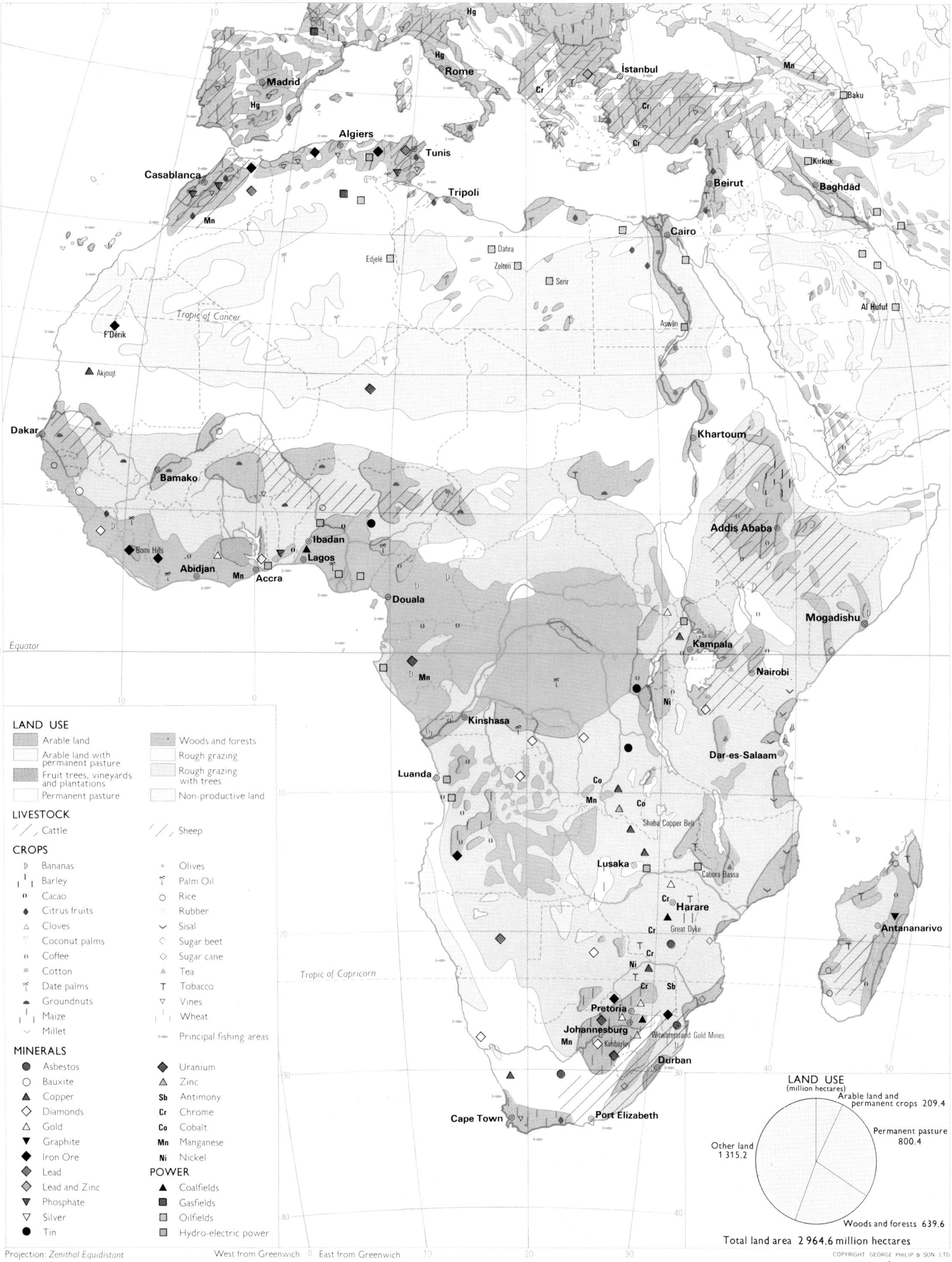

Madrid
Rome
İstanbul
Baku
Algiers
Tunis
Casablanca
Tripoli
Beirut
Kirkuk
Baghdād
Cairo
Edjelé
Dahra
Zelten
Serir
Aswān
Al Hufuf
Tropic of Cancer
F'Dérik
Akjoujt
Dakar
Khartoum
Bamako
Addis Ababa
Ibadan
Bomi Hills
Lagos
Abidjan
Accra
Douala
Mogadishu
Kampala
Equator
Nairobi
Kinshasa
Dar-es-Salaam
Luanda
Shaba Copper Belt
Lusaka
Cabora Bassa
Harare
Great Dyke
Antananarivo
Tropic of Capricorn
Pretoria
Johannesburg
Witwatersrand Gold Mines
Kimberley
Durban
Cape Town
Port Elizabeth

LAND USE

- Arable land
- Arable land with permanent pasture
- Fruit trees, vineyards and plantations
- Permanent pasture
- Woods and forests
- Rough grazing
- Rough grazing with trees
- Non-productive land

LIVESTOCK

- Cattle
- Sheep

CROPS

- Bananas
- Barley
- Cacao
- Citrus fruits
- Cloves
- Coconut palms
- Coffee
- Cotton
- Date palms
- Groundnuts
- Maize
- Millet
- Olives
- Palm Oil
- Rice
- Rubber
- Sisal
- Sugar beet
- Sugar cane
- Tea
- Tobacco
- Vines
- Wheat
- Principal fishing areas

MINERALS

- Asbestos
- Bauxite
- Copper
- Diamonds
- Gold
- Graphite
- Iron Ore
- Lead
- Lead and Zinc
- Phosphate
- Silver
- Tin
- Uranium
- Zinc
- Sb Antimony
- Cr Chrome
- Co Cobalt
- Mn Manganese
- Ni Nickel

POWER

- Coalfields
- Gasfields
- Oilfields
- Hydro-electric power

LAND USE (million hectares)

Category	Million hectares
Arable land and permanent crops	209.4
Permanent pasture	800.4
Woods and forests	639.6
Other land	1 315.2

Total land area 2 964.6 million hectares

Projection: *Zenithal Equidistant* West from Greenwich 0 East from Greenwich

	Population								Land			Agriculture		
	Total	Density	Birth Rate	Death Rate	Life Expectancy	Growth 1965-73	Growth 1973-83	Urban	Area	Arable	Forest	Agricultural Population	Index of Production	Food intake
	th.	persons per km²	per th. popn.	per th. popn.	yrs.	av. % per annum	av. % per annum	%	th. km²	th. km²	th. km²	% of total popn.	1974-76 = 100	calories per day
Algeria	21 272	8.9	47	13	57	2.9	3.1	46	2 382	75	44	47	98	2 586
Angola	8 540	6.8	48	24	43	2.2	2.6	23	1 247	35	536	56	83	2 353
Benin	3 825	34	51	25	48	2.6	2.8	16	111	18	39	45	119	2 174
Botswana	1 051	1.8	51	14	53		4.6	16	585	14	10	78	97	2 352
Burkina Faso	6 582	24	48	24	44	2.0	1.9	11	274	26	71	79	114	2 009
Burundi	4 537	175	42	20	47	1.4	2.2	2	26	13	0.6	82	118	2 353
Cameroon	9 467	20	43	19	54	2.4	3.1	39	469	70	254	79	100	2 295
Central Africa	2 508	4.0	45	24	48	1.6	2.3	44	623	20	397	86	107	2 117
Chad	4 901	3.9	44	24	43	1.8	2.1	20	1 259	32	203	81	114	1 823
Congo	1 695	5.0	45	20	63	2.6	3.1	55	342	6.7	213	32	113	2 433
Egypt	45 657	46	37	10	58	2.3	2.5	45	995	25	0	49	119	3 183
Ethiopia	35 420	32	49	23	43	2.6	2.7	15	1 101	140	265	77	128	2 149
Gabon	1 146	4.4	33	19	40		1.4		258	4.5	200	75	113	2 763
Gambia	630	63	48	30	34		3.7	18	10	1.6	2.0	77	73	2 251
Ghana	13 044	57	47	16	59	2.2	3.1	38	230	28	86	48	76	1 769
Guinea	5 301	22	47	25	37	1.8	2.0	26	246	16	105	79	107	1 880
Guinea-Bissau	875	31	41	22	41		4.6		28	2.9	11	80	92	2 176
Ivory Coast	9 474	30	46	20	52	4.6	4.6	44	318	40	89	78	137	2 613
Kenya	19 536	34	56	16	57	3.7	4.0	17	569	24	25	76	124	2 011
Lesotho	1 481	49	37	15	53	2.1	2.5	13	30	3.0	0	81	95	2 424
Liberia	2 109	22	50	21	49	2.8	3.3	38	96	3.7	38	68	111	2 276
Libya	3 624	2.1	38	13	56	4.1	4.3	61	1 760	21	6.2	12	112	3 812
Madagascar	9 731	17	45	18	49	2.4	2.6	20	582	30	132	81	110	2 491
Malawi	6 839	73	49	25	44	2.9	3.0	11	94	23	43	82	137	2 208
Mali	7 719	6.3	43	18	45	2.6	2.5	19	1 220	206	87	85	117	1 894
Mauritania	1 832	1.8	50	23	46	2.3	2.2	25	1 030	2.1	151	81	119	2 072
Morocco	22 848	51	45	14	52	2.4	2.6	43	446	84	52	49	113	2 607
Mozambique	13 693	17	45	17	46	2.3	2.6	17	784	31	152	61	77	1 881
Namibia	1 507	1.8	45	19	47		2.7		823	6.6	104	46	109	2 197
Niger	5 940	4.7	51	25	45	2.6	3.0	14	1 267	37	28	86	147	2 440
Nigeria	92 037	101	51	19	49	2.5	2.7	22	911	304	143	51	119	2 378
Rwanda	5 903	236	51	22	47	3.1	3.4	5	25	10	2.6	88	138	2 274
Senegal	6 352	33	55	23	46	2.4	2.8	34	192	52	53	73	75	2 346
Sierra Leone	3 536	49	48	32	38	1.7	2.1	23	72	18	21	63	120	1 938
Somalia	5 423	5.9	46	21	45	3.5	2.8	33	927	11	88	78	113	1 986
South Africa	31 586	26	38	15	64	2.6	2.4	35	1 221	136	46	28	91	2 862
Sudan	20 945	8.8	47	19	48	2.6	3.2	20	2 376	124	483	75	113	2 314
Swaziland	649	38	47	19	46		3.5	20	17	1.3	1.0	70	147	2 553
Tanzania	21 062	24	51	17	51	3.1	3.3	14	886	52	419	79	118	1 955
Togo	2 838	53	46	19	49	2.8	2.6	22	54	14	16	66	120	2 126
Tunisia	7 042	45	33	11	62	2.0	2.5	54	155	50	5.6	38	104	2 763
Uganda	15 150	76	50	16	49	3.5	2.8	7	200	58	60	79	119	1 784
Zaire	32 084	14	46	17	51	2.1	2.5	38	2 268	64	1 769	73	115	2 130
Zambia	6 445	8.7	48	17	51	3.0	3.2	47	741	52	206	65	93	2 146
Zimbabwe	7 980	21	47	14	56	3.4	3.2	24	387	28	238	57	90	2 108

For explanations see pages 54-55 or 86-87.

Trade		Education		Health	Energy	Consumer Price Index	G.N.P.		G.D.P. Part formed by		Loans & Debt		
Imports	Exports	Primary	Secondary					Growth per capita	Agric.	Indust.			
US$ per capita		% of age group		Popn. per doctor	Consumption in kgs of oil equiv. per capita	1970 = 100	US$ per capita	% per yr. 1973-82	%		end 1983 US$ millions	as % of GNP	
484	602	93	36	2 630	982	265	2 400	2.4	6	41	12 942	28	Algeria
74	238				226								Angola
97	18	65	21	16 980	39		290	2.7	44	7	615	59	Benin
				7 378		245	920	5.0	12	34			Botswana
45	9	28	3	48 510	22		180	1.6	37	12	398	38	Burkina Faso
41	22	33	3	45 020	17	382	240		51	9	284	26	Burundi
117	93	100	19	13 990	128	448	800	4.6	29	19	1 883	27	Cameroon
53	45	70	14	26 750	35		280	1.3	31	18	215	33	Central Africa
23	12		3	47 640	30	145	80	7.7	41	17	129	44	Chad
488	646		69	5 510	216	383	1 230	3.6	8	46	1 487	76	Congo
224	70	78	54	970	532	459	700	6.6	22	28	15 229	49	Egypt
27	12	46	12	69 390	19	363	140	0.7	45	10	1 223	26	Ethiopia
755	1 748			2 560	941	440	4 250	4.7	5	50			Gabon
156	75			11 632	230	474	290	0.8					Gambia
200	160	76	34	7 160	111	24 648	320	3.8	61	10	1 095	28	Ghana
		33	16	17 110	54		300	0.5			1 216	69	Guinea
59	14			7 306	50		180	2.1					Guinea-Bissau
194	222	76	17	15 234	186	407	720	1.1	27	13	4 824	79	Ivory Coast
73	52	100	20	7 890	109	467	340	1.0	28	13	2 384	43	Kenya
		100	20	18 640		447	470	4.0	24	13	145	23	Lesotho
288	298	66	20	8 550	357	260	470	0.9	17	18	699	72	Liberia
2 155	4 189		67	660	2 769	167	7 500	0.3	2	56	85	0.4	Libya
41	43	100	14	10 220	59	594	290	2.5	33	19	1 490	52	Madagascar
47	33	62	4	41 460	45	182	210	1.1	38	15	719	55	Malawi
46	22	27	9	22 130	22	567	150	2.1	46	11	881	89	Mali
106	161	33	10	14 500	130	150	440	0.7	22	19	1 171	158	Mauritania
169	92	80	28	10 750	258	270	750	2.1	14	23	9 445	70	Morocco
65	18	100	6	39 140	95								Mozambique
							1 760	1.8					Namibia
79	59	23	5	38 790	43	352	240	2.8	50	14	631	49	Niger
151	127	98	16	12 550	150	466	760	0.7	20	32	11 757	18	Nigeria
48	14	70	2	31 340	35	265	270	2.3	46	17	220	14	Rwanda
164	86	48	12	13 780	151	461	440	0.7	18	28	1 496	61	Senegal
47	42	40	12	17 520	102	1 776	380	0.3	31	17	359	35	Sierra Leone
65	39	30	11	15 630	84	217	250	1.9	50	11	1 149	62	Somalia
472	314			1 906	2 278	482	2 450	0.5	7	44			South Africa
67	31	52	18	8 930	66	1 498	400	3.5	34	10	5 726	78	Sudan
				7 000		544	890	0	20	21			Swaziland
40	18	98	3	17 740	38	760	240	0.1	43	8	2 584	59	Tanzania
103	59	100	27	18 100	88	354	280	0.4	27	17	805	114	Togo
452	269	100	32	3 690	473	190	1 290	4.1	14	26	3 427	43	Tunisia
22	26	60	8	26 810	23	730	220	5.6	73	7	623	18	Uganda
16	36	90	23	13 940	77	1 813	160	4.2	26	16	4 022	92	Zaire
88	100	96	16	7 670	432	640	580	2.5	17	27	2 638	84	Zambia
120	136	100	23	5 900	491	192	740	3.3	16	31	1 497	28	Zimbabwe

British Indian Oc. Terr. Land 0.08/Popn. 2; Cape Verde 4.0/317; Comoros 2.2/443; Djibouti 22/354; Eq. Guinea 28/383; Mauritius 1.9/1 011; Reunion 2.5/555; St.Helena 0.3/6; Sao Tome 0.9/94; Seychelles 0.3/65; Western Sahara 266/151

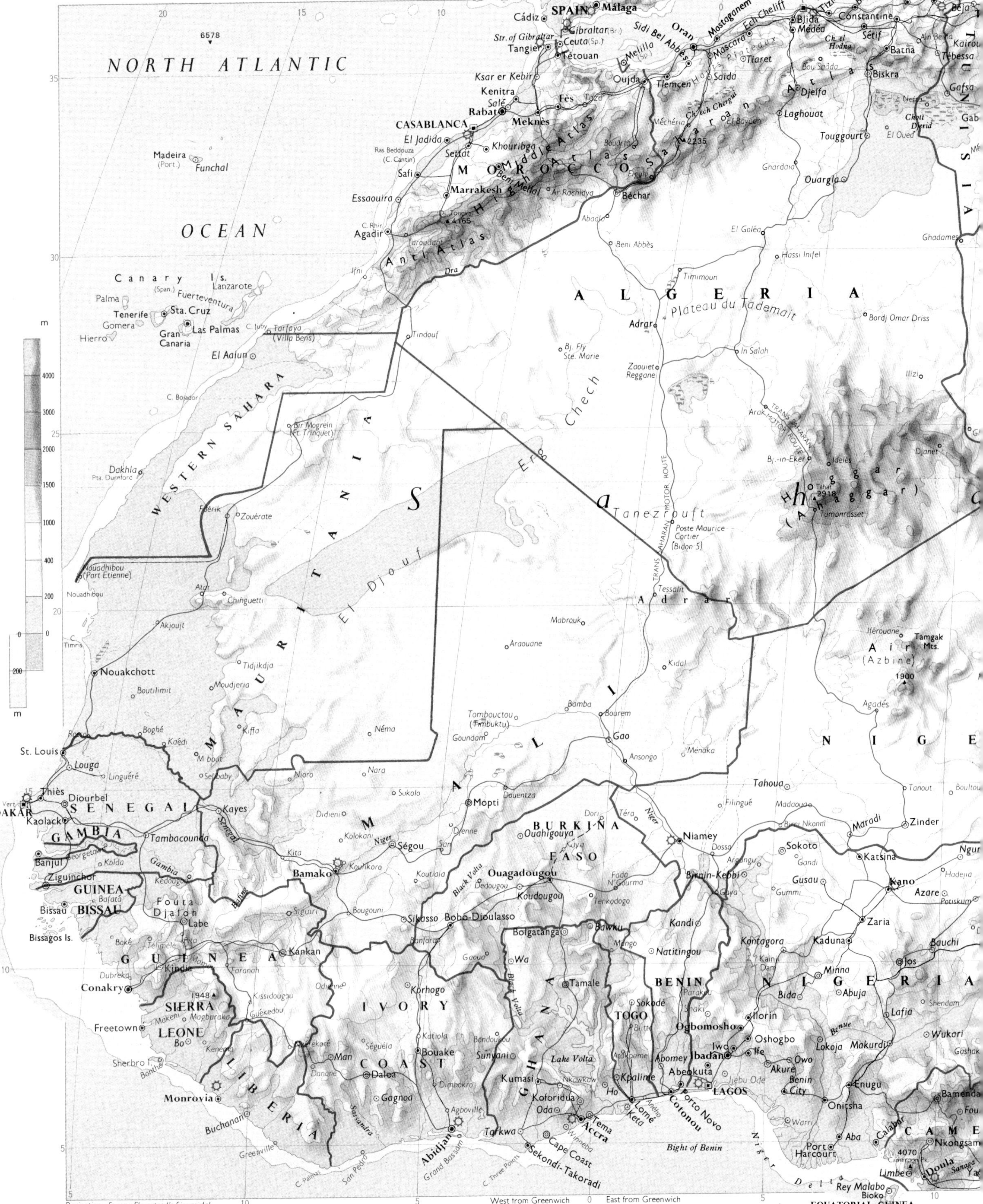
NORTH ATLANTIC
OCEAN
Madeira (Port.)
Funchal
Canary Is.
Lanzarote
Fuerteventura
Palma
Tenerife
Sta. Cruz
Gomera
Las Palmas
Gran Canaria
Hierro
SPAIN
Málaga
Cádiz
Gibraltar (Br.)
Str. of Gibraltar
Ceuta (Sp.)
Tangier
Tétouan
Melilla (Sp.)
Ksar er Kebir
Kenitra
Salé
Rabat
Fès
Taza
Meknès
CASABLANCA
El Jadida
Khouribga
Settat
Safi
Essaouira
Marrakesh
Beni Mellal
Agadir
Taroudant
Ifni
M O R O C C O
Middle Atlas
High Atlas
Anti Atlas
Dra
Oujda
Tlemcen
Sidi Bel Abbès
Oran
Mostaganem
Mascara
Saïda
Tiaret
Ech Cheliff
ALGIERS (Alger)
Blida
Médéa
Tizi-Ouzou
Bejaia
Skikda
Annaba (Bône)
Constantine
Sétif
Batna
Tebessa
Biskra
Djelfa
Laghouat
Touggourt
El Oued
Ouargla
Ghardaia
Méchéria
El Bayadh
Béchar
Figuig
Abadla
Beni Abbès
El Goléa
Hassi Inifel
Timimoun
Adrar
Plateau du Tademait
In Salah
Ghadames
Bordj Omar Driss
Illizi
Tindouf
Tarfaya (Villa Bens)
El Aaiun
C. Bojador
WESTERN SAHARA
Dakhla
Bir Mogrein (Ft. Trinquet)
Bj. Fly Ste. Marie
Zaouiet Reggane
Chech
Erg
A L G E R I A
Tanezrouft
Poste Maurice Cortier (Bidon 5)
Ahaggar
Tahat 2918
Tamanrasset
Djanet
Idelès
Bj.-in-Eker
Arak
TRANS-SAHARAN MOTOR ROUTE
Nouadhibou (Port Etienne)
Zouérate
Atar
Chinguetti
Akjoujt
C. Timris
Nouakchott
Tidjikdja
Boutilimit
Moudjeria
Kiffa
Néma
Boghé
Kaédi
M'bout
Sélibaby
Rosso
M A U R I T A N I A
El Djouf
S a h a r a
Adrar
Tessalit
Mabrouk
Araouane
Kidal
Aïr (Azbine)
Iférouane
Tamgak Mts.
1900
Agadés
Bamba
Bourem
Gao
Ansongo
Ménaka
Tombouctou (Timbuktu)
Goundam
Nioro
Nara
Sokolo
Douentza
Mopti
Djenné
Ségou
Kita
Bamako
Koulikoro
Koutiala
Sikasso
Bougouni
Siguiri
M A L I
N I G E R
Tahoua
Tanout
Zinder
Maradi
Filingué
Niamey
Dosso
Téra
Dori
Birnin-Kebbi
St. Louis
Louga
Linguéré
Thiès
Diourbel
DAKAR
C. Vert
Kaolack
SENEGAL
Kayes
Tambacounda
GAMBIA
Banjul
Georgetown
Kolda
Ziguinchor
GUINEA-BISSAU
Bafatá
Bissau
Bissagos Is.
Fouta Djalon
Labe
Boké
Kindia
Conakry
Faranah
Kankan
G U I N E A
Kissidougou
Guékédou
SIERRA LEONE
Makeni
Freetown
Bo
Kenema
Sherbro I.
Bonthe
1948
LIBERIA
Monrovia
Buchanan
Greenville
C. Palmas
San Pedro
Odienné
Korhogo
Katiola
Bouaké
Séguéla
Man
Daloa
Gagnoa
Dimbokro
Agboville
Abidjan
Grand Bassam
IVORY COAST
Sassandra
BURKINA FASO
Ouahigouya
Ouagadougou
Koudougou
Dédougou
Bobo-Dioulasso
Banfora
Fada N'Gourma
Tenkodogo
Black Volta
Bolgatanga
Bawku
Wa
Tamale
GHANA
Lake Volta
Sunyani
Kumasi
Koforidua
Oda
Tarkwa
Sekondi-Takoradi
Cape Coast
Winneba
Accra
Tema
C. Three Points
Keta
Lomé
TOGO
Sokodé
Kpalimé
Atakpamé
BENIN
Natitingou
Kandi
Parakou
Abomey
Cotonou
Porto Novo
Bight of Benin
LAGOS
Abeokuta
Ibadan
Ijebu Ode
Iwo
Ife
Oshogbo
Ogbomosho
Ilorin
Akure
Owo
Benin City
Warri
Onitsha
Enugu
Aba
Port Harcourt
Calabar
Niger Delta
N I G E R I A
Sokoto
Gusau
Katsina
Kano
Azare
Potiskum
Zaria
Kaduna
Kontagora
Bauchi
Jos
Minna
Abuja
Bida
Lafia
Shendam
Makurdi
Wukari
Lokoja
Bamenda
Nkongsamba
Douala
Limbe
4070
Rey Malabo
Bioko
EQUATORIAL GUINEA
Projection: Sanson Flamsteed's Sinusoidal
West from Greenwich
East from Greenwich

1:15 000 000

100 0 100 200 300 400 500 600 km

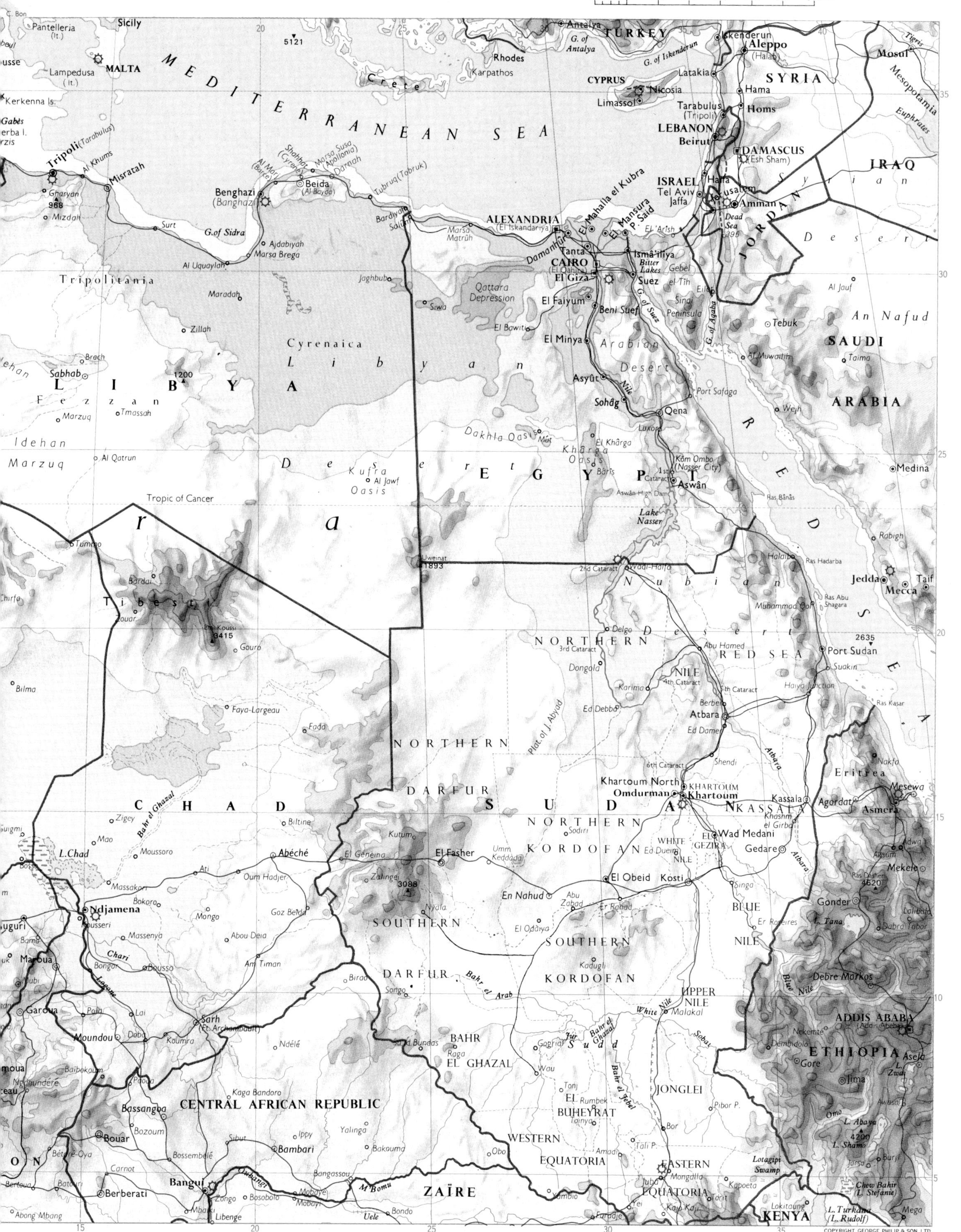

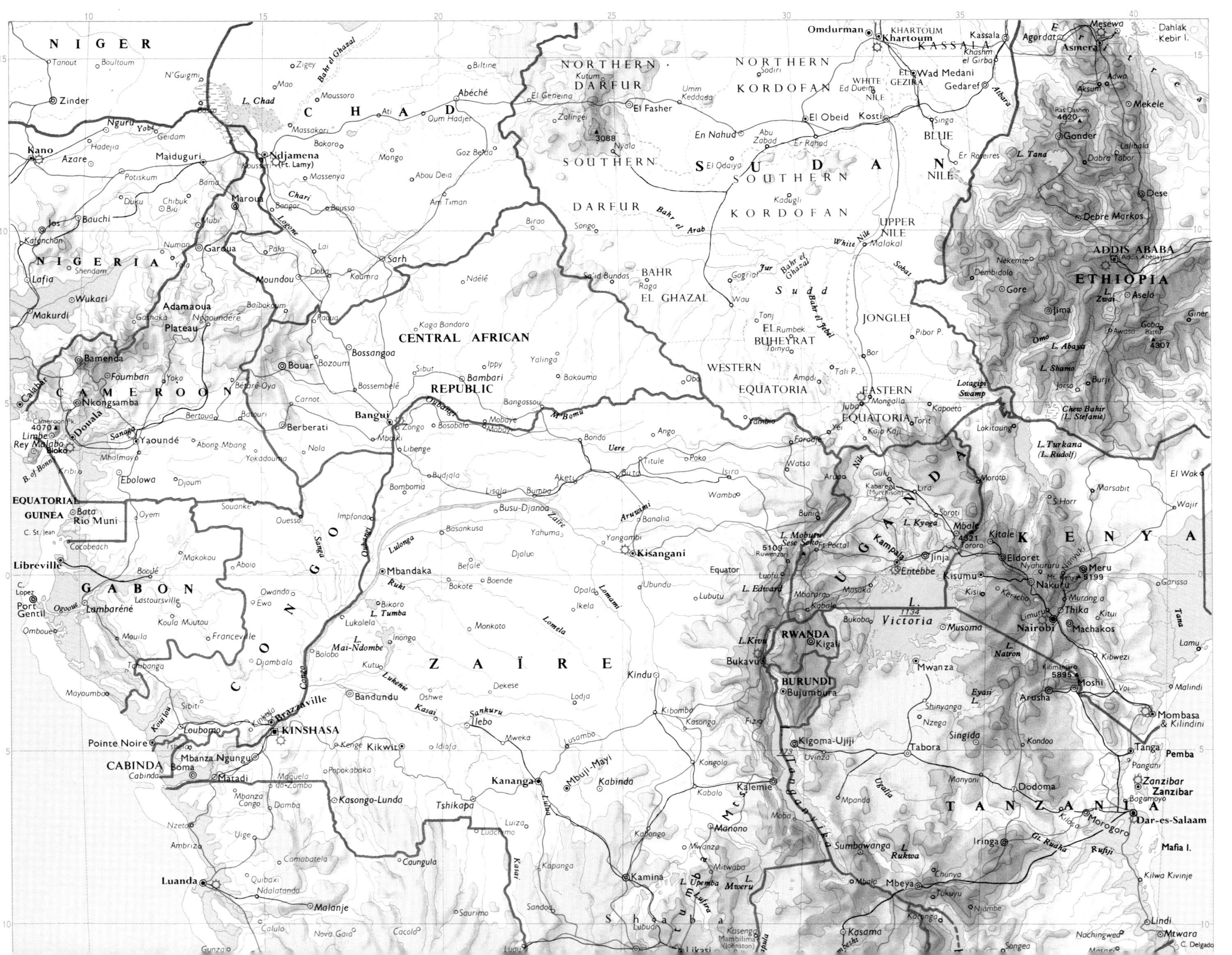

NIGER
NIGERIA
CHAD
CAMEROON
CENTRAL AFRICAN REPUBLIC
SUDAN
ETHIOPIA
Eritrea
KENYA
UGANDA
RWANDA
BURUNDI
TANZANIA
ZAÏRE
CONGO
GABON
EQUATORIAL GUINEA
Rio Muni
CABINDA
NORTHERN DARFUR
SOUTHERN DARFUR
NORTHERN KORDOFAN
SOUTHERN KORDOFAN
KHARTOUM
KASSALA
BLUE NILE
WHITE NILE
GEZIRA
UPPER NILE
JONGLEI
BAHR EL GHAZAL
EL BUHEYRAT
WESTERN EQUATORIA
EASTERN EQUATORIA
Omdurman
Khartoum
Wad Medani
Kassala
Gedaref
Kosti
El Obeid
El Fasher
Asmera
Mekele
Dese
Gonder
ADDIS ABABA
Kano
Zinder
Maiduguri
Ndjamena (Ft. Lamy)
Abéché
Sarh
Bangui
Garoua
Yaoundé
Douala
Malabo
Libreville
Port Gentil
Lambaréné
Pointe Noire
Brazzaville
KINSHASA
Mbandaka
Kisangani
Bukavu
Kampala
Entebbe
Jinja
Nairobi
Mombasa & Kilindini
Tanga
Zanzibar
Dar-es-Salaam
Mafia I.
Pemba
Dodoma
Tabora
Mwanza
Arusha
Mbeya
Iringa
Kigoma-Ujiji
Kigali
Bujumbura
Kananga
Kamina
Luanda
Malanje
L. Chad
L. Tana
L. Turkana (L. Rudolf)
L. Victoria
L. Tanganyika
L. Kivu
L. Edward
L. Mobutu Sese Seko
L. Kyoga
L. Rukwa
Sudd
Bahr el Arab
Bahr el Ghazal
Bahr el Jebel
Atbara
Sobat
Ubangi
Congo
Kasai
Lomami
Sanga
Ogooué
Chari
Logone

1:15 000 000

100 0 100 200 300 400 500 600 km
MADAGASCAR
On same scale as General Map
COPYRIGHT GEORGE PHILIP & SON, LTD
INDIAN OCEAN
ATLANTIC OCEAN
Tropic of Capricorn
East from Greenwich
Projection: Sanson Flamsteed's Sinusoidal
BOTSWANA
Kalahari
NAMIBIA
(SOUTH WEST AFRICA)
SOUTH AFRICA
ZIMBABWE
MOZAMBIQUE
TRANSVAAL
ORANGE FREE STATE
NATAL
CAPE PROVINCE
LESOTHO
SWAZI LAND
Mozambique Channel
Namaland
Damaraland
Owambo
Caprivi Strip
CAPE TOWN
C. of Good Hope
Port Elizabeth
East London
Durban
Pietermaritzburg
Bloemfontein
Kimberley
JOHANNESBURG
Pretoria
Maputo (Lourenço Marques)
Beira
Harare (Salisbury)
Bulawayo
Gaborone
Windhoek
Walvis Bay
Lüderitz
Lusaka
Livingstone
Blantyre
Zomba
Lilongwe
Quelimane
Nampula
Mozambique
Inhambane
Antananarivo (Tananarive)
Toamasina
Antsiranana
Mahajanga
Fianarantsoa
Toliara
Antsirabe
Bassas da India (Réunion)
Île Europa (Réunion)
Is. Glorieuses (Réunion)
Limpopo
Orange
Zambezi
5283
5349
m
6000
4000
3000
2000
1500
1000
400
200
0

1:35 000 000

400 0 400 800 1200 km
ARCTIC OCEAN
Asia
Greenland
Iceland
Beaufort Sea
Bering Sea
Bering Strait
Alaska
Brooks Range
Alaska Range
Mt. McKinley 6194
Alaska Pen.
Gulf of Alaska
Mt. St. Elias 5489
Mt. Logan 6050
Yukon
Porcupine
Mackenzie Mts.
Mackenzie
Great Bear L.
Great Slave L.
Arctic Circle
Queen Elizabeth Islands
Ellesmere I.
Axel Heiberg Land
Sverdrup Is.
Parry Is.
Melville I.
Banks I.
Victoria I.
Prince of Wales I.
Devon I.
Baffin Bay
Baffin Island
Davis Strait
Denmark Strait
Hudson Strait
Hudson Bay
James Bay
Southampton I.
Foxe Basin
Melville Pen.
Gulf of Boothia
Ungava Peninsula
Labrador
Newfoundland
Gulf of St. Lawrence
Nova Scotia
Alexander Archipelago
Queen Charlotte Islands
Vancouver I.
Coast Mountains
Rocky Mountains
Great Plains
Mt. Robson 3954
Edmonton
Calgary
Regina
Winnipeg
Lake Winnipeg
Laurentian Plateau
Quebec
Montreal
Ottawa
Toronto
L. Superior
L. Michigan
L. Huron
L. Erie
L. Ontario
Chicago
Detroit
Minneapolis
New York
Philadelphia
Washington
Chesapeake Bay
Appalachian Mts.
Allegheny Mts.
Blue Ridge 2037
Atlanta
Seattle
Mt. Rainier 4392
Portland
Cascade Range
Coast Range
Mt. Shasta 4317
Sierra Nevada
San Francisco
Mt. Whitney 4418
Los Angeles
Great Basin
Great Salt Lake
Wasatch Mountains
Mt. Elbert 4399
Denver
Colorado Plateau
Llano Estacado
Kansas City
St. Louis
Ozark Plateau
Memphis
Dallas
Houston
New Orleans
Mississippi
Mississippi Delta
Florida
Florida Strait
Bahama Islands
Bermuda
ATLANTIC OCEAN
6399
PACIFIC OCEAN
Mendocino Seascarp
Murray Seascarp
Clarion Fracture Zone
Revilla Gigedo Is.
Tropic of Cancer
Lower California
Gulf of California
C. San Lucas
Western Sierra Madre
Eastern Sierra Madre
Mexican Plateau
Monterrey
Guadalajara
Mexico
Puebla
Popocatepetl 5452
Citlaltepetl 5700
Isthmus of Tehuantepec
Gulf of Mexico
Gulf of Campeche
Yucatán Peninsula
Yucatán Strait
Yucatán Basin
Cuba
Havana
Greater Antilles
Jamaica
Hispaniola
Puerto Rico
Milwaukee Deep 9200
Cayman Trench 7680
Caribbean Sea
Colombian Basin
Venezuelan Basin
Gulf of Honduras
Guatemala
L. Nicaragua
Panama Canal
G. of Panamá
G. of Darién
Guatemala Trench 6662
G. of Tehuantepec
Andes
Sierra de Mérida
Maracaibo
G. of Venezuela
Sa. Nevada de Sta. Marta 5800
Projection: Bonne
West from Greenwich

1:35 000 000

400 0 400 800 1200 km

1:70 000 000

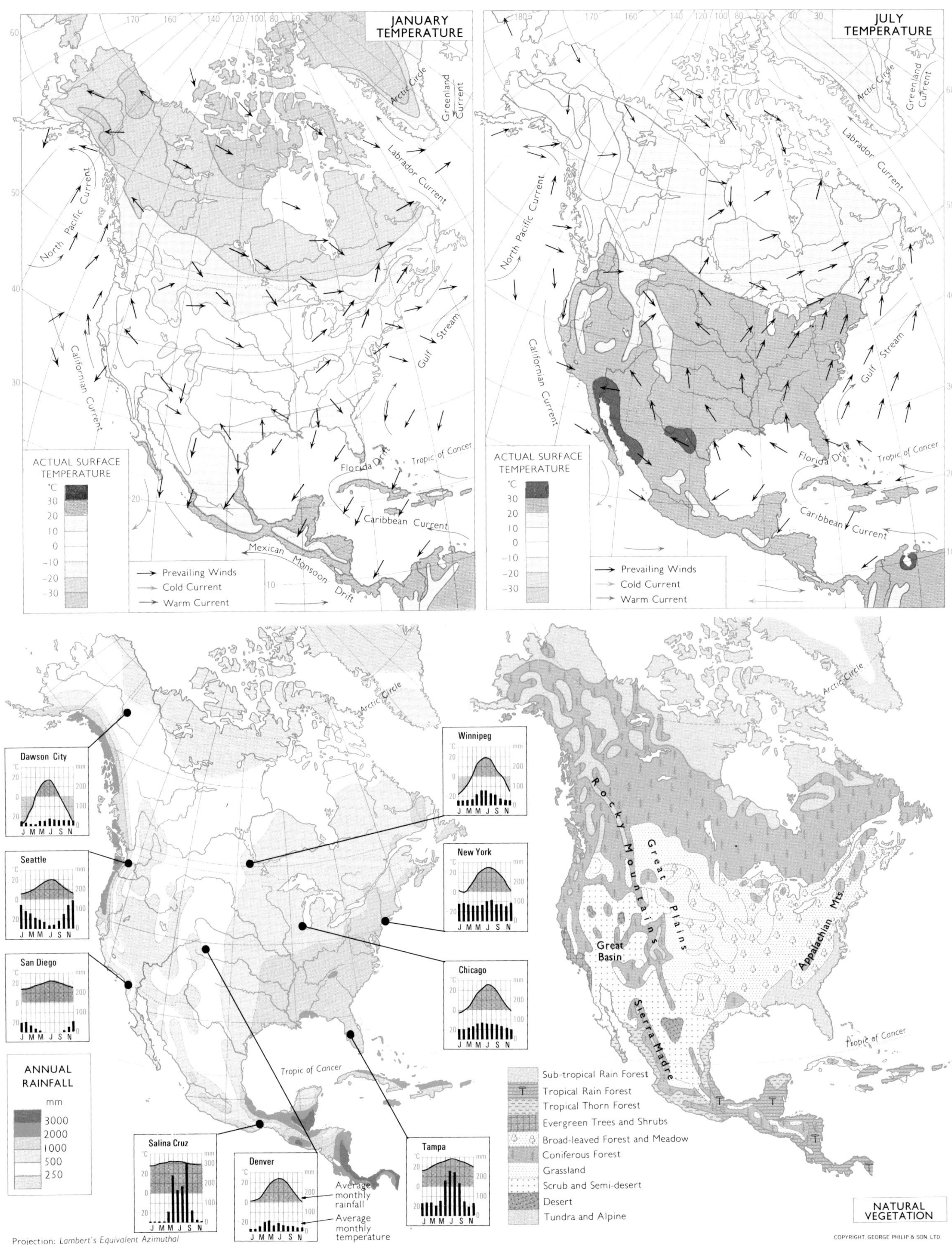

Projection: *Lambert's Equivalent Azimuthal*

1:32 000 000

400 0 400 800 1200 km

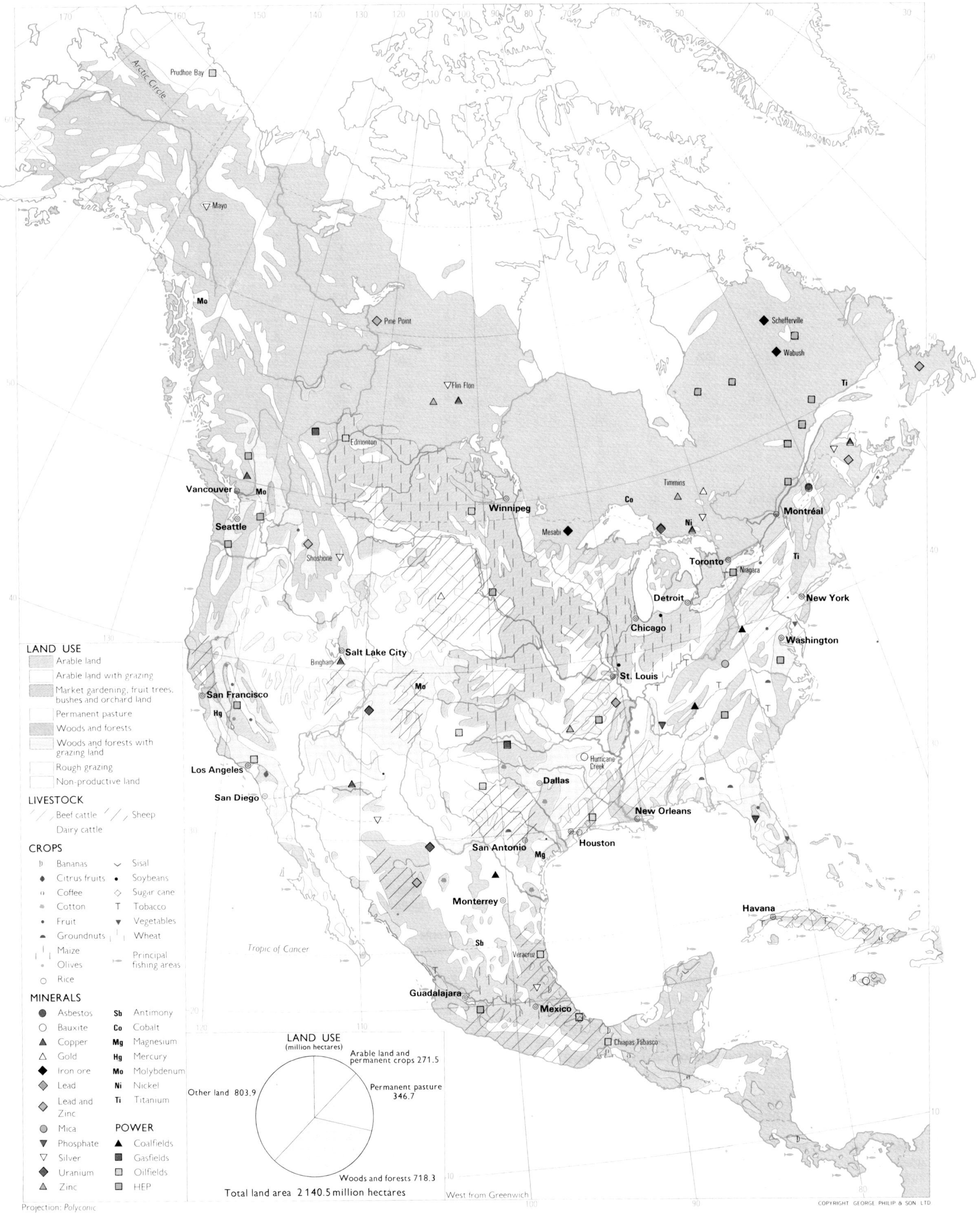

Prudhoe Bay
Arctic Circle
Mayo
Mo
Pine Point
Flin Flon
Schefferville
Wabush
Ti
Edmonton
Vancouver
Mo
Seattle
Winnipeg
Co
Timmins
Ni
Mesabi
Montréal
Shoshone
Toronto
Niagara
Ti
Detroit
New York
Chicago
Washington
Salt Lake City
Bingham
St. Louis
Mo
San Francisco
Hg
Hurricane Creek
Los Angeles
Dallas
San Diego
New Orleans
San Antonio
Houston
Mg
Monterrey
Havana
Tropic of Cancer
Sb
Veracruz
Guadalajara
Mexico
Chiapas Tabasco
West from Greenwich

LAND USE

- Arable land
- Arable land with grazing
- Market gardening, fruit trees, bushes and orchard land
- Permanent pasture
- Woods and forests
- Woods and forests with grazing land
- Rough grazing
- Non-productive land

LIVESTOCK

- Beef cattle
- Sheep
- Dairy cattle

CROPS

- Bananas
- Citrus fruits
- Coffee
- Cotton
- Fruit
- Groundnuts
- Maize
- Olives
- Rice
- Sisal
- Soybeans
- Sugar cane
- Tobacco
- Vegetables
- Wheat
- Principal fishing areas

MINERALS

- Asbestos
- Bauxite
- Copper
- Gold
- Iron ore
- Lead
- Lead and Zinc
- Mica
- Phosphate
- Silver
- Uranium
- Zinc
- Sb Antimony
- Co Cobalt
- Mg Magnesium
- Hg Mercury
- Mo Molybdenum
- Ni Nickel
- Ti Titanium

POWER

- Coalfields
- Gasfields
- Oilfields
- HEP

LAND USE
(million hectares)

- Arable land and permanent crops 271.5
- Permanent pasture 346.7
- Woods and forests 718.3
- Other land 803.9

Total land area 2 140.5 million hectares

Projection: Polyconic

PACIFIC OCEAN
ALASKA
YUKON TERRITORY
NORTHWEST TERRITORIES
BRITISH COLUMBIA
ALBERTA
SASKATCHEWAN
MANITOBA
INUVIK
FORT SMITH
KITIKMEOT
KEEWATIN
Mackenzie Mountains
Rocky Mountains
Coast Mountains
Cassiar Mountains
Columbia Mountains
Selkirk Mts.
St. Elias Mts.
Wrangell Mts.
ALASKA HIGHWAY
Banks Island
Victoria Island
Prince of Wales Island
Melville Sound
Viscount Melville Sound
M'Clintock Channel
Amundsen Gulf
Coronation Gulf
Queen Maud Gulf
Great Bear Lake
Great Slave L.
Lake Athabasca
Wollaston L.
Reindeer Lake
Southern Indian L.
Lake Winnipeg
L. Manitoba
Anchorage
Fairbanks
Juneau
Whitehorse
Dawson
Yellowknife
Edmonton
Calgary
VANCOUVER
Victoria
SEATTLE
Tacoma
Spokane
Kamloops
Kelowna
Prince George
Prince Rupert
Lethbridge
Medicine Hat
Saskatoon
Regina
Moose Jaw
Prince Albert
Winnipeg
Brandon
Fort McMurray
Grande Prairie
Dawson Creek
Churchill
The Pas
Flin Flon
Queen Charlotte Is.
Vancouver I.
Projection: Bonne
WASHINGTON
MONTANA
NORTH DAKOTA
SOUTH DAKOTA
NEBRASKA
WYOMING
MINNESOTA
UNITED STATES
ALASKA
1:30 000 000
0 200 400 600 km
Brooks Range
Alaska Range
Bering Sea
Gulf of Alaska
Aleutian Is.
Alaska Peninsula
Kodiak I.
Nome
Bering Strait
PACIFIC OCEAN
West from Greenwich
m
3000
2000
1500
1000
400
200
0
200
2000
m

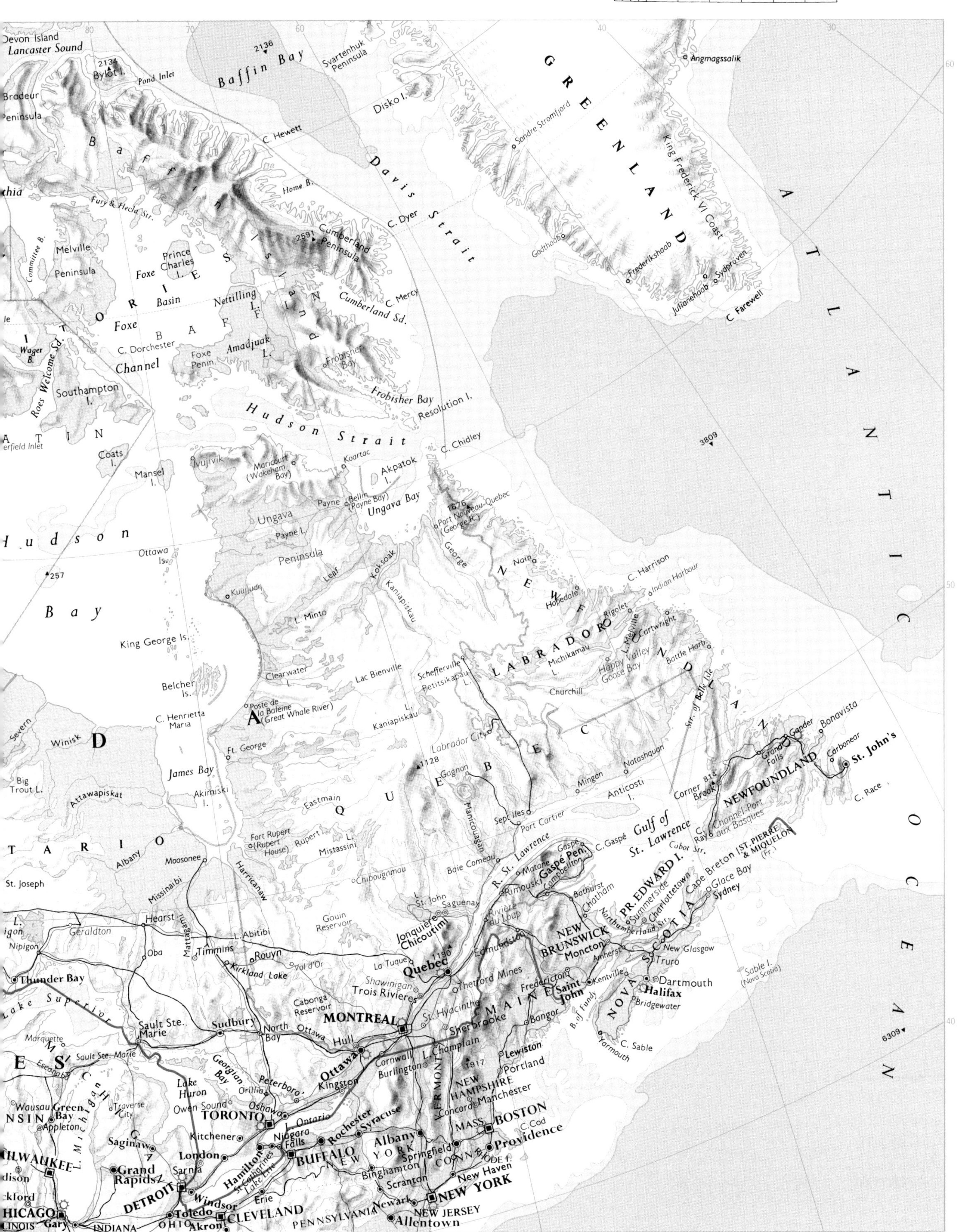

West from Greenwich

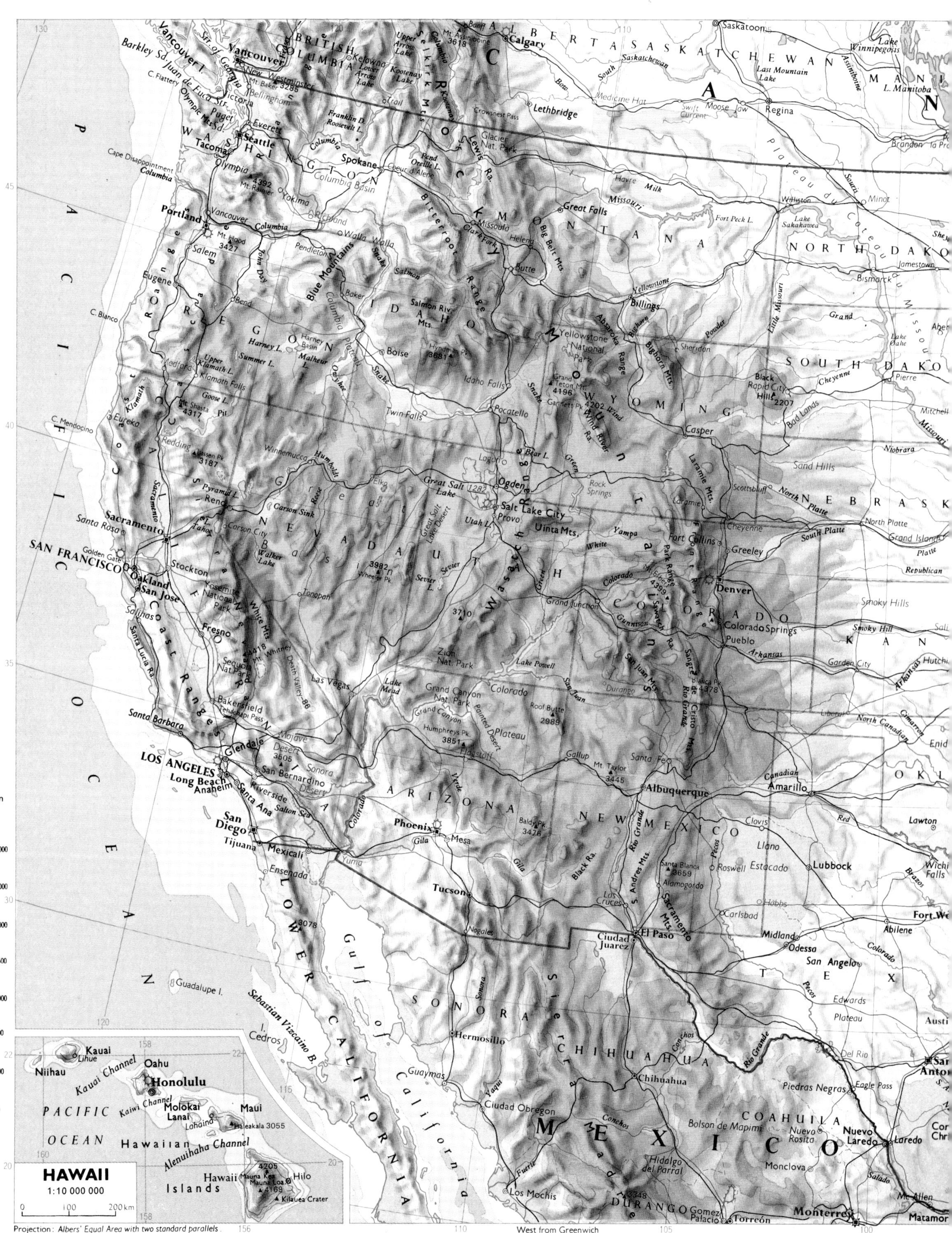
HAWAII
1:10 000 000
Projection: Albers' Equal Area with two standard parallels
West from Greenwich

1:12 000 000

100 0 100 200 300 400 500 km

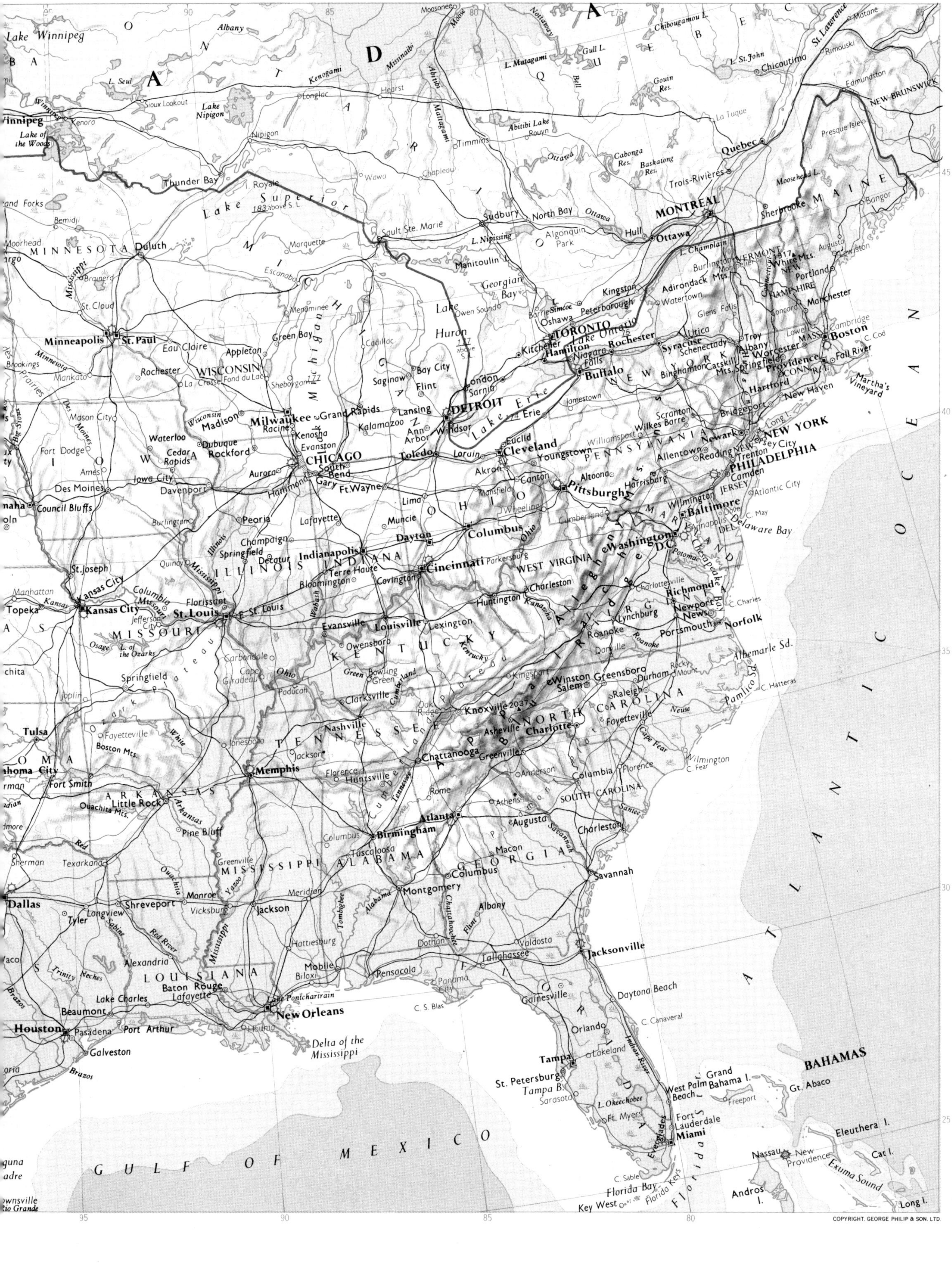

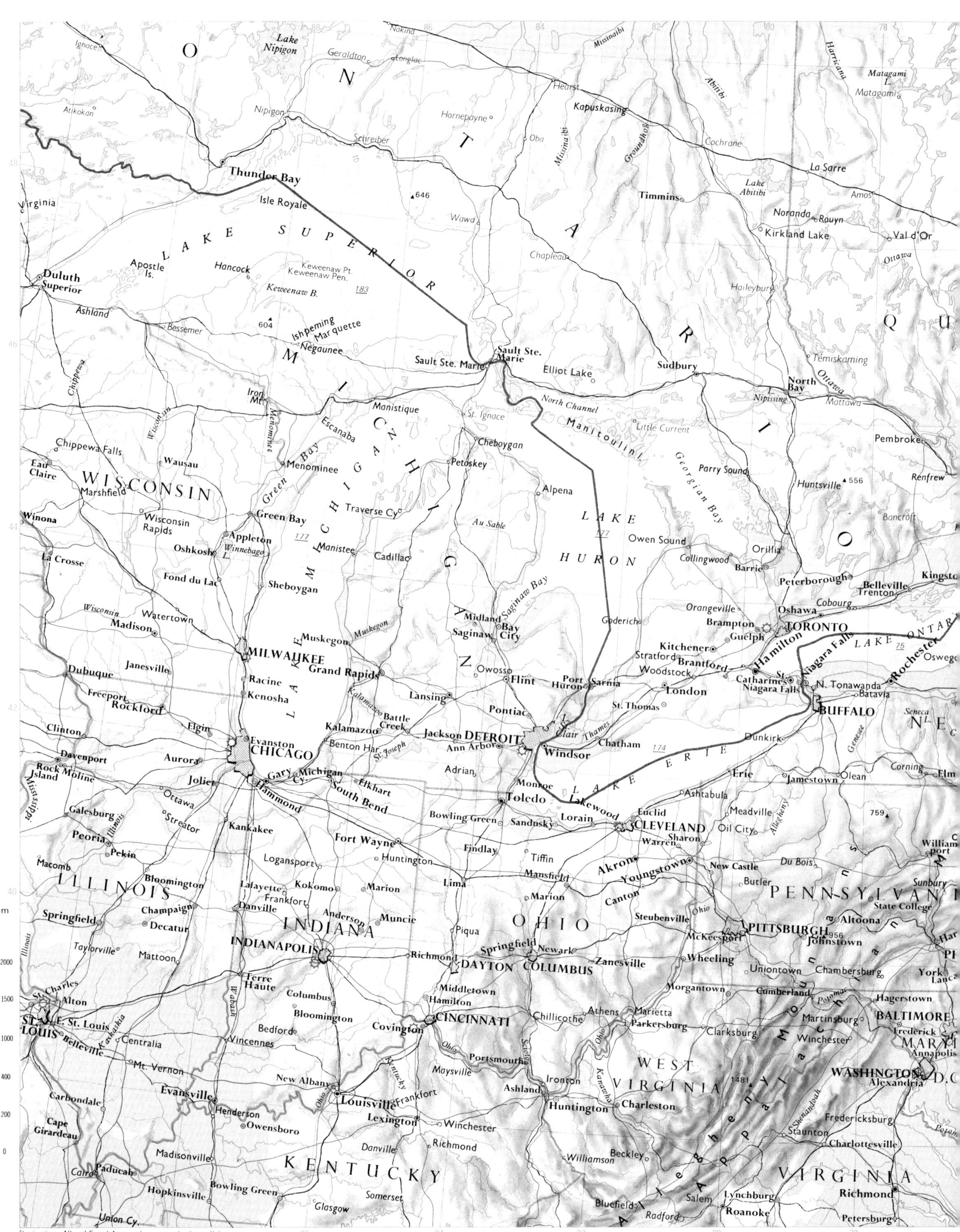

Projection: Albers' Equal Area with two standard parallels

1:6 000 000

Anticosti I.
GULF OF ST. LAWRENCE
PRINCE EDWARD ISLAND
Cape Breton Island
NEW BRUNSWICK
NOVA SCOTIA
MAINE
VERMONT
NEW HAMPSHIRE
MASS.
CONN.
R.I.
NEW JERSEY
DELAWARE
ATLANTIC OCEAN
Quebec
MONTREAL
Ottawa
BOSTON
NEW YORK
Halifax
Saint John
Moncton
Fredericton
Portland
Providence
Hartford
Springfield
Worcester
Sydney
Charlottetown
Gaspé Peninsula
Shickshock Mts.
Bay of Fundy
Massachusetts Bay
Long Island
West from Greenwich

San Diego
Tijuana
Mexicali
Yuma
Ensenada
Phoenix
Tucson
Nogales
Ciudad Juárez
El Paso
Agua Prieta
Carlsbad
Wichita Falls
Fort Worth
Dallas
Abilene
Pecos
San Angelo
Waco
Tyler
Brazos
Trinity
Austin
San Antonio
Houston
Birmingham
Shreveport
Monroe
Jackson
Montgomery
Mississippi
Red
Sabine
Alexandria
Beaumont
Lake Charles
Lafayette
Baton Rouge
Mobile
Pensacola
Alabama
Port Arthur
Galveston
New Orleans
Mississippi Delta
U N I T E D S T A T E S
Pt. Baja
Sebastian Vizcaino Bay
Pt. Sta. Eugenia
Lower California
Gulf of California
3078
3658
3200
Sonora
Tiburón I.
Hermosillo
Empalme
Guaymas
Sta. Rosalia
Ciudad Obregon
Yaqui
Navojoa
Fuerte
Villa Ahumada
Sta. Maria
Conchos
Rio Grande
Chihuahua
Delicias
Sierra Madre
Hidalgo del Parral
3150
2896
Piedras Negras
Eagle Pass
Nueva Rosita
Sabinas
Laredo
Nuevo Laredo
Monclova
Falcon Res.
Sabinas Hidalgo
Matagorda I.
Corpus Christi
Padre I.
Brownsville
Rio Grande del Norte
Matamoros
Reynosa
Monterrey
Los Machis
Guamúchil
Nazas
S. Pedro
Gómez Palacio
Torreón
Saltillo
Culiacan
Aguanaval
Concepción del Oro
Montemorelos
Laguna de la Madre
G U L F O F M E X I C O
2406
C. San Lucas
Elota
Durango
Mazatlán
Rosario
4054
Matehuala
Ciudad Victoria
Fresnillo
Zacatecas
Ciudad Mante
Tropic of Cancer
Yucatan Channel
P A C I F I C
O C E A N
Las Tres Marías
3353
San Luis Potosí
Ciudad Madero
Tampico
Tepic
R. Grande de Santiago
Aguascalientes
Panuco
C. Rojo
C. Corrientes
Guadalajara
Ameca
León
Irapuato
Celaya
Queretaro
Tuxpan
L. de Chapala
Colima Vol.
3960
Zamora
Morelia
MEXICO
Pachuca
Manzanillo
Colima
Toluca
Cuernavaca
Iguala
Citlaltepetl 5700
Jalapa Enriquez
Veracruz
Puebla
Orizaba
Popocatepetl 5452
Balsas
3703
Chilpancingo
Mexcala
Acapulco
Ometepec
Gulf of Campeche
Ciudad del Carmen
Campeche
Progreso
Mérida
Valladolid
Peto
I. de Cozumel
Yucatan
Laguna de Terminos
Chetumal
Minatitlán
Coatzacoalcos
Villahermosa
Usumacinta
3396
Isthmus of Tehuantepec
Oaxaca
Verde
Juchitan
Tuxtla Gutiérrez
San Cristobal
3139
Salina Cruz
Tonala
Chiapa
Belize
Belmopan
BELIZE
Turneffe Is.
Gulf of Honduras
Pto. Barrios
Pto Cortés
Tela
La Ceiba
G. of Tehuantepec
Tapachula
4217
Guatemala
GUATEMALA
Quezaltenang
Zacapa
S. Pedro Sula
HONDURAS
Comayagua
Tegucigalpa
Sta. Ana
San Salvador
EL SALVADOR
S. Miguel
G. of Fonseca
Choluteca
NICARAGUA
Leon
Managua
Nicoya Pen.
Colón
Coco Solo
Fort Limon
Sherman
Cristobal
Puerto Pilón
Margarita
Chagres
Gatun
Gatun Locks
Gatun Dam
Zorra I.
El Limon
Madden L.
Madden Dam
Buenos Aires
Juan Gallegos
Gatun Lake
Frijoles
Escobal
Colorado I.
Darien
Chagres
Gamboa
The Gaillard Cut
Balboa Hill
350
Las Cascadas
Culebra
Paraiso
Pedro Miguel
Pedro Miguel Locks
Miraflores Locks
Fort Clayton
Curundu
Corozal
Ancon
Balboa
Arraijan
Fort Amador
Bay of Panama
PANAMA
La Chorrera
PANAMA CANAL
1:1 000 000
0 10 20 km
Montego Bay
Falmouth
St. Ann's Bay
Galina Point
Annotto Bay
Port Antonio
Savanna la Mar
Mandeville
KINGSTON
2256
Morant Point
May Pen
Spanish Town
Morant Bay
Portland Point
JAMAICA
1:5 000 000
0 50 km
TRINIDAD AND TOBAGO
1:5 000 000
0 50 km
Charlotteville
Tobago
Scarborough
Port of Spain
940
Arima
Sangre Grande
Gulf of Paria
TRINIDAD
Rio Claro
San Fernando
Princes Town
Point Fortin
Siparia
Serpent's Mouth
The Valley
Anguilla (Br.)
Marigot
St. Martin (Fr.)
St. Maarten (Neth.)
St. Barthélemy (Fr.)
Saba (Neth.)
St. Eustatius (Neth.)
Codrington
Barbuda
ANTIGUA & BARBUDA
St. Christopher (St. Kitts)
ST. CHRISTOPHER-NEVIS
Basseterre
Charlestown
Nevis
St. John's
Antigua
Redonda
Montserrat
Plymouth
Guadeloupe Passage
GUADELOUPE (Fr.)
Grande Terre
Ste Rose
Moule
Désirade (Fr.)
Basse Terre
Pointe-à-Pitre
Marie-Galante (Fr.)
I. des Saintes (Fr.)
Dominica Passage
Grand Bourg
Portsmouth
Morne Diablotin
1490
Roseau
DOMINICA (Windward Is.)
LEEWARD ISLANDS
1:5 000 000
0 50 km
Martinique Passage
Mt. Pelée 1397
Ste. Marie
St. Pierre
Fort de France
Le François
Lamentin
MARTINIQUE (Fr.)
Ste. Anne
St. Lucia Channel
Castries
Soufrière
ST. LUCIA
Vieux Fort
St. Vincent Passage
Soufrière
1178
Georgetown
ST. VINCENT
Kingstown
& Bequia
BARBADOS
Speightstown
Bridgetown
THE GRENADINES
Mustique
Canouan
Union
The
Carriacou
Hillsborough
Ronde
Grenadines
840
St. George's
Grenville
GRENADA
WINDWARD ISLANDS
1:5 000 000
0 50 km
Projection: Bonne

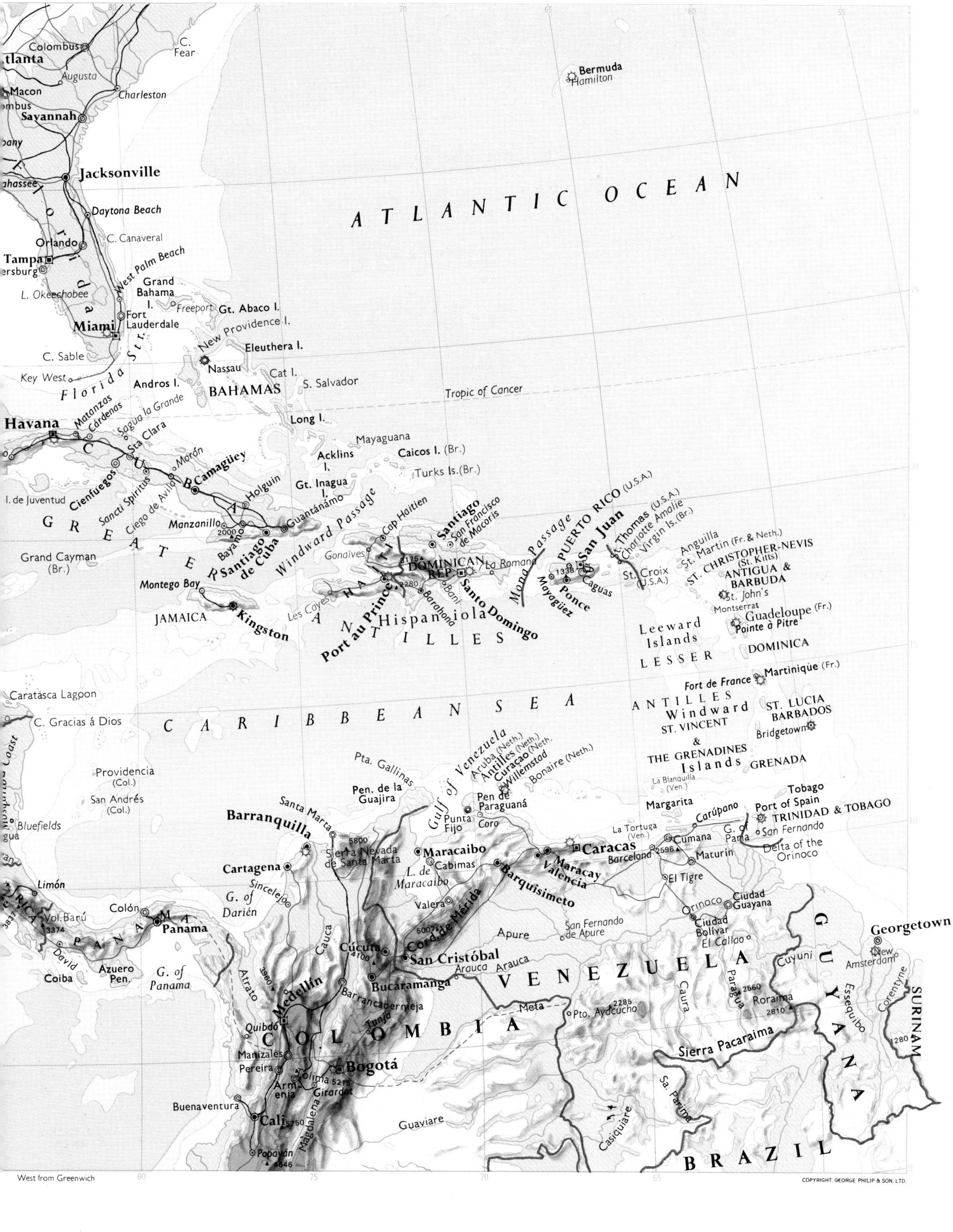

1:15 000 000

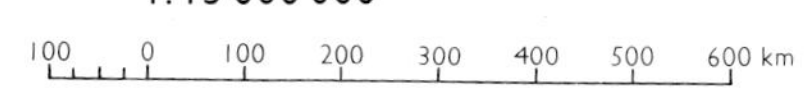

Colombus
Atlanta
C. Fear
Augusta
Macon
Charleston
Bermuda
Hamilton
Savannah
Jacksonville
Florida
Daytona Beach
ATLANTIC OCEAN
Orlando
C. Canaveral
Tampa
West Palm Beach
L. Okeechobee
Grand Bahama I.
Freeport
Gt. Abaco I.
Fort Lauderdale
Miami
New Providence I.
Eleuthera I.
C. Sable
Nassau
Cat I.
Key West
Florida Str.
Andros I.
BAHAMAS
S. Salvador
Tropic of Cancer
Havana
Matanzas
Cárdenas
Sagua la Grande
Sta Clara
Long I.
Mayaguana
CUBA
Acklins I.
Caicos I. (Br.)
Morón
Cienfuegos
Camagüey
Turks Is.(Br.)
Sancti Spiritus
Holguín
Gt. Inagua I.
I. de Juventud
Ciego de Avila
Guantánamo
Windward Passage
Cap Haitien
Santiago
San Francisco de Macoris
PUERTO RICO (U.S.A.)
St. Thomas (U.S.A.)
Charlotte Amalie
Virgin Is. (Br.)
Anguilla
St. Martin (Fr. & Neth.)
ST. CHRISTOPHER-NEVIS (St. Kitts)
Manzanillo
2000
Bayamo
Santiago de Cuba
GREATER ANTILLES
Grand Cayman (Br.)
Gonaïves
HAITI
3175
DOMINICAN REP.
La Romana
Mona Passage
San Juan
1338
Caguas
Mayagüez
Ponce
St. Croix (U.S.A.)
ANTIGUA & BARBUDA
St. John's
Montego Bay
2280
Baní
Barahona
Santo Domingo
Montserrat
Guadeloupe (Fr.)
Pointe à Pitre
JAMAICA
Kingston
Les Cayes
Port au Prince
Hispaniola
Leeward Islands
LESSER ANTILLES
DOMINICA
Fort de France
Martinique (Fr.)
Caratasca Lagoon
CARIBBEAN SEA
Windward Islands
ST. LUCIA
BARBADOS
C. Gracias á Dios
ST. VINCENT & THE GRENADINES
Bridgetown
Coast
Pta. Gallinas
Gulf of Venezuela
Aruba (Neth.)
Antilles (Neth.)
Curaçao (Neth.)
Willemstad
Bonaire (Neth.)
GRENADA
Providencia (Col.)
La Blanquilla (Ven.)
Tobago
San Andrés (Col.)
Pen. de la Guajira
Pen de Paraguaná
Margarita
Carúpano
Port of Spain
TRINIDAD & TOBAGO
Santa Marta
Punta Fijo
Coro
La Tortuga (Ven.)
Cumana
G. of Paria
San Fernando
Bluefields
Barranquilla
5800
Sierra Nevada de Santa Marta
Maracaibo
Cabimas
Caracas
2596
Maturín
Delta of the Orinoco
Cartagena
L. de Maracaibo
Barquisimeto
Maracay
Valencia
Barcelona
El Tigre
Limón
Sincelejo
G. of Darién
Valera
Cord. de Mérida
Orinoco
Ciudad Guayana
Ciudad Bolívar
Colón
Vol. Barú
3374
3837
PANAMA
Panama
5007
Apure
San Fernando de Apure
El Callao
GUYANA
Georgetown
New Amsterdam
Cauca
Cúcuta
4100
San Cristóbal
Arauca
Arauca
David
Azuero Pen.
Coiba
G. of Panama
Atrato
3960
Medellín
Bucaramanga
VENEZUELA
Cuyuni
Caura
Paragua
2560
Roraima
2810
Corentyne
Essequibo
SURINAM
Barrancabermeja
Tunja
Meta
2285
Pto. Ayacucho
Quibdó
COLOMBIA
Manizales
Pereira
Bogotá
Armenia
Tolima
5215
Girardot
Sierra Pacaraima
1280
Sa. Parima
Buenaventura
Cali
5750
Guaviare
Casiquiare
Magdalena
Popayán
4646
BRAZIL

1:30 000 000

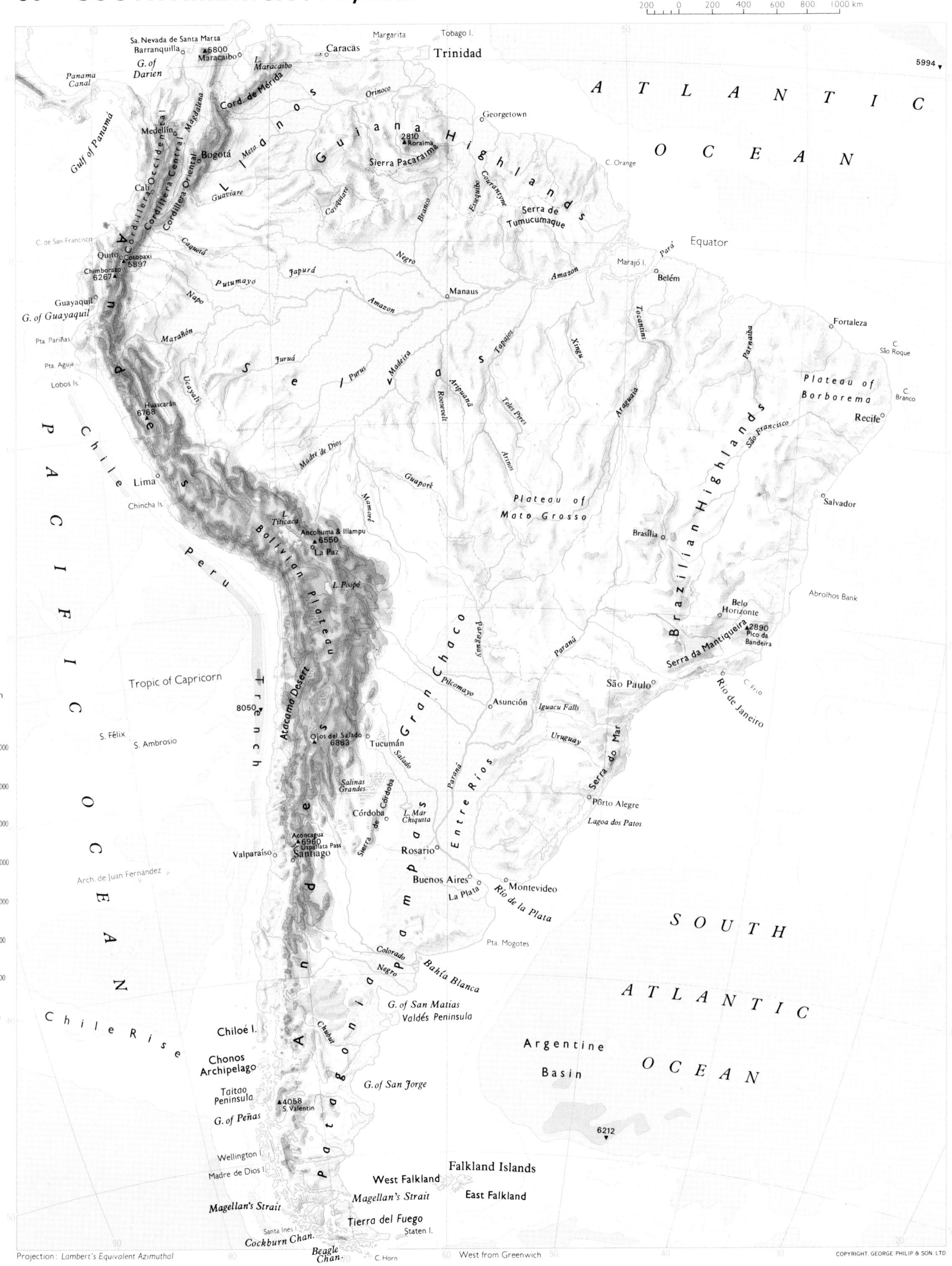

Projection: Lambert's Equivalent Azimuthal

West from Greenwich

1:30 000 000

Projection: *Lambert's Equivalent Azimuthal*

West from Greenwich

BUENOS AIRES Capital Cities

SOUTH AMERICA : Climate and Natural Vegetation

1:70 000 000

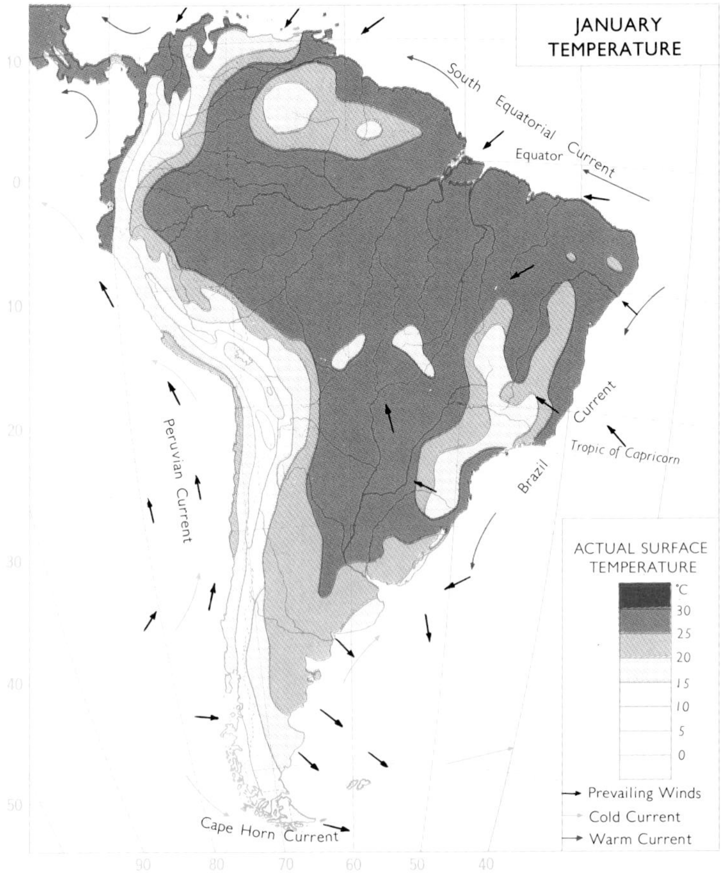
JANUARY TEMPERATURE
South Equatorial Current
Equator
Peruvian Current
Brazil Current
Tropic of Capricorn
Cape Horn Current
ACTUAL SURFACE TEMPERATURE
°C
30
25
20
15
10
5
0
Prevailing Winds
Cold Current
Warm Current
90
80
70
60
50
40

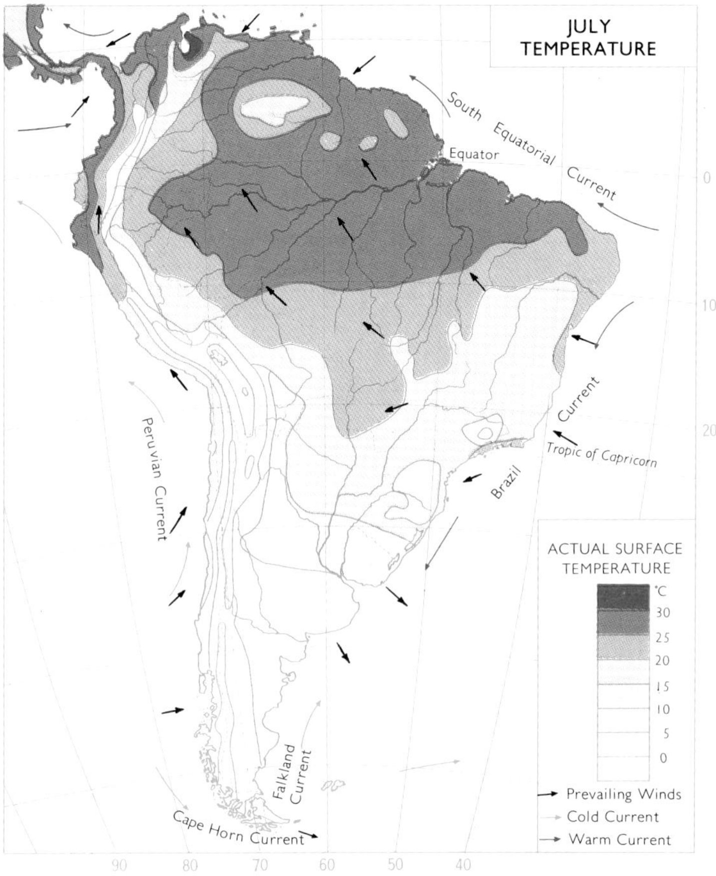
JULY TEMPERATURE
South Equatorial Current
Equator
Peruvian Current
Brazil Current
Tropic of Capricorn
Falkland Current
Cape Horn Current
ACTUAL SURFACE TEMPERATURE
°C
30
25
20
15
10
5
0
Prevailing Winds
Cold Current
Warm Current
90
80
70
60
50
40

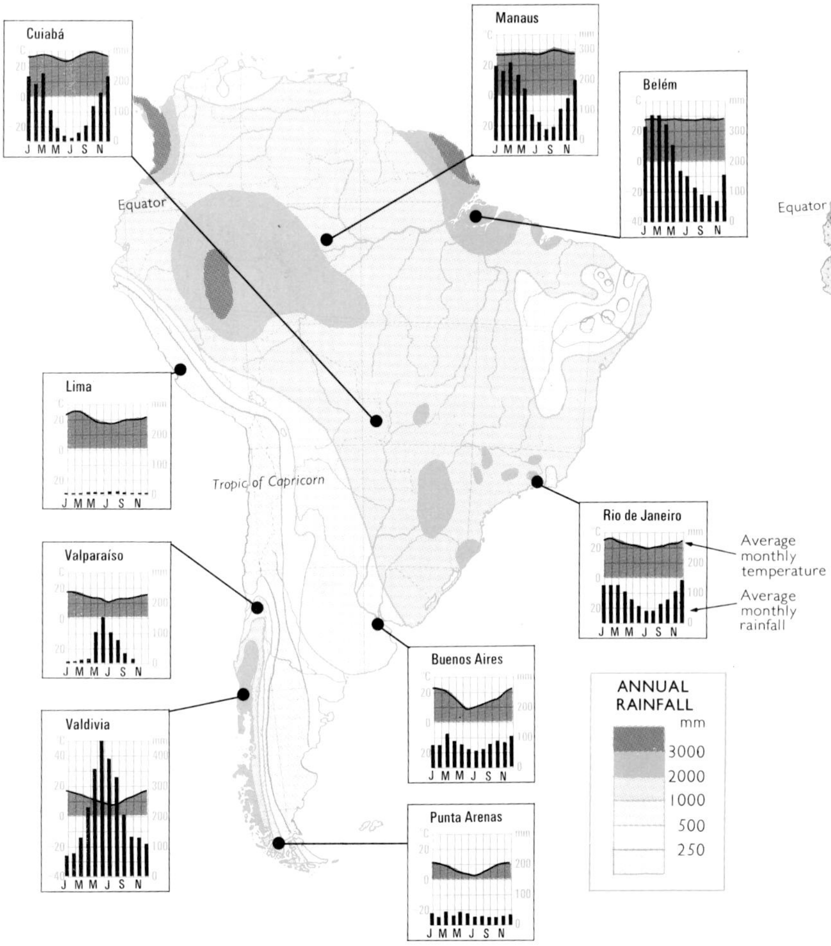
Cuiabá
Manaus
Belém
Equator
Lima
Tropic of Capricorn
Rio de Janeiro
Average monthly temperature
Average monthly rainfall
Valparaíso
Buenos Aires
Valdivia
Punta Arenas
J M M J S N
ANNUAL RAINFALL
mm
3000
2000
1000
500
250

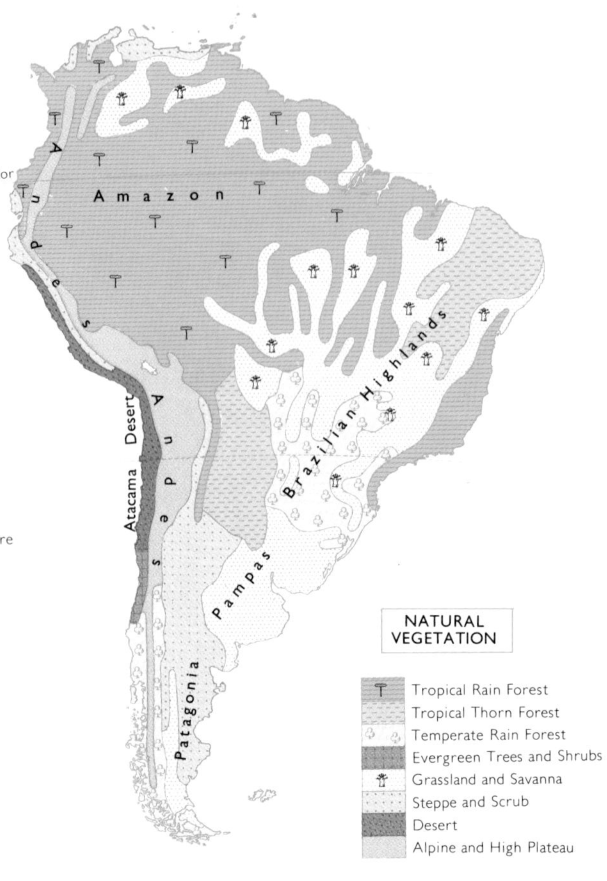
Equator
Amazon
Andes
Atacama Desert
Brazilian Highlands
Pampas
Patagonia
NATURAL VEGETATION
Tropical Rain Forest
Tropical Thorn Forest
Temperate Rain Forest
Evergreen Trees and Shrubs
Grassland and Savanna
Steppe and Scrub
Desert
Alpine and High Plateau

Projection: *Lambert's Equivalent Azimuthal*

1:30 000 000

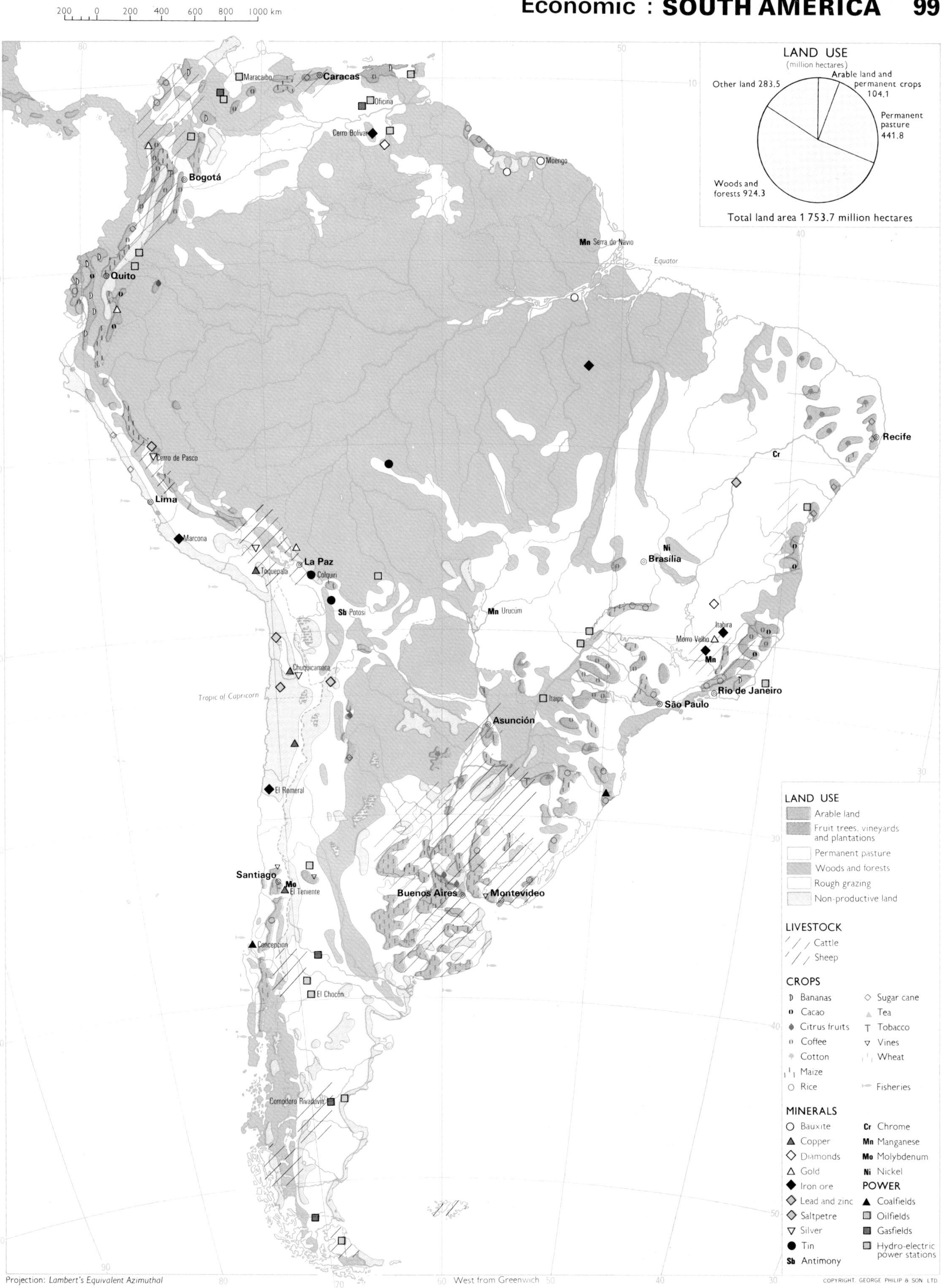

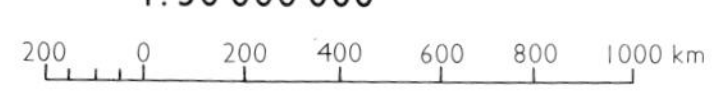

LAND USE
(million hectares)

Other land 283.5
Arable land and permanent crops 104.1
Permanent pasture 441.8
Woods and forests 924.3

Total land area 1 753.7 million hectares

Maracaibo
Caracas
Oficina
Cerro Bolívar
Moengo
Bogotá
Mn Serra do Navio
Equator
Quito
Recife
Cr
Cerro de Pasco
Lima
Marcona
Ni
Brasília
La Paz
Toquepala
Colquiri
Sb Potosí
Mn Urucum
Itabira
Morro Velho
Mn
Chuquicamata
Tropic of Capricorn
Itaipu
Rio de Janeiro
São Paulo
Asunción
El Romeral
Santiago
Mo
El Teniente
Buenos Aires
Montevideo
Concepción
El Chocón
Comodoro Rivadavia

LAND USE
- Arable land
- Fruit trees, vineyards and plantations
- Permanent pasture
- Woods and forests
- Rough grazing
- Non-productive land

LIVESTOCK
- Cattle
- Sheep

CROPS
- Bananas
- Cacao
- Citrus fruits
- Coffee
- Cotton
- Maize
- Rice
- Sugar cane
- Tea
- Tobacco
- Vines
- Wheat
- Fisheries

MINERALS
- Bauxite
- Copper
- Diamonds
- Gold
- Iron ore
- Lead and zinc
- Saltpetre
- Silver
- Tin
- Sb Antimony
- Cr Chrome
- Mn Manganese
- Mo Molybdenum
- Ni Nickel

POWER
- Coalfields
- Oilfields
- Gasfields
- Hydro-electric power stations

Projection: *Lambert's Equivalent Azimuthal*

West from Greenwich

Projection: Sanson-Flamsteed's Sinusoidal

1:16 000 000

200 100 0 200 400 600 km

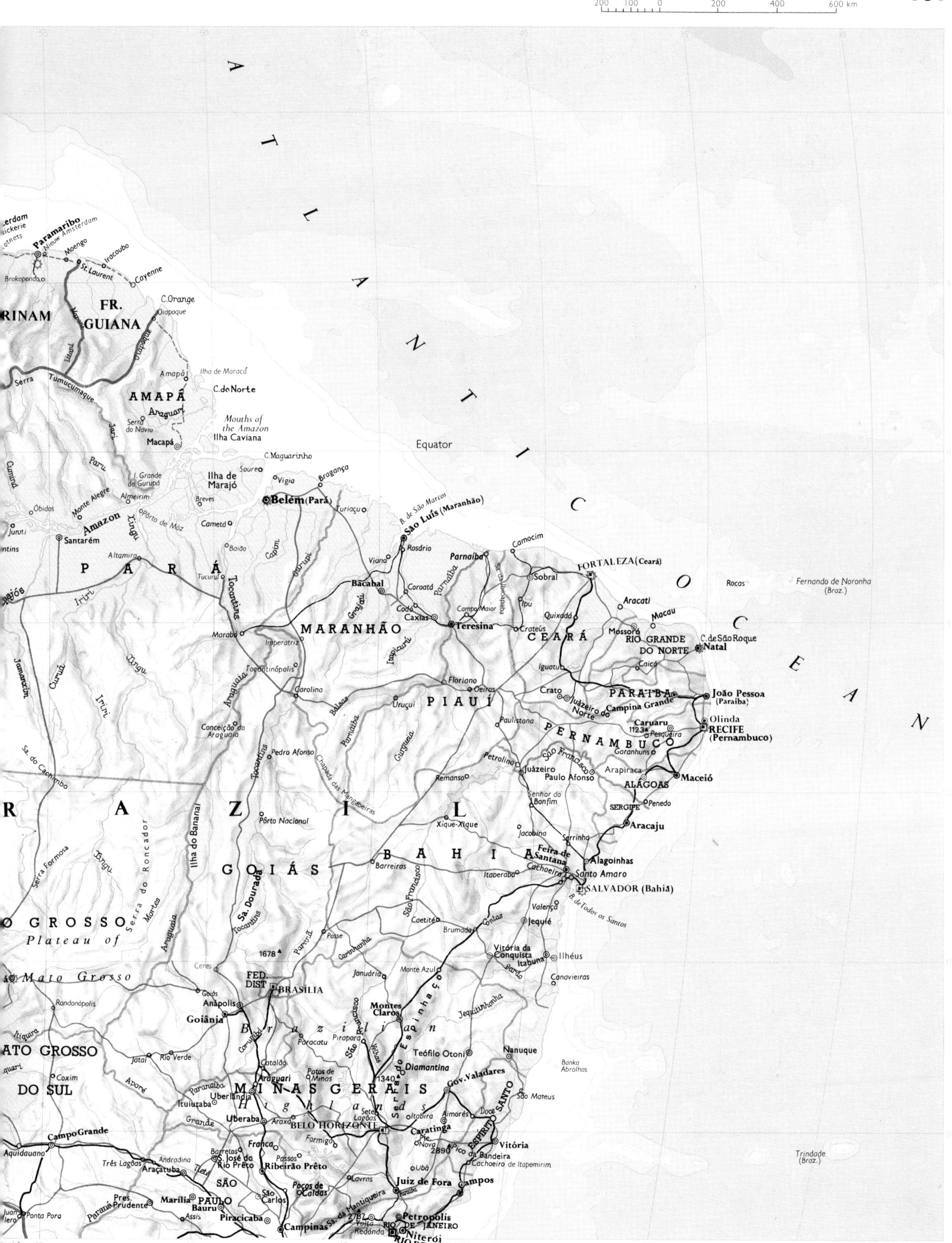

1:16 000 000

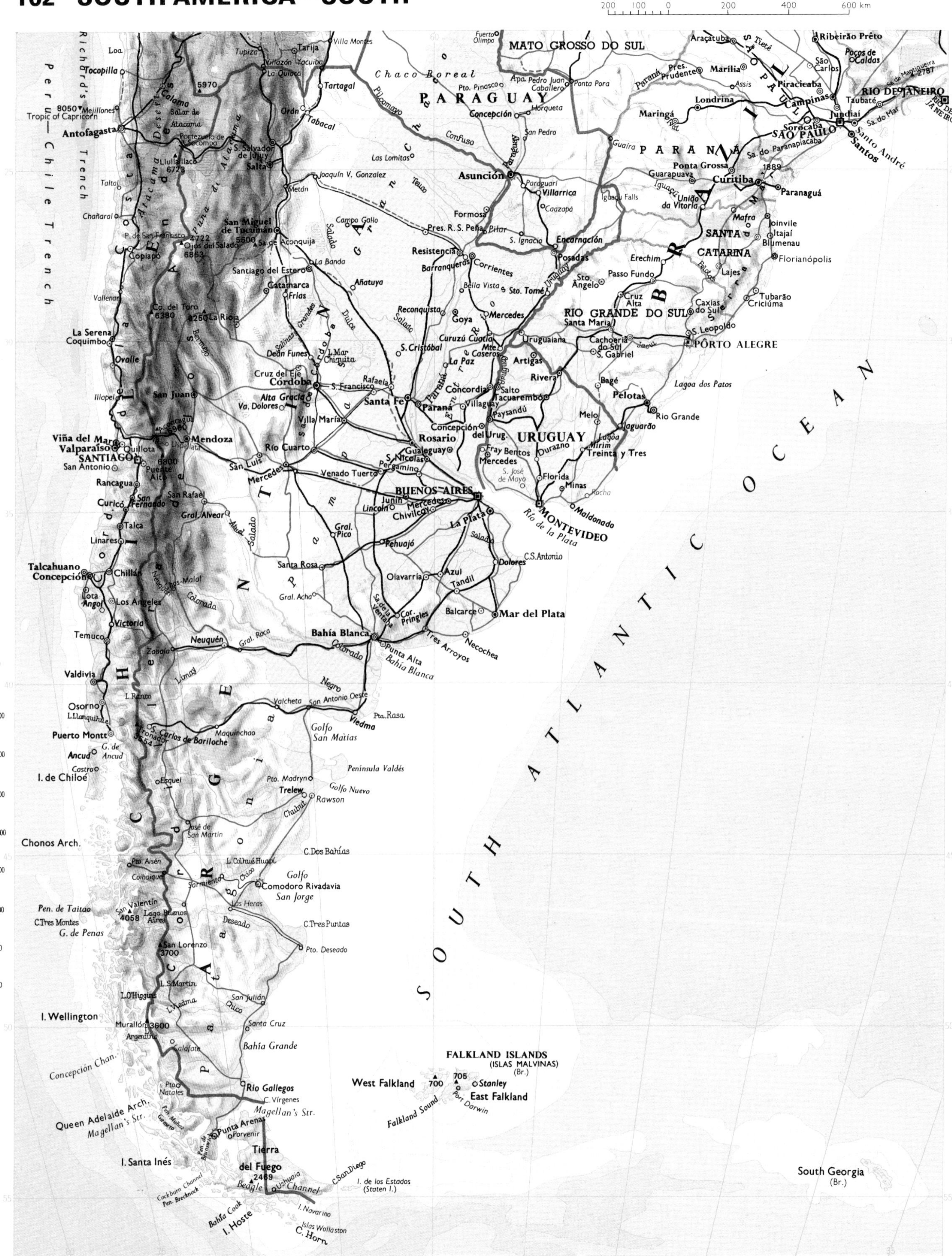

Projection: Sanson-Flamsteed's Sinusoidal

West from Greenwich

1:50 000 000

500 0 500 1000 1500 2000 km

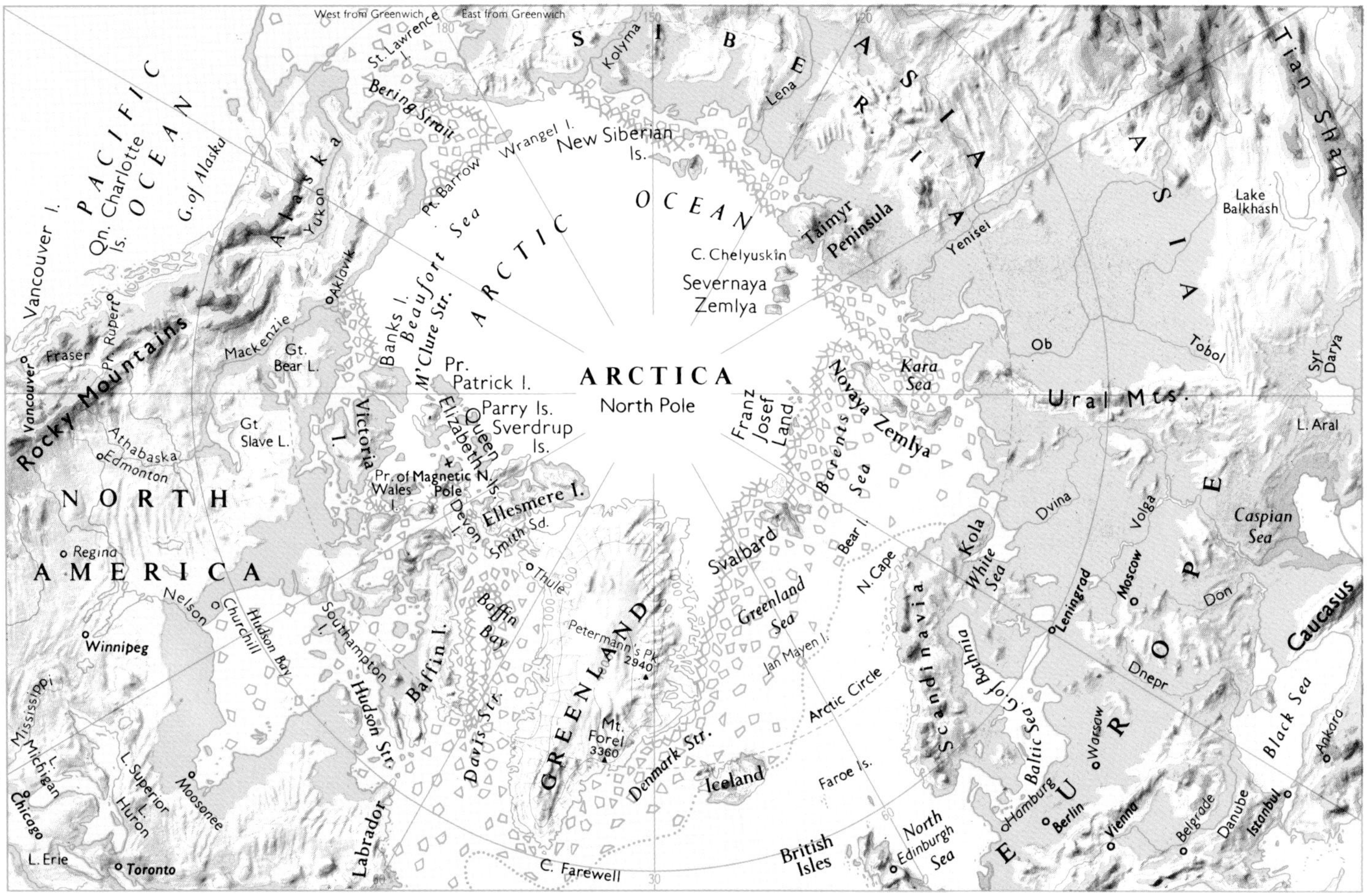

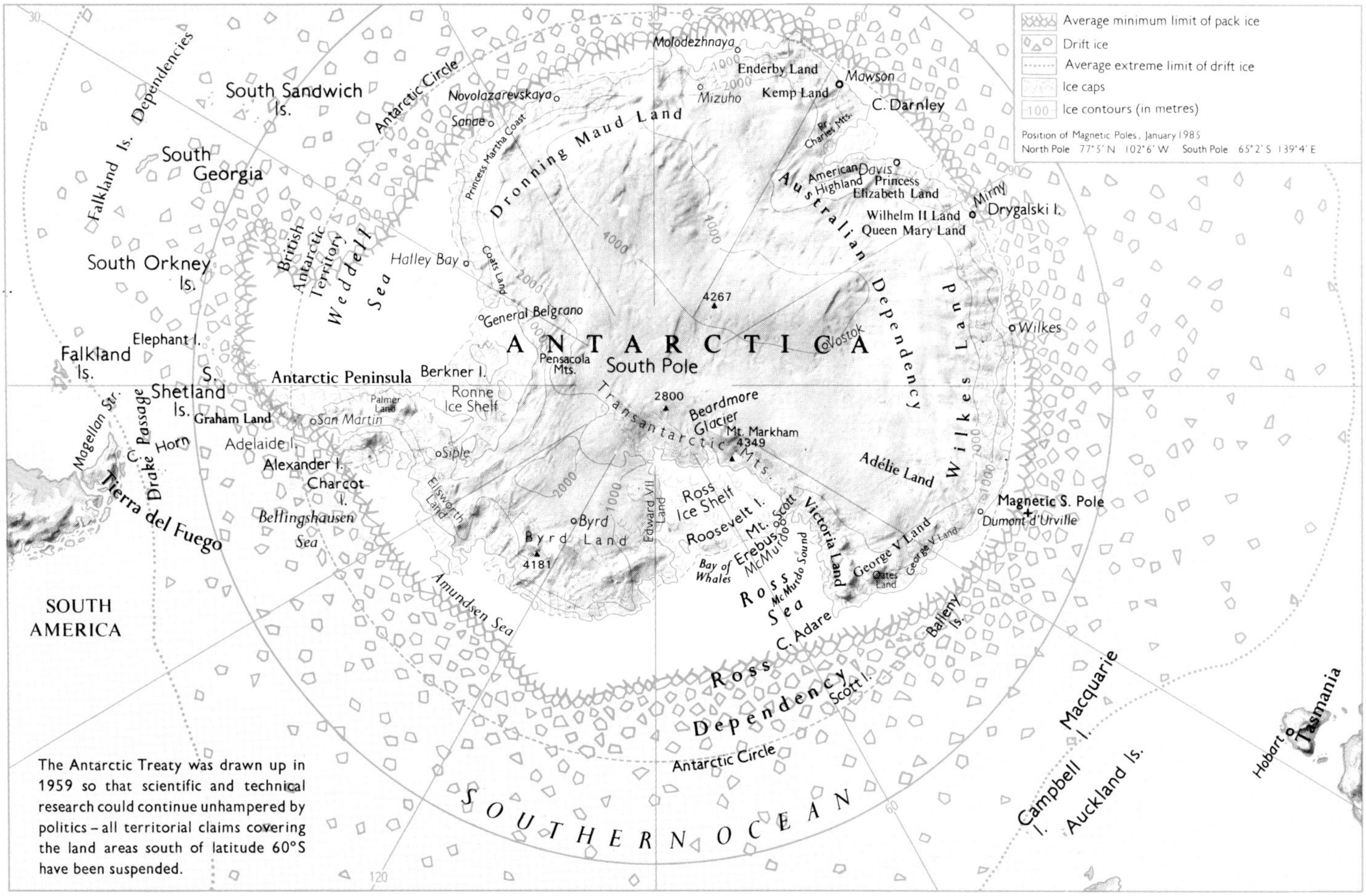

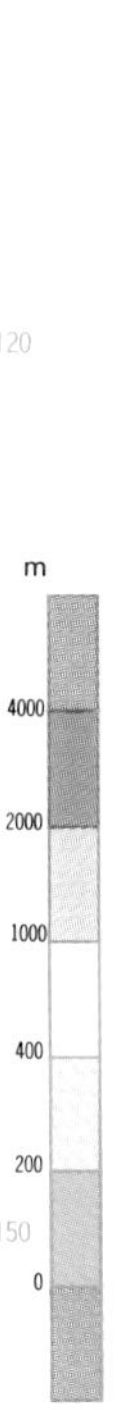

West from Greenwich 180 East from Greenwich

150 120 90 60 30 20

PACIFIC OCEAN
G. of Alaska
Qn. Charlotte Is.
Vancouver I.
Pr. Rupert
Vancouver
Fraser
Rocky Mountains
Alaska
Yukon
Aklavik
Mackenzie
Gt. Bear L.
Gt Slave L.
Athabaska
Edmonton
NORTH AMERICA
Regina
Nelson
Churchill
Winnipeg
Mississippi
L. Michigan
Chicago
L. Superior
L. Huron
L. Erie
Toronto
Moosonee
Hudson Bay
Southampton I.
Hudson Str.
Labrador
Victoria I.
Banks I.
Beaufort Sea
M'Clure Str.
Pr. Patrick I.
Parry Is.
Sverdrup Is.
Pr. of Wales I.
Magnetic N. Pole
Queen Elizabeth Is.
Devon I.
Ellesmere I.
Smith Sd.
Thule
Baffin I.
Baffin Bay
Davis Str.
GREENLAND
Petermann's Pk 2940
Mt. Forel 3360
C. Farewell
Denmark Str.
Iceland
St. Lawrence I.
Bering Strait
Pt. Barrow
Wrangel I.
New Siberian Is.
ARCTIC OCEAN
ARCTICA
North Pole
SIBERIA
Kolyma
Lena
Taimyr Peninsula
C. Chelyuskin
Severnaya Zemlya
Franz Josef Land
Novaya Zemlya
Kara Sea
Barents Sea
Svalbard
Bear I.
Greenland Sea
Jan Mayen I.
N. Cape
Arctic Circle
Faroe Is.
British Isles
North Sea
Edinburgh
ASIA
Yenisei
Ob
Tobol
Lake Balkhash
Tian Shan
Syr Darya
Ural Mts.
L. Aral
Caspian Sea
Volga
Dvina
Kola
White Sea
Scandinavia
Gulf of Bothnia
Leningrad
Moscow
Don
Dnepr
Caucasus
Black Sea
Ankara
Istanbul
Danube
Belgrade
Vienna
Warsaw
Berlin
Hamburg
Baltic Sea
EUROPE

Average minimum limit of pack ice
Drift ice
Average extreme limit of drift ice
Ice caps
Ice contours (in metres)

Position of Magnetic Poles, January 1985
North Pole 77°5' N 102°6' W South Pole 65°2' S 139°4' E

Falkland Is. Dependencies
South Sandwich Is.
South Georgia
Falkland Is.
South Orkney Is.
Elephant I.
Falkland Is.
S. Shetland Is.
Magellan Str.
Drake Passage
C. Horn
Tierra del Fuego
SOUTH AMERICA
British Antarctic Territory
Weddell Sea
Halley Bay
General Belgrano
Antarctic Peninsula
Graham Land
Palmer Land
San Martin
Adelaide I.
Alexander I.
Charcot I.
Bellingshausen Sea
Berkner I.
Ronne Ice Shelf
Siple
Ellsworth Land
Byrd
Byrd Land
4181
Amundsen Sea
Edward VII Land
Ross Ice Shelf
Roosevelt I.
Bay of Whales
Mt. Erebus
McMurdo Sound
Scott
Ross Sea
C. Adare
Balleny Is.
Ross Dependency
Scott I.
Antarctic Circle
SOUTHERN OCEAN
Antarctic Circle
Novolazarevskaya
Sanae
Princess Martha Coast
Dronning Maud Land
Coats Land
Molodezhnaya
Enderby Land
Mizuho
Kemp Land
Mawson
C. Darnley
Pr. Charles Mts.
American Highland
Davis
Princess Elizabeth Land
Australian Dependency
Wilhelm II Land
Queen Mary Land
Mirny
Drygalski I.
4267
ANTARCTICA
Pensacola Mts.
South Pole
Vostok
2800
Beardmore Glacier
Mt. Markham 4349
Transantarctic Mts.
Victoria Land
Wilkes Land
Wilkes
Adélie Land
George V Land
Oates Land
Magnetic S. Pole
Dumont d'Urville
Macquarie I.
Campbell I.
Auckland Is.
Hobart
Tasmania

The Antarctic Treaty was drawn up in 1959 so that scientific and technical research could continue unhampered by politics – all territorial claims covering the land areas south of latitude 60°S have been suspended.

m
4000
2000
1000
400
200
150
0

Projection: *Zenithal Equidistant*

West from Greenwich 180 East from Greenwich

Queen Elizabeth Is.
Ellesmere I.
North Magnetic Pole
Greenland
Bering Str.
Yukon
Mt. McKinley 6199
Mackenzie
Victoria I.
Gt. Bear L.
Baffin Island
Davis Str.
Arctic Ci
Bering Sea
Gt. Slave L.
Hudson Str.
Iceland
Aleutian Is.
Hudson Bay
C. Farewell
British Isles
Coast Ra.
Rocky Mountains
Labrador
Vancouver I.
L. Winnipeg
Great Plains
Great Lakes
St. Lawrence
Newfoundland
C. Race
Cascade Ra.
Sa. Nevada
Missouri
Mt. Whitney 4418
Arkansas
Ohio
Appalachian Mts.
Azores
Colorado
Mississippi
C. Hatteras
Str. of Gibraltar
Bermuda
Lower California
Rio Grande
Canary Is.
Sierra Madre
Gulf of Mexico
Florida Str.
Bahama Islands
ATLANTIC
Hawaiian Is.
Tropic of Ca
Mauna Kea 4202
Cuba
Popocatepetl 5452
Citlaltepetl 5700
Yucatan
Greater Antilles
Hispaniola
Jamaica
Caribbean Sea
Lesser Antilles
C.Verde Is.
C. Verde
Palmyra Is.
PACIFIC
Isthmus of Panama
Orinoco
Llanos
Guiana Highlands
Tabuaeran
Roraima 2772
OCEAN
C. Palmas
Kiritimati
Negro
Equator
Galapagos Is.
Chimborazo 6267
Amazon
Andes
Selvas
C. de São Roque
Phoenix Is.
Madeira
Tocantins
Ascension
Tokelau Is.
Marquesas Is.
OCEAN
Samoa Is.
Mato Grosso
Society Is.
Tuamotu Archipelago
L. Titicaca
St. Helena
Cook Is.
Tahiti
Brazilian Highlands
Gran Chaco
Paraguay
Tonga Is.
Atacama Desert
C. Frio
Tropic of Capric
Tubuai Is.
Pitcairn I.
Easter I.
Ojos del Salado 6863
Parana
Pampas
Aconcagua 6960
R. de la Plata
Kermadec Is.
Tristan da Cu
Negro
Patagonia
Chatham Is.
Falkland Is.
Tierra del Fuego
S. Georgia
Magellan's Str.
C. Horn
Drake Passage
Graham Land
Antarctic Peninsula
Antarctic C
Weddell Sea
Palmer Land
Caird Coast
Coats Land
Ellsworth Land
Byrd Land
Ross Sea
West from Green

HEIGHT OF LAND
in metres

Above 6 000
4 000–6 000
2 000–4 000
1000–2 000
200–1000
0–200
Below Sea-Level

DEPTH OF SEA
in metres

0–200
200–4000
4000–8000
Below 8000

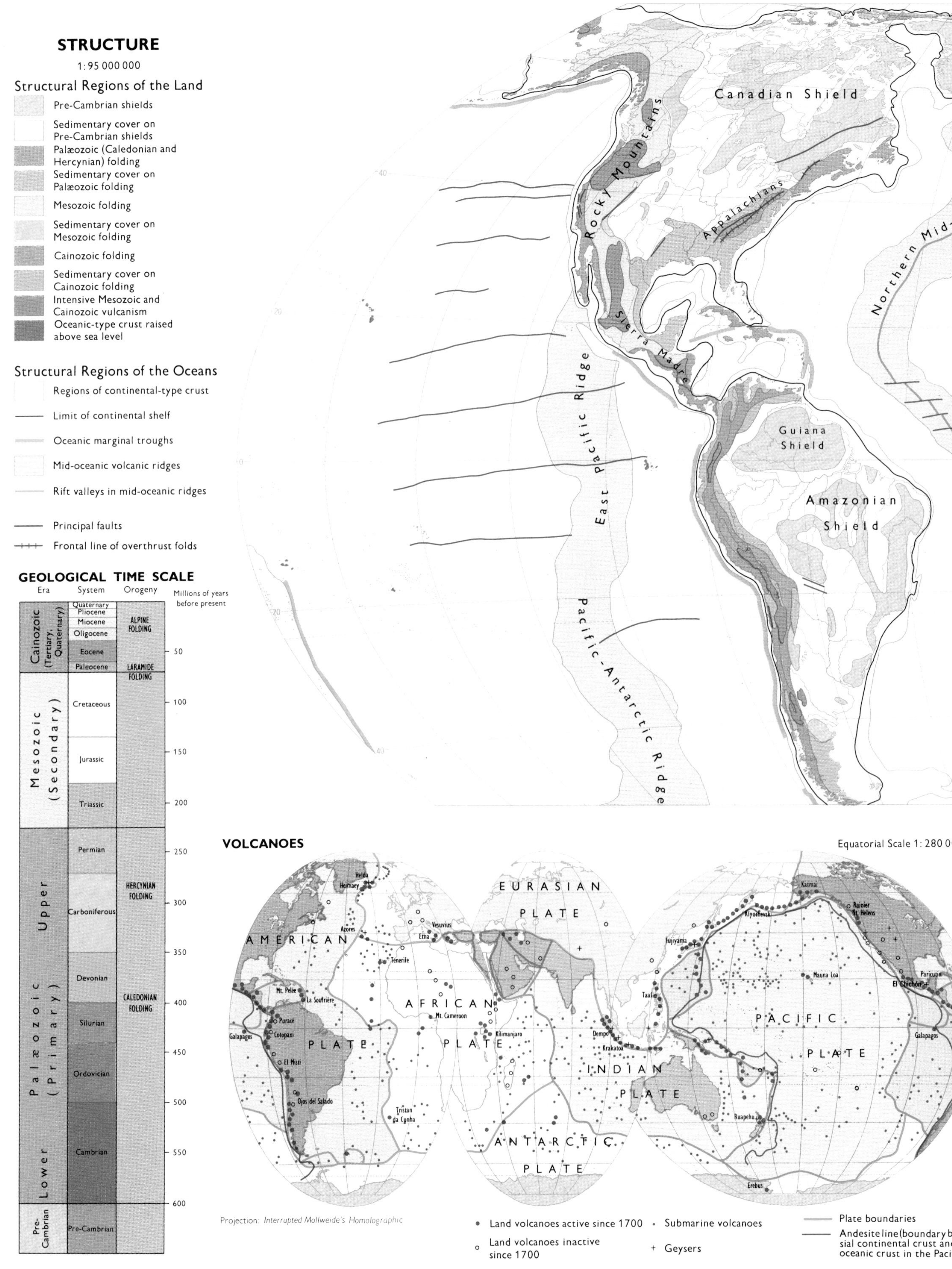
STRUCTURE
1: 95 000 000
Structural Regions of the Land
Pre-Cambrian shields
Sedimentary cover on Pre-Cambrian shields
Palæozoic (Caledonian and Hercynian) folding
Sedimentary cover on Palæozoic folding
Mesozoic folding
Sedimentary cover on Mesozoic folding
Cainozoic folding
Sedimentary cover on Cainozoic folding
Intensive Mesozoic and Cainozoic vulcanism
Oceanic-type crust raised above sea level
Structural Regions of the Oceans
Regions of continental-type crust
Limit of continental shelf
Oceanic marginal troughs
Mid-oceanic volcanic ridges
Rift valleys in mid-oceanic ridges
Principal faults
Frontal line of overthrust folds
GEOLOGICAL TIME SCALE
Era
System
Orogeny
Millions of years before present
Cainozoic (Tertiary, Quaternary)
Quaternary
Pliocene
Miocene
Oligocene
Eocene
Paleocene
ALPINE FOLDING
LARAMIDE FOLDING
Mesozoic (Secondary)
Cretaceous
Jurassic
Triassic
Palæozoic (Primary)
Upper
Permian
Carboniferous
Devonian
HERCYNIAN FOLDING
CALEDONIAN FOLDING
Silurian
Ordovician
Lower
Cambrian
Pre-Cambrian
Pre-Cambrian
50
100
150
200
250
300
350
400
450
500
550
600
Canadian Shield
Rocky Mountains
Appalachians
Northern Mid-A
Sierra Madre
East Pacific Ridge
Guiana Shield
Amazonian Shield
Pacific-Antarctic Ridge
VOLCANOES
Equatorial Scale 1: 280 000
EURASIAN PLATE
AMERICAN PLATE
AFRICAN PLATE
INDIAN PLATE
PACIFIC PLATE
ANTARCTIC PLATE
Hekla
Heimaey
Azores
Vesuvius
Etna
Tenerife
Mt. Pelée
La Soufrière
Puracé
Cotopaxi
Galapagos
El Misti
Ojos del Salado
Tristan da Cunha
Mt. Cameroon
Kilimanjaro
Dempo
Krakatoa
Fujiyama
Taal
Katmai
Klyuchevski
Rainier
St. Helens
Mauna Loa
Paricutin
El Chichón
Ruapehu
Erebus
Projection: Interrupted Mollweide's Homolographic
Land volcanoes active since 1700
Land volcanoes inactive since 1700
Submarine volcanoes
Geysers
Plate boundaries
Andesite line (boundary bet sial continental crust and s oceanic crust in the Pacific

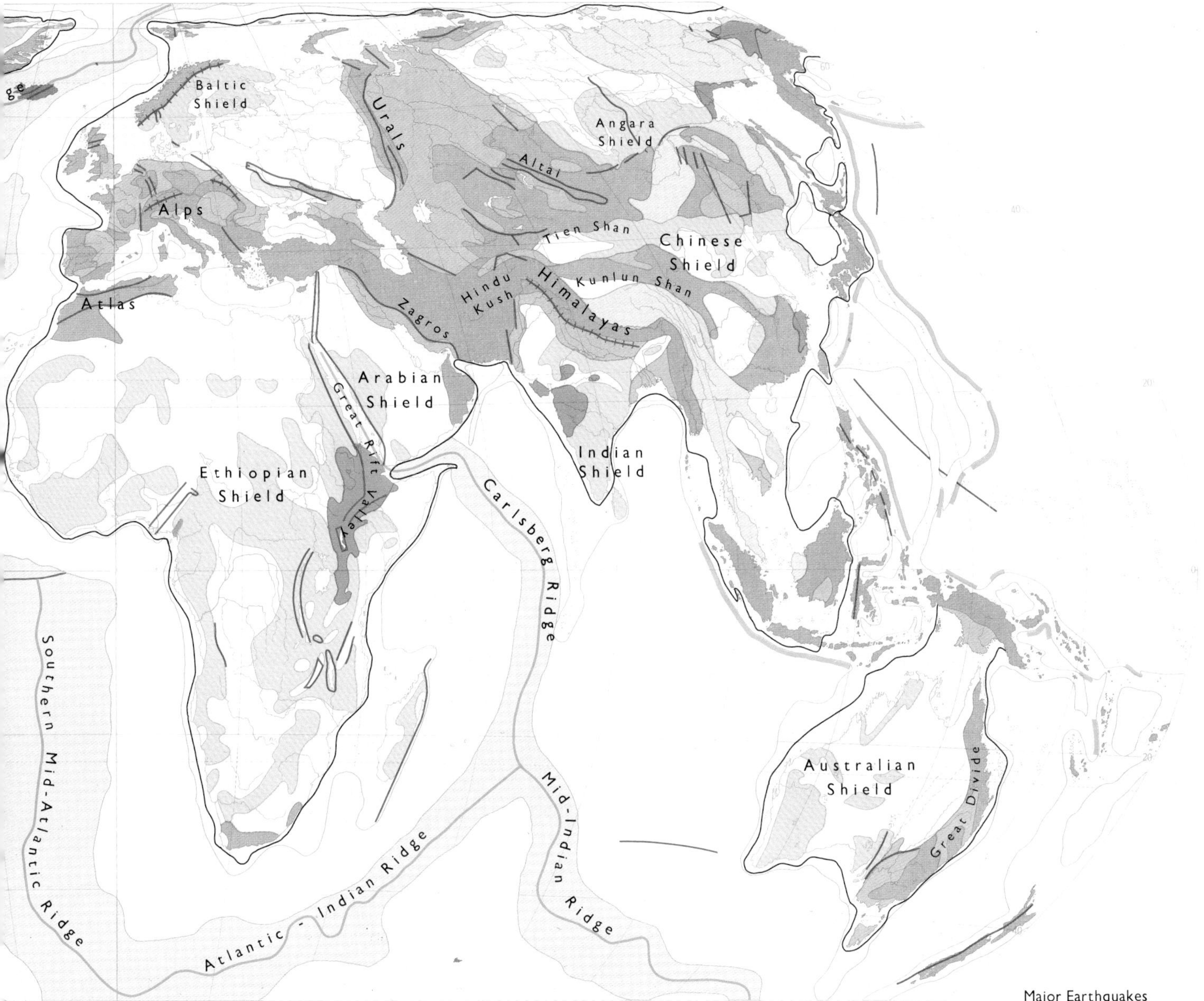

Baltic Shield
Urals
Angara Shield
Altai
Alps
Tien Shan
Chinese Shield
Kunlun Shan
Atlas
Hindu Kush
Himalayas
Zagros
Arabian Shield
Great Rift Valley
Ethiopian Shield
Indian Shield
Carlsberg Ridge
Southern Mid-Atlantic Ridge
Atlantic - Indian Ridge
Mid-Indian Ridge
Australian Shield
Great Divide

Projection: *Hammer Equal Area*

RTHQUAKES

Equatorial Scale 1: 280 000 000

1972
1868
1970
1906
1939
1755
1915
1980
1960
1908
1963
1939
1976
1962
1978
1968
1974
1935
1927
1932
1934
1737
1920
1556
1976
1730
1923
1964
1906
1931
1985
1972
1868
1970
1906

906 Principal earthquakes and their dates
— Oceanic marginal troughs
Mobile land areas
Submarine zones of mobile land areas
Stable land platforms
Submarine extensions of stable land platforms
Mid-oceanic volcanic ridges
Oceanic platforms

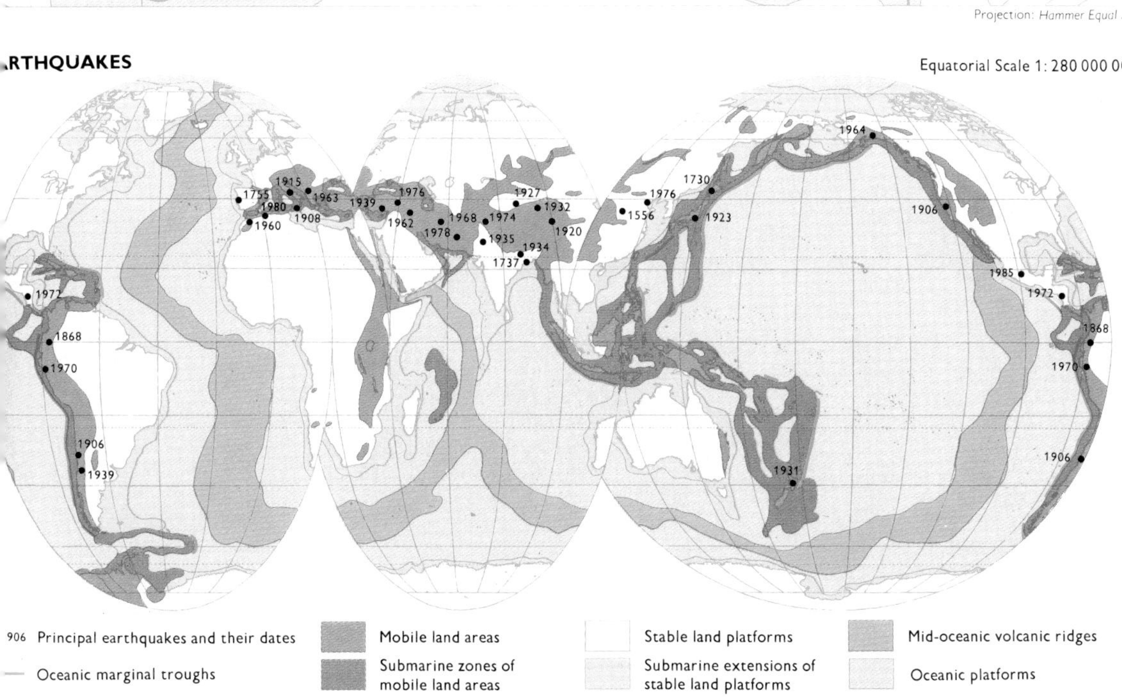

Major Earthquakes

		Nos. killed
1556	Shaanxi, China	830 000
1730	Hokkaido, Japan	137 000
1737	Calcutta, India	300 000
1755	Lisbon, Portugal	60 000
1868	Ecuador and N. Peru	40 000
1906	Valparaiso, Chile	22 000
1906	San Francisco, U.S.A.	450
1908	Messina, Italy	77 000
1915	Avezzano, Italy	30 000
1920	Gansu, China	180 000
1923	Yokohama, Japan	143 000
1927	Nan Shan, China	200 000
1931	Napier, N. Zealand	250
1932	Gansu, China	70 000
1934	Nepal	11 700
1935	Quetta, Pakistan	30 000
1939	Erzincan, Turkey	30 000
1960	Agadir, Morocco	12 000
1962	Khorasan, Iran	10 000
1963	Skopje, Yugoslavia	1000
1964	Anchorage, Alaska	100
1968	N.E. Iran	12 000
1970	N. Peru	67 000
1972	Managua, Nicaragua	7 000
1974	N. Pakistan	10 000
1976	Tangshan, China	650 000
1978	Tabas, Iran	11 000
1980	El Asnam, Algeria	20 000
1985	Mexico	20 000

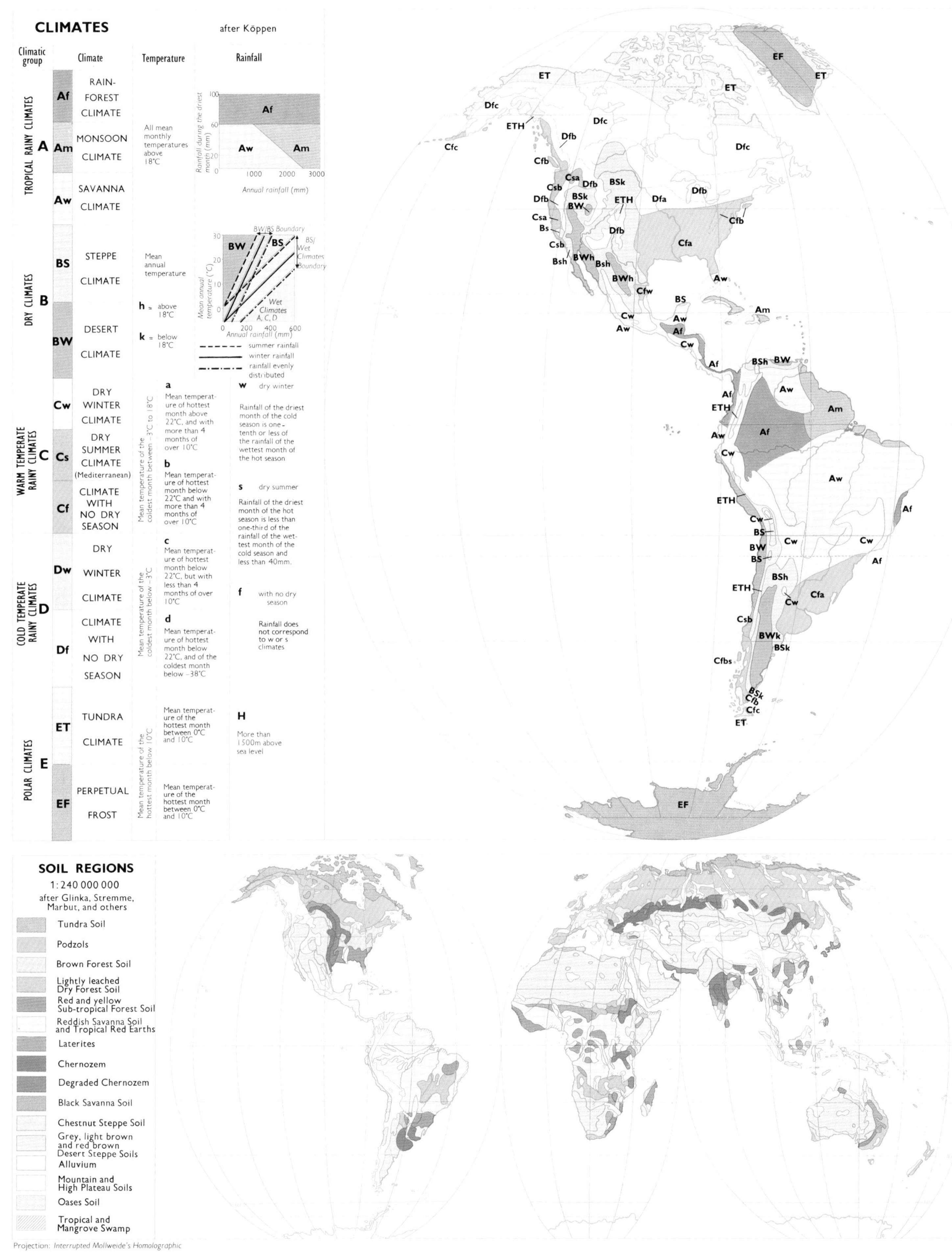
CLIMATES
after Köppen
Climatic group
Climate
Temperature
Rainfall
TROPICAL RAINY CLIMATES
A
Af RAIN-FOREST CLIMATE
Am MONSOON CLIMATE
Aw SAVANNA CLIMATE
All mean monthly temperatures above 18°C
Rainfall during the driest month (mm)
Annual rainfall (mm)
DRY CLIMATES
B
BS STEPPE CLIMATE
BW DESERT CLIMATE
Mean annual temperature
h = above 18°C
k = below 18°C
BW/BS Boundary
BS/Wet Climates Boundary
Wet Climates A, C, D
Mean annual temperature (°C)
Annual rainfall (mm)
summer rainfall
winter rainfall
rainfall evenly distributed
WARM TEMPERATE RAINY CLIMATES
C
Cw DRY WINTER CLIMATE
Cs DRY SUMMER CLIMATE (Mediterranean)
Cf CLIMATE WITH NO DRY SEASON
Mean temperature of the coldest month between -3°C to 18°C
a Mean temperature of hottest month above 22°C, and with more than 4 months of over 10°C
b Mean temperature of hottest month below 22°C and with more than 4 months of over 10°C
w dry winter
Rainfall of the driest month of the cold season is one-tenth or less of the rainfall of the wettest month of the hot season
s dry summer
Rainfall of the driest month of the hot season is less than one-third of the rainfall of the wettest month of the cold season and less than 40mm.
COLD TEMPERATE RAINY CLIMATES
D
Dw DRY WINTER CLIMATE
Df CLIMATE WITH NO DRY SEASON
Mean temperature of the coldest month below -3°C
c Mean temperature of hottest month below 22°C, but with less than 4 months of over 10°C
d Mean temperature of hottest month below 22°C, and of the coldest month below -38°C
f with no dry season
Rainfall does not correspond to w or s climates
POLAR CLIMATES
E
ET TUNDRA CLIMATE
EF PERPETUAL FROST
Mean temperature of the hottest month below 10°C
Mean temperature of the hottest month between 0°C and 10°C
H
More than 1500m above sea level
SOIL REGIONS
1:240 000 000
after Glinka, Stremme, Marbut, and others
Tundra Soil
Podzols
Brown Forest Soil
Lightly leached Dry Forest Soil
Red and yellow Sub-tropical Forest Soil
Reddish Savanna Soil and Tropical Red Earths
Laterites
Chernozem
Degraded Chernozem
Black Savanna Soil
Chestnut Steppe Soil
Grey, light brown and red brown Desert Steppe Soils
Alluvium
Mountain and High Plateau Soils
Oases Soil
Tropical and Mangrove Swamp
Projection: Interrupted Mollweide's Homolographic

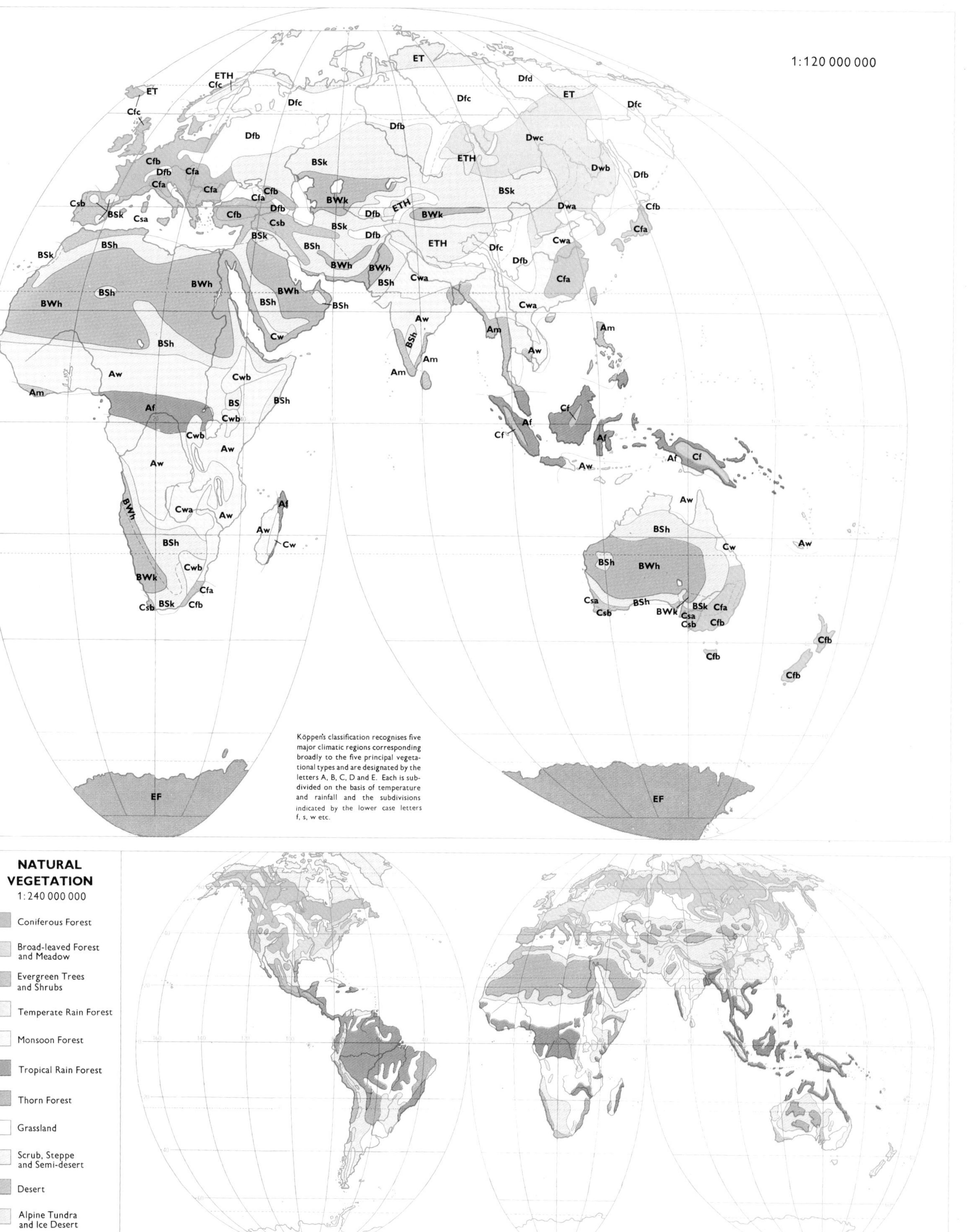
1:120 000 000
Köppen's classification recognises five major climatic regions corresponding broadly to the five principal vegetational types and are designated by the letters A, B, C, D and E. Each is subdivided on the basis of temperature and rainfall and the subdivisions indicated by the lower case letters f, s, w etc.
NATURAL VEGETATION
1: 240 000 000
Coniferous Forest
Broad-leaved Forest and Meadow
Evergreen Trees and Shrubs
Temperate Rain Forest
Monsoon Forest
Tropical Rain Forest
Thorn Forest
Grassland
Scrub, Steppe and Semi-desert
Desert
Alpine Tundra and Ice Desert

THE WORLD : Climate Statistics

These four pages give temperature and precipitation statistics for over 80 stations, which are arranged by listing the continents and the places within each continent in alphabetical order. The elevation of each station, in metres above mean sea level, is stated beneath its name. The average monthly temperature, in degrees Celsius, and the average monthly precipitation, in millimetres, are given. To the right, the average yearly rainfall, the average yearly temperature, and the annual range of temperature (the difference between the warmest and the coldest months) are also stated.

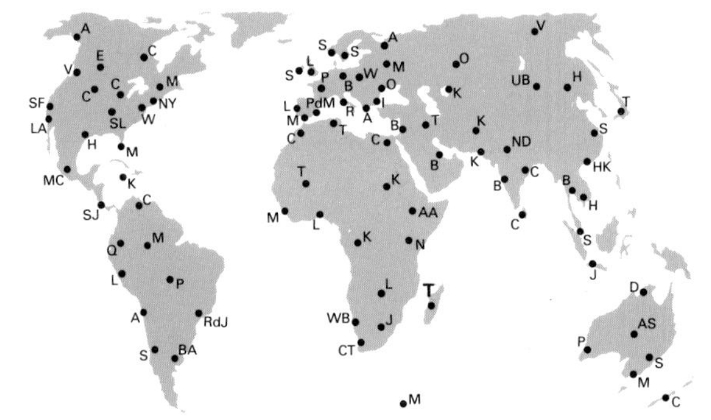

AFRICA

Station		Jan.	Feb.	Mar.	Apr.	May	June	July	Aug.	Sept.	Oct.	Nov.	Dec.	Year	Annual Range
Addis Ababa, Ethiopia	*Precipitation*	201	206	239	102	28	<3	0	<3	3	25	135	213	1 151	
2 450 m	*Temperature*	19	20	20	20	19	18	18	19	21	22	21	20	20	4
Cairo, Egypt	*Precipitation*	5	5	5	3	3	<3	0	0	<3	<3	3	5	28	
116 m	*Temperature*	13	15	18	21	25	28	28	28	26	24	20	15	22	15
Cape Town, South Africa	*Precipitation*	15	8	18	48	79	84	89	66	43	31	18	10	508	
17 m	*Temperature*	21	21	20	17	14	13	12	13	14	16	18	19	17	9
Casablanca, Morocco	*Precipitation*	53	48	56	36	23	5	0	<3	8	38	66	71	404	
50 m	*Temperature*	13	13	14	16	18	20	22	23	22	19	16	13	18	10
Johannesburg, South Africa	*Precipitation*	114	109	89	38	25	8	8	8	23	56	107	125	709	
1 665 m	*Temperature*	20	20	18	16	13	10	11	13	16	18	19	20	16	10
Khartoum, Sudan	*Precipitation*	<3	<3	<3	<3	3	8	53	71	18	5	<3	0	158	
390 m	*Temperature*	24	25	28	31	33	34	32	31	32	32	28	25	29	9
Kinshasa, Zaïre	*Precipitation*	135	145	196	196	158	8	3	3	31	119	221	142	1 354	
325 m	*Temperature*	26	26	27	27	26	24	23	24	25	26	26	26	25	4
Lagos, Nigeria	*Precipitation*	28	46	102	150	269	460	279	64	140	206	69	25	1 836	
3 m	*Temperature*	27	28	29	28	28	26	26	25	26	26	28	28	27	4
Lusaka, Zambia	*Precipitation*	231	191	142	18	3	<3	<3	0	<3	10	91	150	836	
1 277 m	*Temperature*	21	22	21	21	19	16	16	18	22	24	23	22	21	8
Monrovia, Liberia	*Precipitation*	31	56	97	216	516	973	996	373	744	772	236	130	5 138	
23 m	*Temperature*	26	26	27	27	26	25	24	25	25	25	26	26	26	3
Nairobi, Kenya	*Precipitation*	38	64	125	211	158	46	15	23	31	53	109	86	958	
1 820 m	*Temperature*	19	19	19	19	18	16	16	16	18	19	18	18	18	3
Tananarive, Madagascar	*Precipitation*	300	279	178	53	18	8	8	10	18	61	135	287	1 356	
1 372 m	*Temperature*	21	21	21	19	18	15	14	15	17	19	21	21	19	7
Timbuktu, Mali	*Precipitation*	<3	<3	3	<3	5	23	79	81	38	3	<3	<3	231	
301 m	*Temperature*	22	24	28	32	34	35	32	30	32	31	28	23	29	13
Tunis, Tunisia	*Precipitation*	64	51	41	36	18	8	3	8	33	51	48	61	419	
66 m	*Temperature*	10	11	13	16	19	23	26	27	25	20	16	11	18	17
Walvis Bay, South Africa	*Precipitation*	<3	5	8	3	3	<3	<3	3	<3	<3	<3	<3	23	
7 m	*Temperature*	19	19	19	18	17	16	15	14	14	15	17	18	18	5

AMERICA, NORTH

Station		Jan.	Feb.	Mar.	Apr.	May	June	July	Aug.	Sept.	Oct.	Nov.	Dec.	Year	Annual Range
Anchorage, Alaska, U.S.A.	*Precipitation*	20	18	15	10	13	18	41	66	66	56	25	23	371	
40 m	*Temperature*	−11	−8	−5	2	7	12	14	13	9	2	−5	−11	2	25
Cheyenne, Wyo., U.S.A.	*Precipitation*	10	15	25	48	61	41	53	41	31	25	13	13	376	
1 871 m	*Temperature*	−4	−3	1	5	10	16	19	19	14	7	1	−2	7	23
Chicago, Ill., U.S.A.	*Precipitation*	51	51	66	71	86	89	84	81	79	66	61	51	836	
251 m	*Temperature*	−4	−3	2	9	14	20	23	22	19	12	5	−1	10	27
Churchill, Man., Canada	*Precipitation*	15	13	18	23	32	44	46	58	51	43	39	21	402	
13 m	*Temperature*	−28	−26	−20	−10	−2	6	12	11	5	−2	−12	−22	−7	40

		Jan.	Feb.	Mar.	Apr.	May	June	July	Aug.	Sept.	Oct.	Nov.	Dec.	Year	Annual range
Edmonton, Alta., Canada															
	Precipitation	25	19	19	22	43	77	89	78	39	17	16	25	466	
676 m	*Temperature*	−15	−10	−5	4	11	15	17	16	11	6	−4	−10	3	32
Honolulu, Hawaii, U.S.A.															
	Precipitation	104	66	79	48	25	18	23	28	36	48	64	104	643	
12 m	*Temperature*	23	18	19	20	22	24	25	26	26	24	22	19	22	8
Houston, Tex., U.S.A.															
	Precipitation	89	76	84	91	119	117	99	99	104	94	89	109	1 171	
12 m	*Temperature*	12	13	17	21	24	27	28	29	26	22	16	12	21	17
Kingston, Jamaica															
	Precipitation	23	15	23	31	102	89	38	91	99	180	74	36	800	
34 m	*Temperature*	25	25	25	26	26	28	28	28	27	27	26	26	26	3
Los Angeles, Calif., U.S.A.															
	Precipitation	79	76	71	25	10	3	<3	<3	5	15	31	66	381	
95 m	*Temperature*	13	14	14	16	17	19	21	22	21	18	16	14	17	9
Mexico City, Mexico															
	Precipitation	13	5	10	20	53	119	170	152	130	51	18	8	747	
2 309 m	*Temperature*	12	13	16	18	19	19	17	18	18	16	14	13	16	7
Miami, Fla., U.S.A.															
	Precipitation	71	53	64	81	173	178	155	160	203	234	71	51	1 516	
8 m	*Temperature*	20	20	22	23	25	27	28	28	27	25	22	21	24	8
Montreal, Que., Canada															
	Precipitation	72	65	74	74	66	82	90	92	88	76	81	87	946	
57 m	*Temperature*	−10	−9	−3	−6	13	18	21	20	15	9	2	−7	6	31
New York, N.Y., U.S.A.															
	Precipitation	94	97	91	81	81	84	107	109	86	89	76	91	1 092	
96 m	*Temperature*	−1	−1	3	10	16	20	23	23	21	15	7	2	8	24
St. Louis, Mo., U.S.A.															
	Precipitation	58	64	89	97	114	114	89	86	81	74	71	64	1 001	
173 m	*Temperature*	0	1	7	13	19	24	26	26	22	15	8	2	14	26
San Francisco, Calif., U.S.A.															
	Precipitation	119	97	79	38	18	3	<3	<3	8	25	64	112	561	
16 m	*Temperature*	10	12	13	13	14	15	15	15	17	16	14	11	14	7
San José, Costa Rica															
	Precipitation	15	5	20	46	229	241	211	241	305	300	145	41	1 798	
1 146 m	*Temperature*	19	19	21	21	22	21	21	21	21	20	20	19	20	2
Vancouver, B.C., Canada															
	Precipitation	154	115	101	60	52	45	32	41	67	114	150	182	1113	
14 m	*Temperature*	3	5	6	9	12	15	17	17	14	10	6	4	10	14
Washington, D.C., U.S.A.															
	Precipitation	86	76	91	84	94	99	112	109	94	74	66	79	1 064	
22 m	*Temperature*	1	2	7	12	18	23	25	24	20	14	8	3	13	24

AMERICA, SOUTH

		Jan.	Feb.	Mar.	Apr.	May	June	July	Aug.	Sept.	Oct.	Nov.	Dec.	Year	Annual range
Antofagasta, Chile															
	Precipitation	0	0	0	<3	<3	3	5	3	<3	3	<3	0	13	
94 m	*Temperature*	21	21	20	18	16	15	14	14	15	16	18	19	17	7
Buenos Aires, Argentina															
	Precipitation	79	71	109	89	76	61	56	61	79	86	84	99	950	
27 m	*Temperature*	23	23	21	17	13	9	10	11	13	15	19	22	16	14
Caracas, Venezuela															
	Precipitation	23	10	15	33	79	102	109	109	107	109	94	46	836	
1 042 m	*Temperature*	19	19	20	21	22	21	21	21	21	21	20	20	21	3
Lima, Peru															
	Precipitation	3	<3	<3	<3	5	5	8	8	8	3	3	<3	41	
120 m	*Temperature*	23	24	24	22	19	17	17	16	17	18	19	21	20	8
Manaus, Brazil															
	Precipitation	249	231	262	221	170	84	58	38	46	107	142	203	1 811	
44 m	*Temperature*	28	28	28	27	28	28	28	28	29	29	29	28	28	2
Paraná, Brazil															
	Precipitation	287	236	239	102	13	<3	3	5	28	127	231	310	1 582	
260 m	*Temperature*	23	23	23	23	23	21	21	22	24	24	24	23	23	3
Quito, Ecuador															
	Precipitation	99	112	142	175	137	43	20	31	69	112	97	79	1 115	
2 879 m	*Temperature*	15	15	15	15	15	14	14	15	15	15	15	15	15	1
Rio de Janeiro, Brazil															
	Precipitation	125	122	130	107	79	53	41	43	66	79	104	137	1 082	
61 m	*Temperature*	26	26	25	24	22	21	21	21	21	22	23	25	23	5
Santiago, Chile															
	Precipitation	3	3	5	13	64	84	76	56	31	15	8	5	358	
520 m	*Temperature*	21	20	18	15	12	9	9	10	12	15	17	19	15	12

ASIA

Station		Jan.	Feb.	Mar.	Apr.	May	June	July	Aug.	Sept.	Oct.	Nov.	Dec.	Year	Annual range
Bahrain	*Precipitation*	8	18	13	8	< 3	0	0	0	0	0	18	18	81	
5 m	*Temperature*	17	18	21	25	29	32	33	34	31	28	24	19	26	16
Bangkok, Thailand	*Precipitation*	8	20	36	58	198	160	160	175	305	206	66	5	1 397	
2 m	*Temperature*	26	28	29	30	29	29	28	28	28	28	26	25	28	5
Beirut, Lebanon	*Precipitation*	191	158	94	53	18	3	< 3	< 3	5	51	132	185	892	
34 m	*Temperature*	14	14	16	18	22	24	27	28	26	24	19	16	21	14
Bombay, India	*Precipitation*	3	3	3	< 3	18	485	617	340	264	64	13	3	1 809	
11 m	*Temperature*	24	24	26	28	30	29	27	27	27	28	27	26	27	6
Calcutta, India	*Precipitation*	10	31	36	43	140	297	325	328	252	114	20	5	1 600	
6 m	*Temperature*	20	22	27	30	30	30	29	29	29	28	23	19	26	11
Colombo, Sri Lanka	*Precipitation*	89	69	147	231	371	224	135	109	160	348	315	147	2 365	
7 m	*Temperature*	26	26	27	28	28	27	27	27	27	27	26	26	27	2
Harbin, China	*Precipitation*	5	5	10	23	43	94	112	104	46	33	8	5	488	
160 m	*Temperature*	–18	–15	–5	6	13	19	22	21	14	4	–6	–16	3	40
Ho Chi Minh City, Vietnam	*Precipitation*	15	3	13	43	221	330	315	269	335	269	114	56	1 984	
9 m	*Temperature*	26	27	29	30	29	28	28	28	27	27	27	26	28	4
Jakarta, Indonesia	*Precipitation*	300	300	211	147	114	97	64	43	66	112	142	203	1 798	
8 m	*Temperature*	26	26	27	27	27	27	27	27	27	27	27	26	27	1
Hong Kong	*Precipitation*	33	46	74	137	292	394	381	361	257	114	43	31	2 162	
33 m	*Temperature*	16	15	18	22	26	28	28	28	27	25	21	18	23	13
Kabul, Afghanistan	*Precipitation*	31	36	94	102	20	5	3	3	< 3	15	20	10	338	
1 815 m	*Temperature*	–3	–1	6	13	18	22	25	24	20	14	7	3	12	28
Karachi, Pakistan	*Precipitation*	13	10	8	3	3	18	81	41	13	< 3	3	5	196	
4 m	*Temperature*	19	20	24	28	30	31	30	29	28	28	24	20	26	12
New Delhi, India	*Precipitation*	23	18	13	8	13	74	180	172	117	10	3	10	640	
218 m	*Temperature*	14	17	23	28	33	34	31	30	29	26	20	15	25	20
Shanghai, China	*Precipitation*	48	58	84	94	94	180	147	142	130	71	51	36	1 135	
7 m	*Temperature*	4	5	9	14	20	24	28	28	23	19	12	7	16	24
Singapore	*Precipitation*	252	173	193	188	173	173	170	196	178	208	254	257	2 413	
10 m	*Temperature*	26	27	28	28	28	28	28	27	27	27	27	27	27	2
Tehran, Iran	*Precipitation*	46	38	46	36	13	3	3	3	3	8	20	31	246	
1 220 m	*Temperature*	2	5	9	16	21	26	30	29	25	18	12	6	17	28
Tokyo, Japan	*Precipitation*	48	74	107	135	147	165	142	152	234	208	97	56	1 565	
6 m	*Temperature*	3	4	7	13	17	21	25	26	23	17	11	6	14	23
Ulan Bator, Mongolia	*Precipitation*	< 3	< 3	3	5	10	28	76	51	23	5	5	3	208	
1 325 m	*Temperature*	–26	–21	–13	–1	6	14	16	14	8	–1	–13	–22	–3	42

AUSTRALIA, NEW ZEALAND and ANTARCTICA

Station		Jan.	Feb.	Mar.	Apr.	May	June	July	Aug.	Sept.	Oct.	Nov.	Dec.	Year	Annual range
Alice Springs, Australia	*Precipitation*	43	33	28	10	15	13	8	8	8	18	31	38	252	
579 m	*Temperature*	29	28	25	20	15	12	12	14	18	23	26	28	21	17
Christchurch, New Zealand	*Precipitation*	56	43	48	48	66	66	69	48	46	43	48	56	638	
10 m	*Temperature*	16	16	14	12	9	6	6	7	9	12	14	16	11	10
Darwin, Australia	*Precipitation*	386	312	254	97	15	3	< 3	3	13	51	119	239	1 491	
30 m	*Temperature*	29	29	29	29	28	26	25	26	28	29	30	29	28	5
Mawson, Antarctica	*Precipitation*	11	30	20	10	44	180	4	40	3	20	0	0	362	
14 m	*Temperature*	0	–5	–10	–14	–15	–16	–18	–18	–19	–13	–5	–1	–11	18

		Jan.	Feb.	Mar.	Apr.	May	June	July	Aug.	Sept.	Oct.	Nov.	Dec.	Year	Annual Range
Melbourne, Australia															
	Precipitation	48	46	56	58	53	53	48	48	58	66	58	58	653	
35 m	*Temperature*	20	20	18	15	13	10	9	11	13	14	16	18	15	11
Perth, Australia															
	Precipitation	8	10	20	43	130	180	170	149	86	56	20	13	881	
60 m	*Temperature*	23	23	22	19	16	14	13	13	15	16	19	22	18	10
Sydney, Australia															
	Precipitation	89	102	127	135	127	117	117	76	73	71	73	73	1 181	
42 m	*Temperature*	22	22	21	18	15	13	12	13	15	18	19	21	17	10

EUROPE and U.S.S.R.

		Jan.	Feb.	Mar.	Apr.	May	June	July	Aug.	Sept.	Oct.	Nov.	Dec.	Year	Annual Range
Archangel, U.S.S.R.															
	Precipitation	31	19	25	29	42	52	62	56	63	63	47	41	530	
13 m	*Temperature*	–16	–14	–9	0	7	12	15	14	8	2	–4	–11	0	31
Athens, Greece															
	Precipitation	62	37	37	23	23	14	6	7	15	51	56	71	402	
107 m	*Temperature*	10	10	12	16	20	25	28	28	24	20	15	11	18	18
Berlin, Germany															
	Precipitation	46	40	33	42	49	65	73	69	48	49	46	43	603	
55 m	*Temperature*	–1	0	4	9	14	17	19	18	15	9	5	1	9	20
Istanbul, Turkey															
	Precipitation	109	92	72	46	38	34	34	30	58	81	103	119	816	
114 m	*Temperature*	5	6	7	11	16	20	23	23	20	16	12	8	14	18
Kazalinsk, U.S.S.R.															
	Precipitation	10	10	13	13	15	5	5	8	8	10	13	15	125	
63 m	*Temperature*	–12	–11	–3	6	18	23	25	23	16	8	–1	–7	7	37
Lisbon, Portugal															
	Precipitation	111	76	109	54	44	16	3	4	33	62	93	103	708	
77 m	*Temperature*	11	12	14	16	17	20	22	23	21	18	14	12	17	12
London, U.K.															
	Precipitation	54	40	37	37	46	45	57	59	49	57	64	48	593	
5 m	*Temperature*	4	5	7	9	12	16	18	17	15	11	8	5	11	14
Málaga, Spain															
	Precipitation	61	51	62	46	26	5	1	3	29	64	64	62	474	
33 m	*Temperature*	12	13	15	17	19	29	25	26	23	20	16	13	18	17
Moscow, U.S.S.R.															
	Precipitation	39	38	36	37	53	58	88	71	58	45	47	54	624	
156 m	*Temperature*	–13	–10	–4	6	13	16	18	17	12	6	–1	–7	4	31
Odessa, U.S.S.R.															
	Precipitation	57	62	30	21	34	34	42	37	37	13	35	71	473	
64 m	*Temperature*	–3	–1	2	9	15	20	22	22	18	12	9	1	10	25
Omsk, U.S.S.R.															
	Precipitation	15	8	8	13	31	51	51	51	28	25	18	20	318	
85 m	*Temperature*	–22	–19	–12	–1	10	16	18	16	10	1	–11	–18	–1	40
Palma de Mallorca, Spain															
	Precipitation	39	34	51	32	29	17	3	25	55	77	47	40	449	
10 m	*Temperature*	10	11	12	15	17	21	24	25	23	18	14	11	17	15
Paris, France															
	Precipitation	56	46	35	42	57	54	59	64	55	50	51	50	619	
75 m	*Temperature*	3	4	8	11	15	18	20	19	17	12	7	4	12	17
Rome, Italy															
	Precipitation	71	62	57	51	46	37	15	21	63	99	129	93	744	
17 m	*Temperature*	8	9	11	14	18	22	25	25	22	17	13	10	16	17
Shannon, Irish Republic															
	Precipitation	94	67	56	53	61	57	77	79	86	86	96	117	929	
2 m	*Temperature*	5	5	7	9	12	14	16	16	14	11	8	6	10	11
Stavanger, Norway															
	Precipitation	93	56	45	70	49	84	93	118	142	129	125	126	1 130	
85 m	*Temperature*	1	1	3	6	10	13	15	15	13	9	6	3	8	14
Stockholm, Sweden															
	Precipitation	43	30	25	31	34	45	61	76	60	48	53	48	554	
44 m	*Temperature*	–3	–3	–1	5	10	15	18	17	12	7	3	0	7	21
Verkhoyansk, U.S.S.R.															
	Precipitation	5	5	3	5	8	23	28	25	13	8	8	5	134	
100 m	*Temperature*	–50	–45	–32	–15	0	12	14	9	2	–15	–38	–48	–17	64
Warsaw, Poland															
	Precipitation	27	32	27	37	46	69	96	65	43	38	31	44	555	
110 m	*Temperature*	–3	–3	2	7	14	17	19	18	14	9	3	0	8	22

THE WORLD : Temperature and Ocean Currents

1:190 000 000

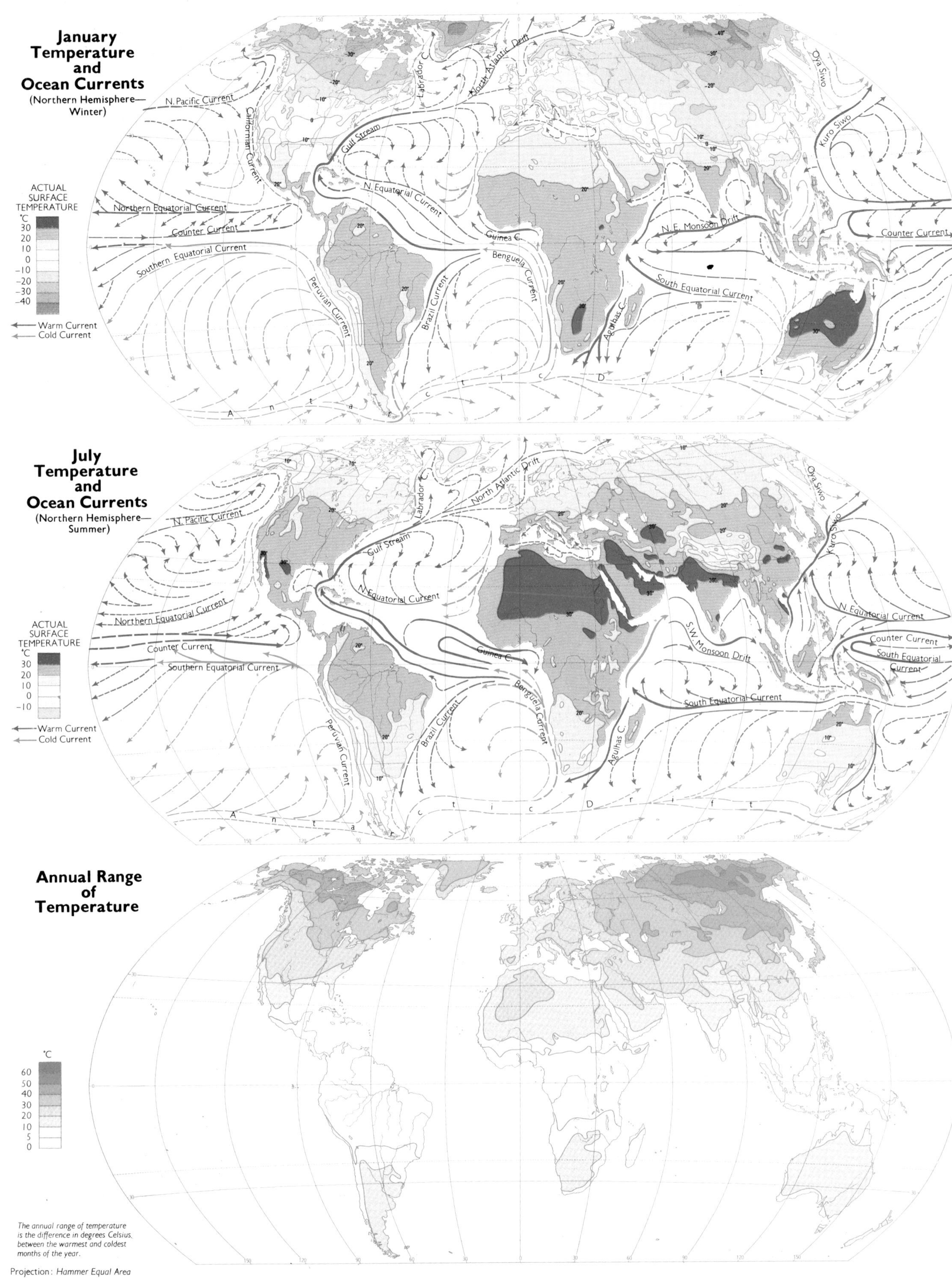

Projection: *Hammer Equal Area*

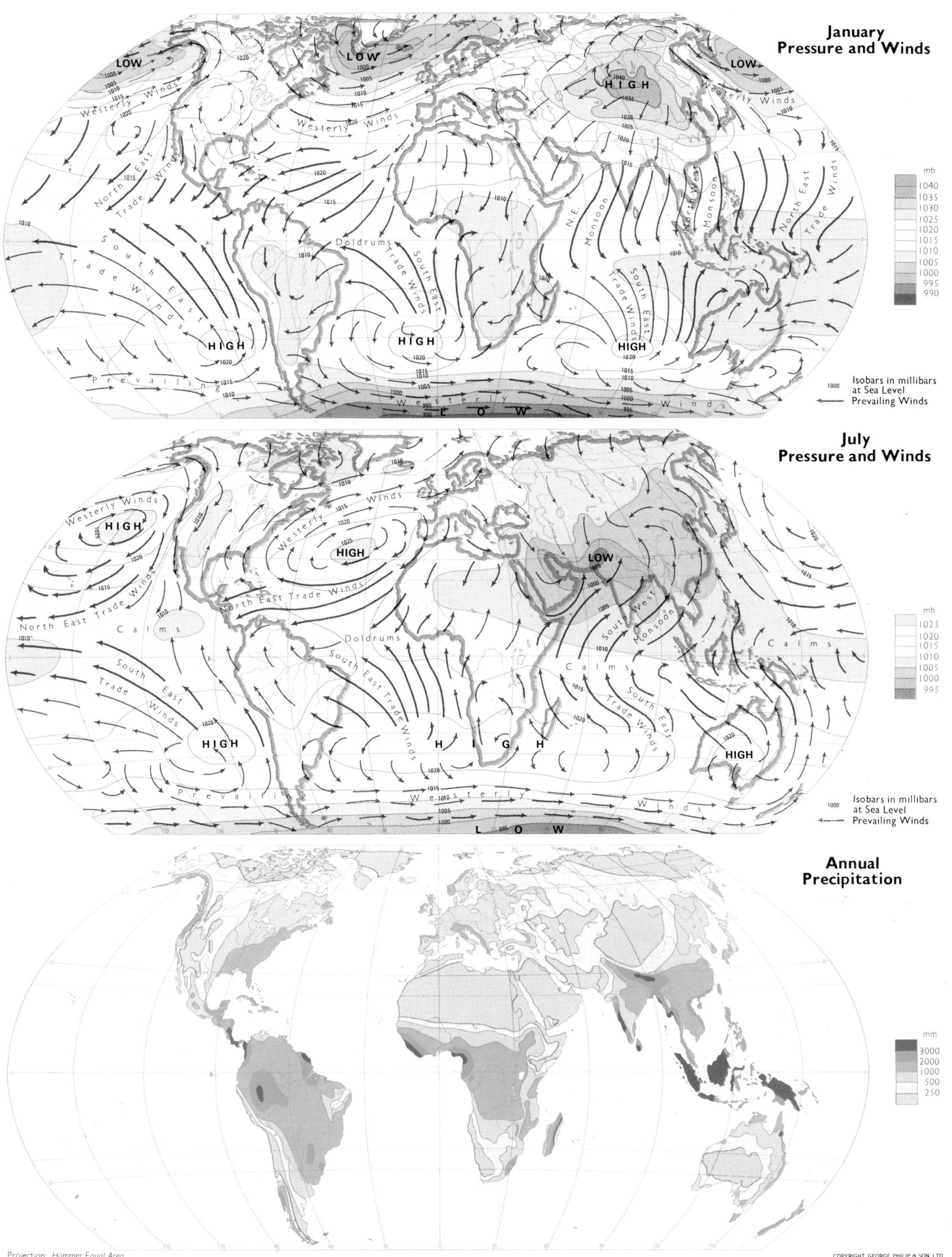

Projection: *Hammer Equal Area*

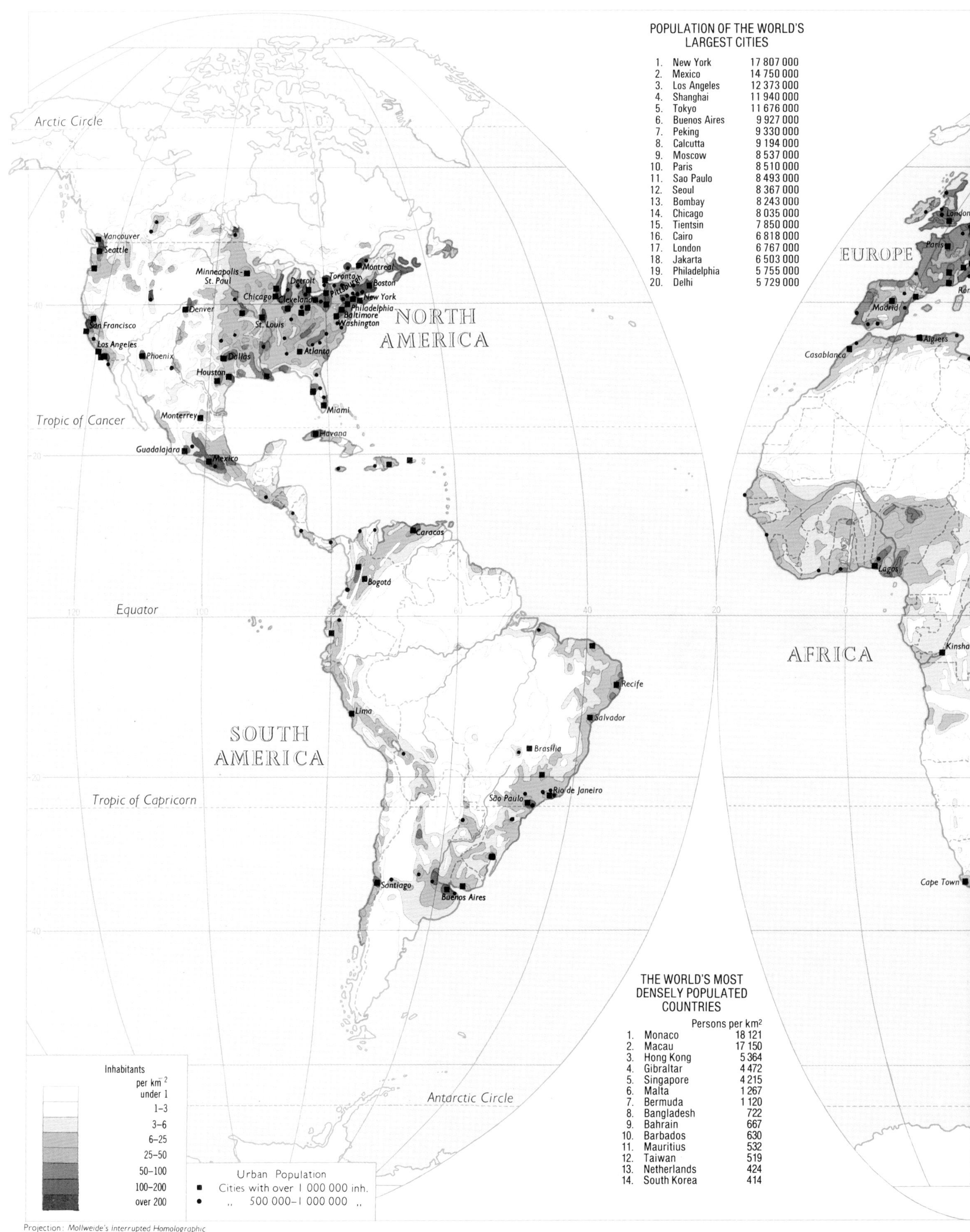

POPULATION OF THE WORLD'S LARGEST CITIES

	City	Population
1.	New York	17 807 000
2.	Mexico	14 750 000
3.	Los Angeles	12 373 000
4.	Shanghai	11 940 000
5.	Tokyo	11 676 000
6.	Buenos Aires	9 927 000
7.	Peking	9 330 000
8.	Calcutta	9 194 000
9.	Moscow	8 537 000
10.	Paris	8 510 000
11.	Sao Paulo	8 493 000
12.	Seoul	8 367 000
13.	Bombay	8 243 000
14.	Chicago	8 035 000
15.	Tientsin	7 850 000
16.	Cairo	6 818 000
17.	London	6 767 000
18.	Jakarta	6 503 000
19.	Philadelphia	5 755 000
20.	Delhi	5 729 000

THE WORLD'S MOST DENSELY POPULATED COUNTRIES

	Country	Persons per km^2
1.	Monaco	18 121
2.	Macau	17 150
3.	Hong Kong	5 364
4.	Gibraltar	4 472
5.	Singapore	4 215
6.	Malta	1 267
7.	Bermuda	1 120
8.	Bangladesh	722
9.	Bahrain	667
10.	Barbados	630
11.	Mauritius	532
12.	Taiwan	519
13.	Netherlands	424
14.	South Korea	414

Projection: Mollweide's Interrupted Homolographic

THE WORLD'S MOST DENSELY POPULATED COUNTRIES

Continuation		Persons per km²
15.	Puerto Rico	382
16.	Grenada	373
17.	San Marino	367
18.	Saint Vincent	347
19.	Belgium	329
20.	Japan	323
21.	Martinique	297
22.	Lebanon	264
23.	El Salvador	257
24.	India	251
25.	West Germany	251
26.	Sri Lanka	240
27.	Rwanda	236
28.	UK	230

Some of the lesser islands have high densities but have been omitted from this table.

For comparison the London urban area has a density of 4 270 persons per km².

POPULATION OF CITIES

The population figures used are from censuses or more recent estimates and are given in thousands for towns and cities over 200,000 (over 250,000 in Brazil and Japan and 500,000 in China, India, United States and U.S.S.R.). Where possible the population of the metropolitan area is given e.g. Greater London, Greater New York etc.

AFRICA

ALGERIA (1977)
Algiers 1 740
Oran 543
Constantine 379
Annaba 246
Tizi-Ouzou 224

ANGOLA (1982)
Luanda 700

BENIN (1982)
Cotonou 487
Porto-Novo 208

BURKINA FASO (1982)
Ouagadougou 286

CAMEROON (1983)
Douala 708
Yaoundé 485

CANARY ISLANDS (1981)
Las Palmas 360

CENTRAL AFRICAN REPUBLIC (1981)
Bangui 387

CHAD (1979)
Ndjamena 303

CONGO (1980)
Brazzaville 422

EGYPT (1976)
Cairo 6 818
Alexandria 2 318
El Giza 1 230
Shubra el Kheima 394
El Mahalla el Kubra 292
Tanta 285
Port Said 263
El Mansûra 259
Asyût 214
Zagazig 203

ETHIOPIA (1983)
Addis Ababa 1 478
Asmera 491

GABON (1983)
Libreville 350

GHANA (1984)
Accra 965
Kumasi 489

GUINEA (1980)
Conakry 763

IVORY COAST (1982)
Abidjan 1 850
Bouaké 640
Man-Danane 450
Korhogo 280

KENYA (1983)
Nairobi (1985) 1 200
Mombasa 410

LIBERIA (1984)
Monrovia 425

LIBYA (1982)
Tripoli 980
Benghazi 650
Misrātah 285

MADAGASCAR (1978)
Antananarivo 400

MALAWI (1977)
Blantyre 219

MALI (1976)
Bamako 419

MOROCCO (1981)
Casablanca 2 409
Rabat-Salé 842
Fès 562
Marrakesh 549
Meknès 487
Oujda 470
Kénitra 450
Tétouan 372
Tangier 304
Safi 256
Agadir 246
Khouribga 229
Béni-Mellal 204

MOZAMBIQUE (1970)
Maputo 384

NIGER (1977)
Niamey 225

NIGERIA (1975)
Lagos 1 477
Ibadan 847
Ogbomosho 432
Kano 399
Ilorin 282
Oshogbo 282
Abeokuta 253
Port Harcourt 242
Ilesha 224
Zaria 224
Onitsha 220
Iwo 214
Ado-Ekiti 213
Kaduna 202

SENEGAL (1979)
Dakar 799

SIERRA LEONE (1982)
Freetown 316

SOMALI REP. (1982)
Mogadishu 600

SOUTH AFRICA (1980)
Johannesburg 1 726
Cape Town 1 491
Durban 961
Pretoria 739
Port Elizabeth 585
Vanderbijlpark/Vereeniging 448

SUDAN (1983)
Omdurman 526
Khartoum 476
Khartoum North 341
Port Sudan 207

TANZANIA (1978)
Dar-es-Salaam 757

TOGO (1980)
Lomé 283

TUNISIA (1984)
Tunis 774
Sfax 232

UGANDA (1975)
Kampala 332

ZAÏRE (1976)
Kinshasa 2 444
Kananga 704
Lubumbashi 451
Mbuji Mayi 383
Kisangani 339
Bukavu 209

ZAMBIA (1980)
Lusaka 538
Kitwe 315
Ndola 282

ZIMBABWE (1983)
Harare 681
Bulawayo 429
Chitungwiza 202

ASIA

AFGHANISTAN (1982)
Kābul 1 127

BANGLADESH (1982)
Dacca 3 459
Chittagong 1 388
Khulna 623
Narayanganj 298

BURMA (1977)
Rangoon (1983) 2 459
Mandalay 458
Kanbe (1973) 254

CAMBODIA (KAMPUCHEA) (1983)
Phnom Penh 500

CHINA (1982)
Shanghai 11 940
Peking 9 330
Tientsin 7 850
Shenyang 4 080
Wuhan 3 280
Canton 3 160
Chungking 2 690
Harbin 2 560
Chengdu 2 510
Zibo 2 264
Sian 2 220
Nanking 2 170
Taiyuan 1 790
Changchun 1 770
Dalian 1 520
Zhengzhou 1 517
Lanzhou 1 430
Jinan 1 360
Tangshan 1 351
Guiyang 1 330
Kunming 1 320
Anshan 1 240
Qiqihar 1 232
Qingdao 1 210
Hangzhou 1 201
Fushun 1 200
Fuzhou 1 142
Changsha 1 100
Jilin 1 099
Shijiazhuang 1 098
Nanchang 1 061
Baotou 1 051
Huainan 1 017
Ürümqi 944
Xuzhou 793
Suzhou (1970) 730
Wuxi (1970) 650
Hefei (1970) 630
Benxi (1970) 600
Luoyang (1970) 580
Nanning (1970) 550
Hohhot (1970) 530
Xining (1970) 500

HONG KONG (1981)
Kowloon 2 450
Hong Kong 1 184
Tsuen Wan 599

INDIA (1981)
Calcutta 9 194
Bombay 8 243
Delhi 5 729
Madras 4 289
Bangalore 2 922
Ahmadabad 2 548
Hyderabad 2 546
Pune 1 686
Kanpur 1 639
Nagpur 1 302
Jaipur 1 015
Lucknow 1 008
Coimbatore 920
Patna 919
Surat 914
Madurai 908
Indore 829
Varanasi 797
Jabalpur 757
Agra 747
Vadodara 744
Cochin 686
Dhanbad 678
Bhopal 671
Jamshedpur 670
Allahabad 650
Ulhasnagar 649
Tiruchchirappalli 610
Ludhiana 606
Srinagar 606
Vishakhapatnam 604
Amritsar 595
Gwalior 556
Calicut 546
Vijayawada 543
Meerut 537
Dharwad 527
Trivandrum 520
Salem 519
Solapur 515
Jodhpur 506
Ranchi 503

INDONESIA (1980)
Jakarta 6 503
Surabaya 2 028
Bandung 1 462
Medan 1 379
Semarang 1 026
Palembang 787
Ujung Pandang 709
Malang 512
Padang 481
Surakarta 470
Yogyakarta 399
Banjarmasin 381
Pontianak 305
Tanjung Karang 284
Balikpapan 281
Samarinda 265
Bogor 247
Jambi 230
Cirebon 224
Kediri 222
Manado 217
Ambon 209

IRAN (1976)
Tehrān 4 589
Esfahān 842
Mashhad 743
Tabrīz 715
Shīrāz 448
Ahvāz 340
Bākhtarān 336
Abadan 308
Qom 247
Hamadan 230
Karaj 214

IRAQ (1970)
Baghdād 2 969
Basra 371
Mosul 293
Kirkūk 208

ISRAEL (1983)
Jerusalem 429
Tel Aviv-Jaffa 327
Haifa 226

JAPAN (1982)
Tōkyō 11 676
Yokohama 2 848
Ōsaka 2 623
Nagoya 2 093
Kyōto 1 480
Sapporo 1 465
Kobe 1 383
Fukuoka 1 121
Kitakyūshū 1 065
Kawasaki 1 055
Hiroshima 898
Sakai 809
Chiba 756
Sendai 662
Okayama 551
Kumamoto 522
Kagoshima 514
Amagasaki 510
Higashiōsaka 501
Hamamatsu 500
Funabashi 488
Shizuoka 462
Niigata 458
Sagamihara 455
Nagasaki 449
Hameji 448
Yokosuka 429
Matsuyama 413
Kanazawa 412
Matsudo 411
Kurashiki 410
Nishinoyama 410
Gifu 409
Wakayama 404
Toyonaka 397
Hachiōji 395
Kawaguchi 391
Utsunomiya 389
Ichikawa 374
Hirakata 368
Oita 367
Urawa 366
Omiya 361
Asahikawa 359
Fukuyama 353
Iwaki 352
Takatsuki 340
Suita 333
Nagano 328
Hakodate 321
Takamatsu 320
Fujisawa 313
Toyohashi 311
Nara 309
Toyama 308
Kōchi 305
Naha 302
Machida 301
Aomori 291
Akita 290
Kōriyama 290
Toyota 287
Maebashi 271
Okazaki 269
Shimonoseki 269
Miyazaki 267
Yao 266
Fukushima 265
Kawagoe 265
Yokkaichi 258
Akashi 257
Neyagawa 255
Ichinomiya 253
Sasebo 253
Tokushima 251

JORDAN (1981)
'Ammān 681
Az-Zarqā 234

KOREA, NORTH (1972)
Pyŏngyang 1 500
Hamhung 420
Chongjin 265
Kimchaek 265

KOREA, SOUTH (1980)
Seoul 8 367
Pusan 3 160
Taegu 1 607
Inchŏn 1 085
Kwangju 728
Taejon 652
Ulsan 418
Masan 387
Songnam 376
Chonju 367
Suwŏn 311

KUWAIT (1980)
Kuwait 775

LEBANON (1980)
Beirut 702

MACAU (1981)
Macau 250

MALAYSIA (1980)
Kuala Lumpur 938
Ipoh 301
Pinang 251

MONGOLIA (1980)
Ulan Bator 419

NEPAL (1981)
Katmandu 235

PAKISTAN (1981)
Karachi 5 103
Lahore 2 922
Faisalabad 1 092
Rawalpindi 806
Hyderabad 795
Multan 730
Gujranwala 597
Peshawar 555
Sialkot 296
Sargodha 294
Quetta 243
Islamabad 201

PHILIPPINES (1980)
Manila 1 630
Quezon City 1 166
Davao 610
Cebu 490
Caloocan 468
Zamboanga 344
Pasay 288
Bacolod 262
Iloilo 245
Cagayan de Oro 227

SAUDI ARABIA (1974)
Riyadh 667
Jedda 561
Mecca 367
Taif 205

SINGAPORE (1983)
Singapore 2 517

SRI LANKA (1982)
Colombo 1 412

SYRIA (1982)
Damascus 1 112
Aleppo 985
Homs 354

TAIWAN (1981)
Taipei 2 271
Kaohsiung 1 227
Taichung 607
Tainan 595
Chilung 348
Sanchung 335
Chiai 252
Hsinchu 243
Fengshan 227
Chunli 215
Yungho 214

THAILAND (1980)
Bangkok (1982) 5 468

TURKEY (1982)
İstanbul 2 949
Ankara 2 276
İzmir 1 083
Adana 864
Konya 691
Bursa 658
Gaziantep 526
Mersin 440
Kayseri 394
Diyarbakir 390
Samsun 354
Balikesir 352
Eskişehir 352
İzmit 328
Zonguldak 321
Erzurum 292
Maras 292
Antalya 290
Urfa 285
Sivas 279
Malatya 245
Denizli 211

UNITED ARAB EMIRATES (1980)
Dubai 266
Abu Dhabi 243

VIETNAM (1973)
Ho Chi Minh City (1979) 3 420
Hanoi (1979) 2 571
Haiphong (1979) 1 279
Da-Nang 492
Nha-Trang 216
Qui-Nhon 214
Hue 209

YEMEN, NORTH (1981)
Sana' 278

YEMEN, SOUTH (1981)
Aden 264

AUSTRALIA AND NEW ZEALAND

AUSTRALIA (1983)
Sydney 3 335
Melbourne 2 865
Brisbane 1 138
Adelaide 969
Perth 969
Newcastle 414
Canberra 256
Wollongong 235

NEW ZEALAND (1983)

City	Population
Auckland	864
Wellington	343
Christchurch	322

EUROPE

ALBANIA (1982)

City	Population
Tiranë	202

AUSTRIA (1984)

City	Population
Vienna	1 531
Graz	243

BELGIUM (1983)

City	Population
Brussels	989
Antwerp	491
Ghent	237
Charleroi	216
Liège	207

BULGARIA (1984)

City	Population
Sofia	1 094
Plovdiv	373
Varna	295

CZECHOSLOVAKIA (1984)

City	Population
Prague	1 190
Bratislava	409
Brno	383
Ostrava	325
Kosice	218

DENMARK (1984)

City	Population
Copenhagen	1 366

FINLAND (1983)

City	Population
Helsinki	932
Turku	257
Tampere	250

FRANCE (1982)

City	Population
Paris	8 510
Lyons	1 170
Marseilles	1 080
Lille	935
Bordeaux	628
Toulouse	523
Nantes	465
Nice	449
Toulon	410
Grenoble	392
Rouen	380
Strasbourg	373
Valenciennes	337
Lens	323
St-Étienne	317
Grasse-Cannes	296
Nancy	278
Clermont-Ferrand	256
Le Havre	255
Tours	255
Rennes	234
Montpellier	221
Mulhouse	220
Orléans	220
Dijon	209
Douai	202

GERMANY, EAST (1982)

City	Population
East Berlin	1 173
Leipzig	557
Dresden	521
Karl-Marx-Stadt	320
Magdeburg	288
Rostock	239
Halle	235
Erfurt	213

GERMANY, WEST (1983)

City	Population
West Berlin	1 860
Hamburg	1 618
Munich	1 284
Cologne	953
Essen	635
Frankfurt	615
Dortmund	595
Düsseldorf	580
Stuttgart	571
Bremen	545
Duisburg	542
Hanover	524
Nuremberg	476
Bochum	391
Wuppertal	386
Bielefeld	308
Mannheim	300
Gelsenkirchen	295
Bonn	293
Munster	273
Wiesbaden	273
Karlsruhe	270
Mönchengladbach	258
Braunschweig	257
Kiel	248
Augsburg	247
Aachen	244
Oberhausen	226
Krefeld	222
Lübeck	216
Hagen	212

GREECE (1981)

City	Population
Athens	3 027
Thessaloníki	871

HUNGARY (1984)

City	Population
Budapest	2 064
Miskolc	211

IRISH REPUBLIC (1981)

City	Population
Dublin	915

ITALY (1983)

City	Population
Rome	2 831
Milan	1 561
Naples	1 209
Turin	1 069
Genoa	747
Palermo	712
Bologna	448
Florence	441
Catánia	380
Bari	370
Venice	341
Messina	264
Verona	262
Trieste	246
Táranto	243
Padua	231
Cágliari	225
Bréscia	204

NETHERLANDS (1984)

City	Population
Rotterdam	1 025
Amsterdam	994
The Hague	672
Utrecht	501
Eindhoven	374
Arnhem	291
Heerlen-Kerkrade	266
Enschede-Hengelo	248
Tilburg	234
Nijmegen	222
Haarlem	217
Groningen	207

NORWAY (1984)

City	Population
Oslo	643
Bergen	208

POLAND (1984)

City	Population
Warsaw	1 649
Łodz	849
Kraków	740
Wrocław	636
Poznań	574
Gdansk	467
Szczecin	391
Katowice	363
Bydgoszcz	361
Lublin	324
Sosnowiec	254
Częstochowa	247
Białystok	245
Gdynia	243
Bytom	238
Radom	213
Gliwice	206

PORTUGAL (1981)

City	Population
Lisbon	1 612
Oporto	1 315

ROMANIA (1982)

City	Population
Bucharest	1 979
Braşov	334
Constanța	307
Timişoara	302
Cluj-Napoca	301
Iasi	295
Galati	279
Craiova	253
Ploieşti	228
Brăila	225
Oradea	201

SPAIN (1981)

City	Population
Madrid	3 188
Barcelona	1 755
Valencia	752
Seville	654
Zaragoza	591
Málaga	503
Bilbao	433
Valladolid	330
Palma de Mallorca	304
Hospitalet	294
Murcia	289
Córdoba	285
Granada	262
Vigo	259
Gijón	256
Alicante	251
La Coruña	232
Badalona	228

SWEDEN (1983)

City	Population
Stockholm	1 420
Göteborg	699
Malmö	455

SWITZERLAND (1983)

City	Population
Zürich	840
Geneva	372
Basle	365
Bern	301
Lausanne	225

U.S.S.R. (1983-84)

City	Population
Moscow	8 537
Leningrad	4 827
Kiev	2 409
Tashkent	1 986
Baku	1 661
Kharkov	1 536
Minsk	1 442
Gorki	1 392
Novosibirsk	1 384
Sverdlovsk	1 286
Kuybyshev	1 250
Dnepropetrovsk	1 140
Tbilisi	1 140
Yerevan	1 114
Odessa	1 113
Omsk	1 094
Chelyabinsk	1 086
Donetsk	1 064
Perm	1 048
Ufa	1 048
Alma-Ata	1 046
Kazan	1 039
Rostov	983
Volgograd	969
Saratov	893
Riga	875
Krasnoyarsk	857
Zaporozhye	844
Voronezh	840
Lvov	728
Krivoy Rog	680
Yaroslavl	623
Karaganda	608
Kishinev	605
Krasnodar	603
Ustinov	603
Frunze	590
Vladivostok	590
Irkutsk	589
Novokuznetsk	572
Barnaul	568
Khabarovsk	568
Dushanbe	539
Vilnius	535
Tula	529
Ulyanovsk	524
Penza	522
Zhdanov	520
Samarkand	515
Orenburg	513

UNITED KINGDOM (1981)

City	Population
London (1985)	6 767
Birmingham (1985)	1 007
Glasgow	762
Liverpool	510
Leeds	449
Manchester	449
Sheffield	447
Edinburgh	419
Bristol	388
Belfast	374
Coventry	314
Leicester	283
Bradford	281
Cardiff	274
Nottingham	271
Hull	268
Stoke-on-Trent	252
Wolverhampton	252
Plymouth	244
Derby	216
Southampton	204

YUGOSLAVIA (1981)

City	Population
Belgrade	1 407
Zagreb	1 175
Skopje	507
Sarajevo	449
Ljubljana	305
Novi Sad	258
Split	236
Niš	231
Priština	216

NORTH AMERICA

CANADA (1983)

City	Population
Toronto	3 067
Montréal	2 862
Vancouver	1 311
Ottawa	738
Edmonton	699
Calgary	634
Winnipeg	601
Québec	580
Hamilton	548
St. Catherines	304
Kitchener	294
London	287
Halifax	281
Windsor	245
Victoria	240

COSTA RICA (1984)

City	Population
San José	245

CUBA (1982)

City	Population
Havana	1 951
Santiago de Cuba	349
Camagüey	251

DOMINICAN REP. (1981)

City	Population
Santo Domingo	1 313
Santiago	279

EL SALVADOR (1983)

City	Population
San Salvador	884

GUATEMALA (1983)

City	Population
Guatemala	1 300

HAITI (1982)

City	Population
Port-au-Prince	888

HONDURAS (1982)

City	Population
Tegucigalpa	534
San Pedro Sula	398

JAMAICA (1980)

City	Population
Kingston	671

MEXICO (1979)

City	Population
Mexico	14 750
Guadalajara	2 468
Netzahualcóyotl	2 331
Monterrey	2 019
Puebla	711
Ciudad Juárez	625
León	625
Tijuana	566
Acapulco	462
Torreón	407
Tampico	390
Chihuahua	386
Mexicali	349
San Luis Potosi	327
Culiacán	324
Hermosillo	319
Veracruz	307
Mérida	270
Saltillo	258
Aguascalientes	257
Morelia	251
Toluca	242
Cuernavaca	241
Reynosa	231
Durango	229
Nuevo Laredo	224
Jalapa	201

NICARAGUA (1981)

City	Population
Managua	615

PANAMA (1981)

City	Population
Panama	655

PUERTO RICO (1980)

City	Population
San Juan	1 086
Ponce	253
Bayamón	209

UNITED STATES (1984)

City	Population
New York	17 807
Los Angeles	12 373
Chicago	8 035
Philadelphia	5 755
San Francisco	5 685
Detroit	4 577
Boston	4 027
Houston	3 566
Washington	3 429
Dallas	3 348
Miami	2 799
Cleveland	2 788
St. Louis	2 398
Atlanta	2 380
Pittsburgh	2 372
Baltimore	2 245
Minneapolis-St. Paul	2 231
Seattle	2 208
San Diego	2 064
Tampa	1 811
Denver	1 791
Phoenix	1 715
Cincinnati	1 673
Milwaukee	1 568
Kansas City	1 477
Portland	1 341
New Orleans	1 319
Columbus	1 279
Sacramento	1 220
Buffalo	1 205
Indianapolis	1 195
San Antonio	1 188
Providence	1 095
Norfolk	1 026
Salt Lake City	1 025
Rochester	989
Louisville	963
Oklahoma	963
Memphis	935
Dayton	930
Birmingham	895
Nashville-Davidson	890
Greensboro	886
Albany	843
Orlando	824
Honolulu	805
Richmond	796
Jacksonville	795
Hartford	729
Scranton	727
Tulsa	726
West Palm Beach	692
Syracuse	650
Charlotte	647
Austin	645
Allentown	635
Grand Rapids	626
Toledo	611
Raleigh	609
Omaha	607
Greenville	593
Knoxville	589
Fresno	565
Baton Rouge	538
Las Vegas	536
Tucson	531
El Paso	526
Youngstown	518
Springfield	516

SOUTH AMERICA

ARGENTINA (1980)

City	Population
Buenos Aires	9 927
Córdoba	982
Rosario	955
Mendoza	597
La Plata	560
San Miguel de Tucuman	497
Mar del Plata	407
San Juan	290
Santa Fé	287
Salta	260
Bahia Blanca	221
Resistencia	218

BOLIVIA (1982)

City	Population
La Paz	881
Santa Cruz	377
Cochabamba	282

BRAZIL (1980)

City	Population
São Paulo	8 493
Rio de Janeiro	5 091
Belo Horizonte	1 781
Salvador	1 502
Fortaleza	1 308
Recife	1 204
Brasilia	1 177
Pôrto Alegre	1 125
Nova Iguaçu	1 095
Curitiba	1 025
Belém	933
Goiánia	717
Campinas	665
Manaus	633
São Gonçalo	615
Duque de Caxias	576
Santo André	553
Guarulhos	533
Osasco	474
São Luis	449
São Bernardo do Campo	426
Natal	417
Santos	417
Maceió	399
São João de Meriti	399
Niterói	397
Teresina	378
Campos	348
Jaboatao	330
João Pessoa	330
Ribeirão Preto	318
Juiz de Fora	307
Londrina	302
Aracaju	293
Campo Grande	292
Feira de Santana	292
São José dos Campos	288
Olinda	282
Sorocaba	269
Pelotas	260
Jundiaí	259

CHILE (1983)

City	Population
Santiago	4 132
Viña del Mar	299
Valparaiso	268
Talcahuano	213
Concepción	210

COLOMBIA (1980)

City	Population
Bogotá	4 486
Medellin	1 812
Cali	1 232
Barranquilla	900
Bucaramanga	459
Cartagena	368
Pereira	309
Manizales	302
Cucuta	272
Ibagué	238

ECUADOR (1982)

City	Population
Guayaquil	1 301
Quito	1 110

PARAGUAY (1983)

City	Population
Asunción	708

PERU (1981)

City	Population
Lima (1983)	5 258
Arequipa	447
Callao	441
Trujillo	355
Chiclayo	280
Chimbote	216

URUGUAY (1981)

City	Population
Montevideo	1 362

VENEZUELA (1980)

City	Population
Caracas	2 944
Maracaibo	901
Valencia	506
Barquisimento	489
Maracay	344
Barcelona-Puerto La Cruz	275
San Cristóbal	272
Ciudad Guayana	206

 1:105 000 000

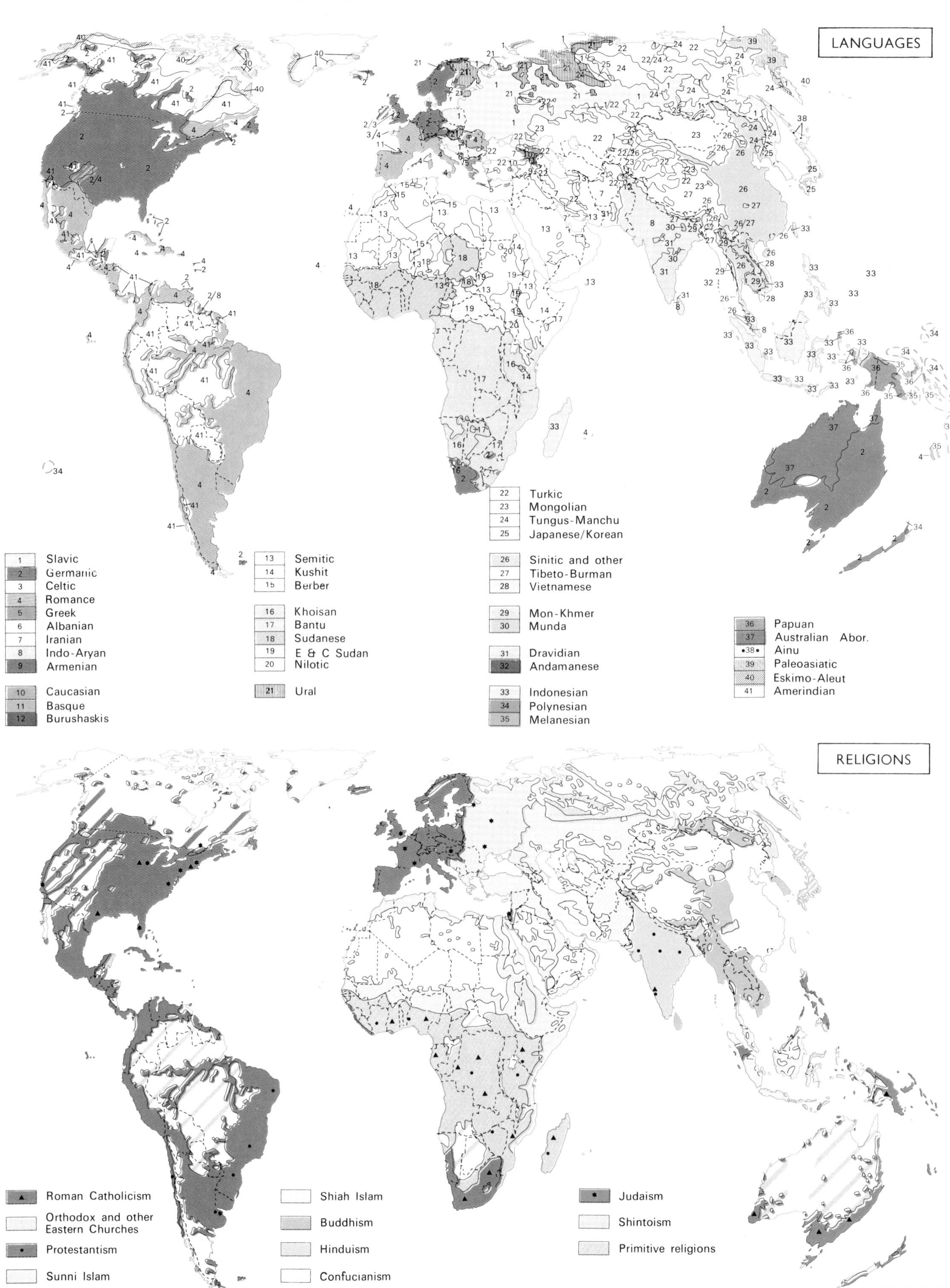
LANGUAGES
1 Slavic
2 Germanic
3 Celtic
4 Romance
5 Greek
6 Albanian
7 Iranian
8 Indo-Aryan
9 Armenian
10 Caucasian
11 Basque
12 Burushaskis
13 Semitic
14 Kushit
15 Berber
16 Khoisan
17 Bantu
18 Sudanese
19 E & C Sudan
20 Nilotic
21 Ural
22 Turkic
23 Mongolian
24 Tungus-Manchu
25 Japanese/Korean
26 Sinitic and other
27 Tibeto-Burman
28 Vietnamese
29 Mon-Khmer
30 Munda
31 Dravidian
32 Andamanese
33 Indonesian
34 Polynesian
35 Melanesian
36 Papuan
37 Australian Abor.
38 Ainu
39 Paleoasiatic
40 Eskimo-Aleut
41 Amerindian
RELIGIONS
Roman Catholicism
Orthodox and other Eastern Churches
Protestantism
Sunni Islam
Shiah Islam
Buddhism
Hinduism
Confucianism
Judaism
Shintoism
Primitive religions
COPYRIGHT GEORGE PHILIP & SON LTD

UNITED NATIONS

The United Nations was created in 1945 to promote world peace and co-operation between nations. It is the largest international organisation in the world. It has 159 members and a budget of over two billion U.S. dollars each year. Member countries meet each year to discuss their problems and disputes in the General Assembly. Each member has one vote. The Security Council consists of 15 members who are responsible for keeping the peace between nations. The Economic and Social Council consists of 54 members who are responsible for economic, social, cultural, educational, health and related matters. The Trusteeship Council is responsible for safeguarding the interests of the inhabitants of territories which are not yet fully self-governing. The Secretariat is the chief administrative officer of the organisation. The United Nations has a number of specialised agencies which help members in many fields such as economic development (UNDP), education (UNESCO), farming (FAO) and medicine (WHO). The United Nations is based in New York.

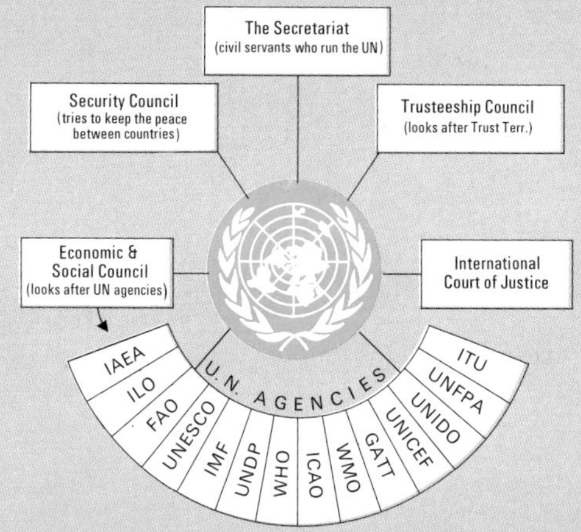

COMMONWEALTH

The Commonwealth maintains many of the ties that were formed in the days of the British Empire. The 49 members are all equal in status. There is no formal treaty or aim. The Commonwealth represents about one quarter of the world's population.

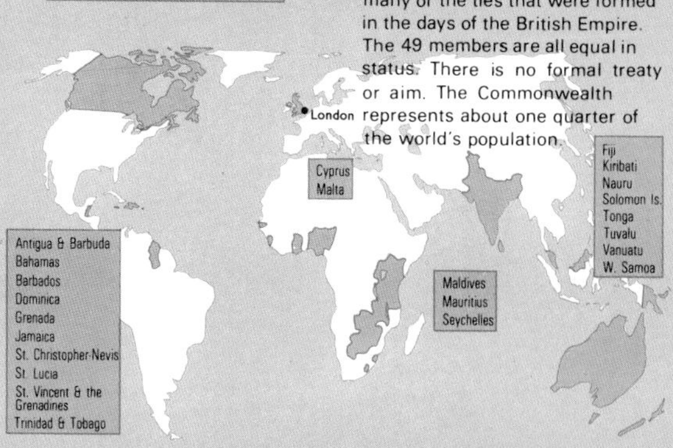

EFTA

The European Free Trade Association was founded in 1960. There are no customs duties between its members and the E.E.C. for industrial goods.

EEC

COMECON

The Council for Mutual Economic Assistance was formed to develop the trade and resources of the Soviet bloc countries.

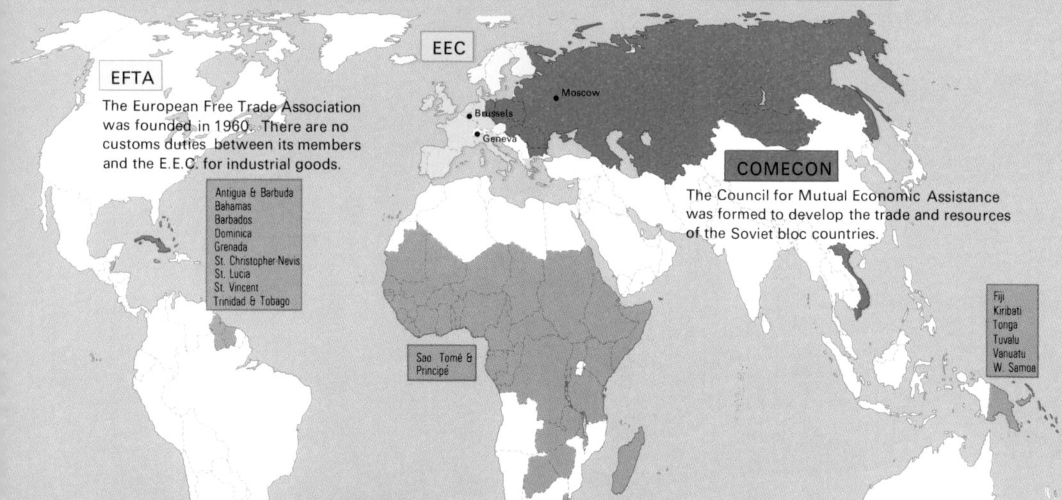

ACP

The African-Caribbean-Pacific countries are mostly former colonies which are associate members of the EEC. They pay low customs duties on their trade with the EEC and receive aid from the EEC. The trading agreement was founded in 1963.

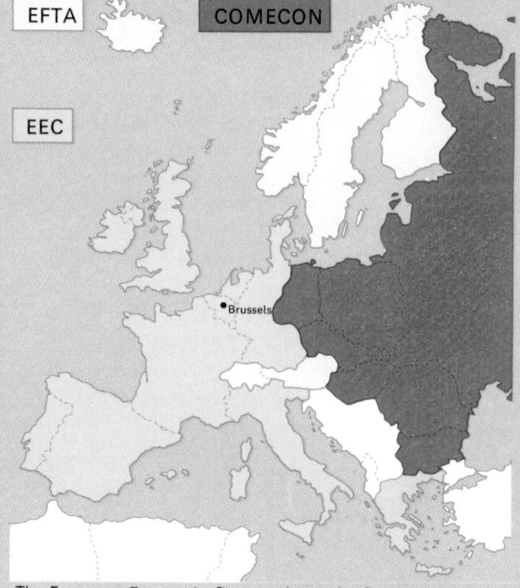

The European Economic Community or the Common Market was founded in 1957 by the Treaty of Rome. The EEC aims to integrate its members' economies, coordinate social developments and to bring about political union of the democratic countries in Europe. Its members share common agricultural and industrial policies and tariffs on external trade. The EEC has over 320 million inhabitants and is one of the wealthiest markets in the world. Some 60 nations in Africa, the Caribbean and the Pacific (ACP) are affiliated with the EEC under the Lomé Convention.

NATO

WARSAW PACT

The North Atlantic Treaty Organisation and the Warsaw Pact countries are opposing military alliances. If any member of an alliance is attacked the other members will go to his defence. The border between the two organisations is known as the Iron Curtain and is heavily defended on both sides.

OAU

The Organisation of African Unity was formed in 1963 between 30 countries. It aims to end colonialism in Africa and to defend the independence of its members. There are now 50 members, representing over 90% of the people in Africa.

ASEAN

The Association of South East Asian Nations was formed to promote political and economic co-operation among the non-communist states of the region.

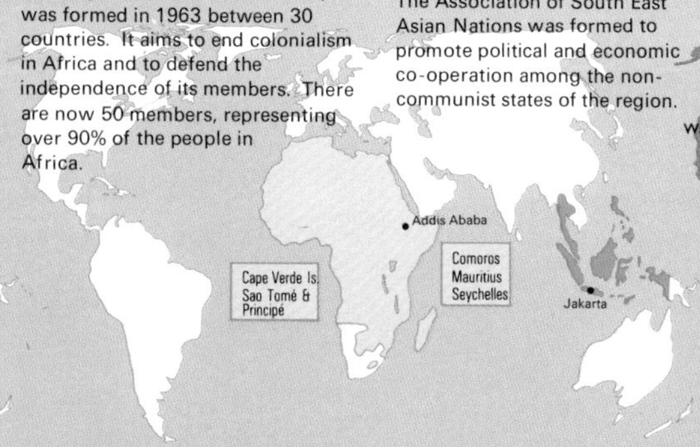

OAS

The Organisation of American States encourages the social and economic growth of the developing countries of Latin America with aid from the developed countries in North America.

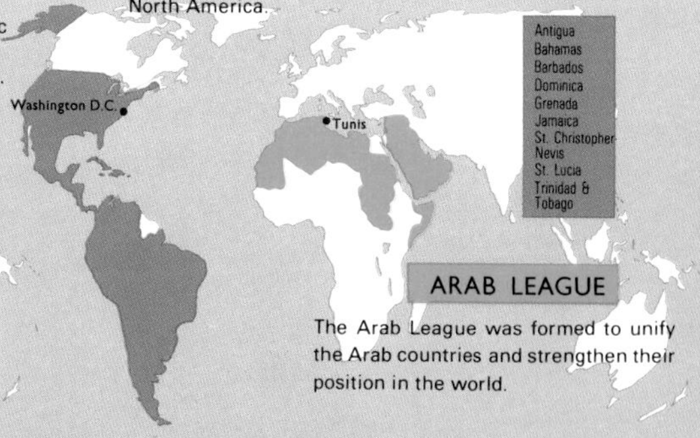

ARAB LEAGUE

The Arab League was formed to unify the Arab countries and strengthen their position in the world.

LAIA

OECD

The Organisation for Economic Co-operation and Development encourages economic growth and trade between developed and developing countries.

LAIA stands for Latin American Integration Association. It was recently formed to replace the Latin American Free Trade Association. It encourages free trade between its members.

COLOMBO PLAN

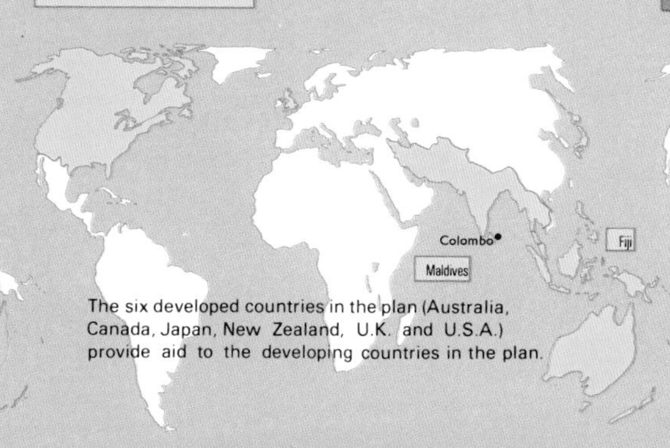

The six developed countries in the plan (Australia, Canada, Japan, New Zealand, U.K. and U.S.A.) provide aid to the developing countries in the plan.

OPEC

The Organisation of Petroleum Exporting Countries was formed in 1960. It maintains the price of oil on the world market. It controls three quarters of the world's oil supply and it is therefore very powerful.

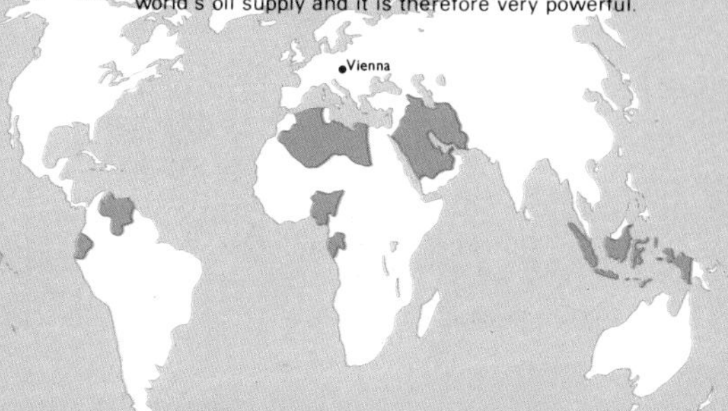

NATURAL INCREASE

The birth rates and death rates are the number of births and deaths per 1000 population each year.

North America
North Europe
West Europe
East Europe
U.S.S.R.
China
Japan
South Europe
South Asia-West
Other East Asia
Caribbean
Middle America
North Africa
Polynesia & Micronesia
West Africa
South Asia-East
Mid Africa
South Asia-Mid
East Africa
Melanesia
Tropical South America
South Africa
Australia & N.Z.
Temperate South America
15 million
10 million
5 million
1 million
Natural increase in population in 1980 per region
BIRTH RATE
High
Medium
Low
DEATH RATE
Low
Medium
High

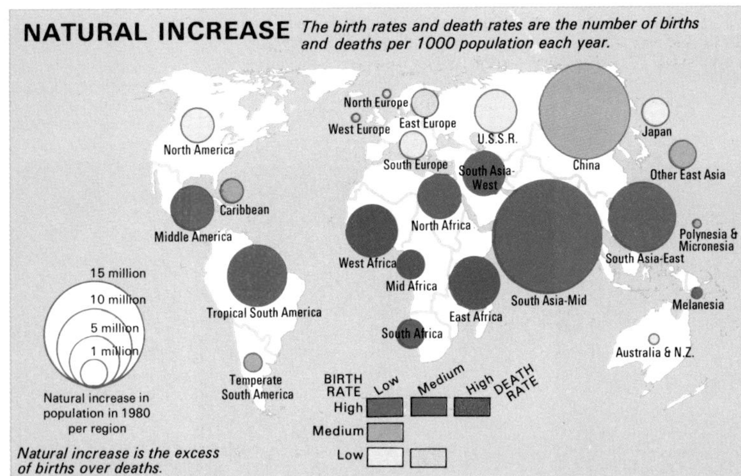

Natural increase is the excess of births over deaths.

FAMILY SIZE

Family size is the total number of children an average woman will bear in her lifetime, for each region. In 1980 the world average wa[illegible] 3.6 children; in 2000 it is expected to be 2.8 children.

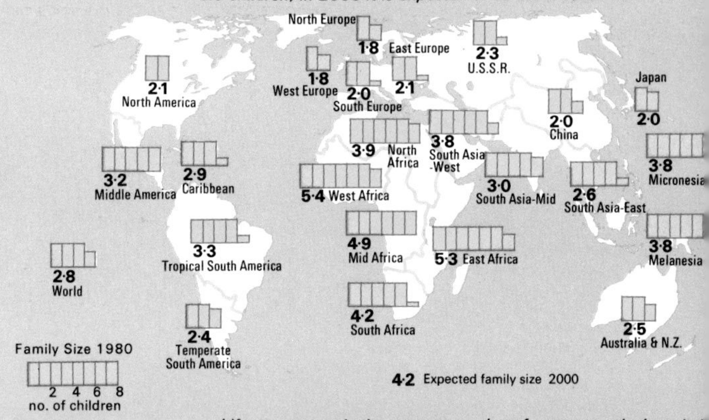

North Europe 1·8
East Europe 2·3
U.S.S.R.
North America 2·1
West Europe 1·8
2·0
2·1
South Europe
Japan 2·0
China 2·0
Middle America 3·2
Caribbean 2·9
3·9 North Africa
3·8 South Asia -West
Micronesia 3·8
5·4 West Africa
3·0 South Asia-Mid
2·6 South Asia-East
Tropical South America 3·3
4·9 Mid Africa
5·3 East Africa
Melanesia 3·8
2·8 World
4·2 South Africa
2·4 Temperate South America
2·5 Australia & N.Z.
Family Size 1980
2 4 6 8
no. of children
4·2 Expected family size 2000

LIFE EXPECTANCY

Life expectancy is the average number of years a newly-born ba[illegible] can expect to live. The world average has risen from 47 years in 1950 to 58 years in 1980, and is expected to be 64 years in 20[illegible]

North Europe
East Europe
North America 74
West Europe 75
75
U.S.S.R. 72
China 73
Japan 77
Polynesia Micronesia
South Europe 74
74
Caribbean 67
North Africa 62
65 South Asia -West
58 South Asia-Mid
Other East Asia 70
70
Middle America 70
West Africa 56
57 Mid Africa
62 South Asia -East
62 Melanesia
Tropical South America 67
59 East Africa
Life expectancy 1980
70 60 50 40 30 20 10
71 Temperate South America
67 South Africa
75 Australia & N.Z.
Increase in life expectancy 1950–1980
0–5 5–9 10–14 15+ years
74 Estimated life expectancy 2000

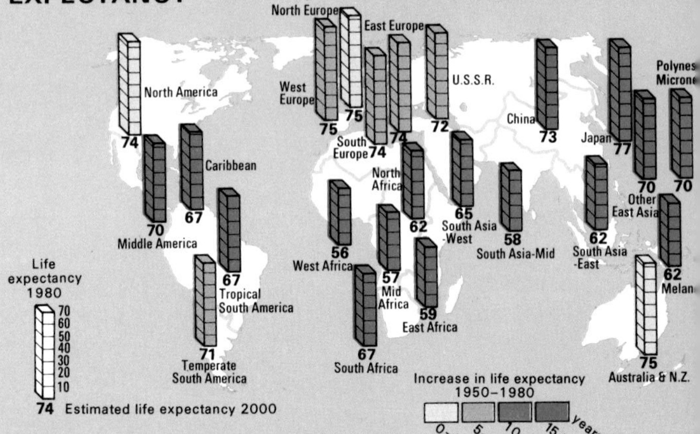

INFANT MORTALITY

The infant mortality rate for the world was 113 in 1960. It is now 81 and is expected to fall to 53 by 2000.

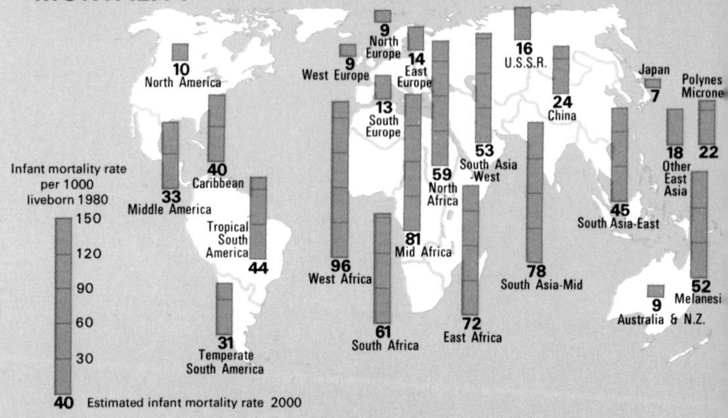

9 North Europe
9 West Europe
14 East Europe
16 U.S.S.R.
10 North America
24 China
Japan 7
Polynesia Micronesia
13 South Europe
18 Other East Asia
22
Infant mortality rate per 1000 liveborn 1980
150 120 90 60 30
33 Middle America
40 Caribbean
59 North Africa
53 South Asia -West
45 South Asia-East
Tropical South America 44
81 Mid Africa
96 West Africa
78 South Asia-Mid
52 Melanesia
9 Australia & N.Z.
61 South Africa
72 East Africa
31 Temperate South America
40 Estimated infant mortality rate 2000

YOUNG AND OLD

Median Age is the age in years w[illegible] divides the population into two eq[illegible] parts, one young and the other ol[illegible] The median age for the world is 2[illegible]

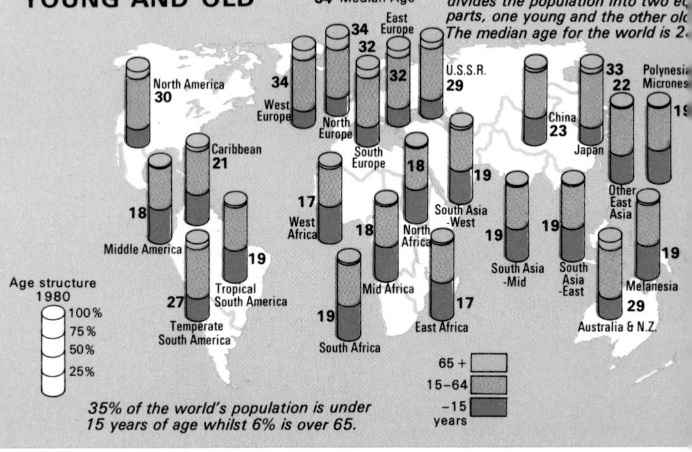

34 Median Age
North America 30
34 West Europe
34 East Europe
32 North Europe
32
U.S.S.R. 29
33 Polynesia Micronesia
22
China 23
Japan
Caribbean 21
18 Middle America
South Europe
18 North Africa
19 South Asia -West
17 West Africa
18
19 South Asia -Mid
19 South Asia -East
Other East Asia
19 Melanesia
19 Tropical South America
27 Temperate South America
Mid Africa
19 South Africa
17 East Africa
29 Australia & N.Z.
Age structure 1980
100% 75% 50% 25%
65+
15–64
–15 years

35% of the world's population is under 15 years of age whilst 6% is over 65.

AGE DISTRIBUTION PYRAMIDS

The bars represent the percentage of the population in the age group shown. The blue bars represent the males, the red bars the females. The developing countries such as India tend to have a higher proportion of young people than the developed countries such as Canada.

See page 8 for age distribution pyramid of the U.K.

World
% Male
% Female
Population in 2025
85+ 80-84 75-79 70-74 65-69 60-64 55-59 50-54 45-49 40-44 35-39 30-34 25-29 20-24 15-19 10-14 5-9 0-4
10 8 6 4 2 0 2 4 6 8 10

Canada
% Male
% Female

France
% Male
% Female

Brazil
% Male
% Female

U.S.S.R.
% Male
% Female

Ghana
% Male
% Female

India
% Male
% Female

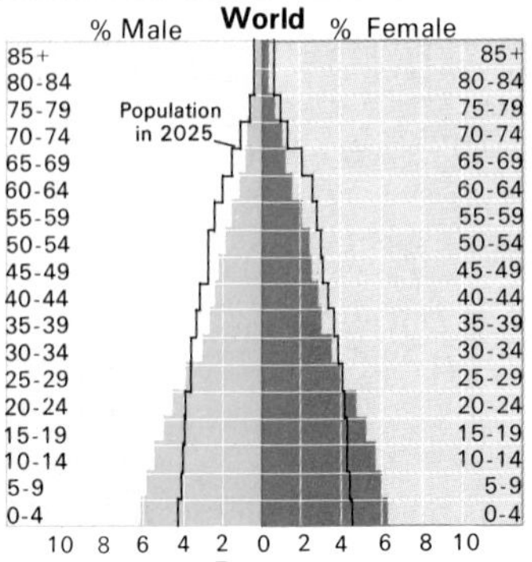

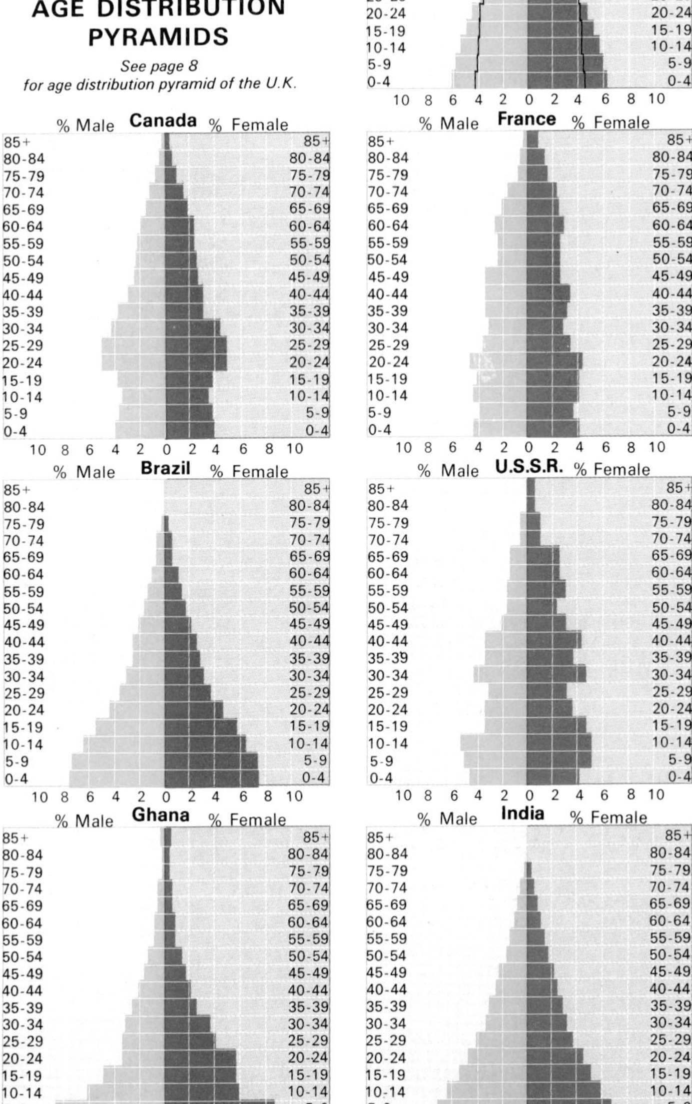

See page 125 for maps of Population Growth and Urbanisation

OPULATION Y COUNTRY

e map on pages 116-117 greater detail.

The most populous country (China) contains a quarter of the world's population. The four most populous countries (China, India, U.S.S.R., and U.S.A.) contain half, and the first eighteen (all those countries named in larger type on the map) contain over three-quarters of the world's population. The remaining 150 countries contain only one quarter.

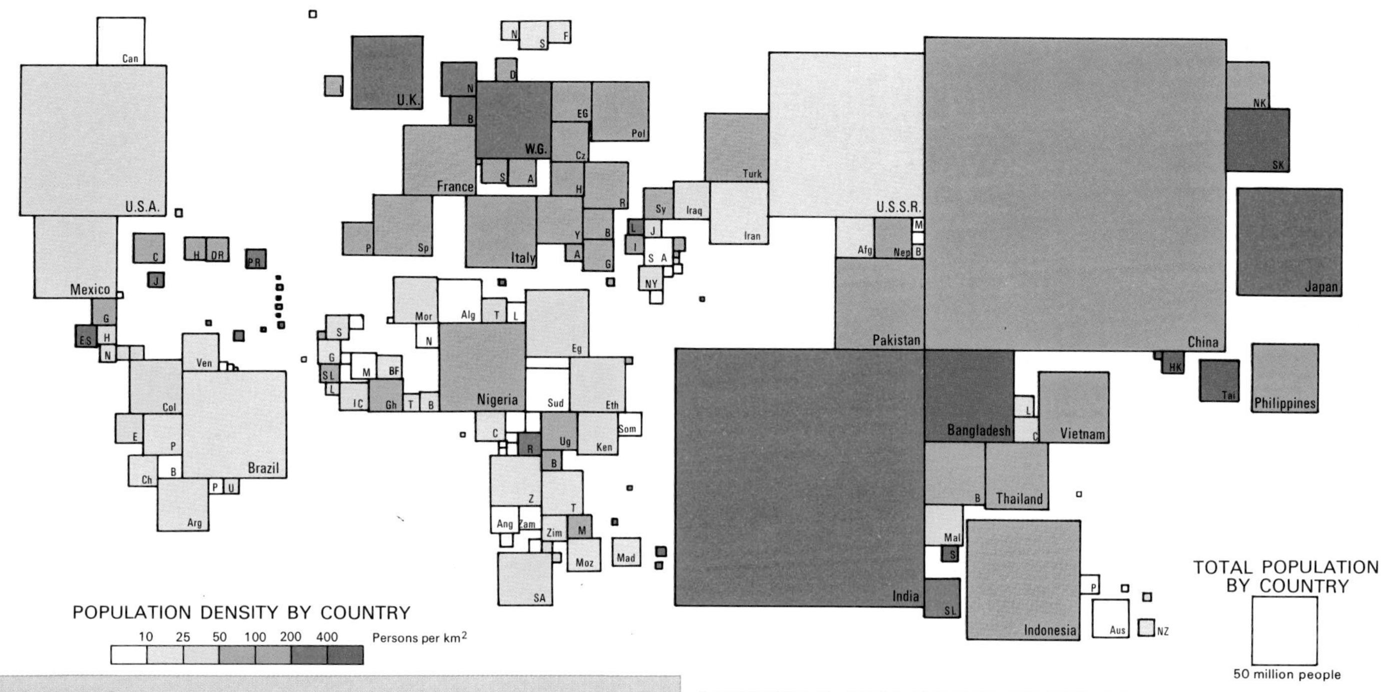

IGRATIONS

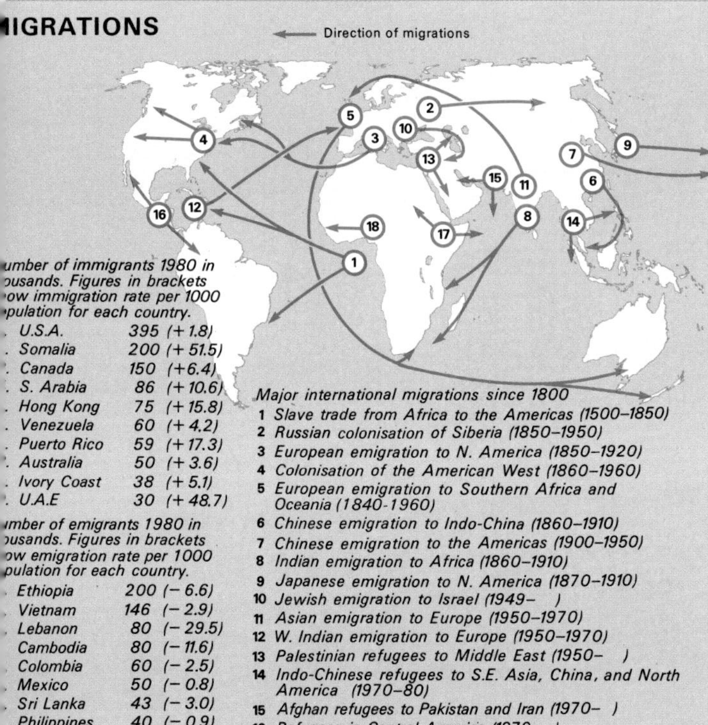

umber of immigrants 1980 in ousands. Figures in brackets ow immigration rate per 1000 pulation for each country.

U.S.A.	395	(+1.8)
Somalia	200	(+51.5)
Canada	150	(+6.4)
S. Arabia	86	(+10.6)
Hong Kong	75	(+15.8)
Venezuela	60	(+4.2)
Puerto Rico	59	(+17.3)
Australia	50	(+3.6)
Ivory Coast	38	(+5.1)
U.A.E	30	(+48.7)

umber of emigrants 1980 in ousands. Figures in brackets ow emigration rate per 1000 pulation for each country.

Ethiopia	200	(−6.6)
Vietnam	146	(−2.9)
Lebanon	80	(−29.5)
Cambodia	80	(−11.6)
Colombia	60	(−2.5)
Mexico	50	(−0.8)
Sri Lanka	43	(−3.0)
Philippines	40	(−0.9)
S. Yemen	36	(−5.4)
U.K.	30	(−0.5)

Major international migrations since 1800

1. Slave trade from Africa to the Americas (1500–1850)
2. Russian colonisation of Siberia (1850–1950)
3. European emigration to N. America (1850–1920)
4. Colonisation of the American West (1860–1960)
5. European emigration to Southern Africa and Oceania (1840–1960)
6. Chinese emigration to Indo-China (1860–1910)
7. Chinese emigration to the Americas (1900–1950)
8. Indian emigration to Africa (1860–1910)
9. Japanese emigration to N. America (1870–1910)
10. Jewish emigration to Israel (1949–)
11. Asian emigration to Europe (1950–1970)
12. W. Indian emigration to Europe (1950–1970)
13. Palestinian refugees to Middle East (1950–)
14. Indo-Chinese refugees to S.E. Asia, China, and North America (1970–80)
15. Afghan refugees to Pakistan and Iran (1970–)
16. Refugees in Central America (1979–)
17. Ethiopian refugees in Somalia and Sudan (1977–)
18. Immigrants evicted from Nigeria (1983)

ABORTION AND BIRTH CONTROL

Poland 75 %
France 79 %
U.S.A. 65 %
China 69 %
Mexico 39 %
Egypt 24 %
India 28 %
Nigeria 6 %
Indonesia 53 %

Status of Abortion
- Abortion legal
- Legal only for certain medical or juridical reasons
- Abortions illegal
- No data

Percentage of married women using contraception, for selected countries.

Legally induced abortions per 1000 live births. Total abortions in thousands are in brackets.

Bulgaria	1216	(152)	Canada	175	(66)
U.S.A.	347	(1 158)	New Zealand	133	(7)
France	207	(171)	Tunisia	77	(16)
Poland	192	(141)	India	27	(346)
Great Britain	189	(137)			

POPULATION IN 2000 A.D.

Percentage of world total is given in brackets.

World	6 119		
South Asia	2 075 (34%)	U.S.S.R.	310 (5%)
East Asia	1 475 (24%)	Europe	512 (8.5%)
Oceania	30 (0.5%)		
Africa	853 (14%)		
South America	566 (9%)		
N. America	299 (5%)		

ntil comparatively recently there was little increase in the population of the world. It is ought there were about 200 million in 600 B.C., 300 million in 1000 A.D. and 500 illion by 1600 A.D.. This diagram shows how the world's population has increased since en at an ever increasing rate. 90% of this increase has been in the less developed regions e world population of 1950 will have doubled by 1990 and if present trends continue will have trebled by 2020.

OPULATION INCREASE SINCE 1650

6000m
5000m
4000m
3000m
South Asia
Oceania
2000m
Africa
East Asia
South America
1000m
North America
Asia pre 1925
U.S.S.R.
Europe pre 1925
Europe
0
1700 1750 1800 1850 1900 1925 1950 1975 2000

NATURAL DISASTERS

EARTHQUAKES AND VOLCANOES

- ○ Major earthquakes with dates
- ▲ Major volcanoes
- Earthquake zones (land and sea)

STORMS AND FLOODS

- * Major storms and floods with dates
- Paths of winter blizzards
- Paths of tropical storms
- Areas liable to flood

PESTS

- Locust invasion areas
- Main tsetse fly areas

MAJOR FAMINES

- ⊙ Sahel 1973

Famine is by far the most destructive of these disasters. Over a quarter million starved to death in the Sahel during the drought of 1968 – 1973. Famine is usually the result of prolonged drought but it can also be caused by war, flood, disease or pests.

Since 1945 there have been over 300 wars. Few countries in the world have been unaffected by war, strife or terrorism.

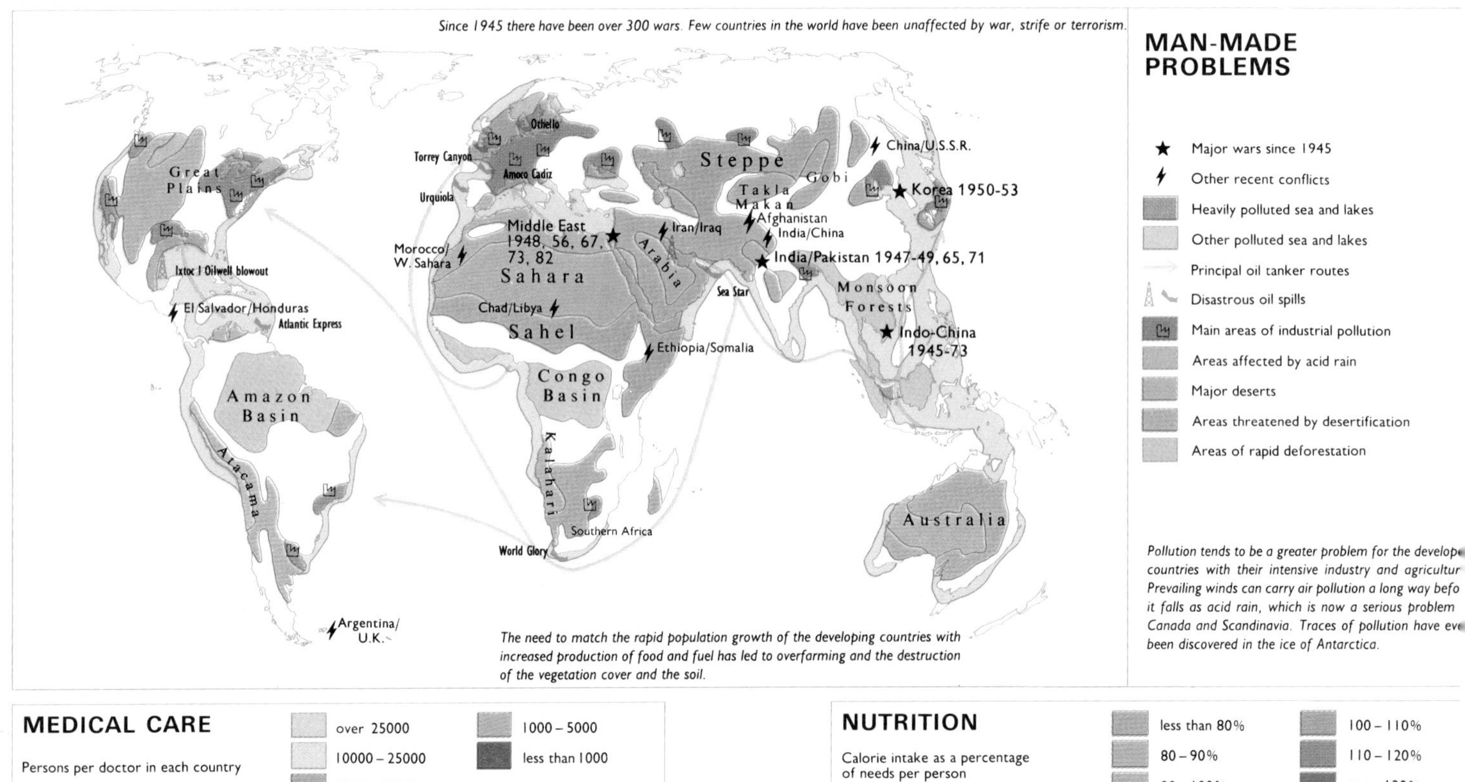

The need to match the rapid population growth of the developing countries with increased production of food and fuel has led to overfarming and the destruction of the vegetation cover and the soil.

MAN-MADE PROBLEMS

- ★ Major wars since 1945
- ϟ Other recent conflicts
- Heavily polluted sea and lakes
- Other polluted sea and lakes
- Principal oil tanker routes
- Disastrous oil spills
- Main areas of industrial pollution
- Areas affected by acid rain
- Major deserts
- Areas threatened by desertification
- Areas of rapid deforestation

Pollution tends to be a greater problem for the develope[d] countries with their intensive industry and agricultur[e]. Prevailing winds can carry air pollution a long way befo[re] it falls as acid rain, which is now a serious problem [in] Canada and Scandinavia. Traces of pollution have eve[n] been discovered in the ice of Antarctica.

MEDICAL CARE

Persons per doctor in each country

- over 25000
- 10000 – 25000
- 5000 – 10000
- 1000 – 5000
- less than 1000

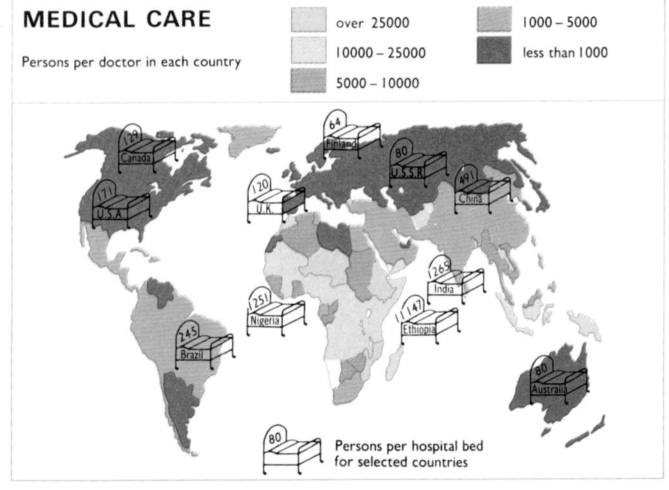

Persons per hospital bed for selected countries

NUTRITION

Calorie intake as a percentage of needs per person

- less than 80%
- 80 – 90%
- 90 – 100%
- 100 – 110%
- 110 – 120%
- over 120%

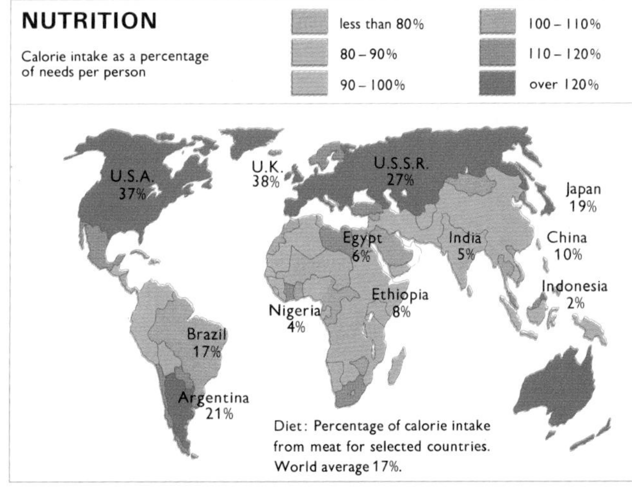

Diet: Percentage of calorie intake from meat for selected countries. World average 17%.

TANDARDS OF LIVING

HE RICH

Countries with more than four times the world's average income

Countries with more than twice the world's average income

Countries with incomes just above the world's average

HE POOR

Countries with incomes just below the world's average

Countries with less than half of the world's average income

Countries with less than one quarter of the world's average income

Data not available

ne world's average income is just under 2200 US$ per num. The richest country on a per capita basis is uwait with an income over 200 times that of the poorest untry, Mali.

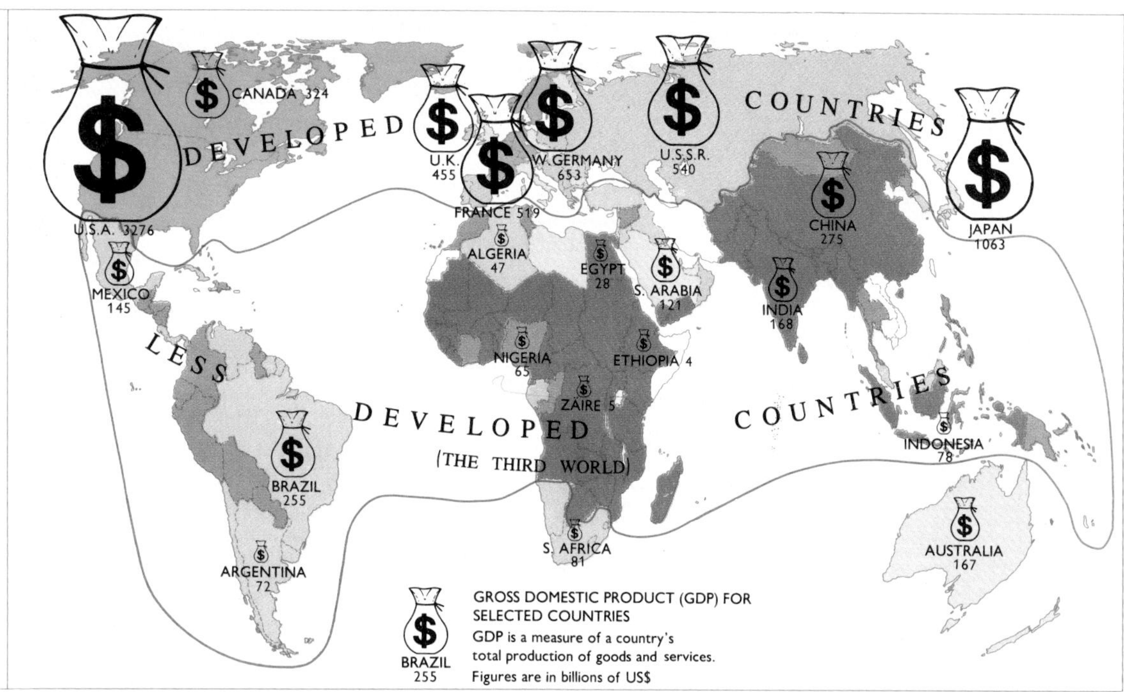

GROSS DOMESTIC PRODUCT (GDP) FOR SELECTED COUNTRIES
GDP is a measure of a country's total production of goods and services.
Figures are in billions of US$

POPULATION EXPLOSION IN THE THIRD WORLD

CURRENT RATE OF INCREASE

less than 1%
1 – 2%
2 – 2½%
2½% – 3%
over 3%

Annual rate of population growth in each country

EXPECTED RATE OF INCREASE

2034 — Date by which 1984 population of selected countries will double if present trends continue.
World = 2025

6167m Population in 2000
WORLD 40% — Expected rate of population increase 1980 – 2000 for each continent (1mm = 2%)
4380m Population in 1980

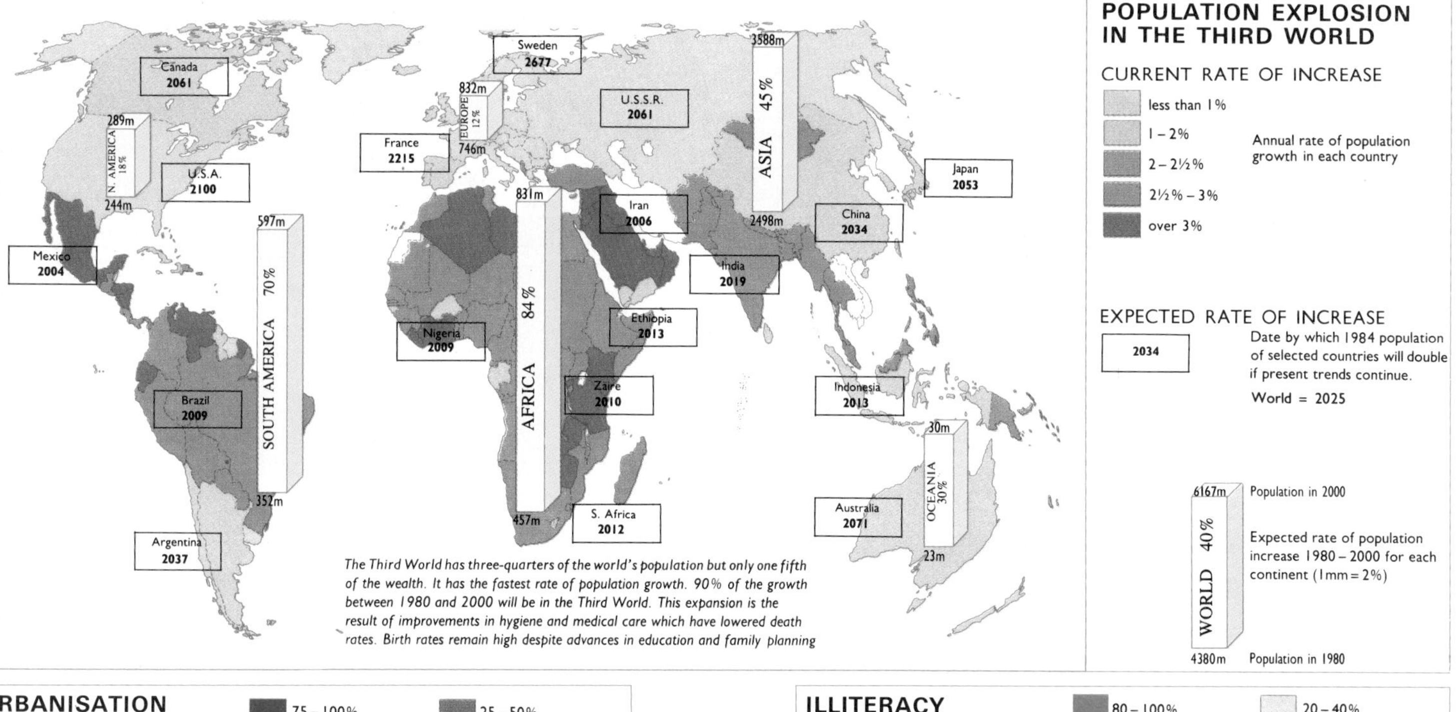

The Third World has three-quarters of the world's population but only one fifth of the wealth. It has the fastest rate of population growth. 90% of the growth between 1980 and 2000 will be in the Third World. This expansion is the result of improvements in hygiene and medical care which have lowered death rates. Birth rates remain high despite advances in education and family planning

RBANISATION

rcentage of population living towns and cities in each country

75 – 100%
50 – 75%
25 – 50%
0 – 25%

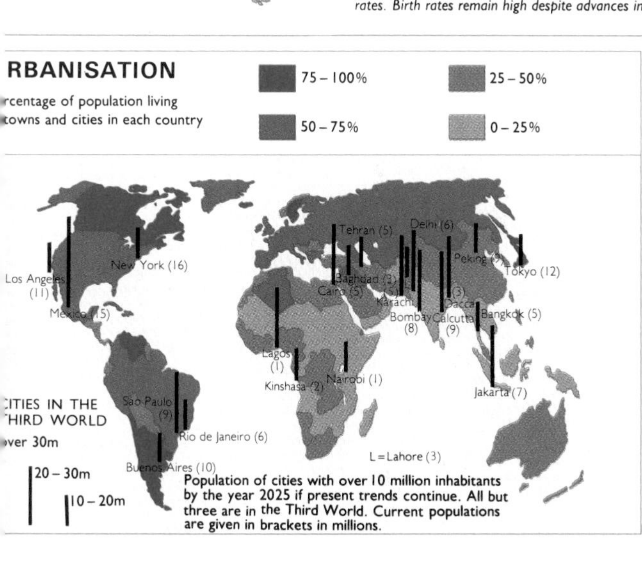

Population of cities with over 10 million inhabitants by the year 2025 if present trends continue. All but three are in the Third World. Current populations are given in brackets in millions.

ILLITERACY

Percentage of population in each country who are illiterate

80 – 100%
60 – 80%
40 – 60%
20 – 40%
0 – 20%

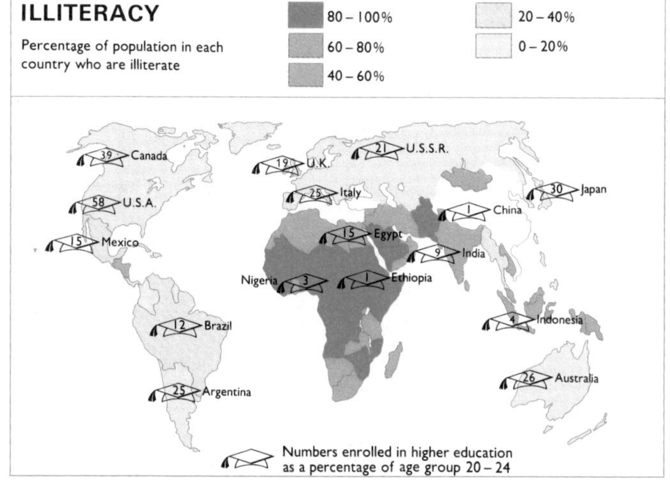

Numbers enrolled in higher education as a percentage of age group 20 – 24

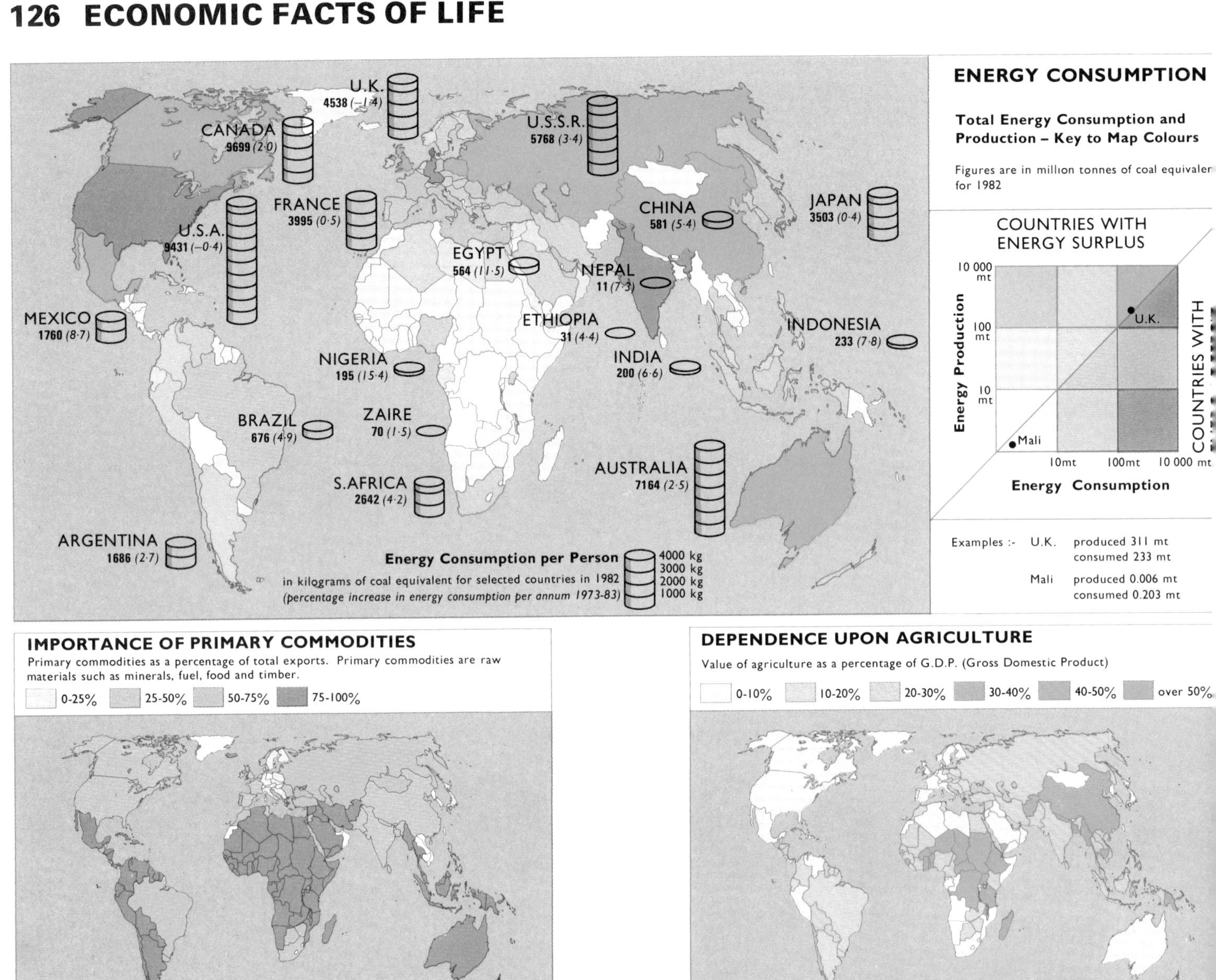

FOOD PRODUCTION

Food production per person

Percentage change from 1974-6 to 1981-3 for each country

INCREASE: over 20%, 15-20%, 10-15%, 5-10%, 0-5%

DECREASE: 0-5%, 5-10%, 10-15%, 15-20%, over 20%

TRADE IN FOOD

60.6 U.K. — Cereal imports per person for selected countries in 1983 (figures in kilograms)

Net exporters of food (value of food exports greater than food imports

U.K. 60·6
U.S.S.R. 117·9
CANADA 18·0
U.S.A. 2·5
JAPAN 212·0
BELGIUM 610·4
CUBA 214·8
CHINA 18·8
EGYPT 180·4
MEXICO 113·1
ISRAEL 364·6
NIGERIA 24·6
S.ARABIA 334·8
INDIA 5·8
ZAIRE 9·2
ETHIOPIA 7·9
INDONESIA 19·2
BRAZIL 38·0
ARGENTINA 0·1
S.AFRICA 48·2
AUSTRALIA 2·1

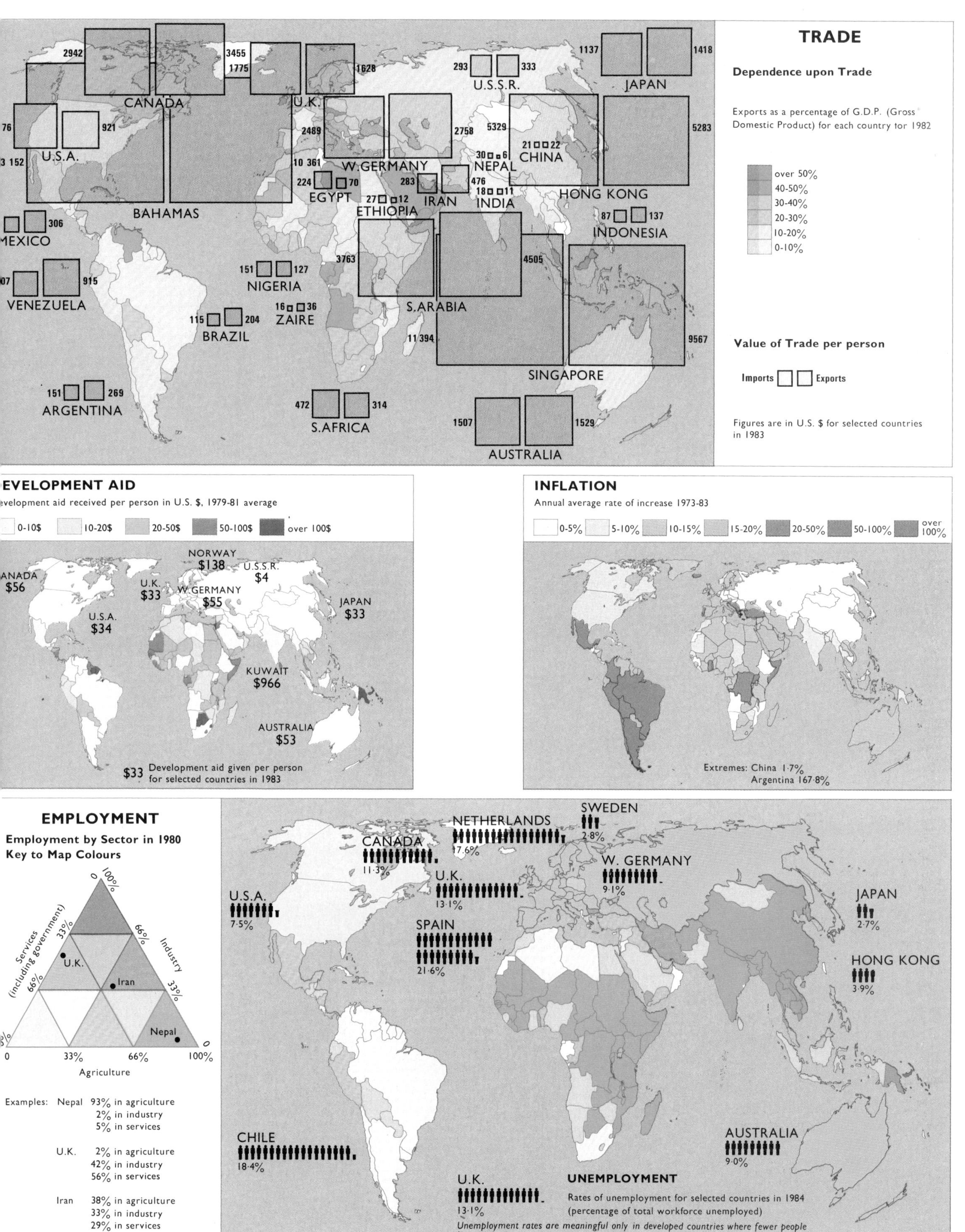

TRADE
Dependence upon Trade
Exports as a percentage of G.D.P. (Gross Domestic Product) for each country for 1982
over 50%
40-50%
30-40%
20-30%
10-20%
0-10%
Value of Trade per person
Imports Exports
Figures are in U.S. $ for selected countries in 1983
CANADA 2942 3455
U.K. 1775 1628
U.S.S.R. 293 333
JAPAN 1137 1418
U.S.A. 921
W.GERMANY 2489 2758
BAHAMAS 10 361
EGYPT 224 70
ETHIOPIA 27 12
IRAN 283 476
NEPAL 30 6
INDIA 18 11
CHINA 21 22
HONG KONG 5329 5283
INDONESIA 87 137
MEXICO 306
VENEZUELA 915
NIGERIA 151 127
ZAIRE 16 36
BRAZIL 115 204
S.ARABIA 3763 4505
SINGAPORE 11 394 9567
ARGENTINA 151 269
S.AFRICA 472 314
AUSTRALIA 1507 1529
DEVELOPMENT AID
Development aid received per person in U.S. $, 1979-81 average
0-10$
10-20$
20-50$
50-100$
over 100$
NORWAY $138
U.S.S.R. $4
CANADA $56
U.K. $33
W.GERMANY $55
JAPAN $33
U.S.A. $34
KUWAIT $966
AUSTRALIA $53
$33 Development aid given per person for selected countries in 1983
INFLATION
Annual average rate of increase 1973-83
0-5%
5-10%
10-15%
15-20%
20-50%
50-100%
over 100%
Extremes: China 1·7%
Argentina 167·8%
EMPLOYMENT
Employment by Sector in 1980
Key to Map Colours
Services (including government)
Industry
Agriculture
0
33%
66%
100%
U.K.
Iran
Nepal
Examples: Nepal 93% in agriculture
2% in industry
5% in services
U.K. 2% in agriculture
42% in industry
56% in services
Iran 38% in agriculture
33% in industry
29% in services
SWEDEN 2·8%
NETHERLANDS 17·6%
CANADA 11·3%
W. GERMANY 9·1%
U.K. 13·1%
U.S.A. 7·5%
JAPAN 2·7%
SPAIN 21·6%
HONG KONG 3·9%
CHILE 18·4%
AUSTRALIA 9·0%
U.K. 13·1%
UNEMPLOYMENT
Rates of unemployment for selected countries in 1984 (percentage of total workforce unemployed)
Unemployment rates are meaningful only in developed countries where fewer people live on the land.

Polar Routes
Pacific Routes
Principal Air Routes
Distances in km
GREENLAND
Queen Elizabeth Is.
Victoria I.
Baffin I.
ICELAND
Anchorage
Churchill
Hudson Bay
Edmonton
C A N A D A
Vancouver
Calgary
Winnipeg
Seattle
Newfoundland
Quebec
Montreal
Toronto
Boston
Chicago
Detroit
New York
Washington
San Francisco
Denver
St. Louis
UNITED STATES
Los Angeles
Dallas
New Orleans
Houston
MEXICO
Gulf of Mexico
Miami
BAHAMAS
Havana
CUBA
West Indies
JAMAICA
HAITI
DOMINICAN REP.
PUERTO RICO
Mexico
BELIZE
GUATEMALA
HONDURAS
EL SALVADOR
NICARAGUA
COSTA RICA
PANAMA
Caribbean Sea
Caracas
VENEZUELA
GUYANA
SURINAM
FR. GUIANA
Bogota
COLOMBIA
Quito
ECUADOR
Galapagos Is. (Ecuador)
Manaus
Belém
B R A Z I L
Recife
PERU
Lima
Salvador
Brasilia
La Paz
BOLIVIA
PARAGUAY
Asunción
Rio de Janeiro
São Paulo
C H I L E
A R G E N T I N A
URUGUAY
Montevideo
Santiago
Buenos Aires
Falkland Is.
Tierra del Fuego
S. Georgia
FALKLAND IS. DEPENDENCIES (Br.)
BRITISH ANTARCTIC TERRITORY
ROSS DEPENDENCY
A T L A N T I C
O C E A N
P A C I F I C
O C E A N
UNITED KINGDOM
Glasgow
IRELAND
PORTUGAL
Lisbon
Azores
Casablanca
MOROCCO
Canary Is.
W. SAHARA
MAURITANIA
C. Verde Is.
SENEGAL
GAMBIA
GUINEA-BISSAU
GUINEA
SIERRA LEONE
LIBERIA
Ascension (Br.)
St. Helena (Br.)
Tristan da Cunha (Br.)
Hawaiian Islands (U.S.)
Tropic of Cancer
Palmyra Is. (U.S.)
Tabuaeran
Kiritimati
Equator
Phoenix Is.
Tokelau Is. (N.Z.)
Samoan Is.
Tonga
Society Is. (Fr.)
Tuamotu Archipelago (Fr.)
Tubuai Is. (Fr.)
Tropic of Capricorn
Easter I.
Kermadec Is. (N.Z.)
Chatham Is. (N.Z.)
West from Greenwich

Principal Sea Routes
Distances in km
Pacific Routes
ARCTIC OCEAN
Novaya Zemlya
New Siberian Is.
Arkhangelsk
UNION OF SOVIET SOCIALIST REPUBLICS
Bering Sea
Helsinki
Leningrad
Oslo
Stockholm
Copenhagen
Moscow
Sverdlovsk
Novosibirsk
Irkutsk
Warsaw
Berlin
Vienna
Kiev
Ulan Bator
MONGOLIA
Vladivostok
Sapporo
Bucharest
Rome
Istanbul
Baku
Tashkent
Peking
Dalian
N. KOREA
S. KOREA
JAPAN
Tokyo
Osaka
Pusan
TURKEY
Athens
Tunis
Tehran
Baghdad
IRAN
IRAQ
Kabul
Islamabad
Lahore
CHINA
Shanghai
Mediterranean Sea
Tripoli
Alexandria
Cairo
KUWAIT
PAKISTAN
NEPAL
Delhi
Chungking
PACIFIC
LIBYA
EGYPT
BAHRAIN
Karachi
BANGLADESH
Dacca
INDIA
Tropic of Cancer
TAIWAN
Hong Kong
SAUDI ARABIA
U.A.E.
Mecca
Red Sea
OMAN
Ahmadabad
Calcutta
BURMA
Hanoi
LAOS
Northern Marianas
Wake I. (U.S.)
NIGER
CHAD
Khartoum
SUDAN
YEMEN
SOUTH YEMEN
Bombay
Arabian Sea
Rangoon
Bay of Bengal
Madras
THAILAND
VIETNAM
Bangkok
CAMBODIA
Phnom Penh
Ho Chi Minh City
Manila
PHILIPPINES
OCEAN
Niamey
Kano
NIGERIA
Ndjamena
DJIB.
Addis Ababa
ETHIOPIA
SOMALI REP.
Marshall Is.
Lagos
CAMEROON
CENTRAL AFRICAN REPUBLIC
Douala
SRI LANKA
Colombo
MALAYSIA
BRUNEI
Federated States of Micronesia
(U.S. Trust Territory)
Kuala Lumpur
Singapore
Mogadishu
Maldives
UGANDA
KENYA
Equator
Kiribati
GABON
CONGO
ZAÏRE
RWANDA
BURUNDI
Nairobi
Mombasa
INDIAN OCEAN
Padang
Sumatra
Borneo
Seychelles
INDONESIA
New Guinea
PAPUA NEW GUINEA
CABINDA
Kinshasa
TANZANIA
Dar-es-Salaam
Jakarta
Surabaya
Solomon Is.
Luanda
ANGOLA
Port Moresby
Tuvalu (Ellice Is.)
ZAMBIA
MALAWI
MOZAMBIQUE
Darwin
Coral Sea
Harare
ZIMBABWE
NAMIBIA
BOTSWANA
Antananarivo
MADAGASCAR
Mauritius
Vanuatu
Fiji
New Caledonia (Fr.)
Alice Springs
AUSTRALIA
Johannesburg
SWAZ.
SOUTH AFRICA
LES.
Durban
Tropic of Capricorn
Brisbane
Cape Town
Perth
Adelaide
Sydney
Canberra
Auckland
Melbourne
Tasmania
NEW ZEALAND
Hobart
Christchurch
Crozet Is. (Fr.)
Kerguelen Is. (Fr.)
Dunedin
SOUTHERN OCEAN
DEPENDENCY
AUSTRALIAN DEPENDENCY
ADELIE LAND
from Greenwich

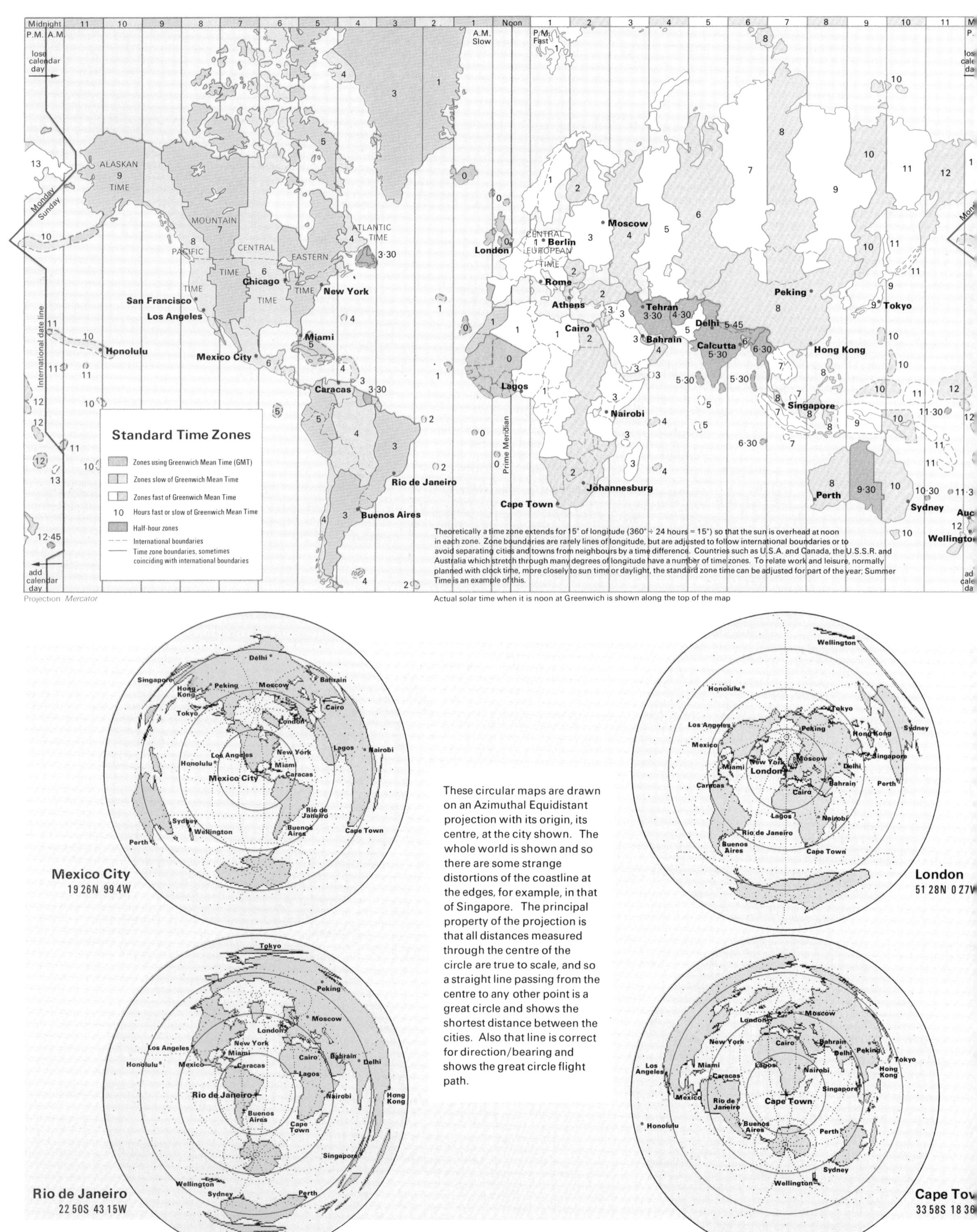

Theoretically a time zone extends for 15° of longitude (360° ÷ 24 hours = 15°) so that the sun is overhead at noon in each zone. Zone boundaries are rarely lines of longitude, but are adjusted to follow international boundaries or to avoid separating cities and towns from neighbours by a time difference. Countries such as U.S.A. and Canada, the U.S.S.R. and Australia which stretch through many degrees of longitude have a number of time zones. To relate work and leisure, normally planned with clock time, more closely to sun time or daylight, the standard zone time can be adjusted for part of the year; Summer Time is an example of this.

These circular maps are drawn on an Azimuthal Equidistant projection with its origin, its centre, at the city shown. The whole world is shown and so there are some strange distortions of the coastline at the edges, for example, in that of Singapore. The principal property of the projection is that all distances measured through the centre of the circle are true to scale, and so a straight line passing from the centre to any other point is a great circle and shows the shortest distance between the cities. Also that line is correct for direction/bearing and shows the great circle flight path.

These distances are in kilometres and are the great circle distances between the cities (international airports). Great circle distances are the shortest distances between two points on the globe. They are the normal flight paths for aircraft where they are free from the restrictions of air corridors or national airspace.

	Bahrain	Buenos Aires	Cairo	Cape Town	Caracas	Delhi	Hong Kong	Honolulu	Lagos	London	Los Angeles	Mexico	Miami	Moscow	Nairobi	New York	Peking	Perth	Rio de Janeiro	Singapore	Sydney	Tokyo
Buenos Aires	13 291																					
Cairo	1 927	11 845																				
Cape Town	7 496	6 880	7 246																			
Caracas	12 121	5 124	10 200	10 254																		
Delhi	2 618	15 784	4 400	9 278	14 186																	
Hong Kong	6 387	18 442	8 121	11 852	16 340	3 768																
Honolulu	13 882	12 158	14 195	18 555	9 671	11 984	8 911															
Lagos	5 454	7 932	3 926	4 783	7 722	8 071	11 832	16 286														
London	5 089	11 128	3 528	9 672	7 465	6 726	9 637	11 617	4 998													
Los Angeles	13 210	9 854	12 206	16 067	5 813	12 863	11 634	4 105	12 408	8 752												
Mexico	13 962	7 391	12 360	13 701	3 572	14 651	12 121	6 096	11 043	8 898	2 498											
Miami	12 182	7 113	10 441	12 334	2 190	13 495	14 430	7 806	9 045	7 102	3 759	2 050										
Moscow	3 466	13 488	2 909	10 150	9 900	4 359	7 148	11 289	6 250	2 505	9 748	10 682	9 191									
Nairobi	3 398	10 413	3 542	4 096	11 545	5 413	8 750	17 255	3 828	6 835	15 560	14 812	12 771	6 365								
New York	10 613	8 526	9 009	12 551	3 402	11 747	12 956	8 000	8 437	5 535	3 968	3 361	1 751	7 476	11 828							
Peking	6 180	19 273	7 526	12 956	14 356	3 804	1 985	8 124	11 452	8 146	10 030	12 426	12 475	5 789	9 217	10 971						
Perth	9 467	12 562	11 256	8 684	17 610	7 874	6 030	10 886	12 517	14 495	14 986	16 247	18 281	12 236	8 889	18 699	8 000					
Rio de Janeiro	11 462	1 990	9 897	6 080	4 522	14 054	17 688	13 330	6 022	9 248	10 132	7 659	6 713	11 528	8 937	7 724	17 306	13 527				
Singapore	6 319	15 860	8 246	9 650	18 332	4 148	2 581	10 789	11 149	10 867	14 099	16 593	16 951	8 437	7 446	15 330	4 489	3 909	15 729			
Sydney	12 502	11 760	14 391	10 982	15 341	10 424	7 370	8 163	15 514	17 005	12 052	12 973	15 012	14 501	12 125	16 001	8 956	3 274	13 512	6 294		
Tokyo	8 271	18 338	9 552	14 710	14 154	5 852	2 874	6 185	13 475	9 584	8 806	11 304	11 991	7 487	11 243	10 869	2 089	7 896	18 557	5 300	7 809	
Wellington	14 678	9 943	16 503	11 287	13 119	12 647	9 424	7 508	16 047	18 816	10 787	11 099	13 054	16 547	13 643	14 406	10 782	5 246	11 865	8 521	2 226	9 258

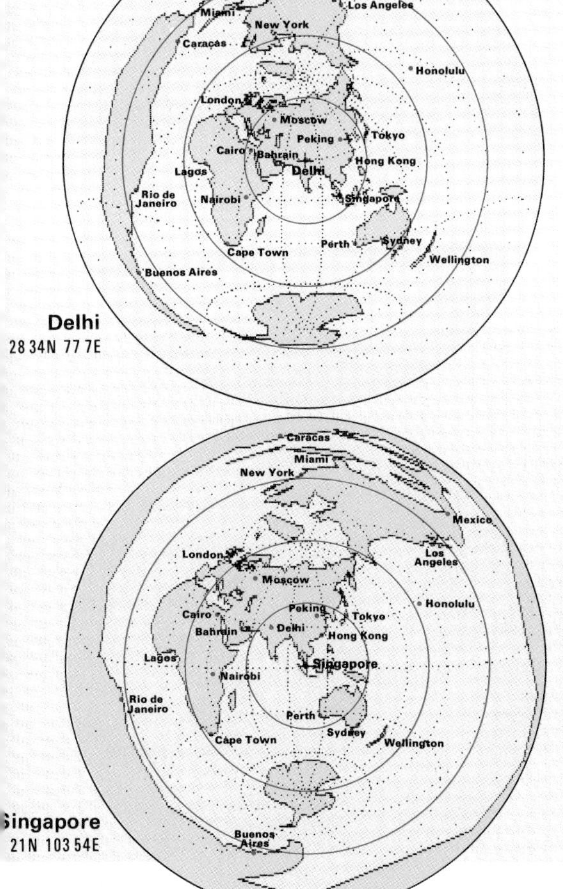

Delhi
28 34N 77 7E

Singapore
1 21N 103 54E

The three circles are drawn at radius 5 000, 10 000 and 15 000 km from the central city

• Cities shown on the distance table

The co-ordinates given for the airport of each city

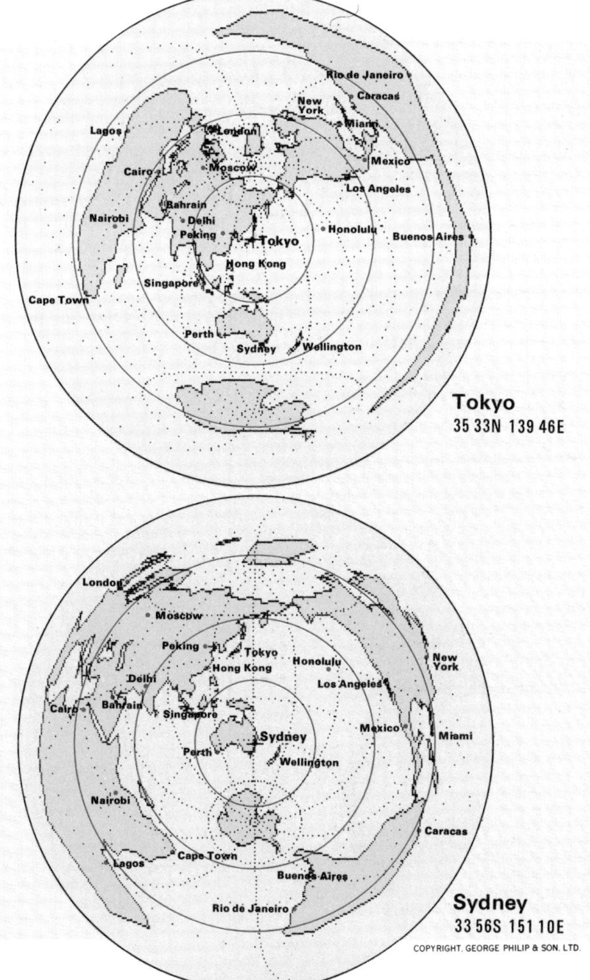

Tokyo
35 33N 139 46E

Sydney
33 56S 151 10E

INDEX

The number in bold type which follows each name in the index refers to the number of the page where that feature or place will be found.

The geographical co-ordinates which follow the place name are sometimes only approximate but are close enough for the place name to be located.

An open square □ signifies that the name refers to an administrative division of a country while a solid square ■ follows the name of a country.

Rivers have been indexed to their mouth or to their confluence.

The alphabetical order of names composed of two or more words is governed primarily by the first word and then by the second. This is an example of the rule:

West Wyalong
West Yorkshire
Westbourne
Westbury
Westbury-on-Severn
Western Australia

Names composed of a proper name (Gibraltar) and a description (Strait of) are positioned alphabetically by the proper name. All river names are followed by →. If the same word occurs in the name of a town and a geographical feature, the town name is listed first followed by the name or names of the geographical features.

Names beginning with M', Mc are all indexed as if they were spelled Mac.

If the same place name occurs twice or more in the index and the places are in different countries they will be followed by the country names and the latter in alphabetical order.

Sydney, Australia
Sydney, Canada

In the index each placename is followed by its geographical co-ordinates which allow the reader to find the place on the map. These co-ordinates give the latitude and longitude of a particular place.

The latitude (or parallel) is the distance of a point north or south of the Equator measured as an angle with the centre of the earth. The Equator is latitude 0°, the North Pole is 90°N and the South Pole 90°S. On a globe the lines could be drawn as concentric circles parallel to the Equator, decreasing in diameter from the Equator until they become a point at the Poles. On the maps these lines of latitude are usually represented as lines running across the map from East to West in smooth curves. They are numbered on the sides of the map; north of the Equator the numbers increase northwards, to the south they increase southwards. The degree interval between them depends on the scale of the map. On a large scale map (for example, 1:2 000 000) the interval is one degree, but on a small scale (for example 1:50 000 000) it will be ten degrees.

Lines of longitude (or meridians) cut the latitude lines at right angles on the globe and intersect with one another at the Poles. Longitude is measured by the angle at the centre of the earth between it and the meridian of origin which runs through Greenwich (0°). It may be a measurement East or West of this line and from 0° to 180° in each direction. The longitude line of 180° runs North – South through the Pacific Ocean. On a particular map the interval between the lines of longitude is always the same as that between the lines of latitude and normally they are drawn vertically. They are numbered in the top and bottom margins and a note states East or West from Greenwich.

The unit of measurement for latitude and longitude is the degree and it is subdivided into 60 minutes. An index entry states the position of a place in degrees and minutes, a space being left between the degrees and minutes. The latitude is followed by N(orth) or S(outh) and the longitude by E(ast) or W(est).

The diagram illustrates how the reader has to estimate the required distance from the nearest line of latitude or longitude. In the diagram there is one degree, or 60 minutes between the lines and so to find the position of Calais an estimate has to be made, 57 parts of 60 north of the 50 degree latitude line and 50 parts of 60, or 50 minutes east of the one degree longitude line.

Where the map is smaller in scale it is more difficult to calculate the position of a place because there are five or ten degree intervals between the lines.

Scale 1:2 000 000

Longitude East from Greenwich
51
1
2
50/60 or
50 minutes
Calais
Latitude
North of
the Equator
57/60 or 57
minutes
50

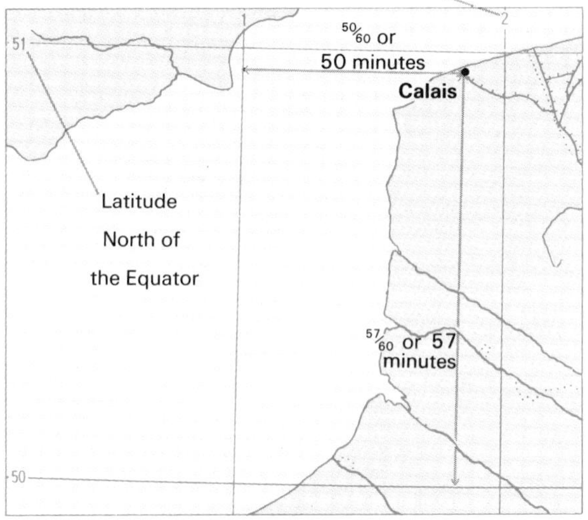

Calais 34 50 57 N 1 50 E
page latitude longitude

The following is a list of the principal abbreviations used in the Index.

A.S.S.R. – Autonomous Soviet Socialist Republic
Afg. – Afghanistan
Afr. – Africa
Alb. – Albania
Alg. – Algeria
Am. – America
Ant. – Antarctica
Arch. – Archipelago
Arg. – Argentina
Atl. Oc. – Atlantic Ocean
B. – Bay
B. Faso – Burkina Faso
Barb. – Barbados
Berm. – Bermuda
Bol. – Bolivia
Bots. – Botswana
Bulg. – Bulgaria
Bur. – Burma
C. – Cape (Cap, Cabo)
C.A.R. – Central African Republic
C.R. – Costa Rica
Cam. – Cameroon
Carib. – Caribbean Sea
Chan. – Channel
Col. – Colombia
Cont. – Continent
Cr. – Creek
Cur. – Curaçao
Dom. – Dominica
Dom. Rep. – Dominican Republic
E. – East
Eq. Guin. – Equatorial Guinea
Eth. – Ethiopia
Falk. – Falkland Is.
Fr. – France
Fr. G. – French Guiana
G. – Gulf (Golf, Golfo)
Ga. – Georgia
Ger. – Germany
Gr. – Great
Green. – Greenland
Gren. – Grenada
Guad. – Guadeloupe
Guat. – Guatemala
Guin. – Guinea
Guy. – Guyana
Hond. – Honduras
Hr. – Harbour
Hts. – Heights
I. – Island (Isle, Ile, Isla)
Ill. – Illinois
Ind. – Indies
Kor. – Korea
Kuw. – Kuwait
L. – Lake (Lac, Loch, Lough, Lago)
Leb. – Lebanon
Les. – Lesotho
Lib. – Liberia
Mart. – Martinique
Mass. – Massachusetts
Maurit. – Mauritania
Minn. – Minnesota
Miss. – Mississippi
Mong. – Mongolia
Mor. – Morocco
Mt. – Mountain (Mount, Mont, Monte, Monti, Montana)
N. – North
N. Cal. – New Caledonia
Nam. – Namibia
Nic. – Nicaragua
Nig. – Nigeria
Nor. – Norway
Oc. – Oceania
P.N.G. – Papua New Guinea
P.R. – Puerto Rico
Pac. Oc. – Pacific Ocean
Pan. – Panama
Par. – Paraguay
Pen. – Peninsula
Pk. – Peak
Pt. – Point (Pointe, Punta)
Ra. – Range
Rom. – Romania
S. – South
S. Oc. – Southern Ocean
Sd. – Sound
Sene. – Senegal
Si. Arab. – Saudi Arabia
Som. – Somalia
St. L. – St. Lucia
Str. – Strait
Swaz. – Swaziland
Tanz. – Tanzania
U.A.E. – United Arab Emirates
Ven. – Venezuela
W. – West
Yem. – Yemen
Zam. – Zambia
Zim. – Zimbabwe

A

Aachen, *W. Ger.* **36** 50 47N 6 4 E
Aalborg, *Den.* **45** 57 2N 9 54 E
Aalst, *Belg.* **36** 50 56N 4 2 E
Aarhus, *Den.* **45** 56 8N 10 11 E
Ābādān, *Iran* **56** 30 22N 48 20 E
Abbey Town, *U.K.* **18** 54 50N 3 18W
Abbots Bromley, *U.K.* **14** 52 50N 1 52W
Abbots Langley, *U.K.* **15** 51 43N 0 25W
Abbotsbury, *U.K.* **14** 50 40N 2 36W
Abéché, *Chad* **79** 13 50N 20 35 E
Aberaeron, *U.K.* **17** 52 15N 4 16W
Aberdare, *U.K.* **17** 51 43N 3 27W
Aberdeen, *U.K.* **23** 57 9N 2 6W
Aberdour, *U.K.* **21** 56 2N 3 18W
Aberdovey, *U.K.* **17** 52 33N 4 3W
Aberfeldy, *U.K.* **23** 56 37N 3 50W
Aberfoyle, *U.K.* **20** 56 10N 4 23W
Abergavenny, *U.K.* **17** 51 49N 3 1W
Abergele, *U.K.* **17** 53 17N 3 35W
Aberlady, *U.K.* **21** 56 0N 2 51W
Abernethy, *U.K.* **21** 56 19N 3 18W
Aberporth, *U.K.* **17** 52 8N 4 32W
Abersoch, *U.K.* **17** 52 50N 4 30W
Abersychan, *U.K.* **17** 51 44N 3 3W
Abertillery, *U.K.* **17** 51 44N 3 9W
Aberystwyth, *U.K.* **17** 52 25N 4 6W
Abidjan, *Ivory C.* **78** 5 26N 3 58W
Abingdon, *U.K.* **14** 51 40N 1 17W
Abington, *U.K.* **21** 55 30N 3 42W
Aboyne, *U.K.* **23** 57 4N 2 48W
Abū Dhabī, *U.A.E.* **57** 24 28N 54 36 E
Acapulco, *Mex.* **94** 16 51N 99 56W
Accra, *Ghana* **78** 5 35N 0 6W
Accrington, *U.K.* **18** 53 46N 2 22W
Achill Hd., *Ire.* **24** 53 59N 10 15W
Achill I., *Ire.* **24** 53 58N 10 5W
Achinsk, *U.S.S.R.* **49** 56 20N 90 20 E
Achnasheen, *U.K.* **22** 57 35N 5 5W
Acklins I., *Baham.* **95** 22 30N 74 0W
Acle, *U.K.* **15** 52 38N 1 32 E
Aconcagua, Cerro, *Arg.* **102** 32 39S 70 0W
Acre, *Isr.* **57** 32 55N 35 4 E
Acton Burnell, *U.K.* **14** 52 37N 2 41W
Adamaoua Plateau, *Cam.* **80** 7 20N 12 20 E
Adam's Bridge, *Sri L.* **58** 9 15N 79 40 E
Adana, *Turk.* **47** 37 0N 35 16 E
Adapazarı, *Turk.* **47** 40 48N 30 25 E
Addis Ababa, *Eth.* **79** 9 2N 38 42 E
Addlestone, *U.K.* **15** 51 22N 0 30W
Adelaide, *Austral.* **67** 34 52S 138 30 E
Adélie Land, *Ant.* **103** 68 0S 140 0 E
Aden, *S. Yem.* **56** 12 45N 45 0 E
Aden, G. of, *Asia* **56** 13 0N 50 0 E
Adirondack Mts., *U.S.A.* **93** 44 0N 74 15W
Admiralty Is., *P.N.G.* **64** 2 0S 147 0 E
Adrar, *Alg.* **78** 27 51N 0 11W
Adriatic Sea, *Europe* **40** 43 0N 16 0 E
Adwick le Street, *U.K.* **19** 53 35N 1 12W
Ægean Sea, *Europe* **41** 37 0N 25 0 E
Afghanistan ■, *Asia* **57** 33 0N 65 0 E
Agadès, *Niger* **78** 16 58N 7 59 E
Agadir, *Mor.* **78** 30 28N 9 35W
Agartala, *India* **59** 23 50N 91 23 E
Agra, *India* **58** 27 17N 77 58 E
Agrigento, *It.* **40** 37 19N 13 33 E
Aguascalientes, *Mex.* **94** 21 53N 102 12W
Ahmadabad, *India* **58** 23 0N 72 40 E
Ahvāz, *Iran* **56** 31 20N 48 40 E
Ahvenanmaa = Åland, *Fin.* **45** 60 15N 20 0 E
Ailsa Craig, *U.K.* **20** 55 15N 5 7W
Ainsdale, *U.K.* **18** 53 37N 3 2W
Airdrie, *U.K.* **21** 55 53N 3 57W
Aire →, *U.K.* **19** 53 42N 0 55W
Aisgill, *U.K.* **18** 54 23N 2 21W
Aix-en-Provence, *Fr.* **35** 43 32N 5 27 E
Ajaccio, *Fr.* **35** 41 55N 8 40 E
Akashi, *Jap.* **62** 34 45N 135 0 E
Akita, *Jap.* **62** 39 45N 140 7 E
Akranes, *Ice.* **44** 64 19N 21 58W
Akron, *U.S.A.* **92** 41 7N 81 31W
Aktyubinsk, *U.S.S.R.* **47** 50 17N 57 10 E
Akure, *Nig.* **78** 7 15N 5 5 E
Akureyri, *Ice.* **44** 65 40N 18 6W
Al Ḥudaydah, *Yem.* **56** 14 50N 43 0 E
Al Hūfuf, *Si. Arab.* **56** 25 25N 49 45 E
Al Jawf, *Si. Arab.* **56** 29 55N 39 40 E
Al Qaṭīf, *Si. Arab.* **56** 26 35N 50 0 E
Al Qunaytirah, *Syria* **57** 32 55N 35 45 E
Alabama □, *U.S.A.* **91** 33 0N 87 0W
Åland, *Fin.* **45** 60 15N 20 0 E
Alaska □, *U.S.A.* **88** 65 0N 150 0W
Alaska, G. of, *Pac. Oc.* **88** 58 0N 145 0W
Alaska Pen., *U.S.A.* **88** 56 0N 160 0W
Alaska Range, *U.S.A.* **88** 62 50N 151 0W
Alba Iulia, *Rom.* **43** 46 8N 23 39 E
Albacete, *Sp.* **37** 39 0N 1 50W
Albania ■, *Europe* **41** 41 0N 20 0 E
Albany, *Austral.* **66** 35 1S 117 58 E
Albany, *Ga., U.S.A.* **90** 31 40N 84 10W
Albany, *N.Y., U.S.A.* **93** 42 35N 73 47W
Albany →, *Canada* **89** 52 17N 81 31W
Alberta □, *Canada* **88** 54 40N 115 0W
Albrighton, *U.K.* **14** 52 38N 2 17W
Albuquerque, *U.S.A.* **90** 35 5N 106 47W
Albury, *Austral.* **70** 36 3S 146 56 E
Alcalá de Henares, *Sp.* **37** 40 28N 3 22W
Alcester, *U.K.* **14** 52 13N 1 52W
Aldan →, *U.S.S.R.* **49** 63 28N 129 35 E
Aldborough, *U.K.* **19** 54 6N 1 21W
Aldbourne, *U.K.* **14** 51 28N 1 38W
Aldbrough, *U.K.* **19** 53 50N 0 7W
Aldeburgh, *U.K.* **15** 52 9N 1 35 E
Alderbury, *U.K.* **14** 51 4N 1 45W
Alderley Edge, *U.K.* **18** 53 18N 2 15W
Alderney, *U.K.* **34** 49 42N 2 12W
Aldershot, *U.K.* **15** 51 15N 0 43W
Aldingham, *U.K.* **18** 54 8N 3 3W
Aleppo, *Syria* **56** 36 10N 37 15 E
Alessándria, *It.* **40** 44 54N 8 37 E
Ålesund, *Nor.* **44** 62 28N 6 12 E
Aleutian Is., *Pac. Oc.* **88** 52 0N 175 0W
Alexander Arch., *U.S.A.* **88** 57 0N 135 0W
Alexandria, *Egypt* **79** 31 0N 30 0 E
Alexandria, *U.K.* **20** 55 59N 4 40W
Alexandria, *U.S.A.* **90** 31 20N 92 30W
Alford, *Grampian, U.K.* **23** 57 13N 2 42W
Alford, *Lincs., U.K.* **19** 53 16N 0 10 E
Alfreton, *U.K.* **19** 53 6N 1 22W
Alfriston, *U.K.* **15** 50 48N 0 10 E
Algarve, *Port.* **37** 36 58N 8 20W
Algeciras, *Sp.* **37** 36 9N 5 28W
Algeria ■, *Africa* **78** 35 10N 3 11 E
Algiers, *Alg.* **78** 36 42N 3 8 E
Alicante, *Sp.* **37** 38 23N 0 30W
Alice Springs, *Austral.* **66** 23 40S 133 50 E
Aligarh, *India* **58** 27 55N 78 10 E
Alkmaar, *Neth.* **36** 52 37N 4 45 E
Allahabad, *India* **59** 25 25N 81 58 E
Allegheny Mts., *U.S.A.* **92** 38 0N 80 0W
Allen →, *U.K.* **21** 54 53N 2 13W
Allen, Bog of, *Ire.* **25** 53 15N 7 0W
Allen, L., *Ire.* **24** 54 12N 8 5W
Allendale, *U.K.* **21** 54 55N 2 15W
Allenheads, *U.K.* **21** 54 49N 2 12W
Allentown, *U.S.A.* **93** 40 36N 75 30W
Alloa, *U.K.* **21** 56 7N 3 49W
Allonby, *U.K.* **18** 54 45N 3 27W
Alma Ata, *U.S.S.R.* **48** 43 15N 76 57 E
Almelo, *Neth.* **36** 52 22N 6 42 E
Almería, *Sp.* **37** 36 52N 2 27W
Almond →, *U.K.* **21** 56 27N 3 27W
Almondsbury, *U.K.* **14** 51 33N 2 34W
Aln →, *U.K.* **21** 55 27N 1 32W
Alness, *U.K.* **23** 57 41N 4 15W
Alnmouth, *U.K.* **21** 55 24N 1 37W
Alnwick, *U.K.* **19** 55 25N 1 42W
Alphen, *Neth.* **36** 51 29N 4 58 E
Alphington, *U.K.* **16** 50 41N 3 32W
Alps, *Europe* **42** 47 0N 8 0 E
Alrewas, *U.K.* **14** 52 43N 1 44W
Alsager, *U.K.* **18** 53 7N 2 20W
Alston, *U.K.* **18** 54 48N 2 26W
Altai Mts., *Asia* **60** 46 40N 92 45 E
Altarnun, *U.K.* **16** 50 35N 4 30W
Altay, *China* **60** 47 48N 88 10 E
Alton, *U.K.* **15** 51 8N 0 59W
Altoona, *U.S.A.* **92** 40 32N 78 24W
Altrincham, *U.K.* **18** 53 25N 2 21W
Altun Shan, *China* **60** 38 30N 88 0 E
Alva, *U.K.* **21** 56 9N 3 49W
Alvechurch, *U.K.* **14** 52 22N 1 58W
Alwinton, *U.K.* **21** 55 20N 2 7W
Alyth, *U.K.* **23** 56 38N 3 15W
Amadjuak L., *Canada* **89** 65 0N 71 8W
Amagasaki, *Jap.* **62** 34 42N 135 20 E
Amarillo, *U.S.A.* **90** 35 14N 101 46W
Amazon →, *S. Am.* **100** 0 5S 50 0W
Amazonas □, *Brazil* **101** 4 0S 62 0W
Amble, *U.K.* **21** 55 20N 1 36W
Ambleside, *U.K.* **18** 54 26N 2 58W
Ambon, *Indon.* **63** 3 35S 128 20 E
American Samoa ■, *Pac. Oc.* **65** 14 20S 170 40W
Amersfoort, *Neth.* **36** 52 9N 5 23 E
Amersham, *U.K.* **15** 51 40N 0 38W
Amesbury, *U.K.* **14** 51 10N 1 46W
Amiens, *Fr.* **34** 49 54N 2 16 E
Amlwch, *U.K.* **17** 53 24N 4 21W
'Ammān, *Jord.* **57** 31 57N 35 52 E
Ammanford, *U.K.* **17** 51 48N 4 0W
Amoy = Xiamen, *China* **61** 24 25N 118 4 E
Ampleforth, *U.K.* **19** 54 13N 1 8W
Ampthill, *U.K.* **15** 52 3N 0 30W
Amravati, *India* **58** 20 55N 77 45 E
Amritsar, *India* **58** 31 35N 74 57 E
Amsterdam, *Neth.* **36** 52 23N 4 54 E
Amudarya →, *U.S.S.R.* **48** 43 40N 59 0 E
Amundsen Gulf, *Canada* **88** 71 0N 124 0W
Amundsen Sea, *Ant.* **103** 72 0S 115 0W
Amur →, *U.S.S.R.* **49** 52 56N 141 10 E
An Nafūd, *Si. Arab.* **56** 28 15N 41 0 E
An Najaf, *Iraq* **56** 32 3N 44 15 E
An Uaimh, *Ire.* **24** 53 39N 6 40W
Anadyr, G. of, *U.S.S.R.* **49** 64 0N 180 0 E
Anaheim, *U.S.A.* **90** 33 50N 118 0W
Anápolis, *Brazil* **101** 16 15S 48 50W
Anatolia, *Turk.* **47** 38 0N 30 0 E
Ancaster, *U.K.* **19** 52 59N 0 32W
Ancholme →, *U.K.* **19** 53 42N 0 32W
Anchorage, *U.S.A.* **88** 61 10N 149 50W
Ancona, *It.* **40** 43 37N 13 30 E
Ancrum, *U.K.* **21** 55 31N 2 35W
Anda, *China* **61** 46 24N 125 19 E
Andalusia, Reg., *Sp.* **37** 37 35N 5 0W
Andaman Is., *India* **51** 12 30N 92 30 E
Anderlecht, *Belg.* **36** 50 50N 4 19 E
Andes, *S. Am.* **96** 20 0S 68 0W
Andhra Pradesh □, *India* **58** 16 0N 79 0 E
Andizhan, *U.S.S.R.* **48** 41 10N 72 0 E
Andorra ■, *Europe* **35** 42 30N 1 30 E
Andover, *U.K.* **14** 51 13N 1 29W
Andreanof Is., *Pac. Oc.* **88** 52 0N 178 0W
Andreas, *U.K.* **18** 54 23N 4 25W
Ándria, *It.* **40** 41 13N 16 17 E
Andropov, *U.S.S.R.* **46** 58 5N 38 50 E
Andros I., *Baham.* **95** 24 30N 78 0W
Angara →, *U.S.S.R.* **49** 58 30N 97 0 E
Angarsk, *U.S.S.R.* **49** 52 30N 104 0 E
Angers, *Fr.* **34** 47 30N 0 35W
Anglesey, *U.K.* **17** 53 17N 4 20W
Angmagssalik, *Green.* **89** 65 40N 37 20W
Angmering, *U.K.* **15** 50 48N 0 28W
Angola ■, *Africa* **81** 12 0S 18 0 E
Angoulême, *Fr.* **35** 45 39N 0 10 E
Anguilla, *W. Ind.* **94** 18 14N 63 5W
Angus, Braes of, *U.K.* **23** 56 51N 3 10W
Anhui □, *China* **61** 32 0N 117 0 E
Anjou, *Fr.* **34** 47 20N 0 15W
Ankara, *Turk.* **47** 40 0N 32 54 E
Ann Arbor, *U.S.A.* **92** 42 17N 83 45W
Annaba, *Alg.* **78** 36 50N 7 46 E
Annalee →, *Ire.* **24** 54 3N 7 15W
Annan, *U.K.* **21** 55 0N 3 17W
Annan →, *U.K.* **21** 54 58N 3 18W
Annandale, *U.K.* **21** 55 10N 3 25W
Annecy, *Fr.* **35** 45 55N 6 8 E
Annfield Plain, *U.K.* **19** 54 52N 1 45W
Annobón, *Atl. Oc.* **73** 1 25S 5 36 E
Anshan, *China* **61** 41 5N 122 58 E
Anshun, *China* **60** 26 18N 105 57 E
Anstey, *U.K.* **14** 52 41N 1 14W
Anstruther, *U.K.* **21** 56 14N 2 40W
Antalya, *Turk.* **47** 36 52N 30 45 E
Antananarivo, *Madag.* **81** 18 55S 47 31 E
Antarctic Pen., *Ant.* **103** 67 0S 60 0W
Antarctica, *Cont.* **103** 90 0S 0 0 E
Anticosti, I. d', *Canada* **93** 49 30N 63 0W
Antigua & Barbuda ■, *W. Ind.* **94** 17 20N 61 48W
Antofagasta, *Chile* **102** 23 50S 70 30W
Antony, *U.K.* **16** 50 22N 4 13W
Antrim, *U.K.* **24** 54 43N 6 13W
Antrim □, *U.K.* **24** 54 55N 6 20W
Antrim, Mts. of, *U.K.* **24** 54 57N 6 8W
Antsiranana, *Madag.* **81** 12 25S 49 20 E
Antwerp, *Belg.* **36** 51 13N 4 25 E
Anyang, *China* **61** 36 5N 114 21 E
Anzhero-Sudzhensk, *U.S.S.R.* **48** 56 10N 86 0 E
Aomori, *Jap.* **62** 40 45N 140 45 E
Apeldoorn, *Neth.* **36** 52 13N 5 57 E
Apennines, *It.* **40** 44 20N 10 20 E
Appalachian Mts., *U.S.A.* **91** 38 0N 80 0W
Appleby, *U.K.* **18** 54 35N 2 29W
Appledore, *Devon, U.K.* **16** 51 3N 4 12W
Appledore, *Kent, U.K.* **15** 51 2N 0 47 E
Arabia, *Asia* **50** 25 0N 45 0 E
Arabian Desert, *Egypt* **79** 26 0N 33 30 E
Arabian Sea, *Ind. Oc.* **50** 16 0N 65 0 E
Aracaju, *Brazil* **101** 10 55S 37 4W
Araçatuba, *Brazil* **101** 21 10S 50 30W
Arad, *Rom.* **43** 46 10N 21 20 E
Arafura Sea, *E. Ind.* **64** 9 0S 135 0 E
Aragón □, *Sp.* **37** 41 25N 1 0W
Araguaia →, *Brazil* **101** 5 21S 48 41W
Arakan Yoma, *Burma* **59** 20 0N 94 40 E
Aral Sea, *U.S.S.R.* **48** 44 30N 60 0 E
Aralsk, *U.S.S.R.* **48** 46 50N 61 20 E
Aran I., *Ire.* **24** 55 0N 8 30W
Aran Is., *Ire.* **25** 53 5N 9 42W
Arapiraca, *Brazil* **101** 9 45S 36 39W
Ararat, *Austral.* **70** 37 16S 143 0 E
Arbroath, *U.K.* **23** 56 34N 2 35W
Arctic Ocean, *Arctic* **103** 78 0N 160 0W
Arctic Red River, *Canada* **88** 67 15N 134 0W
Ardbeg, *U.K.* **20** 55 38N 6 6W
Ardchyle, *U.K.* **20** 56 26N 4 24W
Ardee, *Ire.* **24** 53 51N 6 32W
Ardennes, *Belg.* **36** 50 0N 5 10 E
Ardentinny, *U.K.* **20** 56 3N 4 56W
Ardgour, *U.K.* **22** 56 45N 5 25W
Ardingly, *U.K.* **15** 51 3N 0 3W
Ardlui, *U.K.* **20** 56 19N 4 43W
Ardmore Pt., *U.K.* **20** 55 40N 6 0W
Ardnamurchan, Pt. of, *U.K.* **22** 56 44N 6 14W
Ardnave Pt., *U.K.* **20** 55 54N 6 20W
Ardrishaig, *U.K.* **20** 56 0N 5 27W
Ardrossan, *U.K.* **20** 55 39N 4 50W
Ards □, *U.K.* **24** 54 35N 5 30W
Ards Pen., *U.K.* **24** 54 30N 5 25W
Ardvasar, *U.K.* **22** 57 5N 5 54W
Arendal, *Nor.* **45** 58 28N 8 46 E
Arequipa, *Peru* **100** 16 20S 71 30W
Argentina ■, *S. Am.* **102** 35 0S 66 0W
Argyll, *U.K.* **20** 56 14N 5 10W
Arica, *Chile* **100** 18 32S 70 20W
Arima, *Trin. & Tob.* **94** 10 38N 61 17W
Arinagour, *U.K.* **20** 56 38N 6 31W
Arisaig, *U.K.* **22** 56 55N 5 50W
Arizona □, *U.S.A.* **90** 34 20N 111 30W
Arkaig, L., *U.K.* **22** 56 58N 5 10W
Arkansas □, *U.S.A.* **91** 35 0N 92 30W
Arkansas →, *U.S.A.* **91** 33 48N 91 4W
Arkhangelsk, *U.S.S.R.* **46** 64 40N 41 0 E
Arkle →, *U.K.* **18** 54 25N 1 55W
Arklow, *Ire.* **25** 52 48N 6 10W
Arles, *Fr.* **35** 43 41N 4 40 E
Arlon, *Belg.* **36** 49 42N 5 49 E
Armadale, *U.K.* **21** 55 54N 3 42W
Armagh, *U.K.* **24** 54 22N 6 40W
Armagh □, *U.K.* **24** 54 18N 6 37W
Armenia, *Col.* **100** 4 35N 75 45W
Armenia □, *U.S.S.R.* **47** 40 0N 41 0 E
Armidale, *Austral.* **67** 30 30S 151 40 E
Arnhem, *Neth.* **36** 51 58N 5 55 E
Arnhem Land, *Austral.* **66** 13 10S 134 30 E
Arnold, *U.K.* **19** 53 0N 1 8W
Arnside, *U.K.* **18** 54 12N 2 49W
Arran, *U.K.* **20** 55 34N 5 12W
Arras, *Fr.* **34** 50 17N 2 46 E
Arrochar, *U.K.* **20** 56 12N 4 45W
Arrow, L., *Ire.* **24** 54 3N 8 20W
Arun →, *U.K.* **15** 50 48N 0 33W
Arunachal Pradesh □, *India* **59** 28 0N 95 0 E
Arundel, *U.K.* **15** 50 52N 0 32W
Arusha, *Tanz.* **80** 3 20S 36 40 E
As Salt, *Jord.* **57** 32 2N 35 43 E
As Summān, *Si. Arab.* **56** 25 0N 47 0 E
Asahigawa, *Jap.* **62** 43 46N 142 22 E
Asansol, *India* **59** 23 40N 87 1 E
Ascension I., *Atl. Oc.* **128** 8 0S 14 15W
Ascot, *U.K.* **15** 51 24N 0 41W
Asfordby, *U.K.* **15** 52 45N 0 57W
Ash, *Kent, U.K.* **15** 51 17N 1 16 E
Ash, *Surrey, U.K.* **15** 51 14N 0 43W
Ashbourne, *U.K.* **19** 53 2N 1 44W
Ashburton, *N.Z.* **71** 43 53S 171 48 E
Ashburton, *U.K.* **16** 50 31N 3 45W
Ashburton →, *Austral.* **66** 21 40S 114 56 E
Ashby-de-la-Zouch, *U.K.* **14** 52 45N 1 29W
Ashchurch, *U.K.* **14** 52 0N 2 7W
Ashdown Forest, *U.K.* **15** 51 4N 0 2 E
Ashford, *Derby, U.K.* **19** 53 13N 1 43W
Ashford, *Kent, U.K.* **15** 51 8N 0 53 E
Ashington, *U.K.* **21** 55 12N 1 35W
Ashkhabad, *U.S.S.R.* **48** 38 0N 57 50 E
Ashq'elon, *Isr.* **57** 31 42N 34 35 E
Ashton-in-Makerfield, *U.K.* **18** 53 29N 2 39W
Ashton-under-Lyne, *U.K.* **18** 53 30N 2 8W
Ashurstwood, *U.K.* **15** 51 6N 0 2 E
Ashwater, *U.K.* **16** 50 43N 4 18W
Ashwick, *U.K.* **14** 51 13N 2 31W
'Asīr □, *Si. Arab.* **56** 18 40N 42 30 E
Asir, Ras, *Som.* **73** 11 55N 51 10 E
Askrigg, *U.K.* **18** 54 19N 2 6W
Aslackby, *U.K.* **19** 52 53N 0 23W
Asmera, *Eth.* **79** 15 19N 38 55 E
Aspatria, *U.K.* **18** 54 45N 3 20W
Assam □, *India* **59** 26 0N 93 0 E
Assen, *Neth.* **36** 53 0N 6 35 E
Assynt, L., *U.K.* **22** 58 25N 5 15W
Asti, *It.* **40** 44 54N 8 11 E
Aston Clinton, *U.K.* **15** 51 48N 0 44W
Astrakhan, *U.S.S.R.* **47** 46 25N 48 5 E
Astwood Bank, *U.K.* **14** 52 15N 1 55W
Asunción, *Par.* **102** 25 10S 57 30W
Aswân, *Egypt* **79** 24 4N 32 57 E
Atacama, Desierto de, *Chile* **102** 24 0S 69 20W
Atbara, *Sudan* **79** 17 42N 33 59 E
Athabasca, L., *Canada* **88** 59 15N 109 15W
Athboy, *Ire.* **24** 53 37N 6 55W
Athenry, *Ire.* **25** 53 18N 8 45W
Athens, *Greece* **41** 37 58N 23 46 E
Atherstone, *U.K.* **14** 52 35N 1 32W
Atherton, *U.K.* **18** 53 32N 2 30W
Athínai = Athens, *Greece* **41** 37 58N 23 46 E
Athlone, *Ire.* **24** 53 26N 7 57W
Atholl, Forest of, *U.K.* **23** 56 51N 3 50W
Athy, *Ire.* **25** 53 0N 7 0W
Atlanta, *U.S.A.* **91** 33 50N 84 24W
Atlantic City, *U.S.A.* **93** 39 25N 74 25W
Atlantic Ocean **128** 0 0 20 0W
Atlas Mts., *Mor.* **72** 32 30N 5 0W
Attleborough, *U.K.* **15** 52 32N 1 1 E
Auchencairn, *U.K.* **21** 54 51N 3 52W
Auchinleck, *U.K.* **20** 55 28N 4 18W
Auchterarder, *U.K.* **21** 56 18N 3 43W
Auchterderran, *U.K.* **21** 56 8N 3 16W
Auchtermuchty, *U.K.* **21** 56 18N 3 15W
Auchtertyre, *U.K.* **22** 57 17N 5 35W
Auckland, *N.Z.* **71** 36 52S 174 46 E
Audlem, *U.K.* **18** 52 59N 2 31W
Aughnacloy, *U.K.* **24** 54 25N 6 58W
Augsburg, *W. Ger.* **42** 48 22N 10 54 E
Augusta, *U.S.A.* **90** 33 29N 81 59W
Aurangabad, *India* **58** 19 50N 75 23 E
Aurora, *U.S.A.* **92** 41 42N 88 12W
Austin, *U.S.A.* **90** 30 20N 97 45W
Australia ■, *Oc.* **66** 23 0S 135 0 E
Australian Alps, *Austral.* **70** 36 30S 148 30 E
Australian Cap. Terr. □, *Austral.* **70** 35 30S 149 0 E
Austria ■, *Europe* **42** 47 0N 14 0 E
Auxerre, *Fr.* **34** 47 48N 3 32 E

Place	Page	Lat.	Long.
Avebury, *U.K.*	**14**	51 25N	1 52W
Avellino, *It.*	**40**	40 54N	14 46 E
Aveton Gifford, *U.K.*	**16**	50 17N	3 51W
Avich, L., *U.K.*	**20**	56 17N	5 25W
Aviemore, *U.K.*	**23**	57 11N	3 50W
Avignon, *Fr.*	**35**	43 57N	4 50 E
Ávila, *Sp.*	**37**	40 39N	4 43W
Avoca, *Ire.*	**25**	52 52N	6 13W
Avon □, *U.K.*	**14**	51 30N	2 40W
Avon →, *Avon, U.K.*	**14**	51 30N	2 43W
Avon →, *Hants., U.K.*	**14**	50 44N	1 45W
Avon →, *Warwick, U.K.*	**14**	52 0N	2 9W
Avonmouth, *U.K.*	**14**	51 30N	2 42W
Awe, L., *U.K.*	**20**	56 15N	5 15W
Axbridge, *U.K.*	**14**	51 17N	2 50W
Axe →, *U.K.*	**14**	51 17N	2 52W
Axe Edge, *U.K.*	**18**	53 14N	1 59W
Axholme, Isle of, *U.K.*	**19**	53 30N	0 55W
Axminster, *U.K.*	**16**	50 47N	3 1W
Axmouth, *U.K.*	**16**	50 43N	3 2W
Ayers Rock, *Austral.*	**66**	25 23S	131 5 E
Aylesbury, *U.K.*	**15**	51 48N	0 49W
Aylesford, *U.K.*	**15**	51 18N	0 29 E
Aylsham, *U.K.*	**15**	52 48N	1 16 E
Aynho, *U.K.*	**14**	51 59N	1 15W
Ayr, *U.K.*	**20**	55 28N	4 37W
Ayr →, *U.K.*	**20**	55 29N	4 40W
Ayr, Heads of, *U.K.*	**20**	55 25N	4 43W
Ayre, Pt. of, *U.K.*	**18**	54 27N	4 21W
Aysgarth, *U.K.*	**18**	54 18N	2 0W
Ayton, *Borders, U.K.*	**21**	55 51N	2 6W
Ayton, *N. Yorks., U.K.*	**19**	54 15N	0 29W
Az Zarqā, *Jord.*	**57**	32 5N	36 4 E
Azores, *Atl. Oc.*	**128**	38 44N	29 0W
Azov Sea, *U.S.S.R.*	**47**	46 0N	36 30 E
Azuero, Pen. de, *Pan.*	**95**	7 30N	80 30W

B

Place	Page	Lat.	Long.
Bābol, *Iran*	**56**	36 40N	52 50 E
Bacabal, *Brazil*	**101**	4 15S	44 45W
Bacău, *Rom.*	**43**	46 35N	26 55 E
Back, *U.K.*	**22**	58 17N	6 20W
Bacolod, *Phil.*	**63**	10 40N	122 57 E
Bacton, *U.K.*	**15**	52 50N	1 29 E
Bacup, *U.K.*	**18**	53 42N	2 12W
Badajoz, *Sp.*	**37**	38 50N	6 59W
Badalona, *Sp.*	**37**	41 26N	2 15 E
Baffin B., *Canada*	**89**	72 0N	64 0W
Baffin I., *Canada*	**89**	68 0N	75 0W
Bagenalstown = Muine Bheag, *Ire.*	**25**	52 42N	6 57W
Baggy Pt., *U.K.*	**16**	51 11N	4 12W
Baghdād, *Iraq*	**56**	33 20N	44 30 E
Bagshot, *U.K.*	**15**	51 22N	0 41W
Bahamas ■, *Atl. Oc.*	**95**	24 0N	75 0W
Bahawalpur, *Pak.*	**58**	29 24N	71 40 E
Bahía = Salvador, *Brazil*	**101**	13 0S	38 30W
Bahía Blanca, *Arg.*	**102**	38 35S	62 13W
Bahrain ■, *Asia*	**56**	26 0N	50 35 E
Baia Mare, *Rom.*	**43**	47 40N	23 35 E
Baildon, *U.K.*	**19**	53 52N	1 46W
Baile Atha Cliath = Dublin, *Ire.*	**24**	53 20N	6 18W
Bain →, *U.K.*	**19**	53 10N	0 15W
Bainbridge, *U.K.*	**18**	54 18N	2 7W
Bakersfield, *U.S.A.*	**90**	35 25N	119 0W
Bakewell, *U.K.*	**19**	53 13N	1 40W
Bākhtarān, *Iran*	**56**	34 23N	47 0 E
Baku, *U.S.S.R.*	**47**	40 25N	49 45 E
Bala, *U.K.*	**17**	52 54N	3 36W
Bala, L. = Tegid, L., *U.K.*	**17**	52 53N	3 38W
Balallan, *U.K.*	**22**	58 5N	6 35W
Balaton, *Hung.*	**43**	46 50N	17 40 E
Balbeggie, *U.K.*	**21**	56 26N	3 19W
Balboa, *Pan.*	**94**	9 0N	79 30W
Balbriggan, *Ire.*	**24**	53 35N	6 10W
Balderton, *U.K.*	**19**	53 3N	0 46W
Baldock, *U.K.*	**15**	51 59N	0 11W
Balearic Is., *Sp.*	**37**	39 30N	3 0 E
Balfron, *U.K.*	**20**	56 4N	4 20W
Bali □, *Indon.*	**63**	8 20S	115 0 E
Balikesir, *Turk.*	**47**	39 35N	27 58 E
Balikpapan, *Indon.*	**63**	1 10S	116 55 E
Balkan Mts., *Bulg.*	**41**	43 15N	23 0 E
Balkan Pen., *Europe*	**26**	42 0N	22 0 E
Balkhash, L., *U.S.S.R.*	**48**	46 0N	74 50 E
Ballachulish, *U.K.*	**22**	56 40N	5 10W
Ballantrae, *U.K.*	**20**	55 6N	5 0W
Ballarat, *Austral.*	**70**	37 33S	143 50 E
Ballasalla, *U.K.*	**18**	54 7N	4 36W
Ballater, *U.K.*	**23**	57 2N	3 2W
Ballaugh, *U.K.*	**18**	54 20N	4 32W
Ballina, *Mayo, Ire.*	**24**	54 7N	9 10W
Ballina, *Tipp., Ire.*	**25**	52 49N	8 27W
Ballinasloe, *Ire.*	**25**	53 20N	8 12W
Ballinrobe, *Ire.*	**24**	53 36N	9 13W
Ballinskelligs B., *Ire.*	**25**	51 46N	10 11W
Balloch, *U.K.*	**20**	56 0N	4 35W
Ballycastle, *U.K.*	**24**	55 12N	6 15W
Ballyclare, *U.K.*	**24**	54 46N	6 0W
Ballymena, *U.K.*	**24**	54 53N	6 18W
Ballymena □, *U.K.*	**24**	54 53N	6 18W
Ballymoney, *U.K.*	**24**	55 5N	6 30W
Ballymoney □, *U.K.*	**24**	55 5N	6 23W
Ballynahinch, *U.K.*	**24**	54 24N	5 55W
Ballyshannon, *Ire.*	**24**	54 30N	8 10W
Balmaclellan, *U.K.*	**21**	55 6N	4 5W
Balmoral, *U.K.*	**23**	57 3N	3 13W
Balquhidder, *U.K.*	**20**	56 22N	4 22W
Balsas →, *Mex.*	**94**	17 55N	102 10W
Baltic Sea, *Europe*	**45**	56 0N	20 0 E
Baltimore, *Ire.*	**25**	51 29N	9 22W
Baltimore, *U.S.A.*	**92**	39 18N	76 37W
Baluchistan □, *Pak.*	**58**	27 30N	65 0 E
Balurghat, *India*	**59**	25 15N	88 44 E
Balvicar, *U.K.*	**20**	56 17N	5 38W
Bamako, *Mali*	**78**	12 34N	7 55W
Bamberg, *W. Ger.*	**42**	49 54N	10 53 E
Bamburgh, *U.K.*	**21**	55 36N	1 42W
Bamenda, *Cam.*	**80**	5 57N	10 11 E
Bamford, *U.K.*	**19**	53 21N	1 41W
Bampton, *Devon, U.K.*	**16**	50 59N	3 29W
Bampton, *Oxon., U.K.*	**14**	51 44N	1 33W
Banaras = Varanasi, *India*	**59**	25 22N	83 0 E
Banbridge, *U.K.*	**24**	54 21N	6 17W
Banbridge □, *U.K.*	**24**	54 21N	6 16W
Banbury, *U.K.*	**14**	52 4N	1 21W
Banchory, *U.K.*	**23**	57 3N	2 30W
Banda Aceh, *Indon.*	**63**	5 35N	95 20 E
Banda Sea, *Indon.*	**63**	6 0S	130 0 E
Bandār 'Abbās, *Iran*	**57**	27 15N	56 15 E
Bandar Seri Begawan, *Brunei*	**63**	4 52N	115 0 E
Bandon, *Ire.*	**25**	51 44N	8 45W
Bandon →, *Ire.*	**25**	51 40N	8 41W
Bandundu, *Zaïre*	**80**	3 15S	17 22 E
Bandung, *Indon.*	**63**	6 54S	107 36 E
Banff, *U.K.*	**23**	57 40N	2 32W
Bangalore, *India*	**58**	12 59N	77 40 E
Bangka, Selat, *Indon.*	**63**	2 30S	105 30 E
Bangkok, *Thai.*	**63**	13 45N	100 35 E
Bangladesh ■, *Asia*	**59**	24 0N	90 0 E
Bangor, *N. Ireland, U.K.*	**24**	54 40N	5 40W
Bangor, *Wales, U.K.*	**17**	53 13N	4 9W
Bangor, *U.S.A.*	**93**	44 48N	68 42W
Bangui, *C.A.R.*	**80**	4 23N	18 35 E
Banham, *U.K.*	**15**	52 27N	1 3 E
Banjarmasin, *Indon.*	**63**	3 20S	114 35 E
Banjul, *Gambia*	**78**	13 28N	16 40W
Bankend, *U.K.*	**21**	55 2N	3 31W
Bankfoot, *U.K.*	**21**	56 30N	3 31W
Banks I., *Canada*	**88**	73 15N	121 30W
Banks Pen., *N.Z.*	**71**	43 45S	173 15 E
Bann →, *Down, U.K.*	**24**	54 30N	6 31W
Bann →, *Londonderry, U.K.*	**24**	55 10N	6 34W
Bannockburn, *U.K.*	**21**	56 5N	3 55W
Bantry, *Ire.*	**25**	51 40N	9 28W
Bantry, B., *Ire.*	**25**	51 35N	9 50W
Banwell, *U.K.*	**14**	51 19N	2 51W
Baoding, *China*	**61**	38 50N	115 28 E
Baoji, *China*	**60**	34 20N	107 5 E
Baotou, *China*	**61**	40 32N	110 2 E
Barbados ■, *W. Ind.*	**94**	13 0N	59 30W
Barcaldine, *Austral.*	**67**	23 43S	145 6 E
Barcelona, *Sp.*	**37**	41 21N	2 10 E
Bardney, *U.K.*	**19**	53 13N	0 19W
Bardsey I., *U.K.*	**17**	52 46N	4 47W
Bareilly, *India*	**58**	28 22N	79 27 E
Barents Sea, *Arctic*	**48**	73 0N	39 0 E
Barford, *U.K.*	**14**	52 15N	1 35W
Bargoed, *U.K.*	**17**	51 42N	3 22W
Barham, *U.K.*	**15**	51 12N	1 10 E
Bari, *It.*	**40**	41 6N	16 52 E
Bari Doab, *Pak.*	**58**	30 20N	73 0 E
Barisal, *Bangla.*	**59**	22 45N	90 20 E
Barisan Mts., *Indon.*	**63**	3 30S	102 15 E
Barking, *U.K.*	**15**	51 31N	0 10 E
Barkly Tableland, *Austral.*	**67**	17 50S	136 40 E
Barlborough, *U.K.*	**19**	53 17N	1 17W
Barlby, *U.K.*	**19**	53 48N	1 3W
Barletta, *It.*	**40**	41 20N	16 17 E
Barmby Moor, *U.K.*	**19**	53 55N	0 47W
Barmoor Castle, *U.K.*	**21**	55 38N	2 0W
Barmouth, *U.K.*	**17**	52 44N	4 3W
Barnard Castle, *U.K.*	**18**	54 33N	1 55W
Barnaul, *U.S.S.R.*	**48**	53 20N	83 40 E
Barnet, *U.K.*	**15**	51 37N	0 15W
Barnetby le Wold, *U.K.*	**19**	53 34N	0 24W
Barnoldswick, *U.K.*	**18**	53 55N	2 11W
Barnsley, *U.K.*	**19**	53 33N	1 29W
Barnstaple, *U.K.*	**16**	51 5N	4 3W
Barnstaple B., *U.K.*	**16**	51 5N	4 25W
Baroda = Vadodara, *India*	**58**	22 20N	73 10 E
Barquísimeto, *Ven.*	**100**	10 4N	69 19W
Barr, *U.K.*	**20**	55 13N	4 44W
Barra, *U.K.*	**22**	57 0N	7 30W
Barra, Sd. of, *U.K.*	**22**	57 4N	7 25W
Barra Hd., *U.K.*	**22**	56 47N	7 40W
Barrancabermeja, *Col.*	**100**	7 0N	73 50W
Barranquilla, *Col.*	**100**	11 0N	74 50W
Barrhead, *U.K.*	**20**	55 48N	4 23W
Barrhill, *U.K.*	**20**	55 7N	4 46W
Barrow →, *Ire.*	**25**	52 10N	6 57W
Barrow-in-Furness, *U.K.*	**18**	54 8N	3 15W
Barrow upon Humber, *U.K.*	**19**	53 41N	0 22W
Barrowford, *U.K.*	**18**	53 51N	2 14W
Barry, *S. Glam., U.K.*	**17**	51 23N	3 19W
Barry, *Tayside, U.K.*	**21**	56 29N	2 45W
Barton, *U.K.*	**19**	54 28N	1 38W
Barton-upon-Humber, *U.K.*	**19**	53 41N	0 27W
Barvas, *U.K.*	**22**	58 21N	6 31W
Barwell, *U.K.*	**14**	52 35N	1 22W
Basildon, *U.K.*	**15**	51 34N	0 29 E
Basingstoke, *U.K.*	**14**	51 15N	1 5W
Basle, *Switz.*	**42**	47 35N	7 35 E
Basra, *Iraq*	**56**	30 30N	47 50 E
Bass Rock, *U.K.*	**21**	56 5N	2 40W
Bass Str., *Austral.*	**67**	39 15S	146 30 E
Basse-Terre, *Guad.*	**94**	16 0N	61 40W
Bassein, *Burma*	**59**	16 45N	94 30 E
Bassenthwaite, L., *U.K.*	**18**	54 40N	3 14W
Basseterre, *Guad.*	**94**	17 17N	62 43W
Bastia, *Fr.*	**35**	42 40N	9 30 E
Baston, *U.K.*	**15**	52 43N	0 19W
Bata, *Eq. Guin.*	**80**	1 57N	9 50 E
Batangas, *Phil.*	**63**	13 35N	121 10 E
Bath, *U.K.*	**14**	51 22N	2 22W
Bathford, *U.K.*	**14**	51 23N	2 18W
Bathgate, *U.K.*	**21**	55 54N	3 38W
Bathurst, *Austral.*	**70**	33 25S	149 31 E
Bathurst, *Canada*	**93**	47 37N	65 43W
Batley, *U.K.*	**19**	53 43N	1 38W
Batna, *Alg.*	**78**	35 34N	6 15 E
Baton Rouge, *U.S.A.*	**91**	30 30N	91 5W
Battle, *U.K.*	**15**	50 55N	0 30 E
Batumi, *U.S.S.R.*	**47**	41 30N	41 30 E
Bauru, *Brazil*	**101**	22 10S	49 0W
Bavaria □, *W. Ger.*	**42**	49 7N	11 30 E
Bawdsey, *U.K.*	**15**	52 1N	1 27 E
Bawtry, *U.K.*	**19**	53 25N	1 1W
Bayamo, *Cuba*	**95**	20 20N	76 40W
Bayan Har Shan, *China*	**60**	34 0N	98 0 E
Bayeux, *Fr.*	**34**	49 17N	0 42W
Baykal, L., *U.S.S.R.*	**49**	53 0N	108 0 E
Bayonne, *Fr.*	**35**	43 30N	1 28W
Beachley, *U.K.*	**14**	51 37N	2 39W
Beachy Head, *U.K.*	**15**	50 44N	0 16 E
Beaconsfield, *U.K.*	**15**	51 36N	0 39W
Beadnell, *U.K.*	**21**	55 33N	1 38W
Beagle, Canal, *S. Am.*	**102**	55 0S	68 30W
Beaminster, *U.K.*	**14**	50 48N	2 44W
Bear I., *Ire.*	**25**	51 38N	9 50W
Beardmore Glacier, *Ant.*	**103**	84 30S	170 0 E
Bearsden, *U.K.*	**20**	55 55N	4 21W
Bearsted, *U.K.*	**15**	51 15N	0 35 E
Beattock, *U.K.*	**21**	55 19N	3 27W
Beaufort Sea, *Arctic*	**103**	72 0N	140 0W
Beaulieu, *U.K.*	**14**	50 49N	1 27W
Beauly, *U.K.*	**23**	57 29N	4 27W
Beauly →, *U.K.*	**23**	57 26N	4 28W
Beaumaris, *U.K.*	**17**	53 16N	4 7W
Beaumont, *U.S.A.*	**91**	30 5N	94 8W
Beauvais, *Fr.*	**34**	49 25N	2 8 E
Bebington, *U.K.*	**18**	53 23N	3 1W
Beccles, *U.K.*	**15**	52 27N	1 33 E
Béchar, *Alg.*	**78**	31 38N	2 18W
Beckermet, *U.K.*	**18**	54 26N	3 31W
Beckfoot, *U.K.*	**18**	54 50N	3 25W
Beckingham, *U.K.*	**19**	53 24N	0 49W
Bedale, *U.K.*	**19**	54 18N	1 35W
Beddgelert, *U.K.*	**17**	53 2N	4 8W
Bedford, *U.K.*	**15**	52 8N	0 29W
Bedford □, *U.K.*	**15**	52 4N	0 28W
Bedford Level, *U.K.*	**15**	52 25N	0 5 E
Bedlington, *U.K.*	**21**	55 8N	1 35W
Bedworth, *U.K.*	**14**	52 28N	1 29W
Beeford, *U.K.*	**19**	53 58N	0 18W
Beer, *U.K.*	**16**	50 41N	3 5W
Beersheba, *Isr.*	**57**	31 15N	34 48 E
Beeston, *U.K.*	**19**	52 55N	1 11W
Bei'an, *China*	**61**	48 10N	126 20 E
Beighton, *U.K.*	**19**	53 21N	1 21W
Beijing = Peking, *China*	**61**	39 55N	116 20 E
Beira, *Mozam.*	**81**	19 50S	34 52 E
Beira-Baixa, *Port.*	**37**	40 2N	7 30W
Beirut, *Leb.*	**57**	33 53N	35 31 E
Beith, *U.K.*	**20**	55 45N	4 38W
Bejaïa, Golfe de, *Alg.*	**78**	36 42N	5 13 E
Belbroughton, *U.K.*	**14**	52 23N	2 5W
Belcher Is., *Canada*	**89**	56 15N	78 45W
Belém, *Brazil*	**101**	1 20S	48 30W
Belfast, *U.K.*	**24**	54 35N	5 56W
Belfast □, *U.K.*	**24**	54 35N	5 56W
Belfast, L., *U.K.*	**24**	54 40N	5 50W
Belford, *U.K.*	**21**	55 36N	1 50W
Belfort, *Fr.*	**34**	47 38N	6 50 E
Belgium ■, *Europe*	**36**	50 30N	5 0 E
Belgorod, *U.S.S.R.*	**47**	50 35N	36 35 E
Belgrade, *Yug.*	**41**	44 50N	20 37 E
Beliton, Is., *Indon.*	**63**	3 10S	107 50 E
Belize ■, *Cent. Am.*	**94**	17 0N	88 30W
Belize City, *Belize*	**94**	17 25N	88 0W
Bell Rock = Inchcape Rock, *U.K.*	**21**	56 26N	2 24W
Bellary, *India*	**58**	15 10N	76 56 E
Belle-Ile, *Fr.*	**34**	47 20N	3 10W
Belle Isle, Str. of, *Canada*	**89**	51 30N	56 30W
Belleville, *Canada*	**92**	44 10N	77 23W
Bellingham, *U.K.*	**21**	55 9N	2 16W
Belmopan, *Belize*	**94**	17 18N	88 30W
Belmullet, *Ire.*	**24**	54 13N	9 58W
Belo Horizonte, *Brazil*	**101**	19 55S	43 56W
Beloye More, *U.S.S.R.*	**46**	66 30N	38 0 E
Belper, *U.K.*	**19**	53 2N	1 29W
Belsay, *U.K.*	**21**	55 6N	1 53W
Belton, *Humberside, U.K.*	**19**	53 33N	0 49W
Belton, *Norfolk, U.K.*	**15**	52 35N	1 39 E
Belturbet, *Ire.*	**24**	54 6N	7 28W
Bembridge, *U.K.*	**14**	50 41N	1 4W
Ben Bheigeir, *U.K.*	**20**	55 43N	6 6W
Ben Chonzie, *U.K.*	**21**	56 27N	4 0W
Ben Cruachan, *U.K.*	**20**	56 26N	5 8W
Ben Dearg, *U.K.*	**23**	57 47N	4 58W
Ben Dorain, *U.K.*	**20**	56 30N	4 42W
Ben Hope, *U.K.*	**23**	58 24N	4 36W
Ben Lawers, *U.K.*	**23**	56 33N	4 13W
Ben Lomond, *U.K.*	**20**	56 12N	4 39W
Ben Lui, *U.K.*	**20**	56 24N	4 50W
Ben Macdhui, *U.K.*	**23**	57 4N	3 40W
Ben Mhor, *U.K.*	**22**	57 16N	7 21W
Ben More, *Central, U.K.*	**20**	56 23N	4 31W
Ben More, *Strathclyde, U.K.*	**20**	56 26N	6 2W
Ben More Assynt, *U.K.*	**23**	58 7N	4 51W
Ben Nevis, *U.K.*	**22**	56 48N	5 0W
Ben Venue, *U.K.*	**20**	56 13N	4 28W
Ben Vorlich, *U.K.*	**20**	56 22N	4 15W
Ben Wyvis, *U.K.*	**23**	57 40N	4 35W
Benalla, *Austral.*	**70**	36 30S	146 0 E
Benares = Varanasi, *India*	**59**	25 22N	83 0 E
Benbecula, *U.K.*	**22**	57 26N	7 21W
Bendigo, *Austral.*	**70**	36 40S	144 15 E
Beneraird, *U.K.*	**20**	55 4N	4 57W
Benevento, *It.*	**40**	41 7N	14 45 E
Bengal, Bay of, *Ind. Oc.*	**59**	18 0N	90 0 E
Bengbu, *China*	**61**	32 58N	117 20 E
Benghazi, *Libya*	**79**	32 11N	20 3 E
Beni Suef, *Egypt*	**79**	29 5N	31 6 E
Benin ■, *Africa*	**78**	10 0N	2 0 E
Benin, Bight of, *W. Afr.*	**78**	5 0N	3 0 E
Benin City, *Nig.*	**78**	6 20N	5 31 E
Benington, *U.K.*	**19**	52 59N	0 5 E
Bennane Hd., *U.K.*	**20**	55 9N	5 2W
Benoni, *S. Afr.*	**81**	26 11S	28 18 E
Benson, *U.K.*	**14**	51 37N	1 6W
Bentley, *Hants., U.K.*	**15**	51 12N	0 52W
Bentley, *S. Yorks., U.K.*	**19**	53 33N	1 9W
Benue →, *Nig.*	**78**	7 48N	6 46 E
Benxi, *China*	**61**	41 20N	123 48 E
Berbera, *Som.*	**73**	10 30N	45 2 E
Berbérati, *C.A.R.*	**80**	4 15N	15 40 E
Bere Alston, *U.K.*	**16**	50 29N	4 11W
Bere Regis, *U.K.*	**14**	50 45N	2 13W
Berezniki, *U.S.S.R.*	**46**	59 24N	56 46 E
Bérgamo, *It.*	**40**	45 42N	9 40 E
Bergen, *Nor.*	**45**	60 23N	5 20 E
Bergen-op-Zoom, *Neth.*	**36**	51 30N	4 18 E
Bergerac, *Fr.*	**35**	44 51N	0 30 E
Bergisch-Gladbach, *W. Ger.*	**36**	50 59N	7 9 E
Berhampore, *India*	**59**	24 2N	88 27 E
Berhampur, *India*	**59**	19 15N	84 54 E
Bering Sea, *Pac. Oc.*	**88**	58 0N	167 0 E
Bering Str., *N. Am.*	**103**	66 0N	170 0W
Berkeley, *U.K.*	**14**	51 41N	2 28W
Berkhamsted, *U.K.*	**15**	51 45N	0 33W
Berkshire □, *U.K.*	**14**	51 30N	1 20W
Berkshire Downs, *U.K.*	**15**	51 30N	1 30W
Berlin, *Ger.*	**42**	52 32N	13 24 E
Bermuda ■, *Atl. Oc.*	**95**	32 45N	65 0W
Bern, *Switz.*	**42**	46 57N	7 28 E
Berry Hd., *U.K.*	**16**	50 24N	3 29W
Berwick-upon-Tweed, *U.K.*	**19**	55 47N	2 0W
Berwyn Mts., *U.K.*	**17**	52 54N	3 26W
Besançon, *Fr.*	**34**	47 15N	6 0 E
Bethesda, *U.K.*	**17**	53 11N	4 3W
Bethlehem, *Jord.*	**57**	31 43N	35 12 E
Bethlehem, *U.S.A.*	**93**	40 39N	75 24W
Béthune, *Fr.*	**34**	50 30N	2 38 E
Betws-y-Coed, *U.K.*	**17**	53 4N	3 49W
Beverley, *U.K.*	**19**	53 52N	0 26W
Beverwijk, *Neth.*	**36**	52 28N	4 38 E
Bewdley, *U.K.*	**14**	52 23N	2 19W
Bexhill, *U.K.*	**15**	50 51N	0 29 E
Bexley, *U.K.*	**15**	51 26N	0 10 E
Béziers, *Fr.*	**35**	43 20N	3 12 E
Bhagalpur, *India*	**59**	25 10N	87 0 E
Bhatinda, *India*	**58**	30 15N	74 57 E
Bhatpara, *India*	**59**	22 50N	88 25 E
Bhavnagar, *India*	**58**	21 45N	72 10 E
Bhimavaram, *India*	**59**	16 30N	81 30 E
Bhopal, *India*	**58**	23 20N	77 30 E
Bhubaneshwar, *India*	**59**	20 15N	85 50 E
Bhutan ■, *Asia*	**59**	27 25N	90 30 E
Białystok, *Pol.*	**43**	53 10N	23 10 E
Biarritz, *Fr.*	**34**	43 29N	1 33W
Bibury, *U.K.*	**14**	51 46N	1 50W
Bicester, *U.K.*	**14**	51 53N	1 9W
Bicton, *U.K.*	**14**	52 43N	2 47W
Biddenden, *U.K.*	**15**	51 7N	0 40 E
Biddulph, *U.K.*	**18**	53 8N	2 11W
Bideford, *U.K.*	**16**	51 1N	4 13W
Bideford Bay, *U.K.*	**16**	51 5N	4 20W
Bidford on Avon, *U.K.*	**14**	52 9N	1 53W
Bié Plateau, *Angola*	**81**	12 0S	16 0 E
Biel, *Switz.*	**42**	47 8N	7 14 E
Bielefeld, *W. Ger.*	**42**	52 2N	8 31 E
Bigbury, *U.K.*	**16**	50 17N	3 52W
Bigbury B., *U.K.*	**16**	50 18N	3 58W
Biggar, *U.K.*	**21**	55 38N	3 31W
Biggleswade, *U.K.*	**15**	52 6N	0 16W
Bighorn Mts., *U.S.A.*	**90**	44 30N	107 30W
Bihar □, *India*	**59**	25 0N	86 0 E
Bikaner, *India*	**58**	28 2N	73 18 E

Bikini Atoll, *Pac. Oc.* **64** 12 0N 167 30 E
Bilbao, *Sp.* **37** 43 16N 2 56W
Billericay, *U.K.* **15** 51 38N 0 25 E
Billesdon, *U.K.* **15** 52 38N 0 56W
Billingham, *U.K.* **19** 54 36N 1 18W
Billinghay, *U.K.* **19** 53 5N 0 17W
Billings, *U.S.A.* **90** 45 43N 108 29W
Billingshurst, *U.K.* **15** 51 2N 0 28W
Bilston, *U.K.* **14** 52 34N 2 5W
Binbrook, *U.K.* **19** 53 26N 0 9W
Bingham, *U.K.* **19** 52 57N 0 55W
Binghamton, *U.S.A.* **93** 42 9N 75 54W
Bingley, *U.K.* **18** 53 51N 1 50W
Bioko, *Eq. Guin.* **80** 3 30N 8 40 E
Birch, *U.K.* **15** 51 50N 0 54 E
Birchington, *U.K.* **15** 51 22N 1 18 E
Birdlip, *U.K.* **14** 51 50N 2 7W
Birkdale, *U.K.* **18** 53 38N 3 2W
Birkenhead, *U.K.* **18** 53 24N 3 1W
Birmingham, *U.K.* **14** 52 30N 1 55W
Birmingham, *U.S.A.* **91** 33 31N 86 50W
Birr, *Ire.* **25** 53 7N 7 55W
Birtley, *Northumberland, U.K.* **21** 55 5N 2 12W
Birtley, *Tyne & Wear, U.K.* **21** 54 53N 1 34W
Biscay, B. of, *Atl. Oc.* **35** 45 0N 2 0W
Bishop Auckland, *U.K.* **19** 54 40N 1 40W
Bishop's Castle, *U.K.* **14** 52 29N 3 0W
Bishop's Cleeve, *U.K.* **14** 51 56N 2 3W
Bishop's Frome, *U.K.* **14** 52 8N 2 29W
Bishops Lydeard, *U.K.* **14** 51 4N 3 12W
Bishop's Nympton, *U.K.* **16** 50 58N 3 44W
Bishop's Stortford, *U.K.* **15** 51 52N 0 11 E
Bishop's Waltham, *U.K.* **14** 50 57N 1 13W
Bishopsteignton, *U.K.* **16** 50 32N 3 32W
Bishopstoke, *U.K.* **14** 50 58N 1 19W
Biskra, *Alg.* **78** 34 50N 5 44 E
Bismarck Arch., *P.N.G.* **64** 2 30S 150 0 E
Bissau, *Guin.-Biss.* **78** 11 45N 15 45W
Bitola, *Yug.* **41** 41 5N 21 10 E
Bitton, *U.K.* **14** 51 25N 2 27W
Biwa-Ko, *Jap.* **62** 35 15N 136 10 E
Biysk, *U.S.S.R.* **48** 52 40N 85 0 E
Blaby, *U.K.* **14** 52 34N 1 10W
Black Combe, *U.K.* **18** 54 16N 3 20W
Black Esk ➝, *U.K.* **21** 55 14N 3 13W
Black Forest, Mts., *W. Ger.* **42** 48 0N 8 0 E
Black Hd., *U.K.* **16** 50 1N 5 6W
Black Mt. = Mynydd Du, *U.K.* **17** 51 45N 3 45W
Black Mts., *U.K.* **17** 51 52N 3 5W
Black Sea, *Europe* **47** 43 30N 35 0 E
Black Volta ➝, *Africa* **78** 8 41N 1 33W
Blackall, *Austral.* **67** 24 25S 145 45 E
Blackburn, *U.K.* **18** 53 44N 2 30W
Blackdown Hills, *U.K.* **14** 50 57N 3 15W
Blackford, *U.K.* **21** 56 15N 3 48W
Blackmoor Gate, *U.K.* **16** 51 9N 3 55W
Blackmoor Vale, *U.K.* **14** 50 54N 2 28W
Blackpool, *U.K.* **18** 53 48N 3 3W
Blacksod B., *Ire.* **24** 54 6N 10 0W
Blacktown, *Austral.* **70** 33 48S 150 55 E
Blackwater ➝, *Ire.* **25** 51 55N 7 50W
Blackwater ➝, *Essex, U.K.* **15** 51 44N 0 53 E
Blackwater ➝, *N. Ireland, U.K.* **24** 54 31N 6 35W
Blackwood, *U.K.* **21** 55 40N 3 56W
Blaenau Ffestiniog, *U.K.* **17** 53 0N 3 57W
Blaenavon, *U.K.* **17** 51 46N 3 5W
Blagdon, *U.K.* **14** 51 19N 2 42W
Blagoveshchensk, *U.S.S.R.* **49** 50 20N 127 30 E
Blair Athol, *Austral.* **67** 22 42S 147 31 E
Blair Atholl, *U.K.* **23** 56 46N 3 50W
Blairgowrie, *U.K.* **23** 56 36N 3 20W
Blakeney, *Gloucs., U.K.* **14** 51 45N 2 29W
Blakeney, *Norfolk, U.K.* **15** 52 57N 1 1 E
Blanc, Mont, *Europe* **35** 45 48N 6 50 E
Blandford Forum, *U.K.* **14** 50 52N 2 10W
Blantyre, *Malawi* **81** 15 45S 35 0 E
Blarney, *Ire.* **25** 51 57N 8 35W
Blaydon, *U.K.* **19** 54 56N 1 47W
Bleadon, *U.K.* **14** 51 18N 2 57W
Blean, *U.K.* **15** 51 18N 1 3 E
Bleasdale Moors, *U.K.* **18** 53 57N 2 40W
Blenheim, *N.Z.* **71** 41 38S 173 57 E
Bletchingdon, *U.K.* **14** 51 51N 1 16W
Bletchley, *U.K.* **15** 51 59N 0 44W
Blisworth, *U.K.* **15** 52 11N 0 56W
Blockley, *U.K.* **14** 52 1N 1 45W
Bloemfontein, *S. Afr.* **81** 29 6S 26 14 E
Blofield, *U.K.* **15** 52 38N 1 25 E
Blois, *Fr.* **34** 47 35N 1 20 E
Bloody Foreland, *Ire.* **24** 55 10N 8 18W
Bloxham, *U.K.* **14** 52 1N 1 22W
Blue Mts., *Austral.* **70** 33 40S 150 0 E
Blue Mts., *U.S.A.* **90** 45 15N 119 0W
Blue Nile ➝, *Sudan* **79** 12 30N 34 30 E
Blue Ridge Mts., *U.S.A.* **91** 36 30N 80 15W
Blue Stack Mts., *Ire.* **24** 54 46N 8 5W
Blumenau, *Brazil* **102** 27 0S 49 0W
Blundeston, *U.K.* **15** 52 33N 1 42 E
Blyth, *Northumberland, U.K.* **19** 55 8N 1 32W
Blyth, *Notts., U.K.* **19** 53 22N 1 2W
Blyth ➝, *U.K.* **21** 55 8N 1 30W
Blyth Bridge, *U.K.* **21** 55 41N 3 22W
Blyton, *U.K.* **19** 53 25N 0 42W
Bobo-Dioulasso, *B. Faso* **78** 11 8N 4 13W
Bocholt, *W. Ger.* **36** 51 50N 6 35 E
Bochum, *W. Ger.* **36** 51 28N 7 12 E
Bodenham, *U.K.* **14** 52 9N 2 41W
Bodensee, *W. Ger.* **42** 47 35N 9 25 E
Bodiam, *U.K.* **15** 51 1N 0 33 E
Bodinnick, *U.K.* **16** 50 20N 4 37W
Bodmin, *U.K.* **16** 50 28N 4 44W
Bodmin Moor, *U.K.* **16** 50 33N 4 36W
Bodø, *Nor.* **44** 67 17N 14 24 E
Bogan ➝, *Austral.* **67** 29 59S 146 17 E
Boggeragh Mts., *Ire.* **25** 52 2N 8 55W
Bognor Regis, *U.K.* **15** 50 47N 0 40W
Bogor, *Indon.* **63** 6 36S 106 48 E
Bogota, *Col.* **100** 4 34N 74 0W
Bohemian Forest, *Czech.* **42** 49 20N 13 0 E
Boise, *U.S.A.* **90** 43 43N 116 9W
Bolgatanga, *Ghana* **78** 10 44N 0 53W
Bolivia ■, *S. Am.* **100** 17 6S 64 0W
Bolivian Plateau, *S. Am.* **96** 20 0S 67 30W
Bollington, *U.K.* **18** 53 18N 2 8W
Bolney, *U.K.* **15** 50 59N 0 11W
Bologna, *It.* **40** 44 30N 11 20 E
Bolshevik, I., *U.S.S.R.* **49** 78 30N 102 0 E
Bolshezemelskaya Tundra, *U.S.S.R.* **46** 67 0N 56 0 E
Bolsover, *U.K.* **19** 53 14N 1 18W
Bolt Head, *U.K.* **16** 50 13N 3 48W
Bolt Tail, *U.K.* **16** 50 13N 3 55W
Bolton, *U.K.* **18** 53 35N 2 26W
Bolton Abbey, *U.K.* **18** 53 59N 1 53W
Bolton by Bowland, *U.K.* **18** 53 56N 2 21W
Bolton le Sands, *U.K.* **18** 54 7N 2 49W
Bolungavík, *Ice.* **44** 66 9N 23 15W
Bolzano, *It.* **40** 46 30N 11 20 E
Boma, *Zaïre* **80** 5 50S 13 4 E
Bombay, *India* **58** 18 55N 72 50 E
Bonaparte Archipelago, *Austral.* **66** 14 0S 124 30 E
Bonarbridge, *U.K.* **23** 57 53N 4 20W
Bonchester Bridge, *U.K.* **21** 55 23N 2 36W
Bonchurch, *U.K.* **14** 50 36N 1 11W
Bo'ness, *U.K.* **21** 56 0N 3 38W
Bonifacio, Str. of, *Fr.* **40** 41 12N 9 15 E
Bonn, *W. Ger.* **36** 50 43N 7 6 E
Bonnyrigg, *U.K.* **21** 55 52N 3 8W
Boot, *U.K.* **18** 54 24N 3 18W
Boothia, Gulf of, *Canada* **89** 71 0N 90 0W
Boothia Pen., *Canada* **88** 71 0N 94 0W
Bootle, *Cumbria, U.K.* **18** 54 17N 3 24W
Bootle, *Merseyside, U.K.* **18** 53 28N 3 1W
Borås, *Swed.* **45** 57 43N 12 56 E
Bordeaux, *Fr.* **35** 44 50N 0 36W
Borders □, *U.K.* **21** 55 35N 2 50W
Bordon, *U.K.* **15** 51 6N 0 52W
Borehamwood, *U.K.* **15** 51 40N 0 15W
Boreland, *U.K.* **21** 55 12N 3 16W
Borgarnes, *Ice.* **44** 64 32N 21 55W
Borneo, *E. Ind.* **63** 1 0N 115 0 E
Bornholm, *Den.* **45** 55 10N 15 0 E
Boroughbridge, *U.K.* **19** 54 6N 1 23W
Borrowdale, *U.K.* **18** 54 31N 3 10W
Borth, *U.K.* **17** 52 29N 4 3W
Bosbury, *U.K.* **14** 52 5N 2 27W
Boscastle, *U.K.* **16** 50 42N 4 42W
Bosham, *U.K.* **15** 50 50N 0 51W
Bosporus, *Turk.* **47** 41 10N 29 10 E
Boston, *U.K.* **19** 52 59N 0 2W
Boston, *U.S.A.* **93** 42 20N 71 0W
Botany Bay, *Austral.* **70** 34 0S 151 14 E
Bothel, *U.K.* **18** 54 43N 3 16W
Bothnia, G. of, *Europe* **44** 63 0N 20 0 E
Botswana ■, *Africa* **81** 22 0S 24 0 E
Bottesford, *U.K.* **19** 52 57N 0 48W
Bottrop, *W. Ger.* **36** 51 34N 6 59 E
Bouaké, *Ivory C.* **78** 7 40N 5 2W
Bouar, *C.A.R.* **80** 6 0N 15 40 E
Boulogne-sur-Mer, *Fr.* **34** 50 42N 1 36 E
Bourges, *Fr.* **34** 47 9N 2 25 E
Bourgogne, *Fr.* **34** 47 0N 4 50 E
Bourke, *Austral.* **67** 30 8S 145 55 E
Bourne, *U.K.* **15** 52 46N 0 22W
Bournemouth, *U.K.* **14** 50 43N 1 53W
Bourton-on-the-Water, *U.K.* **14** 51 53N 1 45W
Bovey Tracey, *U.K.* **16** 50 36N 3 40W
Bowen, *Austral.* **67** 20 0S 148 16 E
Bowes, *U.K.* **18** 54 31N 1 59W
Bowland, Forest of, *U.K.* **18** 54 0N 2 30W
Bowmore, *U.K.* **20** 55 45N 6 18W
Bowness, *Solway, U.K.* **18** 54 57N 3 13W
Bowness, *Windermere, U.K.* **18** 54 22N 2 56W
Box, *U.K.* **14** 51 24N 2 16W
Box Hill, *U.K.* **15** 51 16N 0 16W
Boxley, *U.K.* **15** 51 17N 0 34 E
Boyle, *Ire.* **24** 53 58N 8 19W
Boyne ➝, *Ire.* **24** 53 43N 6 15W
Bozeat, *U.K.* **15** 52 14N 0 41W
Bracadale, L., *U.K.* **22** 57 20N 6 30W
Bracebridge Heath, *U.K.* **19** 53 13N 0 32W
Brackley, *U.K.* **14** 52 3N 1 9W
Bracknell, *U.K.* **15** 51 24N 0 45W
Braco, *U.K.* **21** 56 16N 3 55W
Bradda Hd., *U.K.* **18** 54 6N 4 46W
Bradford, *U.K.* **19** 53 47N 1 45W
Bradford-on-Avon, *U.K.* **14** 51 20N 2 15W
Brading, *U.K.* **14** 50 41N 1 9W
Bradwell-on-Sea, *U.K.* **15** 51 44N 0 55 E
Bradworthy, *U.K.* **16** 50 54N 4 22W
Braemar, *U.K.* **23** 57 2N 3 20W
Braga, *Port.* **37** 41 35N 8 25W
Brahmaputra ➝, *India* **59** 24 2N 90 59 E
Braich-y-pwll, *U.K.* **17** 52 47N 4 46W
Brăila, *Rom.* **43** 45 19N 27 59 E
Brailsford, *U.K.* **19** 52 58N 1 35W
Braintree, *U.K.* **15** 51 53N 0 34 E
Bramford, *U.K.* **15** 52 5N 1 6 E
Brampton, *Canada* **92** 43 45N 79 45W
Brampton, *Cambs., U.K.* **15** 52 19N 0 13W
Brampton, *Cumbria, U.K.* **18** 54 56N 2 43W
Bramshott, *U.K.* **15** 51 5N 0 47W
Brancaster, *U.K.* **15** 52 58N 0 40 E
Branco ➝, *Brazil* **100** 1 20S 61 50W
Brander, Pass of, *U.K.* **20** 56 25N 5 10W
Brandon, *Canada* **88** 49 50N 99 57W
Brandon, *Durham, U.K.* **19** 54 46N 1 37W
Brandon, *Suffolk, U.K.* **15** 52 27N 0 37 E
Brandon, Mt., *Ire.* **25** 52 15N 10 15W
Brandon B., *Ire.* **25** 52 17N 10 8W
Branston, *U.K.* **19** 53 13N 0 28W
Brantford, *Canada* **92** 43 10N 80 15W
Brasília, *Brazil* **101** 15 47S 47 55 E
Braşov, *Rom.* **43** 45 38N 25 35 E
Brasted, *U.K.* **15** 51 16N 0 8 E
Bratislava, *Czech.* **43** 48 10N 17 7 E
Bratsk, *U.S.S.R.* **49** 56 10N 101 30 E
Braunton, *U.K.* **16** 51 6N 4 9W
Bray, *Ire.* **25** 53 12N 6 6W
Bray, *U.K.* **15** 51 30N 0 42W
Brazil ■, *S. Am.* **101** 10 0S 50 0W
Brazilian Highlands, *Brazil* **101** 18 0S 46 30W
Brazzaville, *Congo* **80** 4 9S 15 12 E
Breadalbane, *U.K.* **20** 56 30N 4 15W
Breage, *U.K.* **16** 50 6N 5 17W
Breamish ➝, *U.K.* **21** 55 30N 1 55W
Brechin, *U.K.* **23** 56 44N 2 40W
Breckland, *U.K.* **15** 52 30N 0 40 E
Brecon, *U.K.* **17** 51 57N 3 23W
Brecon Beacons, *U.K.* **17** 51 53N 3 27W
Brede, *U.K.* **15** 50 56N 0 37 E
Bredon Hill, *U.K.* **14** 52 3N 2 2W
Breiðafjörður, *Ice.* **44** 65 15N 23 15W
Bremen, *W. Ger.* **42** 53 4N 8 47 E
Bremerhaven, *W. Ger.* **40** 53 34N 8 35 E
Brendon Hills, *U.K.* **14** 51 6N 3 25W
Brenner Pass, *Alps* **42** 47 0N 11 30 E
Brent, *U.K.* **15** 51 33N 0 18W
Brentwood, *U.K.* **15** 51 37N 0 19 E
Bréscia, *It.* **40** 45 33N 10 13 E
Breslau = Wrocław, *Pol.* **43** 51 5N 17 5 E
Bressay I., *U.K.* **22** 60 10N 1 5W
Brest, *Fr.* **34** 48 24N 4 31W
Brest, *U.S.S.R.* **46** 52 10N 23 40 E
Bretagne, *Fr.* **34** 48 0N 3 0W
Brewood, *U.K.* **14** 52 41N 2 10W
Brezhnev, *U.S.S.R.* **46** 55 42N 52 19 E
Bride, *U.K.* **18** 54 24N 4 23W
Bridestowe, *U.K.* **16** 50 41N 4 7W
Bridge, *U.K.* **15** 51 14N 1 8 E
Bridge of Allan, *U.K.* **21** 56 9N 3 57W
Bridge of Earn, *U.K.* **21** 56 20N 3 25W
Bridge of Orchy, *U.K.* **20** 56 29N 4 48W
Bridge of Weir, *U.K.* **20** 55 51N 4 35W
Bridgend, *Islay, U.K.* **20** 55 46N 6 15W
Bridgend, *Mid Glam., U.K.* **17** 51 30N 3 35W
Bridgeport, *U.S.A.* **93** 41 12N 73 12W
Bridgetown, *Barb.* **94** 13 0N 59 30W
Bridgnorth, *U.K.* **14** 52 33N 2 25W
Bridgwater, *U.K.* **14** 51 7N 3 0W
Bridgwater B., *U.K.* **14** 51 15N 3 15W
Bridlington, *U.K.* **19** 54 6N 0 11W
Bridlington B., *U.K.* **19** 54 4N 0 10W
Bridport, *U.K.* **14** 50 43N 2 45W
Brierfield, *U.K.* **18** 53 49N 2 15W
Brierley Hill, *U.K.* **14** 52 29N 2 7W
Brigg, *U.K.* **19** 53 33N 0 30W
Brighouse, *U.K.* **19** 53 42N 1 47W
Brighstone, *U.K.* **15** 50 38N 1 36W
Brightlingsea, *U.K.* **15** 51 49N 1 1 E
Brighton, *U.K.* **15** 50 50N 0 9W
Brightstone, *U.K.* **14** 50 38N 1 23W
Brigstock, *U.K.* **15** 52 27N 0 38W
Brill, *U.K.* **14** 51 49N 1 3W
Brimfield, *U.K.* **14** 52 18N 2 42W
Bríndisi, *It.* **41** 40 39N 17 55 E
Brinklow, *U.K.* **14** 52 25N 1 22W
Brinkworth, *U.K.* **14** 51 33N 1 59W
Brisbane, *Austral.* **67** 27 25S 153 2 E
Bristol, *U.K.* **14** 51 26N 2 35W
Bristol Channel, *U.K.* **16** 51 18N 4 30W
Briston, *U.K.* **15** 52 52N 1 4 E
British Columbia □, *Canada* **88** 55 0N 125 15W
British Guiana = Guyana ■, *S. Am.* **100** 5 0N 59 0W
British Isles, *Europe* **4** 55 0N 4 0W
Brittany = Bretagne, *Fr.* **34** 48 0N 3 0W
Brixham, *U.K.* **16** 50 24N 3 31W
Brixworth, *U.K.* **15** 52 20N 0 54W
Brize Norton, *U.K.* **14** 51 46N 1 35W
Brno, *Czech.* **42** 49 10N 16 35 E
Broad B., *U.K.* **22** 58 14N 6 16W
Broad Chalke, *U.K.* **14** 51 2N 1 54W
Broad Clyst, *U.K.* **16** 50 46N 3 27W
Broad Haven, *Ire.* **24** 54 20N 9 55W
Broad Law, *U.K.* **21** 55 30N 3 22W
Broad Sd., *U.K.* **16** 49 56N 6 19W
Broadford, *U.K.* **22** 57 14N 5 55W
Broadhembury, *U.K.* **16** 50 49N 3 16W
Broads, The, *U.K.* **15** 52 45N 1 30 E
Broadstairs, *U.K.* **15** 51 21N 1 28 E
Broadway, *U.K.* **14** 52 2N 1 51W
Broadwindsor, *U.K.* **14** 50 49N 2 49W
Brockenhurst, *U.K.* **14** 50 49N 1 34W
Brockton, *U.S.A.* **93** 42 25N 79 26W
Brockworth, *U.K.* **14** 51 51N 2 9W
Brodick, *U.K.* **20** 55 34N 5 9W
Broken Hill, *Austral.* **70** 31 58S 141 29 E
Bromborough, *U.K.* **18** 53 20N 3 0W
Bromfield, *U.K.* **14** 52 25N 2 45W
Bromham, *U.K.* **14** 51 23N 2 3W
Bromley, *U.K.* **15** 51 20N 0 5 E
Brompton, *U.K.* **19** 54 22N 1 25W
Bromsgrove, *U.K.* **14** 52 20N 2 3W
Bromyard, *U.K.* **14** 52 12N 2 30W
Brooks, *Canada* **88** 50 35N 111 55W
Brooks Ra., *U.S.A.* **88** 68 40N 147 0W
Broom, L., *U.K.* **22** 57 55N 5 15W
Broomfield, *U.K.* **14** 51 46N 0 28 E
Broomhill, *U.K.* **21** 55 19N 1 36W
Brora, *U.K.* **23** 58 0N 3 50W
Brora ➝, *U.K.* **23** 58 4N 3 52W
Broseley, *U.K.* **14** 52 36N 2 30W
Brosna ➝, *Ire.* **25** 53 8N 8 0W
Brothertoft, *U.K.* **19** 53 0N 0 5W
Brotton, *U.K.* **19** 54 34N 0 55W
Brough, *Cumbria, U.K.* **18** 54 32N 2 19W
Brough, *Humberside, U.K.* **19** 53 44N 0 35W
Broughton, *Borders, U.K.* **21** 55 37N 3 25W
Broughton, *Humberside, U.K.* **19** 53 33N 0 36W
Broughton, *N. Yorks., U.K.* **19** 54 26N 1 8W
Broughton, *Northants., U.K.* **15** 52 22N 0 45W
Broughton-in-Furness, *U.K.* **18** 54 17N 3 12W
Broughty Ferry, *U.K.* **21** 56 29N 2 50W
Brown Willy, *U.K.* **16** 50 35N 4 34W
Brownhills, *U.K.* **14** 52 38N 1 57W
Broxburn, *U.K.* **21** 55 56N 3 23W
Bruay-en-Artois, *Fr.* **34** 50 29N 2 33 E
Bruce, Mt., *Austral.* **66** 22 37S 118 8 E
Brue ➝, *U.K.* **14** 51 10N 2 59W
Bruges, *Belg.* **36** 51 13N 3 13 E
Brunei ■, *E. Ind.* **63** 4 50N 115 0 E
Brunswick, *W. Ger.* **42** 52 17N 10 28 E
Brunton, *U.K.* **21** 55 2N 2 6W
Brussels, *Belg.* **36** 50 51N 4 21 E
Bruton, *U.K.* **14** 51 6N 2 28W
Bryansk, *U.S.S.R.* **46** 53 13N 34 25 E
Bryher I., *U.K.* **16** 49 57N 6 21W
Brynamman, *U.K.* **17** 51 49N 3 52W
Brynmawr, *U.K.* **17** 51 48N 3 11W
Bucaramanga, *Col.* **100** 7 0N 73 0W
Buchan, *U.K.* **23** 57 32N 2 8W
Buchan Ness, *U.K.* **23** 57 29N 1 48W
Bucharest, *Rom.* **43** 44 27N 26 10 E
Buchlyvie, *U.K.* **20** 56 7N 4 20W
Buckden, *U.K.* **15** 52 17N 0 16W
Buckfastleigh, *U.K.* **16** 50 28N 3 47W
Buckhaven, *U.K.* **21** 56 10N 3 2W
Buckie, *U.K.* **23** 57 40N 2 58W
Buckingham, *U.K.* **15** 52 0N 0 59W
Buckingham □, *U.K.* **15** 51 50N 0 55W
Buckland Brewer, *U.K.* **16** 50 56N 4 14W
Buckland Newton, *U.K.* **14** 50 45N 2 25W
Buckley, *U.K.* **17** 53 10N 3 5W
Budapest, *Hung.* **43** 47 29N 19 5 E
Buddon Ness, *U.K.* **21** 56 29N 2 42W
Bude, *U.K.* **16** 50 49N 4 33W
Bude Bay, *U.K.* **16** 50 50N 4 40W
Budle B., *U.K.* **21** 55 37N 1 45W
Budleigh Salterton, *U.K.* **16** 50 37N 3 19W
Buenaventura, *Col.* **100** 3 53N 77 4W
Buenos Aires, *Arg.* **102** 34 30S 58 20W
Buffalo, *U.S.A.* **92** 42 55N 78 50W
Bug ➝, *Pol.* **43** 52 31N 21 5 E
Bug ➝, *U.S.S.R.* **47** 46 59N 31 58 E
Buglawton, *U.K.* **18** 53 12N 2 11W
Bugle, *U.K.* **16** 50 23N 4 46W
Buie L., *U.K.* **20** 56 20N 5 55W
Builth Wells, *U.K.* **17** 52 10N 3 26W
Bujumbura, *Bur.* **80** 3 16S 29 18 E
Bukavu, *Zaïre* **80** 2 20S 28 52 E
Bukhara, *U.S.S.R.* **48** 39 48N 64 25 E
Bulawayo, *Zimb.* **81** 20 7S 28 32 E
Bulford, *U.K.* **14** 51 11N 1 45W
Bulgaria ■, *Europe* **41** 42 35N 25 30 E
Bulwell, *U.K.* **19** 53 1N 1 12W
Bunbury, *Austral.* **66** 33 20S 115 35 E
Buncrana, *Ire.* **24** 55 8N 7 28W
Bundaberg, *Austral.* **67** 24 54S 152 22 E
Bundoran, *Ire.* **24** 54 24N 8 17W

Bunessan, U.K. 20 56 18N 6 15W
Bungay, U.K. 15 52 27N 1 26 E
Buntingford, U.K. 15 51 57N 0 1W
Bunwell, U.K. 15 52 30N 1 9 E
Buraydah, Si. Arab. 56 26 20N 44 8 E
Burbage, Derby, U.K. 18 53 15N 1 55W
Burbage, Leics., U.K. 14 52 31N 1 20W
Burbage, Wilts., U.K. 14 51 21N 1 40W
Burdwan, India 59 23 14N 87 39 E
Bure →, U.K. 15 52 38N 1 45 E
Burford, U.K. 14 51 48N 1 38W
Burgas, Bulg. 41 42 33N 27 29 E
Burgess Hill, U.K. 15 50 57N 0 7W
Burgh-le-Marsh, U.K. 19 53 10N 0 15 E
Burgos, Sp. 37 42 21N 3 41W
Burgundy = Bourgogne, Fr. 34 47 0N 4 50 E
Burkina Faso ■, Africa 78 12 0N 1 0W
Burley, Hants., U.K. 14 50 49N 1 41W
Burley, N. Yorks., U.K. 19 53 55N 1 46W
Burlington, U.S.A. 93 44 27N 73 14W
Burma ■, Asia 59 21 0N 96 30 E
Burnham, Essex, U.K. 15 51 37N 0 50 E
Burnham, Somerset, U.K. 14 51 14N 3 0W
Burnham Market, U.K. 15 52 57N 0 43 E
Burnie, Austral. 67 41 4S 145 56 E
Burnley, U.K. 18 53 47N 2 15W
Burnmouth, U.K. 21 55 50N 2 4W
Burntisland, U.K. 21 56 4N 3 14W
Burrelton, U.K. 21 56 30N 3 16W
Burrow Hd., U.K. 20 54 40N 4 23W
Burry Port, U.K. 17 51 41N 4 17W
Bursa, Turk. 47 40 15N 29 5 E
Burstwick, U.K. 19 53 43N 0 6W
Burton, U.K. 18 54 10N 2 43W
Burton Agnes, U.K. 19 54 4N 0 18W
Burton Bradstock, U.K. 14 50 41N 2 43W
Burton Fleming, U.K. 19 54 8N 0 20W
Burton Latimer, U.K. 15 52 23N 0 41W
Burton upon Stather, U.K. 19 53 39N 0 41W
Burton-upon-Trent, U.K. 14 52 48N 1 39W
Burundi ■, Africa 80 3 15S 30 0 E
Burwash, U.K. 15 50 59N 0 24 E
Burwell, U.K. 15 52 17N 0 20 E
Bury, U.K. 18 53 36N 2 19W
Bury St. Edmunds, U.K. 15 52 15N 0 42 E
Buryat A.S.S.R. □, U.S.S.R. 49 53 0N 110 0 E
Būshehr, Iran 56 28 20N 51 45 E
Bushey, U.K. 15 51 38N 0 20W
Bushmills, U.K. 24 55 14N 6 32W
Bute, U.K. 20 55 48N 5 2W
Bute, Kyles of, U.K. 20 55 55N 5 10W
Bute, Sd. of, U.K. 20 55 43N 5 8W
Buttermere, U.K. 18 54 32N 3 17W
Butuan, Phil. 63 8 57N 125 33 E
Buxton, U.K. 18 53 16N 1 54W
Buzău, Rom. 43 45 10N 26 50 E
Bydgoszcz, Pol. 43 53 10N 18 0 E
Byfield, U.K. 14 52 10N 1 15W
Byrd Land, Ant. 103 79 30S 125 0W
Byrrang Mts., U.S.S.R. 49 75 0N 100 0 E
Bytom, Pol. 43 50 25N 18 54 E

C

Cabimas, Ven. 100 10 23N 71 25W
Cabinda □, Angola 80 5 0S 12 30 E
Čačak, Yug. 41 43 54N 20 20 E
Cáceres, Sp. 37 39 26N 6 23W
Cachoeira do Sul, Brazil 102 30 3S 52 53W
Cader Idris, U.K. 17 52 43N 3 56W
Cádiz, Sp. 37 36 30N 6 20W
Caen, Fr. 34 49 10N 0 22W
Caenby Corner, U.K. 19 53 23N 0 32W
Caernarfon, U.K. 17 53 8N 4 17W
Caernarfon B., U.K. 17 53 4N 4 40W
Caerphilly, U.K. 17 51 34N 3 13W
Caersws, U.K. 17 52 32N 3 27W
Cagayan de Oro, Phil. 63 8 30N 124 40 E
Cágliari, It. 40 39 15N 9 6 E
Caha Mts., Ire. 25 51 45N 9 40W
Caher, Ire. 25 52 23N 7 56W
Cahersiveen, Ire. 25 51 57N 10 13W
Cahore Pt., Ire. 25 52 34N 6 11W
Caicos Is., W. Ind. 95 21 40N 71 40W
Cairn Gorm, U.K. 23 57 7N 3 40W
Cairn Table, U.K. 21 55 30N 4 0W
Cairn Toul, U.K. 23 57 3N 3 44W
Cairngorm Mts., U.K. 23 57 6N 3 42W
Cairnryan, U.K. 20 54 59N 5 0W
Cairns, Austral. 67 16 57S 145 45 E
Cairo, Egypt 79 30 1N 31 14 E
Caister-on-Sea, U.K. 15 52 38N 1 43 E
Caistor, U.K. 19 53 29N 0 20W
Caithness, Ord of, U.K. 23 58 9N 3 37W
Cajamarca, Peru 100 7 5S 78 28W
Calabar, Nig. 78 4 57N 8 20 E
Calábria □, It. 40 39 24N 16 30 E
Calais, Fr. 34 50 57N 1 50 E
Calbayog, Phil. 63 12 4N 124 38 E
Calcutta, India 59 22 36N 88 24 E
Caldbeck, U.K. 18 54 45N 3 3W
Calder →, U.K. 19 53 44N 1 21W
Calder Bridge, U.K. 18 54 27N 3 31W
Caldew →, U.K. 18 54 54N 2 59W
Caledonian Canal, U.K. 23 56 50N 5 6W
Calf of Man, U.K. 18 54 4N 4 48W
Calgary, Canada 88 51 0N 114 10W
Calgary, U.K. 20 56 34N 6 17W
Cali, Col. 100 3 25N 76 35W
Caliach Pt., U.K. 20 56 37N 6 20W
Calicut, India 58 11 15N 75 43 E
California □, U.S.A. 90 37 25N 120 0W
California, G. of, N. Am. 94 27 0N 111 0W
Callan, Ire. 25 52 33N 7 25W
Callander, U.K. 20 56 15N 4 14W
Callao, Peru 100 12 0S 77 0W
Calne, U.K. 14 51 26N 2 0W
Calshot, U.K. 14 50 49N 1 18W
Calstock, U.K. 16 50 30N 4 13W
Caltanissetta, It. 40 37 30N 14 3 E
Cam →, U.K. 15 52 21N 0 16 E
Camagüey, Cuba 95 21 20N 78 0W
Camargue, Fr. 35 43 34N 4 34 E
Cambay, G. of, India 58 20 45N 72 30 E
Camberley, U.K. 15 51 20N 0 44W
Cambo, U.K. 21 55 9N 1 57W
Cambodia ■, Asia 63 12 15N 105 0 E
Camborne, U.K. 16 50 13N 5 18W
Cambrian Mts., U.K. 17 52 25N 3 52W
Cambridge, U.K. 15 52 13N 0 8 E
Cambridge, U.S.A. 93 42 20N 71 8W
Cambridge Bay, Canada 88 69 10N 105 0W
Cambridgeshire □, U.K. 15 52 12N 0 7 E
Camden, U.K. 15 51 33N 0 10W
Camden, U.S.A. 93 39 57N 75 7W
Camel →, U.K. 16 50 28N 4 49W
Camelford, U.K. 16 50 37N 4 41W
Cameroon ■, Africa 80 6 0N 12 30 E
Campbellton, Canada 93 49 17N 54 56W
Campbelltown, Austral. 70 34 53S 138 40 E
Campbeltown, U.K. 20 55 25N 5 36W
Campeche, Mex. 94 19 50N 90 32W
Campeche, G. of, Mex. 94 19 30N 93 0W
Campina Grande, Brazil 101 7 20S 35 47W
Campinas, Brazil 102 22 50S 47 0W
Campo Grande, Brazil 101 20 25S 54 40W
Campos, Brazil 101 21 50S 41 20W
Campsie Fells, U.K. 20 56 2N 4 20W
Camrose, Canada 88 53 0N 112 50W
Can Tho, Viet. 63 10 2N 105 46 E
Canada ■, N. Am. 88 60 0N 100 0W
Canary Is., Atl. Oc. 78 29 30N 17 0W
Canaveral, C., U.S.A. 91 28 28N 80 31W
Canberra, Austral. 70 35 15S 149 8 E
Canik Mts., Turk. 47 40 30N 38 0 E
Canna, U.K. 22 57 3N 6 33W
Cannes, Fr. 35 43 32N 7 0 E
Cannington, U.K. 14 51 8N 3 4W
Cannock, U.K. 14 52 42N 2 2W
Cannock Chase, U.K. 14 52 43N 2 0W
Canonbie, U.K. 21 55 4N 2 58W
Cantabrian Mts., Sp. 37 43 0N 5 10W
Canterbury, U.K. 15 51 17N 1 5 E
Canterbury Plains, N.Z. 71 43 55S 171 22 E
Canton = Guangzhou, China 61 23 5N 113 10 E
Canton, U.S.A. 92 40 47N 81 22W
Canvey, U.K. 15 51 32N 0 35 E
Caoles, U.K. 20 56 32N 6 43W
Caolisport, Loch, U.K. 20 55 54N 5 40W
Cape Breton I., Canada 93 46 0N 60 30W
Cape Coast, Ghana 78 5 5N 1 15W
Cape Province □, S. Afr. 81 32 0S 23 0 E
Cape Town, S. Afr. 81 33 55S 18 22 E
Cape Verde Is. ■, Atl. Oc. 128 17 10N 25 20W
Cape York Peninsula, Austral. 67 12 0S 142 30 E
Capel, U.K. 15 51 8N 0 18W
Caracas, Ven. 100 10 30N 66 55W
Caratinga, Brazil 101 19 50S 42 10W
Carbost, U.K. 22 57 19N 6 21W
Cardiff, U.K. 17 51 28N 3 11W
Cardigan, U.K. 17 52 6N 4 41W
Cardigan B., U.K. 17 52 30N 4 30W
Cardington, U.K. 15 52 7N 0 23W
Carey, L., Austral. 66 29 0S 122 15 E
Caribbean Sea 95 15 0N 75 0W
Carisbrooke, U.K. 14 50 42N 1 19W
Cark, U.K. 18 54 11N 2 59W
Carleton Rode, U.K. 15 52 30N 1 6 E
Carlingford, L., Ire. 24 54 0N 6 5W
Carlisle, U.K. 18 54 54N 2 55W
Carlops, U.K. 21 55 47N 3 20W
Carlow, Ire. 25 52 50N 6 58W
Carlow □, Ire. 25 52 43N 6 50W
Carloway, U.K. 22 58 17N 6 48W
Carlton, U.K. 19 52 58N 1 6W
Carlton Colville, U.K. 15 52 27N 1 41 E
Carlton Miniott, U.K. 19 54 13N 1 22W
Carluke, U.K. 21 55 44N 3 50W
Carmarthen, U.K. 17 51 52N 4 20W
Carmarthen B., U.K. 17 51 40N 4 30W
Carnarvon, Austral. 66 24 51S 113 42 E
Carndonagh, Ire. 24 55 15N 7 16W
Carnegie, L., Austral. 66 26 5S 122 30 E
Carnforth, U.K. 18 54 8N 2 47W
Carno, U.K. 17 52 34N 3 31W
Carnoustie, U.K. 21 56 30N 2 41W
Carnsore Pt., Ire. 25 52 10N 6 20W
Carnwath, U.K. 21 55 42N 3 38W
Caroline Is., Pac. Oc. 64 8 0N 150 0 E
Carpathians, Mts., Europe 43 49 50N 21 0 E
Carpentaria, G. of, Austral. 67 14 0S 139 0 E
Carradale, U.K. 20 55 35N 5 30W
Carrauntoohill, Mt., Ire. 25 52 0N 9 49W
Carrick, U.K. 20 55 12N 4 38W
Carrick-on-Shannon, Ire. 24 53 57N 8 7W
Carrick-on-Suir, Ire. 25 52 22N 7 30W
Carrickfergus, U.K. 24 54 43N 5 50W
Carrickfergus □, U.K. 24 54 43N 5 49W
Carrickmacross, Ire. 24 54 0N 6 43W
Carron →, U.K. 22 57 30N 5 30W
Carron, L., U.K. 22 57 22N 5 35W
Carronbridge, U.K. 21 55 16N 3 46W
Carse of Gowrie, U.K. 21 56 30N 3 10W
Carsphairn, U.K. 20 55 13N 4 15W
Carstairs, U.K. 21 55 42N 3 41W
Cartagena, Col. 100 10 25N 75 33W
Cartagena, Sp. 37 37 38N 0 59W
Cartmel, U.K. 18 54 13N 2 57W
Caruaru, Brazil 101 8 15S 35 55W
Carúpano, Ven. 100 10 39N 63 15W
Casablanca, Mor. 78 33 36N 7 36W
Cascade Ra., U.S.A. 90 47 0N 121 30W
Cashel, Ire. 25 52 31N 7 53W
Casper, U.S.A. 90 42 52N 106 20W
Caspian Sea, U.S.S.R. 47 43 0N 50 0 E
Castellón □, Sp. 37 40 15N 0 5W
Castle Acre, U.K. 15 52 42N 0 42W
Castle Cary, U.K. 14 51 5N 2 32W
Castle Donington, U.K. 14 52 50N 1 20W
Castle Douglas, U.K. 21 54 57N 3 57W
Castle Eden, U.K. 19 54 45N 1 20W
Castlebar, Ire. 24 53 52N 9 17W
Castlebay, U.K. 22 56 57N 7 30W
Castleblaney, Ire. 24 54 7N 6 44W
Castleford, U.K. 19 53 43N 1 21W
Castlereagh, Ire. 24 53 47N 8 30W
Castlereagh □, U.K. 24 54 33N 5 53W
Castlereagh →, Austral. 70 30 12S 147 32 E
Castleside, U.K. 18 54 50N 1 52W
Castleton, Derby, U.K. 19 53 20N 1 47W
Castleton, N. Yorks., U.K. 19 54 27N 0 57W
Castletown, U.K. 18 54 4N 4 40W
Castletown Bearhaven, Ire. 25 51 40N 9 54W
Castries, St. Lucia 94 14 0N 60 50W
Catánia, It. 40 37 31N 15 4 E
Catanzaro, It. 40 38 54N 16 38 E
Catcleugh, U.K. 21 55 19N 2 22W
Caterham, U.K. 15 51 16N 0 4W
Caton, U.K. 18 54 5N 2 41W
Catrine, U.K. 20 55 30N 4 20W
Catsfield, U.K. 15 50 53N 0 28 E
Catterick, U.K. 19 54 23N 1 38W
Catterick Camp, U.K. 19 54 22N 1 43W
Catton, U.K. 21 54 56N 2 16W
Caucasus, U.S.S.R. 47 43 0N 44 0 E
Caulkerbush, U.K. 21 54 54N 3 40W
Cavan, Ire. 24 54 0N 7 22W
Cavan □, Ire. 24 53 58N 7 10W
Cawood, U.K. 19 53 50N 1 7W
Cawston, U.K. 15 52 47N 1 10 E
Caxias, Brazil 101 4 55S 43 20W
Caxias do Sul, Brazil 102 29 10S 51 10W
Cayenne, Fr. G. 101 5 0N 52 18W
Ceanannus Mor, Ire. 24 53 42N 6 53W
Cebu, Phil. 63 10 18N 123 54 E
Cedar Rapids, U.S.A. 90 42 0N 91 38W
Celbridge, Ire. 25 53 20N 6 33W
Celebes = Sulawesi □, Indon. 63 2 0S 120 0 E
Celebes Sea, E. Ind. 63 3 0N 123 0 E
Cemaes Bay, U.K. 17 53 24N 4 27W
Central □, U.K. 20 56 10N 4 30W
Central African Republic ■, Africa 80 7 0N 20 0 E
Central Russian Uplands, U.S.S.R. 26 54 0N 36 0 E
Central Siberian Plateau, U.S.S.R. 49 65 0N 105 0 E
Cephalonia = Kefallinía, Greece 41 38 20N 20 30 E
Ceram, Indon. 63 3 10S 129 0 E
Ceres, U.K. 21 56 18N 2 57W
Cerignola, It. 40 41 17N 15 53 E
Cerne Abbas, U.K. 14 50 49N 2 29W
Cerrig-y-drudion, U.K. 17 53 2N 3 34W
Cessnock, Austral. 70 32 50S 151 21 E
Ceuta, Mor. 78 35 52N 5 18W
Cévennes, Fr. 34 44 10N 3 50 E
Ceylon = Sri Lanka ■, Asia 58 7 30N 80 50 E
Chacewater, U.K. 16 50 15N 5 8W
Chad ■, Africa 78 15 0N 17 15 E
Chad, L., Chad 79 13 30N 14 30 E
Chagford, U.K. 16 50 40N 3 50W
Chale, U.K. 14 50 35N 1 19W
Chalfont St. Peter, U.K. 15 51 36N 0 33W
Châlons-sur-Marne, Fr. 34 48 58N 4 20 E
Chambéry, Fr. 35 45 34N 5 55 E
Champagne, Fr. 34 48 40N 4 20 E
Champlain, L., U.S.A. 93 44 30N 73 20W
Chandigarh, India 58 30 43N 76 47 E
Chandler's Ford, U.K. 14 50 59N 1 23W
Changchun, China 61 43 58N 125 19 E
Changde, China 61 29 4N 111 35 E
Changsha, China 61 28 5N 113 1 E
Changzhou, China 61 31 47N 119 58 E
Channel Is., U.K. 34 49 30N 2 40W
Chao Phraya →, Thai. 63 13 32N 100 36 E
Chapel-en-le-Frith, U.K. 18 53 19N 1 54W
Chapel St. Leonards, U.K. 19 53 13N 0 19 E
Chard, U.K. 14 50 52N 2 59W
Chardzhou, U.S.S.R. 48 39 6N 63 34 E
Charing, U.K. 15 51 12N 0 49 E
Charlbury, U.K. 14 51 52N 1 29W
Charleroi, Belg. 36 50 24N 4 27 E
Charleston, U.S.A. 91 32 47N 79 56W
Charleville = Rath Luirc, Ire. 25 52 21N 8 40W
Charleville, Austral. 67 26 24S 146 15 E
Charleville-Mézières, Fr. 34 49 44N 4 40 E
Charlotte, U.S.A. 91 35 16N 80 46W
Charlottenburg, W. Ger. 42 52 31N 13 15 E
Charlottetown, Canada 93 46 14N 63 8W
Charlton Kings, U.K. 14 51 52N 2 3W
Charlwood, U.K. 15 51 8N 0 12W
Charminster, U.K. 14 50 43N 2 28W
Charmouth, U.K. 14 50 45N 2 54W
Charnwood Forest, U.K. 14 52 43N 1 18W
Charters Towers, Austral. 67 20 5S 146 13 E
Chartham, U.K. 15 51 14N 1 1 E
Chartres, Fr. 34 48 29N 1 30 E
Châteauroux, Fr. 34 46 50N 1 40 E
Chatham, U.K. 15 51 22N 0 32 E
Chattanooga, U.S.A. 91 35 2N 85 17W
Chatteris, U.K. 15 52 27N 0 3 E
Chatton, U.K. 21 55 34N 1 55W
Cheadle, Gr. Manchester, U.K. 18 53 23N 2 14W
Cheadle, Staffs., U.K. 18 52 59N 1 59W
Cheadle Hulme, U.K. 18 53 22N 2 12W
Cheboksary, U.S.S.R. 46 56 8N 47 12 E
Cheddar, U.K. 14 51 16N 2 47W
Cheddleton, U.K. 18 53 5N 2 2W
Chelmarsh, U.K. 14 52 29N 2 25W
Chelmer →, U.K. 15 51 45N 0 42 E
Chelmsford, U.K. 15 51 44N 0 29 E
Cheltenham, U.K. 14 51 55N 2 5W
Chelyabinsk, U.S.S.R. 48 55 10N 61 24 E
Chenab →, Pak. 58 30 23N 71 2 E
Chengdu, China 60 30 38N 104 2 E
Chepstow, U.K. 17 51 38N 2 40W
Cherbourg, Fr. 34 49 39N 1 40W
Cheremkhovo, U.S.S.R. 49 53 8N 103 1 E
Cherepovets, U.S.S.R. 46 59 5N 37 55 E
Cheriton, U.K. 14 51 3N 1 9W
Cheriton Fitzpaine, U.K. 16 50 51N 3 38W
Cherkassy, U.S.S.R. 47 49 27N 32 4 E
Chernigov, U.S.S.R. 46 51 28N 31 20 E
Chernovtsy, U.S.S.R. 47 48 15N 25 52 E
Chertsey, U.K. 15 51 23N 0 30W
Cherwell →, U.K. 14 51 46N 1 18W
Chesapeake Bay, U.S.A. 92 38 0N 76 12W
Chesham, U.K. 15 51 42N 0 36W
Cheshire □, U.K. 18 53 14N 2 30W
Cheshunt, U.K. 15 51 42N 0 1W
Chesil Beach, U.K. 14 50 37N 2 33W
Chester, U.K. 18 53 12N 2 53W
Chester-le-Street, U.K. 19 54 53N 1 34W
Chesterfield, U.K. 19 53 14N 1 26W
Chesterfield Inlet, Canada 88 63 30N 90 45W
Cheviot, The, U.K. 19 55 29N 2 8W
Cheviot Hills, U.K. 19 55 20N 2 30W
Chew Magna, U.K. 14 51 21N 2 37W
Chiai, China 61 23 29N 120 25 E
Chiba, Jap. 62 35 30N 140 7 E
Chicago, U.S.A. 92 41 53N 87 40W
Chichester, U.K. 15 50 50N 0 47W
Chiclayo, Peru 100 6 42S 79 50W
Chicoutimi, Canada 93 48 28N 71 5W
Chiddingfold, U.K. 15 51 6N 0 37W
Chidley, C., Canada 89 60 23N 64 26W
Chieti, It. 40 42 22N 14 10 E
Chihli, G. of, China 61 38 30N 119 0 E
Chihuahua, Mex. 94 28 40N 106 3W
Chile ■, S. Am. 102 35 0S 72 0W
Chilham, U.K. 15 51 15N 0 59 E
Chillán, Chile 102 36 40S 72 10W
Chilpancingo, Mex. 94 17 30N 99 30W
Chiltern Hills, U.K. 15 51 44N 0 42W
Chilung, Taiwan 61 25 3N 121 45 E
Chimborazo, Ecuad. 100 1 29S 78 55W
Chimbote, Peru 100 9 0S 78 35W
Chimkent, U.S.S.R. 48 42 18N 69 36 E
China ■, Asia 60 30 0N 110 0 E
Chincha Alta, Peru 100 13 25S 76 7W
Chingola, Zam. 81 12 31S 27 53 E
Chipata, Zam. 81 13 38S 32 28 E
Chippenham, U.K. 14 51 27N 2 7W
Chipping Campden, U.K. 14 52 4N 1 48W
Chipping Norton, U.K. 14 51 56N 1 32W
Chipping Ongar, U.K. 15 51 43N 0 15 E
Chipping Sodbury, U.K. 14 51 31N 2 23W
Chirbury, U.K. 14 52 35N 3 6W
Chirnside, U.K. 21 55 47N 2 11W
Chisledon, U.K. 14 51 30N 1 44W
Chita, U.S.S.R. 49 52 0N 113 35 E
Chittagong, Bangla. 59 22 19N 91 48 E

Chollerton, *U.K.* **21** 55 4N 2 7W
Cholsey, *U.K.* **14** 51 34N 1 10W
Chongjin, *N. Kor.* **61** 41 47N 129 50 E
Chongqing =
Chungking, *China* **60** 29 35N 106 25 E
Chorley, *U.K.* **18** 53 39N 2 39W
Chorrera, La, *Pan.* **94** 8 50N 79 50W
Chorzów, *Pol.* **43** 50 18N 18 57 E
Choybalsan, *Mong.* **61** 48 4N 114 30 E
Christchurch, *N.Z.* **71** 43 33S 172 47 E
Christchurch, *U.K.* **14** 50 44N 1 33W
Chudleigh, *U.K.* **16** 50 35N 3 36W
Chulmleigh, *U.K.* **16** 50 55N 3 52W
Chungking, *China* **60** 29 35N 106 25 E
Chur, *Switz.* **42** 46 52N 9 32 E
Church Stretton, *U.K.* **14** 52 32N 2 49W
Churchdown, *U.K.* **14** 51 53N 2 9W
Churchill →, *Canada* **88** 58 47N 94 12W
Ciénaga, *Col.* **100** 11 1N 74 15W
Cienfuegos, *Cuba* **95** 22 10N 80 30W
Cincinnati, *U.S.A.* **92** 39 10N 84 26W
Cinderford, *U.K.* **14** 51 49N 2 30W
Cirencester, *U.K.* **14** 51 43N 1 59W
Citlaltépetl, *Mex.* **94** 19 0N 97 20W
Ciudad Bolívar, *Ven.* **100** 8 5N 63 36W
Ciudad Guayana, *Ven.* **100** 8 0N 62 30W
Ciudad Juárez, *Mex.* **94** 31 40N 106 28W
Ciudad Madero, *Mex.* **94** 22 19N 97 50W
Ciudad Obregón, *Mex.* **94** 27 28N 109 59W
Ciudad Real, *Sp.* **37** 38 59N 3 55W
Ciudad Victoria, *Mex.* **94** 23 41N 99 9W
Clabhach, *U.K.* **20** 56 38N 6 36W
Clach Leathad, *U.K.* **20** 56 36N 7 52W
Clachan, *U.K.* **20** 55 45N 5 35W
Clackmannan, *U.K.* **21** 56 10N 3 50W
Clacton-on-Sea, *U.K.* **15** 51 47N 1 10 E
Cladich, *U.K.* **20** 56 21N 5 5W
Clara, *Ire.* **25** 53 20N 7 38W
Clare, *U.K.* **15** 52 5N 0 36 E
Clare □, *Ire.* **25** 52 20N 9 0W
Clare →, *Ire.* **24** 53 22N 9 5W
Clare I., *Ire.* **24** 53 48N 10 0W
Claremorris, *Ire.* **24** 53 45N 9 0W
Clarksville, *U.S.A.* **90** 36 32N 87 20W
Clatteringshaws L., *U.K.* **20** 55 3N 4 17W
Claverley, *U.K.* **14** 52 32N 2 19W
Clay Cross, *U.K.* **19** 53 11N 1 26W
Clay Hd., *U.K.* **18** 54 13N 4 23W
Claydon, *U.K.* **15** 52 6N 1 7 E
Clear, C., *Ire.* **25** 51 26N 9 30W
Clear I., *Ire.* **25** 51 26N 9 30W
Cleator Moor, *U.K.* **18** 54 30N 3 32W
Clee Hills, *U.K.* **14** 52 26N 2 35W
Cleethorpes, *U.K.* **19** 53 33N 0 2W
Cleeve Cloud, *U.K.* **14** 51 56N 2 0W
Clent, *U.K.* **14** 52 25N 2 6W
Cleobury Mortimer, *U.K.* **14** 52 23N 2 28W
Clermont-Ferrand, *Fr.* **34** 45 46N 3 4 E
Clevedon, *U.K.* **14** 51 26N 2 52W
Cleveland, *U.S.A.* **92** 41 28N 81 43W
Cleveland □, *U.K.* **19** 54 35N 1 8 E
Cleveland Hills, *U.K.* **19** 54 25N 1 11W
Clew B., *Ire.* **24** 53 54N 9 50W
Cley, *U.K.* **15** 52 57N 1 3 E
Clifden, *Ire.* **24** 53 30N 10 2W
Cliffe, *U.K.* **15** 51 27N 0 31 E
Clifford, *U.K.* **14** 52 6N 3 6W
Clipston, *U.K.* **15** 52 26N 0 58W
Clitheroe, *U.K.* **18** 53 52N 2 23W
Clonakilty, *Ire.* **25** 51 37N 8 53W
Clonakilty B., *Ire.* **25** 51 33N 8 50W
Cloncurry, *Austral.* **67** 20 40S 140 28 E
Clones, *Ire.* **24** 54 10N 7 13W
Clonmel, *Ire.* **25** 52 22N 7 42W
Closeburn, *U.K.* **21** 55 13N 3 45W
Cloughton, *U.K.* **19** 54 20N 0 27W
Clovelly, *U.K.* **16** 51 0N 4 25W
Clowne, *U.K.* **19** 53 18N 1 16W
Cluj-Napoca, *Rom.* **43** 46 47N 23 38 E
Clun, *U.K.* **14** 52 26N 3 2W
Clun Forest, *U.K.* **14** 52 27N 3 7W
Clunbury, *U.K.* **14** 52 25N 2 55W
Clwyd □, *U.K.* **17** 53 5N 3 20W
Clwyd →, *U.K.* **17** 53 20N 3 30W
Clyde →, *U.K.* **20** 55 56N 4 29W
Clyde, Firth of, *U.K.* **20** 55 20N 5 0W
Clydebank, *U.K.* **20** 55 54N 4 25W
Clydesdale, *U.K.* **21** 55 42N 3 50W
Coalbrookdale, *U.K.* **14** 52 38N 2 30W
Coalburn, *U.K.* **21** 55 35N 3 55W
Coalville, *U.K.* **14** 52 43N 1 21W
Coast Mts., *Canada* **88** 55 0N 129 0W
Coast Ranges, *U.S.A.* **90** 41 0N 123 0W
Coatbridge, *U.K.* **21** 55 52N 4 2W
Coatzacoalcos, *Mex.* **94** 18 7N 94 25W
Cóbh, *Ire.* **25** 51 50N 8 18W
Cobourg Pen., *Austral.* **66** 11 20S 132 15 E
Cochabamba, *Bol.* **100** 17 26S 66 10W
Cochin, *India* **58** 9 59N 76 22 E
Cockburnspath, *U.K.* **21** 55 56N 2 23W
Cockenzie, *U.K.* **21** 55 58N 2 59W
Cockerham, *U.K.* **18** 53 58N 2 49W
Cockermouth, *U.K.* **18** 54 40N 3 22W
Cockfield, *U.K.* **15** 52 8N 0 47 E
Cod, C., *U.S.A.* **93** 42 8N 70 10W
Coddenham, *U.K.* **15** 52 8N 1 8 E
Coffs Harbour, *Austral.* **67** 30 16S 153 5 E
Coggeshall, *U.K.* **15** 51 53N 0 41 E
Coimbatore, *India* **58** 11 2N 76 59 E
Coimbra, *Port.* **37** 40 15N 8 27W
Colac, *Austral.* **70** 38 21S 143 35 E
Colby, *U.K.* **18** 54 6N 4 42W
Colchester, *U.K.* **15** 51 54N 0 55 E
Cold Fell, *U.K.* **18** 54 54N 2 40W
Coldingham, *U.K.* **21** 55 53N 2 10W
Coldstream, *U.K.* **21** 55 39N 2 14W
Colebrooke, *U.K.* **16** 50 45N 3 44W
Coleford, *U.K.* **14** 51 46N 2 38W
Coleraine, *U.K.* **24** 55 8N 6 40W
Coleraine □, *U.K.* **24** 55 8N 6 40 E
Coleshill, *U.K.* **14** 52 30N 1 42W
Colima, *Mex.* **94** 19 14N 103 43W
Colinton, *U.K.* **21** 55 54N 3 17W
Coll, *U.K.* **20** 56 40N 6 35W
Collie, *Austral.* **66** 33 22S 116 8 E
Collier Law Pk., *U.K.* **18** 54 47N 1 59W
Collin, *U.K.* **21** 55 4N 3 30W
Collingbourne, *U.K.* **14** 51 16N 1 39W
Collooney, *Ire.* **24** 54 11N 8 28W
Colmar, *Fr.* **34** 48 5N 7 20 E
Colmonel, *U.K.* **20** 55 8N 4 55W
Colne, *U.K.* **18** 53 51N 2 11W
Colne →, *Essex, U.K.* **15** 51 55N 0 50 E
Colne →, *Herts., U.K.* **15** 51 36N 0 30W
Cologne, *W. Ger.* **36** 50 56N 6 58 E
Colombia ■, *S. Am.* **100** 3 45N 73 0W
Colombo, *Sri L.* **58** 6 56N 79 58 E
Colón, *Mex.* **94** 20 48N 100 3W
Colonsay, *U.K.* **20** 56 4N 6 12W
Colorado □, *U.S.A.* **90** 37 40N 106 0W
Colorado →, *Calif., U.S.A.* **90** 34 45N 114 40W
Colorado →, *Tex., U.S.A.* **90** 28 36N 95 58W
Colorado Plateau, *U.S.A.* **90** 36 40N 110 30W
Colorado Springs, *U.S.A.* **90** 38 55N 104 50W
Colstorworth, *U.K.* **15** 52 48N 0 37W
Coltishall, *U.K.* **15** 52 44N 1 21 E
Columbia, *Miss., U.S.A.* **90** 31 16N 89 50W
Columbia, *S.C., U.S.A.* **91** 34 0N 81 0W
Columbia →, *N. Am.* **90** 46 15N 124 5W
Columbus, *Ga., U.S.A.* **91** 32 30N 84 58W
Columbus, *Ohio, U.S.A.* **92** 39 57N 83 1W
Colwell, *U.K.* **21** 55 4N 2 4W
Colwich, *U.K.* **14** 52 48N 1 58W
Colwyn Bay, *U.K.* **17** 53 17N 3 44W
Colyton, *U.K.* **16** 50 44N 3 4W
Combe Martin, *U.K.* **16** 51 12N 4 2W
Comber, *U.K.* **24** 54 33N 5 45W
Comeragh Mts., *Ire.* **25** 52 17N 7 35W
Comilla, *Bangla.* **59** 23 28N 91 10 E
Comino, *Malta* **40** 36 0N 14 20 E
Communism Pk., *U.S.S.R.* **48** 38 40N 72 20 E
Como, *It.* **40** 45 48N 9 5 E
Como, L., *It.* **40** 46 5N 9 17 E
Comodoro Rivadavia, *Arg.* **102** 45 50S 67 40W
Comorin, C., *India* **58** 8 3N 77 40 E
Comoro Is. ■, *Ind. Oc.* **73** 12 10S 44 15 E
Compiègne, *Fr.* **34** 49 24N 2 50 E
Comrie, *U.K.* **21** 56 22N 4 0W
Conakry, *Guin.* **78** 9 29N 13 49W
Concepción, *Chile* **102** 36 50S 73 0W
Conchos →, *Mex.* **94** 29 32N 104 25W
Concordia, *Arg.* **102** 31 20S 58 2W
Condover, *U.K.* **14** 52 39N 2 46W
Congleton, *U.K.* **18** 53 10N 2 12W
Congo = Zaïre →, *Africa* **80** 6 4S 12 24 E
Congo ■, *Africa* **80** 1 0S 16 0 E
Congo Basin, *Africa* **72** 0 10S 24 30 E
Congresbury, *U.K.* **14** 51 20N 2 49W
Coningsby, *U.K.* **19** 53 7N 0 9W
Conisbrough, *U.K.* **19** 53 29N 1 12W
Coniston, *U.K.* **18** 54 22N 3 6W
Coniston Water, *U.K.* **18** 54 20N 3 5W
Conn, L., *Ire.* **24** 54 3N 9 15W
Connacht, *Ire.* **24** 53 23N 8 40W
Connah's Quay, *U.K.* **17** 53 13N 3 6W
Connecticut □, *U.S.A.* **93** 41 40N 72 40W
Connecticut →, *U.S.A.* **93** 41 17N 72 21W
Connel, *U.K.* **20** 56 27N 5 24W
Connel Park, *U.K.* **20** 55 22N 4 15W
Connemara, *Ire.* **24** 53 29N 9 45W
Conon →, *U.K.* **23** 57 33N 4 28W
Cononbridge, *U.K.* **23** 57 32N 4 30W
Consett, *U.K.* **18** 54 52N 1 50W
Constance, L. =
Bodensee, *W. Ger.* **42** 47 35N 9 25 E
Constanța, *Rom.* **43** 44 14N 28 38 E
Constantine, *Alg.* **78** 36 25N 6 42 E
Conwy, *U.K.* **17** 53 17N 3 50W
Conwy →, *U.K.* **17** 53 18N 3 50W
Cook, Mt., *N.Z.* **71** 43 36S 170 9 E
Cook Is., *Pac. Oc.* **65** 17 0S 160 0W
Cook Strait, *N.Z.* **71** 41 15S 174 29 E
Cookham, *U.K.* **15** 51 33N 0 42W
Cookstown, *U.K.* **24** 54 40N 6 43W
Cookstown □, *U.K.* **24** 54 40N 6 43W
Coolgardie, *Austral.* **66** 30 55S 121 8 E
Cootamundra, *Austral.* **70** 34 36S 148 1 E
Cootehill, *Ire.* **24** 54 5N 7 5W
Copenhagen, *Den.* **45** 55 41N 12 34 E
Coppermine, *Canada* **88** 67 50N 115 5W
Coppermine →, *Canada* **88** 67 49N 116 4W
Copythorne, *U.K.* **14** 50 56N 1 34W
Coquet →, *U.K.* **19** 55 18N 1 45W
Coquet, I., *U.K.* **21** 55 21N 1 30W
Coral Sea, *Pac. Oc.* **64** 15 0S 150 0 E
Coral Sea Islands Terr., *Austral.* **67** 20 0S 155 0 E
Corbridge, *U.K.* **21** 54 58N 2 0W
Corby, *Lincs., U.K.* **15** 52 49N 0 31W
Corby, *Northants., U.K.* **15** 52 29N 0 41W
Córdoba, *Arg.* **102** 31 20S 64 10W
Córdoba, *Sp.* **37** 37 50N 4 50W
Cordova, *U.S.A.* **88** 60 36N 145 45W
Corfe Castle, *U.K.* **14** 50 37N 2 3W
Corfe Mullen, *U.K.* **14** 50 45N 2 0W
Corfu = Kérkira, *Greece* **41** 39 38N 19 50 E
Corinth, G. of, *Greece* **41** 38 16N 22 30 E
Cork, *Ire.* **25** 51 54N 8 30W
Cork □, *Ire.* **25** 51 50N 8 50W
Cork Harbour, *Ire.* **25** 51 46N 8 16W
Corner Brook, *Canada* **89** 48 57N 57 58W
Cornforth, *U.K.* **19** 54 42N 1 28W
Cornwall □, *U.K.* **16** 50 26N 4 40W
Cornwall, C., *U.K.* **16** 50 8N 5 42W
Coro, *Ven.* **100** 11 25N 69 41W
Coromandel Coast, *India* **58** 12 30N 81 0 E
Coronation Gulf, *Canada* **88** 68 25N 110 0W
Corpus Christi, *U.S.A.* **90** 27 50N 97 28W
Corrib, L., *Ire.* **24** 53 5N 9 10W
Corrie, *U.K.* **20** 55 39N 5 10W
Corrientes, *Arg.* **102** 27 30S 58 45W
Corringham, *U.K.* **19** 53 25N 0 42W
Corryvreckan, G. of, *U.K.* **20** 56 10N 5 44W
Corsewall Pt., *U.K.* **20** 55 0N 5 10W
Corsham, *U.K.* **14** 51 25N 2 11W
Corsica, I., *Medit. S.* **35** 42 0N 9 0 E
Corsley, *U.K.* **14** 51 12N 2 14W
Corsock, *U.K.* **21** 55 4N 3 56W
Corton, *U.K.* **15** 52 31N 1 46 E
Corumbá, *Brazil* **100** 19 0S 57 30W
Coruña, La, *Sp.* **37** 43 20N 8 25W
Corve →, *U.K.* **14** 52 22N 2 43W
Coseley, *U.K.* **14** 52 33N 2 6W
Cosenza, *It.* **40** 39 17N 16 14 E
Cosham, *U.K.* **14** 50 51N 1 3W
Costa Rica ■, *Cent. Am.* **95** 10 0N 84 0W
Costessey, *U.K.* **15** 52 40N 1 11 E
Côte d'Or, *Fr.* **34** 47 10N 4 50 E
Cotherstone, *U.K.* **18** 54 34N 1 59W
Cotonou, *Benin* **78** 6 20N 2 25 E
Cotopaxi, Vol., *Ecuad.* **100** 0 40S 78 30W
Cotswold Hills, *U.K.* **14** 51 42N 2 10W
Cottbus, *E. Ger.* **42** 51 44N 14 20 E
Cottenham, *U.K.* **15** 52 18N 0 8 E
Cottingham, *U.K.* **19** 53 47N 0 29W
Coulport, *U.K.* **20** 56 3N 4 53W
Council Bluffs, *U.S.A.* **90** 41 20N 95 50W
Coupar Angus, *U.K.* **21** 56 33N 3 17W
Coventry, *U.K.* **14** 52 25N 1 31W
Cover →, *U.K.* **18** 54 14N 1 45W
Coverack, *U.K.* **16** 50 2N 5 6W
Covington, *U.S.A.* **92** 39 5N 84 30W
Cowal, *U.K.* **20** 56 5N 5 8W
Cowan, L., *Austral.* **66** 31 45S 121 45 E
Cowbridge, *U.K.* **17** 51 28N 3 28W
Cowdenbeath, *U.K.* **21** 56 7N 3 20W
Cowes, *U.K.* **14** 50 45N 1 18W
Cowfold, *U.K.* **15** 50 58N 0 16W
Cowley, *U.K.* **14** 51 43N 1 12W
Cowpen, *U.K.* **21** 55 8N 1 34W
Cowra, *Austral.* **70** 33 49S 148 42 E
Craigavon □, *U.K.* **24** 54 30N 6 25W
Craighouse, *U.K.* **20** 55 50N 5 58W
Craignish, L., *U.K.* **20** 56 11N 5 32W
Crail, *U.K.* **21** 56 16N 2 38W
Craiova, *Rom.* **43** 44 21N 23 48 E
Cramlington, *U.K.* **21** 55 5N 1 36W
Cranborne, *U.K.* **14** 50 55N 1 55W
Cranborne Chase, *U.K.* **14** 50 56N 2 6W
Cranbrook, *Canada* **88** 49 30N 115 46W
Cranbrook, *U.K.* **15** 51 6N 0 33 E
Cranleigh, *U.K.* **15** 51 8N 0 29W
Cranshaws, *U.K.* **21** 55 51N 2 30W
Cranwell, *U.K.* **19** 53 4N 0 29W
Craven Arms, *U.K.* **14** 52 27N 2 49W
Crawford, *U.K.* **21** 55 28N 3 40W
Crawley, *U.K.* **15** 51 7N 0 10W
Credenhill, *U.K.* **14** 52 6N 2 49W
Crediton, *U.K.* **16** 50 47N 3 39W
Cree →, *U.K.* **20** 54 51N 4 24W
Creeside, *U.K.* **20** 55 4N 4 41W
Creetown, *U.K.* **20** 54 54N 4 23W
Cremona, *It.* **40** 45 8N 10 2 E
Crete, I., *Greece* **41** 35 15N 25 0 E
Creusot, Le, *Fr.* **34** 46 48N 4 24 E
Crewe, *U.K.* **18** 53 6N 2 28W
Crewkerne, *U.K.* **14** 50 53N 2 48W
Crianlarich, *U.K.* **20** 56 24N 4 37W
Criccieth, *U.K.* **17** 52 55N 4 15W
Crick, *U.K.* **14** 52 22N 1 9W
Crickhowell, *U.K.* **17** 51 52N 3 8W
Cricklade, *U.K.* **14** 51 38N 1 50W
Crieff, *U.K.* **21** 56 22N 3 50W
Criffell, *U.K.* **21** 54 56N 3 38W
Crimea, *U.S.S.R.* **47** 45 0N 34 0 E
Crinan, *U.K.* **20** 56 6N 5 34W
Crinan Canal, *U.K.* **20** 56 4N 5 30W
Croaghpatrick, *Ire.* **24** 53 46N 9 40W
Crocketford, *U.K.* **21** 55 3N 3 49W
Croglin, *U.K.* **18** 54 50N 2 37W
Cromarty, *U.K.* **23** 57 40N 4 2W
Cromarty Firth, *U.K.* **23** 57 40N 4 15W
Cromer, *U.K.* **15** 52 56N 1 18 E
Crondall, *U.K.* **15** 51 13N 0 51W
Crook, *U.K.* **19** 54 43N 1 45W
Crooklands, *U.K.* **18** 54 16N 2 43W
Crosby, *Cumbria, U.K.* **18** 54 45N 3 25W
Crosby, *Merseyside, U.K.* **18** 53 30N 3 2W
Crosby Ravensworth, *U.K.* **18** 54 34N 2 35W
Cross Fell, *U.K.* **18** 54 44N 2 29W
Crosshaven, *Ire.* **25** 51 48N 8 19W
Crosshill, *U.K.* **20** 55 19N 4 39W
Crouch →, *U.K.* **15** 51 37N 0 53 E
Crow Hd., *Ire.* **25** 51 34N 10 9W
Crow Sound, *U.K.* **16** 49 56N 6 16W
Crowborough, *U.K.* **15** 51 3N 0 9 E
Crowland, *U.K.* **15** 52 41N 0 10W
Crowle, *U.K.* **19** 53 36N 0 49W
Croyde, *U.K.* **16** 51 7N 4 13W
Croydon, *U.K.* **15** 51 18N 0 5W
Crudgington, *U.K.* **14** 52 46N 2 33W
Crummock Water L., *U.K.* **18** 54 33N 3 18W
Cruzeiro do Sul, *Brazil* **100** 7 35S 72 35W
Cuba ■, *W. Ind.* **95** 22 0N 79 0W
Cuckfield, *U.K.* **15** 51 0N 0 8W
Cúcuta, *Col.* **100** 7 54N 72 31W
Cudworth, *U.K.* **19** 53 35N 1 25W
Cuenca, *Ecuad.* **100** 2 50S 79 9W
Cuenca, *Sp.* **37** 40 5N 2 10W
Cuernavaca, *Mex.* **94** 18 55N 99 15W
Cuiabá, *Brazil* **101** 15 30S 56 0W
Cuillin Hills, *U.K.* **22** 57 14N 6 15W
Cuillin Sd., *U.K.* **22** 57 4N 6 20W
Culiacán, *Mex.* **94** 24 50N 107 23W
Cullen, *U.K.* **23** 57 45N 2 50W
Culloden Moor, *U.K.* **23** 57 29N 4 7W
Cullompton, *U.K.* **16** 50 52N 3 23W
Culm →, *U.K.* **16** 50 46N 3 31W
Culrain, *U.K.* **23** 57 55N 4 25W
Culross, *U.K.* **21** 56 4N 3 38W
Cumaná, *Ven.* **100** 10 30N 64 5W
Cumberland Plateau, *U.S.A.* **91** 36 0N 84 30W
Cumbrae Is., *U.K.* **20** 55 46N 4 54W
Cumbria □, *U.K.* **18** 54 35N 2 55W
Cumbrian Mts., *U.K.* **18** 54 30N 3 0W
Cummertrees, *U.K.* **21** 55 0N 3 20W
Cumnock, *U.K.* **20** 55 27N 4 18W
Cumnor, *U.K.* **14** 51 44N 1 20W
Cumwhinton, *U.K.* **18** 54 51N 2 49W
Cúneo, *It.* **40** 44 23N 7 31 E
Cunninghame, *U.K.* **20** 55 38N 4 35W
Cupar, *U.K.* **21** 56 20N 3 0W
Curitiba, *Brazil* **102** 25 20S 49 10W
Currie, *U.K.* **21** 55 53N 3 17W
Curry Rivel, *U.K.* **14** 51 2N 2 52W
Cuttack, *India* **59** 20 25N 85 57 E
Cuzco, *Peru* **100** 13 32S 72 0W
Cwmbran, *U.K.* **17** 51 39N 3 0W
Cyclades = Kikládhes, *Greece* **41** 37 20N 24 30 E
Cyprus ■, *Medit. S.* **47** 35 0N 33 0 E
Czechoslovakia ■, *Europe* **42** 49 0N 17 0 E
Częstochowa, *Pol.* **43** 50 49N 19 7 E

D

Da Lat, *Viet.* **63** 11 56N 108 25 E
Da Nang, *Viet.* **63** 16 4N 108 13 E
Dacca, *Bangla.* **59** 23 43N 90 26 E
Daer →, *U.K.* **21** 55 23N 3 39W
Dailly, *U.K.* **20** 55 16N 4 44W
Daingean, *Ire.* **25** 53 18N 7 15W
Dakar, *Sene.* **78** 14 34N 17 29W
Dakhla, *W. Sah.* **78** 23 50N 15 53W
Dalbeattie, *U.K.* **21** 54 55N 3 50W
Dalian, *China* **61** 38 50N 121 40 E
Dalkeith, *U.K.* **21** 55 54N 3 5W
Dallas, *U.S.A.* **91** 32 50N 96 50W
Dalmally, *U.K.* **20** 56 25N 5 0W
Dalmatia, *Yug.* **41** 43 20N 17 0 E
Dalmellington, *U.K.* **20** 55 20N 4 25W
Daloa, *Ivory C.* **78** 7 0N 6 30W
Dalry, *U.K.* **20** 55 44N 4 42W
Dalrymple, *U.K.* **20** 55 24N 4 36W
Dalton, *Cumbria, U.K.* **18** 54 9N 3 11W
Dalton, *Dumf. & Gall., U.K.* **21** 55 3N 3 22W
Dalton, *N. Yorks., U.K.* **19** 54 28N 1 32W
Dalwhinnie, *U.K.* **23** 56 56N 4 14W
Damascus, *Syria* **57** 33 30N 36 18 E
Damerham, *U.K.* **14** 50 57N 1 52W
Dampier, *Austral.* **66** 20 41S 116 42 E
Dandenong, *Austral.* **70** 38 0S 145 15 E
Dandong, *China* **61** 40 10N 124 20 E
Dannevirke, *N.Z.* **71** 40 12S 176 8 E
Danube →, *Europe* **42** 45 20N 29 40 E
Dar-es-Salaam, *Tanz.* **80** 6 50S 39 12 E
Dar'ā, *Syria* **57** 32 36N 36 7 E
Dardanelles, *Turk.* **47** 40 0N 26 0 E
Darent →, *U.K.* **15** 51 22N 0 12 E

Dargaville, *N.Z.* 71 35 57S 173 52 E
Darién, G. del, *Col.* 95 9 0N 77 0W
Darlaston, *U.K.* 14 52 35N 2 1W
Darling —►, *Austral.* 70 34 4S 141 54 E
Darling Ra., *Austral.* 66 32 30S 116 0 E
Darlington, *U.K.* 19 54 33N 1 33W
Darmstadt, *W. Ger.* 42 49 51N 8 40 E
Dart —►, *U.K.* 16 50 24N 3 36W
Dartford, *U.K.* 15 51 26N 0 15 E
Dartington, *U.K.* 16 50 26N 3 42W
Dartmoor, *U.K.* 16 50 36N 4 0W
Dartmouth, *Canada* 93 44 40N 63 30W
Dartmouth, *U.K.* 16 50 21N 3 35W
Darton, *U.K.* 19 53 36N 1 32W
Darvel, *U.K.* 20 55 37N 4 20W
Darwen, *U.K.* 18 53 42N 2 29W
Darwin, *Austral.* 66 12 25S 130 51 E
Dasht-e Kavīr, *Iran* 57 34 30N 55 0 E
Dasht-e Lūt, *Iran* 57 31 30N 58 0 E
Datong, *China* 61 40 6N 113 18 E
Dauphin, *Canada* 88 51 9N 100 5W
Dauphiné, *Fr.* 35 45 15N 5 25 E
Davao, *Phil.* 63 7 0N 125 40 E
Davenport, *U.S.A.* 92 41 30N 90 40W
Daventry, *U.K.* 14 52 16N 1 10W
David, *Pan.* 95 8 30N 82 30W
Davis Str., *N. Am.* 89 65 0N 58 0W
Dawley, *U.K.* 14 52 40N 2 29W
Dawlish, *U.K.* 16 50 34N 3 28W
Dawson, *Canada* 88 64 10N 139 30W
Dawson Creek, *Canada* 88 55 45N 120 15W
Dayton, *U.S.A.* 92 39 45N 84 10W
De Aar, *S. Afr.* 81 30 39S 24 0 E
De Grey —►, *Austral.* 66 20 12S 119 13 E
Dead Sea, *Asia* 57 31 30N 35 30 E
Deal, *U.K.* 15 51 13N 1 25 E
Dean, Forest of, *U.K.* 14 51 50N 2 35W
Dearham, *U.K.* 18 54 43N 3 28W
Dease Lake, *Canada* 88 58 25N 130 6W
Death Valley, *U.S.A.* 90 36 19N 116 52W
Deben —►, *U.K.* 15 52 4N 1 19 E
Debenham, *U.K.* 15 52 14N 1 10 E
Debrecen, *Hung.* 43 47 33N 21 42 E
Deccan, *India* 58 18 0N 79 0 E
Deddington, *U.K.* 14 51 58N 1 19W
Dee —►, *Scotland, U.K.* 23 57 4N 2 7W
Dee —►, *Wales, U.K.* 17 53 15N 3 7W
Deeping, St. Nicholas, *U.K.* 15 52 44N 0 11W
Deeping Fen, *U.K.* 15 52 45N 0 15W
Dehra Dun, *India* 58 30 20N 78 4 E
Delabole, *U.K.* 16 50 37N 4 45W
Delaware □, *U.S.A.* 93 39 0N 75 40W
Delaware —►, *U.S.A.* 93 39 20N 75 25W
Delft, *Neth.* 36 52 1N 4 22 E
Delhi, *India* 58 28 38N 77 17 E
Den Helder, *Neth.* 36 52 57N 4 45 E
Denbigh, *U.K.* 17 53 12N 3 26W
Denby Dale, *U.K.* 19 53 35N 1 40W
Deniliquin, *Austral.* 70 35 30S 144 58 E
Denizli, *Turk.* 47 37 42N 29 2 E
Denmark ■, *Europe* 45 55 30N 9 0 E
Denmark Str., *Atl. Oc.* 103 66 0N 30 0W
Denny, *U.K.* 21 56 1N 3 55W
Dent, *U.K.* 18 54 17N 2 28W
Denton, *E. Sussex, U.K.* 15 50 48N 0 5 E
Denton, *Gr. Manchester, U.K.* 18 53 26N 2 10W
Denton, *Lincs., U.K.* 19 52 52N 0 42W
Denver, *U.S.A.* 90 39 45N 105 0W
Derby, *U.K.* 19 52 55N 1 28W
Derby □, *U.K.* 19 52 55N 1 28W
Derg —►, *U.K.* 24 54 42N 7 26W
Derg, L., *Ire.* 25 53 0N 8 20W
Derry = Londonderry, *U.K.* 24 55 0N 7 20W
Derryveagh Mts., *Ire.* 24 55 0N 8 40W
Dervaig, *U.K.* 20 56 35N 6 13W
Derwent —►, *Derby, U.K.* 19 52 53N 1 17W
Derwent —►, *N. Yorks., U.K.* 19 53 45N 0 57W
Derwent —►, *Tyne & Wear, U.K.* 21 54 58N 1 40W
Derwent Water, L., *U.K.* 18 54 35N 3 9W
Des Moines, *U.S.A.* 91 41 35N 93 37W
Des Moines —►, *U.S.A.* 91 40 23N 91 25W
Desborough, *U.K.* 15 52 27N 0 50W
Desford, *U.K.* 14 52 38N 1 19W
Dessau, *E. Ger.* 42 51 49N 12 15 E
Detroit, *U.S.A.* 92 42 23N 83 5W
Deurne, *Belg.* 36 51 12N 4 24 E
Deventer, *Neth.* 36 52 15N 6 10 E
Deveron —►, *U.K.* 23 57 40N 2 31W
Devizes, *U.K.* 14 51 21N 2 0W
Devonport, *N.Z.* 71 36 49S 174 49 E
Devonport, *U.K.* 16 50 23N 4 11W
Devonshire □, *U.K.* 16 50 50N 3 40W
Dewsbury, *U.K.* 19 53 42N 1 38W
Dhanbad, *India* 59 23 50N 86 30 E
Dharwad, *India* 58 15 22N 75 15 E
Dhule, *India* 58 20 58N 74 50 E
Diamantina —►, *Austral.* 67 26 45S 139 10 E
Dibden, *U.K.* 14 50 53N 1 24W
Didcot, *U.K.* 14 51 36N 1 14W
Dieppe, *Fr.* 34 49 54N 1 4 E
Dijon, *Fr.* 34 47 20N 5 0 E
Dillingham, *U.S.A.* 88 59 5N 158 30W
Dinaric Alps, *Yug.* 40 44 0N 16 30 E
Dingle, *Ire.* 25 52 9N 10 17W
Dingle B., *Ire.* 25 52 3N 10 20W
Dingwall, *U.K.* 23 57 36N 4 26W
Diss, *U.K.* 15 52 23N 1 6 E
Distington, *U.K.* 18 54 35N 3 33W
Ditchingham, *U.K.* 15 52 28N 1 26 E
Ditchling Beacon, *U.K.* 15 50 49N 0 7W
Dittisham, *U.K.* 16 50 22N 3 36W
Ditton Priors, *U.K.* 14 52 30N 2 33W
Diyarbakir, *Turk.* 47 37 55N 40 18 E
Dizzard Pt., *U.K.* 16 50 46N 4 38W
Djibouti ■, *Africa* 56 12 0N 43 0 E
Dnepr —►, *U.S.S.R.* 46 46 30N 32 18 E
Dneprodzerzhinsk, *U.S.S.R.* 47 48 32N 34 37 E
Dnepropetrovsk, *U.S.S.R.* 47 48 30N 35 0 E
Dnestr —►, *U.S.S.R.* 47 46 18N 30 17 E
Docking, *U.K.* 15 52 55N 0 39 E
Doddington, *Cambs., U.K.* 15 52 29N 0 3 E
Doddington, *Northumberland, U.K.* 21 55 33N 2 0W
Dodecanese, *Greece* 41 36 35N 27 0 E
Dodman Pt., *U.K.* 16 50 13N 4 49W
Dodoma, *Tanz.* 80 6 8S 35 45 E
Dogger Bank, *N. Sea* 26 54 50N 2 0 E
Dolgarrog, *U.K.* 17 53 11N 3 50W
Dolgellau, *U.K.* 17 52 44N 3 53W
Dollar, *U.K.* 21 56 9N 3 41W
Dolomites, *It.* 40 46 30N 11 40 E
Dolphinton, *U.K.* 21 55 42N 3 28W
Dolton, *U.K.* 16 50 53N 4 2W
Dominica ■, *W. Ind.* 94 15 20N 61 20W
Dominican Rep. ■, *W. Ind.* 95 19 0N 70 30W
Don —►, *Humberside, U.K.* 19 53 41N 0 51W
Don —►, *Grampian, U.K.* 23 57 14N 2 5W
Don —►, *U.S.S.R.* 47 47 4N 39 18 E
Donaghadee, *U.K.* 24 54 38N 5 32W
Doncaster, *U.K.* 19 53 31N 1 9W
Dondra Head, *Sri L.* 58 5 55N 80 40 E
Donegal, *Ire.* 24 54 39N 8 8W
Donegal □, *Ire.* 24 54 53N 8 0W
Donegal B., *Ire.* 24 54 30N 8 35W
Donetsk, *U.S.S.R.* 47 48 0N 37 45 E
Dongting Hu, *China* 61 29 18N 112 45 E
Donhead, *U.K.* 14 51 1N 2 8W
Donington, *U.K.* 19 52 54N 0 12W
Donna Nook, Pt., *U.K.* 19 53 29N 0 9 E
Doon —►, *U.K.* 20 55 26N 4 41W
Doon, L., *U.K.* 20 55 15N 4 22W
Dorchester, *Dorset, U.K.* 14 50 42N 2 28W
Dorchester, *Oxon., U.K.* 14 51 38N 1 10W
Dordrecht, *Neth.* 36 51 48N 4 39 E
Dorking, *U.K.* 15 51 14N 0 20W
Dornoch, *U.K.* 23 57 52N 4 0W
Dornoch Firth, *U.K.* 23 57 52N 4 0W
Dorset □, *U.K.* 14 50 48N 2 25W
Dorstone, *U.K.* 14 52 4N 3 0W
Dortmund, *W. Ger.* 36 51 32N 7 28 E
Douai, *Fr.* 34 50 21N 3 4 E
Douala, *Cam.* 80 4 0N 9 45 E
Douglas, *I. of M., U.K.* 18 54 9N 4 29W
Douglas, *Strathclyde, U.K.* 21 55 33N 3 50W
Douglas Hd., *U.K.* 18 54 9N 4 28W
Doune, *U.K.* 21 56 12N 4 3W
Dounreay, *U.K.* 23 58 34N 3 44W
Douro —►, *Port.* 37 41 8N 8 40W
Dove —►, *N. Yorks., U.K.* 19 54 20N 0 55W
Dove —►, *Staffs., U.K.* 18 52 51N 1 36W
Dove Dale, *U.K.* 19 53 10N 1 47W
Dover, *U.K.* 15 51 7N 1 19 E
Dover, Str. of, *Europe* 34 51 0N 1 30 E
Doveridge, *U.K.* 18 52 54N 1 49 E
Dovey —►, *U.K.* 17 52 32N 4 0W
Down □, *U.K.* 24 54 20N 6 0W
Downham, *U.K.* 15 52 26N 0 15 E
Downham Market, *U.K.* 15 52 36N 0 22 E
Downpatrick, *U.K.* 24 54 20N 5 43W
Downpatrick Hd., *Ire.* 24 54 20N 9 21W
Downton, *U.K.* 14 51 0N 1 44W
Drake Passage, *S. Oc.* 103 58 0S 68 0W
Drakensberg, *S. Afr.* 81 31 0S 28 0 E
Drammen, *Nor.* 45 59 42N 10 12 E
Drava —►, *Yug.* 42 45 33N 18 55 E
Dreghorn, *U.K.* 20 55 36N 4 30W
Drenthe □, *Neth.* 36 52 52N 6 40 E
Dresden, *E. Ger.* 42 51 2N 13 45 E
Driffield, *U.K.* 19 54 0N 0 25W
Drina —►, *Yug.* 41 44 53N 19 21 E
Drogheda, *Ire.* 24 53 45N 6 20W
Droichead Nua, *Ire.* 25 53 11N 6 50W
Droitwich, *U.K.* 14 52 16N 2 10W
Dronfield, *U.K.* 19 53 18N 1 29W
Dronning Maud Land, *Ant.* 103 72 30S 12 0 E
Drumheller, *Canada* 88 51 25N 112 40W
Drumjohn, *U.K.* 20 55 14N 4 15W
Drummondville, *Canada* 93 45 55N 72 25W
Drummore, *U.K.* 20 54 41N 4 53W
Druridge B., *U.K.* 21 55 16N 1 32W
Drymen, *U.K.* 20 56 4N 4 28W
Dubai, *U.A.E.* 57 25 18N 55 20 E
Dubbo, *Austral.* 70 32 11S 148 35 E
Dubh Artach, *U.K.* 20 56 8N 6 40W
Dublin, *Ire.* 24 53 20N 6 18W
Dublin □, *Ire.* 24 53 24N 6 20W
Dublin B., *Ire.* 25 53 18N 6 5W
Dubrovnik, *Yug.* 41 42 39N 18 6 E
Duddington, *U.K.* 15 52 36N 0 32W
Duddon —►, *U.K.* 18 54 12N 3 15W
Dudley, *U.K.* 14 52 30N 2 5W
Duero —►, *Sp.* 37 41 8N 8 40W
Duffield, *U.K.* 19 52 59N 1 30W
Dufftown, *U.K.* 23 57 26N 3 9W
Duisburg, *W. Ger.* 36 51 27N 6 42 E
Dukinfield, *U.K.* 18 53 29N 2 7W
Duluth, *U.S.A.* 92 46 48N 92 10W
Dulverton, *U.K.* 14 51 2N 3 33W
Dumbarton, *U.K.* 20 55 58N 4 35W
Dumfries, *U.K.* 21 55 4N 3 37W
Dumfries & Galloway □, *U.K.* 21 55 0N 4 0W
Dun Laoghaire, *Ire.* 25 53 17N 6 9W
Dunans, *U.K.* 20 56 4N 5 9W
Dunbar, *U.K.* 21 56 0N 2 32W
Dunblane, *U.K.* 21 56 10N 3 58W
Duncansby Head, *U.K.* 23 58 39N 3 0W
Dunchurch, *U.K.* 14 52 21N 1 19W
Dundalk, *Ire.* 24 54 1N 6 25W
Dundalk Bay, *Ire.* 24 53 55N 6 15W
Dundee, *U.K.* 21 56 29N 3 0W
Dundrennan, *U.K.* 21 54 49N 3 56W
Dundrum, *U.K.* 24 54 17N 5 50W
Dundrum B., *U.K.* 24 54 12N 5 40W
Dunedin, *N.Z.* 71 45 50S 170 33 E
Dunfermline, *U.K.* 21 56 5N 3 28W
Dungannon, *U.K.* 24 54 30N 6 47W
Dungannon □, *U.K.* 24 54 30N 6 55W
Dungarvan, *Ire.* 25 52 6N 7 40W
Dungarvan Bay, *Ire.* 25 52 5N 7 35W
Dungavel, *U.K.* 21 55 37N 4 7W
Dungeness, *U.K.* 15 50 54N 0 59 E
Dunkeld, *U.K.* 23 56 34N 3 36W
Dunkerque, *Fr.* 34 51 2N 2 20 E
Dunkery Beacon, *U.K.* 14 51 15N 3 37W
Dunkirk = Dunkerque, *Fr.* 34 51 2N 2 20 E
Dúnleary = Dun Laoghaire, *Ire.* 25 53 17N 6 9W
Dunlop, *U.K.* 20 55 43N 4 32W
Dunmanus B., *Ire.* 25 51 31N 9 50W
Dunmore Hd., *Ire.* 25 52 10N 10 35W
Dunnet Hd., *U.K.* 23 58 38N 3 22W
Dunning, *U.K.* 21 56 18N 3 37W
Dunoon, *U.K.* 20 55 57N 4 56W
Duns, *U.K.* 21 55 47N 2 20W
Dunscore, *U.K.* 21 55 8N 3 48W
Dunsford, *U.K.* 16 50 41N 3 40W
Dunstable, *U.K.* 15 51 53N 0 31W
Dunster, *U.K.* 14 51 11N 3 28W
Dunston, *U.K.* 14 52 46N 2 7W
Dunvegan, *U.K.* 22 57 26N 6 35W
Durango, *Mex.* 94 24 3N 104 39W
Durban, *S. Afr.* 81 29 49S 31 1 E
Düren, *W. Ger.* 36 50 48N 6 30 E
Durg, *India* 59 21 15N 81 22 E
Durgapur, *India* 59 23 30N 87 20 E
Durham, *U.K.* 19 54 47N 1 34W
Durham, *U.S.A.* 91 36 0N 78 55W
Durham □, *U.K.* 18 54 42N 1 45W
Durlstone Hd., *U.K.* 14 50 35N 1 58W
Durness, *U.K.* 23 58 34N 4 45W
Durrësi, *Alb.* 41 41 19N 19 28 E
Durrington, *U.K.* 14 51 12N 1 47W
Dursley, *U.K.* 14 51 41N 2 21W
Dushanbe, *U.S.S.R.* 48 38 33N 68 48 E
Düsseldorf, *W. Ger.* 36 51 15N 6 46 E
Duyun, *China* 60 26 18N 107 29 E
Dvina, N. —►, *U.S.S.R.* 46 61 40N 45 30 E
Dyfed □, *U.K.* 17 52 0N 4 30W
Dymchurch, *U.K.* 15 51 2N 1 0 E
Dymock, *U.K.* 14 51 58N 2 27W
Dysart, *U.K.* 21 56 8N 3 8W
Dzerzhinsk, *U.S.S.R.* 46 56 14N 43 30 E
Dzhambul, *U.S.S.R.* 48 42 54N 71 22 E
Dzungaria, *China* 60 44 10N 88 0 E

E

Eaglesfield, *U.K.* 21 55 3N 3 12W
Eagleshan, *U.K.* 20 55 44N 4 18W
Eakring, *U.K.* 19 53 9N 0 59W
Ealing, *U.K.* 15 51 30N 0 19W
Earby, *U.K.* 18 53 55N 2 8W
Eardisland, *U.K.* 14 52 14N 2 50W
Eardisley, *U.K.* 14 52 8N 3 0W
Earith, *U.K.* 15 52 21N 0 1 E
Earl Shilton, *U.K.* 14 52 35N 1 20W
Earl Soham, *U.K.* 15 52 14N 1 15 E
Earls Barton, *U.K.* 15 52 16N 0 44W
Earl's Colne, *U.K.* 15 51 56N 0 43 E
Earlsferry, *U.K.* 21 56 11N 2 50W
Earlston, *U.K.* 21 55 39N 2 40W
Earn —►, *U.K.* 21 56 20N 3 19W
Earn, L., *U.K.* 20 56 23N 4 14W
Earsdon, *U.K.* 21 55 4N 1 30W
Easebourne, *U.K.* 15 51 0N 0 42W
Easington, *Durham, U.K.* 19 54 50N 1 24W
Easington, *Humberside, U.K.* 19 53 40N 0 7 E
Easington Colliery, *U.K.* 19 54 49N 1 19W
Easingwold, *U.K.* 19 54 8N 1 11W
East Anglian Hts., *U.K.* 15 52 10N 0 17 E
East Bergholt, *U.K.* 15 51 58N 1 2 E
East Brent, *U.K.* 14 51 14N 2 55W
East China Sea, *Asia* 61 30 5N 126 0 E
East Cowes, *U.K.* 14 50 45N 1 17W
East Dereham, *U.K.* 15 52 40N 0 57 E
East Fen, *U.K.* 19 53 4N 0 5 E
East Germany ■, *Europe* 42 52 0N 12 0 E
East Grinstead, *U.K.* 15 51 8N 0 1W
East Harling, *U.K.* 15 52 26N 0 55 E
East Ilsley, *U.K.* 14 51 33N 1 15W
East Indies, *Asia* 50 0 0 120 0 E
East Kilbride, *U.K.* 20 55 46N 4 10W
East Kirkby, *U.K.* 19 53 5N 1 15W
East Linton, *U.K.* 21 56 0N 2 40W
East London, *S. Afr.* 81 33 0S 27 55 E
East Markham, *U.K.* 19 53 15N 0 53W
East Moor, *U.K.* 19 53 15N 1 30W
East Retford, *U.K.* 19 53 19N 0 55W
East Siberian Sea, *U.S.S.R.* 49 73 0N 160 0 E
East Sussex □, *U.K.* 15 51 0N 0 20 E
East Wemyss, *U.K.* 21 56 8N 3 5W
East Wittering, *U.K.* 15 50 46N 0 53W
East Woodhay, *U.K.* 14 51 21N 1 26W
Eastbourne, *U.K.* 15 50 46N 0 18 E
Eastchurch, *U.K.* 15 51 23N 0 53 E
Easter Islands, *Pac. Oc.* 65 27 0S 109 0W
Eastern Ghats, *India* 58 14 0N 78 50 E
Eastleigh, *U.K.* 14 50 58N 1 21W
Eastnor, *U.K.* 14 52 2N 2 22W
Easton, *Avon, U.K.* 14 51 28N 2 42W
Easton, *Dorset, U.K.* 14 50 32N 2 27W
Easton, *Northants., U.K.* 15 52 37N 0 31W
Eastry, *U.K.* 15 51 15N 1 19 E
Eastwood, *U.K.* 19 53 2N 1 17W
Eaton, *U.K.* 15 52 52N 0 46W
Eaton Socon, *U.K.* 15 52 13N 0 18W
Eau Claire, *U.S.A.* 92 44 46N 91 30W
Ebberston, *U.K.* 19 54 14N 0 35W
Ebbw Vale, *U.K.* 17 51 47N 3 12W
Ebro —►, *Sp.* 37 40 43N 0 54 E
Ecclefechan, *U.K.* 21 55 3N 3 18W
Eccleshall, *U.K.* 14 52 52N 2 14W
Ech Cheliff, *Alg.* 78 36 10N 1 20 E
Echo Bay, *Canada* 88 66 5N 117 55W
Echuca, *Austral.* 70 36 10S 144 20 E
Eck, L., *U.K.* 20 56 5N 5 0W
Eckington, *U.K.* 19 53 19N 1 21W
Ecuador ■, *S. Am.* 100 2 0S 78 0W
Edam, *Neth.* 36 52 31N 5 3 E
Eday, *U.K.* 23 59 11N 2 47W
Eddrachillis B., *U.K.* 22 58 16N 5 10W
Eddystone, *U.K.* 16 50 11N 4 16W
Ede, *Neth.* 36 52 4N 5 40 E
Eden —►, *U.K.* 18 54 57N 3 2W
Edenbridge, *U.K.* 15 51 12N 0 4 E
Edenderry, *Ire.* 25 53 21N 7 3W
Edge Hill, *U.K.* 14 52 7N 1 28W
Edinburgh, *U.K.* 21 55 57N 3 12W
Edington, *U.K.* 14 51 17N 2 6W
Edmondbyers, *U.K.* 18 54 50N 1 59W
Edmonton, *Canada* 88 53 30N 113 30W
Edmundston, *Canada* 93 47 23N 68 20W
Edward, L., *Africa* 80 0 25S 29 40 E
Egersund, *Nor.* 45 58 26N 6 1 E
Egham, *U.K.* 15 51 25N 0 33W
Egmont, Mt., *N.Z.* 71 39 17S 174 5 E
Egremont, *U.K.* 18 54 28N 3 33W
Egton, *U.K.* 19 54 27N 0 45W
Egypt ■, *Africa* 79 28 0N 31 0 E
Eifel, *W. Ger.* 36 50 10N 6 45 E
Eigg, *U.K.* 22 56 54N 6 10W
Eighty Mile Beach, *Austral.* 66 19 30S 120 40 E
Eil, L., *U.K.* 22 56 50N 5 15W
Eildon, L., *Austral.* 70 37 10S 146 0 E
Eindhoven, *Neth.* 36 51 26N 5 30 E
Eire ■, *Europe* 25 53 0N 8 0W
El Aaiún, *W. Sah.* 78 27 9N 13 12W
El Asnam = Ech Cheliff, *Alg.* 78 36 10N 1 20 E
El Faiyûm, *Egypt* 79 29 19N 30 50 E
El Fâsher, *Sudan* 79 13 33N 25 26 E
El Gîza, *Egypt* 79 30 0N 31 10 E
El Jadida, *Mor.* 78 33 11N 8 17W
El Mahalla el Kubra, *Egypt* 79 31 0N 31 0 E
El Mansûra, *Egypt* 79 31 0N 31 19 E
El Minyâ, *Egypt* 79 28 7N 30 33 E
El Obeid, *Sudan* 79 13 8N 30 10 E
El Paso, *U.S.A.* 90 31 50N 106 30W
El Qâhira = Cairo, *Egypt* 79 30 1N 31 14 E
El Salvador ■, *Cent. Am.* 94 13 50N 89 0W
Elba, *It.* 40 42 48N 10 15 E
Elbasani, *Alb.* 41 41 9N 20 9 E
Elbe —►, *W. Ger.* 42 53 50N 9 0 E
Elbląg, *Pol.* 43 54 10N 19 25 E
Elburz Mts., *Iran* 56 36 0N 52 0 E
Elche, *Sp.* 37 38 15N 0 42W
Eldoret, *Kenya* 80 0 30N 35 17 E
Eleuthera, *Baham.* 95 25 0N 76 20W
Elgin, *U.K.* 23 57 39N 3 20W
Elham, *U.K.* 15 51 9N 1 7 E
Elie, *U.K.* 21 56 11N 2 50W

Elishaw, *U.K.* **21** 55 16N 2 14W
Elizabeth, *Austral.* **67** 34 42S 138 41 E
Elizabeth, *U.S.A.* **93** 40 37N 74 12W
Elland, *U.K.* **19** 53 41N 1 49W
Ellen →, *U.K.* **18** 54 44N 3 30W
Eller Beck Bridge, *U.K.* **19** 54 23N 0 40W
Ellesmere, *U.K.* **18** 52 55N 2 53W
Ellesmere I., *Canada* **103** 79 30N 80 0W
Ellesmere Port, *U.K.* **18** 53 17N 2 55W
Ellice Is. = Tuvalu ■, *Pac. Oc.* **64** 8 0S 178 0 E
Ellington, *U.K.* **21** 55 14N 1 34W
Ellon, *U.K.* **23** 57 21N 2 5W
Elmira, *U.S.A.* **92** 42 8N 76 49W
Elmswell, *U.K.* **15** 52 14N 0 53 E
Eluru, *India* **59** 16 48N 81 8 E
Ely, *U.K.* **15** 52 24N 0 16 E
Emāmrūd, *Iran* **56** 36 30N 55 0 E
Embleton, *U.K.* **21** 55 30N 1 38W
Emden, *W. Ger.* **36** 53 22N 7 12 E
Emerald, *Austral.* **67** 23 32S 148 10 E
Emmeloord, *Neth.* **36** 52 44N 5 46 E
Emmen, *Neth.* **36** 52 48N 6 57 E
Ems →, *W. Ger.* **36** 52 37N 9 26 E
Enard B., *U.K.* **22** 58 5N 5 20W
Enderbury I., *Pac. Oc.* **64** 3 8S 171 5W
Enderby, *U.K.* **14** 52 35N 1 15W
Enderby Land, *Ant.* **103** 66 0S 53 0 E
Enfield, *U.K.* **15** 51 39N 0 4W
England □, *U.K.* **5** 53 0N 2 0W
English Channel, *Europe* **15** 50 0N 2 0W
Ennerdale Water, *U.K.* **18** 54 32N 3 24W
Ennis, *Ire.* **25** 52 51N 8 59W
Enniscorthy, *Ire.* **25** 52 30N 6 35W
Enniskillen, *U.K.* **24** 54 20N 7 40W
Ennistimon, *Ire.* **25** 52 56N 9 18W
Enschede, *Neth.* **36** 52 13N 6 53 E
Ensenada, *Mex.* **94** 31 50N 116 50W
Enstone, *U.K.* **14** 51 55N 1 25W
Entebbe, *Uganda* **80** 0 4N 32 28 E
Enugu, *Nig.* **78** 6 20N 7 30 E
Epping, *U.K.* **15** 51 42N 0 8 E
Epping Forest, *U.K.* **15** 51 40N 0 5 E
Epsom, *U.K.* **15** 51 19N 0 16W
Epworth, *U.K.* **19** 53 30N 0 50W
Equatorial Guinea ■, *Africa* **80** 2 0S 8 0 E
Erebus, Mt., *Ant.* **103** 77 35S 167 0 E
Erfurt, *E. Ger.* **42** 50 58N 11 2 E
Eriboll, L., *U.K.* **23** 58 28N 4 41W
Erie, *U.S.A.* **92** 42 10N 80 7W
Erie, L., *N. Am.* **92** 42 15N 81 0W
Eritrea □, *Eth.* **79** 14 0N 41 0 E
Erlangen, *W. Ger.* **42** 49 35N 11 0 E
Erne →, *U.K.* **24** 54 30N 8 16W
Erne, Lough, *U.K.* **24** 54 26N 7 46W
Erode, *India* **58** 11 24N 77 45 E
Errigal, Mt., *Ire.* **24** 55 2N 8 8W
Erris Hd., *Ire.* **24** 54 19N 10 0W
Errol, *U.K.* **21** 56 24N 3 13W
Erzurum, *Turk.* **47** 39 57N 41 15 E
Esbjerg, *Den.* **45** 55 29N 8 29 E
Esch, *Neth.* **36** 51 37N 5 17 E
Eschweiler, *W. Ger.* **36** 50 49N 6 14 E
Escrick, *U.K.* **19** 53 53N 1 3W
Eşfahān, *Iran* **56** 33 0N 53 0 E
Esk →, *Cumbria, U.K.* **18** 54 23N 3 21W
Esk →, *Dumf. & Gall., U.K.* **21** 54 58N 3 4W
Esk →, *N. Yorks., U.K.* **19** 54 27N 0 36W
Eskdale, *U.K.* **21** 55 12N 3 4W
Eskifjörður, *Ice.* **44** 65 3N 13 55W
Eskilstuna, *Swed.* **45** 59 22N 16 32 E
Eskimo Pt., *Canada* **88** 61 10N 94 15W
Eskişehir, *Turk.* **47** 39 50N 30 35 E
Esmeraldas, *Ecuad.* **100** 1 0N 79 40W
Esperance, *Austral.* **66** 33 45S 121 55 E
Espinhaço, Serra do, *Brazil* **101** 17 30S 43 30W
Essen, *W. Ger.* **36** 51 28N 6 59 E
Essex □, *U.K.* **15** 51 48N 0 30 E
Eston, *U.K.* **19** 54 33N 1 6W
Estonian S.S.R. □, *U.S.S.R.* **46** 58 30N 25 30 E
Etchingham, *U.K.* **15** 51 0N 0 27 E
Ethiopia ■, *Africa* **78** 8 0N 40 0 E
Ethiopian Highlands, *Eth.* **72** 10 0N 37 0 E
Etive, L., *U.K.* **20** 56 30N 5 12W
Etna, *It.* **40** 37 45N 15 0 E
Eton, *U.K.* **15** 51 29N 0 37W
Ettington, *U.K.* **14** 52 8N 1 38W
Ettrick Forest, *U.K.* **21** 55 30N 3 0W
Ettrick Water, *U.K.* **21** 55 31N 2 55W
Eugene, *U.S.A.* **90** 44 0N 123 8W
Euphrates →, *Asia* **56** 31 0N 47 25 E
Euston, *Austral.* **70** 34 30S 142 46 E
Euxton, *U.K.* **18** 53 41N 2 42W
Evansville, *U.S.A.* **92** 38 0N 87 35W
Evercreech, *U.K.* **14** 51 8N 2 30W
Everest, Mt., *Nepal* **60** 28 5N 86 58 E
Evesham, *U.K.* **14** 52 6N 1 57W
Évora, *Port.* **37** 38 33N 7 57W
Évreux, *Fr.* **34** 49 0N 1 8 E
Évvoia, *Greece* **41** 38 30N 24 0 E
Ewe, L., *U.K.* **22** 57 49N 5 38W
Ewell, *U.K.* **15** 51 20N 0 15W
Ewhurst, *U.K.* **15** 51 9N 0 25W
Exe →, *U.K.* **16** 50 38N 3 27W
Exeter, *U.K.* **16** 50 43N 3 31W
Exford, *U.K.* **14** 51 8N 3 39W
Exminster, *U.K.* **16** 50 40N 3 29W
Exmoor, *U.K.* **16** 51 10N 3 59W
Exmouth, *Austral.* **66** 21 54S 114 10 E
Exmouth, *U.K.* **16** 50 37N 3 26W
Exmouth G., *Austral.* **66** 22 15S 114 15 E
Exton, *U.K.* **15** 52 42N 0 38W
Eyam, *U.K.* **19** 53 17N 1 40W
Eye, *Cambs., U.K.* **15** 52 36N 0 11W
Eye, *Suffolk, U.K.* **15** 52 19N 1 9 E
Eye Pen., *U.K.* **22** 58 13N 6 10W
Eyemouth, *U.K.* **21** 55 53N 2 5W
Eynsham, *U.K.* **14** 51 47N 1 21W
Eyre, L., *Austral.* **67** 29 30S 137 26 E
Eyre Cr. →, *Austral.* **67** 26 40S 139 0 E
Eyre Pen., *Austral.* **66** 33 30S 137 17 E

F

Fair Hd., *U.K.* **24** 55 14N 6 10W
Fairbanks, *U.S.A.* **88** 64 50N 147 50W
Fairfield, *Austral.* **70** 33 53S 150 57 E
Fairford, *U.K.* **14** 51 42N 1 48W
Fairlie, *N.Z.* **71** 44 5S 170 49 E
Fairlie, *U.K.* **20** 55 44N 4 52W
Fairlight, *U.K.* **15** 50 53N 0 40 E
Faisalabad, *Pak.* **58** 31 30N 73 5 E
Faizabad, *India* **59** 26 45N 82 10 E
Fakenham, *U.K.* **15** 52 50N 0 51 E
Faldingworth, *U.K.* **19** 53 21N 0 22W
Falkenberg, *Swed.* **45** 56 54N 12 30 E
Falkirk, *U.K.* **21** 56 0N 3 47W
Falkland, *U.K.* **21** 56 15N 3 13W
Falkland Is., *Atl. Oc.* **102** 51 30S 59 0W
Fall River, *U.S.A.* **93** 41 45N 71 5W
Falmouth, *U.K.* **16** 50 9N 5 5W
Falmouth B., *U.K.* **16** 50 7N 5 3W
Falstone, *U.K.* **21** 55 10N 2 26W
Falun, *Swed.* **45** 60 37N 15 37 E
Famagusta, *Cyprus* **47** 35 8N 33 55 E
Fannich, L., *U.K.* **22** 57 40N 5 0W
Fareham, *U.K.* **14** 50 52N 1 11W
Faringdon, *U.K.* **14** 51 39N 1 34W
Farnborough, *U.K.* **15** 51 17N 0 46W
Farne Is., *U.K.* **19** 55 38N 1 37W
Farnham, *U.K.* **15** 51 13N 0 49W
Farnworth, *U.K.* **18** 53 33N 2 24W
Faroe Is., *Atl. Oc.* **26** 62 0N 7 0W
Farrar →, *U.K.* **23** 57 30N 4 30W
Faslane, *U.K.* **20** 56 3N 4 49W
Fastnet Rock, *Ire.* **25** 51 22N 9 37W
Fauldhouse, *U.K.* **21** 55 50N 3 44W
Faversham, *U.K.* **15** 51 18N 0 54 E
Fawley, *U.K.* **14** 50 49N 1 20W
Faya-Largeau, *Chad* **79** 17 58N 19 6 E
Fayetteville, *U.S.A.* **91** 35 0N 78 58W
Fazeley, *U.K.* **14** 52 36N 1 42W
Fdérik, *Maurit.* **78** 22 40N 12 45W
Feale →, *Ire.* **25** 52 26N 9 40W
Feilding, *N.Z.* **71** 40 13S 175 35 E
Feira de Santana, *Brazil* **101** 12 15S 38 57W
Felixstowe, *U.K.* **15** 51 58N 1 22 E
Felpham, *U.K.* **15** 50 47N 0 38W
Felton, *U.K.* **21** 55 18N 1 42W
Feltwell, *U.K.* **15** 52 29N 0 32 E
Fenit, *Ire.* **25** 52 17N 9 51W
Fenny Bentley, *U.K.* **19** 53 4N 1 43W
Fenny Compton, *U.K.* **14** 52 9N 1 20W
Fenny Stratford, *U.K.* **15** 51 59N 0 42W
Fens, The, *U.K.* **15** 52 45N 0 2 E
Fenwick, *U.K.* **20** 55 38N 4 25W
Fergana, *U.S.S.R.* **48** 40 23N 71 19 E
Fermanagh □, *U.K.* **24** 54 21N 7 40W
Fermoy, *Ire.* **25** 52 4N 8 18W
Fernhurst, *U.K.* **15** 51 3N 0 43W
Ferrara, *It.* **40** 44 50N 11 36 E
Ferryhill, *U.K.* **19** 54 42N 1 32W
Fès, *Mor.* **78** 34 0N 5 0W
Fetlar, *U.K.* **22** 60 36N 0 52W
Ffestiniog, *U.K.* **17** 52 58N 3 56W
Fianarantsoa, *Madag.* **81** 21 26S 47 5 E
Fife □, *U.K.* **21** 56 13N 3 2W
Fife Ness, *U.K.* **21** 56 17N 2 35W
Fiji ■, *Pac. Oc.* **64** 17 20S 179 0 E
Filby, *U.K.* **15** 52 40N 1 39 E
Filey, *U.K.* **19** 54 13N 0 18W
Filey B., *U.K.* **19** 54 12N 0 15W
Filton, *U.K.* **14** 51 29N 2 34W
Fincham, *U.K.* **15** 52 38N 0 30 E
Findhorn →, *U.K.* **23** 57 38N 3 38W
Findon, *U.K.* **15** 50 53N 0 24W
Finedon, *U.K.* **15** 52 20N 0 40W
Fingest, *U.K.* **15** 51 35N 0 52W
Finisterre, C., *Sp.* **37** 42 50N 9 19W
Finland ■, *Europe* **44** 63 0N 27 0 E
Finland, G. of, *Europe* **45** 60 0N 26 0 E
Finn →, *Ire.* **24** 54 50N 7 55W
Finnart, *U.K.* **20** 56 7N 4 48W
Finnmark fylke □, *Nor.* **44** 69 30N 25 0 E
Finstown, *U.K.* **23** 59 0N 3 8W
Fionnphort, *U.K.* **20** 56 19N 6 23W
Firozabad, *India* **58** 27 10N 78 25 E
Fishguard, *U.K.* **17** 51 59N 4 59W
Fishtoft, *U.K.* **19** 52 27N 0 2 E
Fitzroy →, *Austral.* **66** 17 31S 123 35 E
Flamborough, *U.K.* **19** 54 7N 0 7W
Flamborough Hd., *U.K.* **19** 54 8N 0 4W
Flanders, *Belg.* **34** 51 10N 3 15 E
Flatey, *Ice.* **44** 65 22N 22 56W
Fleet, *U.K.* **15** 51 16N 0 50W
Fleetwood, *U.K.* **18** 53 55N 3 1W
Flensburg, *W. Ger.* **42** 54 46N 9 28 E
Fletton, *U.K.* **15** 52 34N 0 13W
Flimby, *U.K.* **18** 54 42N 3 31W
Flinders →, *Austral.* **67** 17 36S 140 36 E
Flinders Ranges, *Austral.* **67** 31 30S 138 30 E
Flint, *U.K.* **17** 53 15N 3 7W
Flint, *U.S.A.* **92** 43 5N 83 40W
Flint →, *U.S.A.* **91** 30 52N 84 38W
Flitwick, *U.K.* **15** 51 59N 0 30W
Flodden, *U.K.* **19** 55 37N 2 8W
Florence, *It.* **40** 43 47N 11 15 E
Flores, *Indon.* **63** 8 35S 121 0 E
Flores Sea, *Indon.* **63** 6 30S 124 0 E
Florianópolis, *Brazil* **102** 27 30S 48 30W
Florida □, *U.S.A.* **91** 28 30N 82 0W
Florida, Straits of, *U.S.A.* **95** 25 0N 80 0W
Florida Keys, *U.S.A.* **91** 25 0N 80 40W
Florissant, *U.S.A.* **90** 38 48N 90 20W
Flushing = Vlissingen, *Neth.* **36** 51 26N 3 34 E
Fóggia, *It.* **40** 41 28N 15 31 E
Folkestone, *U.K.* **15** 51 5N 1 11 E
Fontainebleau, *Fr.* **34** 48 24N 2 40 E
Forbach, *Fr.* **34** 49 10N 6 52 E
Ford, *U.K.* **20** 56 10N 5 27W
Fordham, *U.K.* **15** 52 19N 0 23 E
Fordingbridge, *U.K.* **14** 50 56N 1 48W
Forest Row, *U.K.* **15** 51 6N 0 3 E
Forfar, *U.K.* **23** 56 40N 2 53W
Formby, *U.K.* **18** 53 34N 3 4W
Formby Pt., *U.K.* **18** 53 33N 3 7W
Formosa = Taiwan ■, *Asia* **61** 23 30N 121 0 E
Formosa Strait, *Asia* **61** 24 40N 120 0 E
Forres, *U.K.* **23** 57 37N 3 38W
Fort Augustus, *U.K.* **23** 57 9N 4 40W
Fort Collins, *U.S.A.* **90** 40 30N 105 4W
Fort-de-France, *Mart.* **94** 14 36N 61 2W
Fort George, *Canada* **89** 53 50N 79 0W
Fort Lauderdale, *U.S.A.* **91** 26 10N 80 5W
Fort McMurray, *Canada* **88** 56 44N 111 7W
Fort Smith, *U.S.A.* **90** 35 25N 94 25W
Fort Wayne, *U.S.A.* **92** 41 5N 85 10W
Fort William, *U.K.* **22** 56 48N 5 8W
Fort Worth, *U.S.A.* **90** 32 45N 97 25W
Fortaleza, *Brazil* **101** 3 45S 38 35W
Forth, *U.K.* **21** 55 45N 3 42W
Forth, Firth of, *U.K.* **21** 56 5N 2 55W
Forth Bridge, *U.K.* **21** 56 0N 3 24W
Fortrose, *U.K.* **23** 57 35N 4 10W
Foshan, *China* **61** 23 4N 113 5 E
Fothergill, *U.K.* **18** 54 43N 3 30W
Fotheringhay, *U.K.* **15** 52 32N 0 28W
Foulness I., *U.K.* **15** 51 36N 0 55 E
Foulness Pt., *U.K.* **15** 51 36N 0 59 E
Foulsham, *U.K.* **15** 52 48N 1 1 E
Fountainhall, *U.K.* **21** 55 45N 2 55W
Fountains Abbey, *U.K.* **19** 54 8N 1 35W
Fovant, *U.K.* **14** 51 4N 2 0W
Foveaux Str., *N.Z.* **71** 46 42S 168 10 E
Fowey, *U.K.* **16** 50 20N 4 39W
Fowey →, *U.K.* **16** 50 20N 4 39W
Fownhope, *U.K.* **14** 52 0N 2 37W
Foxdale, *U.K.* **18** 54 12N 4 38W
Foxe Chan., *Canada* **89** 65 0N 80 0W
Foyle, Lough, *U.K.* **24** 55 6N 7 8W
Foynes, *Ire.* **25** 52 37N 9 5W
Fraddon, *U.K.* **16** 50 22N 4 55W
Framlingham, *U.K.* **15** 52 14N 1 20 E
France ■, *Europe* **34** 47 0N 3 0 E
Frankfurt am Main, *W. Ger.* **42** 50 7N 8 40 E
Frankston, *Austral.* **70** 38 8S 145 8 E
Frant, *U.K.* **15** 51 5N 0 17 E
Franz Josef Land, *U.S.S.R.* **48** 82 0N 55 0 E
Fraser →, *Canada* **88** 49 7N 123 11W
Fraser I., *Austral.* **67** 25 15S 153 10 E
Fraserburgh, *U.K.* **23** 57 41N 2 0W
Fredericton, *Canada* **93** 45 57N 66 40W
Frederikshavn, *Den.* **45** 57 28N 10 31 E
Fredrikstad, *Nor.* **45** 59 13N 10 57 E
Freetown, *Sa. Leone* **78** 8 30N 13 17W
Freiburg, *W. Ger.* **42** 48 0N 7 52 E
Fremantle, *Austral.* **66** 32 7S 115 47 E
French Guiana ■, *S. Am.* **101** 4 0N 53 0W
French Polynesia □, *Pac. Oc.* **65** 20 0S 145 0 E
Freshwater, *U.K.* **14** 50 42N 1 31W
Fresnillo, *Mex.* **94** 23 10N 103 0W
Fresno, *U.S.A.* **90** 36 47N 119 50W
Freuchie, *U.K.* **21** 56 14N 3 8W
Fridaythorpe, *U.K.* **19** 54 2N 0 40W
Friesland □, *Neth.* **36** 53 5N 5 50 E
Frimley, *U.K.* **15** 51 18N 0 43W
Frinton-on-Sea, *U.K.* **15** 51 50N 1 16 E
Frisa, Loch, *U.K.* **20** 56 34N 6 5W
Frisian Is., *Europe* **36** 53 30N 6 0 E
Frizington, *U.K.* **18** 54 33N 3 30W
Frobisher B., *Canada* **89** 62 30N 66 0W
Frodsham, *U.K.* **18** 53 17N 2 45W
Frome, *U.K.* **14** 51 16N 2 17W
Frome →, *U.K.* **14** 50 44N 2 5W
Frome, L., *Austral.* **67** 30 45S 139 45 E
Frunze, *U.S.S.R.* **48** 42 54N 74 46 E
Fuji-San, *Jap.* **62** 35 22N 138 44 E
Fujian □, *China* **61** 26 0N 118 0 E
Fukui, *Jap.* **62** 36 0N 136 10 E
Fukuoka, *Jap.* **62** 33 39N 130 21 E
Fukushima, *Jap.* **62** 37 44N 140 28 E
Fukuyama, *Jap.* **62** 34 35N 133 20 E
Fulwood, *U.K.* **18** 53 47N 2 41W
Fundy, B. of, *Canada* **93** 45 0N 66 0W
Furneaux Group, *Austral.* **66** 40 10S 147 50 E
Furness, Pen., *U.K.* **18** 54 12N 3 10W
Fürth, *W. Ger.* **42** 49 29N 11 0 E
Fury and Hecla Str., *Canada* **89** 69 56N 84 0W
Fushun, *China* **61** 41 50N 123 56 E
Fuxin, *China* **61** 42 5N 121 48 E
Fuzhou, *China* **61** 26 5N 119 16 E
Fylde, *U.K.* **18** 53 50N 2 58W
Fylingdales Moor, *U.K.* **19** 54 22N 0 32W
Fyn, *Den.* **45** 55 20N 10 30 E
Fyne, L., *U.K.* **20** 56 0N 5 20W
Fyvie, *U.K.* **23** 57 26N 2 24W

G

Gabès, *Tunisia* **78** 33 53N 10 2 E
Gabon ■, *Africa* **80** 0 10S 10 0 E
Gaborone, *Bots.* **81** 24 45S 25 57 E
Gabrovo, *Bulg.* **41** 42 52N 25 19 E
Gainesville, *U.S.A.* **90** 29 38N 82 20W
Gainford, *U.K.* **19** 54 34N 1 44W
Gainsborough, *U.K.* **19** 53 23N 0 46W
Gairdner L., *Austral.* **66** 31 30S 136 0 E
Gairloch, *U.K.* **22** 57 42N 5 40W
Gairloch, L., *U.K.* **22** 57 43N 5 45W
Galápagos, *Pac. Oc.* **65** 0 0 89 0W
Galashiels, *U.K.* **21** 55 37N 2 50W
Galaţi, *Rom.* **43** 45 27N 28 2 E
Galgate, *U.K.* **18** 53 59N 2 47W
Galilee, Sea of = Kinneret, Lake, *Isr.* **57** 32 45N 35 35 E
Galle, *Sri L.* **58** 6 5N 80 10 E
Galley Hd., *Ire.* **25** 51 32N 8 56W
Gällivare, *Swed.* **44** 67 9N 20 40 E
Galloway, *U.K.* **20** 55 0N 4 25W
Galloway, Mull of, *U.K.* **20** 54 38N 4 50W
Galmpton, *U.K.* **16** 50 23N 3 32W
Galston, *U.K.* **20** 55 36N 4 22W
Galty Mts., *Ire.* **25** 52 22N 8 10W
Galtymore, *Ire.* **25** 52 22N 8 12W
Galveston, *U.S.A.* **91** 29 15N 94 48W
Galway, *Ire.* **25** 53 16N 9 4W
Galway □, *Ire.* **24** 53 16N 9 3W
Galway B., *Ire.* **25** 53 10N 9 20W
Gambia ■, *W. Afr.* **78** 13 25N 16 0W
Gamboa, *Pan.* **94** 9 8N 79 42W
Gamlingay, *U.K.* **15** 52 9N 0 11W
Gan Jiang →, *China* **61** 29 15N 116 0 E
Ganga →, *India* **59** 23 20N 90 30 E
Ganganagar, *India* **58** 29 56N 73 56 E
Ganges = Ganga →, *India* **59** 23 20N 90 30 E
Gansu □, *China* **60** 36 0N 104 0 E
Gao, *Mali* **78** 16 15N 0 5W
Gap, *Fr.* **34** 44 33N 6 5 E
Garboldisham, *U.K.* **15** 52 24N 0 57 E
Garda, L. di, *It.* **40** 45 40N 10 40 E
Gare, L., *U.K.* **20** 56 1N 4 50W
Garelochhead, *U.K.* **20** 56 7N 4 50W
Garforth, *U.K.* **19** 53 48N 1 22W
Gargrave, *U.K.* **18** 53 58N 2 7W
Garlieston, *U.K.* **20** 54 47N 4 22W
Garonne →, *Fr.* **35** 45 2N 0 36W
Garoua, *Cam.* **80** 9 19N 13 21 E
Garry →, *U.K.* **23** 56 47N 3 47W
Garsdale Head, *U.K.* **18** 54 19N 2 19W
Garstang, *U.K.* **18** 53 53N 2 47W
Garston, *U.K.* **18** 53 21N 2 55W
Garvald, *U.K.* **21** 55 55N 2 39W
Garvellachs, Is., *U.K.* **20** 56 14N 5 48W
Gary, *U.S.A.* **92** 41 35N 87 20W
Garzê, *China* **60** 31 39N 99 58 E
Gascony, *Fr.* **35** 43 45N 0 20 E
Gascoyne →, *Austral.* **66** 24 52S 113 37 E
Gaspé, Pén. de, *Canada* **93** 48 45N 65 40W
Gatehouse of Fleet, *U.K.* **20** 54 53N 4 10W
Gateshead, *U.K.* **19** 54 57N 1 37W
Gatley, *U.K.* **18** 53 25N 2 15W
Gatun, *Pan.* **94** 9 16N 79 55W
Gatun, L., *Pan.* **94** 9 7N 79 56W
Gävle, *Swed.* **45** 60 40N 17 9 E
Gawthwaite, *U.K.* **18** 54 16N 3 6W
Gaya, *India* **59** 24 47N 85 4 E
Gayton, *U.K.* **15** 52 45N 0 35 E
Gaywood, *U.K.* **15** 52 46N 0 26 E
Gaza, *Egypt* **57** 31 30N 34 28 E
Gaziantep, *Turk.* **47** 37 6N 37 23 E
Gdańsk, *Pol.* **43** 54 22N 18 40 E
Gdańsk Bay, *Pol.* **43** 54 30N 19 20 E
Gdynia, *Pol.* **43** 54 35N 18 33 E
Gedney, *U.K.* **15** 52 47N 0 5 E
Geelong, *Austral.* **70** 38 10S 144 22 E
Gejiu, *China* **60** 23 20N 103 10 E
Gelderland □, *Neth.* **36** 52 5N 6 10 E

Gelsenkirchen, *W. Ger.* **36** 51 30N 7 5 E
Geneva, *Switz.* **42** 46 12N 6 9 E
Geneva, L., *Switz.* **42** 46 26N 6 30 E
Genk, *Belg.* **36** 50 58N 5 32 E
Gennargentu, Mti. del, *It.* **40** 40 0N 9 10 E
Genoa, *It.* **40** 44 24N 8 56 E
Geographe Chan., *Austral.* **66** 24 30S 113 0 E
George, *S. Afr.* **81** 33 58S 22 29 E
George Town, *Malay.* **63** 5 25N 100 15 E
Georgetown, *Guy.* **100** 6 50N 58 12W
Georgia □, *U.S.A.* **91** 32 0N 82 0W
Georgia □, *U.S.S.R.* **47** 42 0N 43 0 E
Georgian B., *Canada* **92** 45 15N 81 0W
Gera, *E. Ger.* **42** 50 53N 12 11 E
Geraldton, *Austral.* **66** 28 48S 114 32 E
Germiston, *S. Afr.* **81** 26 15S 28 10 E
Gerona, *Sp.* **37** 41 58N 2 46 E
Gerrans B., *U.K.* **16** 50 12N 4 57W
Gerrards Cross, *U.K.* **15** 51 35N 0 32W
Ghaghara →, *India* **59** 25 45N 84 40 E
Ghana ■, *W. Afr.* **78** 6 0N 1 0W
Ghaziabad, *India* **58** 28 42N 77 26 E
Ghent, *Belg.* **36** 51 2N 3 42 E
Giant's Causeway, *U.K.* **24** 55 15N 6 30W
Gibraltar, *Europe* **37** 36 7N 5 22W
Gibraltar, Str. of, *Medit. S.* **37** 35 55N 5 40W
Gibraltar Pt., *U.K.* **19** 53 6N 0 20 E
Gibson Desert, *Austral.* **66** 24 0S 126 0 E
Gifford, *U.K.* **21** 55 54N 2 45W
Gifu, *Jap.* **62** 35 30N 136 45 E
Giggleswick, *U.K.* **18** 54 5N 2 19W
Gigha, *U.K.* **20** 55 42N 5 45W
Gijón, *Sp.* **37** 43 32N 5 42W
Gilbert Is. = Kiribati ■, *Pac. Oc.* **65** 1 0N 176 0 E
Gillingham, *Dorset, U.K.* **14** 51 2N 2 15W
Gillingham, *Kent, U.K.* **15** 51 23N 0 34 E
Gilsland, *U.K.* **18** 55 0N 2 34W
Girdle Ness, *U.K.* **23** 57 9N 2 2W
Gironde →, *Fr.* **35** 45 32N 1 7W
Girvan, *U.K.* **20** 55 15N 4 50W
Girvan →, *U.K.* **20** 55 18N 4 51W
Gisborne, *N.Z.* **71** 38 39S 178 5 E
Gisburn, *U.K.* **18** 53 56N 2 16W
Gizhiga, *U.S.S.R.* **49** 62 3N 160 30 E
Gizhiga, G., *U.S.S.R.* **49** 61 0N 158 0 E
Gladstone, *Austral.* **67** 25 57S 114 17 E
Glanton, *U.K.* **21** 55 25N 1 54W
Glasgow, *U.K.* **20** 55 52N 4 14W
Glastonbury, *U.K.* **14** 51 9N 2 42W
Glemsford, *U.K.* **15** 52 6N 0 41 E
Glen →, *U.K.* **15** 52 50N 0 7W
Glen Affric, *U.K.* **22** 57 15N 5 0W
Glen Almond, *U.K.* **21** 56 28N 3 50W
Glen Coe, *U.K.* **19** 56 40N 5 0W
Glen Etive, *U.K.* **20** 56 37N 5 0W
Glen Garry, *U.K.* **22** 57 3N 5 7W
Glen Helen, *U.K.* **18** 54 14N 4 35W
Glen Mor, *U.K.* **23** 57 12N 4 37 E
Glen Moriston, *U.K.* **22** 57 10N 4 58W
Glen Orchy, *U.K.* **20** 56 27N 4 52W
Glen Spean, *U.K.* **23** 56 53N 4 40W
Glenbarr, *U.K.* **20** 55 34N 5 40W
Glendale, *U.S.A.* **90** 34 7N 118 18W
Gleneagles, *U.K.* **21** 56 16N 3 44W
Glengarriff, *Ire.* **25** 51 45N 9 33W
Glenkens, The, *U.K.* **20** 55 10N 4 15W
Glenluce, *U.K.* **20** 54 53N 4 50W
Glenmaye, *U.K.* **18** 54 11N 4 42W
Glenorchy, *Austral.* **67** 31 55S 139 46 E
Glenrothes, *U.K.* **20** 56 12N 3 11W
Glenties, *Ire.* **24** 54 48N 8 18W
Glentrool Village, *U.K.* **20** 55 5N 4 30W
Gliwice, *Pol.* **43** 50 22N 18 41 E
Glossop, *U.K.* **18** 53 27N 1 56W
Gloucester, *U.K.* **14** 51 52N 2 15W
Gloucestershire □, *U.K.* **14** 51 44N 2 10W
Gnosall, *U.K.* **14** 52 48N 2 15W
Goa □, *India* **58** 15 33N 73 59 E
Goat Fell, *U.K.* **20** 55 37N 5 11W
Gobi, *Asia* **60** 44 0N 111 0 E
Godalming, *U.K.* **15** 51 12N 0 37W
Godavari →, *India* **58** 16 25N 82 18 E
Godmanchester, *U.K.* **15** 52 19N 0 11W
Godshill, *U.K.* **14** 50 38N 1 13W
Godstone, *U.K.* **15** 51 15N 0 3W
Goiânia, *Brazil* **101** 16 43S 49 20W
Goil, L., *U.K.* **20** 56 8N 4 52W
Gold Coast, *Austral.* **67** 28 0S 153 25 E
Golden Vale, *Ire.* **25** 52 33N 8 17W
Golspie, *U.K.* **23** 57 58N 3 58W
Gomel, *U.S.S.R.* **46** 52 28N 31 0 E
Gometra I., *U.K.* **20** 56 30N 6 18W
Gómez Palacio, *Mex.* **94** 25 40N 104 0W
Gonder, *Eth.* **79** 12 39N 37 30 E
Good Hope, C. of, *S. Afr.* **81** 34 24S 18 30 E
Goodrich, *U.K.* **14** 51 52N 2 38W
Goodwood, *U.K.* **15** 50 53N 0 44W
Goole, *U.K.* **19** 53 42N 0 52W
Goondiwindi, *Austral.* **67** 28 30S 150 21 E
Gorakhpur, *India* **59** 26 47N 83 23 E
Gordon, *U.K.* **21** 55 41N 2 32W
Gorebridge, *U.K.* **21** 55 51N 3 2W
Gorey, *Ire.* **25** 52 41N 6 18W
Goring, *Oxon., U.K.* **14** 51 31N 1 8W
Goring, *W. Sussex, U.K.* **15** 50 49N 0 26W
Gorki, *U.S.S.R.* **46** 56 20N 44 0 E
Gorleston, *U.K.* **15** 52 35N 1 44 E
Görlitz, *E. Ger.* **42** 51 10N 14 59 E
Gort, *Ire.* **25** 53 4N 8 50W
Gorzów Wielkopolski, *Pol.* **42** 52 43N 15 15 E
Gosberton, *U.K.* **19** 52 52N 0 10W
Gosford, *Austral.* **70** 33 23S 151 18 E
Gosforth, *U.K.* **18** 54 24N 3 27W
Gosport, *U.K.* **14** 50 48N 1 8W
Göteborg, *Swed.* **45** 57 43N 11 59 E
Gotha, *E. Ger.* **42** 50 56N 10 42 E
Gotland, *Swed.* **45** 57 30N 18 33 E
Gouda, *Neth.* **36** 52 1N 4 42 E
Goudhurst, *U.K.* **15** 51 7N 0 28 E
Gouin, Rés., *Canada* **93** 48 35N 74 40W
Goulburn, *Austral.* **70** 34 44S 149 44 E
Gourock, *U.K.* **20** 55 58N 4 49W
Governador Valadares, *Brazil* **101** 18 15S 41 57W
Gower, The, *U.K.* **17** 51 35N 4 10W
Gowna, L., *Ire.* **24** 53 52N 7 35W
Gowrie, Carse of, *U.K.* **21** 56 30N 3 10W
Goya, *Arg.* **102** 29 10S 59 10W
Gozo, *Malta* **40** 36 0N 14 13 E
Grafham Water, *U.K.* **15** 52 18N 0 17W
Grafton, *Austral.* **67** 29 38S 152 58 E
Graham Bell, I., *U.S.S.R.* **48** 80 5N 70 0 E
Graham Land, *Ant.* **103** 65 0S 64 0W
Grainthorpe, *U.K.* **19** 53 27N 0 5 E
Grampian □, *U.K.* **23** 57 0N 3 0W
Grampian Mts., *U.K.* **23** 56 50N 4 0W
Gran Canaria, *Can. Is.* **78** 27 55N 15 35W
Gran Chaco, *S. Am.* **96** 25 0S 61 0W
Granada, *Sp.* **37** 37 10N 3 35W
Granard, *Ire.* **24** 53 47N 7 30W
Grand Bahama, *Baham.* **95** 26 40N 78 30W
Grand Canyon National Park, *U.S.A.* **90** 36 15N 112 20W
Grand Cayman, *W. Ind.* **95** 19 20N 81 20W
Grand Rapids, *U.S.A.* **92** 42 57N 86 40W
Grande de Santiago →, *Mex.* **94** 21 36N 105 26W
Grande Prairie, *Canada* **88** 55 10N 118 50W
Grange-over-Sands, *U.K.* **18** 54 12N 2 55W
Grangemouth, *U.K.* **21** 56 1N 3 43W
Grangetown, *U.K.* **19** 54 36N 1 7W
Grantham, *U.K.* **19** 52 55N 0 39W
Grantown-on-Spey, *U.K.* **23** 57 19N 3 36W
Grantshouse, *U.K.* **21** 55 53N 2 17W
Grasmere, *U.K.* **18** 54 28N 3 2W
Grassington, *U.K.* **18** 54 5N 2 0W
Gravesend, *U.K.* **15** 51 25N 0 22 E
Grayrigg, *U.K.* **18** 54 22N 2 40W
Grays, *U.K.* **15** 51 28N 0 23 E
Graz, *Austria* **42** 47 4N 15 27 E
Great Abaco I., *Baham.* **95** 26 25N 77 10W
Great Australian Bight, *Austral.* **66** 33 30S 130 0 E
Great Ayton, *U.K.* **19** 54 29N 1 8W
Great Baddow, *U.K.* **15** 51 43N 0 31 E
Great Barrier Reef, *Austral.* **67** 18 0S 146 50 E
Great Basin, *U.S.A.* **90** 40 0N 116 30W
Great Bear L., *Canada* **88** 65 30N 120 0W
Great Bentley, *U.K.* **15** 51 51N 1 5 E
Great Blasket I., *Ire.* **25** 52 5N 10 30W
Great Britain, *Europe* **5** 54 0N 2 15W
Great Chesterford, *U.K.* **15** 52 4N 0 11 E
Great Clifton, *U.K.* **18** 54 39N 3 29W
Great Divide, The, *Austral.* **70** 35 0S 149 17 E
Great Dividing Ra., *Austral.* **67** 23 0S 146 0 E
Great Dunmow, *U.K.* **15** 51 52N 0 22 E
Great Falls, *U.S.A.* **90** 47 27N 111 12W
Great Harwood, *U.K.* **18** 53 43N 2 30W
Great Inagua I., *Baham.* **95** 21 0N 73 20W
Great Indian Desert = Thar Desert, *India* **58** 28 0N 72 0 E
Great Malvern, *U.K.* **14** 52 7N 2 19W
Great Massingham, *U.K.* **15** 52 47N 0 41 E
Great Missenden, *U.K.* **15** 51 42N 0 42W
Great Orme's Head, *U.K.* **17** 53 20N 3 52W
Great Ouse →, *U.K.* **15** 52 47N 0 22 E
Great Plains, *N. Am.* **82** 47 0N 105 0W
Great Salt Lake, *U.S.A.* **90** 41 0N 112 30W
Great Sandy Desert, *Austral.* **66** 21 0S 124 0 E
Great Shefford, *U.K.* **14** 51 29N 1 27W
Great Shelford, *U.K.* **15** 52 9N 0 9 E
Great Shunner Fell, *U.K.* **18** 54 22N 2 16W
Great Slave L., *Canada* **88** 61 23N 115 38W
Great Stour = Stour →, *U.K.* **15** 51 15N 1 20 E
Great Torrington, *U.K.* **16** 50 57N 4 9W
Great Victoria Desert, *Austral.* **66** 29 30S 126 30 E
Great Waltham, *U.K.* **15** 51 47N 0 29 E
Great Whernside, *U.K.* **18** 54 9N 1 59W
Great Wyrley, *U.K.* **14** 52 40N 2 1W
Great Yarmouth, *U.K.* **15** 52 40N 1 45 E
Great Yeldham, *U.K.* **15** 52 1N 0 33 E
Greater Antilles, *W. Ind.* **95** 17 40N 74 0W
Greater London □, *U.K.* **15** 51 30N 0 5W
Greater Manchester □, *U.K.* **18** 53 30N 2 15W
Greater Sunda Is., *Indon.* **63** 7 0S 112 0 E
Greatham, *U.K.* **19** 54 38N 1 14W
Greece ■, *Europe* **41** 40 0N 23 0 E
Greeley, *U.S.A.* **90** 40 30N 104 40W
Green B., *U.S.A.* **92** 45 0N 87 30W
Green Bay, *U.S.A.* **92** 44 30N 88 0W
Green Hammerton, *U.K.* **19** 54 2N 1 17W
Green Lowther, *U.K.* **21** 55 22N 3 44W
Greenhead, *U.K.* **21** 54 58N 2 31W
Greenland ■, *N. Am.* **89** 66 0N 45 0W
Greenland Sea, *Arctic* **103** 73 0N 10 0W
Greenlaw, *U.K.* **21** 55 42N 2 28W
Greenock, *U.K.* **20** 55 57N 4 46W
Greenodd, *U.K.* **18** 54 14N 3 3W
Greenore, *Ire.* **24** 54 2N 6 8W
Greenore Pt., *Ire.* **25** 52 15N 6 20W
Greensboro, *U.S.A.* **91** 36 7N 79 46W
Greenwich, *U.K.* **15** 51 28N 0 0 E
Grenada ■, *W. Ind.* **94** 12 10N 61 40W
Grenoble, *Fr.* **35** 45 12N 5 42 E
Greta →, *U.K.* **18** 54 9N 2 36W
Gretna, *U.K.* **21** 54 59N 3 4W
Gretna Green, *U.K.* **21** 55 0N 3 3W
Gretton, *U.K.* **15** 52 33N 0 40W
Grey Range, *Austral.* **67** 27 0S 143 30 E
Greymouth, *N.Z.* **71** 42 29S 171 13 E
Greystoke, *U.K.* **18** 54 39N 2 52W
Gribbin Head, *U.K.* **16** 50 18N 4 41W
Griffith, *Austral.* **70** 34 18S 146 2 E
Grimsby, *U.K.* **19** 53 35N 0 5W
Gris-Nez, C., *Fr.* **34** 50 52N 1 35 E
Grizebeck, *U.K.* **18** 54 16N 3 10W
Grodno, *U.S.S.R.* **46** 53 42N 23 52 E
Groningen, *Neth.* **36** 53 15N 6 35 E
Groote Eylandt, *Austral.* **67** 14 0S 136 40 E
Groznyy, *U.S.S.R.* **47** 43 20N 45 45 E
Gruinard B., *U.K.* **22** 57 56N 5 35W
Guadalajara, *Mex.* **94** 20 40N 103 20W
Guadalajara, *Sp.* **37** 40 37N 3 12W
Guadalete →, *Sp.* **37** 36 35N 6 13W
Guadeloupe ■, *W. Ind.* **94** 16 20N 61 40W
Guadiana →, *Port.* **37** 37 14N 7 22W
Guadix, *Sp.* **37** 37 18N 3 11W
Gualeguay, *Arg.* **102** 33 10S 59 14W
Guam, *Pac. Oc.* **64** 13 27N 144 45 E
Guangdong □, *China* **61** 23 0N 113 0 E
Guangxi Zhuangzu Zizhiqu □, *China* **61** 24 0N 109 0 E
Guangzhou, *China* **61** 23 5N 113 10 E
Guantánamo, *Cuba* **95** 20 10N 75 14W
Guaporé →, *Brazil* **100** 11 55S 65 4W
Guard Bridge, *U.K.* **21** 56 21N 2 52W
Guardafui, C. = Asir, Ras, *Som.* **73** 11 55N 51 10 E
Guatemala, *Guat.* **94** 14 40N 90 22W
Guatemala ■, *Cent. Am.* **94** 15 40N 90 30W
Guaviare →, *Col.* **100** 4 3N 67 44W
Guayaquil, *Ecuad.* **100** 2 15S 79 52W
Guaymas, *Mex.* **94** 27 59N 110 54W
Guelph, *Canada* **92** 43 35N 80 20W
Guernsey, *U.K.* **34** 49 30N 2 35W
Guestling Green, *U.K.* **15** 50 53N 0 40 E
Guildford, *U.K.* **15** 51 14N 0 34W
Guilin, *China* **61** 25 18N 110 15 E
Guinea ■, *W. Afr.* **78** 10 20N 10 0W
Guinea, Gulf of, *Atl. Oc.* **72** 3 0N 2 30 E
Guinea-Bissau ■, *Africa* **78** 12 0N 15 0W
Guisborough, *U.K.* **19** 54 32N 1 2W
Guiyang, *China* **60** 26 32N 106 40 E
Guizhou □, *China* **60** 27 0N 107 0 E
Gujarat □, *India* **58** 23 20N 71 0 E
Gujranwala, *Pak.* **58** 32 10N 74 12 E
Gujrat, *Pak.* **58** 32 40N 74 2 E
Gulbarga, *India* **58** 17 20N 76 50 E
Gulf, The, *Asia* **56** 27 0N 50 0 E
Gullane, *U.K.* **21** 56 2N 2 50W
Guntur, *India* **59** 16 23N 80 30 E
Gurnard's Head, *U.K.* **16** 50 12N 5 37W
Guyana ■, *S. Am.* **100** 5 0N 59 0W
Gwalchmai, *U.K.* **17** 53 16N 4 23W
Gwalior, *India* **58** 26 12N 78 10 E
Gweebarra B., *Ire.* **24** 54 52N 8 21W
Gweedore, *Ire.* **24** 55 4N 8 15W
Gweek, *U.K.* **16** 50 6N 5 12W
Gwennap, *U.K.* **16** 50 12N 5 9W
Gwent □, *U.K.* **17** 51 45N 2 55W
Gweru, *Zimb.* **81** 19 28S 29 45 E
Gwynedd □, *U.K.* **17** 53 0N 4 0W
Gympie, *Austral.* **67** 26 11S 152 38 E
Györ, *Hung.* **43** 47 41N 17 40 E

H

Haarlem, *Neth.* **36** 52 23N 4 39 E
Hachinohe, *Jap.* **62** 40 30N 141 29 E
Hackney, *U.K.* **15** 51 33N 0 2W
Hackthorpe, *U.K.* **18** 54 37N 2 42W
Haddenham, *U.K.* **15** 51 46N 0 56W
Haddington, *U.K.* **21** 55 57N 2 48W
Hadleigh, *U.K.* **15** 52 3N 0 58 E
Hadley, *U.K.* **14** 52 42N 2 28W
Hadlow, *U.K.* **15** 51 12N 0 20 E
Hadrians Wall, *U.K.* **19** 55 0N 2 30W
Haeju, *N. Kor.* **61** 38 3N 125 45 E
Hafnarfjördur, *Ice.* **44** 64 4N 21 57W
Hagen, *W. Ger.* **36** 51 21N 7 29 E
Hags Hd., *Ire.* **25** 52 57N 9 30W
Haifa, *Isr.* **57** 32 46N 35 0 E
Haikou, *China* **61** 20 1N 110 16 E
Ḥa'il, *Si. Arab.* **56** 27 28N 41 45 E
Hailar, *China* **61** 49 12N 119 37 E
Hailsham, *U.K.* **15** 50 52N 0 17 E
Hainan, *China* **61** 19 0N 109 30 E
Hainton, *U.K.* **19** 53 21N 0 13W
Haiphong, *Viet.* **60** 20 47N 106 41 E
Haiti ■, *W. Ind.* **95** 19 0N 72 30W
Hakodate, *Jap.* **62** 41 45N 140 44 E
Halberton, *U.K.* **16** 50 55N 3 24W
Hale, *U.K.* **18** 53 24N 2 21W
Halesowen, *U.K.* **14** 52 27N 2 2W
Halesworth, *U.K.* **15** 52 21N 1 30 E
Halifax, *Canada* **93** 44 38N 63 35W
Halifax, *U.K.* **18** 53 43N 1 51W
Halifax B., *Austral.* **67** 18 50S 147 0 E
Halkirk, *U.K.* **23** 58 30N 3 30W
Halle, *Ger.* **42** 51 29N 12 0 E
Hallow, *U.K.* **14** 52 14N 2 15W
Hallworthy, *U.K.* **16** 50 38N 4 34W
Halmahera, *Indon.* **63** 0 40N 128 0 E
Halmstad, *Swed.* **45** 56 41N 12 52 E
Halstead, *U.K.* **15** 51 59N 0 39 E
Haltwhistle, *U.K.* **21** 54 58N 2 27W
Hamadān, *Iran* **56** 34 52N 48 32 E
Hamāh, *Syria* **56** 35 5N 36 40 E
Hamamatsu, *Jap.* **62** 34 45N 137 45 E
Hambledon, *U.K.* **14** 50 56N 1 6W
Hambleton Hills, *U.K.* **19** 54 17N 1 12W
Hamburg, *W. Ger.* **42** 53 32N 9 59 E
Hämeenlinna, *Fin.* **45** 61 0N 24 28 E
Hamersley Ra., *Austral.* **66** 22 0S 117 45 E
Hamilton, *Berm.* **95** 32 15N 64 45W
Hamilton, *Canada* **92** 43 15N 79 50W
Hamilton, *N.Z.* **71** 37 47S 175 19 E
Hamilton, *U.K.* **21** 55 47N 4 2W
Hamm, *W. Ger.* **36** 51 40N 7 49 E
Hammerfest, *Nor.* **44** 70 39N 23 41 E
Hammersmith, *U.K.* **15** 51 30N 0 15W
Hammond, *U.S.A.* **92** 41 40N 87 30W
Hampshire □, *U.K.* **14** 51 3N 1 20W
Hampshire Downs, *U.K.* **14** 51 10N 1 10W
Hampton in Arden, *U.K.* **14** 52 26N 1 42W
Hangzhou, *China* **61** 30 18N 120 11 E
Hanko, *Fin.* **45** 59 59N 22 57 E
Hanningfield Water, *U.K.* **15** 51 40N 0 30 E
Hanoi, *Viet.* **60** 21 5N 105 55 E
Hanover, *W. Ger.* **42** 52 23N 9 43 E
Haora, *India* **59** 22 37N 88 20 E
Happy Valley, *Canada* **89** 53 15N 60 20W
Harare, *Zimb.* **81** 17 43S 31 2 E
Harbin, *China* **61** 45 46N 126 51 E
Hardangerfjorden, *Nor.* **45** 60 15N 6 0 E
Harewood, *U.K.* **19** 53 54N 1 30W
Haringey, *U.K.* **15** 51 35N 0 7W
Harlech, *U.K.* **17** 52 52N 4 7W
Harleston, *U.K.* **15** 52 25N 1 18 E
Harlingen, *Neth.* **36** 53 11N 5 25 E
Harlow, *U.K.* **15** 51 47N 0 9 E
Harpenden, *U.K.* **15** 51 48N 0 20W
Harrietsham, *U.K.* **15** 51 15N 0 41 E
Harrington, *U.K.* **18** 54 37N 3 55W
Harris, *U.K.* **22** 57 50N 6 55W
Harris, Sd. of, *U.K.* **22** 57 44N 7 6W
Harrisburg, *U.S.A.* **93** 40 18N 76 52W
Harrogate, *U.K.* **19** 53 59N 1 32W
Harrow, *U.K.* **15** 51 35N 0 15W
Hartest, *U.K.* **15** 52 7N 0 41 E
Hartford, *U.S.A.* **93** 41 47N 72 41W
Harthill, *U.K.* **21** 55 52N 3 45W
Hartland, *U.K.* **16** 50 59N 4 29W
Hartland Pt., *U.K.* **16** 51 2N 4 32W
Hartlebury, *U.K.* **14** 52 20N 2 13W
Hartlepool, *U.K.* **19** 54 42N 1 11W
Hartley, *U.K.* **21** 55 5N 1 27W
Hartpury, *U.K.* **14** 51 55N 2 18W
Harwell, *U.K.* **15** 51 40N 1 17W
Harwich, *U.K.* **15** 51 56N 1 18 E
Harz, *Europe* **26** 51 40N 10 40 E
Hasa, *Si. Arab.* **56** 26 0N 49 0 E
Haslemere, *U.K.* **15** 51 5N 0 41W
Haslingden, *U.K.* **18** 53 43N 2 20W
Hasselt, *Belg.* **36** 50 56N 5 21 E
Hastings, *N.Z.* **71** 39 39S 176 52 E
Hastings, *U.K.* **15** 50 51N 0 36 E
Hatfield, *U.K.* **15** 51 46N 0 11W
Hatfield Broad Oak, *U.K.* **15** 51 48N 0 16 E
Hatherleigh, *U.K.* **16** 50 49N 4 4W
Hathersage, *U.K.* **19** 53 20N 1 39W
Hatteras, C., *U.S.A.* **91** 35 10N 75 30W
Haugh of Urr, *U.K.* **21** 55 0N 3 51W
Haughley, *U.K.* **15** 52 13N 0 59 E
Hauraki Gulf, *N.Z.* **71** 36 35S 175 5 E
Hauxley, *U.K.* **21** 55 21N 1 35W
Havana, *Cuba* **95** 23 8N 82 22W
Havant, *U.K.* **15** 50 51N 0 59W
Haverfordwest, *U.K.* **17** 51 48N 4 59W
Haverhill, *U.K.* **15** 52 6N 0 27 E
Haverigg, *U.K.* **18** 54 12N 3 16W
Havering, *U.K.* **15** 51 33N 0 20 E
Havre, Le, *Fr.* **34** 49 30N 0 5 E
Hawaiian Is., *Pac. Oc.* **90** 20 30N 156 0W
Hawera, *N.Z.* **71** 39 35S 174 19 E
Hawes, *U.K.* **18** 54 18N 2 12W
Haweswater, *U.K.* **18** 54 32N 2 48W
Hawick, *U.K.* **21** 55 25N 2 48W
Hawkchurch, *U.K.* **16** 50 47N 2 56W

Hawke B., N.Z. 71 39 25S 177 20 E
Hawkesbury Upton, U.K. 14 51 34N 2 19W
Hawkhurst, U.K. 15 51 2N 0 31 E
Hawkshead, U.K. 18 54 23N 3 0W
Haworth, U.K. 18 53 50N 1 57W
Hawsker, U.K. 19 54 27N 0 34W
Haxby, U.K. 19 54 1N 1 4W
Hay-on-Wye, U.K. 17 52 4N 3 9W
Hay River, Canada 88 60 51N 115 44W
Hayburn Wyke, U.K. 19 54 22N 0 28W
Haydon Bridge, U.K. 21 54 58N 2 15W
Hayle, U.K. 16 50 12N 5 25W
Hayton, U.K. 18 54 55N 2 45W
Hayward's Heath, U.K. 15 51 0N 0 5W
Heacham, U.K. 15 52 55N 0 30 E
Headcorn, U.K. 15 51 10N 0 39 E
Heanor, U.K. 19 53 1N 1 20W
Heathfield, U.K. 15 50 58N 0 18 E
Hebburn, U.K. 21 54 59N 1 30W
Hebden Bridge, U.K. 18 53 45N 2 0W
Hebei □, China 61 39 0N 116 0 E
Hebrides, U.K. 22 57 30N 7 0W
Hechuan, China 60 30 2N 106 12 E
Heckington, U.K. 19 52 59N 0 17W
Hedmark fylke □, Nor. 44 61 17N 11 40 E
Hednesford, U.K. 14 52 43N 2 0W
Hedon, U.K. 19 53 44N 0 11W
Heerlen, Neth. 36 50 55N 6 0 E
Hefei, China 61 31 52N 117 18 E
Hegang, China 61 47 20N 130 19 E
Heidelberg, W. Ger. 42 49 23N 8 41 E
Heilbronn, W. Ger. 42 49 8N 9 13 E
Heilongjiang □, China 61 48 0N 126 0 E
Hekla, Ice. 44 63 56N 19 35W
Helensburgh, U.K. 20 56 0N 4 44W
Heligoland, W. Ger. 42 54 10N 7 51 E
Hellifield, U.K. 18 54 0N 2 13W
Helmond, Neth. 36 51 29N 5 41 E
Helmsdale, U.K. 23 58 7N 3 40W
Helmsley, U.K. 19 54 15N 1 2W
Helperby, U.K. 19 54 8N 1 20W
Helsby, U.K. 18 53 16N 2 47W
Helsingborg, Swed. 45 56 3N 12 42 E
Helsingør, Den. 45 56 2N 12 35 E
Helsinki, Fin. 45 60 15N 25 3 E
Helston, U.K. 16 50 7N 5 17W
Helvellyn, U.K. 18 54 31N 3 1W
Hemel Hempstead, U.K. 15 51 45N 0 28W
Hempton, U.K. 15 52 50N 0 49 E
Hemsworth, U.K. 19 53 37N 1 21W
Hemyock, U.K. 16 50 50N 3 15W
Henan □, China 61 34 0N 114 0 E
Henfield, U.K. 15 50 56N 0 17W
Hengelo, Neth. 36 52 16N 6 48 E
Hengyang, China 61 26 51N 112 30 E
Henley-in-Arden, U.K. 14 52 18N 1 47W
Henley-on-Thames, U.K. 15 51 32N 0 53W
Henlow, U.K. 15 52 2N 0 18W
Henstridge, U.K. 14 50 59N 2 24W
Henzada, Burma 59 17 38N 95 26 E
Herāt, Afg. 57 34 20N 62 7 E
Hereford, U.K. 14 52 4N 2 42W
Hereford and Worcester □, U.K. 14 52 10N 2 30W
Hermosillo, Mex. 94 29 4N 110 58W
Herne, W. Ger. 36 51 33N 7 12 E
Herne Bay, U.K. 15 51 22N 1 8 E
Herning, Den. 45 56 8N 8 58 E
Herstmonceux, U.K. 15 50 53N 0 21 E
Hertford, U.K. 15 51 47N 0 4W
Hertford □, U.K. 15 51 51N 0 5W
's-Hertogenbosch, Neth. 36 51 42N 5 17 E
Hesse □, W. Ger. 42 50 40N 9 20 E
Hessle, U.K. 19 53 44N 0 28 E
Hethersett, U.K. 15 52 35N 1 10 E
Hetton-le-Hole, U.K. 21 54 49N 1 26W
Hexham, U.K. 19 54 58N 2 7W
Heybridge, U.K. 15 51 44N 0 42 E
Heysham, U.K. 18 54 5N 2 53W
Heytesbury, U.K. 14 51 11N 2 7W
Heywood, U.K. 18 53 36N 2 13W
High Atlas, Mor. 72 32 30N 5 0W
High Bentham, U.K. 18 54 8N 2 31W
High Borrow Bridge, U.K. 18 54 26N 2 43W
High Ercall, U.K. 14 52 46N 2 37W
High Hesket, U.K. 18 54 47N 2 49W
High Pike, U.K. 18 54 43N 3 4W
High Willhays, U.K. 16 50 41N 3 59W
High Wycombe, U.K. 15 51 37N 0 45W
Higham Ferrers, U.K. 15 52 18N 0 36W
Highbridge, U.K. 14 51 13N 2 59W
Highclere, U.K. 14 51 20N 1 22W
Highland □, U.K. 22 57 30N 5 0W
Highley, U.K. 14 52 25N 2 23W
Hightae, U.K. 21 55 5N 3 27W
Highworth, U.K. 14 51 38N 1 42W
Hilgay, U.K. 15 52 34N 0 23 E
Hillingdon, U.K. 15 51 33N 0 29W
Hillsborough, U.K. 24 54 28N 6 6W
Hilo, U.S.A. 90 19 44N 155 5W
Hilpsford Pt., U.K. 18 54 4N 3 12W
Hilversum, Neth. 36 52 14N 5 10 E
Himachal Pradesh □, India 58 31 30N 77 0 E
Himalaya, Mts., Asia 60 29 0N 84 0 E
Himeji, Jap. 62 34 50N 134 40 E
Hinckley, U.K. 14 52 33N 1 21W
Hinderwell, U.K. 19 54 32N 0 45W
Hindhead, U.K. 15 51 6N 0 42W
Hindley, U.K. 18 53 32N 2 35W
Hindu Kush, Asia 57 36 0N 71 0 E
Hingham, U.K. 15 52 35N 0 59 E
Hinkley Pt., U.K. 14 50 59N 3 32W
Hinstock, U.K. 14 52 50N 2 28W
Hiroshima, Jap. 62 34 24N 132 30 E
Hispaniola, W. Ind. 95 19 0N 71 0W
Histon, U.K. 15 52 15N 0 6 E
Hitchin, U.K. 15 51 57N 0 16W
Ho Chi Minh City, Viet. 63 10 58N 106 40 E
Hobart, Austral. 66 42 50S 147 21 E
Hodder —►, U.K. 18 53 57N 2 27W
Hoddesdon, U.K. 15 51 45N 0 1W
Hodge —►, U.K. 19 54 14N 0 55W
Hoff, U.K. 18 54 34N 2 31W
Hoggar, Mts., Alg. 78 23 0N 6 30 E
Hog's Back, U.K. 15 51 13N 0 40W
Hohhot, China 61 40 52N 111 40 E
Hokitika, N.Z. 71 42 42S 171 0 E
Hokkaidô □, Jap. 62 43 30N 143 0 E
Holbeach, U.K. 15 52 48N 0 1 E
Holbeach Marsh, U.K. 15 52 52N 0 5 E
Holderness, U.K. 19 53 45N 0 5W
Holguín, Cuba 95 20 50N 76 20W
Holkham, U.K. 15 52 57N 0 48 E
Holland Fen, U.K. 19 53 0N 0 8W
Holland-on-Sea, U.K. 15 51 48N 1 12 E
Holme, Humberside, U.K. 19 53 50N 0 48W
Holme, N. Yorks., U.K. 18 53 34N 1 50W
Holmes Chapel, U.K. 18 53 13N 2 21W
Holmfirth, U.K. 19 53 34N 1 48W
Holmwood, U.K. 15 51 12N 0 19W
Holsworthy, U.K. 16 50 48N 4 21W
Holt, U.K. 15 52 55N 1 4 E
Holy I., England, U.K. 19 55 42N 1 48W
Holy I., Scotland, U.K. 20 55 31N 5 4W
Holy I., Wales, U.K. 17 53 17N 4 37W
Holyhead, U.K. 17 53 18N 4 38W
Holywell, U.K. 17 53 16N 3 14W
Holywood, U.K. 24 54 38N 5 50W
Homs, Syria 56 34 40N 36 45 E
Honduras ■, Cent. Am. 94 14 40N 86 30W
Honduras, G. de, Cent. Am. 94 16 50N 87 0W
Hong —►, Viet. 60 20 17N 106 34 E
Hong Kong ■, Asia 61 22 11N 114 14 E
Honington, U.K. 19 52 58N 0 35W
Honiton, U.K. 16 50 48N 3 11W
Honolulu, U.S.A. 90 21 19N 157 52W
Honshū, Jap. 62 36 0N 138 0 E
Hoo, U.K. 15 51 25N 0 33 E
Hook, U.K. 15 51 17N 0 55W
Hook Hd., Ire. 25 52 8N 6 57W
Hoorn, Neth. 36 52 38N 5 4 E
Horden, U.K. 19 54 45N 1 17W
Horley, U.K. 15 51 10N 0 10W
Horn, C., Chile 102 55 50S 67 30W
Horn Head, Ire. 24 55 13N 8 0W
Horncastle, U.K. 19 53 13N 0 8W
Horndean, U.K. 15 50 50N 0 59W
Horningsham, U.K. 14 51 11N 2 16W
Hornsby, Austral. 70 33 42S 151 2 E
Hornsea, U.K. 19 53 55N 0 10W
Horsens, Den. 45 55 52N 9 51 E
Horsforth, U.K. 19 53 50N 1 39W
Horsham, Austral. 70 36 44S 142 13 E
Horsham, U.K. 15 51 4N 0 20W
Horsham St. Faith, U.K. 15 52 41N 1 15 E
Horsted Keynes, U.K. 15 51 2N 0 1W
Horton-in-Ribblesdale, U.K. 18 54 9N 2 19W
Horwich, U.K. 18 53 37N 2 33W
Hospitalet de Llobregat, Sp. 37 41 21N 2 6 E
Hotan, China 60 37 25N 79 55 E
Houghton-le-Spring, U.K. 19 54 51N 1 28W
Houghton Regis, U.K. 15 51 54N 0 32W
Hounslow, U.K. 15 51 29N 0 20W
Houston, U.S.A. 91 29 50N 95 20W
Hovd, Mong. 60 48 2N 91 37 E
Hove, U.K. 15 50 50N 0 10W
Hoveton, U.K. 15 52 45N 1 23 E
Hovingham, U.K. 19 54 10N 0 59W
Hövsgöl Nuur, Mong. 60 51 0N 100 30 E
Howden, U.K. 19 53 45N 0 52W
Howth Hd., Ire. 24 53 21N 6 0W
Hoxne, U.K. 15 52 22N 1 11 E
Hoy I., U.K. 23 58 50N 3 15W
Hoylake, U.K. 18 53 24N 3 11W
Hrádec Králové, Czech. 42 50 15N 15 50 E
Hron —►, Czech. 43 47 49N 18 45 E
Huainan, China 61 32 39N 117 2 E
Huambo, Angola 81 12 42S 15 54 E
Huancayo, Peru 100 12 5S 75 12W
Huang He —►, China 60 37 55N 118 50 E
Huangshi, China 61 30 10N 115 3 E
Huánuco, Peru 100 9 55S 76 15W
Hubei □, China 61 31 0N 112 0 E
Hucknall, U.K. 19 53 3N 1 12W
Huddersfield, U.K. 19 53 38N 1 49W
Hudson —►, U.S.A. 93 40 42N 74 2W
Hudson Bay, Canada 89 52 51N 102 23W
Hudson Str., Canada 89 62 0N 70 0W
Hue, Viet. 63 16 30N 107 35 E
Huelva, Sp. 37 37 18N 6 57W
Huesca, Sp. 37 42 8N 0 25W
Hugh Town, U.K. 16 49 55N 6 19W
Hughenden, Austral. 67 20 52S 144 10 E
Hughes, U.S.A. 88 66 0N 154 20W
Hull, Canada 93 45 25N 75 44W
Hull = Kingston-upon-Hull, U.K. 19 53 45N 0 20W
Hull —►, U.K. 19 53 43N 0 25W
Hullavington, U.K. 14 51 31N 2 9W
Hulme End, U.K. 18 53 8N 1 51W
Humber —►, U.K. 19 53 40N 0 10W
Humber, Mouth of the, U.K. 19 53 32N 0 8 E
Humberside □, U.K. 19 53 50N 0 30W
Humboldt —►, U.S.A. 90 40 2N 118 31W
Hume, L., Austral. 70 36 0S 147 0 E
Humshaugh, U.K. 21 55 3N 2 8W
Húnaflói, Ice. 44 65 50N 20 50W
Hunan □, China 61 27 30N 111 30 E
Hungary ■, Europe 43 47 20N 19 20 E
Hungary, Plain of, Europe 26 47 0N 20 0 E
Hungerford, U.K. 14 51 25N 1 30W
Hŭngnam, N. Kor. 61 39 49N 127 45 E
Hunmanby, U.K. 19 54 12N 0 19W
Hunstanton, U.K. 15 52 57N 0 30 E
Hunter —►, Austral. 70 32 52S 151 46 E
Hunterston, U.K. 20 55 43N 4 55W
Huntingdon, U.K. 15 52 20N 0 11W
Huntington, U.S.A. 92 38 20N 82 30W
Huntly, U.K. 23 57 27N 2 48W
Huntsville, U.S.A. 91 34 45N 86 35W
Hurlford, U.K. 20 55 35N 4 29W
Huron, L., N. Am. 92 45 0N 83 0W
Hursley, U.K. 14 51 1N 1 23W
Hurstbourne Tarrant, U.K. 14 51 17N 1 27W
Hurstpierpoint, U.K. 15 50 56N 0 11W
Húsavík, Ice. 44 66 3N 17 21W
Husband's Bosworth, U.K. 14 52 27N 1 3W
Huyton, U.K. 18 53 25N 2 52W
Hyde, U.K. 18 53 26N 2 6W
Hyderabad, India 58 17 22N 78 29 E
Hyderabad, Pak. 58 25 23N 68 24 E
Hynish, U.K. 20 56 27N 6 54W
Hynish B., U.K. 20 56 29N 6 40W
Hythe, U.K. 15 51 4N 1 5 E

I

Iaşi, Rom. 43 47 10N 27 40 E
Ibadan, Nig. 78 7 22N 3 58 E
Ibagué, Col. 100 4 20N 75 20W
Iberian Peninsula, Europe 26 40 0N 5 0W
Ibiza, Sp. 37 38 54N 1 26 E
Ibstock, U.K. 14 52 42N 1 23W
Icá, Peru 100 14 0S 75 48W
Iceland ■, Atl. Oc. 44 65 0N 19 0W
Ichinomiya, Jap. 62 35 18N 136 48 E
Idaho □, U.S.A. 90 44 10N 114 0W
Idar-Oberstein, W. Ger. 36 49 43N 7 19 E
Idle —►, U.K. 19 53 27N 0 49W
Idmiston, U.K. 14 51 8N 1 43W
Idsworth, U.K. 15 50 56N 0 56W
Igarka, U.S.S.R. 49 67 30N 86 33 E
Iglésias, It. 40 39 19N 8 27 E
Iguaçu Falls, Brazil 102 25 41S 54 26W
IJsselmeer, Neth. 36 52 45N 5 20 E
Ilchester, U.K. 14 51 0N 2 41W
Île-de-France, Fr. 34 49 0N 2 20 E
Ilfracombe, U.K. 16 51 13N 4 8W
Ilhéus, Brazil 101 14 49S 39 2W
Ilkeston, U.K. 19 52 59N 1 19W
Ilkley, U.K. 18 53 56N 1 49W
Illinois □, U.S.A. 91 40 15N 89 30W
Ilminster, U.K. 14 50 55N 2 56W
Iloilo, Phil. 63 10 45N 122 33 E
Immingham, U.K. 19 53 37N 0 12W
Imphal, India 59 24 48N 93 56 E
Inari, Fin. 44 68 54N 27 5 E
Ince, U.K. 18 53 32N 2 38W
Inchcape Rock, U.K. 21 56 26N 2 24W
Inchkeith, I., U.K. 21 56 2N 3 8W
Inchon, S. Kor. 61 37 27N 126 40 E
Inchture, U.K. 21 56 26N 3 8W
Indaal, L., U.K. 20 55 44N 6 20W
India ■, Asia 58 20 0N 78 0 E
Indian Ocean 129 5 0S 75 0 E
Indiana □, U.S.A. 92 40 0N 86 0W
Indianapolis, U.S.A. 92 39 42N 86 10W
Indonesia ■, Asia 63 5 0S 115 0 E
Indore, India 58 22 42N 75 53 E
Indus —►, Pak. 58 24 20N 67 47 E
Ingatestone, U.K. 15 51 40N 0 23W
Ingleborough, U.K. 18 54 11N 2 23W
Ingleton, U.K. 18 54 9N 2 29W
Ingoldmells, Pt., U.K. 19 53 11N 0 21 E
Inishbofin, Ire. 24 53 35N 10 12W
Inishmore, Ire. 25 53 8N 9 45W
Inishowen, Ire. 24 55 14N 7 15W
Inkberrow, U.K. 14 52 13N 1 59W
Inkpen Beacon, U.K. 14 51 22N 1 28W
Inn —►, Austria 40 48 35N 13 28 E
Innellan, U.K. 20 55 54N 4 58W
Inner Hebrides, U.K. 22 57 0N 6 30W
Inner Mongolia □, China 61 42 0N 112 0 E
Inner Sound, U.K. 22 57 30N 5 55W
Innerleithen, U.K. 21 55 37N 3 4W
Innsbruck, Austria 42 47 16N 11 23 E
Inny —►, Ire. 25 53 30N 7 50W
Interlaken, Switz. 42 46 41N 7 50 E
Inuvik, Canada 88 68 16N 133 40W
Inveraray, U.K. 20 56 13N 5 5W
Inverbervie, U.K. 23 56 50N 2 17W
Invercargill, N.Z. 71 46 24S 168 24 E
Inverell, Austral. 67 29 45S 151 8 E
Invergarry, U.K. 23 57 5N 4 48W
Invergordon, U.K. 23 57 41N 4 10W
Invergowrie, U.K. 21 56 29N 3 5W
Inverkeithing, U.K. 21 56 2N 3 24W
Invermoriston, U.K. 23 57 13N 4 38W
Inverness, U.K. 23 57 29N 4 12W
Inverurie, U.K. 23 57 15N 2 21W
Iona, U.K. 20 56 20N 6 25W
Ionian Is., Greece 41 38 40N 20 0 E
Ionian Sea, Greece 41 37 30N 17 30 E
Iowa □, U.S.A. 91 42 18N 93 30W
Iowa City, U.S.A. 90 41 40N 91 35W
Ipoh, Malay. 63 4 35N 101 5 E
Ipswich, U.K. 15 52 4N 1 9 E
Iquique, Chile 100 20 19S 70 5W
Iquitos, Peru 100 3 45S 73 10W
Iráklion, Greece 41 35 20N 25 12 E
Iran ■, Asia 57 33 0N 53 0 E
Irapuato, Mex. 94 20 40N 101 30W
Iraq ■, Asia 56 33 0N 44 0 E
Irchester, U.K. 15 52 17N 0 40W
Ireland ■, Europe 24 53 0N 8 0W
Ireland's Eye, Ire. 24 53 25N 6 4W
Irian Jaya □, Indon. 64 4 0S 137 0 E
Iringa, Tanz. 80 7 48S 35 43 E
Irish Republic ■, Europe 25 53 0N 8 0W
Irish Sea, Europe 18 54 0N 5 0W
Irkutsk, U.S.S.R. 49 52 18N 104 20 E
Irlam, U.K. 18 53 26N 2 27W
Ironbridge, U.K. 14 52 38N 2 29W
Irrawaddy —►, Burma 59 15 50N 95 6 E
Irt —►, U.K. 18 54 24N 3 25W
Irthing —►, U.K. 21 54 55N 2 55W
Irthlingborough, U.K. 15 52 20N 0 37W
Irtysh —►, U.S.S.R. 48 61 4N 68 52 E
Irvine, U.K. 20 55 37N 4 40W
Irvine —►, U.K. 20 55 35N 4 40W
Irvinestown, U.K. 24 54 28N 7 38W
Isabela, Phil. 63 10 12N 122 59 E
Ísafjörður, Ice. 44 66 5N 23 9W
Ishim —►, U.S.S.R. 48 57 45N 71 10 E
İskenderun, Turk. 47 36 32N 36 10 E
Isla —►, U.K. 23 56 32N 3 20W
Islamabad, Pak. 58 33 40N 73 10 E
Islay, U.K. 20 55 46N 6 10W
Islay Sound, U.K. 20 55 45N 6 5W
Isle of Whithorn, U.K. 20 54 42N 4 22W
Isle of Wight □, U.K. 14 50 40N 1 20W
Isleham, U.K. 15 52 21N 0 24 E
Islip, U.K. 14 51 49N 1 12W
Ismâ'ilîya, Egypt 79 30 37N 32 18 E
Israel ■, Asia 57 32 0N 34 50 E
İstanbul, Turk. 47 41 0N 29 0 E
Itabuna, Brazil 101 14 48S 39 16W
Italy ■, Europe 40 42 0N 13 0 E
Itchen —►, U.K. 14 50 57N 1 20W
Ivanovo, U.S.S.R. 46 52 7N 25 29 E
Ivinghoe, U.K. 15 51 50N 0 38W
Ivory Coast ■, Africa 78 7 30N 5 0W
Ivugivik, Canada 89 62 24N 77 55W
Ivybridge, U.K. 16 50 24N 3 56W
Iwaki, Jap. 62 37 3N 140 55 E
Ixworth, U.K. 15 52 18N 0 50 E
Izhevsk = Ustinov, U.S.S.R. 46 56 51N 53 14 E
İzmir, Turk. 47 38 25N 27 8 E

J

Jabalpur, India 58 23 9N 79 58 E
Jackson, U.S.A. 91 32 20N 90 10W
Jacksonville, U.S.A. 91 30 15N 81 38W
Jaén, Sp. 37 37 44N 3 43W
Jaffna, Sri L. 58 9 45N 80 2 E
Jaipur, India 58 27 0N 75 50 E
Jakarta, Indon. 63 6 9S 106 49 E
Jamaica ■, W. Ind. 94 18 10N 77 30W
Jambi, Indon. 63 1 38S 103 30 E
James B., Canada 89 51 30N 80 0W
Jammu, India 58 32 43N 74 54 E
Jammu & Kashmir □, India 58 34 25N 77 0 E
Jamnagar, India 58 22 30N 70 6 E
Jamshedpur, India 59 22 44N 86 12 E
Japan ■, Asia 62 36 0N 136 0 E
Japan, Sea of, Asia 62 40 0N 135 0 E
Japurá —►, Brazil 100 3 8S 64 46W
Jarrow, U.K. 21 54 58N 1 28W
Java, I., Indon. 63 7 0S 110 0 E
Java Sea, E. Ind. 63 4 35S 107 15 E
Jedburgh, U.K. 21 55 28N 2 33W
Jedda, Si. Arab. 56 21 29N 39 10 E
Jena, E. Ger. 42 50 56N 11 33 E
Jequié, Brazil 101 13 51S 40 5W
Jerez de la Frontera, Sp. 37 36 41N 6 7W
Jericho, Jord. 57 31 52N 35 27 E
Jersey, I., U.K. 34 49 13N 2 7W

Jersey City, *U.S.A.* **93** 40 41N 74 8W
Jerusalem, *Asia* **57** 31 47N 35 10 E
Jervaulx, *U.K.* **19** 54 19N 1 41W
Jervis Bay, *Austral.* **70** 35 8S 150 43 E
Jhansi, *India* **58** 25 30N 78 36 E
Jhelum →, *Pak.* **58** 31 20N 72 10 E
Jiamusi, *China* **61** 46 40N 130 26 E
Ji'an, *China* **61** 27 6N 114 59 E
Jiangsu □, *China* **61** 33 0N 120 0 E
Jiangxi □, *China* **61** 27 30N 116 0 E
Jilin, *China* **61** 43 44N 126 30 E
Jilin □, *China* **61** 44 0N 124 0 E
Jima, *Eth.* **79** 7 40N 36 47 E
Jinan, *China* **61** 36 38N 117 1 E
Jinja, *Uganda* **80** 0 25N 33 12 E
Jinzhou, *China* **61** 41 5N 121 3 E
Jixi, *China* **61** 45 20N 130 50 E
João Pessoa, *Brazil* **101** 7 10S 34 52W
Johannesburg, *S. Afr.* **81** 26 10S 28 2 E
John o' Groats, *U.K.* **23** 58 39N 3 3W
Johnstone, *U.K.* **20** 55 50N 4 31W
Johnstown, *U.S.A.* **92** 40 19N 78 53W
Johor Baharu, *Malay.* **63** 1 28N 103 46 E
Jönköping, *Swed.* **45** 57 45N 14 10 E
Jonquière, *Canada* **93** 48 27N 71 14W
Jordan ■, *Asia* **57** 31 0N 36 0 E
Jordan →, *Asia* **57** 31 48N 35 32 E
Jos, *Nig.* **78** 9 53N 8 51 E
Joseph Bonaparte G., *Austral.* **66** 14 35S 128 50 E
Jotunheimen, *Nor.* **44** 61 35N 8 25 E
Juan de Fuca Str., *Canada* **90** 48 15N 124 0W
Juàzeiro do Norte, *Brazil* **101** 7 10S 39 18W
Juiz de Fora, *Brazil* **101** 21 43S 43 19W
Juliaca, *Peru* **100** 15 25S 70 10W
Julianehåb, *Green.* **89** 60 43N 46 0W
Jullundur, *India* **58** 31 20N 75 40 E
Jundiaí, *Brazil* **102** 24 30S 47 0W
Juneau, *U.S.A.* **88** 58 20N 134 20W
Jura, *U.K.* **20** 56 0N 5 50W
Jura, Mts., *Europe* **42** 46 40N 6 5 E
Jura, Paps of, *U.K.* **20** 55 55N 6 0W
Jura, Sd. of, *U.K.* **20** 55 57N 5 45W
Jurby Hd., *U.K.* **18** 54 23N 4 31W
Juruá →, *Brazil* **100** 2 37S 65 44W
Jutland = Jylland, *Den.* **45** 56 25N 9 30 E
Jylland, *Den.* **45** 56 25N 9 30 E
Jyväskylä, *Fin.* **44** 62 14N 25 50 E

K

Kābul, *Afg.* **57** 34 28N 69 11 E
Kabwe, *Zam.* **81** 14 30S 28 29 E
Kaduna, *Nig.* **78** 10 30N 7 21 E
Kaesŏng, *N. Kor.* **61** 37 58N 126 35 E
Kagoshima, *Jap.* **62** 31 35N 130 33 E
Kaifeng, *China* **61** 34 49N 114 30 E
Kaiserslautern, *W. Ger.* **36** 49 30N 7 43 E
Kaitaia, *N.Z.* **71** 35 8S 173 17 E
Kajaani, *Fin.* **44** 64 17N 27 46 E
Kakinada, *India* **59** 16 57N 82 11 E
Kalahari, *Africa* **81** 24 0S 21 30 E
Kalamazoo, *U.S.A.* **92** 42 20N 85 35W
Kalemie, *Zaïre* **80** 5 55S 29 9 E
Kalgoorlie-Boulder, *Austral.* **66** 30 40S 121 22 E
Kalimantan, *Indon.* **63** 0 0 114 0 E
Kalinin, *U.S.S.R.* **46** 56 55N 35 55 E
Kaliningrad, *U.S.S.R.* **46** 54 42N 20 32 E
Kaluga, *U.S.S.R.* **46** 54 35N 36 10 E
Kamchatka Pen., *U.S.S.R.* **49** 57 0N 160 0 E
Kamensk Uralskiy, *U.S.S.R.* **48** 56 25N 62 2 E
Kames, *U.K.* **20** 55 53N 5 15W
Kamina, *Zaïre* **80** 8 45S 25 0 E
Kamloops, *Canada* **88** 50 40N 120 20W
Kampala, *Uganda* **80** 0 20N 32 30 E
Kampuchea = Cambodia ■, *Asia* **63** 12 15N 105 0 E
Kananga, *Zaïre* **80** 5 55S 22 18 E
Kanazawa, *Jap.* **62** 36 30N 136 38 E
Kanchenjunga, *Nepal* **59** 27 50N 88 10 E
Kandy, *Sri L.* **58** 7 18N 80 43 E
Kangaroo I., *Austral.* **67** 35 45S 137 0 E
Kanin, Pen., *U.S.S.R.* **46** 68 0N 45 0 E
Kankan, *Guin.* **78** 10 23N 9 15W
Kano, *Nig.* **78** 12 2N 8 30 E
Kanpur, *India* **58** 26 28N 80 20 E
Kansas □, *U.S.A.* **90** 38 40N 98 0W
Kansas City, *Kans., U.S.A.* **91** 39 0N 94 40W
Kansas City, *Mo., U.S.A.* **91** 39 3N 94 30W
Kansk, *U.S.S.R.* **49** 56 20N 95 37 E
Kanturk, *Ire.* **25** 52 10N 8 55W
Kaohsiung, *Taiwan* **61** 22 35N 120 16 E
Kaolack, *Sene.* **78** 14 5N 16 8W
Kara Bogaz Gol, Zaliv, *U.S.S.R.* **47** 41 0N 53 30 E
Kara Kalpak A.S.S.R. □, *U.S.S.R.* **48** 43 0N 60 0 E
Kara Kum, *U.S.S.R.* **48** 39 30N 60 0 E
Kara Sea, *U.S.S.R.* **48** 75 0N 70 0 E
Karachi, *Pak.* **58** 24 53N 67 0 E
Karaganda, *U.S.S.R.* **48** 49 50N 73 10 E
Karakoram Ra., *Asia* **58** 35 30N 77 0 E
Karbalā, *Iraq* **56** 32 36N 44 3 E
Karl-Marx-Stadt, *E. Ger.* **42** 50 50N 12 55 E
Karlskrona, *Swed.* **45** 56 10N 15 35 E
Karlsruhe, *W. Ger.* **42** 49 3N 8 23 E
Karlstad, *Swed.* **45** 59 23N 13 30 E
Karratha, *Austral.* **66** 20 53S 116 40 E
Karsakpay, *U.S.S.R.* **48** 47 55N 66 40 E
Karshi, *U.S.S.R.* **48** 38 53N 65 48 E
Kāshān, *Iran* **56** 34 5N 51 30 E
Kashi, *China* **60** 39 30N 76 2 E
Kassala, *Sudan* **79** 16 0N 36 0 E
Kassel, *W. Ger.* **42** 51 19N 9 32 E
Katmandu, *Nepal* **59** 27 45N 85 20 E
Katoomba, *Austral.* **70** 33 41S 150 19 E
Katowice, *Pol.* **43** 50 17N 19 5 E
Katrine, L., *U.K.* **20** 56 15N 4 30W
Katsina, *Nig.* **78** 13 0N 7 32 E
Kattegatt, *Den.* **45** 57 0N 11 20 E
Kauai, *U.S.A.* **90** 22 0N 159 30W
Kaunas, *U.S.S.R.* **46** 54 54N 23 54 E
Kaválla, *Greece* **41** 40 57N 24 28 E
Kawagoe, *Jap.* **62** 35 55N 139 29 E
Kawasaki, *Jap.* **62** 35 35N 139 42 E
Kawthoolei □, *Burma* **59** 18 0N 97 30 E
Kayes, *Mali* **78** 14 25N 11 30W
Kayseri, *Turk.* **47** 38 45N 35 30 E
Kazakhstan □, *U.S.S.R.* **48** 50 0N 70 0 E
Kazan, *U.S.S.R.* **46** 55 48N 49 3 E
Kea, *U.K.* **16** 50 13N 5 4W
Keady, *U.K.* **24** 54 15N 6 42W
Keal, Loch na, *U.K.* **20** 56 30N 6 5W
Kecskemét, *Hung.* **43** 46 57N 19 42 E
Kediri, *Indon.* **63** 7 51S 112 1 E
Keelby, *U.K.* **19** 53 34N 0 15W
Keele, *U.K.* **18** 53 0N 2 17W
Keeper Hill, *Ire.* **25** 52 46N 8 17W
Keewatin, *Canada* **88** 49 46N 94 34W
Kefallinía, *Greece* **41** 38 20N 20 30 E
Keflavík, *Ice.* **44** 64 2N 22 35W
Kegworth, *U.K.* **14** 52 50N 1 17W
Keighley, *U.K.* **18** 53 52N 1 54W
Keith, *U.K.* **23** 57 33N 2 58W
Keld, *U.K.* **18** 54 24N 2 11W
Kellerberrin, *Austral.* **66** 31 36S 117 38 E
Kells = Ceanannus Mor, *Ire.* **24** 53 42N 6 53W
Kells, Rhinns of, *U.K.* **20** 55 9N 4 22W
Kelowna, *Canada* **88** 49 50N 119 25W
Kelsale, *U.K.* **15** 52 15N 1 30 E
Kelsall, *U.K.* **18** 53 14N 2 44W
Kelso, *U.K.* **21** 55 36N 2 27W
Kelvedon, *U.K.* **15** 51 50N 0 43 E
Kemble, *U.K.* **14** 51 40N 2 1W
Kemerovo, *U.S.S.R.* **48** 55 20N 86 5 E
Kemi, *Fin.* **44** 65 44N 24 34 E
Kempsey, *U.K.* **14** 52 8N 2 11W
Kempston, *U.K.* **15** 52 7N 0 30W
Ken, L., *U.K.* **21** 55 0N 4 8W
Kendal, *U.K.* **18** 54 19N 2 44W
Kenilworth, *U.K.* **14** 52 22N 1 35W
Kenitra, *Mor.* **78** 34 15N 6 40W
Kenmare, *Ire.* **25** 51 52N 9 35W
Kenmare →, *Ire.* **25** 51 40N 10 0W
Kennet →, *U.K.* **14** 51 24N 0 58W
Kenninghall, *U.K.* **15** 52 26N 1 0 E
Kenora, *Canada* **88** 49 47N 94 29W
Kent □, *U.K.* **15** 51 12N 0 40 E
Kentisbeare, *U.K.* **16** 50 51N 3 18W
Kenton, *U.K.* **16** 50 37N 3 28W
Kentucky □, *U.S.A.* **91** 37 20N 85 0W
Kenya ■, *Africa* **80** 1 0N 38 0 E
Kerala □, *India* **58** 11 0N 76 15 E
Kerch, *U.S.S.R.* **47** 45 20N 36 20 E
Kérkira, *Greece* **41** 39 38N 19 50 E
Kermān, *Iran* **57** 30 15N 57 1 E
Kerrera I., *U.K.* **20** 56 24N 5 32W
Kerry □, *Ire.* **25** 52 7N 9 35W
Kerry Hd., *Ire.* **25** 52 26N 9 56W
Kessingland, *U.K.* **15** 52 25N 1 41 E
Keswick, *U.K.* **18** 54 35N 3 9W
Ketchikan, *U.S.A.* **88** 55 25N 131 40W
Kettering, *U.K.* **15** 52 24N 0 44W
Kettle Ness, *U.K.* **19** 54 32N 0 41W
Kettlewell, *U.K.* **18** 54 8N 2 2W
Keweenaw Pen., *U.S.A.* **92** 47 30N 88 0W
Kexby, *U.K.* **19** 53 21N 0 41W
Key West, *U.S.A.* **91** 24 33N 82 0W
Keyingham, *U.K.* **19** 53 42N 0 7W
Keymer, *U.K.* **15** 50 55N 0 5W
Keynsham, *U.K.* **14** 51 25N 2 30W
Keyworth, *U.K.* **14** 52 52N 1 8W
Khabarovsk, *U.S.S.R.* **49** 48 30N 135 5 E
Khaniá, *Greece* **41** 35 30N 24 4 E
Kharagpur, *India* **59** 22 20N 87 25 E
Kharkov, *U.S.S.R.* **47** 49 58N 36 20 E
Khartoum, *Sudan* **79** 15 31N 32 35 E
Khaskovo, *Bulg.* **41** 41 56N 25 30 E
Kherson, *U.S.S.R.* **47** 46 35N 32 35 E
Khíos, I., *Greece* **41** 38 20N 26 0 E
Khorrāmshahr, *Iran* **56** 30 29N 48 15 E
Khouribga, *Mor.* **78** 32 58N 6 57W
Khulna, *Bangla.* **59** 22 45N 89 34 E
Khulna □, *Bangla.* **59** 22 25N 89 35 E
Khurasan, *Iran* **57** 34 0N 57 0 E
Kibworth Beauchamp, *U.K.* **15** 52 33N 0 59W
Kicking Horse Pass, *Canada* **88** 51 28N 116 16W
Kidderminster, *U.K.* **14** 52 24N 2 13W
Kidlington, *U.K.* **14** 51 49N 1 18W
Kidsgrove, *U.K.* **18** 53 6N 2 15W
Kidstones, *U.K.* **18** 54 15N 2 2W
Kidwelly, *U.K.* **17** 51 44N 4 20W
Kiel, *W. Ger.* **42** 54 16N 10 8 E
Kielce, *Pol.* **43** 50 52N 20 42 E
Kielder, *U.K.* **21** 55 14N 2 35W
Kiev, *U.S.S.R.* **47** 50 30N 30 28 E
Kigali, *Rwanda* **80** 1 59S 30 4 E
Kigoma-Ujiji, *Tanz.* **80** 4 55S 29 36 E
Kikládhes, *Greece* **41** 37 20N 24 30 E
Kikwit, *Zaïre* **80** 5 5S 18 45 E
Kilbirnie, *U.K.* **20** 55 46N 4 42W
Kilbrannan Sd., *U.K.* **20** 55 40N 5 23W
Kilcreggan, *U.K.* **20** 55 59N 4 50W
Kildare, *Ire.* **25** 53 10N 6 50W
Kildare □, *Ire.* **25** 53 10N 6 50W
Kildonan, *U.K.* **23** 58 10N 3 50W
Kilfinan, *U.K.* **20** 55 57N 5 19W
Kilham, *U.K.* **19** 54 4N 0 22W
Kilimanjaro, *Tanz.* **80** 3 7S 37 20 E
Kilkee, *Ire.* **25** 52 41N 9 40W
Kilkeel, *U.K.* **24** 54 4N 6 0W
Kilkenny, *Ire.* **25** 52 40N 7 17W
Kilkenny □, *Ire.* **25** 52 35N 7 15W
Kilkhampton, *U.K.* **16** 50 53N 4 30W
Kilkieran B., *Ire.* **25** 53 18N 9 45W
Killala, *Ire.* **24** 54 13N 9 12W
Killala B., *Ire.* **24** 54 20N 9 12W
Killaloe, *Ire.* **25** 52 48N 8 28W
Killarney, *Ire.* **25** 52 2N 9 30W
Killarney, Lakes of, *Ire.* **25** 52 0N 9 30W
Killary Harbour, *Ire.* **24** 53 38N 9 52W
Killchianaig, *U.K.* **20** 56 2N 5 48W
Killean, *U.K.* **20** 55 38N 5 40W
Killiecrankie, Pass of, *U.K.* **23** 56 44N 3 46W
Killin, *U.K.* **20** 56 28N 4 20W
Killinghall, *U.K.* **19** 54 1N 1 33W
Killybegs, *Ire.* **24** 54 38N 8 26W
Kilmacolm, *U.K.* **20** 55 54N 4 39W
Kilmarnock, *U.K.* **20** 55 36N 4 30W
Kilmartin, *U.K.* **20** 56 8N 5 29W
Kilmaurs, *U.K.* **20** 55 37N 4 33W
Kilmelford, *U.K.* **20** 56 16N 5 30W
Kilninver, *U.K.* **20** 56 20N 5 30W
Kilrenny, *U.K.* **21** 56 15N 2 40W
Kilrush, *Ire.* **25** 52 39N 9 30W
Kilsby, *U.K.* **14** 52 20N 1 11W
Kilsyth, *U.K.* **21** 55 58N 4 3W
Kilwinning, *U.K.* **20** 55 40N 4 41W
Kimberley, *Austral.* **66** 16 20S 127 0 E
Kimberley, *S. Afr.* **81** 28 43S 24 46 E
Kimbolton, *U.K.* **15** 52 17N 0 23W
Kincardine, *U.K.* **21** 56 4N 3 43W
Kindu, *Zaïre* **80** 2 55S 25 50 E
Kineton, *U.K.* **14** 52 10N 1 30W
King Frederick VI Coast, *Green.* **89** 63 0N 43 0W
King Sd., *Austral.* **66** 16 50S 123 20 E
Kingarth, *U.K.* **20** 55 45N 5 2W
Kinghorn, *U.K.* **21** 56 4N 3 10W
King's Lynn, *U.K.* **15** 52 45N 0 25 E
King's Sutton, *U.K.* **14** 52 1N 1 16W
King's Worthy, *U.K.* **14** 51 6N 1 18W
Kingsbarns, *U.K.* **21** 56 18N 2 40W
Kingsbridge, *U.K.* **16** 50 17N 3 46W
Kingsbury, *U.K.* **14** 52 33N 1 41W
Kingscourt, *Ire.* **24** 53 55N 6 48W
Kingskerswell, *U.K.* **16** 50 30N 3 34W
Kingsland, *U.K.* **14** 52 15N 2 49W
Kingsteignton, *U.K.* **16** 50 32N 3 35W
Kingston, *Canada* **92** 44 14N 76 30W
Kingston, *Jam.* **94** 18 0N 76 50W
Kingston, *U.K.* **14** 51 18N 1 40W
Kingston-upon-Hull, *U.K.* **19** 53 45N 0 20W
Kingston-upon-Thames, *U.K.* **15** 51 23N 0 20W
Kingstown, *St. Vinc.* **94** 13 10N 61 10W
Kingswear, *U.K.* **16** 50 21N 3 33W
Kingswood, *U.K.* **14** 51 26N 2 31W
Kington, *U.K.* **14** 52 12N 3 2W
Kingussie, *U.K.* **23** 57 5N 4 2W
Kinlochewe, *U.K.* **22** 57 37N 5 20W
Kinlochleven, *U.K.* **22** 56 42N 4 59W
Kinnairds Hd., *U.K.* **23** 57 40N 2 0W
Kinneret, Lake, *Isr.* **57** 32 45N 35 35 E
Kinross, *U.K.* **21** 56 13N 3 25W
Kinsale, *Ire.* **25** 51 42N 8 31W
Kinsale, Old Hd. of, *Ire.* **25** 51 37N 8 32W
Kinshasa, *Zaïre* **80** 4 20S 15 15 E
Kintyre, *U.K.* **20** 55 30N 5 35W
Kintyre, Mull of, *U.K.* **20** 55 17N 5 55W
Kippen, *U.K.* **20** 56 8N 4 12W
Kippure, *Ire.* **25** 53 11N 6 23W
Kirensk, *U.S.S.R.* **49** 57 50N 107 55 E
Kirgizia □, *U.S.S.R.* **48** 42 0N 75 0 E
Kirgiziya Steppe, *U.S.S.R.* **47** 50 0N 55 0 E
Kiribati ■, *Pac. Oc.* **65** 1 0N 176 0 E
Kirk Michael, *U.K.* **18** 54 17N 4 35W
Kirkbean, *U.K.* **21** 54 56N 3 35W
Kirkbride, *U.K.* **18** 54 54N 3 13W
Kirkburton, *U.K.* **19** 53 36N 1 42W
Kirkby, *U.K.* **18** 53 29N 2 54W
Kirkby-in-Ashfield, *U.K.* **19** 53 6N 1 15W
Kirkby Lonsdale, *U.K.* **18** 54 13N 2 36W
Kirkby Malzeard, *U.K.* **19** 54 10N 1 38W
Kirkby Moorside, *U.K.* **19** 54 16N 0 56W
Kirkby Stephen, *U.K.* **18** 54 27N 2 23W
Kirkby Thore, *U.K.* **18** 54 38N 2 34W
Kirkcaldy, *U.K.* **21** 56 7N 3 10W
Kirkcolm, *U.K.* **20** 54 59N 5 4W
Kirkconnel, *U.K.* **21** 55 23N 4 0W
Kirkcowan, *U.K.* **20** 54 53N 4 38W
Kirkcudbright, *U.K.* **21** 54 50N 4 3W
Kirkcudbright B., *U.K.* **21** 54 46N 4 0W
Kirkham, *U.K.* **18** 53 47N 2 52W
Kirkinner, *U.K.* **20** 54 49N 4 28W
Kirkintilloch, *U.K.* **21** 55 57N 4 10W
Kirkland Lake, *Canada* **92** 48 9N 80 2W
Kirkliston, *U.K.* **21** 55 55N 3 27W
Kirkoswald, *U.K.* **18** 54 46N 2 41W
Kirkoswold, *U.K.* **20** 55 19N 4 48W
Kirkstone P., *U.K.* **18** 54 29N 2 55W
Kirkūk, *Iraq* **56** 35 30N 44 21 E
Kirkwall, *U.K.* **23** 58 59N 2 59W
Kirkwhelpington, *U.K.* **21** 55 9N 2 0W
Kirov, *U.S.S.R.* **46** 58 35N 49 40 E
Kirovabad, *U.S.S.R.* **47** 40 45N 46 20 E
Kirovograd, *U.S.S.R.* **47** 48 35N 32 20 E
Kirovsk, *U.S.S.R.* **46** 48 35N 38 30 E
Kirriemuir, *U.K.* **23** 56 41N 3 0W
Kirtling, *U.K.* **15** 52 11N 0 27 E
Kirtlington, *U.K.* **14** 51 54N 1 9W
Kirton, *U.K.* **19** 52 56N 0 3W
Kirton-in-Lindsey, *U.K.* **19** 53 29N 0 35W
Kiruna, *Swed.* **44** 67 52N 20 15 E
Kisangani, *Zaïre* **80** 0 35N 25 15 E
Kishinev, *U.S.S.R.* **47** 47 0N 28 50 E
Kismayu, *Som.* **73** 0 22S 42 32 E
Kisumu, *Kenya* **80** 0 3S 34 45 E
Kitakyūshū, *Jap.* **62** 33 50N 130 50 E
Kitchener, *Canada* **92** 43 27N 80 29W
Kíthira, *Greece* **41** 36 9N 23 0 E
Kitikmeot □, *Canada* **88** 70 0N 110 0W
Kitimat, *Canada* **88** 54 3N 128 38W
Kitwe, *Zam.* **81** 12 54S 28 13 E
Klagenfurt, *Austria* **42** 46 38N 14 20 E
Klerksdorp, *S. Afr.* **81** 26 51S 26 38 E
Klondike, *Canada* **88** 64 0N 139 26W
Knapdale, *U.K.* **20** 55 55N 5 30W
Knaresborough, *U.K.* **19** 54 1N 1 29W
Knebworth, *U.K.* **15** 51 52N 0 11W
Knighton, *U.K.* **17** 52 21N 3 2W
Knockmealdown Mts., *Ire.* **25** 52 16N 8 0W
Knossos, *Greece* **41** 35 16N 25 10 E
Knott End, *U.K.* **18** 53 55N 3 0W
Knottingley, *U.K.* **19** 53 42N 1 15W
Knowle, *U.K.* **14** 52 23N 1 43W
Knoxville, *U.S.A.* **91** 35 58N 83 57W
Knutsford, *U.K.* **18** 53 18N 2 22W
Kōbe, *Jap.* **62** 34 45N 135 10 E
København = Copenhagen, *Den.* **45** 55 41N 12 34 E
Koblenz, *W. Ger.* **36** 50 21N 7 36 E
Kodiak I., *U.S.A.* **88** 57 30N 152 45W
Koforidua, *Ghana* **78** 6 3N 0 17W
Kokand, *U.S.S.R.* **48** 40 30N 70 57 E
Kokchetav, *U.S.S.R.* **48** 53 20N 69 25 E
Kokkola, *Fin.* **44** 63 50N 23 8 E
Kola Pen., *U.S.S.R.* **46** 67 30N 38 0 E
Kolding, *Den.* **45** 55 30N 9 29 E
Kolguyev, I., *U.S.S.R.* **46** 69 20N 48 30 E
Kolomna, *U.S.S.R.* **46** 55 8N 38 45 E
Kolwezi, *Zaïre* **80** 10 40S 25 25 E
Kolyma →, *U.S.S.R.* **49** 69 30N 161 0 E
Kolyma Ra., *U.S.S.R.* **49** 63 0N 157 0 E
Komandorskiye, Is., *U.S.S.R.* **49** 55 0N 167 0 E
Komsomolets I., *U.S.S.R.* **49** 80 30N 95 0 E
Komsomolsk, *U.S.S.R.* **49** 50 30N 137 0 E
Konya, *Turk.* **47** 37 52N 32 35 E
Kópavogur, *Ice.* **44** 64 6N 21 55W
Korce, *Alb.* **41** 40 37N 20 50 E
Korea, North ■, *Asia* **61** 40 0N 127 0 E
Korea, South ■, *Asia* **61** 36 0N 128 0 E
Korea Strait, *Asia* **61** 34 0N 129 30 E
Kōriyama, *Jap.* **62** 37 24N 140 23 E
Korla, *China* **60** 41 45N 86 4 E
Kortrijk, *Belg.* **36** 50 50N 3 17 E
Koryak Range, *U.S.S.R.* **49** 61 0N 171 0 E
Kos, *Greece* **41** 36 50N 27 15 E
Košice, *Czech.* **43** 48 42N 21 15 E
Kôstī, *Sudan* **79** 13 8N 32 43 E
Kostroma, *U.S.S.R.* **46** 57 50N 40 58 E
Kota, *India* **58** 25 14N 75 49 E
Kota Baharu, *Malay.* **63** 6 7N 102 14 E
Kota Kinabalu, *Malay.* **63** 6 0N 116 4 E
Kotka, *Fin.* **45** 60 28N 26 58 E
Kra, Isthmus of, *Thai.* **63** 10 15N 99 30 E
Kragujevac, *Yug.* **41** 44 2N 20 56 E
Krakatau, *Indon.* **63** 6 10S 105 20 E
Kraków, *Pol.* **43** 50 4N 19 57 E
Krasnodar, *U.S.S.R.* **47** 45 5N 39 0 E
Krasnoturinsk, *U.S.S.R.* **46** 59 46N 60 12 E
Krasnovodsk, *U.S.S.R.* **48** 40 0N 52 52 E
Krasnoyarsk, *U.S.S.R.* **49** 56 8N 93 0 E
Krefeld, *W. Ger.* **36** 51 20N 6 32 E
Kremenchug, *U.S.S.R.* **47** 49 5N 33 25 E
Krishna →, *India* **59** 15 57N 80 59 E
Kristiansand, *Nor.* **45** 58 9N 8 1 E
Kristianstad, *Swed.* **45** 56 2N 14 9 E
Kristiansund, *Nor.* **44** 63 7N 7 45 E
Krivoy Rog, *U.S.S.R.* **47** 47 51N 33 20 E
Kroonstad, *S. Afr.* **81** 27 43S 27 19 E
Krung Thep = Bangkok, *Thai.* **63** 13 45N 100 35 E
Kruševac, *Yug.* **41** 43 35N 21 28 E
Kuala Lumpur, *Malay.* **63** 3 9N 101 41 E

Kuala Trengganu, *Malay.* 63 5 20N 103 8 E
Kuangchou = Guangzhou, *China* 61 23 5N 113 10 E
Kuantan, *Malay.* 63 3 49N 103 20 E
Kucing, *Malay.* 63 1 33N 110 25 E
Kueiyang = Guiyang, *China* 60 26 32N 106 40 E
Kumanovo, *Yug.* 41 42 9N 21 42 E
Kumasi, *Ghana* 78 6 41N 1 38W
Kunlun Shan, *Asia* 60 36 0N 86 30 E
Kunming, *China* 60 25 1N 102 41 E
Kuopio, *Fin.* 44 62 53N 27 35 E
Kura →, *U.S.S.R.* 47 39 50N 49 20 E
Kurashiki, *Jap.* 62 34 40N 133 50 E
Kure, *Jap.* 62 34 14N 132 32 E
Kurgan, *U.S.S.R.* 48 55 26N 65 18 E
Kuria Maria Is., *Ind. Oc.* 57 17 30N 55 58 E
Kuril Is., *U.S.S.R.* 49 45 0N 150 0 E
Kurnool, *India* 58 15 45N 78 0 E
Kurri Kurri, *Austral.* 70 32 50S 151 28 E
Kursk, *U.S.S.R.* 46 51 42N 36 11 E
Kurume, *Jap.* 62 33 15N 130 30 E
Kushiro, *Jap.* 62 43 0N 144 25 E
Kustanay, *U.S.S.R.* 48 53 10N 63 35 E
Kütahya, *Turk.* 47 39 30N 30 2 E
Kutaisi, *U.S.S.R.* 47 42 19N 42 40 E
Kutch, Gulf of, *India* 58 22 50N 69 15 E
Kutch, Rann of, *India* 58 24 0N 70 0 E
Kuwait, *Kuw.* 56 29 30N 47 30 E
Kuwait ■, *Asia* 56 29 30N 47 30 E
Kuybyshev, *U.S.S.R.* 46 53 8N 50 6 E
Kwangju, *S. Kor.* 61 35 9N 126 54 E
Kyle, *U.K.* 20 55 32N 4 25W
Kyle of Lochalsh, *U.K.* 22 57 17N 5 43W
Kyōto, *Jap.* 62 35 0N 135 45 E
Kyūshū, *Jap.* 62 33 0N 131 0 E
Kzyl-Orda, *U.S.S.R.* 48 44 48N 65 28 E

L

Labe = Elbe →, *Ger.* 42 53 50N 9 0 E
Labé, *Guin.* 78 11 24N 12 16W
Labrador, Coast of □, *Canada* 89 53 20N 61 0W
Labrador City, *Canada* 89 52 57N 66 55W
Laccadive Is. = Lakshadweep Is., *Ind. Oc.* 51 10 0N 72 30 E
Laceby, *U.K.* 19 53 32N 0 10W
Lachlan →, *Austral.* 70 34 22S 143 55 E
Lacock, *U.K.* 14 51 24N 2 8W
Ladock, *U.K.* 16 50 19N 4 58W
Ladoga, L., *U.S.S.R.* 46 61 15N 30 30 E
Ladybank, *U.K.* 21 56 16N 3 8W
Lafayette, *U.S.A.* 90 30 18N 92 0W
Lagan →, *U.K.* 24 54 35N 5 55W
Lagg, *U.K.* 20 55 51N 5 50W
Laggan B., *U.K.* 20 55 40N 6 20W
Lagos, *Nig.* 78 6 25N 3 27 E
Lagos, *Port.* 37 37 5N 8 41W
Lahore, *Pak.* 58 31 32N 74 22 E
Lahti, *Fin.* 45 60 58N 25 40 E
Lairg, *U.K.* 23 58 1N 4 24W
Lake Charles, *U.S.A.* 90 30 15N 93 10W
Lake District, *U.K.* 18 54 30N 3 10W
Lakenheath, *U.K.* 15 52 25N 0 30 E
Lakewood, *U.S.A.* 92 41 28N 81 50W
Lakshadweep Is., *Ind. Oc.* 51 10 0N 72 30 E
Lambay I., *Ire.* 24 53 30N 6 0W
Lamberhurst, *U.K.* 15 51 5N 0 21 E
Lambeth, *U.K.* 15 51 27N 0 7W
Lambley, *U.K.* 21 54 56N 2 30W
Lambourn, *U.K.* 14 51 31N 1 31W
Lamlash, *U.K.* 20 55 32N 5 8W
Lammermuir, *U.K.* 21 55 50N 2 25W
Lammermuir Hills, *U.K.* 21 55 50N 2 40W
Lampeter, *U.K.* 17 52 6N 4 6W
Lanark, *U.K.* 21 55 40N 3 48W
Lancashire □, *U.K.* 18 53 40N 2 30W
Lancaster, *U.K.* 18 54 3N 2 48W
Lancaster Sd., *Canada* 89 74 13N 84 0W
Lanchester, *U.K.* 19 54 50N 1 44W
Lancing, *U.K.* 15 50 49N 0 19W
Landkey, *U.K.* 16 51 2N 4 0W
Land's End, *U.K.* 16 50 4N 5 43W
Langholm, *U.K.* 21 55 9N 2 59W
Langness, *U.K.* 18 54 3N 4 37W
Langport, *U.K.* 14 51 2N 2 51W
Langstrothdale Chase, *U.K.* 18 54 14N 2 13W
Langtoft, *U.K.* 15 52 42N 0 19W
Langtree, *U.K.* 16 50 55N 4 11W
Lansing, *U.S.A.* 92 42 47N 84 40W
Lanzhou, *China* 60 36 1N 103 52 E
Laoag, *Phil.* 63 18 7N 120 34 E
Laois □, *Ire.* 25 53 0N 7 20W
Laos ■, *Asia* 63 17 45N 105 0 E
Lapford, *U.K.* 16 50 52N 3 49W
Lapland, *Europe* 44 68 7N 24 0 E
Laptev Sea, *U.S.S.R.* 49 76 0N 125 0 E
Larbert, *U.K.* 21 56 2N 3 50W
Laredo, *U.S.A.* 90 27 34N 99 29W
Largs, *U.K.* 20 55 48N 4 51W
Lárisa, *Greece* 41 39 49N 22 28 E
Larkhall, *U.K.* 21 55 44N 4 0W
Larne, *U.K.* 24 54 52N 5 50W
Las Palmas, *Can. Is.* 78 28 7N 15 26W
Las Vegas, *U.S.A.* 90 36 10N 115 5W
Laskill, *U.K.* 19 54 19N 1 6W
Lasswade, *U.K.* 21 55 53N 3 8W
Latakia, *Syria* 56 35 30N 35 45 E
Latina, *It.* 40 41 26N 12 53 E
Latvia □, *U.S.S.R.* 46 56 50N 24 0 E
Lauder, *U.K.* 21 55 43N 2 45W
Lauderdale, *U.K.* 21 55 43N 2 44W
Launceston, *Austral.* 67 41 24S 147 8 E
Launceston, *U.K.* 16 50 38N 4 21W
Laune →, *Ire.* 25 52 5N 9 40W
Laurencekirk, *U.K.* 23 56 50N 2 30W
Laurentian Plateau, *Canada* 82 52 0N 70 0W
Laurieston, *U.K.* 21 54 57N 4 2W
Lausanne, *Switz.* 42 46 32N 6 38 E
Laval, *Fr.* 34 48 4N 0 48W
Lavendon, *U.K.* 15 52 11N 0 39W
Lavenham, *U.K.* 15 52 7N 0 48 E
Lawers, *U.K.* 21 56 31N 4 9W
Lawrence, *U.S.A.* 93 42 40N 71 9W
Laxey, *U.K.* 18 54 15N 4 23W
Laxfield, *U.K.* 15 52 18N 1 23 E
Laxford, L., *U.K.* 22 58 25N 5 10W
Lazonby, *U.K.* 18 54 45N 2 42W
Lea, *U.K.* 19 53 22N 0 45W
Lea →, *U.K.* 15 51 30N 0 10W
Leadenham, *U.K.* 19 53 5N 0 33W
Leadhills, *U.K.* 21 55 25N 3 47W
Leamington, *U.K.* 14 52 18N 1 32W
Leatherhead, *U.K.* 15 51 18N 0 20W
Lebanon ■, *Asia* 56 34 0N 36 0 E
Lecce, *It.* 41 40 20N 18 10 E
Lechlade, *U.K.* 14 51 42N 1 40W
Ledbury, *U.K.* 14 52 3N 2 25W
Leduc, *Canada* 88 53 15N 113 30W
Lee, *U.K.* 14 50 47N 1 11W
Lee →, *Ire.* 25 51 50N 8 30W
Leeds, *U.K.* 19 53 48N 1 34W
Leek, *U.K.* 18 53 7N 2 2W
Leer, *W. Ger.* 36 53 13N 7 29 E
Leeton, *Austral.* 70 34 33S 146 23 E
Leeuwarden, *Neth.* 36 53 15N 5 48 E
Leeuwin, C., *Austral.* 66 34 20S 115 9 E
Leghorn, *It.* 40 43 32N 10 18 E
Legnica, *Pol.* 42 51 12N 16 10 E
Leicester, *U.K.* 14 52 39N 1 9W
Leicester □, *U.K.* 14 52 40N 1 10W
Leiden, *Neth.* 36 52 9N 4 30 E
Leigh, *Gr. Manchester, U.K.* 18 53 29N 2 31W
Leigh, *Hereford & Worcs., U.K.* 14 52 10N 2 21W
Leighton Buzzard, *U.K.* 15 51 55N 0 39W
Leinster □, *Ire.* 25 53 0N 7 10W
Leinster, Mt., *Ire.* 25 52 38N 6 47W
Leintwardine, *U.K.* 14 52 22N 2 51W
Leipzig, *E. Ger.* 42 51 20N 12 23 E
Leiston, *U.K.* 15 52 13N 1 35 E
Leith, *U.K.* 21 55 59N 3 10W
Leith Hill, *U.K.* 15 51 10N 0 23W
Leitholm, *U.K.* 21 55 42N 2 16W
Leitrim, *Ire.* 24 54 0N 8 5W
Leitrim □, *Ire.* 24 54 8N 8 0W
Lek →, *Neth.* 36 51 54N 4 35 E
Lelant, *U.K.* 16 50 11N 5 26W
Lelystad, *Neth.* 36 52 30N 5 25 E
Lena →, *U.S.S.R.* 49 72 52N 126 40 E
Lendalfoot, *U.K.* 20 55 12N 4 55W
Lenham, *U.K.* 15 51 14N 0 44 E
Leninakan, *U.S.S.R.* 47 40 47N 43 50 E
Leningrad, *U.S.S.R.* 46 59 55N 30 20 E
Leninsk-Kuznetskiy, *U.S.S.R.* 48 54 44N 86 10 E
Lennox Hills, *U.K.* 20 56 3N 4 12W
Lennoxtown, *U.K.* 20 55 58N 4 14W
Lens, *Fr.* 34 50 26N 2 50 E
Leominster, *U.K.* 14 52 15N 2 43W
León, *Mex.* 94 21 7N 101 40W
León, *Sp.* 37 42 38N 5 34W
Lérida, *Sp.* 37 41 37N 0 39 E
Lerwick, *U.K.* 22 60 10N 1 10W
Lesbos, I. = Lésvos, *Greece* 41 39 10N 26 20 E
Lesbury, *U.K.* 21 55 25N 1 37W
Leskovac, *Yug.* 41 43 0N 21 58 E
Leslie, *U.K.* 21 56 12N 3 12W
Lesmahagow, *U.K.* 21 55 38N 3 55W
Lesotho ■, *Africa* 81 29 40S 28 0 E
Lésvos, *Greece* 41 39 10N 26 20 E
Leswalt, *U.K.* 20 54 56N 5 6W
Letchworth, *U.K.* 15 51 58N 0 13W
Lethbridge, *Canada* 88 49 45N 112 45W
Letterkenny, *Ire.* 24 54 57N 7 42W
Leuchars, *U.K.* 21 56 23N 2 53W
Leven, *Fife, U.K.* 21 56 12N 3 0W
Leven, *Humberside, U.K.* 19 53 54N 0 18W
Leven →, *U.K.* 19 54 27N 1 15W
Leven, L., *U.K.* 21 56 12N 3 22W
Leverburgh, *U.K.* 22 57 46N 7 0W
Leverkusen, *W. Ger.* 36 51 2N 6 59 E
Lewes, *U.K.* 15 50 53N 0 2 E
Lewis, *U.K.* 22 58 10N 6 40W
Lewis, Butt of, *U.K.* 22 58 30N 6 12W
Lewisham, *U.K.* 15 51 27N 0 1W
Lexington, *U.S.A.* 92 38 6N 84 30W
Leyburn, *U.K.* 19 54 19N 1 50W
Leyland, *U.K.* 18 53 41N 2 42W
Leysdown on Sea, *U.K.* 15 51 23N 0 57 E
Lhasa, *China* 60 29 50N 91 3 E
Liaodong, Gulf of, *China* 61 40 20N 121 10 E
Liaoning □, *China* 61 41 40N 122 30 E
Liaoyang, *China* 61 41 15N 123 10 E
Liaoyüan, *China* 61 42 55N 125 10 E
Liberia ■, *W. Afr.* 78 6 30N 9 30W
Libreville, *Gabon* 80 0 25N 9 26 E
Libya ■, *N. Afr.* 79 27 0N 17 0 E
Libyan Desert, *Africa* 79 25 0N 25 0 E
Lichfield, *U.K.* 14 52 40N 1 50W
Lichinga, *Mozam.* 81 13 13S 35 11 E
Liechtenstein ■, *Europe* 42 47 8N 9 35 E
Liège, *Belg.* 36 50 38N 5 35 E
Liepaja, *U.S.S.R.* 46 56 30N 21 0 E
Liffey →, *Ire.* 25 53 21N 6 20W
Lifford, *Ire.* 24 54 50N 7 30W
Ligurian Sea, *It.* 40 43 20N 9 0 E
Likasi, *Zaïre* 80 10 55S 26 48 E
Lille, *Fr.* 34 50 38N 3 3 E
Lille Bælt, *Den.* 45 55 20N 9 45 E
Lillehammer, *Nor.* 45 61 8N 10 30 E
Lilleshall, *U.K.* 14 52 45N 2 22W
Lilongwe, *Malawi* 81 14 0S 33 48 E
Lima, *Peru* 100 12 0S 77 0W
Limassol, *Cyprus* 47 34 42N 33 1 E
Limavady, *U.K.* 24 55 3N 6 58W
Limavady □, *U.K.* 24 55 0N 6 55W
Limburg □, *Neth.* 36 51 20N 5 55 E
Limerick, *Ire.* 25 52 40N 8 38W
Limerick □, *Ire.* 25 52 30N 8 50W
Límnos, *Greece* 41 39 50N 25 5 E
Limoges, *Fr.* 35 45 50N 1 15 E
Limpopo →, *Mozam.* 81 25 15S 33 30 E
Limpsfield, *U.K.* 15 51 15N 0 1 E
Linares, *Sp.* 37 38 10N 3 40W
Lincluden, *U.K.* 21 55 5N 3 40W
Lincoln, *U.K.* 19 53 14N 0 32W
Lincoln, *U.S.A.* 90 40 50N 96 42W
Lincoln □, *U.K.* 19 53 14N 0 32W
Lincoln Wolds, *U.K.* 19 53 20N 0 5W
Lindale, *U.K.* 18 54 14N 2 54W
Lingfield, *U.K.* 15 51 11N 0 1W
Linkinhorne, *U.K.* 16 50 31N 4 22W
Linköping, *Swed.* 45 58 28N 15 36 E
Linlithgow, *U.K.* 21 55 58N 3 38W
Linnhe, L., *U.K.* 20 56 36N 5 25W
Linslade, *U.K.* 15 51 55N 0 40W
Linton, *U.K.* 15 52 6N 0 19 E
Linxia, *China* 60 35 36N 103 10 E
Linz, *Austria* 42 48 18N 14 18 E
Lion, G. du, *Fr.* 35 43 0N 4 0 E
Lípari, Is., *It.* 40 38 30N 14 50 E
Lipetsk, *U.S.S.R.* 46 52 37N 39 35 E
Lisbon, *Port.* 37 38 42N 9 10W
Lisburn, *U.K.* 24 54 30N 6 9W
Liscannor, B., *Ire.* 25 52 57N 9 24W
Liskeard, *U.K.* 16 50 27N 4 29W
Lismore, *Austral.* 67 28 44S 153 21 E
Lismore, *Ire.* 25 52 8N 7 58W
Lismore I., *U.K.* 20 56 30N 5 30W
Liss, *U.K.* 15 51 3N 0 53W
Listowel, *Ire.* 25 52 27N 9 30W
Litcham, *U.K.* 15 52 43N 0 49 E
Litherland, *U.K.* 18 53 29N 3 0W
Lithgow, *Austral.* 70 33 25S 150 8 E
Lithuania □, *U.S.S.R.* 46 55 30N 24 0 E
Little Minch, *U.K.* 22 57 35N 6 45W
Little Ouse →, *U.K.* 15 52 25N 0 50 E
Little Rock, *U.S.A.* 91 34 41N 92 10W
Little Walsingham, *U.K.* 15 52 53N 0 51 E
Littleborough, *U.K.* 18 53 38N 2 8W
Littlehampton, *U.K.* 15 50 48N 0 32W
Littleport, *U.K.* 15 52 27N 0 18 E
Littlestone-on-Sea, *U.K.* 15 50 59N 0 59 E
Liuzhou, *China* 61 24 22N 109 22 E
Liverpool, *Austral.* 70 33 54S 150 58 E
Liverpool, *U.K.* 18 53 25N 3 0W
Liverpool Plains, *Austral.* 70 31 15S 150 15 E
Livingston, *U.K.* 21 55 52N 3 33W
Livingstone, *Zam.* 81 17 46S 25 52 E
Lizard, *U.K.* 16 49 58N 5 10W
Lizard Pt., *U.K.* 16 49 57N 5 11W
Ljubljana, *Yug.* 40 46 4N 14 33 E
Llandeilo, *U.K.* 17 51 53N 4 0W
Llandovery, *U.K.* 17 51 59N 3 49W
Llandrindod Wells, *U.K.* 17 52 15N 3 23W
Llandudno, *U.K.* 17 53 19N 3 51W
Llanelli, *U.K.* 17 51 41N 4 11W
Llanerchymedd, *U.K.* 17 53 20N 4 22W
Llanfair Caereinion, *U.K.* 17 52 39N 3 20W
Llanfair Talhaiarn, *U.K.* 17 53 13N 3 37W
Llanfairfechan, *U.K.* 17 53 15N 3 58W
Llangefni, *U.K.* 17 53 15N 4 20W
Llangollen, *U.K.* 17 52 58N 3 10W
Llanidloes, *U.K.* 17 52 28N 3 31W
Llanllyfni, *U.K.* 17 53 2N 4 18W
Llanos, *S. Am.* 100 5 0N 71 35W
Llanrhystyd, *U.K.* 17 52 19N 4 9W
Llantrisant, *U.K.* 17 51 33N 3 22W
Llantwit-Major, *U.K.* 17 51 24N 3 29W
Llanwrtyd Wells, *U.K.* 17 52 6N 3 39W
Llanybloddwel, *U.K.* 14 52 47N 3 8W
Llanymynech, *U.K.* 14 52 48N 3 6W
Lleyn Peninsula, *U.K.* 17 52 55N 4 35W
Loanhead, *U.K.* 21 55 53N 3 10W
Lobito, *Angola* 81 12 18S 13 35 E
Lochaber, *U.K.* 22 56 55N 5 0W
Lochans, *U.K.* 20 54 52N 5 1W
Lochboisdale, *U.K.* 22 57 10N 7 20W
Lochbuie, *U.K.* 20 56 21N 5 52W
Lochcarron, *U.K.* 22 57 25N 5 30W
Lochdonhead, *U.K.* 20 56 27N 5 40W
Lochearnhead, *U.K.* 20 56 24N 4 19W
Lochgelly, *U.K.* 21 56 7N 3 18W
Lochgilphead, *U.K.* 20 56 2N 5 37W
Lochgoilhead, *U.K.* 20 56 10N 4 54W
Lochinver, *U.K.* 22 58 9N 5 15W
Lochmaben, *U.K.* 21 55 8N 3 27W
Lochmaddy, *U.K.* 22 57 36N 7 10W
Lochnagar, *U.K.* 23 56 57N 3 14W
Lochranza, *U.K.* 20 55 42N 5 18W
Lochwinnoch, *U.K.* 20 55 47N 4 39W
Lochy →, *U.K.* 22 56 52N 5 3W
Lockerbie, *U.K.* 21 55 7N 3 21W
Lod, *Isr.* 57 31 57N 34 54 E
Loddon, *U.K.* 15 52 32N 1 29 E
Łódź, *Pol.* 43 51 45N 19 27 E
Lofoten, *Nor.* 44 68 30N 15 0 E
Loftus, *U.K.* 19 54 33N 0 52W
Logan, Mt., *Canada* 88 60 31N 140 22W
Logroño, *Sp.* 37 42 28N 2 27W
Loire →, *Fr.* 34 47 16N 2 10W
Lolland, *Den.* 45 54 45N 11 30 E
Lombardy □, *It.* 40 45 35N 9 45 E
Lomé, *Togo* 78 6 9N 1 20 E
Lomond, L., *U.K.* 20 56 8N 4 38W
Łomza, *Pol.* 43 53 10N 22 2 E
London, *Canada* 92 42 59N 81 15W
London, *U.K.* 15 51 30N 0 5W
London, Greater □, *U.K.* 15 51 30N 0 5W
Londonderry, *U.K.* 24 55 0N 7 20W
Londonderry □, *U.K.* 24 55 0N 7 20W
Londrina, *Brazil* 102 23 18S 51 10W
Long, L., *U.K.* 20 56 4N 4 50W
Long Beach, *U.S.A.* 90 33 46N 118 12W
Long Bennington, *U.K.* 19 52 59N 0 45W
Long Clawson, *U.K.* 15 52 51N 0 56W
Long Crendon, *U.K.* 15 51 47N 1 0W
Long Eaton, *U.K.* 19 52 54N 1 16W
Long I., *Baham.* 95 23 20N 75 10W
Long I., *U.S.A.* 93 40 50N 73 20W
Long Itchington, *U.K.* 14 52 16N 1 24W
Long Melford, *U.K.* 15 52 5N 0 44 E
Long Mynd, *U.K.* 14 52 35N 2 50W
Long Preston, *U.K.* 18 54 0N 2 16W
Long Sutton, *U.K.* 15 52 47N 0 9 E
Longford, *Ire.* 24 53 43N 7 50W
Longford, *U.K.* 14 51 53N 2 14W
Longford □, *Ire.* 24 53 42N 7 45W
Longforgan, *U.K.* 21 56 28N 3 8W
Longframlington, *U.K.* 21 55 18N 1 47W
Longhorsley, *U.K.* 21 55 15N 1 46W
Longhoughton, *U.K.* 21 55 26N 1 36W
Longridge, *U.K.* 18 53 50N 2 37W
Longton, *U.K.* 18 53 43N 2 48W
Longtown, *Cumbria, U.K.* 18 55 1N 2 59W
Longtown, *Hereford & Worcs., U.K.* 14 51 58N 2 59W
Löningen, *W. Ger.* 36 52 43N 7 44 E
Looe, *U.K.* 16 50 24N 4 25W
Loop Hd., *Ire.* 25 52 34N 9 55W
Lop Nor, *China* 60 40 20N 90 10 E
Lorca, *Sp.* 37 37 41N 1 42W
Lorient, *Fr.* 34 47 45N 3 23W
Lorn, *U.K.* 20 56 26N 5 10W
Lorn, Firth of, *U.K.* 20 56 20N 5 40W
Los Angeles, *Chile* 102 37 28S 72 23W
Los Angeles, *U.S.A.* 90 34 0N 118 10W
Los Mochis, *Mex.* 94 25 45N 108 57W
Lossiemouth, *U.K.* 23 57 43N 3 17W
Lostwithiel, *U.K.* 16 50 24N 4 41W
Lothian □, *U.K.* 21 55 50N 3 0W
Loughborough, *U.K.* 14 52 46N 1 11W
Loughrea, *Ire.* 25 53 11N 8 33W
Loughros More B., *Ire.* 24 54 48N 8 30W
Louisiana □, *U.S.A.* 91 30 50N 92 0W
Louisville, *U.S.A.* 92 38 15N 85 45W
Lourdes, *Fr.* 35 43 6N 0 3W
Louth, *Ire.* 24 53 47N 6 33W
Louth, *U.K.* 19 53 23N 0 0 E
Louth □, *Ire.* 24 53 55N 6 30W
Louvière, La, *Belg.* 36 50 27N 4 10 E
Lowell, *U.S.A.* 93 42 38N 71 19W
Lower Beeding, *U.K.* 15 51 2N 0 15W
Lower California, *Mex.* 94 31 10N 115 12W
Lower Hutt, *N.Z.* 71 41 10S 174 55 E
Lower Tunguska →, *U.S.S.R.* 49 64 20N 93 0 E
Lowes Water L., *U.K.* 18 54 35N 3 23W
Lowestoft, *U.K.* 15 52 29N 1 44 E
Lowick, *U.K.* 21 55 38N 1 57W
Lowther Hills, *U.K.* 21 55 20N 3 40W
Luanda, *Angola* 80 8 50S 13 15 E
Luanshya, *Zam.* 81 13 3S 28 28 E
Lubbock, *U.S.A.* 90 33 40N 101 53W
Lübeck, *W. Ger.* 42 53 52N 10 41 E
Lublin, *Pol.* 43 51 12N 22 38 E
Lubumbashi, *Zaïre* 81 11 40S 27 28 E
Luce Bay, *U.K.* 20 54 45N 4 48W
Lucknow, *India* 59 26 50N 81 0 E
Lüda = Dalian, *China* 61 38 50N 121 40 E
Ludgershall, *U.K.* 14 51 15N 1 38W
Ludgvan, *U.K.* 16 50 9N 5 30W
Ludhiana, *India* 58 30 57N 75 56 E
Ludlow, *U.K.* 14 52 23N 2 42W
Ludwigshafen, *W. Ger.* 42 49 27N 8 27 E

Lugano, Switz. 42 46 0N 8 57 E
Lugnaquilla, Ire. 25 52 58N 6 28W
Lugo, Sp. 37 43 2N 7 35W
Lugwardine, U.K. 14 52 4N 2 38W
Luing I., U.K. 20 56 15N 5 40W
Luleå, Swed. 44 65 35N 22 10 E
Lundy, U.K. 16 51 10N 4 41W
Lune →, U.K. 18 54 0N 2 51W
Lünen, W. Ger. 36 51 36N 7 31 E
Luoyang, China 61 34 40N 112 26 E
Lurgan, U.K. 24 54 28N 6 20W
Lusaka, Zam. 81 15 28S 28 16 E
Luss, U.K. 20 56 6N 4 40W
Luton, U.K. 15 51 53N 0 24W
Lutterworth, U.K. 14 52 28N 1 12W
Luxembourg, Lux. 36 49 37N 6 9 E
Luxembourg ■, Europe 36 50 0N 6 0 E
Luzern, Switz. 42 47 3N 8 18 E
Luzhou, China 60 28 52N 105 20 E
Luzon, Phil. 63 16 0N 121 0 E
Lvov, U.S.S.R. 47 49 50N 24 0 E
Lyakhov Is., U.S.S.R. 49 73 40N 141 0 E
Lybster, U.K. 23 58 18N 3 16W
Lydd, U.K. 15 50 57N 0 56 E
Lydford, U.K. 16 50 38N 4 7W
Lydham, U.K. 14 52 31N 2 59W
Lyell Range, N.Z. 71 41 38S 172 20 E
Lyme Bay, U.K. 16 50 36N 2 55W
Lyme Regis, U.K. 16 50 44N 2 57W
Lyminge, U.K. 15 51 7N 1 6 E
Lymington, U.K. 14 50 46N 1 32W
Lymm, U.K. 18 53 23N 2 30W
Lympne, U.K. 15 51 4N 1 2 E
Lynchburg, U.S.A. 92 37 23N 79 10W
Lyndhurst, U.K. 14 50 53N 1 33W
Lyneham, U.K. 14 51 30N 1 57W
Lynemouth, U.K. 21 55 15N 1 29W
Lynmouth, U.K. 16 51 14N 3 50W
Lynn Lake, Canada 88 56 51N 101 3W
Lynton, U.K. 16 51 14N 3 50W
Lyons, Fr. 35 45 46N 4 50 E
Lytchett Minster, U.K. 14 50 44N 2 3W
Lytham St. Anne's, U.K. 18 53 45N 2 58W
Lythe, U.K. 19 54 30N 0 40W

M

Ma'ān, Jord. 56 30 12N 35 44 E
Maarianhamina, Fin. 45 60 5N 19 55 E
Maastricht, Neth. 36 50 50N 5 40 E
Mablethorpe, U.K. 19 53 21N 0 14 E
Macapá, Brazil 101 0 5N 51 4W
Macau ■, Asia 61 22 16N 113 35 E
Macclesfield, U.K. 18 53 16N 2 9W
McClure Str., Canada 103 75 0N 119 0W
Macdonnell Ranges, Austral. 66 23 40S 133 0 E
Macduff, U.K. 23 57 40N 2 30W
Macedonia □, Greece 41 40 39N 22 0 E
Macedonia □, Yug. 41 41 53N 21 40 E
Maceió, Brazil 101 9 40S 35 41W
Macgillycuddy's Reeks, Ire. 25 52 2N 9 45W
Machakos, Kenya 80 1 30S 37 15 E
Machala, Ecuad. 100 3 20S 79 57W
Machars, The, U.K. 20 54 46N 4 30W
Machrihanish, U.K. 20 55 25N 5 42W
Machynlleth, U.K. 17 52 36N 3 51W
Macintyre →, Austral. 67 28 37S 150 47 E
Mackay, Austral. 67 21 8S 149 11 E
Mackay, L., Austral. 66 22 30S 129 0 E
McKeesport, U.S.A. 92 40 21N 79 50W
Mackenzie →, Austral. 67 23 38S 149 46 E
Mackenzie →, Canada 88 69 10N 134 20W
Mackenzie Mts., Canada 88 64 0N 130 0W
McKinley, Mt., U.S.A. 88 63 2N 151 0W
M'Clintock Chan., Canada 88 72 0N 102 0W
Macon, U.S.A. 90 32 50N 83 37W
Macquarie →, Austral. 70 30 5S 147 30 E
Macquarie Harbour, Austral. 67 42 15S 145 23 E
Macquarie Is., S. Oc. 64 54 36S 158 55 E
Macroom, Ire. 25 51 54N 8 57W
Madadeni, S. Afr. 81 27 43S 30 3 E
Madagascar ■, Africa 81 20 0S 47 0 E
Madeira, Atl. Oc. 78 32 50N 17 0W
Madeira →, Brazil 100 3 22S 58 45W
Madeley, Salop, U.K. 14 52 38N 2 28W
Madeley, Staffs., U.K. 18 52 59N 2 20W
Madhya Pradesh □, India 59 21 50N 81 0 E
Madīnat ash Sha'b, S. Yem. 56 12 50N 45 0 E
Madison, U.S.A. 92 43 5N 89 25W
Madiun, Indon. 63 7 38S 111 32 E
Madley, U.K. 14 52 3N 2 51W
Madras, India 58 13 8N 80 19 E
Madre, L., U.S.A. 91 26 0N 97 40W
Madre, Sierra, Mex. 94 16 0N 93 0W
Madrid, Sp. 37 40 25N 3 45W
Madurai, India 58 9 55N 78 10 E
Maesteg, U.K. 17 51 36N 3 40W
Magadan, U.S.S.R. 49 59 38N 150 50 E
Magdalena →, Col. 100 11 6N 74 51W
Magdeburg, E. Ger. 42 52 8N 11 36 E
Magee, I., U.K. 24 54 48N 5 44W
Magelang, Indon. 63 7 29S 110 13 E
Magellan's Str., Chile 102 52 30S 75 0W
Maggiore, L., It. 40 46 0N 8 35 E
Magherafelt, U.K. 24 54 44N 6 37W
Maghull, U.K. 18 53 31N 2 56W
Magnitogorsk, U.S.S.R. 46 53 27N 59 4 E
Mahajanga, Madag. 81 17 0S 47 0 E
Maiden Bradley, U.K. 14 51 9N 2 18W
Maiden Newton, U.K. 14 50 46N 2 35W
Maidenhead, U.K. 15 51 31N 0 42W
Maidstone, U.K. 15 51 16N 0 31 E
Maiduguri, Nig. 79 12 0N 13 20 E
Main →, U.K. 24 54 49N 6 20W
Maine □, U.S.A. 93 45 20N 69 0W
Maine →, Ire. 25 52 10N 9 40W
Mainland, Orkney, U.K. 23 59 0N 3 10W
Mainland, Shetland, U.K. 22 60 15N 1 22W
Mainz, W. Ger. 36 50 0N 8 17 E
Maitland, Austral. 70 32 33S 151 36 E
Majorca, I. = Mallorca, Sp. 37 39 30N 3 0 E
Makasar, Str. of, Indon. 63 1 0S 118 20 E
Maker, U.K. 16 50 20N 4 10W
Makeyevka, U.S.S.R. 47 48 0N 38 0 E
Makhachkala, U.S.S.R. 47 43 0N 47 30 E
Makran Coast Range, Pak. 58 25 40N 64 0 E
Mal B., Ire. 25 52 50N 9 30W
Malabar Coast, India 58 11 0N 75 0 E
Malacca, Str. of, Indon. 63 3 0N 101 0 E
Málaga, Sp. 37 36 43N 4 23W
Malang, Indon. 63 7 59S 112 45 E
Malanje, Angola 80 9 36S 16 17 E
Mälaren, Swed. 45 59 30N 17 10 E
Malatya, Turk. 47 38 25N 38 20 E
Malawi ■, Africa 81 13 0S 34 0 E
Malay Pen., Asia 63 7 25N 100 0 E
Malaysia ■, Asia 63 5 0N 110 0 E
Maldives ■, Ind. Oc. 129 7 0N 73 0 E
Maldon, U.K. 15 51 43N 0 41 E
Malham Tarn, U.K. 18 54 6N 2 11W
Mali ■, Africa 78 15 0N 2 0W
Mallaig, U.K. 22 57 0N 5 50W
Mallorca, Sp. 37 39 30N 3 0 E
Mallow, Ire. 25 52 8N 8 40W
Malmédy, Belg. 36 50 25N 6 2 E
Malmesbury, U.K. 14 51 35N 2 5W
Malmö, Swed. 45 55 36N 12 59 E
Malpas, U.K. 18 53 3N 2 47W
Malta ■, Europe 40 35 50N 14 30 E
Maltby, U.K. 19 53 25N 1 12W
Malton, U.K. 19 54 9N 0 48W
Malvern, U.K. 14 52 7N 2 19W
Malvern Hills, U.K. 14 52 0N 2 19W
Malvern Wells, U.K. 14 52 4N 2 19W
Malvinas, Is. = Falkland Is., Atl. Oc. 102 51 30S 59 0W
Man, I. of, U.K. 18 54 15N 4 30W
Manaar, Gulf of, Asia 58 8 30N 79 0 E
Manacles, The, U.K. 16 50 3N 5 5W
Manado, Indon. 63 1 29N 124 51 E
Managua, Nic. 94 12 6N 86 20W
Manaus, Brazil 100 3 0S 60 0W
Manby, U.K. 19 53 22N 0 6 E
Manchester, U.K. 18 53 30N 2 15W
Manchester, U.S.A. 93 42 58N 71 29W
Manchuria, China 61 42 0N 125 0 E
Mandalay, Burma 59 22 0N 96 4 E
Manea, U.K. 15 52 29N 0 10 E
Mangalore, India 58 12 55N 74 47 E
Mangotsfield, U.K. 14 51 29N 2 29W
Manila, Phil. 63 14 40N 121 3 E
Manitoba □, Canada 88 55 30N 97 0W
Manizales, Col. 100 5 5N 75 32W
Manly, Austral. 70 33 48S 151 17 E
Mannheim, W. Ger. 42 49 28N 8 29 E
Manningtree, U.K. 15 51 56N 1 3 E
Mans, Le, Fr. 34 48 0N 0 10 E
Mansfield, U.K. 19 53 8N 1 12W
Mansfield, U.S.A. 92 40 45N 82 30W
Mansfield Woodhouse, U.K. 19 53 11N 1 11W
Mantes-la-Jolie, Fr. 34 49 0N 1 41 E
Manton, U.K. 15 52 37N 0 41W
Mantua, It. 40 45 20N 10 42 E
Manukau, N.Z. 71 37 1S 174 55 E
Manzhouli, China 61 49 35N 117 25 E
Maoming, China 61 21 50N 110 54 E
Maputo, Mozam. 81 25 58S 32 32 E
Mar del Plata, Arg. 102 38 0S 57 30W
Maracaibo, Ven. 100 10 40N 71 37W
Maracaibo, L., Ven. 100 9 40N 71 30W
Maracay, Ven. 100 10 15N 67 28W
Marajó, I. de, Brazil 101 1 0S 49 30W
Maranhão = São Luís, Brazil 101 2 39S 44 15W
Marañón →, Peru 100 4 30S 73 35W
Marazion, U.K. 16 50 8N 5 29W
March, U.K. 15 52 33N 0 5 E
Marden, U.K. 14 52 7N 2 42W
Maree L., U.K. 22 57 40N 5 30W
Mareeba, Austral. 67 16 59S 145 28 E
Mareham le Fen, U.K. 19 53 7N 0 3W
Marfleet, U.K. 19 53 45N 0 15W
Margarita I., Ven. 100 11 0N 64 0W
Margate, U.K. 15 51 23N 1 24 E
Maribor, Yug. 40 46 36N 15 40 E
Maricourt, Canada 89 56 34N 70 49W
Marie-Galante, W. Ind. 94 15 56N 61 16W
Marília, Brazil 101 22 13S 50 0W
Maringá, Brazil 102 23 26S 52 2W
Mark, U.K. 20 55 2N 5 1W
Market Bosworth, U.K. 14 52 37N 1 24W
Market Deeping, U.K. 15 52 40N 0 20W
Market Drayton, U.K. 18 52 55N 2 30W
Market Harborough, U.K. 15 52 29N 0 55W
Market Lavington, U.K. 14 51 17N 1 59W
Market Rasen, U.K. 19 53 24N 0 20W
Market Weighton, U.K. 19 53 52N 0 40W
Markfield, U.K. 14 52 42N 1 18W
Markinch, U.K. 21 56 12N 3 9W
Marks Tey, U.K. 15 51 53N 0 48 E
Marlborough, U.K. 14 51 26N 1 44W
Marlborough □, N.Z. 71 41 45S 173 33 E
Marlborough Downs, U.K. 14 51 25N 1 55W
Marlow, U.K. 15 51 34N 0 47W
Marmara, Sea of, Turk. 47 40 45N 28 15 E
Marne →, Fr. 34 48 48N 2 24 E
Marnhull, U.K. 14 50 58N 2 20W
Maroua, Cam. 80 10 40N 14 20 E
Marple, U.K. 18 53 23N 2 5W
Marquesas Is., Pac. Oc. 65 9 30S 140 0W
Marrakech, Mor. 78 31 9N 8 0W
Marseilles, Fr. 35 43 18N 5 23 E
Marshall Is., Pac. Oc. 64 9 0N 171 0 E
Marshfield, U.K. 14 51 27N 2 18W
Marske by the Sea, U.K. 19 54 35N 1 0W
Marston Moor, U.K. 19 53 58N 1 17W
Martaban, G. of, Burma 59 16 5N 96 30 E
Martham, U.K. 15 52 42N 1 38 E
Martinique, W. Ind. 94 14 40N 61 0W
Martley, U.K. 14 52 14N 2 22W
Martock, U.K. 14 50 58N 2 47W
Mary Kathleen, Austral. 67 20 44S 139 48 E
Maryborough, Austral. 67 37 0S 143 44 E
Maryland □, U.S.A. 93 39 10N 76 40W
Maryport, U.K. 18 54 43N 3 30W
Marytavy, U.K. 16 50 34N 4 6W
Masan, S. Kor. 61 35 11N 128 32 E
Maseru, Les. 81 29 18S 27 30 E
Masham, U.K. 19 54 15N 1 40W
Mashhad, Iran 57 36 20N 59 35 E
Mask, L., Ire. 24 53 36N 9 24W
Massachusetts □, U.S.A. 93 42 25N 72 0W
Massif Central, Fr. 35 45 30N 3 0 E
Masterton, N.Z. 71 40 56S 175 39 E
Masvingo, Zimb. 81 20 8S 30 49 E
Matadi, Zaïre 80 5 52S 13 31 E
Matamoros, Mex. 94 25 33N 103 15W
Matera, It. 40 40 40N 16 37 E
Matlock, U.K. 19 53 8N 1 32W
Mato Grosso □, Brazil 101 14 0S 55 0W
Matsue, Jap. 62 35 25N 133 10 E
Matsuyama, Jap. 62 33 45N 132 45 E
Matterhorn, Switz. 42 45 58N 7 39 E
Maturín, Ven. 100 9 45N 63 11W
Maubeuge, Fr. 34 50 17N 3 57 E
Mauchline, U.K. 20 55 31N 4 23W
Maughold, U.K. 18 54 18N 4 17W
Maughold Hd., U.K. 18 54 18N 4 17W
Maui, U.S.A. 90 20 45N 156 20 E
Mauna Loa, U.S.A. 90 21 8N 157 10W
Mauritania ■, Africa 78 20 50N 10 0W
Mauritius ■, Ind. Oc. 129 20 0S 57 0 E
Mawgan, U.K. 16 50 4N 5 10W
Mawlaik, Burma 59 23 40N 94 26 E
Maxwellheugh, U.K. 21 55 35N 2 23W
May, I. of, U.K. 21 56 11N 2 32W
May Pen, Jam. 94 17 58N 77 15W
Maybole, U.K. 20 55 21N 4 41W
Mayfield, Derby, U.K. 19 53 1N 1 47W
Mayfield, E. Sussex, U.K. 15 51 1N 0 17 E
Maynooth, Ire. 24 53 22N 6 38W
Mayo □, Ire. 24 53 47N 9 7W
Mazar-e Sharīf, Afg. 57 36 41N 67 0 E
Mazatlán, Mex. 94 23 13N 106 25W
Mbabane, Swaz. 81 26 18S 31 6 E
Mbandaka, Zaïre 80 0 1N 18 18 E
Mbanza Ngungu, Zaïre 80 5 12S 14 53 E
Mbeya, Tanz. 80 8 54S 33 29 E
Mbini □, Eq. Guin. 80 1 30N 10 0 E
Mbuji-Mayi, Zaïre 80 6 9S 23 40 E
Mdantsane, S. Afr. 81 32 56S 27 46 E
Mealsgate, U.K. 18 54 46N 3 14W
Measham, U.K. 14 52 43N 1 30W
Meath □, Ire. 24 53 32N 6 40W
Mecca, Si. Arab. 56 21 30N 39 54 E
Mechelen, Belg. 36 50 58N 5 41 E
Medan, Indon. 63 3 40N 98 38 E
Medellín, Col. 100 6 15N 75 35W
Medicine Hat, Canada 88 50 0N 110 45W
Medina, Si. Arab. 56 24 35N 39 52 E
Mediterranean Sea, Europe 38 35 0N 15 0 E
Medley, Canada 88 54 25N 110 16W
Medstead, U.K. 14 51 7N 1 4W
Medway →, U.K. 15 51 28N 0 45 E
Meekatharra, Austral. 66 26 32S 118 29 E
Meerut, India 58 29 1N 77 42 E
Mei Xian, China 61 24 16N 116 6 E
Meknès, Mor. 78 33 57N 5 33W
Mekong →, Asia 63 9 30N 106 15 E
Melanesia, Pac. Oc. 64 4 0S 155 0 E
Melbourn, U.K. 15 52 5N 0 1 E
Melbourne, Austral. 70 37 50S 145 0 E
Melbourne, U.K. 14 52 50N 1 25W
Melfort, Loch, U.K. 20 56 13N 5 33W
Melitopol, U.S.S.R. 47 46 50N 35 22 E
Melksham, U.K. 14 51 22N 2 9W
Melmerby, U.K. 18 54 44N 2 35W
Melrose, U.K. 21 53 35N 2 44W
Melsonby, U.K. 19 54 28N 1 41W
Melton, U.K. 15 52 51N 1 1 E
Melton Constable, U.K. 15 52 52N 1 1 E
Melton Mowbray, U.K. 15 52 46N 0 52W
Melvich, U.K. 23 58 33N 3 55W
Melville I., Austral. 66 11 30S 131 0 E
Melville Pen., Canada 89 68 0N 84 0W
Memphis, U.S.A. 91 35 7N 90 0W
Menai Bridge, U.K. 17 53 14N 4 11W
Menai Strait, U.K. 17 53 14N 4 10W
Menan = Chao Phraya →, Thai. 63 13 32N 100 36 E
Mendip Hills, U.K. 14 51 17N 2 40W
Mendlesham, U.K. 15 52 15N 1 4 E
Mendoza, Arg. 102 32 50S 68 52W
Menindee, Austral. 70 32 20S 142 25 E
Menorca, Sp. 37 40 0N 4 0 E
Mere, U.K. 14 51 5N 2 16W
Mérida, Mex. 94 20 58N 89 37W
Mérida, Ven. 100 8 24N 71 8W
Meriden, U.K. 14 52 27N 1 36W
Merrick, U.K. 20 55 8N 4 30W
Merse, U.K. 21 55 40N 2 30W
Mersea I., U.K. 15 51 48N 0 55 E
Mersey →, U.K. 18 53 20N 2 56W
Merseyside □, U.K. 18 53 25N 2 55W
Mersin, Turk. 47 36 51N 34 36 E
Merthyr Tydfil, U.K. 17 51 45N 3 23W
Merton, U.K. 15 51 25N 0 13W
Meru, Tanz. 80 3 15S 36 46 E
Mesa, U.S.A. 90 33 20N 111 56W
Mesopotamia, Asia 56 33 30N 44 0 E
Messina, It. 40 38 10N 15 32 E
Messina, Str. of, It. 40 38 5N 15 35 E
Metheringham, U.K. 19 53 9N 0 22W
Methil, U.K. 21 56 10N 3 1W
Methven, U.K. 21 56 25N 3 35W
Methwold, U.K. 15 52 30N 0 33 E
Metz, Fr. 34 49 8N 6 10 E
Meuse →, Europe 34 50 45N 5 41 E
Mevagissey, U.K. 16 50 16N 4 48W
Mevagissey Bay, U.K. 16 50 15N 4 40W
Mexborough, U.K. 19 53 29N 1 18W
Mexicali, Mex. 94 32 40N 115 29W
México, Mex. 94 19 20N 99 10W
Mexico ■, Cent. Am. 94 20 0N 100 0W
Mexico, G. of, Cent. Am. 94 25 0N 90 0W
Miami, U.S.A. 91 25 45N 80 15W
Micheldever, U.K. 14 51 7N 1 17W
Michigan □, U.S.A. 92 44 40N 85 40W
Michigan, L., U.S.A. 92 44 0N 87 0W
Mickle Fell, U.K. 18 54 38N 2 16W
Mickleover, U.K. 19 52 55N 1 32W
Mickleton, Durham, U.K. 18 54 36N 2 3W
Mickleton, Oxon., U.K. 14 52 5N 1 45W
Micronesia, Pac. Oc. 64 11 0N 160 0 E
Mid Calder, U.K. 21 55 53N 3 23W
Mid Glamorgan □, U.K. 17 51 40N 3 25W
Middle Zoy, U.K. 14 51 5N 2 54W
Middleham, U.K. 19 54 17N 1 49W
Middlemarsh, U.K. 14 50 51N 2 29W
Middlesbrough, U.K. 19 54 35N 1 14W
Middleton, Gr. Manchester, U.K. 18 53 33N 2 12W
Middleton, Norfolk, U.K. 15 52 43N 0 29 E
Middleton Cheney, U.K. 14 52 4N 1 17W
Middleton-in-Teesdale, U.K. 18 54 38N 2 5W
Middleton on the Wolds, U.K. 19 53 56N 0 35W
Middlewich, U.K. 18 53 12N 2 28W
Midhurst, U.K. 15 50 59N 0 44W
Midland, U.S.A. 90 32 0N 102 3W
Midleton, Ire. 25 51 52N 8 12W
Midsomer Norton, U.K. 14 51 17N 2 29W
Midway Is., Pac. Oc. 64 28 13N 177 22W
Mieres, Sp. 37 43 18N 5 48W
Mikkeli, Fin. 44 61 43N 27 15 E
Milan, It. 40 45 28N 9 10 E
Milborne Port, U.K. 14 50 58N 2 28W
Mildenhall, U.K. 15 52 20N 0 30 E
Mildura, Austral. 70 34 13S 142 9 E
Milford Haven, U.K. 17 51 43N 5 2W
Milford Haven, B., U.K. 17 51 40N 5 10W
Milford on Sea, U.K. 14 50 44N 1 36W
Milk →, U.S.A. 90 48 5N 106 15W
Millbrook, U.K. 16 50 19N 4 12W
Milleur Pt., U.K. 20 55 2N 5 5W
Millom, U.K. 18 54 13N 3 16W
Millport, U.K. 20 55 45N 4 55W
Milltown Malbay, Ire. 25 52 51N 9 25W
Milnathort, U.K. 21 56 14N 3 25W
Milngavie, U.K. 20 55 57N 4 20W
Milnthorpe, U.K. 18 54 14N 2 47W
Milton, Dumf. & Gall., U.K. 20 55 18N 4 50W
Milton, Hants., U.K. 14 50 45N 1 40W
Milton, Highland, U.K. 23 57 18N 4 32W
Milton Abbot, U.K. 16 50 35N 4 16W
Milton Keynes, U.K. 15 52 3N 0 42W

Milverton, *U.K.* **14** 51 2N 3 15W
Milwaukee, *U.S.A.* **92** 43 9N 87 58W
Minas Gerais □, *Brazil* **101** 18 50S 46 0W
Minatitlán, *Mex.* **94** 17 59N 94 31W
Minchinghampton, *U.K.* **14** 51 42N 2 10W
Mindanao, *Phil.* **63** 8 0N 125 0 E
Mindoro, *Phil.* **63** 13 0N 121 0 E
Minehead, *U.K.* **14** 51 12N 3 29W
Minneapolis, *U.S.A.* **91** 44 58N 93 20W
Minnesota □, *U.S.A.* **91** 46 40N 94 0W
Minnigaff, *U.K.* **20** 54 58N 4 30W
Minorca = Menorca, *Sp.* **37** 40 0N 4 0 E
Minsk, *U.S.S.R.* **46** 53 52N 27 30 E
Minster, *U.K.* **15** 51 20N 1 20 E
Minster-on-Sea, *U.K.* **15** 51 25N 0 50 E
Minsterley, *U.K.* **14** 52 38N 2 56W
Mirfield, *U.K.* **19** 53 37N 1 54W
Mirzapur, *India* **59** 25 10N 82 34 E
Miskolc, *Hung.* **43** 48 7N 20 50 E
Misrātah, *Libya* **79** 32 24N 15 3 E
Mississippi □, *U.S.A.* **91** 33 0N 90 0W
Mississippi →, *U.S.A.* **91** 29 0N 89 15W
Mississippi, Delta of the, *U.S.A.* **91** 29 15N 90 30W
Missouri □, *U.S.A.* **91** 38 25N 92 30W
Missouri →, *U.S.A.* **91** 38 50N 90 8W
Misterton, *Notts., U.K.* **19** 53 27N 0 49W
Misterton, *Somerset, U.K.* **14** 50 51N 2 46W
Mitcheldean, *U.K.* **14** 51 51N 2 29W
Mitchell →, *Austral.* **67** 15 12S 141 35 E
Mitchelstown, *Ire.* **25** 52 16N 8 18W
Mittelland Kanal, *W. Ger.* **36** 52 23N 7 45 E
Mitumba, Mts., *Zaïre* **80** 6 0S 29 0 E
Miyazaki, *Jap.* **62** 31 56N 131 30 E
Mizen Hd., *Cork, Ire.* **25** 51 27N 9 50W
Mizen Hd., *Wicklow, Ire.* **25** 52 52N 6 4W
Mizoram □, *India* **59** 23 30N 92 40 E
Mmabatho, *S. Afr.* **81** 25 49S 25 30 E
Mo i Rana, *Nor.* **44** 66 15N 14 7 E
Mobile, *U.S.A.* **91** 30 41N 88 3W
Mobutu Sese Seko, L., *Africa* **80** 1 30N 31 0 E
Moçâmedes = Namibe, *Angola* **81** 15 7S 12 11 E
Modbury, *U.K.* **16** 50 21N 3 53W
Módena, *It.* **40** 44 39N 10 55 E
Moe, *Austral.* **70** 38 12S 146 19 E
Moffat, *U.K.* **21** 55 20N 3 27W
Mogadishu, *Som.* **73** 2 2N 45 25 E
Mogilev, *U.S.S.R.* **46** 53 55N 30 18 E
Moidart, L., *U.K.* **22** 56 47N 5 40W
Mojave Desert, *U.S.A.* **90** 35 0N 116 30W
Mold, *U.K.* **17** 53 10N 3 10W
Moldavia □, *U.S.S.R.* **47** 47 0N 28 0 E
Mole →, *U.K.* **15** 51 13N 0 15W
Mollendo, *Peru* **100** 17 0S 72 0W
Mölndal, *Swed.* **45** 57 40N 12 3 E
Molokai, *U.S.A.* **90** 21 8N 157 0W
Moluccas, *Indon.* **63** 1 0S 127 0 E
Mombasa, *Kenya* **80** 4 2S 39 43 E
Mona Passage, *W. Ind.* **95** 18 0N 67 40W
Monach Is., *U.K.* **22** 57 32N 7 40W
Monaco ■, *Europe* **35** 43 46N 7 23 E
Monadhliath Mts., *U.K.* **23** 57 10N 4 4W
Monaghan, *Ire.* **24** 54 15N 6 58W
Monaghan □, *Ire.* **24** 54 10N 7 0W
Monastir = Bitola, *Yug.* **41** 41 5N 21 10 E
Monclova, *Mex.* **94** 26 50N 101 30W
Moncton, *Canada* **93** 46 7N 64 51W
Moneymore, *U.K.* **24** 54 42N 6 40W
Monghyr, *India* **59** 25 23N 86 30 E
Mongolia ■, *Asia* **60** 47 0N 103 0 E
Mongu, *Zam.* **81** 15 16S 23 12 E
Moniaive, *U.K.* **21** 55 11N 3 55W
Monifieth, *U.K.* **21** 56 30N 2 48W
Monkton, *U.K.* **20** 55 30N 4 37W
Monmouth, *U.K.* **17** 51 48N 2 43W
Monnow →, *U.K.* **14** 51 54N 2 48W
Monroe, *U.S.A.* **90** 32 32N 92 4W
Monrovia, *Lib.* **78** 6 18N 10 47W
Mons, *Belg.* **36** 50 27N 3 58 E
Montana □, *U.S.A.* **90** 47 0N 110 0W
Montbéliard, *Fr.* **34** 47 31N 6 48 E
Montceau-les-Mines, *Fr.* **34** 46 40N 4 23 E
Monte-Carlo, *Monaco* **35** 43 46N 7 23 E
Montego Bay, *Jam.* **94** 18 30N 78 0W
Montería, *Col.* **100** 8 46N 75 53W
Monterrey, *Mex.* **94** 25 40N 100 30W
Montes Claros, *Brazil* **101** 16 30S 43 50W
Montevideo, *Urug.* **102** 34 50S 56 11W
Montgomery, *U.K.* **17** 52 34N 3 9W
Montgomery, *U.S.A.* **91** 32 20N 86 20W
Montluçon, *Fr.* **35** 46 22N 2 36 E
Montpelier, *U.S.A.* **93** 44 15N 72 38W
Montpellier, *Fr.* **35** 43 37N 3 52 E
Montréal, *Canada* **93** 45 31N 73 34W
Montrose, *U.K.* **23** 56 43N 2 28W
Montserrat, *W. Ind.* **94** 16 40N 62 10W
Moonie →, *Austral.* **67** 29 19S 148 43 E
Moorfoot Hills, *U.K.* **21** 55 44N 3 8W
Moose Jaw, *Canada* **88** 50 24N 105 30W
Moosehead L., *U.S.A.* **93** 45 34N 69 40W
Mopti, *Mali* **78** 14 30N 4 0W
Moradabad, *India* **58** 28 50N 78 50 E
Morar L., *U.K.* **22** 56 57N 5 40W
Moray Firth, *U.K.* **23** 57 50N 3 30W
Morebattle, *U.K.* **21** 55 30N 2 20W
Morecambe, *U.K.* **18** 54 5N 2 52W
Morecambe B., *U.K.* **18** 54 7N 3 0W
Morelia, *Mex.* **94** 19 42N 101 7W
Morena, Sierra, *Sp.* **37** 38 20N 4 0W
Moreton-in-Marsh, *U.K.* **14** 51 59N 1 42W
Moretonhampstead, *U.K.* **16** 50 39N 3 45W
Morley, *U.K.* **19** 53 45N 1 36W
Morocco ■, *N. Afr.* **78** 32 0N 5 50W
Morogoro, *Tanz.* **80** 6 50S 37 40 E
Morpeth, *U.K.* **19** 55 11N 1 41W
Morte Bay, *U.K.* **16** 51 10N 4 13W
Morte Pt., *U.K.* **16** 51 13N 4 14W
Mortehoe, *U.K.* **16** 51 21N 4 12W
Mortimer's Cross, *U.K.* **14** 52 17N 2 50W
Morton Fen, *U.K.* **15** 52 45N 0 23W
Morvern, *U.K.* **22** 56 38N 5 44W
Morwell, *Austral.* **70** 38 10S 146 22 E
Morwenstow, *U.K.* **16** 50 53N 4 32W
Moscow, *U.S.S.R.* **46** 55 45N 37 35 E
Moselle →, *Europe* **34** 50 22N 7 36 E
Moshi, *Tanz.* **80** 3 22S 37 18 E
Mossley, *U.K.* **18** 53 31N 2 1W
Mossoró, *Brazil* **101** 5 10S 37 15W
Mostaganem, *Alg.* **78** 35 54N 0 5 E
Mostar, *Yug.* **41** 43 22N 17 50 E
Mosul, *Iraq* **56** 36 15N 43 5 E
Motcombe, *U.K.* **14** 51 1N 2 12W
Motherwell, *U.K.* **21** 55 48N 4 0W
Mottisfont, *U.K.* **14** 51 22N 1 32W
Moulmein, *Burma* **59** 16 30N 97 40 E
Moulton, *U.K.* **15** 52 17N 0 51W
Mount Barker, *Austral.* **66** 34 38S 117 40 E
Mount Gambier, *Austral.* **70** 37 50S 140 46 E
Mount Isa, *Austral.* **67** 20 42S 139 26 E
Mount Lofty Ra., *Austral.* **67** 34 35S 139 5 E
Mountain Ash, *U.K.* **17** 51 42N 3 22W
Mountmellick, *Ire.* **25** 53 7N 7 20W
Mounts Bay, *U.K.* **16** 50 3N 5 27W
Mountsorrel, *U.K.* **14** 52 43N 1 9W
Mourne →, *U.K.* **24** 54 45N 7 39W
Mourne Mts., *U.K.* **24** 54 10N 6 0W
Mouscron, *Belg.* **36** 50 45N 3 12 E
Moville, *Ire.* **24** 55 11N 7 3W
Moy →, *Ire.* **24** 54 5N 8 50W
Moyle □, *U.K.* **24** 55 10N 6 15W
Mozambique ■, *Africa* **81** 19 0S 35 0 E
Mozambique Chan., *Africa* **81** 20 0S 39 0 E
Mu Us Shamo, *China* **61** 39 0N 109 0 E
Mubarraz, *Si. Arab.* **56** 25 29N 49 40 E
Much Dewchurch, *U.K.* **14** 51 58N 2 45W
Much Marcle, *U.K.* **14** 51 59N 2 27W
Much Wenlock, *U.K.* **14** 52 36N 2 34W
Muck, *U.K.* **22** 56 50N 6 15W
Mudanjiang, *China* **61** 44 38N 129 30 E
Mudgee, *Austral.* **70** 32 32S 149 31 E
Mufulira, *Zam.* **81** 12 32S 28 15 E
Muine Bheag, *Ire.* **25** 52 42N 6 57W
Muir of Ord, *U.K.* **23** 57 30N 4 35W
Muirdrum, *U.K.* **21** 56 31N 2 40W
Muirhead, *U.K.* **21** 55 54N 4 5W
Muirkirk, *U.K.* **21** 55 31N 4 6W
Mülheim, *W. Ger.* **36** 51 26N 6 53 E
Mulhouse, *Fr.* **34** 47 40N 7 20 E
Mull, *U.K.* **20** 56 27N 6 0W
Mull, Ross of, *U.K.* **20** 56 20N 6 15W
Mull, Sound of, *U.K.* **20** 56 30N 5 50W
Mullet Pen., *Ire.* **24** 54 10N 10 2W
Mullingar, *Ire.* **24** 53 31N 7 20W
Mullion, *U.K.* **16** 50 1N 5 15W
Multan, *Pak.* **58** 30 15N 71 36 E
Mumbles Hd., *U.K.* **17** 51 33N 4 0W
Munchen-Gladbach, *W. Ger.* **36** 51 12N 6 23 E
Mundesley, *U.K.* **15** 52 53N 1 24 E
Munich, *W. Ger.* **42** 48 8N 11 33 E
Münster, *W. Ger.* **36** 51 58N 7 37 E
Munster □, *Ire.* **25** 52 20N 8 40W
Murchison →, *Austral.* **66** 27 45S 114 0 E
Murcia, *Sp.* **37** 38 20N 1 10W
Mureş →, *Rom.* **43** 46 15N 20 13 E
Murmansk, *U.S.S.R.* **46** 68 57N 33 10 E
Murray →, *S. Austral., Austral.* **70** 35 20S 139 22 E
Murray →, *W. Austral., Austral.* **67** 32 33S 115 45 E
Murrumbidgee →, *Austral.* **70** 34 43S 143 12 E
Murton, *U.K.* **19** 54 51N 1 22W
Murwillumbah, *Austral.* **67** 28 18S 153 27 E
Muscat, *Oman* **57** 23 40N 58 38 E
Musgrave Ras., *Austral.* **66** 26 0S 132 0 E
Musselburgh, *U.K.* **21** 55 57N 3 3W
Muswellbrook, *Austral.* **70** 32 16S 150 56 E
Mutare, *Zimb.* **81** 18 58S 32 38 E
Muthill, *U.K.* **21** 56 20N 3 50W
Muzaffarpur, *India* **59** 26 7N 85 23 E
Mwanza, *Tanz.* **80** 2 30S 32 58 E
Mweelrea, *Ire.* **24** 53 37N 9 48W
My Tho, *Viet.* **63** 10 29N 106 23 E
Myddle, *U.K.* **14** 52 49N 2 47W
Myitkyina, *Burma* **59** 25 24N 97 26 E
Mymensingh, *Bangla.* **59** 24 45N 90 24 E
Mynydd Du, *U.K.* **17** 51 45N 3 45W
Mynydd Prescelly, *U.K.* **17** 51 57N 4 48W
Mysore, *India* **58** 12 17N 76 41 E

N

Naas, *Ire.* **25** 53 12N 6 40W
Nābulus, *Jord.* **57** 32 14N 35 15 E
Nafferton, *U.K.* **19** 54 1N 0 24W
Nagaland □, *India* **59** 26 0N 94 30 E
Nagano, *Jap.* **62** 36 40N 138 10 E
Nagaoka, *Jap.* **62** 37 27N 138 51 E
Nagasaki, *Jap.* **62** 32 47N 129 50 E
Nagoya, *Jap.* **62** 35 10N 136 50 E
Nagpur, *India* **58** 21 8N 79 10 E
Naha, *Jap.* **62** 26 13N 127 42 E
Nailsea, *U.K.* **14** 51 25N 2 44W
Nailsworth, *U.K.* **14** 51 41N 2 12W
Nairn, *U.K.* **23** 57 35N 3 54W
Nairobi, *Kenya* **80** 1 17S 36 48 E
Nakuru, *Kenya* **80** 0 15S 36 4 E
Nalchik, *U.S.S.R.* **47** 43 30N 43 33 E
Nam Co, *China* **60** 30 30N 90 45 E
Namangan, *U.S.S.R.* **48** 41 0N 71 40 E
Namib Desert, *Nam.* **81** 22 30S 15 0 E
Namibe, *Angola* **81** 15 7S 12 11 E
Namibia ■, *Africa* **81** 22 0S 18 9 E
Nampula, *Mozam.* **81** 15 6N 39 15 E
Namur, *Belg.* **36** 50 27N 4 52 E
Nan Shan, *China* **60** 38 30N 99 0 E
Nanaimo, *Canada* **88** 49 10N 124 0W
Nanchang, *China* **61** 28 42N 115 55 E
Nanchong, *China* **60** 30 43N 106 2 E
Nancy, *Fr.* **34** 48 42N 6 12 E
Nanda Devi, *India* **58** 30 23N 79 59 E
Nanjing = Nanking, *China* **61** 32 2N 118 47 E
Nanking, *China* **61** 32 2N 118 47 E
Nanning, *China* **60** 22 48N 108 20 E
Nanping, *China* **61** 26 38N 118 10 E
Nantes, *Fr.* **34** 47 12N 1 33W
Nantong, *China* **61** 32 1N 120 52 E
Nantucket Sd., *U.S.A.* **93** 41 30N 70 15W
Nantwich, *U.K.* **18** 53 5N 2 31W
Napier, *N.Z.* **71** 39 30S 176 56 E
Naples, *It.* **40** 40 50N 14 17 E
Nappa, *U.K.* **18** 53 58N 2 14W
Nara, *Jap.* **62** 34 40N 135 49 E
Narayanganj, *Bangla.* **59** 23 40N 90 33 E
Narberth, *U.K.* **17** 51 48N 4 45W
Narborough, *U.K.* **14** 52 34N 1 12W
Nare Head, *U.K.* **16** 50 12N 4 55W
Narmada →, *India* **58** 21 38N 72 36 E
Narrandera, *Austral.* **70** 34 42S 146 31 E
Narrogin, *Austral.* **66** 32 58S 117 14 E
Narromine, *Austral.* **70** 32 12S 148 12 E
Narvik, *Nor.* **44** 68 28N 17 26 E
Naseby, *U.K.* **15** 52 24N 0 59W
Nashua, *U.S.A.* **93** 42 50N 71 25W
Nashville, *U.S.A.* **91** 36 12N 86 46W
Nasik, *India* **58** 19 58N 73 50 E
Nassau, *Baham.* **95** 25 0N 77 20W
Nasser, L., *Egypt* **79** 23 0N 32 30 E
Nässjö, *Swed.* **45** 57 39N 14 42 E
Natal, *Brazil* **81** 5 47S 35 13W
Natal □, *S. Afr.* **101** 28 30S 30 30 E
Nauru ■, *Pac. Oc.* **64** 1 0S 166 0 E
Navan = An Uaimh, *Ire.* **24** 53 39N 6 40W
Navenby, *U.K.* **19** 53 7N 0 32W
Naver →, *U.K.* **23** 58 34N 4 15W
Náxos, *Greece* **41** 37 8N 25 25 E
Nazareth, *Isr.* **57** 32 42N 35 17 E
Naze, The, *U.K.* **15** 51 53N 1 19 E
Ndjamena, *Chad* **79** 12 10N 14 59 E
Ndola, *Zam.* **81** 13 0S 28 34 E
Neagh, L., *U.K.* **24** 54 35N 6 25W
Neath, *U.K.* **17** 51 39N 3 49W
Nebraska □, *U.S.A.* **90** 41 30N 100 0W
Needham Market, *U.K.* **15** 52 9N 1 2 E
Needles, The, *U.K.* **14** 50 39N 1 35W
Negro →, *Arg.* **102** 41 2S 62 47W
Negro →, *Brazil* **100** 3 0S 60 0W
Negros, *Phil.* **63** 9 30N 122 40 E
Neijiang, *China* **60** 29 35N 104 55 E
Neilston, *U.K.* **20** 55 47N 4 27W
Neiva, *Col.* **100** 2 56N 75 18W
Nellore, *India* **58** 14 27N 79 59 E
Nelson, *N.Z.* **71** 41 18S 173 16 E
Nelson, *U.K.* **18** 53 50N 2 14W
Nelson →, *Canada* **88** 54 33N 98 2W
Nelspruit, *S. Afr.* **81** 25 29S 30 59 E
Nenagh, *Ire.* **25** 52 52N 8 11W
Nene →, *U.K.* **15** 52 38N 0 13 E
Nepal ■, *Asia* **59** 28 0N 84 30 E
Nephin, *Ire.* **24** 54 1N 9 21W
Ness, Loch, *U.K.* **23** 57 15N 4 30W
Neston, *U.K.* **18** 53 17N 3 3W
Netanya, *Isr.* **57** 32 20N 34 51 E
Nether Stowey, *U.K.* **14** 51 0N 3 10W
Netherbury, *U.K.* **14** 50 46N 2 45W
Netherlands ■, *Europe* **36** 52 0N 5 30 E
Netley, *U.K.* **14** 50 53N 1 21W
Netley Marsh, *U.K.* **14** 50 55N 1 32W
Nettlebed, *U.K.* **15** 51 34N 0 54W
Nettleham, *U.K.* **19** 53 15N 0 28W
Neuchâtel, *Switz.* **42** 47 0N 6 55 E
Neukirchen, *W. Ger.* **36** 54 52N 8 44 E
Neuss, *W. Ger.* **36** 51 12N 6 39 E
Neustadt, *W. Ger.* **36** 49 21N 8 10 E
Neuwied, *W. Ger.* **36** 50 26N 7 29 E
Nevada □, *U.S.A.* **90** 39 20N 117 0W
Nevada, Sierra, *Sp.* **37** 37 3N 3 15W
Nevada, Sierra, *U.S.A.* **90** 39 0N 120 30W
Nevers, *Fr.* **34** 47 0N 3 9 E
New Abbey, *U.K.* **21** 54 59N 3 38W
New Alresford, *U.K.* **14** 51 6N 1 10W
New Amsterdam, *Guy.* **101** 6 15N 57 36W
New Bedford, *U.S.A.* **93** 41 40N 70 52W
New Brighton, *N.Z.* **71** 43 29S 172 43 E
New Brighton, *U.K.* **18** 53 27N 3 2W
New Brunswick □, *Canada* **93** 46 50N 66 30W
New Caledonia, *Pac. Oc.* **64** 21 0S 165 0 E
New Castile, *Sp.* **37** 39 45N 3 20W
New Cumnock, *U.K.* **20** 55 24N 4 13W
New Forest, *U.K.* **14** 50 53N 1 40W
New Galloway, *U.K.* **21** 55 4N 4 10W
New Guinea, *Pac. Oc.* **64** 4 0S 136 0 E
New Hampshire □, *U.S.A.* **93** 43 40N 71 40W
New Haven, *U.S.A.* **93** 41 20N 72 54W
New Hebrides = Vanuatu ■, *Pac. Oc.* **64** 15 0S 168 0 E
New Holland, *U.K.* **19** 53 42N 0 22W
New Jersey □, *U.S.A.* **93** 40 30N 74 10W
New London, *U.S.A.* **93** 41 23N 72 8W
New Luce, *U.K.* **20** 54 57N 4 50W
New Mexico □, *U.S.A.* **90** 34 30N 106 0W
New Mills, *U.K.* **18** 53 22N 2 0W
New Orleans, *U.S.A.* **91** 30 0N 90 5W
New Plymouth, *N.Z.* **71** 39 4S 174 5 E
New Quay, *U.K.* **17** 52 13N 4 21W
New Radnor, *U.K.* **17** 52 15N 3 10W
New Romney, *U.K.* **15** 50 59N 0 57 E
New Ross, *Ire.* **25** 52 24N 6 58W
New Rossington, *U.K.* **19** 53 30N 1 4W
New Siberian Is., *U.S.S.R.* **49** 75 0N 142 0 E
New South Wales □, *Austral.* **70** 33 0S 146 0 E
New York □, *U.S.A.* **93** 42 40N 76 0W
New York City, *U.S.A.* **93** 40 45N 74 0W
New Zealand ■, *Pac. Oc.* **71** 40 0S 176 0 E
Newark, *U.S.A.* **93** 40 41N 74 12W
Newark-on-Trent, *U.K.* **19** 53 6N 0 48W
Newbiggin-by-the-Sea, *U.K.* **21** 55 12N 1 31W
Newbigging, *U.K.* **21** 55 42N 3 33W
Newburgh, *U.K.* **21** 56 21N 3 15W
Newburn, *U.K.* **21** 54 57N 1 45W
Newbury, *U.K.* **14** 51 24N 1 19W
Newby Bridge, *U.K.* **18** 54 16N 2 59W
Newcastle, *Austral.* **70** 33 0S 151 46 E
Newcastle, *U.K.* **24** 54 13N 5 54W
Newcastle Emlyn, *U.K.* **17** 52 2N 4 29W
Newcastle-under-Lyme, *U.K.* **18** 53 2N 2 15W
Newcastle-upon-Tyne, *U.K.* **19** 54 59N 1 37W
Newcastleton, *U.K.* **21** 55 10N 2 50W
Newent, *U.K.* **14** 51 56N 2 24W
Newfoundland □, *Canada* **89** 53 0N 58 0W
Newham, *U.K.* **15** 51 31N 0 2 E
Newhaven, *U.K.* **15** 50 47N 0 4 E
Newington, *Kent, U.K.* **15** 51 5N 1 8 E
Newington, *Kent, U.K.* **15** 51 21N 0 40 E
Newlyn, *U.K.* **16** 50 6N 5 33W
Newlyn East, *U.K.* **16** 50 22N 5 3W
Newman, *Austral.* **66** 23 18S 119 45 E
Newmarket, *Ire.* **25** 52 13N 9 0W
Newmarket, *Lewis, U.K.* **22** 58 14N 6 24W
Newmarket, *Suffolk, U.K.* **15** 52 15N 0 23 E
Newmilns, *U.K.* **20** 55 36N 4 20W
Newnham, *U.K.* **14** 51 48N 2 27W
Newport, *Dyfed, U.K.* **17** 52 1N 4 53W
Newport, *Essex, U.K.* **15** 51 58N 0 13 E
Newport, *Gwent, U.K.* **17** 51 35N 3 0W
Newport, *I. of W., U.K.* **14** 50 42N 1 18W
Newport, *Salop, U.K.* **14** 52 47N 2 22W
Newport News, *U.S.A.* **91** 37 2N 76 30W
Newport on Tay, *U.K.* **21** 56 27N 2 56W
Newport Pagnell, *U.K.* **15** 52 5N 0 42W
Newquay, *U.K.* **16** 50 24N 5 6W
Newry, *U.K.* **24** 54 10N 6 20W
Newry & Mourne □, *U.K.* **24** 54 10N 6 15W
Newton Abbot, *U.K.* **16** 50 32N 3 37W
Newton Arlosh, *U.K.* **18** 54 53N 3 15W
Newton-Aycliffe, *U.K.* **19** 54 36N 1 33W
Newton Ferrers, *U.K.* **16** 50 19N 4 3W
Newton le Willows, *U.K.* **18** 53 28N 2 40W
Newton St. Cyres, *U.K.* **16** 50 46N 3 35W
Newton Stewart, *U.K.* **20** 54 57N 4 30W
Newtongrange, *U.K.* **21** 55 52N 3 4W
Newtonmore, *U.K.* **23** 57 4N 4 7W
Newtown, *Scotland, U.K.* **21** 55 34N 2 38W
Newtown, *Wales, U.K.* **17** 52 31N 3 19W
Newtownabbey, *Ire.* **24** 54 40N 5 55W
Newtownabbey □, *U.K.* **24** 54 45N 6 0W
Newtownards, *U.K.* **24** 54 37N 5 40W
Nha Trang, *Viet.* **63** 12 16N 109 10 E
Niagara Falls, *Canada* **92** 43 7N 79 5W
Niagara Falls, *U.S.A.* **92** 43 5N 79 0W
Niamey, *Niger* **78** 13 27N 2 6 E
Nicaragua ■, *Cent. Am.* **94** 11 40N 85 30W
Nicaragua, L., *Nic.* **94** 12 0N 85 30W
Nice, *Fr.* **35** 43 42N 7 14 E
Nicobar Is., *Ind. Oc.* **51** 9 0N 93 0 E
Nicosia, *Cyprus* **47** 35 10N 33 25 E
Nicoya, Pen. de, *C.R.* **94** 9 45N 85 40W

Nidd →, *U.K.* **19** 54 1N 1 32W
Nidderdale, *U.K.* **19** 54 5N 1 46W
Niger ■, *W. Afr.* **78** 13 30N 10 0 E
Niger →, *W. Afr.* **78** 5 33N 6 33 E
Nigeria ■, *W. Afr.* **78** 8 30N 8 0 E
Niigata, *Jap.* **62** 37 58N 139 0 E
Niihau, *U.S.A.* **90** 21 55N 160 10W
Nijmegen, *Neth.* **36** 51 50N 5 52 E
Nikolayev, *U.S.S.R.* **47** 46 58N 32 0 E
Nikolayevsk, *U.S.S.R.* **49** 50 0N 45 35 E
Nile →, *Africa* **79** 30 10N 31 6 E
Nîmes, *Fr.* **35** 43 50N 4 23 E
Ninety Mile Beach, The, *Austral.* **70** 38 15S 147 24 E
Ninfield, *U.K.* **15** 50 53N 0 26 E
Ningbo, *China* **61** 29 51N 121 28 E
Ningxia Huizu Zizhiqu □, *China* **60** 38 0N 106 0 E
Niort, *Fr.* **35** 46 19N 0 29W
Nipigon, L., *Canada* **92** 49 50N 88 30W
Niš, *Yug.* **41** 43 19N 21 58 E
Niterói, *Brazil* **101** 22 52S 43 0W
Nith →, *U.K.* **21** 55 20N 3 5W
Nithsdale, *U.K.* **21** 55 14N 3 50W
Niton, *U.K.* **14** 50 35N 1 14W
Nizhniy Tagil, *U.S.S.R.* **46** 57 55N 59 57 E
Nkongsamba, *Cam.* **80** 4 55N 9 55 E
Nobeoka, *Jap.* **62** 32 36N 131 41 E
Nogales, *Mex.* **94** 31 20N 110 56W
Nordelph, *U.K.* **15** 52 34N 0 18 E
Nordhorn, *W. Ger.* **36** 52 27N 7 4 E
Nordvik, *U.S.S.R.* **49** 74 2N 111 32 E
Nore →, *Ire.* **25** 52 40N 7 20W
Norfolk, *U.S.A.* **91** 36 40N 76 15W
Norfolk □, *U.K.* **15** 52 39N 1 0 E
Norfolk Broads, *U.K.* **15** 52 30N 1 15 E
Norfolk I., *Pac. Oc.* **64** 28 58S 168 3 E
Norham, *U.K.* **21** 55 44N 2 9W
Norilsk, *U.S.S.R.* **49** 69 20N 88 6 E
Norman, *U.S.A.* **90** 35 12N 97 30W
Normandy, *Fr.* **34** 48 45N 0 10 E
Normanton, *U.K.* **19** 53 41N 1 26W
Norrbotten □, *Swed.* **44** 66 30N 22 30 E
Norrköping, *Swed.* **45** 58 37N 16 11 E
Norrland □, *Swed.* **44** 66 50N 18 0 E
Norseman, *Austral.* **66** 32 8S 121 43 E
North Battleford, *Canada* **88** 52 50N 108 17W
North Bay, *Canada* **92** 46 20N 79 30W
North Berwick, *U.K.* **21** 56 4N 2 44W
North Cape, *Nor.* **44** 71 15N 25 40 E
North Carolina □, *U.S.A.* **91** 35 30N 80 0W
North Cerney, *U.K.* **14** 51 45N 1 58W
North Channel, *U.K.* **20** 55 0N 5 30W
North Collingham, *U.K.* **19** 53 8N 0 46W
North Dakota □, *U.S.A.* **90** 47 30N 100 0W
North Dorset Downs, *U.K.* **14** 50 50N 2 30W
North Down □, *U.K.* **24** 54 40N 5 45W
North Downs, *U.K.* **15** 51 17N 0 30 E
North Esk →, *U.K.* **23** 56 44N 2 25W
North European Plain **26** 55 0N 20 0 E
North Foreland, *U.K.* **15** 51 22N 1 28 E
North Hill, *U.K.* **16** 50 33N 4 26W
North Hykeham, *U.K.* **19** 53 10N 0 35W
North I., *N.Z.* **71** 38 0S 175 0 E
North Minch, *U.K.* **22** 58 5N 5 55W
North Molton, *U.K.* **16** 51 3N 3 48W
North Petherton, *U.K.* **14** 51 6N 3 1W
North Pole, *Arctic* **103** 90 0N 0 0 E
North Queensferry, *U.K.* **21** 56 1N 3 22W
North Rhine Westphalia □, *W. Ger.* **42** 51 55N 7 0 E
North Ronaldsay, *U.K.* **23** 59 20N 2 30W
North Sea, *Europe* **26** 56 0N 4 0 E
North Somercotes, *U.K.* **19** 53 28N 0 9 E
North Sunderland, *U.K.* **21** 55 35N 1 40W
North Tawton, *U.K.* **16** 50 48N 3 55W
North Thoresby, *U.K.* **19** 53 27N 0 3W
North Tidworth, *U.K.* **14** 51 14N 1 40W
North Tyne →, *U.K.* **19** 54 59N 2 7W
North Uist, *U.K.* **22** 57 40N 7 15W
North Walsham, *U.K.* **15** 52 49N 1 22 E
North West Highlands, *U.K.* **22** 57 35N 5 2W
North West Territories □, *Canada* **89** 67 0N 110 0W
North York Moors, *U.K.* **19** 54 25N 0 50W
North Yorkshire □, *U.K.* **19** 54 15N 1 25W
Northallerton, *U.K.* **19** 54 20N 1 26W
Northam, *Austral.* **66** 31 35S 116 42 E
Northam, *U.K.* **16** 51 2N 4 13W
Northampton, *U.K.* **15** 52 14N 0 54W
Northampton □, *U.K.* **15** 52 16N 0 55W
Northern Ireland □, *U.K.* **24** 54 45N 7 0W
Northern Marianas, *Pac. Oc.* **64** 17 0N 145 0 E
Northern Territory □, *Austral.* **66** 16 0S 133 0 E
Northfleet, *U.K.* **15** 51 26N 0 20 E
Northiam, *U.K.* **15** 50 59N 0 39 E
Northland □, *N.Z.* **71** 35 30S 173 30 E
Northleach, *U.K.* **14** 51 49N 1 50W
Northrepps, *U.K.* **15** 52 53N 1 20 E
Northumberland □, *U.K.* **19** 55 12N 2 0W
Northumberland Str., *Canada* **93** 46 20N 64 0W
Northwich, *U.K.* **18** 53 16N 2 30W
Northwold, *U.K.* **15** 52 33N 0 37 E
Norton, *N. Yorks., U.K.* **19** 54 9N 0 48W
Norton, *Suffolk, U.K.* **15** 52 15N 0 52 E
Norton Fitzwarren, *U.K.* **14** 51 1N 3 10W
Norway ■, *Europe* **44** 63 0N 11 0 E
Norwegian Sea, *Atl. Oc.* **44** 66 0N 1 0 E
Norwich, *U.K.* **15** 52 38N 1 17 E
Noss Hd., *U.K.* **23** 58 29N 3 4W
Nottingham, *U.K.* **19** 52 57N 1 10W
Nottingham □, *U.K.* **19** 53 10N 1 0W
Nouâdhibou, *Maurit.* **78** 20 54N 17 0W
Nouakchott, *Maurit.* **78** 18 9N 15 58W
Nouméa, *N. Cal.* **64** 22 17S 166 30 E
Nova Scotia □, *Canada* **93** 45 10N 63 0W
Novara, *It.* **40** 45 27N 8 36 E
Novaya Zemlya, *U.S.S.R.* **48** 75 0N 56 0 E
Novi Sad, *Yug.* **41** 45 18N 19 52 E
Novocherkassk, *U.S.S.R.* **47** 47 27N 40 5 E
Novokuznetsk, *U.S.S.R.* **48** 53 45N 87 10 E
Novomoskovsk, *U.S.S.R.* **46** 54 5N 38 15 E
Novorossiysk, *U.S.S.R.* **47** 44 43N 37 46 E
Novoshakhtinsk, *U.S.S.R.* **47** 47 46N 39 58 E
Novosibirsk, *U.S.S.R.* **48** 55 0N 83 5 E
Nubian Desert, *Sudan* **79** 21 30N 33 30 E
Nuevo Laredo, *Mex.* **94** 27 30N 99 30W
Nullarbor Plain, *Austral.* **66** 30 45S 129 0 E
Nuneaton, *U.K.* **14** 52 32N 1 29W
Nunney, *U.K.* **14** 51 13N 2 20W
Nuremburg, *W. Ger.* **42** 49 26N 11 5 E
Nyasa, L., *Africa* **81** 12 30S 34 30 E
Nyíregyháza, *Hung.* **43** 47 58N 21 47 E
Nykøbing, *Den.* **45** 56 48N 8 51 E

O

Oa, Mull of, *U.K.* **20** 55 35N 6 20W
Oa, The, Pen., *U.K.* **20** 55 36N 6 17W
Oadby, *U.K.* **14** 52 37N 1 7W
Oahe L., *U.S.A.* **90** 45 30N 100 25W
Oahu, *U.S.A.* **90** 21 30N 158 0W
Oakengates, *U.K.* **14** 52 42N 2 29W
Oakham, *U.K.* **15** 52 40N 0 43W
Oakland, *U.S.A.* **90** 37 50N 122 18W
Oakleigh, *Austral.* **70** 37 54S 145 6 E
Oamaru, *N.Z.* **71** 45 5S 170 59 E
Oaxaca, *Mex.* **94** 17 2N 96 40W
Ob →, *U.S.S.R.* **48** 66 45N 69 30 E
Ob, G. of, *U.S.S.R.* **48** 70 0N 73 0 E
Oban, *U.K.* **20** 56 25N 5 30W
Oberhausen, *W. Ger.* **36** 51 28N 6 50 E
Ochil Hills, *U.K.* **21** 56 14N 3 40W
Ochiltree, *U.K.* **20** 55 26N 4 23W
October Revolution I., *U.S.S.R.* **49** 79 30N 97 0 E
Odense, *Den.* **45** 55 22N 10 23 E
Odessa, *U.S.A.* **90** 31 51N 102 23W
Odessa, *U.S.S.R.* **47** 46 30N 30 45 E
Odiham, *U.K.* **15** 51 16N 0 56W
Odra →, *Pol.* **42** 53 33N 14 38 E
Offaly □, *Ire.* **25** 53 15N 7 30W
Offenbach, *W. Ger.* **42** 50 6N 8 46 E
Ogbomosho, *Nig.* **78** 8 1N 4 11 E
Ogden, *U.S.A.* **90** 41 13N 112 1W
Ohio □, *U.S.A.* **92** 40 20N 14 10 E
Ohio →, *U.S.A.* **92** 38 0N 86 0W
Ōita, *Jap.* **62** 33 14N 131 36 E
Okavango Swamps, *Bots.* **81** 18 45S 22 45 E
Okayama, *Jap.* **62** 34 40N 133 54 E
Okazaki, *Jap.* **62** 34 57N 137 10 E
Okehampton, *U.K.* **16** 50 44N 4 1W
Okhotsk, *U.S.S.R.* **49** 59 20N 143 10 E
Okhotsk, Sea of, *Asia* **49** 55 0N 145 0 E
Oklahoma □, *U.S.A.* **90** 35 20N 97 30W
Oklahoma City, *U.S.A.* **91** 35 25N 97 30W
Ólafsfjörður, *Ice.* **44** 66 4N 18 39W
Öland, *Swed.* **45** 56 45N 16 38 E
Old Basing, *U.K.* **14** 51 16N 1 3W
Old Castile, *Sp.* **37** 41 55N 4 0W
Old Castle, *Ire.* **24** 53 46N 7 10W
Old Kilpatrick, *U.K.* **20** 55 56N 4 34W
Old Leake, *U.K.* **19** 53 2N 0 6 E
Oldbury, *Gloucs., U.K.* **14** 51 38N 2 30W
Oldbury, *W. Midlands, U.K.* **14** 52 30N 2 0W
Oldenburg, *W. Ger.* **36** 53 10N 8 10 E
Oldham, *U.K.* **18** 53 33N 2 8W
Oldmeldrum, *U.K.* **23** 57 20N 2 19W
Olekminsk, *U.S.S.R.* **49** 60 25N 120 30 E
Olinda, *Brazil* **101** 8 1S 34 51W
Ollerton, *U.K.* **19** 53 12N 1 1W
Olney, *U.K.* **15** 52 9N 0 42W
Olomouc, *Czech.* **42** 49 38N 17 12 E
Olsztyn, *Pol.* **43** 53 48N 20 29 E
Olympia, *Greece* **41** 37 39N 21 39 E
Olympus, Mt., *Greece* **41** 40 6N 22 23 E
Omagh, *U.K.* **24** 54 36N 7 20W
Omagh □, *U.K.* **24** 54 35N 7 15W
Omaha, *U.S.A.* **91** 41 15N 96 0W
Oman ■, *Si. Arab.* **57** 23 0N 58 0 E
Oman, G. of, *Asia* **57** 24 30N 58 30 E
Ombersley, *U.K.* **14** 52 17N 2 12W
Omdurmân, *Sudan* **79** 15 40N 32 28 E
Ōmiya, *Jap.* **62** 35 54N 139 38 E
Omsk, *U.S.S.R.* **48** 55 0N 73 12 E
Ōmuta, *Jap.* **62** 33 0N 130 26 E
Onchan, *U.K.* **18** 54 11N 4 27W
Onega →, *U.S.S.R.* **46** 63 58N 37 55 E
Onega, G. of, *U.S.S.R.* **46** 64 30N 37 0 E
Onega, L., *U.S.S.R.* **46** 62 0N 35 30 E
Onehunga, *N.Z.* **71** 36 55S 174 48 E
Onny →, *U.K.* **14** 52 30N 2 50W
Ontario □, *Canada* **88** 52 0N 88 10W
Ontario, L., *N. Am.* **92** 43 40N 78 0W
Opole, *Pol.* **43** 50 42N 17 58 E
Oporto, *Port.* **37** 41 8N 8 40W
Oradea, *Rom.* **43** 47 2N 21 58 E
Oran, *Alg.* **78** 35 45N 0 39W
Orange, *Austral.* **70** 33 15S 149 7 E
Orange →, *S. Afr.* **81** 28 41S 16 28 E
Orange Free State □, *S. Afr.* **81** 28 30S 27 0 E
Ord, Mt., *Austral.* **66** 17 20S 125 34 E
Ordos = Mu Us Shamo, *China* **61** 39 0N 109 0 E
Ordzhonikidze, *U.S.S.R.* **47** 43 0N 44 35 E
Örebro, *Swed.* **45** 59 20N 15 18 E
Oregon □, *U.S.A.* **90** 44 0N 121 0W
Orekhovo-Zuyevo, *U.S.S.R.* **46** 55 50N 38 55 E
Orel, *U.S.S.R.* **46** 52 57N 36 3 E
Orenburg, *U.S.S.R.* **46** 51 45N 55 6 E
Orense, *Sp.* **37** 42 19N 7 55W
Orford, *U.K.* **15** 52 6N 1 31 E
Orford Ness, *U.K.* **15** 52 6N 1 31 E
Orinoco →, *Ven.* **100** 9 15N 61 30W
Orissa □, *India* **59** 20 0N 84 0 E
Oristano, *It.* **40** 39 54N 8 35 E
Orizaba, *Mex.* **94** 18 51N 97 6W
Orkney □, *U.K.* **23** 59 0N 3 0W
Orkney Is., *U.K.* **23** 59 0N 3 0W
Orlando, *U.S.A.* **91** 28 30N 81 25W
Orléans, *Fr.* **34** 47 54N 1 52 E
Ormesby St. Margaret, *U.K.* **15** 52 39N 1 42 E
Ormskirk, *U.K.* **18** 53 35N 2 53W
Örnsköldsvik, *Swed.* **44** 63 17N 18 40 E
Oronsay, Pass of, *U.K.* **20** 56 0N 6 10W
Oronsay I., *U.K.* **20** 56 0N 6 14W
Orsk, *U.S.S.R.* **46** 51 12N 58 34 E
Orton Tebay, *U.K.* **18** 54 28N 2 35W
Oruro, *Bol.* **100** 18 0S 67 9W
Orwell →, *U.K.* **15** 52 2N 1 12 E
Ōsaka, *Jap.* **62** 34 40N 135 30 E
Osh, *U.S.S.R.* **48** 40 37N 72 49 E
Oshawa, *Canada* **92** 43 50N 78 50W
Oshogbo, *Nig.* **78** 7 48N 4 37 E
Osijek, *Yug.* **41** 45 34N 18 41 E
Osizweni, *S. Afr.* **81** 27 49S 30 7 E
Oslo, *Nor.* **45** 59 55N 10 45 E
Oslo Fjord, *Nor.* **45** 58 30N 10 0 E
Osmotherley, *U.K.* **19** 54 22N 1 18W
Osnabrück, *W. Ger.* **36** 52 16N 8 2 E
Osorno, *Chile* **102** 40 25S 73 0W
Ossett, *U.K.* **19** 53 40N 1 35W
Ostend, *Belg.* **36** 51 15N 2 50 E
Östersund, *Swed.* **44** 63 10N 14 38 E
Ostrava, *Czech.* **43** 49 51N 18 18 E
Osumi, Is., *Jap.* **62** 30 30N 130 45 E
Oswaldtwistle, *U.K.* **18** 53 44N 2 27W
Oswestry, *U.K.* **14** 52 52N 3 3W
Otago □, *N.Z.* **71** 44 44S 169 10 E
Otaru, *Jap.* **62** 43 10N 141 0 E
Otley, *U.K.* **19** 53 54N 1 41W
Otranto, Str. of, *It.* **41** 40 15N 18 40 E
Ōtsu, *Jap.* **62** 35 0N 135 50 E
Ottawa, *Canada* **93** 45 27N 75 42W
Ottawa →, *Canada* **93** 45 27N 74 8W
Otter →, *U.K.* **16** 50 47N 3 12W
Otter Ferry, *U.K.* **20** 56 1N 5 20W
Otterburn, *U.K.* **21** 55 14N 2 12W
Ottery St. Mary, *U.K.* **16** 50 45N 3 16W
Ouagadougou, *B. Faso* **78** 12 25N 1 30W
Oujda, *Mor.* **78** 34 41N 1 55W
Oulton, *U.K.* **15** 52 29N 1 40 E
Oulton Broad, *U.K.* **15** 52 28N 1 43 E
Oulu, *Fin.* **44** 65 1N 25 29 E
Oulu, L., *Fin.* **44** 64 25N 27 0 E
Oundle, *U.K.* **15** 52 28N 0 28W
Ouse →, *E. Sussex, U.K.* **15** 50 43N 0 3 E
Ouse →, *N. Yorks., U.K.* **19** 54 3N 0 7 E
Outer Hebrides, *U.K.* **22** 57 30N 7 40W
Outwell, *U.K.* **15** 52 36N 0 14 E
Over Wallop, *U.K.* **14** 51 9N 1 35W
Overstand, *U.K.* **15** 52 55N 1 20W
Overton, *U.K.* **14** 51 14N 1 16W
Oviedo, *Sp.* **37** 43 25N 5 50W
Owston Ferry, *U.K.* **19** 53 28N 0 47W
Ox Mts., *Ire.* **24** 54 6N 9 0W
Oxford, *U.K.* **14** 51 45N 1 15W
Oxford □, *U.K.* **14** 51 45N 1 15W
Oykel →, *U.K.* **23** 57 55N 4 26W
Ozark Plateau, *U.S.A.* **91** 37 20N 91 40W

P

Paarl, *S. Afr.* **81** 33 45S 18 56 E
Pacaraima, Sierra, *Ven.* **100** 4 0N 62 30W
Pachuca, *Mex.* **94** 20 10N 98 40W
Pacific Ocean **64** 10 0N 140 0W
Padang, *Indon.* **63** 1 0S 100 20 E
Paddock Wood, *U.K.* **15** 51 13N 0 24 E
Padiham, *U.K.* **18** 53 48N 2 20W
Padstow, *U.K.* **14** 50 33N 4 57W
Padstow Bay, *U.K.* **16** 50 35N 4 58W
Padua, *It.* **40** 45 24N 11 52 E
Pagalu = Annobón, *Atl. Oc.* **73** 1 25S 5 36 E
Paignton, *U.K.* **16** 50 26N 3 33W
Painswick, *U.K.* **14** 51 47N 2 11W
Paisley, *U.K.* **20** 55 51N 4 27W
Pakistan ■, *Asia* **58** 30 0N 70 0 E
Palawan, *Phil.* **63** 9 30N 118 30 E
Palembang, *Indon.* **63** 3 0S 104 50 E
Palencia, *Sp.* **37** 42 1N 4 34W
Palermo, *It.* **40** 38 8N 13 20 E
Palgrave, *U.K.* **15** 52 22N 1 7 E
Palk Strait, *Asia* **58** 10 0N 79 45 E
Palma de Mallorca, *Sp.* **37** 39 35N 2 39 E
Palmer →, *Austral.* **66** 24 46S 133 25 E
Palmerston North, *N.Z.* **71** 40 21S 175 39 E
Palmira, *Col.* **100** 3 32N 76 16W
Pamirs, *U.S.S.R.* **48** 37 40N 73 0 E
Pamlico Sd., *U.S.A.* **91** 35 20N 76 0W
Pampas, *Arg.* **96** 35 0S 63 0W
Pamplona, *Sp.* **37** 42 48N 1 38W
Panamá, *Pan.* **94** 9 0N 79 25W
Panama ■, *Cent. Am.* **95** 8 48N 79 55W
Panamá, G. de, *Pan.* **95** 8 4N 79 20W
Panama Canal, *Pan.* **94** 9 10N 79 37W
Panay, *Phil.* **63** 11 10N 122 30 E
Pančevo, *Yug.* **41** 44 52N 20 41 E
Pangbourne, *U.K.* **14** 51 28N 1 5W
Pantelleria, *It.* **40** 36 52N 12 0 E
Papua New Guinea ■, *Oc.* **64** 8 0S 145 0 E
Pará □, *Brazil* **101** 3 20S 52 0W
Paraguay ■, *S. Am.* **102** 23 0S 57 0W
Paraguay →, *Par.* **102** 27 18S 58 38W
Paramaribo, *Surinam* **101** 5 50N 55 10W
Paraná, *Arg.* **102** 31 45S 60 30W
Paraná →, *Arg.* **102** 33 43S 59 15W
Parecis, Serra dos, *Brazil* **100** 13 0S 60 0W
Parepare, *Indon.* **63** 4 0S 119 40 E
Paris, *Fr.* **34** 48 50N 2 20 E
Parkes, *Austral.* **70** 33 9S 148 11 E
Parma, *It.* **40** 44 50N 10 20 E
Parnaíba →, *Brazil* **101** 3 0S 41 50W
Parracombe, *U.K.* **16** 51 11N 3 55W
Parramatta, *Austral.* **70** 33 48S 151 1 E
Parrett →, *U.K.* **14** 51 7N 2 58W
Partney, *U.K.* **19** 53 12N 0 7 E
Parton, *U.K.* **18** 54 34N 3 35W
Passage West, *Ire.* **25** 51 52N 8 20W
Pasto, *Col.* **100** 1 13N 77 17W
Patagonia, *Arg.* **102** 45 0S 69 0W
Patcham, *U.K.* **15** 50 52N 0 9W
Pateley Bridge, *U.K.* **19** 54 5N 1 45W
Paterson, *U.S.A.* **93** 40 55N 74 10W
Patna, *India* **59** 25 35N 85 12 E
Patna, *U.K.* **20** 55 21N 4 30W
Pátrai, *Greece* **41** 38 14N 21 47 E
Patrick, *U.K.* **18** 54 13N 4 41W
Patrington, *U.K.* **19** 53 41N 0 1W
Patterdale, *U.K.* **18** 54 33N 2 55W
Pau, *Fr.* **35** 43 19N 0 25W
Paull, *U.K.* **19** 53 42N 0 12W
Pavia, *It.* **40** 45 10N 9 10 E
Pavlodar, *U.S.S.R.* **48** 52 33N 77 0 E
Pawtucket, *U.S.A.* **93** 41 51N 71 22W
Paz, La, *Bol.* **100** 16 20S 68 10W
Pazardzhik, *Bulg.* **41** 42 12N 24 20 E
Peace →, *Canada* **88** 59 0N 111 25W
Peacehaven, *U.K.* **15** 50 47N 0 1 E
Peak, The, *U.K.* **18** 53 24N 1 53W
Peasenhall, *U.K.* **15** 52 17N 1 24 E
Pechora →, *U.S.S.R.* **46** 68 13N 54 15 E
Pécs, *Hung.* **43** 46 5N 18 15 E
Peebles, *U.K.* **21** 55 40N 3 12W
Peel, *U.K.* **18** 54 14N 4 40W
Peel Fell, *U.K.* **21** 55 17N 2 35W
Pegasus Bay, *N.Z.* **71** 43 20S 173 10 E
Pegswood, *U.K.* **21** 55 12N 1 38W
Pegu, *Burma* **59** 17 20N 96 29 E
Pegu Yoma, *Burma* **59** 19 0N 96 0 E
Pegwell Bay, *U.K.* **15** 51 18N 1 22 E
Pekanbaru, *Indon.* **63** 0 30N 101 15 E
Peking, *China* **61** 39 55N 116 20 E
Peloponnese □, *Greece* **41** 37 10N 22 0 E
Pelotas, *Brazil* **102** 31 42S 52 23W
Pelvoux, Massif de, *Fr.* **35** 44 52N 6 20 E
Pematangsiantar, *Indon.* **63** 2 57N 99 5 E
Pemba, *Tanz.* **80** 5 0S 39 45 E
Pembridge, *U.K.* **14** 52 13N 2 54W
Pembroke, *U.K.* **17** 51 41N 4 57W
Pembury, *U.K.* **15** 51 8N 0 20 E
Pen-y-Ghent, *U.K.* **18** 54 10N 2 15W
Pen-y-groes, *U.K.* **17** 53 3N 4 18W
Penang = Pinang, *Malay.* **63** 5 25N 100 15 E
Penarth, *U.K.* **17** 51 26N 3 11W
Pendeen, *U.K.* **16** 50 10N 5 39W
Pendle Hill, *U.K.* **18** 53 53N 2 18W
Penicuik, *U.K.* **21** 55 50N 3 14W
Peninsular Malaysia □, *Malay.* **63** 4 0N 102 0 E
Penistone, *U.K.* **19** 53 31N 1 38W
Penkridge, *U.K.* **14** 52 44N 2 8W
Pennines, *U.K.* **18** 54 50N 2 20W
Pennsylvania □, *U.S.A.* **92** 40 50N 78 0W
Penpont, *U.K.* **21** 55 14N 3 49W

Penrith, Austral. 70 33 43S 150 38 E
Penrith, U.K. 18 54 40N 2 45W
Penryn, U.K. 16 50 10N 5 7W
Pensacola, U.S.A. 90 30 30N 87 10W
Penshurst, U.K. 15 51 10N 0 12 E
Pentire Pt., U.K. 16 50 35N 4 57W
Pentland Firth, U.K. 23 58 43N 3 10W
Pentland Hills, U.K. 21 55 48N 3 25W
Penwortham, U.K. 18 53 45N 2 44W
Penza, U.S.S.R. 46 53 15N 45 5 E
Penzance, U.K. 16 50 7N 5 32W
Peoria, U.S.A. 92 40 40N 89 40W
Pereira, Col. 100 4 49N 75 43W
Perm, U.S.S.R. 46 58 0N 57 10 E
Perouse Str., La, Jap. 64 45 40N 142 0 E
Perpignan, Fr. 35 42 42N 2 53 E
Perranporth, U.K. 16 50 21N 5 9W
Perranzabuloe, U.K. 16 50 18N 5 7W
Pershore, U.K. 14 52 7N 2 4W
Persian Gulf = Gulf, The, Asia 56 27 0N 50 0 E
Perth, Austral. 66 31 57S 115 52 E
Perth, U.K. 21 56 24N 3 27W
Peru ■, S. Am. 100 8 0S 75 0W
Perúgia, It. 40 43 6N 12 24 E
Pescara, It. 40 42 28N 14 13 E
Peshawar, Pak. 58 34 2N 71 37 E
Peterborough, Canada 92 44 20N 78 20W
Peterborough, U.K. 15 52 35N 0 14W
Peterchurch, U.K. 14 52 3N 2 57W
Peterhead, U.K. 23 57 30N 1 49W
Peterlee, U.K. 19 54 45N 1 18W
Petersfield, U.K. 15 51 0N 0 56W
Petropavlovsk, U.S.S.R. 48 54 53N 69 13 E
Petropavlovsk-Kamchatskiy, U.S.S.R. 49 53 3N 158 43 E
Petrópolis, Brazil 101 22 33S 43 9W
Petrozavodsk, U.S.S.R. 46 61 41N 34 20 E
Petworth, U.K. 15 50 59N 0 37W
Pevensey, U.K. 15 50 49N 0 20 E
Pevensey Levels, U.K. 15 50 50N 0 20 E
Pewsey, U.K. 14 51 20N 1 46W
Pewsey, Vale of, U.K. 14 51 20N 1 46W
Pforzheim, W. Ger. 42 48 53N 8 43 E
Philadelphia, U.S.A. 93 40 0N 75 10W
Philippines ■, Asia 63 12 0N 123 0 E
Phnom Penh, Cambod. 63 11 33N 104 55 E
Phoenix, U.S.A. 90 33 30N 112 10W
Phoenix Is., Pac. Oc. 65 3 30S 172 0W
Piacenza, It. 40 45 2N 9 42 E
Piatra Neamţ, Rom. 43 46 56N 26 21 E
Picardie, Fr. 34 49 50N 3 0 E
Picardy = Picardie, Fr. 34 49 50N 3 0 E
Pickering, U.K. 19 54 15N 0 46W
Pickering, Vale of, U.K. 19 54 0N 0 45W
Pidley, U.K. 15 52 33N 0 4W
Piedmont □, It. 40 45 0N 7 30 E
Piedras Negras, Mex. 94 28 42N 100 31W
Pierowall, U.K. 23 59 20N 3 0W
Pietermaritzburg, S. Afr. 81 29 35S 30 25 E
Pilbara, Austral. 66 21 15S 118 16 E
Pilcomayo →, Par. 102 25 21S 57 42W
Pilling, U.K. 18 53 55N 2 54W
Pilton, U.K. 14 51 0N 2 35W
Pinang, Malay. 63 5 25N 100 15 E
Pinchbeck, U.K. 15 52 48N 0 9W
Pindus Mts., Greece 41 40 0N 21 0 E
Pine Bluff, U.S.A. 90 34 10N 92 0W
Pingxiang, China 60 22 6N 106 46 E
Pinhoe, U.K. 16 50 44N 3 29W
Pinjarra, Austral. 66 32 37S 115 52 E
Pinwherry, U.K. 20 55 9N 4 50W
Piotrków Trybunalski, Pol. 43 51 23N 19 43 E
Piracicaba, Brazil 102 22 45S 47 40W
Piraiévs, Greece 41 37 57N 23 42 E
Pirbright, U.K. 15 51 17N 0 40W
Pirmasens, W. Ger. 36 49 12N 7 30 E
Pisa, It. 40 43 43N 10 23 E
Pistóia, It. 40 43 57N 10 53 E
Pitcairn I., Pac. Oc. 65 25 5S 130 5W
Piteşti, Rom. 43 44 52N 24 54 E
Pitlochry, U.K. 23 56 43N 3 43W
Pittenweem, U.K. 21 56 13N 2 43W
Pittsburgh, U.S.A. 92 40 25N 79 55W
Pittsfield, U.S.A. 93 42 28N 73 17W
Piura, Peru 100 5 15S 80 38W
Pladda, I., U.K. 20 55 25N 5 7W
Plata, La, Arg. 102 35 0S 57 55W
Plata, Río de la, S. Am. 102 34 45S 57 30W
Plauen, E. Ger. 42 50 29N 12 9 E
Plenty, Bay of, N.Z. 71 37 45S 177 0 E
Pleven, Bulg. 41 43 26N 24 37 E
Płock, Pol. 43 52 32N 19 40 E
Ploieşti, Rom. 43 44 57N 26 5 E
Plovdiv, Bulg. 41 42 8N 24 44 E
Plymouth, U.K. 16 50 23N 4 9W
Plymouth Sd., U.K. 16 50 20N 4 10W
Plympton, U.K. 16 50 24N 4 2W
Plymstock, U.K. 16 50 22N 4 6W
Plynlimon = Pumlumon Fawr, U.K. 17 52 29N 3 47W
Plzen, Czech. 42 49 45N 13 22 E
Po →, It. 40 44 57N 12 4 E
Pocklington, U.K. 19 53 56N 0 48W
Podolsk, U.S.S.R. 46 55 25N 37 30 E
Pointe-à-Pitre, Guad. 94 16 10N 61 30W
Pointe Noire, Congo 80 4 48S 11 53 E
Poitiers, Fr. 34 46 35N 0 20 E
Poland ■, Europe 43 52 0N 20 0 E
Polden Hills, U.K. 14 51 7N 2 50W
Polegate, U.K. 15 50 49N 0 15 E
Polesworth, U.K. 14 52 37N 1 37W
Polperro, U.K. 16 50 19N 4 31W
Polruan, U.K. 16 50 17N 4 36W
Poltava, U.S.S.R. 47 49 35N 34 35 E
Polynesia, Pac. Oc. 64 10 0S 162 0W
Ponce, P.R. 95 18 1N 66 37W
Pondicherry, India 58 11 59N 79 50 E
Ponta Grossa, Brazil 102 25 7S 50 10W
Pontardawe, U.K. 17 51 43N 3 51W
Pontardulais, U.K. 17 51 42N 4 3W
Pontchartrain, L., U.S.A. 90 30 12N 90 0W
Pontefract, U.K. 19 53 42N 1 19W
Ponteland, U.K. 21 55 7N 1 45W
Pontevedra, Sp. 37 42 26N 8 40W
Pontianak, Indon. 63 0 3S 109 15 E
Pontrilas, U.K. 14 51 56N 2 53W
Pontypool, U.K. 17 51 42N 3 1W
Pontypridd, U.K. 17 51 36N 3 21W
Poole, U.K. 14 50 42N 1 58W
Poole Harbour, U.K. 14 50 41N 2 0W
Pooley Bridge, U.K. 18 54 37N 2 49W
Poona = Pune, India 58 18 29N 73 57 E
Poopó, L., Bol. 100 18 30S 67 35W
Popayán, Col. 100 2 27N 76 36W
Popocatépetl, Volcán, Mex. 94 19 2N 98 38W
Pori, Fin. 45 61 29N 21 48 E
Porirua, N.Z. 71 41 8S 174 52 E
Porlock, U.K. 14 51 13N 3 36W
Porlock B., U.K. 14 51 14N 3 37W
Porlock Hill, U.K. 14 51 12N 3 40W
Porsangen Fjord, Nor. 44 70 45N 25 0 E
Port Antonio, Jam. 94 18 10N 76 30W
Port Arthur, U.S.A. 90 30 0N 94 0W
Port Askaig, U.K. 20 55 51N 6 8W
Port-au-Prince, Haiti 95 18 40N 72 20W
Port Augusta, Austral. 67 32 30S 137 50 E
Port Bannatyne, U.K. 20 55 51N 5 4W
Port Carlisle, U.K. 18 54 56N 3 12W
Port-Cartier, Canada 89 50 2N 66 50W
Port Charlotte, U.K. 20 55 44N 6 22W
Port Elizabeth, S. Afr. 81 33 58S 25 40 E
Port Ellen, U.K. 20 55 38N 6 10W
Port Erin, U.K. 18 54 5N 4 45W
Port-Gentil, Gabon 80 0 40S 8 50 E
Port Glasgow, U.K. 20 55 57N 4 40W
Port Harcourt, Nig. 78 4 40N 7 10 E
Port Hedland, Austral. 66 20 25S 118 35 E
Port Isaac, U.K. 16 50 35N 4 50W
Port Isaac B., U.K. 16 50 36N 4 50W
Port Laoise, Ire. 25 53 2N 7 20W
Port Logan, U.K. 20 54 42N 4 57W
Port Macquarie, Austral. 67 31 25S 152 25 E
Port Moresby, P.N.G. 64 9 24S 147 8 E
Port of Spain, Trin. & Tob. 94 10 40N 61 31W
Port Phillip B., Austral. 70 38 10S 144 50 E
Port Pirie, Austral. 67 33 10S 138 1 E
Port Said, Egypt 79 31 16N 32 18 E
Port St. Mary, U.K. 18 54 5N 4 45W
Port Sudan, Sudan 79 19 32N 37 9 E
Port Sunlight, U.K. 18 53 22N 3 0W
Port Talbot, U.K. 17 51 35N 3 48W
Port William, U.K. 20 54 46N 4 35W
Portadown, U.K. 24 54 27N 6 26W
Portaferry, U.K. 24 54 23N 5 32W
Portage La Prairie, Canada 88 49 58N 98 18W
Portarlington, Ire. 25 53 10N 7 10W
Porthcawl, U.K. 17 51 28N 3 42W
Porthleven, U.K. 16 50 5N 5 19W
Porthmadog, U.K. 17 52 55N 4 13W
Portishead, U.K. 14 51 29N 2 46W
Portland, Austral. 70 38 20S 141 35 E
Portland, Maine, U.S.A. 93 43 40N 70 15W
Portland, Oreg., U.S.A. 90 45 35N 122 40W
Portland, Bill of, U.K. 14 50 31N 2 27W
Portland, I. of, U.K. 14 50 32N 2 25W
Portnacroish, U.K. 20 56 34N 5 24W
Portnahaven, U.K. 20 55 40N 6 30W
Pôrto Alegre, Brazil 102 30 5S 51 10W
Porto Novo, Benin 78 6 23N 2 42 E
Pôrto Velho, Brazil 100 8 46S 63 54W
Porton, U.K. 14 51 8N 1 42W
Portoviejo, Ecuad. 100 1 7S 80 28W
Portpatrick, U.K. 20 54 50N 5 7W
Portree, U.K. 22 57 25N 6 11W
Portrush, U.K. 24 55 13N 6 40W
Portslade, U.K. 15 50 50N 0 11W
Portsmouth, U.K. 14 50 48N 1 6W
Portsmouth, U.S.A. 93 43 5N 70 45W
Portsoy, U.K. 23 57 41N 2 41W
Portstewart, U.K. 24 55 12N 6 43W
Portugal ■, Europe 37 40 0N 7 0W
Portumna, Ire. 25 53 5N 8 12W
Posadas, Arg. 102 27 30S 55 50W
Postbridge, U.K. 16 50 36N 3 54W
Potchefstroom, S. Afr. 81 26 41S 27 7 E
Potenza, It. 40 40 40N 15 50 E
Potomac →, U.S.A. 92 38 0N 76 23W
Potosí, Bol. 100 19 38S 65 50W
Potsdam, E. Ger. 42 52 23N 13 4 E
Potter Heigham, U.K. 15 52 44N 1 33 E
Potterne, U.K. 14 51 19N 2 0W
Potters Bar, U.K. 15 51 42N 0 11W
Potterspury, U.K. 15 52 5N 0 52W
Poulaphouca Res., Ire. 25 53 8N 6 30W
Poulton le Fylde, U.K. 18 53 51N 2 59W
Poundstock, U.K. 16 50 44N 4 34W
Powell, L., U.S.A. 90 37 25N 110 45W
Powick, U.K. 14 52 9N 2 15W
Powys □, U.K. 17 52 20N 3 20W
Poyang Hu, China 61 29 10N 116 10 E
Poznań, Pol. 42 52 25N 16 55 E
Prague, Czech. 42 50 5N 14 22 E
Prato, It. 40 43 53N 11 5 E
Prawle Pt., U.K. 16 50 13N 3 41W
Prees, U.K. 18 52 54N 2 40W
Preesall, U.K. 18 53 55N 2 58W
Prescot, U.K. 18 53 27N 2 49W
Preshute, U.K. 14 51 24N 1 45W
Presidente Prudente, Brazil 101 22 5S 51 25W
Presque Isle, U.S.A. 93 46 40N 68 0W
Prestatyn, U.K. 17 53 20N 3 24W
Prestbury, U.K. 14 51 54N 2 2W
Presteigne, U.K. 17 52 17N 3 0W
Preston, Borders, U.K. 21 55 48N 2 18W
Preston, Dorset, U.K. 14 50 38N 2 26W
Preston, Lancs., U.K. 18 53 46N 2 42W
Prestonpans, U.K. 21 55 58N 3 0W
Prestwich, U.K. 18 53 32N 2 18W
Prestwick, U.K. 20 55 30N 4 38W
Pretoria, S. Afr. 81 25 44S 28 12 E
Prince Albert, Canada 88 53 15N 105 50W
Prince Edward I. □, Canada 93 46 20N 63 20W
Prince George, Canada 88 53 55N 122 50W
Prince of Wales I., Canada 88 73 0N 99 0W
Prince Rupert, Canada 88 54 20N 130 20W
Princes Risborough, U.K. 15 51 43N 0 50W
Princess Charlotte B., Austral. 67 14 25S 144 0 E
Princetown, U.K. 16 50 33N 4 0W
Pripyat Marshes, U.S.S.R. 46 52 0N 28 10 E
Priština, Yug. 41 42 40N 21 13 E
Prizren, Yug. 41 42 13N 20 45 E
Probus, U.K. 16 50 17N 4 55W
Prokopyevsk, U.S.S.R. 48 54 0N 86 45 E
Prome, Burma 59 18 49N 95 13 E
Provence, Fr. 35 43 40N 5 46 E
Providence, U.S.A. 93 41 50N 71 28W
Prudhoe, U.K. 21 54 57N 1 52W
Prudhoe Bay, U.S.A. 88 70 20N 148 20W
Prut →, Rom. 41 46 3N 28 10 E
Przemyśl, Pol. 43 49 50N 22 45 E
Puddletown, U.K. 14 50 45N 2 21W
Pudsey, U.K. 19 53 47N 1 40W
Puebla, Mex. 94 19 3N 98 12W
Pueblo, U.S.A. 90 38 20N 104 40W
Puerto La Cruz, Ven. 100 10 13N 64 38W
Puerto Montt, Chile 102 41 28S 73 0W
Puerto Rico ■, W. Ind. 95 18 15N 66 45W
Pula, It. 40 39 0N 9 0 E
Pulborough, U.K. 15 50 58N 0 30W
Pulham Market, U.K. 15 52 25N 1 15 E
Pulham St. Mary, U.K. 15 52 25N 1 14 E
Pumlumon Fawr, U.K. 17 52 29N 3 47W
Pune, India 58 18 29N 73 57 E
Punjab □, India 58 31 0N 76 0 E
Punjab □, Pak. 58 30 0N 72 0 E
Punta Arenas, Chile 102 53 10S 71 0W
Punto Fijo, Ven. 100 11 50N 70 13W
Purbeck, Isle of, U.K. 14 50 40N 2 5W
Purfleet, U.K. 15 51 29N 0 15 E
Purley, U.K. 14 51 29N 1 4W
Purnia, India 59 25 45N 87 31 E
Purus →, Brazil 100 3 42S 61 28W
Pusan, S. Kor. 61 35 5N 129 0 E
Puy-de-Dôme, Fr. 35 45 46N 2 57 E
Pwllheli, U.K. 17 52 54N 4 26W
Pyŏngyang, N. Kor. 61 39 0N 125 30 E
Pyrenees, Europe 35 42 45N 0 18 E

Q

Qandahār, Afg. 57 31 32N 65 30 E
Qatar ■, Asia 56 25 30N 51 15 E
Qattâra Depression, Egypt 79 29 30N 27 30 E
Qazvin, Iran 56 36 15N 50 0 E
Qena, Egypt 79 26 10N 32 43 E
Qingdao, China 61 36 5N 120 20 E
Qinghai □, China 60 36 0N 98 0 E
Qinghai Hu, China 60 36 40N 100 10 E
Qingjiang, China 61 33 30N 119 2 E
Qiqihar, China 61 47 26N 124 0 E
Qom, Iran 56 34 40N 51 0 E
Quadring, U.K. 19 52 53N 0 9W
Quainton, U.K. 15 51 51N 0 53W
Quantock Hills, U.K. 14 51 8N 3 10W
Queanbeyan, Austral. 70 35 17S 149 14 E
Québec, Canada 93 46 52N 71 13W
Québec □, Canada 89 50 0N 70 0W
Queen Charlotte Is., Canada 88 53 20N 132 10W
Queen Elizabeth Is., Canada 103 76 0N 95 0W
Queen Maud G., Canada 88 68 15N 102 30W
Queenborough, U.K. 15 51 24N 0 46 E
Queensbury, U.K. 18 53 46N 1 50W
Queensferry, U.K. 21 56 0N 3 25W
Queensland □, Austral. 67 22 0S 142 0 E
Queenstown, N.Z. 71 45 1S 168 40 E
Queenstown, S. Afr. 81 31 52S 26 52 E
Querétaro, Mex. 94 20 36N 100 23W
Quetta, Pak. 58 30 15N 66 55 E
Quezon City, Phil. 63 14 38N 121 0 E
Qui Nhon, Viet. 63 13 40N 109 13 E
Quimper, Fr. 34 48 0N 4 9W
Quito, Ecuad. 100 0 15S 78 35W
Quorndon, U.K. 14 52 45N 1 10W

R

Raasay, U.K. 22 57 25N 6 4W
Raasay, Sd. of, U.K. 22 57 30N 6 8W
Rabat, Malta 40 35 53N 14 25 E
Rabat, Mor. 78 34 2N 6 48W
Rackheath, U.K. 15 52 41N 1 22 E
Radcliffe, Gr. Manchester, U.K. 18 53 35N 2 19W
Radcliffe, Notts., U.K. 19 52 57N 1 3W
Radley, U.K. 14 51 42N 1 14W
Radnor Forest, U.K. 17 52 17N 3 10W
Radom, Pol. 43 51 23N 21 12 E
Radstock, U.K. 14 51 17N 2 25W
Ragusa, It. 40 36 56N 14 42 E
Rainham, U.K. 15 51 22N 0 36 E
Rainworth, U.K. 19 53 8N 1 6W
Raipur, India 59 21 17N 81 45 E
Rajahmundry, India 59 17 1N 81 48 E
Rajasthan □, India 58 26 45N 73 30 E
Rajkot, India 58 22 15N 70 56 E
Raleigh, U.S.A. 91 35 47N 78 39W
Rame Head, U.K. 16 50 19N 4 14W
Rampside, U.K. 18 54 6N 3 10W
Rampur, India 58 28 50N 79 5 E
Ramree Kyun, Burma 59 19 0N 94 0 E
Ramsbottom, U.K. 18 53 36N 2 20W
Ramsbury, U.K. 14 51 26N 1 37W
Ramsey, Cambs., U.K. 15 52 27N 0 6W
Ramsey, Essex, U.K. 15 51 55N 1 12 E
Ramsey, I. of M., U.K. 18 54 20N 4 21W
Ramsey Bay, U.K. 18 54 23N 4 20W
Ramsgate, U.K. 15 51 20N 1 25 E
Rancagua, Chile 102 34 10S 70 50W
Ranchi, India 59 23 19N 85 27 E
Rangoon, Burma 59 16 45N 96 20 E
Rannoch, L., U.K. 23 56 41N 4 20W
Rannoch Moor, U.K. 20 56 38N 4 48W
Rasht, Iran 56 37 20N 49 40 E
Rath Luirc, Ire. 25 52 21N 8 40W
Rathdrum, Ire. 25 52 57N 6 13W
Rathfriland, U.K. 24 54 12N 6 12W
Rathkeale, Ire. 25 52 32N 8 57W
Rathlin I., U.K. 24 55 18N 6 14W
Rathlin O'Birne I., Ire. 24 54 40N 8 50W
Rattray Hd., U.K. 23 57 38N 1 50W
Raukumara Ra., N.Z. 71 38 5S 177 55 E
Raunds, U.K. 15 52 20N 0 32W
Raurkela, India 59 22 14N 84 50 E
Ravenglass, U.K. 18 54 21N 3 25W
Ravenna, It. 40 44 28N 12 15 E
Ravenstonedale, U.K. 18 54 26N 2 26W
Rawalpindi, Pak. 58 33 38N 73 8 E
Rawmarsh, U.K. 19 53 27N 1 20W
Rawtenstall, U.K. 18 53 42N 2 18W
Rayleigh, U.K. 15 51 36N 0 38 E
Reading, U.K. 15 51 27N 0 57W
Reading, U.S.A. 93 40 20N 75 53W
Recife, Brazil 101 8 0S 35 0W
Reculver, U.K. 15 51 22N 1 12 E
Red → = Hong Viet. 60 20 17N 106 34 E
Red →, U.S.A. 91 31 0N 91 40W
Red Deer, Canada 88 52 20N 113 50W
Red Dial, U.K. 18 54 48N 3 9W
Red Sea, Asia 56 25 0N 36 0 E
Redbridge, U.K. 15 51 35N 0 7 E
Redcar, U.K. 19 54 37N 1 4W
Redditch, U.K. 14 52 18N 1 57W
Rede →, U.K. 21 55 8N 2 12W
Redesmouth, U.K. 21 55 7N 2 12W
Redhill, U.K. 15 51 14N 0 10W
Redlynch, U.K. 14 50 59N 1 42W
Redmile, U.K. 19 52 54N 0 48W
Redmire, U.K. 18 54 19N 1 55W
Redruth, U.K. 16 50 14N 5 14W
Ree, L., Ire. 24 53 35N 8 0W
Reedham, U.K. 15 52 34N 1 33 E
Reepham, U.K. 15 52 46N 1 6 E
Reeth, U.K. 18 54 23N 1 56W
Regensburg, W. Ger. 42 49 1N 12 7 E
Réggio di Calábria, It. 40 38 7N 15 38 E
Réggio nell' Emília, It. 40 44 42N 10 38 E
Regina, Canada 88 50 27N 104 35W
Reigate, U.K. 15 51 14N 0 11W
Reims, Fr. 34 49 15N 4 1 E
Reindeer L., Canada 88 57 15N 102 15W
Remscheid, W. Ger. 36 51 11N 7 12 E
Renfrew, U.K. 20 55 52N 4 24W
Renmark, Austral. 67 34 11S 140 43 E
Rennes, Fr. 34 48 7N 1 41W
Reno, U.S.A. 90 39 30N 119 50W
Repton, U.K. 14 52 50N 1 32W
Resistencia, Arg. 102 27 30S 59 0W
Reston, U.K. 21 55 51N 2 11W
Réthímnon, Greece 41 35 18N 24 30 E
Reykjavík, Ice. 44 64 10N 21 57W
Reynosa, Mex. 94 26 5N 98 18W

Rhayader, *U.K.* **17** 52 19N 3 30W
Rheidol →, *U.K.* **17** 52 25N 4 5W
Rhein →, *W. Ger.* **36** 51 52N 6 20 E
Rheine, *W. Ger.* **36** 52 17N 7 25 E
Rhine = Rhein →, *W. Ger.* **36** 51 52N 6 20 E
Rhineland-Palatinate □, *W. Ger.* **42** 50 0N 7 0 E
Rhins, The, *U.K.* **20** 54 52N 5 3W
Rhode Island □, *U.S.A.* **93** 41 38N 71 37W
Rhodes = Ródhos, *Greece* **41** 36 15N 28 10 E
Rhodesia = Zimbabwe ■, *Africa* **81** 20 0S 30 0 E
Rhodope Mts., *Bulg.* **41** 41 40N 24 20 E
Rhondda, *U.K.* **17** 51 39N 3 30W
Rhône →, *Fr.* **35** 43 28N 4 42 E
Rhosllanerchrugog, *U.K.* **17** 53 3N 3 4W
Rhossili, *U.K.* **17** 51 34N 4 18W
Rhum, *U.K.* **22** 57 0N 6 20W
Rhyl, *U.K.* **17** 53 19N 3 29W
Rhymney, *U.K.* **17** 51 32N 3 7W
Ribble →, *U.K.* **18** 54 13N 2 20W
Ribeirão Prêto, *Brazil* **101** 21 10S 47 50W
Riccall, *U.K.* **19** 53 50N 1 4W
Riccarton, *N.Z.* **71** 43 32S 172 37 E
Riccarton Junc., *U.K.* **21** 55 16N 2 43W
Richmond, *N. Yorks., U.K.* **19** 54 24N 1 43W
Richmond, *Surrey, U.K.* **15** 51 28N 0 18W
Richmond, *U.S.A.* **92** 37 33N 77 27W
Rickmansworth, *U.K.* **15** 51 38N 0 28W
Ridsdale, *U.K.* **21** 55 9N 2 8W
Rievaulx, *U.K.* **19** 54 16N 1 7W
Riga, *U.S.S.R.* **46** 56 53N 24 8 E
Riga, G. of, *U.S.S.R.* **46** 57 40N 23 45 E
Rijeka, *Yug.* **40** 45 20N 14 21 E
Rijswijk, *Neth.* **36** 52 4N 4 22 E
Rillington, *U.K.* **19** 54 10N 0 41W
Rímini, *It.* **40** 44 3N 12 33 E
Rîmnicu Vîlcea, *Rom.* **43** 45 9N 24 21 E
Rimouski, *Canada* **93** 48 27N 68 30W
Rineanna, *Ire.* **25** 52 42N 85 7W
Ringford, *U.K.* **21** 54 55N 4 3W
Ringmer, *U.K.* **15** 50 53N 0 5 E
Ringwood, *U.K.* **14** 50 50N 1 48W
Rio Branco, *Brazil* **100** 9 58S 67 49W
Río Cuarto, *Arg.* **102** 33 10S 64 25W
Rio de Janeiro, *Brazil* **101** 23 0S 43 12W
Río Gallegos, *Arg.* **102** 51 35S 69 15W
Rio Grande, *Brazil* **102** 32 0S 52 20W
Rio Grande →, *U.S.A.* **90** 25 57N 97 9W
Rio Grande do Norte □, *Brazil* **94** 5 40S 36 0W
Río Muni = Mbini □, *Eq. Guin.* **80** 1 30N 10 0 E
Riobamba, *Ecuad.* **100** 1 50S 78 45W
Ripley, *Derby, U.K.* **19** 53 3N 1 24W
Ripley, *N. Yorks., U.K.* **19** 54 3N 1 34W
Ripon, *U.K.* **19** 54 8N 1 31W
Risca, *U.K.* **17** 51 36N 3 6W
Rishton, *U.K.* **18** 53 46N 2 26W
Riverside, *U.S.A.* **90** 34 0N 117 22W
Riyadh, *Si. Arab.* **56** 24 41N 46 42 E
Roade, *U.K.* **15** 52 10N 0 53W
Roadhead, *U.K.* **18** 55 4N 2 44W
Roag, L., *U.K.* **22** 58 10N 6 55W
Roanne, *Fr.* **35** 46 3N 4 4 E
Roanoke, *U.S.A.* **92** 37 19N 79 55W
Robe →, *Ire.* **24** 53 38N 9 10W
Roberton, *U.K.* **21** 55 24N 2 53W
Robin Hood's Bay, *U.K.* **19** 54 26N 0 31W
Rocester, *U.K.* **18** 52 56N 1 50W
Rochdale, *U.K.* **18** 53 36N 2 10W
Roche, *U.K.* **16** 50 24N 4 50W
Rochelle, La, *Fr.* **35** 46 10N 1 9W
Rochester, *Kent, U.K.* **15** 51 22N 0 30 E
Rochester, *Northumberland, U.K.* **21** 55 16N 2 16W
Rochester, *Minn., U.S.A.* **90** 44 1N 92 28W
Rochester, *N.Y., U.S.A.* **92** 43 10N 77 40W
Rochford, *U.K.* **15** 51 36N 0 42 E
Rockall, *Atl. Oc.* **26** 57 37N 13 42W
Rockcliffe, *U.K.* **18** 54 58N 3 0W
Rockford, *U.S.A.* **92** 42 20N 89 0W
Rockhampton, *Austral.* **67** 23 22S 150 32 E
Rockingham, *U.K.* **15** 52 32N 0 43W
Rockingham Forest, *U.K.* **15** 52 28N 0 42W
Rocky Mts., *N. Am.* **90** 55 0N 121 0W
Ródhos, *Greece* **41** 36 15N 28 10 E
Roding →, *U.K.* **15** 51 31N 0 7 E
Roe →, *U.K.* **24** 55 10N 6 59W
Roeselare, *Belg.* **36** 50 57N 3 7 E
Rogaland fylke □, *Nor.* **45** 59 12N 6 20 E
Rogans Seat, *U.K.* **18** 54 25N 2 10W
Rogate, *U.K.* **15** 51 0N 0 51W
Roma, *Austral.* **67** 26 32S 148 49 E
Roma = Rome, *It.* **40** 41 54N 12 30 E
Romania ■, *Europe* **43** 46 0N 25 0 E
Rome, *It.* **40** 41 54N 12 30 E
Romney Marsh, *U.K.* **15** 51 0N 1 0 E
Romsey, *U.K.* **14** 51 0N 1 29W
Rona, *U.K.* **22** 57 33N 6 0W
Ronse, *Belg.* **36** 50 45N 3 35 E
Roosendaal, *Neth.* **36** 51 32N 4 29 E
Roper →, *Austral.* **67** 14 43S 135 27 E
Ropsley, *U.K.* **19** 52 53N 0 31W
Roraima, Mt., *Ven.* **101** 5 10N 60 40W
Rosario, *Arg.* **102** 33 0S 60 40W
Roscommon, *Ire.* **24** 53 38N 8 11W
Roscommon □, *Ire.* **24** 53 40N 8 15W
Roscrea, *Ire.* **25** 52 58N 7 50W
Roseau, *Dom.* **94** 15 20N 61 24W
Rosedale Abbey, *U.K.* **19** 54 22N 0 51W
Roskilde, *Den.* **45** 55 38N 12 3 E
Rosneath, *U.K.* **20** 56 1N 4 49W
Ross Ice Shelf, *Ant.* **103** 80 0S 180 0 E
Ross on Wye, *U.K.* **14** 51 55N 2 34W
Ross Sea, *Ant.* **103** 74 0S 178 0 E
Rossall Pt., *U.K.* **18** 53 55N 3 2W
Rossan Pt., *Ire.* **24** 54 42N 8 47W
Rosslare, *Ire.* **25** 52 17N 6 23W
Rostock, *E. Ger.* **42** 54 4N 12 9 E
Rostov, *U.S.S.R.* **47** 47 15N 39 45 E
Rosyth, *U.K.* **21** 56 2N 3 26W
Rothbury, *U.K.* **21** 55 19N 1 55W
Rothbury Forest, *U.K.* **21** 55 19N 1 50W
Rother →, *U.K.* **15** 50 59N 0 40 E
Rotherham, *U.K.* **19** 53 26N 1 21W
Rothes, *U.K.* **23** 57 31N 3 12W
Rothesay, *U.K.* **20** 55 50N 5 3W
Rothwell, *Northants., U.K.* **15** 52 25N 0 48W
Rothwell, *W. Yorks., U.K.* **19** 53 46N 1 29W
Rotorua, *N.Z.* **71** 38 9S 176 16 E
Rotorua, L., *N.Z.* **71** 38 5S 176 18 E
Rotterdam, *Neth.* **36** 51 55N 4 30 E
Rottingdean, *U.K.* **15** 50 48N 0 3W
Roubaix, *Fr.* **34** 50 40N 3 10 E
Rouen, *Fr.* **34** 49 27N 1 4 E
Rousay, *U.K.* **23** 59 10N 3 2W
Rowanburn, *U.K.* **21** 55 5N 2 54W
Rowrah, *U.K.* **18** 54 34N 3 26W
Roxburgh, *U.K.* **21** 55 34N 2 30W
Roxby, *U.K.* **19** 53 38N 0 37W
Royston, *U.K.* **15** 52 3N 0 1W
Royton, *U.K.* **18** 53 34N 2 7W
Ruahine Ra., *N.Z.* **71** 39 55S 176 2 E
Rub' al Khali, *Si. Arab.* **56** 18 0N 48 0 E
Rubery, *U.K.* **14** 52 24N 1 59W
Rubh a' Mhail, *U.K.* **20** 55 55N 6 10W
Rubha Hunish, *U.K.* **22** 57 42N 6 20W
Rudgwick, *U.K.* **15** 51 7N 0 54W
Rudston, *U.K.* **19** 54 6N 0 19W
Rufford, *U.K.* **18** 53 37N 2 50W
Rugby, *U.K.* **14** 52 23N 1 16W
Rugeley, *U.K.* **14** 52 47N 1 56W
Rum Jungle, *Austral.* **66** 13 0S 130 59 E
Runcorn, *U.K.* **18** 53 20N 2 44W
Ruse, *Bulg.* **41** 43 48N 25 59 E
Rushden, *U.K.* **15** 52 17N 0 37W
Ruskington, *U.K.* **19** 53 5N 0 23W
Russian S.F.S.R. □, *U.S.S.R.* **46** 62 0N 105 0 E
Rutherglen, *U.K.* **20** 55 50N 4 11W
Ruthin, *U.K.* **17** 53 7N 3 20W
Ruthwell, *U.K.* **21** 55 0N 3 24W
Rwanda ■, *Africa* **80** 2 0S 30 0 E
Ryan, L., *U.K.* **20** 55 0N 5 2W
Ryazan, *U.S.S.R.* **46** 54 40N 39 40 E
Rybinsk = Andropov, *U.S.S.R.* **46** 58 5N 38 50 E
Rybinsk Res., *U.S.S.R.* **46** 58 30N 38 0 E
Rydal, *U.K.* **18** 54 28N 2 59W
Ryde, *U.K.* **14** 50 44N 1 9W
Rye, *U.K.* **15** 50 57N 0 46 E
Rye →, *U.K.* **19** 54 12N 0 53W
Rye Bay, *U.K.* **15** 50 50N 0 50 E
Ryhope, *U.K.* **21** 54 52N 1 22W
Ryton, *Tyne & Wear, U.K.* **21** 54 58N 1 44W
Ryton, *Warwick, U.K.* **14** 52 23N 1 25W
Ryūkyū Is., *Jap.* **62** 26 0N 128 0 E
Rzeszów, *Pol.* **43** 50 5N 21 58 E

S

Saarbrücken, *W. Ger.* **36** 49 15N 6 58 E
Saaremaa, *U.S.S.R.* **46** 58 30N 22 30 E
Saarland □, *W. Ger.* **36** 49 15N 7 0 E
Saba, *W. Ind.* **94** 17 42N 63 26W
Sabadell, *Sp.* **37** 41 28N 2 7 E
Sabah □, *Malay.* **63** 6 0N 117 0 E
Sabhah, *Libya* **79** 27 9N 14 29 E
Sacramento, *U.S.A.* **90** 38 33N 121 30 E
Sacriston, *U.K.* **19** 54 49N 1 38W
Saddell, *U.K.* **20** 55 31N 5 30W
Saffron Walden, *U.K.* **15** 52 2N 0 15 E
Safi, *Mor.* **78** 32 18N 9 20W
Sagar, *India* **58** 14 14N 75 6 E
Saginaw, *U.S.A.* **92** 43 26N 83 55W
Saginaw B., *U.S.A.* **92** 43 50N 83 40W
Sahara, *Africa* **78** 23 0N 5 0 E
Saharan Atlas, *Alg.* **78** 34 9N 3 29 E
Saharanpur, *India* **58** 29 58N 77 33 E
Saigon = Ho Chi Minh City, *Viet.* **63** 10 58N 106 40 E
St. Abb's, *U.K.* **21** 55 54N 2 7W
St. Abb's Head, *U.K.* **21** 55 55N 2 10W
St. Agnes, *U.K.* **16** 50 18N 5 13W
St. Agnes Hd., *U.K.* **16** 50 19N 5 14W
St. Agnes I., *U.K.* **16** 49 53N 6 20W
St. Albans, *U.K.* **15** 51 44N 0 19W
St. Alban's Head, *U.K.* **14** 50 34N 2 3W
St. Andrews, *U.K.* **21** 56 20N 2 48W
St. Ann's, *U.K.* **21** 55 14N 3 28W
St. Asaph, *U.K.* **17** 53 15N 3 27W
St. Austell, *U.K.* **16** 50 20N 4 48W
St. Bees, *U.K.* **18** 54 29N 3 36W
St. Bee's Hd., *U.K.* **18** 54 30N 3 38 E
St. Blazey, *U.K.* **16** 50 22N 4 48W
St. Boniface, *Canada* **88** 49 53N 97 5W
St. Boswells, *U.K.* **21** 55 34N 2 39W
St. Briavels, *U.K.* **14** 51 44N 2 39W
St. Brides B., *U.K.* **17** 51 48N 5 15W
St.-Brieuc, *Fr.* **34** 48 30N 2 46W
St. Budeaux, *U.K.* **16** 50 23N 4 10W
St. Buryan, *U.K.* **16** 50 4N 5 34W
St. Catharines, *Canada* **92** 43 10N 79 15W
St. Catherine's Pt., *U.K.* **14** 50 34N 1 18W
St. Christopher-Nevis ■, *W. Ind.* **94** 17 20N 62 40W
St. Clair, L., *Canada* **92** 42 30N 82 45W
St.-Claude, *Fr.* **35** 46 22N 5 52 E
St. Clears, *U.K.* **17** 51 48N 4 30W
St. Columb Major, *U.K.* **16** 50 26N 4 56W
St. David's, *U.K.* **17** 51 54N 5 16W
St. David's Head, *U.K.* **17** 51 55N 5 16W
St. Dennis, *U.K.* **16** 50 23N 4 53W
St. Dominick, *U.K.* **16** 50 28N 4 15W
St. Elias Mts., *Canada* **88** 60 33N 139 28W
St. Endellion, *U.K.* **16** 50 33N 4 49W
St. Enoder, *U.K.* **16** 50 22N 4 57W
St. Erth, *U.K.* **16** 50 10N 5 26W
St.-Étienne, *Fr.* **35** 45 27N 4 22 E
St. Fillans, *U.K.* **21** 56 25N 4 7W
St. Gallen, *Switz.* **42** 47 25N 9 20 E
St. George's, *Gren.* **94** 12 5N 61 43W
St. George's Channel, *U.K.* **25** 52 0N 6 0W
St. Germans, *U.K.* **16** 50 24N 4 19W
St. Helena, *Atl. Oc.* **128** 15 55S 5 44W
St. Helena B., *S. Afr.* **81** 32 40S 18 10 E
St. Helens, *I. of W., U.K.* **14** 50 42N 1 6W
St. Helens, *Merseyside, U.K.* **18** 53 28N 2 44W
St. Helier, *U.K.* **34** 49 11N 2 6W
St-Hyacinthe, *Canada* **93** 45 40N 72 58W
St. Issey, *U.K.* **16** 50 30N 4 55W
St. Ives, *Cambs., U.K.* **15** 52 20N 0 5W
St. Ives, *Cornwall, U.K.* **16** 50 13N 5 29W
St. Ives Bay, *U.K.* **16** 50 15N 5 27W
St-Jean, L., *Canada* **93** 48 40N 72 0W
St-Jérôme, *Canada* **93** 45 47N 74 0W
St. John, *Canada* **93** 45 20N 66 8W
St. John's, *Antigua* **94** 17 6N 61 51W
St. John's, *Canada* **89** 47 35N 52 40W
St. John's, *U.K.* **18** 54 13N 4 38W
St. Johns Chapel, *U.K.* **18** 54 43N 2 10W
St. Joseph, *U.S.A.* **90** 39 46N 94 50W
St. Just, *U.K.* **16** 50 7N 5 41W
St. Keverne, *U.K.* **16** 50 3N 5 5W
St. Kew, *U.K.* **16** 50 34N 4 48W
St. Lawrence →, *Canada* **93** 49 30N 66 0W
St. Lawrence, Gulf of, *Canada* **89** 48 25N 62 0W
St. Leonards, *U.K.* **15** 50 51N 0 34 E
St. Levan, *U.K.* **16** 50 3N 5 36W
St.-Lô, *Fr.* **34** 49 7N 1 5W
St-Louis, *Sene.* **78** 16 8N 16 27W
St. Louis, *U.S.A.* **92** 38 40N 90 12W
St. Lucia ■, *W. Ind.* **94** 14 0N 60 50W
St. Maarten, *W. Ind.* **94** 18 0N 63 5W
St. Mabyn, *U.K.* **16** 50 30N 4 45W
St.-Malo, *Fr.* **34** 48 39N 2 1W
St. Margaret's-at-Cliffe, *U.K.* **15** 51 10N 1 23 E
St. Margaret's Hope, *U.K.* **23** 58 49N 2 58W
St-Martin, I., *W. Ind.* **94** 18 0N 63 0W
St. Martin's I., *U.K.* **16** 49 58N 6 16W
St. Mary Bourne, *U.K.* **14** 51 16N 1 24W
St. Mary's, *U.K.* **16** 49 55N 6 17W
St. Mary's Sd., *U.K.* **16** 49 53N 6 19W
St. Mawes, *U.K.* **16** 50 10N 5 1W
St. Merryn, *U.K.* **16** 50 31N 4 58W
St. Michael's Mt., *U.K.* **16** 50 7N 5 30W
St. Minver, *U.K.* **16** 50 34N 4 52W
St. Monance, *U.K.* **21** 56 13N 2 46W
St.-Nazaire, *Fr.* **34** 47 17N 2 12W
St. Neots, *U.K.* **15** 52 14N 0 16W
St-Niklaas, *Belg.* **36** 51 10N 4 8 E
St. Osyth, *U.K.* **15** 51 47N 1 4 E
St. Paul, *U.S.A.* **91** 44 54N 93 5W
St. Peter Port, *U.K.* **34** 49 27N 2 31W
St. Petersburg, *U.S.A.* **91** 27 45N 82 40W
St.-Pierre et Miquelon □, *N. Am.* **89** 46 55N 56 10W
St.-Quentin, *Fr.* **34** 49 50N 3 16 E
St. Stephen, *U.K.* **16** 50 20N 4 52W
St. Teath, *U.K.* **16** 50 34N 4 45W
St.-Tropez, *Fr.* **35** 43 17N 6 38 E
St. Tudy, *U.K.* **16** 50 33N 4 45W
St. Vincent and the Grenadines ■, *W. Ind.* **94** 13 0N 61 10W
Saintfield, *U.K.* **24** 54 28N 5 50W
Sakai, *Jap.* **62** 34 30N 135 30 E
Sakhalin, *U.S.S.R.* **49** 51 0N 143 0 E
Salado →, *Arg.* **102** 31 40S 60 41W
Salamanca, *Sp.* **37** 40 58N 5 39W
Salcombe, *U.K.* **16** 50 14N 3 47W
Salcombe Regis, *U.K.* **16** 50 41N 3 11W
Sale, *Austral.* **70** 38 6S 147 6 E
Sale, *U.K.* **18** 53 26N 2 19W
Salem, *India* **58** 11 40N 78 11 E
Salen, *U.K.* **20** 56 31N 5 57W
Salerno, *It.* **40** 40 40N 14 44 E
Salford, *U.K.* **18** 53 30N 2 17W
Salford Priors, *U.K.* **14** 52 10N 1 52W
Salisbury = Harare, *Zimb.* **81** 17 43S 31 2 E
Salisbury, *U.K.* **14** 51 4N 1 48W
Salisbury Plain, *U.K.* **14** 51 13N 1 50W
Salonica = Thessaloníki, *Greece* **41** 40 38N 22 58 E
Salop = Shropshire □, *U.K.* **14** 52 36N 2 45W
Salt Lake City, *U.S.A.* **90** 40 45N 111 58W
Salta, *Arg.* **102** 24 57S 65 25W
Saltash, *U.K.* **16** 50 25N 4 13W
Saltburn by the Sea, *U.K.* **19** 54 35N 0 58W
Saltcoats, *U.K.* **20** 55 38N 4 47W
Saltee Is., *Ire.* **25** 52 7N 6 37W
Saltergate, *U.K.* **19** 54 20N 0 40W
Saltfleet, *U.K.* **19** 53 25N 0 11 E
Saltfleetby, *U.K.* **19** 53 23N 0 10 E
Saltillo, *Mex.* **94** 25 25N 101 0W
Salto, *Urug.* **102** 31 27S 57 50W
Saltwood, *U.K.* **15** 51 4N 1 5 E
Salvador, *Brazil* **101** 13 0S 38 30W
Salween →, *Burma* **59** 16 31N 97 37 E
Salzburg, *Austria* **42** 47 48N 13 2 E
Salzgitter, *W. Ger.* **42** 52 13N 10 22 E
Samarinda, *Indon.* **63** 0 30S 117 9 E
Samarkand, *U.S.S.R.* **48** 39 40N 66 55 E
Sámos, *Greece* **41** 37 45N 26 50 E
Sampford Courtenay, *U.K.* **16** 50 47N 3 58W
Samsun, *Turk.* **47** 41 15N 36 22 E
San Angelo, *U.S.A.* **90** 31 30N 100 30W
San Antonio, *U.S.A.* **90** 29 30N 98 30W
San Bernardino, *U.S.A.* **90** 34 7N 117 18W
San Carlos, *Phil.* **63** 15 55N 120 20 E
San Cristóbal, *Ven.* **100** 16 50N 92 40W
San Diego, *U.S.A.* **90** 32 43N 117 10W
San Fernando, *Mex.* **94** 30 0N 115 10W
San Francisco, *U.S.A.* **90** 37 47N 122 30W
San Jorge, G., *Arg.* **102** 46 0S 66 0W
San José, *C.R.* **95** 10 0N 84 2W
San Jose, *U.S.A.* **90** 37 20N 121 53W
San Juan, *Arg.* **102** 31 30S 68 30W
San Juan, *P.R.* **95** 18 28N 66 8W
San Luis Potosí, *Mex.* **94** 22 9N 100 59W
San Marino ■, *Europe* **40** 43 56N 12 25 E
San Matías, G., *Arg.* **102** 41 30S 64 0W
San Miguel de Tucumán, *Arg.* **102** 26 50S 65 20W
San Pedro Sula, *Hond.* **94** 15 30N 88 0W
San Salvador, *El Salv.* **94** 13 40N 89 10W
San Salvador de Jujuy, *Arg.* **102** 24 10S 64 48W
San Sebastián, *Sp.* **37** 43 17N 1 58W
Sana', *Yem.* **56** 15 27N 44 12 E
Sanda I., *U.K.* **20** 55 17N 5 35W
Sanday, *U.K.* **23** 59 15N 2 30W
Sandbach, *U.K.* **18** 53 9N 2 23W
Sandbank, *U.K.* **20** 55 58N 4 57W
Sandgate, *U.K.* **15** 51 5N 1 9 E
Sandhead, *U.K.* **20** 54 48N 4 58W
Sandhurst, *U.K.* **15** 51 21N 0 48W
Sandness, *U.K.* **22** 60 18N 1 38W
Sandown, *U.K.* **14** 50 39N 1 9W
Sandringham, *U.K.* **15** 52 50N 0 30 E
Sandwich, *U.K.* **15** 51 16N 1 21 E
Sandy, *U.K.* **15** 52 8N 0 18W
Sangli, *India* **58** 16 55N 74 33 E
Sanquhar, *U.K.* **21** 55 21N 3 56W
Santa Ana, *Mex.* **94** 30 33N 111 7W
Santa Ana, *U.S.A.* **90** 33 48N 117 55W
Santa Clara, *Cuba* **95** 22 20N 80 0W
Santa Cruz, *Bol.* **100** 17 43S 63 10W
Santa Cruz de Tenerife, *Can. Is.* **78** 28 28N 16 15W
Santa Fe, *Arg.* **102** 31 35S 60 41W
Santa Fe, *U.S.A.* **90** 35 40N 106 0W
Santa Maria, *Brazil* **102** 29 40S 53 48W
Santa Marta, *Col.* **100** 11 15N 74 13W
Santander, *Sp.* **37** 43 27N 3 51W
Santarém, *Brazil* **101** 2 25S 54 42W
Santarém, *Port.* **37** 39 12N 8 42W
Santiago, *Chile* **102** 33 24S 70 40W
Santiago de Compostela, *Sp.* **37** 42 52N 8 37W
Santiago de Cuba, *Cuba* **95** 20 0N 75 49W
Santiago de los Cabelleros, *Dom. Rep.* **95** 19 30N 70 40W
Santo André, *Brazil* **102** 23 39S 46 29W
Santo Domingo, *Dom. Rep.* **95** 18 30N 64 54W
Santos, *Brazil* **102** 24 0S 46 20W
São Francisco →, *Brazil* **101** 10 30S 36 24W
São José do Rio Prêto, *Brazil* **101** 20 50S 49 20W
São Luís, *Brazil* **101** 2 39S 44 15W
São Paulo, *Brazil* **102** 23 32S 46 37W
São Roque, C. de, *Brazil* **101** 5 30S 35 16W
São Tomé & Principe ■, *Africa* **73** 0 12N 6 39 E
Saône →, *Fr.* **34** 45 44N 4 50 E
Sapporo, *Jap.* **62** 43 0N 141 21 E

Sarajevo, *Yug.* **41** 43 52N 18 26 E
Saransk, *U.S.S.R.* **46** 54 10N 45 10 E
Saratov, *U.S.S.R.* **46** 51 30N 46 2 E
Sarawak □, *Malay.* **63** 2 0N 113 0 E
Sardinia, I., *It.* **40** 40 0N 9 0 E
Sargodha, *Pak.* **58** 32 10N 72 40 E
Sarh, *Chad* **79** 9 5N 18 23 E
Sarnia, *Canada* **92** 42 58N 82 23W
Sasebo, *Jap.* **62** 33 10N 129 43 E
Saskatchewan □, *Canada* **88** 54 40N 106 0W
Saskatchewan →, *Canada* **88** 53 37N 100 40W
Saskatoon, *Canada* **88** 52 10N 106 38W
Sássari, *It.* **40** 40 44N 8 33 E
Satpura Ra., *India* **58** 21 25N 76 10 E
Satu Mare, *Rom.* **43** 47 46N 22 55 E
Sauðarkrókur, *Ice.* **44** 65 45N 19 40W
Saudi Arabia ■, *Asia* **56** 26 0N 44 0 E
Sault Ste. Marie, *Canada* **92** 46 30N 84 20W
Saundersfoot, *U.K.* **17** 51 43N 4 42W
Sava →, *Yug.* **41** 44 50N 20 26 E
Savanna la Mar, *Jam.* **94** 18 10N 78 10W
Savannah, *U.S.A.* **91** 32 4N 81 4W
Savona, *It.* **40** 44 19N 8 29 E
Savonlinna, *Fin.* **44** 61 52N 28 53 E
Sawbridgeworth, *U.K.* **15** 51 49N 0 10 E
Sawel, Mt., *U.K.* **24** 54 48N 7 5W
Sawston, *U.K.* **15** 52 7N 0 11 E
Sawtry, *U.K.* **15** 52 26N 0 17W
Saxilby, *U.K.* **19** 53 16N 0 40W
Saxlingham Nethergate, *U.K.* **15** 52 33N 1 16 E
Saxmundham, *U.K.* **15** 52 13N 1 29 E
Saydā, *Leb.* **57** 33 35N 35 25 E
Scafell Pikes, *U.K.* **18** 54 26N 3 14W
Scalasaig, *U.K.* **20** 56 4N 6 10W
Scalby, *U.K.* **19** 54 18N 0 26W
Scalby Ness, *U.K.* **19** 54 18N 0 25W
Scalloway, *U.K.* **22** 60 9N 1 16W
Scalpay, *U.K.* **22** 57 51N 6 40W
Scamblesby, *U.K.* **19** 53 17N 0 5W
Scandinavia, *Europe* **44** 64 0N 12 0 E
Scapa Flow, *U.K.* **23** 58 52N 3 6W
Scarba, I., *U.K.* **20** 56 10N 5 42W
Scarborough, *U.K.* **19** 54 17N 0 24W
Scarinish, *U.K.* **20** 56 30N 6 48W
Scarning, *U.K.* **15** 52 40N 0 53W
Schefferville, *Canada* **89** 54 48N 66 50W
Schenectady, *U.S.A.* **93** 42 50N 73 58W
Schiedam, *Neth.* **36** 51 55N 4 25 E
Schleswig-Holstein □, *W. Ger.* **42** 54 10N 9 40 E
Schwerin, *E. Ger.* **42** 53 37N 11 22 E
Scilly, Isles of, *U.K.* **16** 49 55N 6 15W
Scole, *U.K.* **15** 52 22N 1 10 E
Scone, *U.K.* **21** 56 25N 3 26W
Scopwick, *U.K.* **19** 53 6N 0 24W
Scotland □, *U.K.* **20** 57 0N 4 0W
Scranton, *U.S.A.* **93** 41 22N 75 41W
Scremerston, *U.K.* **21** 55 44N 1 59W
Scridain, L., *U.K.* **20** 56 23N 6 7W
Scunthorpe, *U.K.* **19** 53 35N 0 38W
Seaford, *U.K.* **15** 50 46N 0 8 E
Seaham, *U.K.* **21** 54 51N 1 20W
Seahouses, *U.K.* **21** 55 35N 1 39W
Seamer, *U.K.* **19** 54 14N 0 27W
Seascale, *U.K.* **18** 54 24N 3 29W
Seaton, *Cumbria, U.K.* **18** 54 40N 3 31W
Seaton, *Devon, U.K.* **16** 50 42N 3 3W
Seaton Delaval, *U.K.* **21** 55 5N 1 33W
Seattle, *U.S.A.* **90** 47 41N 122 15W
Sedbergh, *U.K.* **18** 54 20N 2 31W
Sedgefield, *U.K.* **19** 54 40N 1 27W
Seend, *U.K.* **14** 51 20N 2 2W
Segovia, *Sp.* **37** 40 57N 4 10W
Seil, I., *U.K.* **20** 56 17N 5 37W
Seine →, *Fr.* **34** 49 26N 0 26 E
Sekondi-Takoradi, *Ghana* **78** 4 58N 1 45W
Selborne, *U.K.* **15** 51 5N 0 55W
Selby, *U.K.* **19** 53 47N 1 5W
Selkirk, *U.K.* **21** 55 33N 2 50W
Selsey, *U.K.* **15** 50 44N 0 47W
Selsey Bill, *U.K.* **15** 50 44N 0 47W
Selvas, *Brazil* **100** 6 30S 67 0W
Selwyn Ra., *Austral.* **67** 21 10S 140 0 E
Semarang, *Indon.* **63** 7 0S 110 26 E
Semipalatinsk, *U.S.S.R.* **48** 50 30N 80 10 E
Sendai, *Jap.* **62** 38 15N 140 53 E
Senegal ■, *W. Afr.* **78** 14 30N 14 30W
Senegal →, *W. Afr.* **78** 15 48N 16 32W
Sennen, *U.K.* **16** 50 4N 5 42W
Seoul, *S. Kor.* **61** 37 31N 126 58 E
Seph →, *U.K.* **19** 54 17N 1 9W
Sequoia Nat. Park, *U.S.A.* **90** 36 30N 118 30W
Serbia □, *Yug.* **41** 43 30N 21 0 E
Seremban, *Malay.* **63** 2 43N 101 53 E
Serena, La, *Chile* **102** 29 55S 71 10W
Serpukhov, *U.S.S.R.* **46** 54 55N 37 28 E
Sétif, *Alg.* **78** 36 9N 5 26 E
Settat, *Mor.* **78** 33 0N 7 40W
Settle, *U.K.* **18** 54 5N 2 18W
Setúbal, *Port.* **37** 38 30N 8 58W
Sevastopol, *U.S.S.R.* **47** 44 35N 33 30 E
Seven →, *U.K.* **19** 54 11N 0 51W
Sevenoaks, *U.K.* **15** 51 16N 0 11 E
Severn →, *U.K.* **14** 51 35N 2 38W
Severn Beach, *U.K.* **14** 51 34N 2 39W
Severn Stoke, *U.K.* **14** 52 5N 2 13W
Severnaya Zemlya, *U.S.S.R.* **49** 79 0N 100 0 E
Seville, *Sp.* **37** 37 23N 6 0W
Seward Pen., *U.S.A.* **88** 65 0N 164 0W
Seychelles ■, *Ind. Oc.* **129** 5 0S 56 0 E
Seyðisfjörður, *Ice.* **44** 65 16N 14 0W
Sfax, *Tunisia* **79** 34 49N 10 48 E
Shaanxi □, *China* **61** 35 0N 109 0 E
Shache, *China* **60** 38 20N 77 10 E
Shaftesbury, *U.K.* **14** 51 0N 2 12W
Shahjahanpur, *India* **58** 27 54N 79 57 E
Shakhty, *U.S.S.R.* **47** 47 40N 40 16 E
Shaldon, *U.K.* **16** 50 32N 3 31W
Shan □, *Burma* **59** 21 30N 98 30 E
Shandong □, *China* **61** 36 0N 118 0 E
Shanghai, *China* **61** 31 15N 121 26 E
Shangrao, *China* **61** 28 25N 117 59 E
Shanklin, *U.K.* **14** 50 39N 1 9W
Shannon →, *Ire.* **25** 52 35N 9 30W
Shantou, *China* **61** 23 18N 116 40 E
Shanxi □, *China* **61** 37 0N 112 0 E
Shaoguan, *China* **61** 24 48N 113 35 E
Shaoyang, *China* **61** 27 14N 111 25 E
Shap, *U.K.* **18** 54 32N 2 40W
Shapinsay, *U.K.* **23** 59 2N 2 50W
Shark B., *Austral.* **66** 11 20S 130 30 E
Sharpness, *U.K.* **14** 51 43N 2 28W
Shawbury, *U.K.* **14** 52 48N 2 40W
Shawinigan, *Canada* **93** 46 35N 72 50W
Shebbear, *U.K.* **16** 50 52N 4 12W
Sheelin, Lough, *Ire.* **24** 53 48N 7 20W
Sheep Haven, *Ire.* **24** 55 12N 7 55W
Sheerness, *U.K.* **15** 51 26N 0 47 E
Sheffield, *U.K.* **19** 53 23N 1 28W
Shefford, *U.K.* **15** 52 2N 0 20W
Shelekhov G., *U.S.S.R.* **49** 59 30N 157 0 E
Shellharbour, *Austral.* **70** 34 31S 150 51 E
Shelling Rocks, *Ire.* **25** 51 45N 10 35W
Shenfield, *U.K.* **15** 51 39N 0 21 E
Shenyang, *China* **61** 41 50N 123 25 E
Shepparton, *Austral.* **70** 36 23S 145 26 E
Sheppey, I. of, *U.K.* **15** 51 23N 0 50 E
Shepshed, *U.K.* **14** 52 47N 1 18W
Shepton Mallet, *U.K.* **14** 51 11N 2 31W
Sherborne, *U.K.* **14** 50 56N 2 31W
Sherborne St. John, *U.K.* **14** 51 18N 1 7W
Sherbrooke, *Canada* **93** 45 28N 71 57W
Sherburn, *N. Yorks., U.K.* **19** 54 12N 0 32W
Sherburn, *N. Yorks., U.K.* **19** 53 47N 1 15W
Shere, *U.K.* **15** 51 13N 0 28W
Sherfield English, *U.K.* **14** 51 1N 1 35W
Sheriff Hutton, *U.K.* **19** 54 5N 1 0W
Sheriff Muir, *U.K.* **21** 56 12N 3 53W
Sheringham, *U.K.* **15** 52 56N 1 11 E
Sherston, *U.K.* **14** 51 35N 2 13W
Sherwood Forest, *U.K.* **19** 53 5N 1 5W
Shetland □, *U.K.* **22** 60 30N 1 30W
Shetland Is., *U.K.* **22** 60 30N 1 30W
Shiel, L., *U.K.* **22** 56 48N 5 32W
Shieldaig, *U.K.* **22** 57 31N 5 39W
Shifnal, *U.K.* **14** 52 40N 2 23W
Shijiazhuang, *China* **61** 38 2N 114 28 E
Shikoku, *Jap.* **62** 33 30N 133 30 E
Shilbottle, *U.K.* **21** 55 23N 1 42W
Shildon, *U.K.* **19** 54 37N 1 39W
Shiliguri, *India* **59** 26 45N 88 25 E
Shillelagh, *Ire.* **25** 52 46N 6 32W
Shillingstone, *U.K.* **14** 50 54N 2 15W
Shillong, *India* **59** 25 35N 91 53 E
Shimonoseki, *Jap.* **62** 33 58N 131 0 E
Shin, L., *U.K.* **23** 58 7N 4 30W
Shipbourne, *U.K.* **15** 51 13N 0 19 E
Shipdham, *U.K.* **15** 52 38N 0 53 E
Shipley, *U.K.* **19** 53 50N 1 47W
Shipston-on-Stour, *U.K.* **14** 52 4N 1 38W
Shipton-under-Wychwood, *U.K.* **14** 51 51N 1 35W
Shīrāz, *Iran* **56** 29 42N 52 30 E
Shirebrook, *U.K.* **19** 53 13N 1 11W
Shizuoka, *Jap.* **62** 35 0N 138 24 E
Shkoder, *Alb.* **41** 42 6N 19 20 E
Shoeburyness, *U.K.* **15** 51 31N 0 49 E
Shoreham-by-Sea, *U.K.* **15** 50 50N 0 17W
Shotts, *U.K.* **21** 55 49N 3 47W
Shreveport, *U.S.A.* **91** 32 30N 93 50W
Shrewsbury, *U.K.* **14** 52 42N 2 45W
Shrewton, *U.K.* **14** 51 11N 1 55W
Shrivenham, *U.K.* **14** 51 36N 1 39W
Shropshire □, *U.K.* **14** 52 36N 2 45W
Shuangyashan, *China* **61** 46 28N 131 5 E
Siam = Thailand ■, *Asia* **63** 16 0N 102 0 E
Sian, *China* **61** 34 2N 109 0 E
Siberia, *U.S.S.R.* **50** 60 0N 100 0 E
Sibiu, *Rom.* **43** 45 45N 24 9 E
Sible Hedingham, *U.K.* **15** 51 58N 0 37 E
Sibsey, *U.K.* **19** 53 3N 0 1 E
Sichuan □, *China* **60** 31 0N 104 0 E
Sicily, *It.* **40** 37 30N 14 30 E
Sidbury, *U.K.* **16** 50 43N 3 12W
Sidlaw Hills, *U.K.* **21** 56 32N 3 10W
Sidlesham, *U.K.* **15** 50 46N 0 46W
Sidmouth, *U.K.* **16** 50 40N 3 13W
Sidon = Saydā, *Leb.* **57** 33 35N 35 25 E
Siegen, *W. Ger.* **36** 50 52N 8 2 E
Siena, *It.* **40** 43 20N 11 20 E
Sierra Leone ■, *W. Afr.* **78** 9 0N 12 0W
Sighty Crag, *U.K.* **21** 55 8N 2 37W
Siglufjörður, *Ice.* **44** 66 12N 18 55W
Sikhote Alin Ra., *U.S.S.R.* **49** 46 0N 136 0 E
Sikkim □, *India* **59** 27 50N 88 30 E
Silloth, *U.K.* **18** 54 53N 3 25W
Silsden, *U.K.* **18** 53 55N 1 55W
Silverstone, *U.K.* **14** 52 5N 1 3W
Silverton, *U.K.* **16** 50 49N 3 29W
Simferopol, *U.S.S.R.* **47** 44 55N 34 3 E
Simonsbath, *U.K.* **14** 51 8N 3 45W
Simonside, *U.K.* **21** 55 17N 2 0W
Simpson Desert, *Austral.* **67** 25 0S 137 0 E
Sinai Peninsula, *Egypt* **79** 29 30N 34 0 E
Sind Sagar Doab, *Pak.* **58** 32 0N 71 30 E
Singapore ■, *Asia* **63** 1 17N 103 51 E
Singleton, *U.K.* **15** 50 55N 0 45W
Sioux Falls, *U.S.A.* **91** 43 35N 96 40W
Siping, *China* **61** 33 25N 114 10 E
Siracusa, *It.* **40** 37 4N 15 17 E
Sittingbourne, *U.K.* **15** 51 20N 0 43 E
Sittwe, *Bur.* **59** 20 18N 92 45 E
Sivas, *Turk.* **47** 39 43N 36 58 E
Siwalik Range, *Nepal* **59** 28 0N 83 0 E
Sizewell, *U.K.* **15** 52 13N 1 38 E
Sjælland, *Den.* **45** 55 30N 11 30 E
Skagerrak, *Den.* **45** 57 30N 9 0 E
Skagway, *U.S.A.* **88** 59 23N 135 20W
Skegness, *U.K.* **19** 53 9N 0 20 E
Skellefteå, *Swed.* **44** 64 45N 20 58 E
Skellingthorpe, *U.K.* **19** 53 14N 0 37W
Skelmersdale, *U.K.* **18** 53 34N 2 49W
Skelmorlie, *U.K.* **20** 55 52N 4 53W
Skelton, *Cleveland, U.K.* **19** 54 33N 0 59W
Skelton, *Cumbria, U.K.* **18** 54 42N 2 50W
Skerries, The, *U.K.* **17** 53 27N 4 40W
Skibbereen, *Ire.* **25** 51 33N 9 16W
Skiddaw, *U.K.* **18** 54 39N 3 9W
Skien, *Nor.* **45** 59 12N 9 35 E
Skikda, *Alg.* **78** 36 50N 6 58 E
Skipness, *U.K.* **20** 55 46N 5 20W
Skipsea, *U.K.* **19** 53 58N 0 13W
Skipton, *U.K.* **18** 53 57N 2 1W
Skopje, *Yug.* **41** 42 1N 21 32 E
Skull, *Ire.* **25** 51 32N 9 40W
Skye, *U.K.* **22** 57 15N 6 10W
Slaidburn, *U.K.* **18** 53 57N 2 28W
Slaley, *U.K.* **21** 54 55N 2 4W
Slaney →, *Ire.* **25** 52 52N 6 45W
Sleaford, *U.K.* **19** 53 0N 0 22W
Sleat, Sd. of, *U.K.* **22** 57 5N 5 47W
Sledmere, *U.K.* **19** 54 4N 0 35W
Sleights, *U.K.* **19** 54 27N 0 40W
Slieve Aughty, *Ire.* **25** 53 4N 8 30W
Slieve Bloom, *Ire.* **25** 53 4N 7 40W
Slieve Donard, *U.K.* **24** 54 10N 5 57W
Slieve Gullion, *U.K.* **24** 54 8N 6 26W
Slieve Mish, *Ire.* **25** 52 12N 9 50W
Slievenamon, *Ire.* **25** 52 25N 7 37W
Sligo, *Ire.* **24** 54 17N 8 28W
Sligo □, *Ire.* **24** 54 10N 8 35W
Sligo B., *Ire.* **24** 54 20N 8 40W
Sliven, *Bulg.* **41** 42 42N 26 19 E
Slough, *U.K.* **15** 51 30N 0 35W
Slovenská Socialisticka Republika □, *Czech.* **43** 48 30N 20 0 E
Slyne Hd., *Ire.* **24** 53 25N 10 10W
Smederevo, *Yug.* **41** 44 40N 20 57 E
Smethwick, *U.K.* **14** 52 29N 1 58W
Smithfield, *U.K.* **18** 54 59N 2 51W
Smolensk, *U.S.S.R.* **46** 54 45N 32 0 E
Snaefell, *U.K.* **18** 54 18N 4 26W
Snainton, *U.K.* **19** 54 14N 0 33W
Snaith, *U.K.* **19** 53 42N 1 1W
Snake →, *U.S.A.* **90** 46 12N 119 2W
Snape, *U.K.* **15** 52 11N 1 29 E
Snettisham, *U.K.* **15** 52 52N 0 30 E
Snizort, L., *U.K.* **22** 57 33N 6 28W
Snowdon, *U.K.* **17** 53 4N 4 8W
Snowy Mts., *Austral.* **70** 36 30S 148 20 E
Sobral, *Brazil* **101** 3 50S 40 20W
Sochi, *U.S.S.R.* **47** 43 35N 39 40 E
Society Is., *Pac. Oc.* **65** 17 0S 151 0W
Socotra, *Ind. Oc.* **57** 12 30N 54 0 E
Söderhamn, *Swed.* **45** 61 18N 17 10 E
Sofia, *Bulg.* **41** 42 45N 23 20 E
Sogn og Fjordane fylke □, *Nor.* **44** 61 40N 6 0 E
Sognefjorden, *Nor.* **45** 61 10N 5 50 E
Sohâg, *Egypt* **79** 26 33N 31 43 E
Soham, *U.K.* **15** 52 20N 0 20 E
Sokoto, *Nig.* **78** 13 2N 5 16 E
Solapur, *India* **58** 17 43N 75 56 E
Solent, The, *U.K.* **14** 50 45N 1 25W
Solihull, *U.K.* **14** 52 26N 1 47W
Solimões → = Amazon →, *S. Am.* **100** 0 5S 50 0W
Solingen, *W. Ger.* **36** 51 10N 7 4 E
Solomon Is. ■, *Oc.* **64** 6 0S 155 0 E
Solway Firth, *U.K.* **18** 54 45N 3 38W
Somali Rep. ■, *E. Afr.* **73** 7 0N 47 0 E
Somerby, *U.K.* **15** 52 42N 0 49W
Somerset □, *U.K.* **14** 51 9N 3 0W
Somersham, *U.K.* **15** 52 24N 0 0 E
Somerton, *U.K.* **14** 51 3N 2 45W
Sompting, *U.K.* **15** 50 51N 0 20W
Søndre Strømfjord, *Green.* **89** 66 59N 50 40W
Sonning, *U.K.* **15** 51 28N 0 53W
Sorbie, *U.K.* **20** 54 46N 4 26W
Soria, *Sp.* **37** 41 43N 2 32W
Sorisdale, *U.K.* **20** 56 40N 6 28W
Sorn, *U.K.* **20** 55 31N 4 18W
Sorocaba, *Brazil* **102** 23 31S 47 27W
Sosnowiec, *Pol.* **43** 50 20N 19 10 E
Sousse, *Tunisia* **79** 35 50N 10 38 E
South Africa, Rep. of ■, *Africa* **81** 32 0S 17 0 E
South Australia □, *Austral.* **66** 32 0S 139 0 E
South Barrule, *U.K.* **18** 54 9N 4 36W
South Bend, *U.S.A.* **92** 41 38N 86 20W
South Benfleet, *U.K.* **15** 51 33N 0 34 E
South Brent, *U.K.* **16** 50 26N 3 50W
South Carolina □, *U.S.A.* **91** 33 45N 81 0W
South Cave, *U.K.* **19** 53 46N 0 37W
South China Sea, *Asia* **63** 10 0N 113 0 E
South Dakota □, *U.S.A.* **90** 45 0N 100 0W
South Dorset Downs, *U.K.* **14** 50 40N 2 26W
South Downs, *U.K.* **15** 50 53N 0 10W
South Elkington, *U.K.* **19** 53 22N 0 5W
South Esk →, *U.K.* **23** 56 44N 3 3W
South Foreland, *U.K.* **15** 51 7N 1 23 E
South Georgia, *Atl. Oc.* **102** 54 30S 37 0W
South Glamorgan □, *U.K.* **17** 51 30N 3 20W
South Hayling, *U.K.* **15** 50 47N 0 56W
South I., *N.Z.* **71** 44 0S 170 0 E
South Korea ■, *Asia* **61** 36 0N 128 0 E
South Molton, *U.K.* **16** 51 1N 3 50W
South Orkney Is., *Ant.* **103** 63 0S 45 0W
South Petherton, *U.K.* **14** 50 57N 2 49W
South Petherwin, *U.K.* **16** 50 35N 4 22W
South Platte →, *U.S.A.* **90** 41 7N 100 42W
South Pole, *Ant.* **103** 90 0S 0 0 E
South Ronaldsay, *U.K.* **23** 58 46N 2 58W
South Sandwich Is., *Ant.* **103** 57 0S 27 0W
South Shetland Is., *Ant.* **103** 62 0S 59 0W
South Shields, *U.K.* **19** 54 59N 1 26W
South Tawton, *U.K.* **16** 50 44N 3 55W
South Tyne →, *U.K.* **19** 54 46N 2 25W
South Uist, *U.K.* **22** 57 20N 7 15W
South West Africa = Namibia ■, *Africa* **81** 22 0S 18 9 E
South Woodham Ferrers, *U.K.* **15** 51 40N 0 37 E
South Yemen ■, *Asia* **56** 15 0N 48 0 E
South Yorkshire □, *U.K.* **19** 53 30N 1 20W
Southam, *U.K.* **14** 52 16N 1 24W
Southampton, *U.K.* **14** 50 54N 1 23W
Southampton I., *Canada* **89** 64 30N 84 0W
Southampton Water, *U.K.* **14** 50 52N 1 21W
Southborough, *U.K.* **15** 51 10N 0 15 E
Southend, *U.K.* **20** 55 18N 5 38W
Southend-on-Sea, *U.K.* **15** 51 32N 0 42 E
Southern Alps, *N.Z.* **71** 43 41S 170 11 E
Southern Ocean **103** 62 0S 60 0 E
Southern Uplands, *U.K.* **21** 55 30N 3 3W
Southery, *U.K.* **15** 52 32N 0 23 E
Southland □, *N.Z.* **71** 45 51S 168 13 E
Southminster, *U.K.* **15** 51 40N 0 51 E
Southport, *U.K.* **18** 53 38N 3 1W
Southwark, *U.K.* **15** 51 29N 0 5W
Southwell, *U.K.* **19** 53 4N 0 57W
Southwick, *U.K.* **15** 50 50N 0 14W
Southwold, *U.K.* **15** 52 19N 1 41 E
Sovetskaya Gavan, *U.S.S.R.* **49** 48 50N 140 0 E
Soviet Union ■ = Union of Soviet Socialist Republics ■, *Eurasia* **48** 60 0N 100 0 E
Sowerby, *U.K.* **19** 54 13N 1 19W
Soweto, *S. Afr.* **81** 26 14S 27 54 E
Spain ■, *Europe* **37** 40 0N 5 0W
Spalding, *U.K.* **15** 52 47N 0 9W
Spanish Town, *Jam.* **94** 18 0N 76 57W
Sparkford, *U.K.* **14** 51 2N 2 33W
Spean Bridge, *U.K.* **22** 56 53N 4 55W
Speke, *U.K.* **18** 53 21N 2 51W
Spelve, L., *U.K.* **20** 56 22N 5 45W
Spencer G., *Austral.* **67** 34 0S 137 20 E
Spennymoor, *U.K.* **19** 54 43N 1 35W
Sperrin Mts., *U.K.* **24** 54 50N 7 0W
Spey →, *U.K.* **23** 57 26N 3 25W
Spézia, La, *It.* **40** 44 8N 9 50 E
Spilsby, *U.K.* **19** 53 10N 0 6 E
Spithead, *U.K.* **15** 50 43N 1 5W
Spitzbergen = Svalbard, *Arctic* **103** 78 0N 17 0 E
Split, *Yug.* **40** 43 31N 16 26 E
Spofforth, *U.K.* **19** 53 57N 1 28W
Spokane, *U.S.A.* **90** 47 45N 117 25W
Springfield, *Ill., U.S.A.* **92** 39 48N 89 40W
Springfield, *Mass., U.S.A.* **93** 42 8N 72 37W
Springfield, *Mo., U.S.A.* **91** 37 15N 93 20W
Springfield, *Ohio, U.S.A.* **92** 39 58N 83 48W
Sproatley, *U.K.* **19** 53 46N 0 9W
Spurn Hd., *U.K.* **19** 53 34N 0 8 E
Sredinnyy Ra., *U.S.S.R.* **49** 57 0N 160 0 E
Srednekolymsk, *U.S.S.R.* **49** 67 27N 153 40 E
Sri Lanka ■, *Asia* **58** 7 30N 80 50 E
Srinagar, *India* **58** 34 5N 74 50 E

Staffa, U.K. 20 56 26N 6 21W
Stafford, U.K. 14 52 49N 2 9W
Stafford □, U.K. 14 52 53N 2 10W
Staindrop, U.K. 19 54 35N 1 49W
Staines, U.K. 15 51 26N 0 30W
Stainforth, U.K. 19 53 37N 0 59W
Stainmore For., U.K. 18 54 29N 2 5W
Stainton, U.K. 19 53 17N 0 23W
Staithes, U.K. 19 54 33N 0 47W
Stalbridge, U.K. 14 50 57N 2 22W
Stalham, U.K. 15 52 46N 1 31 E
Stalingrad = Volgograd, U.S.S.R. 47 48 40N 44 25 E
Stallingborough, U.K. 19 53 36N 0 11W
Stalybridge, U.K. 18 53 29N 2 4W
Stamford, U.K. 15 52 39N 0 29W
Stamford, U.S.A. 93 41 5N 73 30W
Stamford Bridge, U.K. 19 53 59N 0 53W
Stamfordham, U.K. 21 55 3N 1 53W
Standish, U.K. 18 53 35N 2 39W
Standon, U.K. 15 51 53N 0 2 E
Stanford on Teme, U.K. 14 52 17N 2 26W
Stanhope, U.K. 18 54 45N 2 0W
Stanley, Falk. 102 51 40S 59 51W
Stanley, Durham, U.K. 19 54 53N 1 42W
Stanley, Tayside, U.K. 21 56 29N 3 28W
Stannington, U.K. 21 55 7N 1 41W
Stanovoy Ra., U.S.S.R. 49 55 0N 130 0 E
Stansted Mountfitchet, U.K. 15 51 54N 0 13 E
Stanwix, U.K. 18 54 54N 2 56W
Stapleford, U.K. 19 52 56N 1 16W
Staplehurst, U.K. 15 51 9N 0 35 E
Stara Zagora, Bulg. 41 42 26N 25 39 E
Start Bay, U.K. 16 50 15N 3 35W
Start Pt., U.K. 16 50 13N 3 38W
Staunton, U.K. 14 51 58N 2 19W
Stavanger, Nor. 45 58 57N 5 40 E
Staveley, Cumbria, U.K. 18 54 24N 2 49W
Staveley, Derby, U.K. 19 53 16N 1 20W
Stavropol, U.S.S.R. 47 45 5N 42 0 E
Stenhousemuir, U.K. 21 56 2N 3 46W
Sterlitamak, U.S.S.R. 46 53 40N 56 0 E
Stevenage, U.K. 15 51 54N 0 11W
Stevenston, U.K. 20 55 38N 4 46W
Stewart I., N.Z. 71 46 58S 167 54 E
Stewarton, U.K. 20 55 40N 4 30W
Steyning, U.K. 15 50 54N 0 19W
Stillington, U.K. 19 54 7N 1 5W
Stinchar →, U.K. 20 55 10N 4 50W
Stiperstones Mt., U.K. 14 52 36N 2 57W
Stirling, U.K. 21 56 7N 3 57W
Stobo, U.K. 21 55 38N 3 18W
Stockbridge, U.K. 14 51 7N 1 30W
Stockholm, Swed. 45 59 20N 18 3 E
Stockport, U.K. 18 53 25N 2 11W
Stocksbridge, U.K. 19 53 30N 1 36W
Stockton, U.S.A. 90 38 0N 121 20W
Stockton-on-Tees, U.K. 19 54 34N 1 20W
Stoke, U.K. 15 51 26N 0 41 E
Stoke Ferry, U.K. 15 52 34N 0 31 E
Stoke Fleming, U.K. 16 50 19N 3 36W
Stoke Mandeville, U.K. 15 51 46N 0 47W
Stoke-on-Trent, U.K. 18 53 1N 2 11W
Stoke Prior, U.K. 14 52 18N 2 5W
Stokenham, U.K. 16 50 15N 3 40W
Stokesley, U.K. 19 54 27N 1 12W
Stone, Bucks., U.K. 15 51 48N 0 52W
Stone, Staffs., U.K. 18 52 55N 2 10W
Stonehaven, U.K. 23 56 58N 2 11W
Stonehouse, Gloucs., U.K. 14 51 45N 2 18W
Stonehouse, Strathclyde, U.K. 21 55 42N 4 0W
Stonham Aspall, U.K. 15 52 11N 1 7 E
Stony Stratford, U.K. 15 52 4N 0 51W
Storm B., Austral. 67 43 10S 147 30 E
Stornoway, U.K. 22 58 12N 6 23W
Stort →, U.K. 15 51 50N 0 7 E
Stotfold, U.K. 15 52 2N 0 13W
Stour →, Dorset, U.K. 14 50 48N 2 7W
Stour →, Hereford & Worcs., U.K. 14 52 25N 2 13W
Stour →, Kent, U.K. 15 51 15N 1 20 E
Stour →, Suffolk, U.K. 15 51 55N 1 5 E
Stourbridge, U.K. 14 52 28N 2 8W
Stourport, U.K. 14 52 21N 2 18W
Stow, U.K. 21 55 41N 2 50W
Stow Bardolph, U.K. 15 52 38N 0 24 E
Stow-on-the-Wold, U.K. 14 51 55N 1 42W
Stowmarket, U.K. 15 52 11N 1 0 E
Strabane, U.K. 24 54 50N 7 28W
Strabane □, U.K. 24 54 45N 7 25W
Strachur, U.K. 20 56 10N 5 5W
Stradbroke, U.K. 15 52 19N 1 16 E
Stralsund, E. Ger. 42 54 17N 13 5 E
Strangford, L., U.K. 24 54 30N 5 37W
Stranraer, U.K. 20 54 54N 5 0W
Strasbourg, Fr. 34 48 35N 7 42 E
Stratford-on-Avon, U.K. 14 52 12N 1 42W
Stratford St. Mary, U.K. 15 51 58N 0 59 E
Strath Earn, U.K. 21 56 20N 3 50W
Strath Spey, U.K. 23 57 15N 3 40W
Strathaven, U.K. 21 55 40N 4 4W
Strathclyde □, U.K. 20 56 0N 4 50W
Strathmore, U.K. 23 56 40N 3 4W
Strathpeffer, U.K. 23 57 35N 4 32W
Strathy Pt., U.K. 23 58 35N 4 0W
Strathyre, U.K. 20 56 14N 4 20W
Stratmiglo, U.K. 21 56 16N 3 15W
Stratton, Cornwall, U.K. 16 50 49N 4 31W
Stratton, Wilts., U.K. 14 51 41N 1 45W
Stratton St. Margaret, U.K. 14 51 35N 1 45W
Streatley, U.K. 14 51 31N 1 9W
Street, U.K. 14 51 7N 2 43W
Strensall, U.K. 19 54 3N 1 2W
Stretford, U.K. 18 53 27N 2 19W
Stretton, U.K. 18 53 21N 2 34W
Strichen, U.K. 23 57 35N 2 5W
Striven, L., U.K. 20 55 58N 5 9W
Stromeferry, U.K. 22 57 20N 5 33W
Stromness, U.K. 23 58 58N 3 18W
Stronachlachar, U.K. 20 56 15N 4 35W
Strone, U.K. 20 55 59N 4 54W
Stronsay, U.K. 23 59 8N 2 38W
Stroud, U.K. 14 51 44N 2 12W
Studland, U.K. 14 50 39N 1 58W
Studley, U.K. 14 52 16N 1 54W
Sturminster Marshall, U.K. 14 50 48N 2 4W
Sturminster Newton, U.K. 14 50 56N 2 18W
Sturt Cr. →, Austral. 66 20 8S 127 24 E
Sturton, U.K. 19 53 22N 0 39W
Stuttgart, W. Ger. 42 48 46N 9 10 E
Subotica, Yug. 41 46 6N 19 49 E
Suck →, Ire. 25 53 17N 8 18W
Sucre, Bol. 100 19 0S 65 15W
Sudan ■, Africa 78 15 0N 30 0 E
Sudbury, Canada 92 46 30N 81 0W
Sudbury, Derby, U.K. 19 52 53N 1 43W
Sudbury, Suffolk, U.K. 15 52 2N 0 44 E
Suez, Egypt 79 29 58N 32 31 E
Suffolk □, U.K. 15 52 16N 1 0 E
Suir →, Ire. 25 52 15N 7 10W
Sukkur, Pak. 58 27 42N 68 54 E
Sulawesi □, Indon. 63 2 0S 120 0 E
Sulby, U.K. 18 54 18N 4 29W
Sullom Voe, U.K. 22 60 30N 1 20W
Sulu Sea, E. Ind. 63 8 0N 120 0 E
Sumatra □, Indon. 63 0 40N 100 20 E
Sumbawa, Indon. 63 8 26S 117 30 E
Sumburgh Hd., U.K. 22 59 52N 1 17W
Summer Is., U.K. 22 58 0N 5 27W
Sumy, U.S.S.R. 47 50 57N 34 50 E
Sunart, L., U.K. 22 56 42N 5 43W
Sunda Str., Indon. 63 6 20S 105 30 E
Sundarbans, The, Asia 59 22 0N 89 0 E
Sunderland, U.K. 19 54 54N 1 22W
Sundsvall, Swed. 44 62 23N 17 17 E
Sunk Island, U.K. 19 53 38N 0 7W
Sunninghill, U.K. 15 51 25N 0 40W
Sunshine, Austral. 70 37 48S 144 52 E
Superior, L., N. Am. 92 47 40N 87 0W
Sūr, Leb. 57 33 19N 35 16 E
Surabaya, Indon. 63 7 17S 112 45 E
Surakarta, Indon. 63 7 35S 110 48 E
Surat, India 58 21 12N 72 55 E
Surgut, U.S.S.R. 48 61 14N 73 20 E
Surinam ■, S. Am. 101 4 0N 56 0W
Surrey □, U.K. 15 51 16N 0 30W
Surtsey, Ice. 44 63 20N 20 30W
Sutlej →, Pak. 58 29 23N 71 3 E
Sutterton, U.K. 19 52 54N 0 8W
Sutton, U.K. 15 51 22N 0 13W
Sutton Bridge, U.K. 15 52 46N 0 12 E
Sutton Coldfield, U.K. 14 52 33N 1 50W
Sutton Courtenay, U.K. 14 51 39N 1 16W
Sutton-in-Ashfield, U.K. 19 53 7N 1 20W
Sutton-on-Sea, U.K. 19 53 18N 0 18 E
Sutton Scotney, U.K. 14 51 9N 1 20W
Suva, Fiji 64 18 6S 178 30 E
Suzhou, China 61 31 19N 120 38 E
Svalbard, Arctic 103 78 0N 17 0 E
Svendborg, Den. 45 55 4N 10 35 E
Sverdlovsk, U.S.S.R. 46 56 50N 60 30 E
Sverdrup Is., Canada 103 79 0N 97 0W
Swadlincote, U.K. 14 52 47N 1 34W
Swaffham, U.K. 15 52 38N 0 42 E
Swale →, U.K. 19 54 5N 1 20W
Swan Hill, Austral. 70 35 20S 143 33 E
Swanage, U.K. 14 50 36N 1 59W
Swansea, U.K. 17 51 37N 3 57W
Swaziland ■, Africa 81 26 30S 31 30 E
Sweden ■, Europe 44 57 0N 15 0 E
Swift Current, Canada 88 50 20N 107 45W
Swilly, L., Ire. 24 55 12N 7 35W
Swindon, U.K. 15 51 33N 1 47W
Swineshead, U.K. 19 52 56N 0 11W
Swinton, Borders, U.K. 21 55 43N 2 14W
Swinton, Gr. Manchester, U.K. 18 53 31N 2 21W
Swinton, S. Yorks., U.K. 19 53 28N 1 20W
Switzerland ■, Europe 42 46 30N 8 0 E
Swords, Ire. 24 53 27N 6 15W
Sydney, Austral. 70 33 53S 151 10 E
Sydney, Canada 93 46 7N 60 7W
Syktyvkar, U.S.S.R. 46 61 45N 50 40 E
Symington, U.K. 21 55 35N 3 36W
Symonds Yat, U.K. 14 51 50N 2 38W
Syracuse, U.S.A. 93 43 4N 76 11W
Syrdarya →, U.S.S.R. 48 46 3N 61 0 E
Syria ■, Asia 56 35 0N 38 0 E
Syrian Desert, Asia 56 31 0N 40 0 E
Syston, U.K. 14 52 42N 1 5W
Syzran, U.S.S.R. 46 53 12N 48 30 E
Szczecin, Pol. 42 53 27N 14 27 E
Szeged, Hung. 43 46 16N 20 10 E
Székesfehérvár, Hung. 43 47 15N 18 25 E

T

Tabora, Tanz. 80 5 2S 32 50 E
Tabrīz, Iran 56 38 7N 46 20 E
Tabūk, Si. Arab. 56 28 23N 36 36 E
Tacna, Peru 100 18 0S 70 20W
Tacoma, U.S.A. 90 47 15N 122 30W
Tacuarembó, Urug. 102 31 45S 56 0W
Tadcaster, U.K. 19 53 53N 1 16W
Tadley, U.K. 14 51 21N 1 8W
Tadzhikistan □, U.S.S.R. 48 35 30N 70 0 E
Taegu, S. Kor. 61 35 50N 128 37 E
Taejŏn, S. Kor. 61 36 20N 127 28 E
Taganrog, U.S.S.R. 47 47 12N 38 50 E
Tagus = Tajo →, Sp. 37 38 40N 9 24W
Tahiti, Pac. Oc. 65 17 37S 149 27W
Taichung, Taiwan 61 24 10N 120 35 E
Taimyr Pen., U.S.S.R. 49 75 0N 100 0 E
Tain, U.K. 23 57 49N 4 4W
Tainan, Taiwan 61 23 17N 120 18 E
Taipei, Taiwan 61 25 2N 121 30 E
Taiwan ■, Asia 61 23 30N 121 0 E
Taiyuan, China 61 37 52N 112 33 E
Ta'izz, Yem. 56 13 35N 44 2 E
Tajo →, Sp. 37 38 40N 9 24W
Tak, Thai. 59 16 52N 99 8 E
Takamatsu, Jap. 62 34 20N 134 5 E
Takaoka, Jap. 62 36 47N 137 0 E
Takapuna, N.Z. 71 36 47S 174 47 E
Takasaki, Jap. 62 36 20N 139 0 E
Takeley, U.K. 15 51 52N 0 16 E
Takla Makan, China 60 39 0N 83 0 E
Talca, Chile 102 35 28S 71 40W
Talcahuano, Chile 102 36 40S 73 10W
Talgarth, U.K. 17 51 59N 3 15W
Tallahassee, U.S.A. 91 30 25N 84 15W
Tallinn, U.S.S.R. 46 59 22N 24 48 E
Tamar →, U.K. 16 50 33N 4 15W
Tambov, U.S.S.R. 46 52 45N 41 28 E
Tame →, U.K. 14 52 43N 1 45W
Tamerton Foliot, U.K. 16 50 25N 4 10W
Tamil Nadu □, India 58 11 0N 77 0 E
Tampa, U.S.A. 91 27 57N 82 38W
Tampere, Fin. 44 61 30N 23 50 E
Tampico, Mex. 94 22 20N 97 50W
Tamworth, Austral. 67 31 7S 150 58 E
Tamworth, U.K. 14 52 38N 1 41W
Tana, L., Eth. 79 13 5N 37 30 E
Tanami Desert, Austral. 66 18 50S 132 0 E
Tandragee, U.K. 24 54 22N 6 23W
Tanga, Tanz. 80 5 5S 39 2 E
Tanganyika, L., E. Afr. 80 6 40S 30 0 E
Tangier, Mor. 78 35 50N 5 49W
Tangshan, China 61 39 38N 118 10 E
Tanworth, U.K. 14 52 20N 1 50W
Tanzania ■, E. Afr. 80 6 40S 34 0 E
Tapajós →, Brazil 101 2 24S 54 41W
Tarābulus, Leb. 56 34 31N 35 50 E
Tarābulus, Libya 79 32 49N 13 7 E
Taranaki □, N.Z. 71 39 5S 174 51 E
Táranto, It. 40 40 30N 17 11 E
Táranto, G. di, It. 40 40 0N 17 15 E
Tarbat Ness, U.K. 23 57 52N 3 48W
Tarbert, Strathclyde, U.K. 20 55 55N 5 25W
Tarbert, W. Isles, U.K. 22 57 54N 6 49W
Tarbes, Fr. 35 43 15N 0 3 E
Tarbet, U.K. 20 56 13N 4 44W
Tarbolton, U.K. 20 55 30N 4 30W
Taree, Austral. 70 31 50S 152 30 E
Tarija, Bol. 100 21 30S 64 40W
Tarim Basin, China 60 40 0N 84 0 E
Tarleton, U.K. 18 53 41N 2 50W
Tarnów, Pol. 43 50 3N 21 0 E
Tarporley, U.K. 18 53 10N 2 42W
Tarragona, Sp. 37 41 5N 1 17 E
Tarrasa, Sp. 37 41 34N 2 1 E
Tashkent, U.S.S.R. 48 41 20N 69 10 E
Tasman B., N.Z. 71 40 59S 173 25 E
Tasman Sea, Pac. Oc. 71 36 0S 160 0 E
Tasmania □, Austral. 67 42 0S 146 30 E
Tatar A.S.S.R. □, U.S.S.R. 46 55 30N 51 30 E
Tattenhall, U.K. 18 53 7N 2 47W
Taunton, U.K. 14 51 1N 3 7W
Taupo, N.Z. 71 38 41S 176 7 E
Taupo, L., N.Z. 71 38 46S 175 55 E
Tauranga, N.Z. 71 37 42S 176 11 E
Taurus Mts., Turk. 47 37 0N 35 0 E
Tavistock, U.K. 16 50 33N 4 9W
Tavoy, Burma 59 14 2N 98 12 E
Taw →, U.K. 16 17 37S 177 55 E
Tay →, U.K. 21 56 37N 3 38W
Tay, Firth of, U.K. 21 56 25N 3 8W
Tay, L., U.K. 21 56 30N 4 10W
Tay Bridge, U.K. 21 56 28N 3 0W
Taynuilt, U.K. 20 56 25N 5 15W
Tayport, U.K. 21 56 27N 2 52W
Tayside □, U.K. 21 56 25N 3 30W
Tbilisi, U.S.S.R. 47 41 43N 44 50 E
Te Anau, L., N.Z. 71 45 15S 167 45 E
Te Aroha, N.Z. 71 37 32S 175 44 E
Tebay, U.K. 18 54 25N 2 35W
Tees →, U.K. 19 54 36N 1 25W
Teesdale, U.K. 18 54 37N 2 10W
Teesside, U.K. 19 54 37N 1 13W
Tegid, L., U.K. 17 52 53N 3 38W
Tegucigalpa, Hond. 94 14 5N 87 14W
Tehrān, Iran 56 35 44N 51 30 E
Tehuantepec, Gulf of, Mex. 94 15 50N 95 0W
Tehuantepec, Isthmus of, Mex. 94 17 0N 94 30W
Teifi →, U.K. 17 52 4N 4 14W
Teign →, U.K. 16 50 41N 3 42W
Teignmouth, U.K. 16 50 33N 3 30W
Tejo →, Port. 37 38 40N 9 24W
Tel Aviv-Jaffa, Isr. 57 32 4N 34 48 E
Telemark fylke □, Nor. 45 59 25N 8 30 E
Telford, U.K. 14 52 42N 2 31W
Teluk Betung, Indon. 63 5 20S 105 10 E
Tema, Ghana 78 5 41N 0 0 E
Teme →, U.K. 14 52 23N 2 15W
Temirtau, U.S.S.R. 48 50 5N 72 56 E
Temora, Austral. 70 34 30S 147 30 E
Temple Combe, U.K. 14 51 0N 2 25W
Temple Ewell, U.K. 15 51 9N 1 15 E
Temple Sowerby, U.K. 18 54 38N 2 33W
Templemore, Ire. 25 52 48N 7 50W
Tenbury, U.K. 14 52 18N 2 35W
Tenby, U.K. 17 51 40N 4 42W
Tenerife, Can. Is. 78 28 15N 16 35W
Tennessee □, U.S.A. 91 36 0N 86 30W
Tennessee →, U.S.A. 91 37 4N 88 34W
Tenterden, U.K. 15 51 4N 0 42 E
Teófilo Otoni, Brazil 101 17 50S 41 30W
Tepic, Mex. 94 21 30N 104 54W
Téramo, It. 40 42 40N 13 40 E
Teresina, Brazil 101 5 9S 42 45W
Terni, It. 40 42 34N 12 38 E
Terre Haute, U.S.A. 92 39 28N 87 24W
Teruel, Sp. 37 40 22N 1 8W
Test →, U.K. 14 51 7N 1 30W
Tetbury, U.K. 14 51 37N 2 9W
Tetlin, U.S.A. 88 63 14N 142 50W
Tetney, U.K. 19 53 30N 0 1W
Tétouan, Mor. 78 35 35N 5 21W
Tetovo, Yug. 41 42 1N 21 2 E
Tettenhall, U.K. 14 52 35N 2 7W
Teviot →, U.K. 21 55 21N 2 51W
Teviotdale, U.K. 21 55 25N 2 50W
Teviothead, U.K. 21 55 19N 2 55W
Tewkesbury, U.K. 14 51 59N 2 8W
Texas □, U.S.A. 90 31 40N 98 30W
Texel, Neth. 36 53 5N 4 50 E
Teynham, U.K. 15 51 19N 0 50 E
Thailand ■, Asia 63 16 0N 102 0 E
Thailand, G. of, Asia 63 11 30N 101 0 E
Thal Desert, Pak. 58 31 10N 71 30 E
Thame, U.K. 15 51 44N 0 58W
Thame →, U.K. 15 51 35N 1 8W
Thames →, U.K. 15 51 30N 0 35 E
Thanet, I. of, U.K. 15 51 21N 1 20 E
Thar Desert, India 58 28 0N 72 0 E
Thatcham, U.K. 14 51 24N 1 17W
Thaxted, U.K. 15 51 57N 0 20 E
The Entrance, Austral. 70 33 21S 151 30 E
The Grenadines, Is., W. Ind. 94 12 40N 61 20W
The Hague, Neth. 36 52 7N 4 17 E
The Pas, Canada 88 53 45N 101 15W
Theale, U.K. 14 51 26N 1 5W
Thessaloníki, Greece 41 40 38N 22 58 E
Thessaloníki, Gulf of, Greece 41 40 15N 22 45 E
Thessaly □, Greece 41 39 30N 22 0 E
Thetford, U.K. 15 52 25N 0 44 E
Thies, Sene. 78 14 50N 16 51W
Thimphu, Bhutan 59 27 31N 89 45 E
Thionville, Fr. 34 49 20N 6 10 E
Thirlmere, L., U.K. 18 54 32N 3 4W
Thirsk, U.K. 19 54 15N 1 20W
Thirston, U.K. 21 55 20N 1 34W
Thisted, Den. 45 56 58N 8 40 E
Thompson →, Canada 88 50 15N 121 24W
Thornaby on Tees, U.K. 19 54 36N 1 19W
Thornbury, U.K. 14 51 36N 2 31W
Thorndon, U.K. 15 52 16N 1 8 E
Thorne, U.K. 19 53 36N 0 56W
Thorney, U.K. 15 52 37N 0 8W
Thornham, U.K. 15 52 59N 0 35 E
Thornhill, U.K. 21 55 15N 3 46W
Thornthwaite, U.K. 18 54 36N 3 13W
Thornton, U.K. 18 53 52N 3 1W
Thornton Dale, U.K. 19 54 14N 0 41W
Thorpe, U.K. 15 52 38N 1 20 E
Thorpe le Soken, U.K. 15 51 50N 1 11 E
Thrace □, Greece 41 41 9N 25 30 E
Thrapston, U.K. 15 52 24N 0 32W
Threlkeld, U.K. 18 54 37N 3 2W
Threshfield, U.K. 18 54 5N 2 2W
Thule, Green. 103 77 40N 69 0W
Thunder Bay, Canada 92 48 20N 89 15W
Thurlby, U.K. 15 52 45N 0 21W
Thurles, Ire. 25 52 40N 7 53W
Thurmaston, U.K. 14 52 40N 1 8W
Thursby, U.K. 18 54 40N 3 3W
Thurso, U.K. 23 58 34N 3 31W
Tian Shan, China 60 43 0N 84 0 E
Tianshui, China 60 34 32N 105 40 E
Tiber →, It. 40 41 44N 12 14 E
Tiberias, Isr. 57 32 47N 35 32 E
Tibesti, Chad 79 21 0N 17 30 E
Ticehurst, U.K. 15 51 2N 0 23 E
Tickhill, U.K. 19 53 25N 1 8W
Tideswell, U.K. 19 53 17N 1 46W
Tientsin, China 61 39 10N 117 15 E
Tierra del Fuego □, Arg. 102 54 0S 67 45W
Tighnabruaich, U.K. 20 55 55N 5 13W
Tigris →, Iraq 56 37 0N 42 30 E

Tijuana, *Mex.* **94** 32 30N 117 10W
Tiksi, *U.S.S.R.* . . . . **49** 71 40N 128 45 E
Tilburg, *Neth.* . . . . **36** 51 31N 5 6 E
Tilbury, *U.K.* . . . . **15** 51 27N 0 24 E
Till →, *U.K.* **19** 55 35N 2 3W
Tillicoultry, *U.K.* **21** 56 9N 3 44W
Tilmanstone, *U.K.* . . . . . **15** 51 13N 1 18 E
Tilt →, *U.K.* **23** 56 50N 3 50W
Timaru, *N.Z.* . . . . **71** 44 23S 171 14 E
Timbuktu =
Tombouctou, *Mali* . . **78** 16 50N 3 0W
Timişoara, *Rom.* . . . . . **43** 45 43N 21 15 E
Timmins, *Canada* **92** 48 28N 81 25W
Timor, *Indon.* . . . . **63** 9 0S 125 0 E
Timor Sea, *E. Ind.* . . . . **66** 10 0S 127 0 E
Tingewick, *U.K.* **14** 51 59N 1 4W
Tintagel, *U.K.* **16** 50 40N 4 45W
Tintagel Hd., *U.K.* **16** 50 40N 4 46W
Tipperary, *Ire.* **25** 52 28N 8 10W
Tipperary □, *Ire.* **25** 52 37N 7 55W
Tipton, *U.K.* **14** 52 32N 2 4W
Tiptree, *U.K.* . . . . **15** 51 48N 0 46 E
Tiranë, *Alb.* . . . . **41** 41 18N 19 49 E
Tiree, *U.K.* **20** 56 31N 6 55W
Tiree, Passage of, *U.K.* **20** 56 30N 6 30W
Tîrgu Mureş, *Rom.* . . . **43** 46 31N 24 38 E
Tiruchchirappalli, *India* **58** 10 45N 78 45 E
Tisbury, *U.K.* **14** 51 4N 2 4W
Tisza →, *Hung.* . . . . . **43** 46 8N 20 2 E
Titchfield, *U.K.* **14** 50 51N 1 13W
Titicaca, L., *Peru* **100** 15 30S 69 30W
Titograd, *Yug.* . . . . **41** 42 30N 19 19 E
Tiverton, *U.K.* **16** 50 54N 3 30W
Tizi-Ouzou, *Alg.* . . . . . . **78** 36 42N 4 3 E
Toamasina, *Madag.* . . **81** 18 10S 49 25 E
Tobago, *W. Ind.* **94** 11 10N 60 30W
Tobermory, *U.K.* **20** 56 37N 6 4W
Tobol →, *U.S.S.R.* . . . **48** 58 10N 68 12 E
Tocantins →, *Brazil* . **101** 1 45S 49 10W
Toddington, *U.K.* **15** 51 57N 0 31W
Todmorden, *U.K.* **18** 53 43N 2 7W
Togliatti, *U.S.S.R.* . . . . **46** 53 32N 49 24 E
Togo ■, *W. Afr.* . . . . . . **78** 6 15N 1 35 E
Tokelau Is., *Pac. Oc.* . **64** 9 0S 171 45W
Tōkyō, *Jap.* . . . . **62** 35 45N 139 45 E
Tolageak, *U.S.A.* **88** 70 2N 162 50W
Tolbukhin, *Bulg.* . . . . . . **41** 43 37N 27 49 E
Toledo, *Sp.* **37** 39 50N 4 2W
Toledo, *U.S.A.* **92** 41 37N 83 33W
Toliara, *Madag.* . . . . . . **81** 23 21S 43 40 E
Tollesbury, *U.K.* . . . . . . **15** 51 46N 0 51 E
Toluca, *Mex.* **94** 19 20N 99 40W
Tom Price, *Austral.* . . . . **66** 22 40S 117 48 E
Tombouctou, *Mali* **78** 16 50N 3 0W
Tomnavoulin, *U.K.* **23** 57 19N 3 18W
Tomsk, *U.S.S.R.* . . . . . . **48** 56 30N 85 5 E
Tonbridge, *U.K.* . . . . . . **15** 51 12N 0 18 E
Tone →, *U.K.* **16** 50 59N 3 15W
Tong, *U.K.* **14** 52 39N 2 18W
Tonga ■, *Pac. Oc.* . . . **64** 19 50S 174 30W
Tonga Trench, *Pac. Oc.* **64** 18 0S 175 0W
Tongue, *U.K.* **23** 58 29N 4 25W
Tonkin, G. of, *Asia* . . . **60** 20 0N 108 0 E
Toowoomba, *Austral.* . . **67** 27 32S 151 56 E
Topeka, *U.S.A.* **91** 39 3N 95 40W
Topsham, *U.K.* **16** 50 40N 3 27W
Tor Bay, *U.K.* **16** 50 26N 3 31W
Torbay, *U.K.* **16** 50 26N 3 31W
Torne älv →, *Swed.* . . **44** 65 50N 24 12 E
Toronto, *Canada* **92** 43 39N 79 20W
Torpoint, *U.K.* **16** 50 23N 4 12W
Torquay, *U.K.* **16** 50 27N 3 31W
Torran Rocks, *U.K.* **20** 56 14N 6 24W
Torrens, L., *Austral.* . . **67** 31 0S 137 50 E
Torreón, *Mex.* **94** 25 33N 103 26W
Torridge →, *U.K.* **16** 50 51N 4 10W
Torridon, L., *U.K.* **22** 57 35N 5 50W
Torthorwald, *U.K.* **21** 55 7N 3 30W
Tortosa, *Sp.* . . . . **37** 40 49N 0 31 E
Toruń, *Pol.* . . . . **43** 53 0N 18 39 E
Torver, *U.K.* **18** 54 20N 3 7W
Tory I., *Ire.* **24** 55 17N 8 12W
Totland, *U.K.* **14** 50 41N 1 32W
Totley, *U.K.* **19** 53 18N 1 32W
Totnes, *U.K.* **16** 50 26N 3 41W
Totton, *U.K.* **14** 50 55N 1 29W
Toulon, *Fr.* . . . . **35** 43 10N 5 55 E
Toulouse, *Fr.* . . . . **35** 43 37N 1 27 E
Tournai, *Belg.* . . . . **36** 50 35N 3 25 E
Tours, *Fr.* . . . . **34** 47 22N 0 40 E
Towcester, *U.K.* **15** 52 7N 0 56W
Town Yetholm, *U.K.* . . . **21** 55 33N 2 19W
Townsville, *Austral.* . . . **67** 19 15S 146 45 E
Toyama, *Jap.* . . . . **62** 36 40N 137 15 E
Toyohashi, *Jap.* . . . . . . **62** 34 45N 137 25 E
Trabzon, *Turk.* . . . . **47** 41 0N 39 45 E
Trail, *Canada* **88** 49 5N 117 40W
Tralee, *Ire.* **25** 52 16N 9 42W
Tralee B., *Ire.* **25** 52 17N 9 55W
Tramore, *Ire.* **25** 52 10N 7 10W
Tranent, *U.K.* **21** 55 57N 2 58W
Transcaucasia, *U.S.S.R.* **47** 42 0N 44 0 E
Transvaal □, *S. Afr.* . . **81** 25 0S 29 0 E
Transylvanian Alps,
Rom. . . . . **43** 45 30N 25 0 E
Trápani, *It.* . . . . **40** 38 1N 12 30 E
Traralgon, *Austral.* . . . . **70** 38 12S 146 34 E
Trawsfynydd, *U.K.* **17** 52 54N 3 55W
Tredegar, *U.K.* **17** 51 47N 3 16W
Tregaron, *U.K.* **17** 52 14N 3 56W
Trent →, *U.K.* **19** 53 33N 0 44W
Trentham, *U.K.* **18** 52 59N 2 12W
Trentino-Alto Adige □,
It. . . . . **40** 46 30N 11 0 E
Trento, *It.* . . . . **40** 46 5N 11 8 E
Trenton, *U.S.A.* **93** 40 15N 74 41W
Tresco I., *U.K.* **16** 49 57N 6 20W
Treshnish Is., *U.K.* **20** 56 30N 6 25W
Trevose Hd., *U.K.* **16** 50 33N 5 3W
Trier, *W. Ger.* . . . . **36** 49 45N 6 37 E
Trieste, *It.* . . . . **40** 45 39N 13 45 E
Trim, *Ire.* **24** 53 34N 6 48W
Trimdon, *U.K.* **19** 54 43N 1 23W
Trimley, *U.K.* . . . . **15** 51 59N 1 19 E
Trincomalee, *Sri L.* . . . **58** 8 38N 81 15 E
Trinidad, *W. Ind.* **94** 10 30N 61 15W
Trinidad & Tobago ■,
W. Ind. **94** 10 30N 61 20W
Tripoli = Tarābulus,
Leb. . . . . **56** 34 31N 35 50 E
Tripoli = Tarābulus,
Libya . . . . **79** 32 49N 13 7 E
Tristan da Cunha,
Atl. Oc. **128** 37 6S 12 20W
Trivandrum, *India* . . . . **58** 8 41N 77 0 E
Trois-Riviéres, *Canada* **93** 46 25N 72 34W
Trollhättan, *Swed.* . . . . **45** 58 17N 12 20 E
Troms fylke □, *Nor.* . . **44** 68 56N 19 0 E
Tromsø, *Nor.* . . . . **44** 69 40N 18 56 E
Trondheim, *Nor.* . . . . . **44** 63 36N 10 25 E
Troon, *U.K.* **20** 55 33N 4 40W
Trossachs, The, *U.K.* . **20** 56 14N 4 24W
Trostan, *U.K.* **24** 55 4N 6 10W
Trotternish, *U.K.* **22** 57 32N 6 15W
Trowbridge, *U.K.* **14** 51 18N 2 12W
Troy, *U.S.A.* **93** 42 45N 73 39W
Troyes, *Fr.* . . . . **34** 48 19N 4 3 E
Trujillo, *Peru* **100** 8 6S 79 0W
Truk, *Pac. Oc.* . . . . **64** 7 25N 151 46 E
Trull, *U.K.* **14** 50 58N 3 8W
Trumpington, *U.K.* . . . . **15** 52 11N 0 6 E
Truro, *U.K.* **16** 50 17N 5 2W
Tselinograd, *U.S.S.R.* . **48** 51 10N 71 30 E
Tsimlyansk Res.,
U.S.S.R. . . . . **47** 48 0N 43 0 E
Tsu, *Jap.* . . . . **62** 34 45N 136 25 E
Tsugaru Str., *Jap.* . . . . **62** 41 30N 140 30 E
Tuam, *Ire.* **24** 53 30N 8 50W
Tuamotu Arch.,
Pac. Oc. **65** 17 0S 144 0W
Tuath, Loch, *U.K.* **20** 56 30N 6 15W
Tubuai Is., *Pac. Oc.* . . **65** 25 0S 150 0W
Tucson, *U.S.A.* **90** 32 14N 110 59W
Tula, *U.S.S.R.* . . . . **46** 54 13N 37 38 E
Tulcán, *Ecuad.* **100** 0 48N 77 43W
Tulla, L., *U.K.* **20** 56 33N 4 47W
Tullamore, *Ire.* **25** 53 17N 7 30W
Tullow, *Ire.* **25** 52 48N 6 45W
Tulsa, *U.S.A.* **91** 36 10N 96 0W
Tulua, *Col.* **100** 4 6N 76 11W
Tumaco, *Col.* **100** 1 50N 78 45W
Tummel, L., *U.K.* **23** 56 43N 3 55W
Tunbridge Wells, *U.K.* . **15** 51 7N 0 16 E
Tuncurry, *Austral.* . . . . **70** 32 17S 152 29 E
Tunis, *Tunisia* . . . . **78** 36 50N 10 11 E
Tunisia ■, *Africa* . . . . . **78** 33 30N 9 10 E
Tunja, *Col.* **100** 5 33N 73 25W
Tunstall, *U.K.* . . . . **15** 52 7N 1 28 E
Tura, *India* . . . . **59** 25 30N 90 16 E
Turfan Depression,
China . . . . **50** 42 40N 89 25 E
Turin, *It.* . . . . **40** 45 4N 7 40 E
Turkana, L., *Kenya* . . . **80** 3 30N 36 5 E
Turkey ■, *Eurasia* . . . . **47** 39 0N 36 0 E
Turkmenistan □,
U.S.S.R. . . . . **48** 39 0N 59 0 E
Turks Is., *W. Ind.* **95** 21 20N 71 20W
Turku, *Fin.* . . . . **45** 60 30N 22 19 E
Turnberry, *U.K.* **20** 55 19N 4 50W
Turnu-Severin, *Rom.* . . **43** 44 39N 22 41 E
Turriff, *U.K.* **23** 57 32N 2 28W
Tuskar Rock, *Ire.* **25** 52 12N 6 10W
Tutbury, *U.K.* **14** 52 52N 1 41W
Tuticorin, *India* . . . . . . **58** 8 50N 78 12 E
Tuvalu ■, *Pac. Oc.* . . . **64** 8 0S 178 0 E
Tuxford, *U.K.* **19** 53 14N 0 52W
Tuxtla Gutiérrez, *Mex.* **94** 16 50N 93 10W
Tuz Gölü, *Turk.* . . . . . . **47** 38 45N 33 30 E
Tuzla, *Yug.* . . . . **41** 44 34N 18 41 E
Twatt, *U.K.* **23** 59 6N 3 15W
Tweed →, *U.K.* **21** 55 42N 2 10W
Tweedmouth, *U.K.* **21** 55 46N 2 1W
Tweedshawe, *U.K.* **21** 55 26N 3 29W
Twenty, *U.K.* **15** 52 43N 0 20W
Twyford, *Berks., U.K.* . . **15** 51 29N 0 51W
Twyford, *Hants., U.K.* . . **14** 51 1N 1 19W
Tychy, *Pol.* . . . . **43** 50 9N 18 59 E
Tydd St. Mary, *U.K.* . . . **15** 52 45N 0 9 E
Tyldesley, *U.K.* **18** 53 31N 2 29W
Tyler, *U.S.A.* **90** 32 18N 95 18W
Tyndrum, *U.K.* **20** 56 26N 4 41W
Tyne →, *Tyne & Wear,*
U.K. **19** 54 58N 1 28W
Tyne →, *Lothian, U.K.* . **21** 55 58N 2 45W
Tyne & Wear □, *U.K.* . . **19** 54 55N 1 35W
Tynemouth, *U.K.* **19** 55 1N 1 27W
Tyre = Sūr, *Leb.* . . . . . . **57** 33 19N 35 16 E
Tyrol □, *Austria* . . . . . . **42** 47 3N 10 43 E
Tyrrhenian Sea, *Europe* **40** 40 0N 12 30 E
Tyumen, *U.S.S.R.* . . . . . **48** 57 11N 65 29 E
Tywardreath, *U.K.* **16** 50 21N 4 40W
Tywi →, *U.K.* **17** 51 48N 4 20W
Tywyn, *U.K.* **17** 52 36N 4 5W

U

Ube, *Jap.* . . . . **62** 33 56N 131 15 E
Uberaba, *Brazil* **101** 19 50S 47 55W
Uberlândia, *Brazil* **101** 19 0S 48 20W
Ucayali →, *Peru* **100** 4 30S 73 30W
Uckfield, *U.K.* . . . . **15** 50 58N 0 6 E
Udaipur, *India* . . . . **58** 24 36N 73 44 E
Uddevalla, *Swed.* . . . . . **45** 58 21N 11 55 E
Uddingston, *U.K.* **21** 55 50N 4 3W
Údine, *It.* . . . . **40** 46 5N 13 10 E
Ufa, *U.S.S.R.* . . . . **46** 54 45N 55 55 E
Uffculme, *U.K.* **16** 50 54N 3 19W
Ufford, *U.K.* . . . . **15** 52 6N 1 22 E
Uganda ■, *E. Afr.* . . . . **80** 2 0N 32 0 E
Ugborough, *U.K.* **16** 50 22N 3 53W
Uig, *U.K.* **22** 57 35N 6 20W
Uitenhage, *S. Afr.* . . . . **81** 33 40S 25 28 E
Ujung Pandang, *Indon.* **63** 5 10S 119 20 E
Ukraine □, *U.S.S.R.* . . **47** 49 0N 32 0 E
Ulan Bator, *Mong.* . . . . **60** 47 55N 106 53 E
Ulan Ude, *U.S.S.R.* . . . **49** 51 45N 107 40 E
Ulceby Cross, *U.K.* . . . **19** 53 14N 0 6 E
Ulhasnagar, *India* . . . . **58** 19 15N 73 10 E
Ullapool, *U.K.* **22** 57 54N 5 10W
Ullswater, *U.K.* **18** 54 35N 2 52W
Ulm, *W. Ger.* . . . . **42** 48 23N 10 0 E
Ulster □, *U.K.* **24** 54 35N 6 30W
Ulva, I., *U.K.* **20** 56 30N 6 12W
Ulverston, *U.K.* **18** 54 13N 3 7W
Ulyanovsk, *U.S.S.R.* . . . **46** 54 20N 48 25 E
Ulyasutay, *Mong.* . . . . . **60** 47 56N 97 28 E
Umbria □, *It.* . . . . **40** 42 53N 12 30 E
Umeå, *Swed.* . . . . **44** 63 45N 20 20 E
Umtata, *S. Afr.* . . . . **81** 31 36S 28 49 E
Ungava B., *Canada* . . . **89** 59 30N 67 30W
Ungava Pen., *Canada* . **89** 60 0N 74 0W
Union of Soviet
Socialist
Republics ■, *Eurasia* **48** 60 0N 100 0 E
United Arab
Emirates ■, *Asia* . . . **57** 23 50N 54 0 E
United Kingdom ■,
Europe **5** 55 0N 3 0W
United States of
America ■, *N. Am.* . . **90** 37 0N 96 0W
United States Trust
Terr. of the Pacific
Is. □, *Pac. Oc.* . . . . . **64** 10 0N 160 0 E
Unst, *U.K.* **22** 60 50N 0 55W
Upavon, *U.K.* **14** 51 17N 1 49W
Upington, *S. Afr.* . . . . . **81** 28 25S 21 15 E
Upper Heyford, *U.K.* . . . **14** 51 54N 1 16W
Upper L. Erne, *U.K.* . . . **24** 54 14N 7 22W
Upper Volta ■ =
Burkina Faso ■,
Africa **78** 12 0N 1 0W
Uppingham, *U.K.* **15** 52 36N 0 43W
Uppsala, *Swed.* . . . . . . **45** 59 53N 17 38 E
Upton, *U.K.* **18** 53 14N 2 52W
Upton-upon-Severn,
U.K. **14** 52 4N 2 12W
Upwey, *U.K.* **14** 50 40N 2 29W
Ural Mts., *U.S.S.R.* . . . . **46** 60 0N 59 0 E
Uralsk, *U.S.S.R.* . . . . . . **46** 51 20N 51 20 E
Uranium City, *Canada* . **88** 59 34N 108 37W
Ure →, *U.K.* **19** 54 20N 1 25W
Urgench, *U.S.S.R.* . . . . **48** 41 40N 60 41 E
Urmia, L., *Iran* . . . . **56** 37 50N 45 30 E
Urmston, *U.K.* **18** 53 28N 2 22W
Uruguay ■, *S. Am.* **102** 32 30S 56 30W
Uruguay →, *S. Am.* . . . **102** 34 12S 58 18W
Ürümqi, *China* . . . . **60** 43 45N 87 45 E
Usk →, *U.K.* **17** 51 37N 2 56W
Üsküdar, *Turk.* . . . . **47** 41 0N 29 5 E
Usselby, *U.K.* **19** 53 25N 0 21W
Ust-Kamenogorsk,
U.S.S.R. . . . . **48** 50 0N 82 36 E
Ust Urt Plateau,
U.S.S.R. . . . . **48** 44 0N 55 0 E
Ustinov, *U.S.S.R.* . . . . . **46** 56 51N 53 14 E
Utah □, *U.S.A.* **90** 39 30N 111 30W
Utica, *U.S.A.* **93** 43 5N 75 18W
Utrecht, *Neth.* . . . . **36** 52 5N 5 8 E
Utsunomiya, *Jap.* . . . . . **62** 36 30N 139 50 E
Uttar Pradesh □, *India* **58** 27 0N 80 0 E
Uttoxeter, *U.K.* **18** 52 53N 1 50W
Uzbekistan □, *U.S.S.R.* **48** 41 30N 65 0 E

V

Vaasa, *Fin.* . . . . **44** 63 6N 21 38 E
Vadodara, *India* . . . . . . **58** 22 20N 73 10 E
Vadsø, *Nor.* . . . . **44** 70 3N 29 50 E
Val d'Or, *Canada* **92** 48 7N 77 47W
Valdez, *U.S.A.* **88** 61 14N 146 17W
Valdivia, *Chile* **102** 39 50S 73 14W
Valence, *Fr.* . . . . **35** 44 57N 4 54 E
Valencia, *Sp.* **37** 39 27N 0 23W
Valencia, *Ven.* **100** 10 11N 68 0W
Valenciennes, *Fr.* . . . . . **34** 50 20N 3 34 E
Valentia Hr., *Ire.* **25** 51 56N 10 17W
Valentia I., *Ire.* **25** 51 54N 10 22W
Valladolid, *Sp.* **37** 41 38N 4 43W
Valledupar, *Col.* **100** 10 29N 73 15W
Valletta, *Malta* . . . . **40** 35 54N 14 30 E
Valley, *U.K.* **17** 53 17N 4 31W
Valparaíso, *Chile* **102** 33 2S 71 40W
Van, L., *Turk.* . . . . **47** 38 30N 43 0 E
Van Diemen G., *Austral.* **66** 11 45S 132 0 E
Vancouver, *Canada* . . . **88** 49 15N 123 10W
Vancouver I., *Canada* . **88** 49 50N 126 0W
Vänern, *Swed.* . . . . **45** 58 47N 13 30 E
Vanua Levu, *Fiji* . . . . . . **64** 16 33S 179 15 E
Vanuatu ■, *Pac. Oc.* . . **64** 15 0S 168 0 E
Varanasi, *India* . . . . **59** 25 22N 83 0 E
Varangar Fjord, *Nor.* . . **44** 70 3N 29 25 E
Vardar →, *Yug.* . . . . . **41** 40 35N 22 50 E
Värmlands län □, *Swed.* **45** 60 0N 13 20 E
Varna, *Bulg.* . . . . **41** 43 13N 27 56 E
Västerås, *Swed.* . . . . . . **45** 59 37N 16 38 E
Västmanlands län □,
Swed. . . . . **45** 59 45N 16 20 E
Vatnajökull, *Ice.* **44** 64 30N 16 48W
Vättern, *Swed.* . . . . **45** 58 25N 14 30 E
Växjö, *Swed.* . . . . **45** 56 52N 14 50 E
Vendée □, *Fr.* **34** 46 50N 1 35W
Venezuela ■, *S. Am.* . . **100** 8 0N 65 0W
Venice, *It.* . . . . **40** 45 27N 12 20 E
Venlo, *Neth.* . . . . **36** 51 22N 6 11 E
Ventnor, *U.K.* **14** 50 35N 1 12W
Veracruz, *Mex.* **94** 19 10N 96 10W
Vercelli, *It.* . . . . **40** 45 19N 8 25 E
Vereeniging, *S. Afr.* . . . **81** 26 38S 27 57 E
Verkhoyansk, *U.S.S.R.* **49** 67 35N 133 25 E
Verkhoyansk Ra.,
U.S.S.R. . . . . **49** 66 0N 129 0 E
Vermont □, *U.S.A.* . . . **93** 43 40N 72 50W
Verona, *It.* . . . . **40** 45 27N 11 0 E
Versailles, *Fr.* . . . . **34** 48 48N 2 8 E
Verviers, *Belg.* . . . . **36** 50 37N 5 52 E
Verwood, *U.K.* **14** 50 53N 1 53W
Veryan, *U.K.* **16** 50 13N 4 56W
Veryan Bay, *U.K.* **16** 50 12N 4 51W
Vestmannaeyjar, *Ice.* . . **44** 63 27N 20 15W
Vesuvius, Mt., *It.* . . . . . **40** 40 50N 14 22 E
Viborg, *Den.* . . . . **45** 56 27N 9 23 E
Vickerstown, *U.K.* **18** 54 8N 3 17W
Victoria, *Canada* **88** 48 30N 123 25W
Victoria □, *Austral.* . . . **70** 37 0S 144 0 E
Victoria →, *Austral.* . . **66** 15 10S 129 40 E
Victoria, L., *Austral.* . . . **70** 33 57S 141 15 E
Victoria, L., *E. Afr.* . . . . **80** 1 0S 33 0 E
Victoria Falls, *Zimb.* . . **81** 17 58S 25 52 E
Victoria I., *Canada* . . . **88** 71 0N 111 0W
Victoria Ld., *Ant.* . . . . . **103** 75 0S 160 0 E
Vienna, *Austria* . . . . . . **42** 48 12N 16 22 E
Vientiane, *Laos* . . . . . . **51** 17 58N 102 36 E
Vietnam ■, *Asia* . . . . . **63** 19 0N 106 0 E
Vigo, *Sp.* **37** 42 12N 8 41W
Vijayawada, *India* . . . . **59** 16 31N 80 39 E
Villahermosa, *Mex.* . . . **94** 17 59N 92 55W
Villefranche-sur-Saône,
Fr. . . . . **35** 45 59N 4 43 E
Vilnius, *U.S.S.R.* . . . . . **46** 54 38N 25 19 E
Vilyuysk, *U.S.S.R.* . . . . **49** 63 40N 121 35 E
Viña del Mar, *Chile* . . . **102** 33 0S 71 30W
Vineland, *U.S.A.* **93** 39 30N 75 0W
Vinnitsa, *U.S.S.R.* . . . . **47** 49 15N 28 30 E
Virgin Is., *W. Ind.* **95** 18 40N 64 30W
Virginia □, *U.S.A.* **91** 37 45N 78 0W
Viscount Melville Sd.,
Canada **88** 74 10N 108 0W
Vishakhapatnam, *India* **59** 17 45N 83 20 E
Vistula = Wisła →,
Pol. . . . . **43** 54 22N 18 55 E
Vitebsk, *U.S.S.R.* . . . . . **46** 55 10N 30 15 E
Viterbo, *It.* . . . . **40** 42 25N 12 8 E
Viti Levu, *Fiji* . . . . **64** 17 30S 177 30 E
Vitim →, *U.S.S.R.* . . . . **49** 59 26N 112 34 E
Vitória, *Brazil* **101** 20 20S 40 22W
Vitoria, *Sp.* **37** 42 50N 2 41W
Vitória da Conquista,
Brazil **101** 14 51S 40 51W
Vlaardingen, *Neth.* . . . . **36** 51 55N 4 21 E
Vladimir, *U.S.S.R.* . . . . **46** 56 15N 40 30 E
Vladivostok, *U.S.S.R.* . **49** 43 10N 131 53 E
Vlissingen, *Neth.* . . . . . **36** 51 26N 3 34 E
Vlórë, *Alb.* . . . . **41** 40 32N 19 28 E
Voil, L., *U.K.* **20** 56 20N 4 25W
Volga →, *U.S.S.R.* . . . **46** 48 30N 46 0 E
Volga Hts., *U.S.S.R.* . . **47** 51 0N 46 0 E
Volgograd, *U.S.S.R.* . . **47** 48 40N 44 25 E
Vologda, *U.S.S.R.* . . . . **46** 59 10N 40 0 E
Vólos, *Greece* . . . . **41** 39 24N 22 59 E
Volta, L., *Ghana* . . . . . **78** 7 30N 0 15 E
Volta Redonda, *Brazil* . **101** 22 31S 44 5W
Volzhskiy, *U.S.S.R.* . . . **47** 48 56N 44 46 E
Voorburg, *Neth.* . . . . . . **36** 52 5N 4 24 E
Vorkuta, *U.S.S.R.* . . . . **46** 67 48N 64 20 E
Voronezh, *U.S.S.R.* . . . **46** 51 40N 39 10 E
Voroshilovgrad,
U.S.S.R. . . . . **47** 48 38N 39 15 E
Vosges, *Fr.* . . . . **34** 48 20N 7 10 E
Vryburg, *S. Afr.* . . . . . . **81** 26 55S 24 45 E
Vyrnwy, L., *U.K.* **17** 52 48N 3 30W

W

Waal →, *Neth.* . . . . . . **36** 51 59N 4 30 E
Wabash →, *U.S.A.* . . . **92** 37 46N 88 2W
Waco, *U.S.A.* **91** 31 33N 97 5W
Wâd Medanî, *Sudan* . . **79** 14 28N 33 30 E
Waddenzee, *Neth.* . . . . **36** 53 6N 5 10 E
Waddesdon, *U.K.* **15** 51 50N 0 54W

Waddingham, *U.K.* ... **19** 53 28N 0 31W
Waddington, *U.K.* **19** 53 10N 0 31W
Waddington, Mt., *Canada* **88** 51 23N 125 15W
Wadebridge, *U.K.* **16** 50 31N 4 51W
Wadhurst, *U.K.* ...... **15** 51 3N 0 21 E
Wagga Wagga, *Austral.* **70** 35 7S 147 24 E
Wagin, *Austral.* ...... **66** 33 17S 117 25 E
Wainfleet All Saints, *U.K.* .... **19** 53 7N 0 16 E
Waipara, *N.Z.* .... **71** 43 3S 172 46 E
Waitaki →, *N.Z.* ..... **71** 44 56S 171 7 E
Wakatipu, L., *N.Z.* .... **71** 45 5S 168 33 E
Wakayama, *Jap.* ..... **62** 34 15N 135 15 E
Wakefield, *U.K.* **19** 53 41N 1 31W
Walberswick, *U.K.* .... **15** 52 18N 1 39 E
Wałbrzych, *Pol.* ...... **42** 50 45N 16 18 E
Walbury Hill, *U.K.* **14** 51 22N 1 28W
Waldron, *U.K.* .... **15** 50 56N 0 13 E
Wales □, *U.K.* **17** 52 30N 3 30W
Walgett, *Austral.* ..... **67** 30 0S 148 5 E
Wallachia, *Rom.* ..... **43** 44 35N 25 0 E
Wallasey, *U.K.* **18** 53 26N 3 2W
Wallingford, *U.K.* **14** 51 40N 1 15W
Wallis & Futuna, *Pac. Oc.* **64** 13 18S 176 10W
Wallsend, *U.K.* **19** 54 59N 1 30W
Walmer, *U.K.* .... **15** 51 12N 1 23 E
Walney, Isle of, *U.K.* .. **18** 54 5N 3 15W
Walpole, *U.K.* .... **15** 52 44N 0 13 E
Walsall, *U.K.* **14** 52 36N 1 59W
Walsoken, *U.K.* ...... **15** 52 41N 0 12 E
Waltham, *U.K.* **19** 53 32N 0 6W
Waltham Abbey, *U.K.* . **15** 51 40N 0 1 E
Waltham Forest, *U.K.* . **15** 51 37N 0 2 E
Waltham on the Wolds, *U.K.* **15** 52 49N 0 48W
Walton-on-the-Naze, *U.K.* .... **15** 51 52N 1 17 E
Walvis Bay, *S. Afr.* ... **81** 23 0S 14 28 E
Wanborough, *U.K.* ... **14** 51 33N 1 40W
Wandsworth, *U.K.* **15** 51 28N 0 15W
Wanganui, *N.Z.* ...... **71** 39 56S 175 3 E
Wangaratta, *Austral.* .. **70** 36 21S 146 19 E
Wansbeck, *U.K.* **21** 55 12N 1 28W
Wantage, *U.K.* **14** 51 35N 1 25W
Warboys, *U.K.* **15** 52 25N 0 5W
Warburton →, *Austral.* **67** 28 4S 137 28 E
Wardington, *U.K.* **14** 52 8N 1 17W
Wardle, *U.K.* **18** 53 7N 2 35W
Ward's Stone, *U.K.* ... **18** 54 2N 2 39W
Ware, *U.K.* **15** 51 48N 0 2W
Wareham, *U.K.* **14** 50 41N 2 8W
Wark, *U.K.* **21** 55 5N 2 14W
Warkworth, *U.K.* **21** 55 22N 1 38W
Warley, *U.K.* **14** 52 30N 2 0W
Warminster, *U.K.* **14** 51 12N 2 11W
Warracknabeal, *Austral.* **70** 36 9S 142 26 E
Warrego →, *Austral.* . **67** 30 24S 145 21 E
Warrenpoint, *U.K.* **24** 54 7N 6 15W
Warrington, *U.K.* **18** 53 25N 2 38W
Warrnambool, *Austral.* **70** 38 25S 142 30 E
Warsaw, *Pol.* .... **43** 52 13N 21 0 E
Warsop, *U.K.* **19** 53 13N 1 9W
Warta →, *Pol.* .... **43** 52 35N 14 39 E
Warthe = Warta →, *Pol.* .... **43** 52 35N 14 39 E
Warwick, *Austral.* .... **67** 28 10S 152 1 E
Warwick, *U.K.* **14** 52 17N 1 36W
Warwick □, *U.K.* **14** 52 20N 1 30W
Wasatch Ra., *U.S.A.* .. **90** 40 30N 111 15W
Wash, The, *U.K.* ..... **19** 52 58N 0 20 E
Washford, *U.K.* **14** 51 9N 3 22W
Washington, *U.K.* **21** 54 55N 1 30W
Washington, *U.S.A.* ... **92** 38 52N 77 0W
Washington □, *U.S.A.* . **90** 47 45N 120 30W
Wast Water, L., *U.K.* .. **18** 54 26N 3 18W
Watchet, *U.K.* **14** 51 10N 3 20W
Waterbeach, *U.K.* .... **15** 52 16N 0 11 E
Waterbury, *U.S.A.* **93** 41 32N 73 0W
Waterford, *Ire.* **25** 52 16N 7 8W
Waterford □, *Ire.* **25** 52 10N 7 40W
Waterford Harb., *Ire.* ... **25** 52 10N 6 58W
Watergate Bay, *U.K.* .. **16** 50 26N 5 4W
Waterloo, *U.K.* **18** 53 29N 3 2W
Watford, *U.K.* **15** 51 38N 0 23W
Wath, *U.K.* **19** 53 29N 1 20W
Watlington, *Norfolk, U.K.* .... **15** 52 40N 0 24 E
Watlington, *Oxon., U.K.* **15** 51 38N 1 0W
Watton, *U.K.* .... **15** 52 35N 0 50 E
Waveney →, *U.K.* .... **15** 52 24N 1 20 E
Waver →, *U.K.* **18** 54 50N 3 15W
Weald, The, *U.K.* ..... **15** 51 7N 0 9 E
Wear →, *U.K.* **19** 54 55N 1 22W
Weardale, *U.K.* **18** 54 44N 2 5W
Wearhead, *U.K.* **18** 54 45N 2 14W
Weaver →, *U.K.* **18** 53 17N 2 35W
Weaverham, *U.K.* **18** 53 15N 2 30W
Weddell Sea, *Ant.* **103** 72 30S 40 0W
Wedmore, *U.K.* **14** 51 14N 2 50W
Wednesbury, *U.K.* **14** 52 33N 2 1W
Wednesfield, *U.K.* **14** 52 36N 2 3W
Weedon Bec, *U.K.* ... **14** 52 14N 1 6W
Weifang, *China* ...... **61** 36 47N 119 10 E
Weldon, *U.K.* **21** 55 16N 1 46W
Welford, *Berks., U.K.* . **14** 51 28N 1 24W
Welford, *Northants., U.K.* **14** 52 26N 1 5W
Welkom, *S. Afr.* ...... **81** 28 0S 26 50 E
Welland →, *U.K.* **15** 52 43N 0 10W
Wellesley Is., *Austral.* . **67** 16 42S 139 30 E
Wellingborough, *U.K.* . **15** 52 18N 0 41W
Wellington, *Austral.* ... **70** 32 35S 148 59 E
Wellington, *N.Z.* ...... **71** 41 19S 174 46 E
Wellington, *Salop, U.K.* **14** 52 42N 2 31W
Wellington, *Somerset, U.K.* **14** 50 58N 3 13W
Wellow, *U.K.* **14** 51 20N 2 22W
Wells, *Norfolk, U.K.* ... **15** 52 57N 0 51 E
Wells, *Somerset, U.K.* . **14** 51 12N 2 39W
Welney, *U.K.* .... **15** 52 31N 0 15 E
Wels, *Austria* .... **42** 48 9N 14 1 E
Welshpool, *U.K.* **17** 52 40N 3 9W
Welton, *U.K.* **19** 53 19N 0 29W
Welwyn Garden City, *U.K.* **15** 51 49N 0 11W
Wem, *U.K.* **14** 52 52N 2 45W
Wembury, *U.K.* **16** 50 19N 4 6W
Wemyss Bay, *U.K.* ... **20** 55 52N 4 54W
Wendover, *U.K.* **15** 51 46N 0 45W
Wenhaston, *U.K.* ..... **15** 52 17N 1 35 E
Wenlock Edge, *U.K.* .. **14** 52 30N 2 43W
Wensleydale, *U.K.* **18** 54 18N 2 0W
Wensum →, *U.K.* .... **15** 52 35N 1 20 E
Wenzhou, *China* ..... **61** 28 0N 120 38 E
Weobley, *U.K.* **14** 52 9N 2 52W
Werribee, *Austral.* .... **70** 37 54S 144 40 E
Werrington, *U.K.* **16** 50 40N 4 22W
Weser →, *W. Ger.* ... **42** 53 33N 8 30 E
West Auckland, *U.K.* .. **19** 54 38N 1 42W
West Bengal □, *India* . **59** 23 0N 88 0 E
West Bridgford, *U.K.* .. **19** 52 56N 1 8W
West Bromwich, *U.K.* . **14** 52 32N 2 1W
West Calder, *U.K.* **21** 55 51N 3 34W
West Coker, *U.K.* **14** 50 55N 2 40W
West Fen, *U.K.* **19** 53 5N 0 5W
West Germany ■, *Europe* .... **42** 52 0N 9 0 E
West Glamorgan □, *U.K.* **17** 51 40N 3 55W
West Grinstead, *U.K.* . **15** 50 58N 0 19W
West Haddon, *U.K.* ... **14** 52 21N 1 5W
West Kilbride, *U.K.* ... **20** 55 41N 4 50W
West Kirby, *U.K.* **18** 53 22N 3 11W
West Linton, *U.K.* **21** 55 45N 3 24W
West Lulworth, *U.K.* .. **14** 50 37N 2 14W
West Malling, *U.K.* ... **15** 51 16N 0 25 E
West Meon, *U.K.* **14** 51 2N 1 3W
West Mersea, *U.K.* ... **15** 51 46N 0 55 E
West Midlands □, *U.K.* **14** 52 30N 1 55W
West Moors, *U.K.* **14** 50 49N 1 50W
West Parley, *U.K.* **14** 50 46N 1 52W
West Rasen, *U.K.* **19** 53 23N 0 23W
West Schelde →, *Neth.* .... **36** 51 23N 3 50 E
West Siberian Plain, *U.S.S.R.* .... **48** 62 0N 75 0 E
West Sussex □, *U.K.* . **15** 50 55N 0 30W
West Tarbert, L., *U.K.* . **20** 55 58N 5 30W
West Virginia □, *U.S.A.* **92** 39 0N 81 0W
West Wyalong, *Austral.* **70** 33 56S 147 10 E
West Yorkshire □, *U.K.* **19** 53 45N 1 40W
Westbourne, *U.K.* **15** 50 53N 0 55W
Westbury, *Salop, U.K.* **14** 52 40N 2 57W
Westbury, *Wilts., U.K.* . **14** 51 16N 2 11W
Westbury-on-Severn, *U.K.* **14** 51 49N 2 24W
Westerham, *U.K.* ..... **15** 51 16N 0 5 E
Western Australia □, *Austral.* .... **66** 25 0S 118 0 E
Western Ghats, *India* . **58** 14 0N 75 0 E
Western Isles □, *U.K.* . **22** 57 30N 7 10W
Western Sahara ■, *Africa* **78** 25 0N 13 0W
Western Samoa ■, *Pac. Oc.* **64** 14 0S 172 0W
Westfield, *U.K.* ...... **15** 50 53N 0 30 E
Westhoughton, *U.K.* .. **18** 53 34N 2 30W
Westland Bight, *N.Z.* .. **71** 42 55S 170 5 E
Westmeath □, *Ire.* **24** 53 30N 7 30W
Weston, *U.K.* **14** 52 51N 2 2W
Weston-super-Mare, *U.K.* **14** 51 20N 2 59W
Westport, *Ire.* **24** 53 44N 9 31W
Westport, *N.Z.* .... **71** 41 46S 171 37 E
Westray, *U.K.* **23** 59 18N 3 0W
Westruther, *U.K.* **21** 55 45N 2 34W
Westward Ho!, *U.K.* .. **16** 51 2N 4 16W
Wetherby, *U.K.* **19** 53 56N 1 23W
Wetwang, *U.K.* **19** 54 2N 0 35W
Wexford, *Ire.* **25** 52 20N 6 28W
Wexford □, *Ire.* **25** 52 20N 6 25W
Wexford Harb., *Ire.* ... **25** 52 20N 6 25W
Wey →, *U.K.* **15** 51 19N 0 29W
Weybourne, *U.K.* .... **15** 52 57N 1 9 E
Weybridge, *U.K.* **15** 51 22N 0 28W
Weymouth, *U.K.* **14** 50 36N 2 28W
Whakatane, *N.Z.* ..... **71** 37 57S 177 1 E
Whaley Bridge, *U.K.* .. **18** 53 20N 2 0W
Whalley, *U.K.* **18** 53 49N 2 25W
Whalsay, *U.K.* **22** 60 22N 1 0W
Whalton, *U.K.* **21** 55 7N 1 46W
Whangarei, *N.Z.* ..... **71** 35 43S 174 21 E
Whaplode, *U.K.* **15** 52 42N 0 3W
Wharfe →, *U.K.* **19** 53 55N 1 30W
Wharfedale, *U.K.* **18** 54 7N 2 4W
Whauphill, *U.K.* **20** 54 48N 4 31W
Wheatley Hill, *U.K.* ... **19** 54 45N 1 23W
Whernside, *U.K.* **18** 54 14N 2 24W
Whichham, *U.K.* **18** 54 14N 3 22W
Whimple, *U.K.* **16** 50 46N 3 21W
Whipsnade, *U.K.* **15** 51 51N 0 32W
Whissendine, *U.K.* **15** 52 43N 0 46W
Whiston, *U.K.* **18** 53 25N 2 45W
Whitburn, *U.K.* **21** 55 52N 3 41W
Whitby, *U.K.* **19** 54 29N 0 37W
Whitchurch, *Devon, U.K.* **16** 50 31N 4 7W
Whitchurch, *Hants., U.K.* **14** 51 14N 1 20W
Whitchurch, *Hereford & Worcs., U.K.* **14** 51 51N 2 41W
Whitchurch, *Salop, U.K.* **18** 52 58N 2 42W
White Esk →, *U.K.* .. **21** 55 14N 3 11W
White Horse Hill, *U.K.* . **14** 51 35N 1 35W
White Nile →, *Sudan* **79** 15 38N 32 31 E
White Russia □, *U.S.S.R.* .... **46** 53 30N 27 0 E
White Sea, *U.S.S.R.* .. **46** 66 30N 38 0 E
Whiteadder Water →, *U.K.* **21** 55 47N 2 20W
Whitehaven, *U.K.* **18** 54 33N 3 35W
Whitehead, *U.K.* **24** 54 45N 5 42W
Whitehorse, *Canada* .. **88** 60 43N 135 3W
Whitehorse, Vale of, *U.K.* **14** 51 37N 1 30W
Whitekirk, *U.K.* **21** 56 2N 2 36W
Whitesand B., *U.K.* ... **16** 50 18N 4 20W
Whithorn, *U.K.* **20** 54 44N 4 25W
Whitley Bay, *U.K.* **21** 55 4N 1 28W
Whitney, Mt., *U.S.A.* .. **90** 36 35N 118 14W
Whitstable, *U.K.* ..... **15** 51 21N 1 2 E
Whittington, *Derby, U.K.* **19** 53 17N 1 26W
Whittington, *Salop, U.K.* **14** 52 53N 3 0W
Whittlesey, *U.K.* **15** 52 34N 0 8W
Whittlesford, *U.K.* .... **15** 52 6N 0 9 E
Whitton, *U.K.* **19** 53 42N 0 39W
Whitwell, *Derby, U.K.* . **19** 53 16N 1 11W
Whitwell, *I. of W., U.K.* **14** 50 35N 1 19W
Whitwick, *U.K.* **14** 52 45N 1 23W
Whitworth, *U.K.* **18** 53 40N 2 11W
Whixley, *U.K.* **19** 54 2N 1 19W
Whyalla, *Austral.* ..... **67** 33 2S 137 30 E
Wichita, *U.S.A.* **91** 37 40N 97 20W
Wichita Falls, *U.S.A.* .. **90** 33 57N 98 30W
Wick, *U.K.* **23** 58 26N 3 5W
Wickford, *U.K.* ...... **15** 51 37N 0 31 E
Wickham, *U.K.* **14** 50 54N 1 11W
Wickham Market, *U.K.* **15** 52 9N 1 21 E
Wicklow, *Ire.* **25** 53 0N 6 2W
Wicklow □, *Ire.* **25** 52 59N 6 25W
Wicklow Mts., *Ire.* **25** 53 0N 6 30W
Wickwar, *U.K.* **14** 51 35N 2 23W
Widdrington, *U.K.* **21** 55 15N 1 35W
Widecombe, *U.K.* **16** 50 34N 3 48W
Widemouth, *U.K.* **16** 50 45N 4 34W
Widnes, *U.K.* **18** 53 22N 2 44W
Wiesbaden, *W. Ger.* .. **36** 50 7N 8 17 E
Wigan, *U.K.* **18** 53 33N 2 38W
Wight, I. of, *U.K.* **14** 50 40N 1 20W
Wigmore, *U.K.* **14** 52 19N 2 51W
Wigston, *U.K.* **14** 52 35N 1 6W
Wigton, *U.K.* **18** 54 50N 3 9W
Wigtown, *U.K.* **20** 54 52N 4 27W
Wigtown B., *U.K.* **20** 54 46N 4 15W
Wilhelm II Land, *Ant.* . **103** 68 0S 90 0 E
Wilhelmshaven, *W. Ger.* **42** 53 30N 8 9 E
Wilkes Barre, *U.S.A.* .. **93** 41 15N 75 52W
Wilkes Land, *Ant.* .... **103** 69 0S 120 0 E
Willemstad, *Cur.* **94** 12 5N 69 0W
Willenhall, *U.K.* **14** 52 36N 2 3W
Willesborough, *U.K.* .. **15** 51 8N 0 55 E
Williamstown, *Austral.* **70** 37 51S 144 52 E
Willingdon, *U.K.* ..... **15** 50 47N 0 17 E
Williton, *U.K.* **14** 51 9N 3 20W
Willoughby, *U.K.* ..... **19** 53 14N 0 12 E
Wilmington, *U.K.* **16** 50 46N 3 8W
Wilmington, *U.S.A.* ... **93** 39 45N 75 32W
Wilmslow, *U.K.* **18** 53 19N 2 14W
Wilnecote, *U.K.* **14** 52 36N 1 40W
Wilsons Promontory, *Austral.* .... **70** 38 55S 146 25 E
Wilton, *U.K.* **14** 51 5N 1 52W
Wiltshire □, *U.K.* **14** 51 20N 2 0W
Wimblington, *U.K.* .... **15** 52 31N 0 5 E
Wimborne Minster, *U.K.* **14** 50 48N 2 0W
Wimmera →, *Austral.* **70** 36 8S 141 56 E
Wincanton, *U.K.* **14** 51 3N 2 24W
Winchelsea, *U.K.* .... **15** 50 55N 0 43 E
Winchester, *U.K.* **14** 51 4N 1 19W
Windermere, *U.K.* **18** 54 24N 2 56W
Windermere, L., *U.K.* . **18** 54 20N 2 57W
Windhoek, *Nam.* ..... **81** 22 35S 17 4 E
Windrush →, *U.K.* ... **14** 51 48N 1 35W
Windsor, *Canada* **92** 42 18N 83 0W
Windsor, *U.K.* **15** 51 28N 0 36W
Windward Passage, *W. Ind.* **95** 20 0N 74 0W
Windygates, *U.K.* **21** 56 12N 3 1W
Wing, *U.K.* **15** 51 54N 0 41W
Wingham, *Austral.* .... **70** 31 48S 152 22 E
Wingham, *U.K.* ...... **15** 51 16N 1 12 E
Winkleigh, *U.K.* **16** 50 49N 3 57W
Winnipeg, *Canada* **88** 49 54N 97 9W
Winnipeg, L., *Canada* . **88** 52 0N 97 0W
Winsford, *U.K.* **18** 53 12N 2 31W
Winslow, *U.K.* **15** 51 57N 0 52W
Winster, *U.K.* **19** 53 9N 1 42W
Winston-Salem, *U.S.A.* **91** 36 7N 80 15W
Winterborne Abbas, *U.K.* **14** 50 43N 2 30W
Winterthur, *Switz.* .... **42** 47 30N 8 44 E
Winterton, *Humberside, U.K.* **19** 53 39N 0 37W
Winterton, *Norfolk, U.K.* **15** 52 43N 1 43 E
Wirksworth, *U.K.* **19** 53 5N 1 34W
Wirral, *U.K.* **18** 53 25N 3 0W
Wisbech, *U.K.* .... **15** 52 39N 0 10 E
Wisborough Green, *U.K.* **15** 51 2N 0 30W
Wisconsin □, *U.S.A.* .. **92** 44 30N 90 0W
Wishaw, *U.K.* **21** 55 46N 3 55W
Wiske →, *U.K.* **19** 54 26N 1 27W
Wisła →, *Pol.* .... **43** 54 22N 18 55 E
Witbank, *S. Afr.* ...... **81** 25 51S 29 14 E
Witham, *U.K.* .... **15** 51 48N 0 39 E
Witham →, *U.K.* **19** 53 3N 0 8W
Withern, *U.K.* .... **19** 53 19N 0 9 E
Withernsea, *U.K.* ..... **19** 53 43N 0 2 E
Witley, *U.K.* **15** 51 9N 0 39W
Witney, *U.K.* **14** 51 47N 1 29W
Witten, *W. Ger.* ...... **36** 51 26N 7 19 E
Wittersham, *U.K.* ..... **15** 51 1N 0 42 E
Wiveliscombe, *U.K.* ... **14** 51 2N 3 20W
Wivenhoe, *U.K.* ...... **15** 51 51N 0 59 E
Włocławek, *Pol.* ...... **43** 52 40N 19 3 E
Woburn, *U.K.* **15** 51 59N 0 37W
Woburn Sands, *U.K.* .. **15** 52 1N 0 38W
Wodonga, *Austral.* ... **70** 36 5S 146 50 E
Woking, *U.K.* **15** 51 18N 0 33W
Wokingham, *U.K.* **15** 51 25N 0 50W
Wolf Rock, *U.K.* **16** 49 56N 5 50W
Wolfsburg, *W. Ger.* ... **42** 52 27N 10 49 E
Wollongong, *Austral.* . **70** 34 25S 150 54 E
Wolsingham, *U.K.* **18** 54 44N 1 52W
Wolverhampton, *U.K.* . **14** 52 35N 2 6W
Wolverton, *U.K.* **15** 52 3N 0 48W
Wolviston, *U.K.* **19** 54 39N 1 25W
Wombwell, *U.K.* **19** 53 31N 1 23W
Wŏnsan, *N. Kor.* ..... **61** 39 11N 127 27 E
Wonston, *U.K.* **14** 51 9N 1 18W
Woodbridge, *U.K.* .... **15** 52 6N 1 19 E
Woodbury, *U.K.* **16** 50 40N 3 24W
Woodhall Spa, *U.K.* ... **19** 53 10N 0 12W
Woodhouse, *U.K.* **19** 53 23N 1 21W
Woodley, *U.K.* **15** 51 26N 0 54W
Woods, L. of the, *Canada* **88** 49 15N 94 45W
Woodstock, *U.K.* **14** 51 51N 1 20W
Wookey, *U.K.* **14** 51 13N 2 41W
Wookey Hole, *U.K.* ... **14** 51 13N 2 41W
Wool, *U.K.* **14** 50 41N 2 13W
Woolacombe, *U.K.* ... **16** 51 10N 4 12W
Wooler, *U.K.* **21** 55 33N 2 0W
Wootton Bassett, *U.K.* **14** 51 32N 1 55W
Wootton Wawen, *U.K.* **14** 52 16N 1 47W
Worcester, *S. Afr.* ... **81** 33 39S 19 27 E
Worcester, *U.K.* **14** 52 12N 2 12W
Worcester, *U.S.A.* ... **93** 42 14N 71 49W
Worfield, *U.K.* **14** 52 34N 2 22W
Workington, *U.K.* **18** 54 39N 3 34W
Worksop, *U.K.* **19** 53 19N 1 9W
Wormit, *U.K.* **21** 56 26N 2 59W
Worms, *W. Ger.* ...... **42** 49 37N 8 21 E
Worplesdon, *U.K.* **15** 51 16N 0 36W
Wortham, *U.K.* .... **15** 52 22N 1 3 E
Worthing, *U.K.* **15** 50 49N 0 21W
Wotton-under-Edge, *U.K.* **14** 51 37N 2 20W
Woy Woy, *Austral.* ... **70** 33 30S 151 19 E
Wragby, *U.K.* **19** 53 17N 0 18W
Wrangel I., *U.S.S.R.* .. **49** 71 0N 180 0 E
Wrangle, *U.K.* .... **19** 53 3N 0 9 E
Wrath, C., *U.K.* **22** 58 38N 5 0W
Wrekin, The, *U.K.* ... **14** 52 41N 2 35W
Wrentham, *U.K.* ..... **15** 52 24N 1 39 E
Wrexham, *U.K.* **17** 53 5N 3 0W
Writtle, *U.K.* .... **15** 51 44N 0 27 E
Wrocław, *Pol.* .... **43** 51 5N 17 5 E
Wrotham, *U.K.* ...... **15** 51 18N 0 20 E
Wroughton, *U.K.* **14** 51 31N 1 47W
Wroxham, *U.K.* ...... **15** 52 42N 1 23 E
Wuhan, *China* .... **61** 30 31N 114 18 E
Wuhu, *China* .... **61** 31 22N 118 21 E
Wuppertal, *W. Ger.* ... **36** 51 15N 7 8 E
Würzburg, *W. Ger.* ... **42** 49 46N 9 55 E
Wutongqiao, *China* ... **60** 29 22N 103 50 E
Wuxi, *China* .... **61** 31 30N 120 30 E
Wuzhou, *China* ...... **61** 23 30N 111 18 E
Wye, *U.K.* .... **15** 51 11N 0 56 E
Wye →, *U.K.* **14** 51 36N 2 40W
Wylye →, *U.K.* **14** 51 8N 1 53W
Wymondham, *Leics., U.K.* **15** 52 45N 0 42W
Wymondham, *Norfolk, U.K.* .... **15** 52 34N 1 7 E
Wyndham, *Austral.* ... **66** 15 33S 128 3 E
Wyoming □, *U.S.A.* ... **90** 42 48N 109 0W
Wyre →, *U.K.* **18** 53 52N 2 57W
Wyre Forest, *U.K.* **14** 52 24N 2 24W

X

Xiaguan, *China* ...... **60** 25 32N 100 16 E
Xiamen, *China* .... **61** 24 25N 118 4 E
Xiangfan, *China* ...... **61** 32 2N 112 8 E
Xiangtan, *China* ...... **61** 27 51N 112 54 E
Xiangyang, *China* .... **61** 32 1N 112 8 E
Xingu →, *Brazil* **101** 1 30S 51 53W
Xining, *China* .... **60** 36 34N 101 40 E
Xinjiang Uygur Zizhiqu □, *China* ... **60** 42 0N 86 0 E
Xuzhou, *China* .... **61** 34 18N 117 10 E

Y

Yablonovy Ra., *U.S.S.R.* **49** 53 0N 114 0 E
Yakut A.S.S.R. □, *U.S.S.R.* **49** 62 0N 130 0 E
Yakutsk, *U.S.S.R.* **49** 62 5N 129 50 E
Yamagata, *Jap.* **62** 38 15N 140 15 E
Yamal, Peninsula, *U.S.S.R.* **48** 71 0N 70 0 E
Yambol, *Bulg.* **41** 42 30N 26 36 E
Yamuna →, *India* **59** 25 30N 81 53 E
Yana →, *U.S.S.R.* **49** 71 30N 136 0 E
Yangtze Kiang →, *China* **60** 31 40N 122 0 E
Yanji, *China* **61** 42 59N 129 30 E
Yantai, *China* **61** 37 34N 121 22 E
Yaoundé, *Cam.* **80** 3 50N 11 35 E
Yarcombe, *U.K.* **16** 50 51N 3 6W
Yare →, *U.K.* **15** 52 36N 1 28 E
Yarm, *U.K.* **19** 54 31N 1 21W
Yarmouth, *U.K.* **14** 50 42N 1 29W
Yaroslavl, *U.S.S.R.* **46** 57 35N 39 55 E
Yarrow, *U.K.* **21** 55 32N 3 0W
Yate, *U.K.* **14** 51 32N 2 26W
Yatsushiro, *Jap.* **62** 32 30N 130 40 E
Yatton, *U.K.* **14** 51 23N 2 50W
Yaxley, *U.K.* **15** 52 31N 0 14W
Yazd, *Iran* **56** 31 55N 54 27 E
Yealmpton, *U.K.* **16** 50 21N 4 0W
Yell, *U.K.* **22** 60 35N 1 5W
Yell Sd., *U.K.* **22** 60 33N 1 15W
Yellow Sea, *China* **61** 35 0N 123 0 E
Yellowknife, *Canada* **88** 62 27N 114 29W
Yellowstone →, *U.S.A.* **90** 47 58N 103 59W
Yellowstone National Park, *U.S.A.* **90** 44 35N 110 0W
Yemen ■, *Si. Arab.* **56** 15 0N 44 0 E
Yenisey →, *U.S.S.R.* **48** 71 50N 82 40 E
Yeo →, *U.K.* **14** 51 10N 3 0W
Yeovil, *U.K.* **14** 50 57N 2 38W
Yerevan, *U.S.S.R.* **47** 40 10N 44 31 E
Yes Tor, *U.K.* **16** 50 41N 3 59W
Yibin, *China* **60** 28 45N 104 32 E
Yichang, *China* **61** 30 40N 111 20 E
Yichuan, *China* **60** 36 2N 110 10 E
Yining, *China* **60** 43 58N 81 10 E
Yogyakarta, *Indon.* **63** 7 49S 110 22 E
Yokkaichi, *Jap.* **62** 35 0N 136 38 E
Yokohama, *Jap.* **62** 35 27N 139 28 E
Yokosuka, *Jap.* **62** 35 20N 139 40 E
Yonkers, *U.S.A.* **93** 40 57N 73 51W
York, *U.K.* **19** 53 58N 1 7W
York, *U.S.A.* **92** 39 57N 76 43W
York, Vale of, *U.K.* **19** 54 15N 1 25W
Yorkshire Wolds, *U.K.* **19** 54 0N 0 30W
Yosemite National Park, *U.S.A.* **90** 38 0N 119 30W
Yoshkar Ola, *U.S.S.R.* **46** 56 38N 47 55 E
Youghal, *Ire.* **25** 51 58N 7 51W
Youghal B., *Ire.* **25** 51 55N 7 50W
Youlgreave, *U.K.* **19** 53 12N 1 50W
Youngstown, *U.S.A.* **92** 41 7N 80 41W
Yoxall, *U.K.* **14** 52 45N 1 49W
Yoxford, *U.K.* **15** 52 16N 1 30 E
Ypres, *Belg.* **36** 50 51N 2 53 E
Ystalyfera, *U.K.* **17** 51 46N 3 48W
Ythan →, *U.K.* **23** 57 26N 2 12W
Yuan Jiang →, *China* **61** 28 55N 111 50 E
Yucatán, Península de, *Mex.* **94** 19 30N 89 0W
Yucatan Str., *Carib.* **94** 22 0N 86 30W
Yugoslavia ■, *Europe* **41** 44 0N 20 0 E
Yukon →, *N. Am.* **88** 65 30N 150 0W
Yukon Territory □, *Canada* **88** 63 0N 135 0W
Yunnan □, *China* **60** 25 0N 102 30 E
Yuzhno-Sakhalinsk, *U.S.S.R.* **49** 46 58N 142 45 E

Z

Zaandam, *Neth.* **36** 52 26N 4 49 E
Zabrze, *Pol.* **43** 50 18N 18 50 E
Zagorsk, *U.S.S.R.* **46** 56 20N 38 10 E
Zagreb, *Yug.* **40** 45 50N 16 0 E
Zagros Mts., *Iran* **56** 33 45N 47 0 E
Zahlah, *Leb.* **57** 33 52N 35 50 E
Zaïre ■, *Africa* **80** 3 0S 23 0 E
Zaïre →, *Africa* **80** 6 4S 12 24 E
Zákinthos, *Greece* **41** 37 47N 20 57 E
Zambezi →, *Africa* **81** 18 55S 36 4 E
Zambia ■, *Africa* **81** 15 0S 28 0 E
Zamboanga, *Phil.* **63** 6 59N 122 3 E
Zamora, *Sp.* **37** 41 30N 5 45W
Zante = Zákinthos, *Greece* **41** 37 47N 20 57 E
Zanzibar, *Tanz.* **80** 6 12S 39 12 E
Zaporozhye, *U.S.S.R.* **47** 47 50N 35 10 E
Zaragoza, *Sp.* **37** 41 39N 0 53W
Zaria, *Nig.* **78** 11 0N 7 40 E
Zeebrugge, *Belg.* **36** 51 19N 3 12 E
Zeist, *Neth.* **36** 52 5N 5 15 E
Zhangjiakou, *China* **61** 40 48N 114 55 E
Zhangzhou, *China* **61** 24 30N 117 35 E
Zhanjiang, *China* **61** 21 15N 110 20 E
Zhdanov, *U.S.S.R.* **47** 47 5N 37 31 E
Zhejiang □, *China* **61** 29 0N 120 0 E
Zhengzhou, *China* **61** 34 45N 113 34 E
Zhitomir, *U.S.S.R.* **47** 50 20N 28 40 E
Zibo, *China* **61** 36 47N 118 3 E
Zielona Góra □, *Pol.* **42** 51 57N 15 30 E
Zigong, *China* **60** 29 15N 104 48 E
Ziguinchor, *Sene.* **78** 12 35N 16 20W
Žilina, *Czech.* **43** 49 12N 18 42 E
Zimbabwe ■, *Africa* **81** 20 0S 30 0 E
Zion Nat. Park, *U.S.A.* **90** 37 25N 112 50W
Zlatoust, *U.S.S.R.* **46** 55 10N 59 40 E
Zonguldak, *Turk.* **47** 41 28N 31 50 E
Zrenjanin, *Yug.* **41** 45 22N 20 23 E
Zug, *Switz.* **42** 47 10N 8 31 E

MAP PROJECTIONS

MAP PROJECTIONS

A map projection is the systematic depiction on a plane surface of the imaginary lines of latitude or longitude from a globe of the earth. This network of lines is called the graticule and forms the framework upon which an accurate depiction of the earth is made. The map graticule, which is the basis of any map, is constructed sometimes by graphical means, but often by using mathematical formulae to give the intersections of the graticule plotted as x and y co-ordinates. The choice between projections is based upon which properties the cartographer wishes the map to possess, the map scale and also the extent of the area to be mapped. Since the globe is three dimensional, it is not possible to depict its surface on a two dimensional plane without distortion. Preservation of one of the basic properties listed below can only be secured at the expense of the others and the choice of projection is often a compromise solution.

Correct Area

In these projections the areas from the globe are to scale on the map. For example, if you look at the diagram at the top right, areas of 10° x 10° are shown from the equator to the poles. The proportion of this area at the extremities are approximately 11:1. An equal area projection will retain that proportion in its portrayal of those areas. This is particularly useful in the mapping of densities and distributions. Projections with this property are termed **Equal Area, Equivalent or Homolographic.**

Correct Distance

In these projections the scale is correct along the meridians, or in the case of the Azimuthal Equidistant scale is true along any line drawn from the centre of the projection. They are called **Equidistant**.

Correct Shape

This property can only be true within small areas as it is achieved only by having a uniform scale distortion along both x and y axes of the projection. The projections are called **Conformal** or **Orthomorphic.**

In order to minimise the distortions at the edges of some projections, central portions of them are often selected for atlas maps. Below are listed some of the major types of projection.

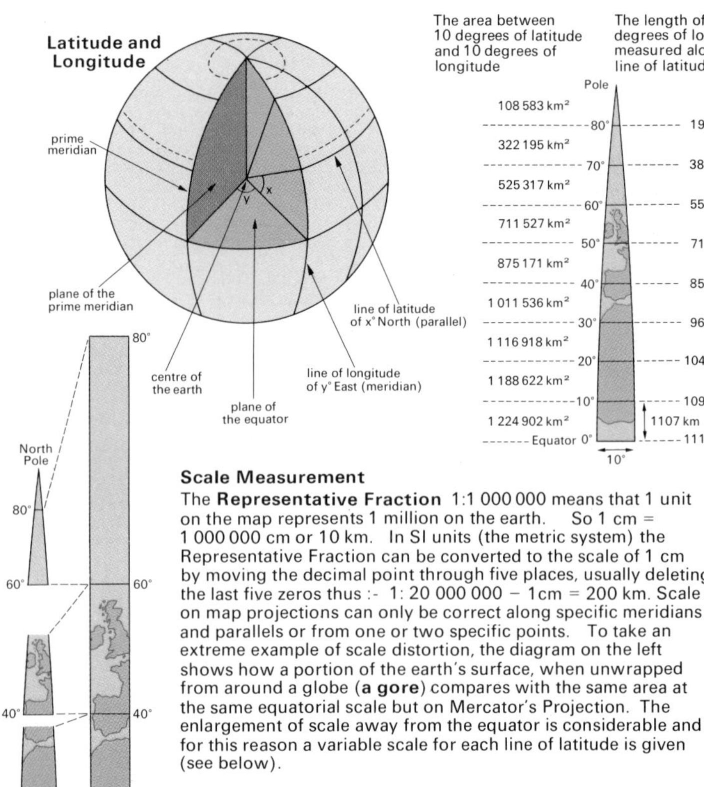

Scale Measurement

The **Representative Fraction** 1:1 000 000 means that 1 unit on the map represents 1 million on the earth. So 1 cm = 1 000 000 cm or 10 km. In SI units (the metric system) the Representative Fraction can be converted to the scale of 1 cm by moving the decimal point through five places, usually deleting the last five zeros thus :- 1: 20 000 000 – 1cm = 200 km. Scale on map projections can only be correct along specific meridians and parallels or from one or two specific points. To take an extreme example of scale distortion, the diagram on the left shows how a portion of the earth's surface, when unwrapped from around a globe (**a gore**) compares with the same area at the same equatorial scale but on Mercator's Projection. The enlargement of scale away from the equator is considerable and for this reason a variable scale for each line of latitude is given (see below).

80° 60° 40° 20° 0°
0 800 1600 km

AZIMUTHAL OR ZENITHAL PROJECTIONS

These are constructed by the projection of part of the graticule from the globe onto a plane tangential to any single point on it. This plane may be tangential to the equator (**equatorial case**), the poles (**polar case**) or any other point (**oblique case**). Any straight line drawn from the point at which the plane touches the globe is the shortest distance from that point and is known as a **great circle**. In its **Gnomonic** construction *any* straight line on the map is a great circle, but there is great exaggeration towards the edges and this reduces its general uses. There are five different ways of transferring the graticule onto the plane and these are shown on the right. The central diagram below shows how the graticules vary, using the polar case as the example.

Equidistant — Equal-Area — Orthographic — Gnomonic — Stereographic (conformal)

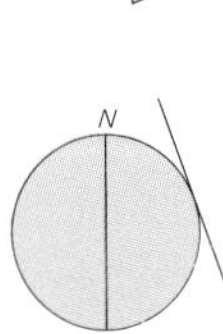

Oblique Case

The plane touches the globe at any point between the equator and poles. The oblique orthographic uses the distortion in azimuthal projections away from the centre to give a graphic depiction of the earth as seen from any desired point in space. It can also be used in both Polar and Equatorial cases. It is used not only for the earth but also for the moon and planets.

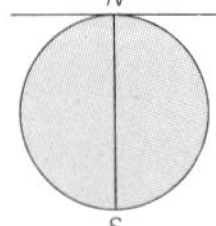

Polar Case

The polar case is the simplest to construct and the diagram below shows the differing effects of all five methods of construction comparing their coverage, distortion etc., using North America as the example.

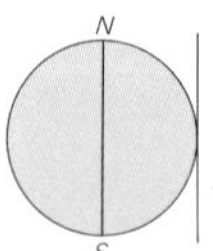

Equatorial Case

The example shown here is Lambert's Equivalent Azimuthal. It is the only projection which is both equal area and where bearing is true from the centre.

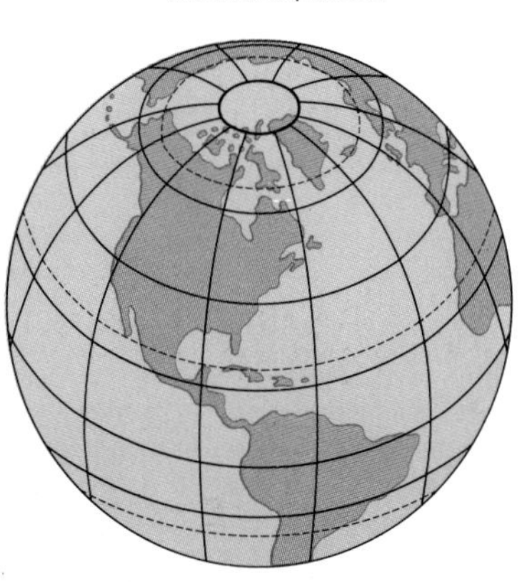

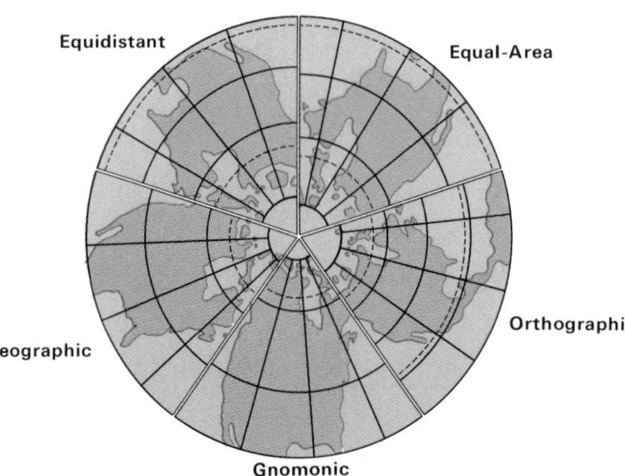

CONICAL PROJECTIONS

These use the projection of the graticule from the globe onto a cone which is tangential to a line of latitude (termed the **standard parallel**). This line is always an arc and scale is always true along it. Because of its method of construction it is used mainly for depicting the temperate latitudes around the standard parallel i.e. where there is least distortion. To reduce the distortion and include a larger range of latitudes, the projection may be constructed with the cone bisecting the surface of the globe so that there are two standard parallels each of which is true to scale. The distortion is thus spread more evenly between the two chosen parallels.

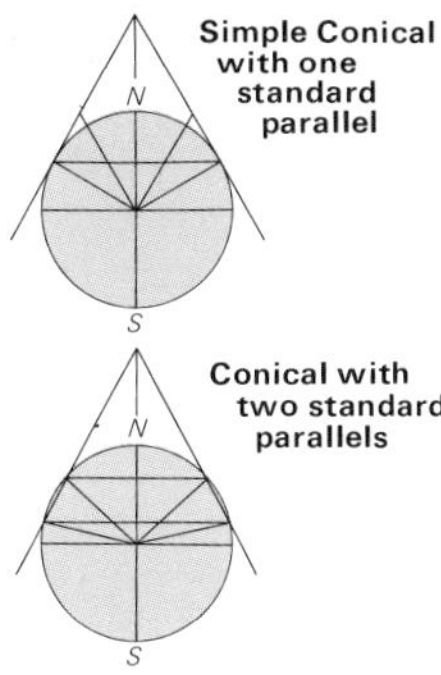

Bonne

This is a modification of the simple conic whereby the true scale along the meridians is sacrificed to enable the accurate representation of areas. However scale is true along each parallel but shapes are distorted at the edges.

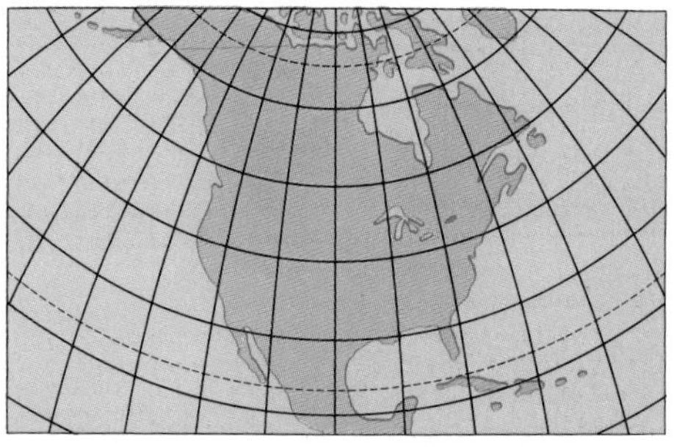

mple Conic

ale is correct not only along the standard parallel t also along all meridians. The selection of the ndard parallel used is crucial because of the stortion away from it. The projection is usually ed to portray regions or continents at small scales.

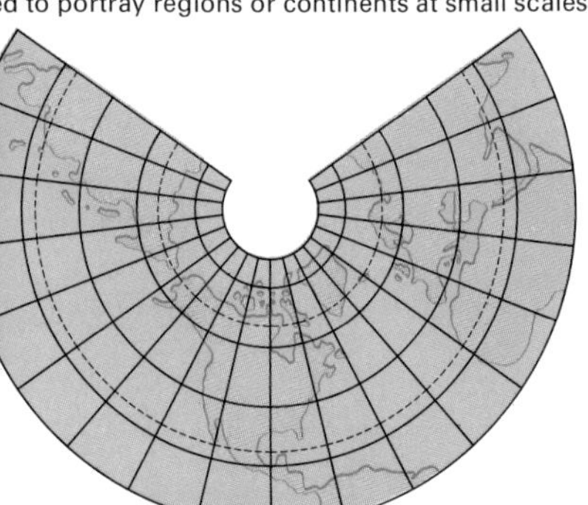

Lambert's Conformal Conic

This projection uses two standard parallels but instead of being equal area as Albers, it is Conformal. Because it has comparatively small distortion, direction and distances can be readily measured and it is therefore used for some navigational charts.

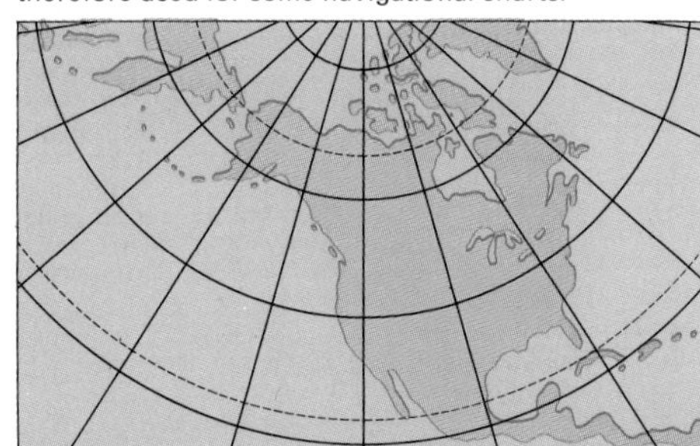

Albers Conical Equal Area

This projection uses two standard parallels and once again the selection of the two specific ones relative to the land area to be mapped is very important. It is equal area and is especially useful for large land masses oriented East-West, for example the U.S.A.

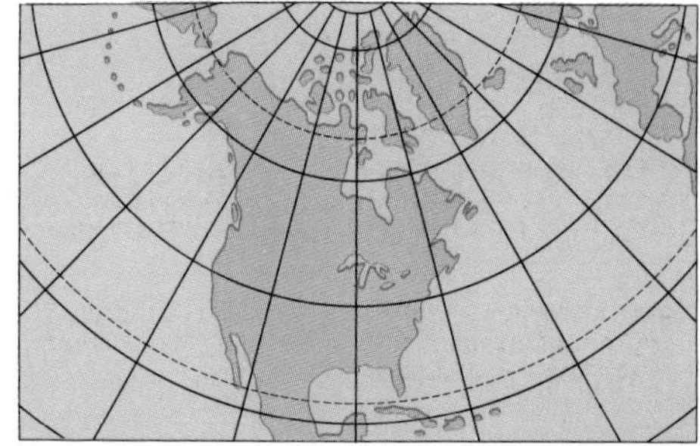

CYLINDRICAL AND OTHER WORLD PROJECTIONS

This group of projections are those which permit the whole of the Earth's surface to be depicted on one map. They are a very large group of projections and the following are only a few of them. Cylindrical projections are constructed by the projection of the graticule from the globe onto a cylinder tangential to the globe. In the examples shown here the cylinder touches the equator, but it can be moved through 90° so it touches the poles - this is called the **Transverse Aspect**. If the cylinder is twisted so that it touches anywhere between the equator and poles it is called the **Oblique Aspect.** Although cylindrical projections can depict all the main land masses, there is considerable distortion of shape and area towards the poles. One cylindrical projection, **Mercator** overcomes this shortcoming by possessing the unique navigational property that any straight drawn on it is a line of constant bearing (**loxodrome**), i.e. a straight line route on the globe crosses the parallels and meridians on the map at the same angles as on the globe. It is used for maps and charts between 15° either side of the equator. Beyond this enlargement of area is a serious drawback, although it is used for navigational charts at all latitudes.

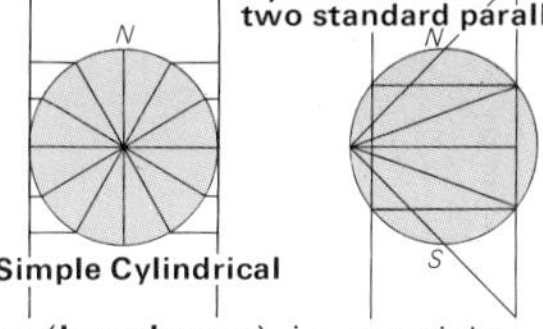

Mercator

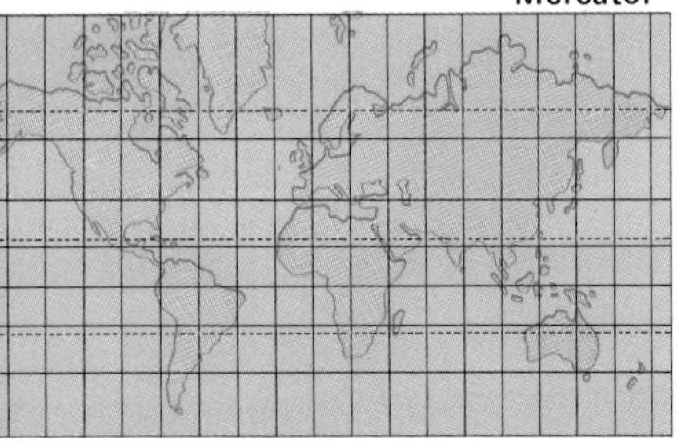

Mollweide

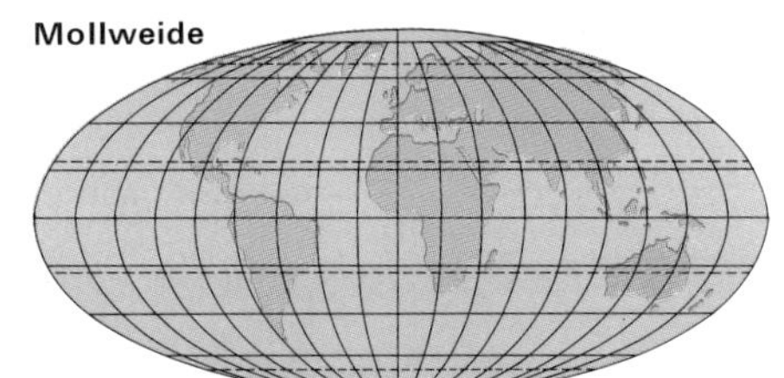

Sanson-Flamsteed

Mollweide and Sanson-Flamsteed

Both of these projections are termed **pseudo-cylindrical**. They are basically cylindrical projections where parallels have been progressively shortened and drawn to scale towards the poles. This allows them to overcome the gross distortions exhibited by the ordinary cylindrical projections and they are in fact Equal Area, Mollweide's giving a slightly better shape. To improve the shape of the continents still further they, like some other projections can be **Interrupted** as can be seen below, but this is at the expense of contiguous sea areas. These projections can have any central meridian and so can be 'centred' on the Atlantic, Pacific, Asia, America etc. In this form both projections are suitable for any form of mapping statistical distributions.

mmer

is is not a cylindrical projection, but is developed m the Lambert Azimuthal Equal Area by doubling the East-West distances along the parallels from central meridian. Like both Sanson–Flamsteed d Mollweide it is distorted towards its edges but s curved parallels to lessen the distortion.

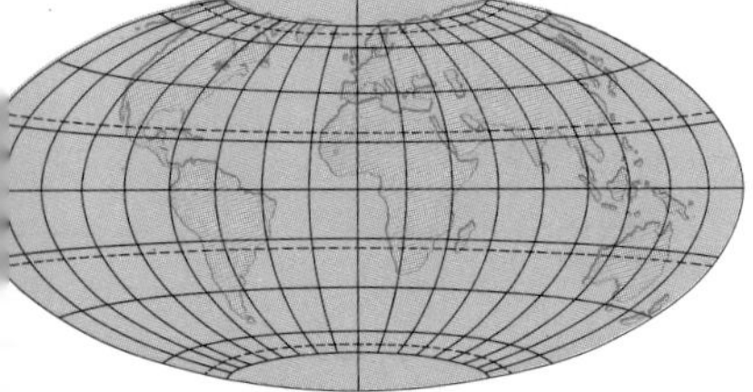

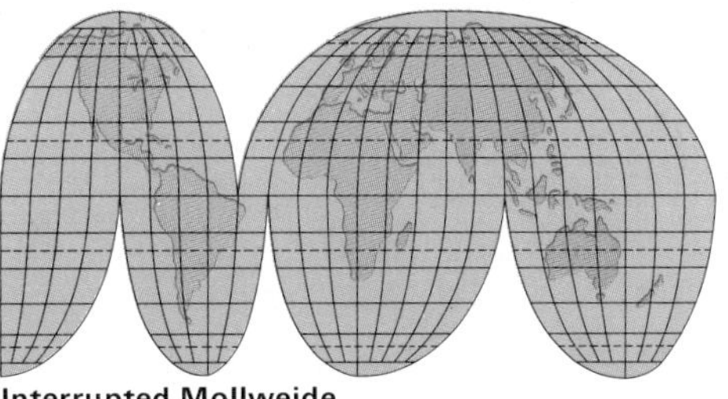

Interrupted Mollweide

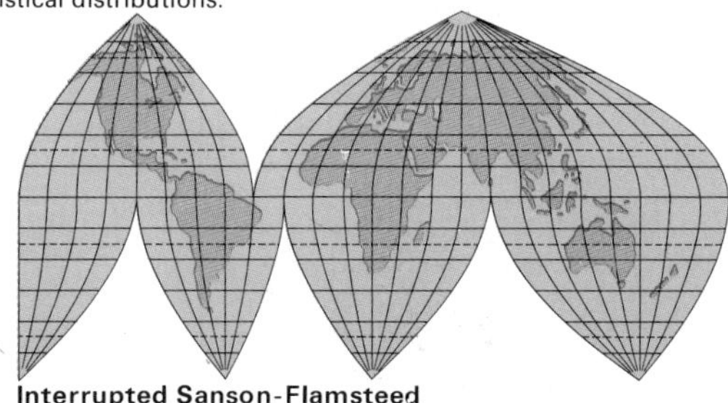

Interrupted Sanson-Flamsteed